WITHDRAWN

Creating and Contesting Carolina

The Carolina Lowcountry and the Atlantic World

Sponsored by the Program in the Carolina Lowcountry and the Atlantic World of the College of Charleston

Money, Trade, and Power
Edited by Jack P. Greene, Rosemary Brana-Shute, and Randy J. Sparks

The Impact of the Haitian Revolution in the Atlantic World
Edited by David P. Geggus

London Booksellers and American Customers
James Raven

Memory and Identity
Edited by Bertrand Van Ruymbeke and Randy J. Sparks

This Remote Part of the World
Bradford J. Wood

The Final Victims
James A. McMillin

The Atlantic Economy during the Seventeenth and Eighteenth Centuries
Edited by Peter A. Coclanis

From New Babylon to Eden
Bertrand Van Ruymbeke

Saints and Their Cults in the Atlantic World
Edited by Margaret Cormack

Who Shall Rule at Home?
Jonathan Mercantini

To Make This Land Our Own
Arlin C. Migliazzo

Votaries of Apollo
Nicholas Michael Butler

Fighting for Honor
T. J. Desch Obi

Paths to Freedom
Edited by Rosemary Brana-Shute and Randy J. Sparks

Material Culture in Anglo-America
Edited by David S. Shields

The Fruits of Exile
Edited by Richard Bodek and Simon Lewis

The Irish in the Atlantic World
Edited by David T. Gleeson

Ambiguous Anniversary
Edited by David T. Gleeson and Simon Lewis

Creating and Contesting Carolina
Edited by Michelle LeMaster and Bradford J. Wood

CREATING and CONTESTING *Carolina*

Proprietary Era Histories

Edited by
Michelle LeMaster *and* Bradford J. Wood

The University of South Carolina Press

© 2013 University of South Carolina

Published by the University of South Carolina Press
Columbia, South Carolina 29208

www.sc.edu/uscpress

Manufactured in the United States of America

22 21 20 19 18 17 16 15 14 13
10 9 8 7 6 5 4 3 2 1

Library of Congress Cataloging-in-Publication Data

Creating and contesting Carolina : proprietary era histories /
edited by Michelle LeMaster and Bradford J. Wood.
pages cm. — (The Carolina lowcountry and the Atlantic world)
Includes bibliographical references and index.
ISBN 978-1-61117-272-0 (hardbound :
alk. paper) — ISBN 978-1-61117-273-7 (ebook)
1. South Carolina—History—Colonial period, ca. 1600–1775.
2. North Carolina—History—Colonial period, ca . 1600–1775.
3. Tuscarora Indians—Wars, 1711–1713. 4. Indians of North
America—South Carolina—History. 5. Indians of North America—
North Carolina—History. I. LeMaster, Michelle, 1970– author, editor of
compilation. II. Wood, Bradford J., 1970– author, editor of compilation.
F272.C895 2013
975.7'02—dc23
2013011562

Portion of "Cutting one another's throats" appears
courtesy of the University of Tennesee Press.

CONTENTS

Acknowledgments vii
Note on Maps x
List of Maps xi
Abbreviations xv

Introduction: Creating and Contesting Carolina 1
Michelle LeMaster and Bradford J. Wood

PART I

Backgrounds

Defining Carolina: Cartography and Colonization
in the North American Southeast, 1657–1733 27
S. Max Edelson

Venturing Out: The Barbadian Diaspora and
the Carolina Colony, 1650–1685 49
Justin Roberts and Ian Beamish

Dr. Henry Woodward's Role in
Early Carolina Indian Relations 73
Eric E. Bowne

PART II

Violence and Conflict

The Economic Philosophies of Indian Trade
Regulation Policy in Early South Carolina 97
Jessica Stern

"Cutting one anothers throats": British, Native,
and African Violence in Early Carolina 118
Matthew Jennings

"Before long to be good friends":
Diplomatic Perspectives of the Tuscarora War 140
Stephen Feeley

War, Masculinity, and Alliances
on the Carolina Frontiers   164
Michelle LeMaster

Histories of the "Tuscarora War"   186
James Taylor Carson

PART III

Building Plantations, Challenging Authority

Thomas Pollock and the Making of an
Albemarle Plantation World   211
Bradford J. Wood

Diversity in the Slave Trade to the Colonial Carolinas   234
Gregory E. O'Malley

Marooned: Politics and Revolution in the
Bahamas Islands and Carolina   256
Alexander Moore

"The Proprietors can't undertake for what
they will do": A Political Interpretation of the
South Carolina Revolution of 1719   273
Hanno T. Scheerer

Protecting the Rights of Englishmen:
The Rise and Fall of Carolina's Piratical State   295
Mark G. Hanna

PART IV

Aftermaths

Forging Alliances: The Impact of the Tuscarora War
on North Carolina's Political Leadership   321
Christine Styrna Devine

"The Indians that live about Pon Pon": John and
Mary Musgrove and the Making of a Creek Indian
Community in South Carolina, 1717–1732   343
Steven C. Hahn

List of Contributors   367
Index   371

Acknowledgments

This book emerged out of conversations between the editors while they stayed with a group of friends at a rented beach house on Oak Island, North Carolina in May 2009. Conversation threads about seafood restaurants, water temperatures, and bird watching became interwoven with conversations about historiographies and about the relations between natives and settlers. If references to the Tuscarora or the Yamasee became tedious for the others in the beach house, they bore it with the easygoing patience of good friends on a vacation. The pleasant and supportive company of that beach house turned out to be a harbinger of things to come for a volume that has been built on the willing assistance and cooperative spirit of many others. In fact, while the editors like to think that this volume provides evidence of many important findings, it may above all else be a testimony to the value of collaboration in academic research and writing. Both editors had already learned about working as part of a community of talented, generous, and hardworking scholars when they began doctoral work and became participants in the Johns Hopkins Seminar on Colonial British America in 1995, and, in many ways, this volume also grew out of that earlier positive experience.

Whatever experiences and ideas the editors brought to this volume, they have been blessed with an outstanding and cooperative group of contributors who have made the book their own. Putting together a collection of essays on a few especially neglected decades in the history of two relatively neglected colonies may sound like a good decision, but it can only work if other scholars are ready and willing to address challenging and understudied issues. Initially, the editors did not know whether they would be able to find enough other scholars to make this volume a reality, but the essays included here have substantially exceeded their expectations. Some of the contributors, such as Stephen Feeley, included work in progress that had helped inspire the editors' initial planning. Others, such as Greg O'Malley and Jamey Carson, were persuaded to undertake new work and pursue new lines of inquiry at the request of the editors. All are appreciated.

As the editors sought contributors and attempted to define the parameters of the volume, they recognized the limits of their own scholarly expertise and distinctive perspectives and asked many others for input and advice. We were struck by the many great suggestions and helpful comments we received from a wide range of scholars. In addition to the editors and contributors, some of those who participated in various conversations about this volume included Denise Bossy, Jeff Crow, Alec Haskell, Wayne Lee, Brendan McConville, Matt Mulcahy, Alex Moore, David Preston, Bill Ramsey, Daniel Richter, Kristi Rutz-Robbins, Peter Wood, Craig Yirush, and Natalie Zacek. We hope that they will be pleased by some of the decisions we made and will forgive us if we did not always benefit sufficiently from their good advice. Members of the Kentucky Early American Studies Seminar also provided comments on the volume's initial project description, a draft of the introduction, and one of the chapters.

One of the volume's contributors, Max Edelson, provided special expertise to make maps available to the readers of this volume. As the foregoing pages explain, he created the MapScholar website which includes a variety of relevant maps that are referenced in the book. We feel that access to this project has been a significant asset to the book, and we appreciate Max's considerable efforts. He received assistance from Lee Wilson Bowden, Rebecca Green, and Bill Ferster.

Any substantial academic publication requires support from institutions as well as from individuals. At Eastern Kentucky University, Bradford Wood benefitted from the resources of the Department of History, ably chaired first by David Coleman and then by Chris Taylor, and of the College of Arts and Sciences under the supportive direction of Dean John Wade. Helpful comments and advice also came from Thomas H. Appleton, Jr. and from John Bowes. Diane Tyer assisted with some administrative tasks. At Lehigh University, Michelle LeMaster received funding for travel related to this project through a Faculty Research Grant. The History Department, under the chairmanship of Steve Cutcliffe, has also supplied resources as well as the invaluable administrative support of Janet Walters. Monica Najar and Jean Soderlund provide a simulating environment for research in early American history. At the University of South Carolina Press, thanks go to Alex Moore and Linda Fogle for working with us and seeing the volume through the publication process.

Most of the essays in this volume were presented and discussed at a conference hosted by the Program in the Carolina Lowcountry and Atlantic World at the College of Charleston in October, 2010. The editors are indebted to the Carolina Lowcountry program for their willingness to host a conference at our request and according to our specifications, while laboring under their own budget constraints and limited resources, and without any institutional affiliation with the editors or the conference's presenters. Specific thanks go to Simon Lewis, John White, Sandy Slater, and Lisa Randle. Lisa Randle handled much of the conference's basic organization and logistics with an impressive level of efficiency and energy. As part of the conference, the editors invited five prominent scholars, Alan Gallay, Tom Hatley, Charles Lesser, Greg O'Brien, and Robert Olwell, to comment on the papers. Their thought-provoking and expert comments have no doubt improved the book in innumerable ways. Both

Eastern Kentucky University's Department of History and Lehigh University provided some additional resources for this conference.

The editors dedicate their work on this volume to three scholars whose foundational work and leadership helped to make these essays possible: Alan Gallay, Jack P. Greene, and Philip D. Morgan. This dedication reflects their enormous influence on scholarship relevant to the volume. It also expresses our appreciation, because all three have provided valuable professional advice and guidance to the editors over some years.

During the work on this book, the editors have also incurred some debts that are more personal than professional. Michelle LeMaster thanks her parents, as well as her supportive friends from YACS (they will know who they are). Bradford Wood extends his thanks to Susan Kroeg, who makes everything in his life better, and to Clare Catharine Wood, who has been surprisingly patient with her father during her first two years of life.

NOTE ON MAPS

"Defining Carolina": An Online MapScholar Collection

The maps featured in this volume have been brought together to view online at mapscholar.org/carolina. MapScholar is a visualization tool for historical map collections. Readers can open the collection in any web browser and will find an intuitive visualization that shows the maps as artifacts as well as representations of geographic space. By dragging and clicking its buttons and images, readers can change the display to explore the maps in greater detail. These images have been numbered to correspond to the printed bibliography included in the volume. MapScholar was developed by associate professor of history S. Max Edelson and senior scientist Bill Ferster at the University of Virginia's Sciences, Humanities, and Arts Network of Technology Initiatives (SHANTI). It has received support from the National Endowment for the Humanities and the American Council of Learned Societies.

LIST OF MAPS

A digital visualization of these maps is available at mapscholar.org/carolina.

References: Philip D. Burden, *The Mapping of North America: A List of Printed Maps, 1511–1670* (Rickmansworth, Eng.: Raleigh, 1996) (hereafter Burden I); Philip D. Burden, *The Mapping of North America II: A List of Printed Maps, 1670–1700* (Rickmansworth, Eng.: Raleigh, 2007) (Burden II); William P. Cumming, *The Southeast in Early Maps,* 3rd ed., edited by Louis de Vorsey Jr. (Chapel Hill: University of North Carolina Press, 1998); Archer B. Hulbert, *The Crown Collection of Photographs of American Maps* (Cleveland: Arthur H. Clark, 1915).

1. P[ierre] Duval, *La Floride Françoise* ([Paris, 1665?]). From Florida Map Collection, University of South Florida Digital Collections, http://digital.lib.usf.edu/?u15.9042. Cumming, 158; Burden I, 485–86.
2. Nicolas Comberford, "The south part of Virginia, now the north part of Carolina" (1657). Manuscripts and Archives Division, New York Public Library. NYPL Digital Gallery, http://digitalgallery.nypl.org/nypldigital/id?ps_mss_cd18_271. Cumming, 152–54.
3. Joseph Moxon, *Americae septentrionalis pars* (London, 1664). From Print Collection, Miriam and Ira D. Wallach Division of Art, Prints and Photographs, New York Public Library. NYPL Digital Gallery, http://digitalgallery.nypl.org/nypldigital/id?54684. Cumming, 157; Burden I, 484–85.
4. Robert Horne, "Carolina Described," in *A Brief Description of the Province of Carolina on the Coasts of Floreda* (London, 1666). From Albert and Shirley Small Special Collections Library, University of Virginia. Cumming, 157–58; Burden I, 497–98.
5. Richard Blome, *A Generall Mapp of Carolina Describeing its Sea Coast and Rivers* (London, 1672). From John Carter Brown Library, Brown University. JCB Archive of Early American Images, http://jcb.lunaimaging.com/luna/servlet/s/s274gn. Cumming, 162–63; Burden II, 14–15.
6. John Ogilby, "A new discription of Carolina by the order of the Lords Proprietors," in *America* ([London, ca. 1671]). From North Carolina Collection, Wilson Library, University of North Carolina at Chapel Hill. North Carolina Maps, http://dc.lib.unc.edu/u?/ncmaps,498. Cumming, 163; Burden II, 41–43.
7. John Culpeper, copy of "Culpeper's Draught of Ashley River, 1671." *Collections of the South Carolina Historical Society,* vol. 5 (Charleston: S. G. Courtney, 1897). Cumming, 160.

8. Joel Gascoyne, *A New Map of the Country of Carolina* ([S.l.], 1682). From Geography and Map Division, Library of Congress. American Memory, http://hdl.loc.gov/loc.gmd/g3870.np000146. Cumming, 174–75; Burden II, 193, 195–97.

9. John Thornton, Robert Morden, and Philip Lea, *A New Map of Carolina* (London, [ca. 1685]). From Albert and Shirley Small Special Collections Library, University of Virginia, http://search.lib.virginia.edu/catalog/uva-lib:616779/view. Cumming, 180–81; Burden II, 282–84.

10. John Thornton and Robert Morden, *To the Right Honorable William Earl of Craven Palatine . . . This New Map of the Cheif [sic] Rivers, Bayes, Creeks, Harbours, and Settlements in South Carolina* (London, [ca. 1685]). From John Carter Brown Library, Brown University. JCB Archive of Early American Images, http://jcb.lunaimaging.com/luna/servlet/s/508801. Cumming, 186–87; Burden II, 419, 420.

11. John Lawson, "To His Excellency William Lord Palatine . . . And the rest of the True and Absolute Lords Proprietors of Carolina in America This Map . . . ," in *A New Voyage to Carolina* (London, 1709). From North Carolina Collection, Wilson Library, University of North Carolina at Chapel Hill. North Carolina Maps, http://dc.lib.unc.edu/u?/ncmaps,2641. Cumming, 201–2.

12. Vincenzo Corenelli, ["America settentrionale Colle Nuovo Scoperte fin all' Anno 1688"], in *Altante Veneto* ([Venice, 1693]). From John Carter Brown Library, Brown University. JCB Archive of Early American Images, http://jcb.lunaimaging.com/luna/servlet/s/wpa3go (sheet 1), http://jcb.lunaimaging.com/luna/servlet/s/spn500 (sheet 2). Burden II, 323–27.

13. Guillaume de Lisle, "Carte du Mexique et de la Floride" (1708; orig. 1703), in [*Atlas de Geographie*] (Paris, 1731). From David Rumsey Historical Map Collection, http://www.davidrumsey.com/luna/servlet/s/mwvvv9. Cumming, 193–95.

14. Ed[ward] Crisp, *A compleat description of the province of Carolina in 3 parts* ([London, 1711?]). From Geography and Map Division, Library of Congress. American Memory, http://hdl.loc.gov/loc.gmd/g3870.ct001123. Cumming, 202–3.

15. Thomas Nairne, "A map of South Carolina shewing the settlements of the English, French, & Indian nations from Charles Town to the River Missisipi," inset from Ed[ward] Crisp, *A compleat description of the province of Carolina in 3 parts* ([London, 1711?]). From Geography and Map Division, Library of Congress. American Memory, http://hdl.loc.gov/loc.gmd/g3870.ct001123. Cumming, 203.

16. Ed[ward] Crisp, "A new chart of the coast of Carolina and Florida from Cape Henry to the Havana in the Island of Cuba," inset from *A compleat description of the province of Carolina in 3 parts* ([London, 1711?]). From Geography and Map Division, Library of Congress. American Memory, http://hdl.loc.gov/loc.gmd/g3870.ct001123. Cumming, 203.

17. "Map of Carolina. Showing the route of the forces sent in the years 1711, 1712, and 1713, from South Carolina to the relief of North Carolina, and in 1715 of the forces sent from North Carolina to the assistance of South Carolina, also showing the controverted bounds between Virginia and Carolina" (ca. 1715). U.K. National Archives, CO 700/Carolina 4. Early Maps of the American South, Research Laboratories of Archaeology, University of North Carolina at Chapel Hill, http://images.dcr.state.nc.us/images1/maps/vol1/mc_150_1716u1_inverted.jpg. Cumming, 208; Hulbert, ser. 3, 17–18.

18. Herman Moll, *A new and exact map of the dominions of the King of Great Britain on ye continent of North America* ([London], 1715). From Geography and Map Division, Library of Congress. American Memory, http://hdl.loc.gov/loc.gmd/g3300.ct000232. Cumming, 206–8.

19. Herman Moll, "A draught of ye town and harbour of Charles-town," inset from *A new and exact map of the dominions of the King of Great Britain on ye continent of North America* ([London], 1715). From Geography and Map Division, Library of Congress. American Memory, http://hdl.loc.gov/loc.gmd/g3300.ct000232. Cumming, 207.

20. Herman Moll, "A map of the improved part of Carolina with the settlements &c.," inset from *A new and exact map of the dominions of the King of Great Britain on ye continent of North America* ([London], 1715). From Geography and Map Division, Library of Congress. American Memory, http://hdl.loc.gov/loc.gmd/g3300.ct000232. Cumming, 206–7.

21. Herman Moll, [Map of southeastern North America], inset from *A new and exact map of the dominions of the King of Great Britain on ye continent of North America* ([London], 1715). From Geography and Map Division, Library of Congress. American Memory, http://hdl.loc.gov/loc.gmd/g3300.ct000232. Cumming, 206.

22. Herman Moll, "A map of the principal part of North America," inset from *A new and exact map of the dominions of the King of Great Britain on ye continent of North America* ([London], 1715). From Geography and Map Division, Library of Congress. American Memory, http://hdl.loc.gov/loc.gmd/g3300.ct000232. Cumming, 207.

23. Sir Robert Montgomery, "A plan representing the form of setling the districts, or county divisions in the Margravate of Azilia," in *A Discourse Concerning the Design'd Establishment of a New Colony to the South of Carolina* (London, 1717). From Albert and Shirley Small Special Collections Library, University of Virginia. Cumming, 210–11.

24. Herman Moll, *A new map of the north parts of America claimed by France under ye names of Louisiana, Mississipi, Canada and New France* ([London], 1720). From Special Collections, University of South Florida Libraries. Florida Map Collection, USF Digital Collections, http://digital.lib.usf.edu/?u15.55.

25. John Herbert, "The Ichnography or plann of the fortification of Charlestown and the streets" (1721). U.K. National Archives, CO 700/Carolina 6. Early Maps of the American South, Research Laboratories of Archaeology, University of North Carolina at Chapel Hill, http://rla.unc.edu/Mapfiles/CC3/CC3.021.jpg. Cumming, 217; Hulbert, ser. 3, 21.

26. W. H. Toms, *The ichnography of Charles-town. At high water* (n.p., 1739). I. N. Phelps Stokes Collection of American Historical Prints, New York Public Library. NYPL Digital Gallery, http://digitalgallery.nypl.org/nypldigital/id?54693. Cumming, 250.

27. John Barnwell, [Map of part of North America from Cape Charles to the Mouth of the River Mississipi] ([ca. 1721]). U.K. National Archives, CO 700/North American Colonies General 7. Early Maps of the American South, Research Laboratories of Archaeology, University of North Carolina at Chapel Hill, http://rla.unc.edu/Mapfiles/SEM/Barnwell%201721~.SEM.jpg. Cumming, 218.

28. John Barnwell, [Southeastern North America] (ca. 1744). Hargrett Rare Book and Manuscript Library, University of Georgia Libraries. Historical Maps Database, http://dlg.galileo.usg.edu/hmap/id:hmap1721-1724b3. Cumming, 256–57.

29. J[ohn] Barnwell, "Map of part of the north branch of the River Alatamaha" (1721). U.K. National Archives, CO 700/Georgia 2. Wikimedia Commons, http://upload.wikimedia.org/wikipedia/commons/2/2c/John_Barnwell_Altamaha_River_Map.jpg. Cumming, 216.

30. "A Plan of King George's Fort at Allatamaha, South Carolina. Latitude 31°12' North" ([ca. 1722]). U.K. National Archives, CO 700/Georgia 4/1. Early Maps of the American South, Research Laboratories of Archaeology, University of North Carolina at Chapel Hill, http://rla.unc.edu/Mapfiles/CC3/CC3.132.jpg. Cumming, 219; Hulbert, ser. 3, 132.

31. Captain Stollard, "Plan of Fort King George and part of the Alatamaha River" ([ca. 1722]). U.K. National Archives, CO 700/Georgia 5. Early Maps of the American South, Research Laboratories of Archaeology, University of North Carolina at Chapel Hill, (part 1) http://rla.unc.edu/Mapfiles/CC3/CC3.133.jpg, (part 2) http://rla.unc.edu/Mapfiles/CC3/CC3.134.jpg. Cumming, 219; Hulbert, ser. 3, 133–34.

32. "The Ishnography or plan of Fort King George" (1722). U.K. National Archives, CO 700/Georgia 7. Early Maps of the American South, Research Laboratories of Archaeology, University of North Carolina at Chapel Hill, (part 1) http://rla.unc.edu/Mapfiles/CC3/CC3.135.jpg, (part 2) http://rla.unc.edu/Mapfiles/CC3/CC3.136.jpg. Cumming, 219–20; Hulbert, ser. 3, 135.

33. "Sketch plan of Fort King George in Georgia" ([ca. 1722?]). U.K. National Archives, CO 700/Georgia 8. Early Maps of the American South, Research Laboratories of Archaeology, University of North Carolina at Chapel Hill, http://rla.unc.edu/Mapfiles/CC3/CC3.137.jpg. Cumming, 220; Hulbert, ser. 3, 137.

34. "A Map Describing the Situation of the several Nations of Indians between South Carolina and the Massisipi River" [1725?]. U.K. National Archives, CO 700/North American Colonies General 6/2. Cumming, 221–22; Hulbert, ser. 3, 7–8.

35. Copy of [Map of the several nations of Indians to the Northwest of South Carolina] (1929; orig. ca. 1721?). Geography and Map Division, Library of Congress. American Memory, http://hdl.loc.gov/loc.gmd/g3860.ct000734. Cumming, 222; Hulbert, ser. 2, vol. 3, 37.

36. Henry Popple, *A Map of the British Empire in America with the French and Spanish Settlements adjacent thereto* (London, 1733). From David Rumsey Historical Map Collection, http://www.davidrumsey.com/luna/servlet/s/h103u7. Cumming, 233–34.

Abbreviations

AHR — *American Historical Review*

BPRO-SC — Sainsbury, Noel, ed. *Records in the British Public Record Office Relating to South Carolina, 1663–1782*, 36 vols. London: 1860–1919.

CHJ — Commons House Journal, South Carolina, Green transcripts, at the South Carolina Department of Archives and History, Columbia.

CO — Colonial Office, National Archives, Great Britain.

CRNC — Saunders, William L., Stephen B. Weeks, and Walter Clark, eds. *The Colonial and State Records of North Carolina*, 30 vols. Raleigh: State of North Carolina, 1886–1912.

CRNC (2nd ser.) — Parker, Mattie Erma Edward, et al., eds. *The Colonial Records of North Carolina*, 2nd ser., 11 vols. Raleigh: Carolina Charter Tercentenary Commission, 1963–.

CSPC — Sainsbury, Noel J., et al., eds. *Great Britain Public Record Office, Calendar of State Papers, Colonial Series: America and the West Indies*, 38 vols. London: 1860–1919.

CVSP — Palmer, William P., ed., *Calendar of Virginia State Papers and Other Manuscripts, 1652–1781*, 11 vols. Richmond: Virginia State Library, 1875–93.

Cumming, *Early Maps* — Cumming, William P., *The Southeast in Early Maps*, 3rd ed., ed. Louis de Vorsey Jr. Chapel Hill: University of North Carolina Press, 1998.

DNCB — Powell, William S., ed. *Dictionary of North Carolina Biography*, 6 vols. Chapel Hill: University of North Carolina Press, 1979–96.

EJCCV — McIlwaine, Henry. R., ed. *Executive Journals of the Council of Colonial Virginia*, 6 vols. Richmond: Virginia State Library, 1925.

GHQ — *Georgia Historical Quarterly*

JAH — *Journal of American History*

JCHA — Salley, A. S., ed. *Journals of the Commons House of Assembly (1692–1734)*. Columbia: Historical Commission of South Carolina, 1907–47.

JCIT McDowell, William L., ed. *The Colonial Records of South Carolina: Journals of the Commissioners of the Indian Trade, September 20, 1710–August 29, 1718.* Columbia: South Carolina Department of Archives and History, 1955.

JGC Salley, A. S., ed. *Journal of the Grand Council of South Carolina,* 2 vols. Columbia: Historical Commission of South Carolina, 1907.

JHBV McIlwaine, Henry Read, ed. *Journals of the House of Burgesses of Virginia,* 12 vols. Richmond: Colonial Press, E. Waddey, 1910.

JSH *Journal of Southern History*

Lawson, *New Voyage* Lawson, John, *A New Voyage to Carolina,* ed. Hugh Talmadge Lefler. Chapel Hill: University of North Carolina Press, 1967.

Nairne, *Muskogean Journals* Nairne, Thomas, *Nairne's Muskogean Journals: The 1708 Expedition to the Mississippi River,* ed. Alexander Moore, Jackson: University Press of Mississippi, 1988.

NCHR *North Carolina Historical Review*

NCHGR Hathaway, J. R. B., ed. *The North Carolina Historical and Genealogical Register,* 3 vols. Edenton, North Carolina, 1900–1903.

NCSA State Archives of North Carolina, Raleigh.

Salley, *Narratives* Salley, A. S., ed. *Narratives of Early Carolina 1650–1674,* New York: Scribner, 1911.

SCDAH South Carolina Department of Archives and History, Columbia.

SCHM *South Carolina Historical Magazine*

SCHGM *South Carolina Historical and Genealogical Magazine*

SCHS South Carolina Historical Society, Charleston.

Shaftesbury Papers *The Shaftesbury Papers and Other Records Relating to Carolina and the First Settlement on Ashley River Prior to the Year 1676,* Collections of the South Carolina Historical Society 5, ed. Langdon Cheves, Richmond, Va.: William Ellis Jones, 1897.

Statutes *Statutes at Large of South Carolina,* ed. Thomas Cooper. *at Large* Columbia, S.C.: A. S. Johnson, 1836–41.

VMHB *Virginia Magazine of History and Biography*

WMQ *William and Mary Quarterly, 3rd Series*

Introduction

Creating and Contesting Carolina

**MICHELLE LEMASTER AND
BRADFORD J. WOOD**

A Decade of Strife: The Carolinas in the 1710s

In the fall of 1711, six men traveled up the Neuse River in North Carolina in quest of wild grapes and to discover how far inland the river remained navigable. The adventurers—the Swiss baron and founder of the New Bern settlement, Christoph von Graffenried; the colony's surveyor general and sometime Indian agent, John Lawson; two black slaves; and two Indians—alarmed residents of Catechna, a leading Tuscarora town, prompting its chief to seize them. A terrified Graffenried managed to broker a separate peace with his captors, but Lawson met his end at the hands of warriors (and women) frustrated with the colonists' corrupt trading practices.[1] Lawson's execution and Graffenried's capture precipitated a conflict known to colonists as the Tuscarora War, which proved to be the most violent and destructive episode in the colonial history of North Carolina. In the space of two hours, 130 colonists were killed. The Indians targeted men, women, and children, slave and free alike, then set fire to homes, destroyed crops, and slaughtered or drove off livestock. Colonists retaliated ruthlessly. Military forces from South Carolina (made up of a few white soldiers and a much larger contingent of allied Indian warriors) enslaved hundreds of Tuscaroras. A second expedition, led by Colonel James Moore Jr., burned several hundred people, including women and children, to death in Fort Neoheroka.[2]

Less than four years later, on the night of April 14, 1715, events at the leading Yamasee town of Pocotaligo, in what British colonists considered South Carolina, showed an eerie similarity to those of Catechna. A British delegation, including former Indian agent John Wright and current agent to the Yamasee, Thomas Nairne, claimed to be delivering a peaceful message, but many Yamasee suspected that they had come not to make peace but rather to spy.[3] In the end, only two of the British ambassadors survived the night; the rest were put to death by torture.[4] More important, the events at Pocotaligo presaged the outbreak of another wrenching and devastating war, this time in the southern Carolina and later called the Yamasee War by the British victors.

The second decade of the eighteenth century was a period of great upheaval in the Carolina colonies; the Tuscarora and Yamasee Wars were the most dramatic and bloody incidents, but they were hardly isolated. Internal and external political disputes also erupted, dividing one colony while uniting the other in opposition to the proprietors. In Cary's Rebellion in North Carolina (1708–11), a dispute over competing claims for the office of governor steadily escalated, as factions maneuvered for position, and rival governments emerged. The dispute had to be resolved with violence, and for a variety of reasons questions of political legitimacy lingered for years. The South Carolina "Revolution of 1719" resulted in a political coup instead of violence. Charles Town elites decided that their grievances against the Carolina Proprietors had become intolerable, leading them—in a move without precedent in British America—to seize control of the government from the proprietors and place South Carolina directly under Crown control. The crises that characterized the decade dramatically reshaped the region and in some ways marked the triumph of the settlers over both native opponents and imperial authorities. They were also, though, the logical outcome of British actions during the previous five decades of settlement in the region.

Scholars have yet to comment on the interrelationship between these events, and they remain neglected stories in the overall narrative of British colonization in America. While some of the striking similarities between the events at Catechna and Pocotaligo may have been coincidental, many of them reflected the common dynamics of interaction between Carolina colonists and the indigenous peoples of the southeast. In hindsight the Tuscarora and Yamasee Wars seem distinct from each other and from political disputes between Europeans, but contemporaries recognized that Cary's Rebellion contributed to the outbreak of the Tuscarora War, that the Tuscarora War had connections to the Yamasee War, and that the Yamasee War played a major role in South Carolina's revolt against the Carolina Proprietors. In addition these four events related to other challenges facing the various peoples who inhabited both Carolina colonies. From a variety of perspectives, then, these turbulent years exposed "Carolinians" of European, Native American, and African descent to one of the most trying collective ordeals in the history of British America.

Shared Histories

For all the peoples living in the geographic space that the British called Carolina, the Proprietary Period brought challenging and dramatic changes to the region. Depending on one's vantage point, those alterations could be perceived as disaster, crisis, or progress, but few could be neutral about them. Some occurrences, such as the violent warfare between British and Indians or British and Spanish, could be obvious and dramatic, while others, such as the development of the plantation system or the decline of proprietary authority, could be much more subtle but perhaps equally significant. All involved contestation, whether through violence or debate. Indeed the very idea of a place called Carolina was challenged by Native Americans (and Spaniards), and many colonists and metropolitan authorities differed in their visions for Carolina. The stakes were high in many of these contests, because they occurred in an early American world often characterized by brutal warfare, rigid hierarchies, labor exploitation, cultural dislocation, and struggles for power. While Native Americans and colonists shed each other's blood in an effort to define the place called Carolina in their own terms, colonists and officials built their own version of Carolina on paper and in the discourse of early modern empires. These seemingly more abstract efforts also involved struggles for power and could be destructive and harrowing in their own way. But new tensions also provided a powerful incentive for creativity. The peoples of the early Carolinas reimagined places, reconceptualized cultures, realigned their loyalties, and adapted in a wide variety of other ways. Again the idea of Carolina itself proves instructive, because it illustrates perhaps the most conspicuous attempt to reconsider the geography of the southeast during these years. The main goal of the essays in *Creating and Contesting Carolina* is to shed light on how the various peoples of the Carolinas responded to these tumultuous changes. In doing so, the essays focus attention on some of the most important and dramatic watersheds in the histories of any colonies in America.

Three major groups of peoples, European colonists, Native Americans, and enslaved Africans, shared these experiences of change in the Carolinas, but their histories have usually been written separately. European colonists are typically positioned within a narrative that emphasizes the growth of the colonies leading toward the ultimate triumph of the American nation-state. Scholarship on Native Americans has flowered in recent years, demonstrating the complex ways native peoples adapted to the arrival of Europeans, but their story is still often relegated to the separate domain of ethnohistory. Enslaved Africans more frequently receive attention in scholarship that describes the evolution of plantation systems and the eventual emergence of southern distinctiveness. None of these groups should be treated as monolithic, but they represent three important categories of experience. Scholarship on the Carolinas during the early decades of the eighteenth century has usually paid attention to European settlers, Native Americans, and Africans in roughly that order, and for a variety of reasons this volume cannot fully depart from that imbalance, but it moves toward more a more sensitive and complex understanding of all these peoples. Unfortunately scholars who concentrate on these three groups do not always engage with each other's work. These disparate but closely related strands of scholarship must be connected in order to make the early Carolinas intelligible. Similarly, separate colonial historiographies prevent scholars from understanding the relationships between colonies, even when they are as closely tied as North and South Carolina. Carolina never functioned as one coherent colony, but the proprietorship itself still insured some commonality and connection through politics, metropolitan influence, and shared perspectives. Scholars must strive to understand the fluid and diverse world of the early southeast by paying less attention to borders and teleologies and more attention to subjective experiences and contingencies. Consequently the essays in this volume focus on the shared histories of the Carolinas—North and South, European, Native American, and African—from early settlement to the end of the proprietorship in the 1720s. They do so by exploring important sources of tension, both in the colonial worlds shared by Europeans and Africans and in the indigenous worlds outside colonial settlement.

So far scholars have devoted relatively little attention to these histories. Indeed in recent years, King Philip's War in New England, an incident somewhat similar to the Tuscarora War or the Yamasee War, has received more attention than the entire proprietary histories of both Carolinas. Calls for more attention to the region broadly referred to as the Lower South have yielded a number of important books, but they have primarily focused on the period after about 1740.[5] The field of Native American history has seen some of the most significant advances. Two recent books on the Yamasee War by Stephen Oatis and William Ramsey mark a promising start and, along with the especially valuable work in Steven Hahn's *The Invention of the Creek Nation* and Alan Gallay's prize-winning work, *The Indian Slave Trade,* have done a great deal to clarify and draw attention to interactions between colonists and Native Americans in the southeast.[6] These and other books on South Carolina have only begun to compensate for decades of scholarly neglect.[7] Work on proprietary North Carolina lags even further. Noeleen McIlvenna recently published the first modern book-length account of the early proprietary period in North Carolina, in a brief study that stops with the Tuscarora War.[8] A fuller account of this period in North Carolina history must reach back at least forty years to the generation of Hugh T. Lefler and William S. Powell.[9] Surprisingly little is known about the native peoples of the North Carolina tidewater, and the first full scholarly treatment of the Tuscarora War is in progress but not yet published.[10] Thus the essays in this volume reveal valuable findings about a formative period in the cultural history of the southeast, when native peoples lost dominance, the plantation complex took deep root, and imperial systems were realigned. An analysis of the experience of early Carolina reveals the uneven and contested means by which the British gradually solidified their claim to the region and succeeded in building more stable, workable communities in a contested borderland.

The essays in *Creating and Contesting Carolina* address an ambitious range of issues and topics, but they represent difficult choices about emphasis. Some of these choices were imposed by the time necessary to complete research and writing and by the space available in one volume shared by many authors. Consequently these essays do not attempt a comprehensive narrative history of the Carolinas during this period, or even a comprehensive treatment of any one group of people, event, or issue. Instead they offer provocative and original approaches to some important questions. In addition the essays necessarily devote more attention to some topics than others. In almost every area, South Carolina has been included more fully than North Carolina. While the settler populations of both Carolinas included religious and ethnic minorities of considerable importance, historians have had comparatively little to say about them in recent decades. There is considerably more potential for work on gender history and environmental history in this time and these places. Somewhat surprisingly, after serving as a focal point in the study of American slavery for a generation, the Carolina lowcountry now gets less of the attention focused on Africans in British America. All these opportunities await other publications and perhaps other authors.

The Carolinas in Context

In the generation after the Glorious Revolution, the British Empire in America underwent a dramatic expansion. The full significance of this transition has only recently become clear to scholars of the British Empire, who have focused more on earlier origins of settlement and major events later in the eighteenth century. Colonists and others adapted to a rapidly growing population combined with increasingly vast territorial aspirations, much greater diversity accompanied by new and increasingly pluralistic attitudes, and an unprecedented level of commercial complexity and economic possibilities. The expansion in the British colonies during this period marked a change in kind as well as scale, because immigration and growing creole populations created colonies that were more fully the product of settler initiatives, efforts, and perspectives than were previous European colonies. Whatever benefits some settlers and metropolitan authorities garnered from this growth came at the expense of bound laborers and of indigenous peoples, who faced increasing pressures from colonial expansion. Under these circumstances change could only take place through struggle and constant negotiation. Rapid transitions and cultural differences encouraged innovation and created new opportunities but also almost inevitably led to violent confrontations that played out in warfare, internal revolts, resistance to authority, and exploitation. During the first decades of the eighteenth century, a new imperial order emerged in British America, and it had far more to do with colonial adaptations to adversity than with metropolitan projections or bureaucratic visions.[11]

Neither rapid expansion nor its sometimes violent consequences played out evenly across the British colonies. Some older colonies had already achieved some stability and therefore did not change as fundamentally.[12] More culturally homogenous populations felt less need to confront issues of division and dissent. Colonies unsuited to profitable export crops discovered fewer routes to prosperity but also experienced a less powerful drive toward coerced labor and commercial competition. Above all else the characteristics and choices of each region's native populations shaped its history during these years.

The vast area that Charles II gave to the Carolina Proprietors in the late seventeenth century proved to be an especially turbulent theater for British expansion. Settlement there lagged through the last decades of the seventeenth century, only to burgeon in the early eighteenth century, despite political dissension, high mortality rates, and other challenges.[13] The complex makeup of this growing population only exacerbated tensions. Both Carolinas, like other new colonies during these years, attracted religiously and culturally diverse immigrants, including Protestant dissenters of various denominations and national backgrounds, such as German and Swiss Lutherans and Calvinists and French Huguenots, as well as Quakers.[14] Religious disputes and ethnic tensions were common.[15]

Economic opportunities played an especially important role in the Carolinas. South Carolina followed the example of Caribbean sugar colonies in developing the most brutal and profitable plantation system in British mainland America, and North Carolina, while less wealthy, showed a similar commitment to the plantation complex and coerced labor, despite significant obstacles.[16] The growing importation of African slaves resulted in the emergence, by 1708, of an enslaved black majority in the southern colony, producing concerns about slave rebellions. Although North Carolina had not developed a black majority like its southern neighbor, and planters still struggled to attract a suitable labor force, slavery permeated the colony. Over the course of forty years, both Carolinas had evolved as multiracial and multiethnic societies that relied on cooperation between vastly disparate groups of people. Such challenging dynamics contributed to unstable political situations, weakening the colonial governments and leaving them ill-prepared to respond when crisis arrived.

Consequently conflict was endemic to the early Carolinas. Disputes among settlers, and between leading colonists and the proprietors, made the political climate contentious. In the northern colony, proprietary neglect, a struggling economy, and relative isolation caused by a treacherous coastline made for an antiauthoritarian political culture and slowed the establishment of a stable and cohesive governing elite. While the proprietors played an active role in organizing and promoting the settlement around Charles Town that became known as South Carolina, North Carolina grew out of a small, unorganized, unimpressive, and poorly documented movement south from Virginia. At least a handful of these settlers along Albemarle Sound arrived even before the Carolina Proprietary existed and, after the proprietors discovered that these settlers resided within the bounds of their jurisdiction, they were never treated as more than an afterthought.[17] The proprietors' comprehensive plans for the government of all Carolina, known as the Fundamental Constitutions, arrived in both colonies stillborn because of their impracticality and elitism. No one ever made a sustained effort to fully implement them despite repeated revisions. When the proprietors bothered to pay specific attention to North Carolina, their comments revealed not only neglect and detachment but an ignorance of even the most basic details of geography and colonial life. Both the limited abilities of the proprietors and their perception of the Albemarle settlements as insignificant and unpromising contributed to their mistakes, but their missteps might also be considered as an extreme example of some of the problems that afflicted most European efforts to govern effectively across the Atlantic. North Carolina was far away and difficult to access by sea, it was settled by people with little interest in the proprietary or other metropolitan authorities, and it offered no clear route to wealth or power. The proprietors, meanwhile, wanted to limit the cost of their investment, lacked the means to coerce settlers, and faced repeated challenges to their legal title and constitutional authority. Tensions finally culminated in the so-called Cary's Rebellion of 1708. These circumstances may have resembled a perfect storm in colonial government by the early eighteenth century, but they were hardly distinctive to North Carolina.

Even in South Carolina, where the proprietors focused much more of their attention, energy, and resources, and where settlers achieved greater levels of wealth, proprietary government went awry. Prominent settlers with wealthy West Indian connections, known as the Goose Creek men, contested proprietary control of the colony and flouted the proprietors' instructions regarding everything from religious freedom to regulation of the Indian trade. By the 1710s, forty years of tensions between the proprietors and colonists in both colonies made stable and legitimate government difficult. Some members of South Carolina's wealthy and assertive elite responded to ongoing disputes with the proprietors about the authority of colonial legislation and military defense during the Yamasee War by contemplating the overthrow of proprietary rule. By 1719, lowcountry planters had begun to articulate colonial political arguments that could ultimately pose a significant challenge to the authority of the British Empire in America.

Early Carolina colonists lived on the periphery of a British imperial system that was adapting to changing circumstances, and some of these changes radiated out from the center of the empire. Consequently attention to the early development and growth of the Carolinas speaks to broad narratives about the making of the British Empire. In the early decades of the eighteenth century, British people on both sides of the Atlantic lived in a political and constitutional world still transitioning in the wake of England's Glorious Revolution of 1688. Steven Pincus has recently characterized the overthrow of James II and the far-reaching political settlement that followed as the first modern revolution.[18] These events carried mixed consequences for the British colonists in America, partly because, while James II clearly intended to exert more control over the colonies than any of his predecessors, new efforts to centralize and govern the colonies did not lose all their momentum with his defeat. Also, in the decades after the Glorious Revolution, these changes forced Britain to reconceptualize its place within the European order and wage frequent wars against its continental and imperial rivals, increasing debt and requiring larger revenues.[19] In response Parliament implemented a program of heavier taxation, established a newly funded and permanent national debt, and sought to exert greater influence over financial matters with the creation of the Bank of England. These measures were dramatic enough to be labeled a "financial revolution" and, together with almost unremitting conflict with European powers over the quarter of a century after 1688, led to the creation of a fiscal-military state capable of, and to some degree committed to, supporting continuing warfare and expansion.[20]

At the same time, metropolitan authorities sought greater involvement in the American colonies even after Parliament vanquished James II and consolidated its position. These efforts at centralization included the growth of a more extensive imperial bureaucracy; the creation of the Board of Trade and Plantations to supervise the colonies; attempts to place proprietary colonies more fully under government control; a new Navigation Act; and other measures to effect more strict control over trade and to eradicate piracy.[21] Chartered enterprises such as the Carolina Proprietary had been preferred in London a generation earlier before the Glorious Revolution but had become less accepted by the end of the seventeenth century. As metropolitan politicians and bureaucrats, led by William Blathwayt, sought to centralize and reform imperial governance, they called the rights of proprietary government into question and made repeated efforts to revoke proprietary charters. The decline of proprietary governments involved both disputes over the extent of prerogative power and new approaches to empire.[22] This context insured a sympathetic hearing among some London officials when South Carolina revolted against the Carolina Proprietors in 1719.[23] By the first years of the eighteenth century, the influence of commercial interests on Parliament made piracy—a practice that was more tolerated and valuable to the colonists in general and which ran rampant in the early Carolinas—another target for metropolitan politicians, who waged and won a "war against pirates" by 1730.[24] In the Carolinas and elsewhere on the fringes of empire, these changes played out in a variety of issues, including increased concerns about defense, disruptions and reorientations of trade, and conflict related to piracy. Imperial power struggles made their mark even while Carolinians confronted significant internal challenges related to unpromising demographic circumstances, the management of a restive bound labor force, and efforts to build a stable and prosperous export economy.

Yet London authorities ultimately could exercise only limited control over the colonies. To some extent this failure was the usual and predictable outcome when early modern states attempted to exert power over colonies at great distances, because they lacked the necessary resources and coercive power to achieve their goals.²⁵ Colonists also found a variety of ways to protect their interests. As scholars of British American politics have long been aware, colonial assemblies rose in importance and gained considerable constitutional and political power in the generations after the Glorious Revolution.²⁶ As Craig Yirush has recently demonstrated, during the same decades American colonists worked at constructing "an alternate account of their place within the empire," thereby countering metropolitan arguments for centralization and colonial subordination and asserting their own claim to traditional English rights.²⁷ Even if the colonists won some of these political struggles, however, they did so through an ongoing process of negotiation and redefinition that involved considerable challenges for settlers on the periphery of a changing empire. Of course part of their identity as colonists also involved strong ties and feelings. They recognized the advantages of autonomy but also sought further integration into metropolitan culture and imperial projects without any sense of contradiction.

Britain's ambitious program of fiscal and military expansion put new pressures on the entire empire. Throughout the colonies war with other imperial powers became the most obvious hallmark of this imperial reorganization, as efforts at mobilization eclipsed other political concerns, shipping disruptions constrained commercial opportunities, and valuable resources had to be reallocated. In the Carolinas, Britain's engagement in the War of the Spanish Succession (Queen Anne's War) led to increased conflict with the Spanish in Florida and the French in Louisiana, revealing the British settlers' precarious position on the southern frontier and necessitating regular attention to defense.²⁸ The presence of the Spanish in particular had been a source of anxiety for Carolinians from the beginning.²⁹ Having preceded the British in the region by nearly one hundred years, the Spanish still claimed much of the territory that British settlers sought to appropriate. Although early attempts by forces from St. Augustine to dislodge the interlopers had failed, Carolinians constantly feared invasions by Spaniards or their Indian allies. In the end, though, it would be Floridians who came out as the losers. Raids by James Moore Sr. during Queen Anne's War (accomplished primarily by Britain's native allies) all but wiped out the mission system in Florida and greatly decreased Spanish power. St. Augustine, although greatly weakened, would survive for another sixty years and would serve as a haven for runaway Carolina slaves.³⁰

Increased imperial competition quickly embroiled the region's native peoples, who occupied the majority of the territory claimed by the European powers and outnumbered them all. Large inland sedentary groups such as the Cherokee and the Muskogean-speaking groups that soon came to be known as the Creek constituted a dense and formidable population that could not be ignored. A wide range of coastal peoples, including the Tuscarora, Yamasee, Meherrin, Westo, Cusabo, and others, posed a more immediate challenge. Weak

British settlements relied on their native neighbors for defense, encouraging allied groups to settle near them in order to provide a protective buffer against enemy Europeans. The Indian trade, in both furs and Indian slaves, constituted a major part of the colonial economy in both settlements, increasing British dependence on their native allies.[31] British success against the Spanish depended on the willingness of native warriors to participate in slave raiding. For native peoples, however, a desire for British manufactures (especially firearms) all too quickly led to dependency, enmeshing them in a vicious cycle of debt-inspired violence. The slave trade was responsible for most of the conflict involving native peoples during the proprietary period. Warriors who needed to pay debts to British traders could easily be turned into proxies for British raids. The British recruited a succession of new allies to wage wars against the Cusabo (1673), Westo (1680), Spanish mission villages (1702–4), Savannah (1707), Tuscarora (1711–13), and Yamasee (1713–15). The constant conflict, though, reflected Carolina settlers' own anxieties about their dependence on native confederates and frustration at their inability to control the trade to the degree they would have liked. Playing one group against another allowed the British to clear a series of tribes from the area and weaken Spanish control, increasing their own security while appropriating additional territory for an expanding plantation system.

Tensions related to the expansion of the Carolina societies emerged gradually at first, and the growing fissures in the social order may have been especially evident among the area's Africans, and, even more so, its Native Americans. African slaves remained few in number in North Carolina, but in South Carolina they were numerous, and in both colonies they more often found themselves confronting both the oppression of chattel slavery and the new work regimes and requirements of plantation agriculture. By contrast, for Native Americans, the challenges related to disease, conflicts between tribal groups, ecological change, and the Indian slave trade underscored a changing power balance and provided powerful incentives to launch successive wars against the two Carolina colonies. Repeated Indian wars in turn threatened outlying settlements and exacerbated divisions between settlers and the proprietors. In the wake of these conflicts, the Native American populations of the Carolinas found themselves forced to retrench and renegotiate their relationships with the British and with each other. Portions of defeated tribes like the Tuscarora fled the region, while others like the newly coalescing Creek nation withdrew and confederated to try to counterbalance British power. Although indigenous peoples continued to occupy large portions of southern territory for more than a century and continued to be major power players, they never again posed the kind of threat to British hegemony that they had during the Proprietary Period.

Together, however, the various Indian wars revealed the vulnerability of the southern colonies. Unable to restrain the behavior of their traders, the governments of the Carolinas had been lax in governing the Indian trade, allowing significant abuses to threaten long-standing trading relationships. The two colonies also lacked the ability to mount a defense without outside help. The weaker northern colony relied almost entirely on its stronger southern neighbor and its Indian allies for manpower during the Tuscarora War. Even the more populous South Carolina had to turn to other Indian allies (in succession, the Westo, Savannah, and Cherokee) in order to avert disaster. In both the Tuscarora War and Yamasee War, native peoples did most of the fighting. These wars focused greater attention on the significance of the Indian trade and Indian alliances, spurring a reorientation of both trade policies and diplomacy. Shell-shocked traders abandoned the Indian slave trade while officials increased trade regulations. Future diplomatic efforts were much more cautious, as each side sought to make the boundaries separating them more distinct and impermeable.

The crises that shook the Carolinas in the 1710s were rooted in long-standing tensions and challenges. They were in many ways a logical outcome of decades of contestation between different ethnic groups and political factions, between settlers and metropolitan officials, and between competing imperial powers. The Tuscarora and Yamasee Wars resulted from years of trading abuses and a slave trade that had mushroomed out of control. Nor were these conflicts between people unfamiliar with one another. Outraged warriors turned their hostility first on those whom they had known the best, the agents and traders who lived among them and who mediated their relationships with colonial capitals. The Cary's Rebellion and the 1719 revolution against the proprietors also drew on deeply rooted divisions between different interest groups within the colonies, as well as a relationship with the proprietors that combined incredible neglect with disconcerting moments of intrusion. The pressures of rapid expansion, the shift to commercial rice agriculture and plantation slavery, and an aggressive foreign policy combined in a series of related events that rocked the two colonies and all the different communities of people living in them and provoked a reorganization of political systems, alliances, and economic ties. In the years that followed, Indian peoples retrenched and withdrew but were far from defeated. The Indian trade had to be reconstructed on a new basis, and although it remained crucial for Indian societies, it declined in importance as a source of economic prosperity for colonists. The plantation system experienced only a brief hiccup before resuming and in fact accelerating its dramatic growth, with devastating consequences for Africans and Indians alike. The revolt against the proprietorship ushered in a period of South Carolina politics remembered for its harmony.[32] In North Carolina regional divisions and economic challenges undermined the legitimacy of colonial elites and politics remained fractious and tense for decades.[33] In both colonies leaders attempted to maintain and expand their autonomy in their interactions with metropolitan elites, and the first few decades of royal rule marked a shift toward greater stability after the more turbulent early years in the Carolinas. By the eve of the American Revolution, Charles Town, South Carolina, had become one of the principal cities in the British colonies. Its leading families were probably the wealthiest and most genteel of mainland residents.[34] Scholars should not forget, though, that this gentility was a very recent acquisition and that the Carolinas' later stability and confidence had been forged in decades of tension, violence, and rapid growth as part of the British Empire.

Creation and Contestation

As the essays in this volume demonstrate, the proprietary period inspired both the creation of new approaches and contests over existing relationships. When the English first arrived in the 1660s and 1670s, they spurred the creation of a new world for all involved.[35] They landed in a region that of course had a long history of its own. Native populations had created and contested their own world for centuries. This was also a region with an existing colonial history, one of Spanish efforts at missionization that foundered during the late sixteenth and seventeenth centuries. The English, though, came in large enough numbers to force a reconfiguration of life in the region. Over the course of the next several decades, they created new settlements; alliances and rivalries; economies (complete with trading ties to the existing coastal Indian populations); labor systems; governments; and local cultures. Colonization represented an effort to impose British worldviews and lifeways on the region. The path to the realization of such a vision was never smooth. Realities on the ground, as well as the responses of other players (natives, Spaniards, and slaves) forced a reworking of the colonizers' expectations. Inherited cultural notions and plans had to be adapted to the environment and existing geopolitical realities. The native populations, as well, had to adapt to the expanding presence of British settlers, who upset older ways of doing things. They formed new alliances and trading ties; relocated settlements and reoriented subsistence patterns; and incorporated new material goods and ideas. Africans, brought unwillingly to the region to supply the insatiable need for labor, created new communities and tried to build lives under the worst of conditions, while adapting to the unfamiliar realities of racial slavery. At the same time, slave owners could use brutal force and other means of power over their slaves but still had to adapt to cultural differences, new plantation strategies, and the recalcitrance of bound labor.

Of course differing groups often contested the worlds that others were trying to create. Multiple visions of what the region should be could not fail to lead to conflict. Indians (and to a lesser extent the Spanish) contested British claims to the region. Native people tried to control how the trade operated and vied with one another and with settlers in a quest to maintain a favorable balance of power. Violent clashes were common. Slaves sought their own relief from the oppressive slave regime that by the first decade of the eighteenth century had come to dominate the lowcountry. The British were no more monolithic as a group than the multitude of Indian groups. Colonists struggled with one another over how the colonies should develop and who should rule. Different religious groups and political factions advocated different legal and constitutional systems, while different economic priorities shaped trading and land policies. Colonists also resisted proprietary efforts to control and regulate the region, often ignoring or evading proprietary orders.

The English and Scottish—or, after 1707, British—settlers, not surprisingly, envisioned Carolina according to their own wishes and aspirations, then struggled to realize their sometimes unrealistic goals. Britain as a nation, and in many cases the settlers themselves, were not new to colonization. They brought with them lessons learned earlier elsewhere. They also brought with them imperial notions that shaped how they sought to develop the region. In the first essay, S. Max Edelson investigates how the English (in the most literal of terms) envisioned their colony in the form of producing maps of the region, and how that changed over the course of the proprietary period. He argues that the perceptions of territorial space illustrated by these maps were rooted in the aspirations, imaginations, and fears of English colonizers. What began as an effort to envision a region that was unfamiliar to the English matured over time to reflect a much greater familiarity with the region and as mapmakers came to see it as part of an increasingly integrated mainland empire.

The presence of Indians presented perhaps the greatest challenge that the British faced in the early years. Outnumbered and militarily weak, early settlers had to rely on neighboring tribes for food and military support. Until a successful staple crop could be identified and developed, the Indian trade drove the economic growth of the region, forcing the British to seek out Indian alliances. Eric E. Bowne demonstrates some of the earliest British efforts to form intercultural ties through the person of Henry Woodward. As one of the first settlers to learn native languages and cultures, Woodward played a crucial role in the development of the Indian trade. He exemplifies the prevalence of boundary crossing and cross-cultural cooperation, as well as the importance of Indian alliances, during the early years of British settlement. His life also demonstrates the changing nature of the Indian trade as the colonists gained experience and became more established. Although in the early years Woodward's ability to establish kinships ties and his linguistic talents gave him an advantage over other traders, he lost his influence as others gradually gained similar skills and ties. Nevertheless the kinds of intensely personal relationships and kinship networks that traders like Woodward created survived the conflicts that plagued British-Indian relations in the region. Steven C. Hahn carries the story of these relationships and networks into a later period in his study of the Pon Pon community of South Carolina. Hahn demonstrates that pre–Yamasee War patterns of cross-cultural interaction persisted into the postwar period, and that the frontier remained permeable despite efforts to solidify boundaries between the British and Indians. The mostly biracial population of this frontier town literally embodied the kinds of persistent interpersonal connections that continued to bind peoples of different backgrounds in colonial Carolina.

The Indian inhabitants of the region were forced to reenvision the world in light of the presence of Europeans. They did so through strategic migration and the creation of trading networks and alliances that bound them in complex ways to one another and to one of the competing European powers. Native peoples quite naturally envisioned their relationships with the British in accordance with their own priorities and viewed their relationships with the newcomers through their own cultural lenses. They were handicapped, though, by the demographic disaster produced by the introduction of foreign diseases and by growing dependence on imported manufactures. Indian efforts to control their own destinies resulted in violent conflicts that destabilized the region for decades. In the process, though, both native peoples and British settlers developed new cultural forms and practices. Michelle LeMaster investigates the importance of joint military endeavors for Anglo-Indian diplomacy. English soldiers and native warriors fought together as allies as often as they fought against one another as enemies. For all their differences they learned to work together toward a common goal, building relationships of mutual reliance that grew out of necessity. Military alliances draw on commonalities in ideas about manhood and created a homosocial world of masculine comradery that facilitated intercultural cooperation. Although misunderstandings could and did arise and each might blame the other for wartime failures, the experience of fighting alongside one another created intensely personal bonds that greatly influenced the southern geopolitical landscape. Matthew Jennings argues that the collision of British, African, and Indian cultures of violence reshaped all three. Indeed new cultures of violence emerged out of the conflicts that rent the region. Even though conflict was widespread and destructive, warfare continued to reflect diverse motives and a degree of interreliance that prevents us from viewing intercultural contests in a monolithic way, and demonstrates both the weakness of the British and the ambiguity inherent in cross-cultural interactions. Stephen Feeley explores the complexity of a war in which some Tuscaroras and other Indian allies fought against some European settlers, even while other Tuscaroras strove for neutrality. Regardless of their military stance, all Tuscaroras undertook vigorous diplomatic efforts to position themselves for an eventual peace. Rather than focus on battles and skirmishes, he analyzes the diplomatic swings in a multisided contest to establish terms of orderly contact, trade, and occupation of land. James Taylor Carson further demonstrates the difficulties that arise if modern scholars try to see the parties of this complex war as part of two unitary and naturally opposing groups. Historians, he argues, need to rethink categories such as Indian and European, because these are themselves a creation of colonization and do not reflect the reality that people lived.

For the British the importance of the Indian trade to the economy raised additional concerns. Early settlers struggled to find ways of making the economy a success, when crops with which they were more familiar like tobacco and sugar failed to thrive in the region. Consequently the Indian trade played a significant role in the development of the new colonies, and its political significance should not be underestimated. Jessica Stern focuses her study on the problems of regulating the trade. She demonstrates that Carolina's changing policies regarding the trade reflected differing economic ideologies. Free-trade philosophies, favored by many settlers interested in making quick profits from the Indian trade, initially allowed for a loosely regulated system of exchange. As a reaction to the uncertainty and violence that stemmed from such a trade, though, other factions pushed for stricter laws based on balance of trade ideology and a suspicion of traders.

In addition to the Indian trade, settlers pursued a variety of other economic options. The story of the evolution of rice cultivation in South Carolina is relatively well known. Yet other strategies have often remained neglected. The North Carolina economy in particular is often overlooked or written off as a failure. Bradford J. Wood, however, reevaluates this approach in his study of the career of Thomas Pollock. Although not as successful as wealthier South Carolina elites, Pollock and other planters tried to make the Albemarle more like other plantation societies and followed models developed elsewhere. They failed to secure enough bound labor or to develop a valuable export staple but did manage to build plantations that, if not as large as they desired, still operated on a significant scale and were at least partly integrated into the larger Atlantic economy. They were ultimately more successful in creating a unified settler society and establishing a racial hierarchy that more closely resembled that of other plantation societies. Mark G. Hanna further integrates the Carolina economy into the Atlantic World by demonstrating the importance of clandestine trade and piracy to the nascent marketplaces of the region. In the early period, pirates, like unscrupulous traders, were welcomed by settlers desperate for goods and willing to deal with anyone who could advance their economy. The settlers' extralegal trading produced conflicts between leading settlers and the proprietors, while masking more serious animosities between those for and against proprietary rule.

Political conflicts were as prevalent as economic ones (and of course the two could not be separated from one another). Colonists competed with one another for control of local governments and battled with the proprietors over who should be able to shape the development of their societies and economies. Christine Styrna Devine turns her attention to the often-neglected story of political strife in North Carolina. North Carolina was particularly riven by factions. The Cary's Rebellion left the colony vulnerable to Indian war and unable to defend itself. Devine argues though that in the wake of the war, a faction of prominent Anglican merchant-planters from the Albemarle managed to establish a relatively stable and cohesive political bloc that dominated the colony's political scene for nearly two decades. This stability may have contributed to North Carolina's ability to avoid the constitutional upheaval that struck its southern neighbor in the wake of its Indian war. South Carolina, in contrast, saw a major revolt against the proprietors in 1719. Hanno T. Scheerer argues that the overthrow of the proprietors was not actually about the need for military protection in the wake of the Yamasee War. Instead colonists were upset about efforts by the proprietors to repeal laws favored by local elites that allowed them to pay off debts from the war and to provide for their own security. The revolt, at its core, was about protecting the assembly's constitutional position and political power.

The Carolinas cannot be separated from the larger British Empire of which they were a part, or from the even broader Atlantic World in which they struggled for a place. Integration into this larger matrix of relationships and contests shaped how the British approached colonization. The Carolinas maintained particularly close ties to other British colonies. In addition to trading relationships, the colonies drew settlers and laborers who came from other places and brought their experiences and cultures to their new communities. The connection between South Carolina and Barbados is well known. Justin Roberts and Ian Beamish expand on this familiar tale, though, demonstrating that South Carolina was in fact part of a larger circum-Caribbean world. Carolina was just one of several colonies created by the Barbadians, and these earlier colonizing efforts informed the ways that Barbadians approached settlement in the Carolinas. In addition, although Barbadians were never a majority among settlers, they played a more significant role in the creation of the colony than their numbers would suggest. Barbadian migrants possessed substantial social and economic capital, which allowed them to emerge as leading planters, while other island residents who did not migrate contributed capital and designs for settlement that shaped the evolution of the colony. Less well known than the Barbadian connection is the relationship between the Carolinas and the Bahamas. Alexander Moore illustrates the close ties between the colonies, which shared the same proprietors and interacted regularly. The colonies suffered similar problems of proprietary mismanagement and threats from international rivals and pirates, and they overthrew their proprietors about the same time. Indeed the successful 1719 "revolution" in South Carolina against the proprietors had a precedent in the earlier Bahamas antiproprietary revolt. Carolina's wide-reaching connections were not limited to other British territories however. Ultimately the largest number of migrants to arrive in South Carolina in the eighteenth century came not from British territories but from Africa. Gregory E. O'Malley reevaluates the migration of Africans to the Carolinas based on information available through the Transatlantic Slave Trade Database and his own research on the intercolonial slave trade. He argues that the movement of Africans to the colonies followed convoluted lines that changed over time. No one particular African ethnic group was dominant in shaping slave culture. As a result, adaptation, negotiation and hybridization must have been vital parts of the transfer of African folkways to the Carolinas.

As these essays often illustrate, the early Carolinas shared much with other places on the shores of the Atlantic. Along the treacherous coast of North Carolina, in interior areas dominated by indigenous populations, and even in Charles Town before the takeoff of the rice economy, transatlantic connections may have seemed relatively limited. Still, the Atlantic served as an important conduit, and the Carolinas had much in common with other Atlantic colonies. After all, without the ocean itself, it is impossible to imagine the cultural collisions that inspired so much innovation and so much tension. Connections to Atlantic and British imperial historiographies also serve as reminders that these essays tell us about the dynamics of the early modern world, even as they focus on specific case studies in the early history of two British colonies. In many ways, the difficulties faced by the peoples of Carolina in the early decades of the eighteenth century functioned as a microcosm of the challenges involved in early modern imperial expansion. Early modern empires struggled with many uncertainties in a contingent world, but to the detriment of many of their subjects, they ultimately succeeded in consolidating and rationalizing the processes of colonization and conquest. As we examine colonists and natives fighting one another, metropolitan governance unraveling, economic opportunities shifting, and people adapting to the changes of these years in myriad ways, it becomes possible to see both the precariousness of European dominance and the emergence of a new imperial order. In other words, three hundred years ago the existence of Carolina could not be taken for granted, because Carolina had to be created, and its place and meaning remained contested.

Notes

1. Christoph von Graffenried, *Account of the Founding of New Bern*, ed. Vincent H. Todd (Raleigh, N.C.: Edwards and Brougton, 1920), 263–70; Christopher Gale to an unnamed sibling, November 2, 1711, in *CRNC*, 1:826. See also Stephen Delbert Feeley, "Tuscarora Trails: Indian Migrations, War, and Constructions of Colonial Frontiers" (Ph.D. diss., College of William and Mary, 2007).

2. The geography of these events can be found in contemporary maps. See especially maps 11 and 17. Map 17 refers to Catechna as "Hancock's Town."

3. Steven J. Oatis, *A Colonial Complex: South Carolina's Frontiers in the Era of the Yamasee War, 1680–1730* (Lincoln: University of Nebraska Press, 2004), 124–26.

4. Oatis, *Colonial Complex*, 126. On the Yamasee War, see also: Verner W. Crane, *The Southern Frontier, 1670–1732* (1928; reprint, Tuscaloosa: University of Alabama Press, 2004), 162–86; Alan Gallay, *The Indian Slave Trade: The Rise of the English Empire in the American South, 1670–1717* (New Haven: Yale University Press, 2002), 315–44; Steven C. Hahn, *The Invention of the Creek Nation, 1670–1763* (Lincoln: University of Nebraska Press, 2004), 81–120; Joseph M. Hall Jr., *Zamumo's Gifts: Indian-European Exchange in the Colonial Southeast* (Philadelphia: University of Pennsylvania Press, 2009), 117–44; William L. Ramsey, *The Yamasee War: A Study of Culture, Economy, and Conflict in the Colonial South* (Lincoln: University of Nebraska Press, 2008); Bradley Scott Schrager, "Yamasee

Indians and the Challenge of Spanish and English Colonialism in the North American Southeast, 1660–1715" (Ph.D. diss., Northwestern University, 2001).

5. See, among others: Philip D. Morgan, *Slave Counterpoint: Black Culture in the Eighteenth-Century Chesapeake and Lowcountry* (Chapel Hill: University of North Carolina Press, 1998); Peter A. Coclanis, *The Shadow of A Dream: Economic Life and Death in the South Carolina Low Country, 1760–1920* (New York: Oxford University Press, 1989); S. Max Edelson, *Plantation Enterprise in Colonial South Carolina* (Cambridge: Harvard University Press, 2006); Joyce E. Chaplin, *"An Anxious Pursuit": Agricultural Innovation and Modernity in the Lower South, 1730–1815* (Chapel Hill: University of North Carolina Press, 1993); Robert Olwell, *Masters, Slaves, and Subjects: The Culture of Power in the South Carolina Low Country, 1740–1790* (Ithaca: Cornell University Press, 1998); Emma Hart, *Building Charleston: Town and Society in the Eighteenth-Century British Atlantic World* (Charlottesville: University of Virginia Press, 2010); Bradford J. Wood, *This Remote Part of the World: Regional Formation in Lower Cape Fear, North Carolina, 1725–1775* (Columbia: University of South Carolina Press, 2004); and Jon Sensbach, *A Separate Canaan: The Making of An Afro-Moravian World in North Carolina, 1763–1840* (Chapel Hill: University of North Carolina Press, 1998).

6. Gallay, *Indian Slave Trade;* Hahn, *Invention of the Creek Nation;* Oatis, *Colonial Complex;* Ramsey, *Yamasee War.* In addition to these works directly related to the Yamasee War, other important scholarly works have focused more attention on the native peoples of the southeast. Some recent examples include: Eric E. Bowne, *The Westo Indians: Slave Traders of the Early Colonial South* (Tuscaloosa: University of Alabama Press, 2005); Robbie Ethridge and Sheri M. Shuck-Hall, eds., *Mapping the Mississippian Shatter Zone: Colonial Indian Slave Trade and Regional Instability in the American South* (Lincoln: University of Nebraska Press, 2009); Hall, *Zamumo's Gifts;* Matthew Jennings, *New Worlds of Violence: Cultures and Conquests in the Early American Southeast* (Knoxville: University of Tennessee Press, 2011); Michelle LeMaster, *Brothers Born of One Mother: British–Native American Relations in the Colonial Southeast* (Charlottesville: University of Virginia Press, 2012). A number of older works remain important as well. See: James H. Merrell, *The Indians' New World: Catawbas and Their Neighbors from European Contact through the Era of Removal* (Chapel Hill: University of North Carolina Press, 1989); J. Leitch Wright Jr., *The Only Land They Knew: The Tragic Story of the American Indians in the Old South* (New York: Macmillan, 1981); Gregory A. Waselkov, Peter H. Wood, and Tom Hatley, eds., *Powhatan's Mantle: Indians in the Colonial Southeast,* rev. and expanded ed. (Lincoln: University of Nebraska Press, 2006).

7. On South Carolina during these years, see Peter H. Wood, *Black Majority: Negroes in Colonial South Carolina from 1670 through the Stono Rebellion* (New York: Norton, 1975); Jack P. Greene, Rosemary Brana-Shute, and Randy J. Sparks, eds., *Money, Trade, and Power: The Evolution of Colonial South Carolina's Plantation Society* (Columbia: University of South Carolina Press, 2001); Converse D. Clowse, *Economic Beginnings in Colonial South Carolina* (Columbia: University of South Carolina Press, 1971); M. Eugene Sirmans, *Colonial South Carolina: A Political History, 1663–1763* (Chapel Hill: University of North Carolina Press, 1966);

L. H. Roper, *Conceiving Carolina: Proprietors, Planters, and Plots, 1662–1729* (New York: Palgrave MacMillan, 2004); Robert M. Weir, *Colonial South Carolina: A History* (Columbia: University of South Carolina Press, 1983). On North Carolina during the same period, see: Hugh T. Lefler and William S. Powell, *Colonial North Carolina: A History* (New York: Scribner's and Sons, 1973); Donna J. Spindel, *Crime and Society in North Carolina, 1663–1776* (Baton Rouge: Louisiana State University Press, 1989); Kirsten Fischer, *Suspect Relations: Sex, Race, and Resistance in Colonial North Carolina* (Ithaca: Cornell University Press, 2002).

8. Noeleen McIlvenna, *A Very Mutinous People: The Struggle for North Carolina, 1660–1713* (Chapel Hill: University of North Carolina Press, 2009). For a critique of McIlvenna's problematic work, see Bradford J. Wood, "Struggling to Find Proprietary North Carolina," *Reviews in American History* 38, no. 4 (December 2010): 601–6.

9. Lefler and Powell, *Colonial North Carolina*. A number of well-researched and helpful but unpublished dissertations also cover this period. Some of these include Herbert Paschal, "Proprietary North Carolina: A Study in Colonial Government" (Ph.D. diss., University of North Carolina, 1961); Charles B. Lowry, "Class, Politics, Rebellion, and Regional Development in Proprietary North Carolina" (Ph.D. diss., University of Florida, 1975); Jacquelyn Wolf, "The Proud and the Poor: The Social Organization of Leadership in Proprietary North Carolina, 1663–1729" (Ph.D. diss., University of Pennsylvania, 1977); Christine Styrna Devine, "The Winds of War and Change: The Impact of the Tuscarora War on Proprietary North Carolina, 1690–1729" (Ph.D. diss., College of William and Mary, 1990); Charles Greer Suttlemyre, "Proprietary Policies and the Development of North Carolina, 1663–1729" (Ph.D. diss., Oxford University, 1991); Kristi Rutz-Robbins, "Colonial Commerce: Race, Class and Gender in a Local Economy, Albemarle, North Carolina, 1663–1729" (Ph.D. diss., Michigan State University, 2003); and Feeley, "Tuscarora Trails."

10. For work on native groups in the North Carolina tidewater, see Shannon Lee Dawdy, "The Meherrin's Secret History of the Dividing Line," *NCHR* 72 (October 1995): 386–415; Patrick Garrow, *The Mattamuskett Documents: A Study in Social History* (Raleigh: Office of State Archaeology, Division of Archives and History, North Carolina Department of Cultural Resources, 1975); Michelle LeMaster, "In the 'Scolding Houses': Indians and the Law in Eastern North Carolina, 1684–1760," *NCHR* 83 (April 2006): 193–232. On the Tuscarora War, see Feeley, "Tuscarora Trails."

11. The historiography on the expansion of the British Empire after 1689 is far too substantial to list here, but a good overview can be found in the essays contained in P. J. Marshall, ed., *The Oxford History of the British Empire: The Eighteenth Century* (Oxford: Oxford University Press, 1998). For a few important studies that emphasize the significance of changes within the empire in the decades after 1689, see: Linda Colley, *Britons: Forging the Nation, 1707–1837* (London: Yale University Press, 1992); John Brewer, *The Sinews of Power: War, Money, and the English State, 1688–1783* (London: Routledge, 1989); P. J. Cain and A. G. Hopkins, *British Imperialism, Innovation, and Expansion, 1688–1914* (London: Longman, 1994).

12. This does not mean that all the older British colonies had become static or stable by every measure by this time but over time the colonies generally tended toward stability. This interpretation follows the logic articulated in Jack P. Greene, *Pursuits of Happiness: The Social Development of Early Modern British Colonies and the Formation of American Culture* (Chapel Hill: University of North Carolina Press, 1988). For example, the Chesapeake colonies appeared to be considerably more stable by the end of the seventeenth century. The less typical New England colonies seemed to have achieved a relatively high degree of stability at an earlier point.

13. On populations in the Carolinas, see: Peter H. Wood, "The Changing Population of the Colonial South: An Overview by Race and Region, 1685–1790," in *Powhatan's Mantle*, rev. and expanded ed., ed. Waselkov et al. (Lincoln: University of Nebraska Press, 2006), 57–132.

14. The presence of a culturally diverse free immigrant population underscores some of the many significant similarities between the Carolinas and the settlements referred to as the Middle Colonies, which were also established at roughly the same time and share some of the same issues with proprietary government. Scholarship on the Middle Colonies has flourished in recent years. The best work on the Middle Colonies has been illuminating to all scholars who study British American colonies, but some historians have made assertions about the distinctiveness of the Middle Colonies that may not be sustainable once the Carolinas have been more fully studied. For a recent synthesis of work on the Middle Colonies, see: Ned Landsman, *Crossroad of Empire: The Middle Colonies in British North America* (Baltimore: Johns Hopkins University Press, 2010). On the Middle Colonies, see: John Smolenski, *Friends and Strangers: The Making of a Creole Culture in Colonial Pennsylvania* (Philadelphia: University of Pennsylvania, 2012); David Preston, *The Texture of Contact: European and Indian Settlers Communities on the Frontiers of Iroquoia, 1667–1783* (Lincoln: University of Nebraska Press, 2009); Brendan McConville, *These Daring Disturbers of the Peace: The Struggle for Property and Power in Early New Jersey* (Philadelphia: University of Pennsylvania Press, 2003); Patricia Bonomi, *The Lord Cornbury Scandal: The Politics of Reputation in British America* (Chapel Hill: University of North Carolina Press, 2000); James H. Merrell, *Into the American Woods: Negotiators on the Pennsylvania Frontier* (New York: Norton, 2000); Marianne S. Wokeck, *Trade in Strangers: The Beginnings of Mass Migration to North America* (Philadelphia: University of Pennsylvania Press, 1999); Alan Tully, *Forming American Politics: Ideals, Interests, and Institutions in Colonial New York and Pennsylvania* (Baltimore: Johns Hopkins University Press, 1994).

15. One outstanding study of a European cultural minority in the Carolinas during this period can be found in Bertrand Van Ruymbeke, *From New Babylon to Eden: The Huguenots and Their Migration to Colonial South Carolina* (Columbia: University of South Carolina Press, 2006). No other religious or ethnic minority among the settler population of the Carolinas during this period has received comparable attention.

16. Wood, *Black Majority*; Morgan, *Slave Counterpoint*; Edelson, *Plantation Enterprise*; Gregory E. O'Malley, "Beyond the Middle Passage: Slave Migration from the Caribbean to North America, 1619–1807," *WMQ* 64, no. 1 (January 2009):

125–72; Jeffrey D. Crow, Paul D. Escott, and Flora J. Hatley, *A History of African Americans in North Carolina* (Raleigh: Division of Archives and History, 1992).

17. Some of the most valuable evidence about these earliest settlements comes from map 2, but for other early maps showing these settlements, see maps 6, 8, and 9.

18. Steven C. A. Pincus, *1688: The First Modern Revolution* (New Haven: Yale University Press, 2009). On the reorientation of the British Empire as a result of the Glorious Revolution, see also Owen Stanwood, *The English Empire Reformed: English America in the Age of the Glorious Revolution* (Philadelphia: University of Pennsylvania Press, 2011).

19. For some discussions of the aftermath of the Glorious Revolution in the colonies, see: Jack P. Greene, "The Glorious Revolution and the British Empire," in *The Revolution of 1688–89: Changing Perspectives*, ed. Lois Schwoerer (Cambridge, U.K.: Cambridge University Press, 1992), 260–71; Richard S. Dunn, "The Glorious Revolution and America," in *The Oxford History of the British Empire: The Origins of Empire*, ed. Nicholas Canny (Oxford: Oxford University Press, 1998), 445–66; Craig Yirush, *Settlers, Liberty, and Empire: The Roots of Early American Political Theory, 1675–1775* (Cambridge, U.K.: Cambridge University Press, 2011), 51–80.

20. The most detailed discussion of the fiscal-military state is John Brewer, *The Sinews of Power: War, Money, and the English State, 1688–1783* (Cambridge: Harvard University Press, 1988). A concise discussion of some of these developments can be found in Patrick O'Brien, "Inseparable Connections: Trade, Economy, Fiscal State, and the Expansion of Empire, 1688–1815," in *The Oxford History of the British Empire: The Eighteenth Century*, ed. Marshall, 53–77. The classic study of the financial revolution is P. G. M. Dickson, *The Financial Revolution in England: A Study in the Development of Popular Credit, 1688–1756* (New York: St. Martin's, 1967). For a broader interpretation that emphasizes the centrality of these developments for the history of the British Empire, see Cain and Hopkins, *British Imperialism: Innovation and Expansion*, esp. 60–75, 84–91, 101–3.

21. On some of these efforts at centralization, see Ian K. Steele, *Politics of Colonial Policy: The Board of Trade in Colonial Administration, 1696–1720* (Oxford: Clarendon, 1968); Michael Garibaldi Hall, *Edward Randolph and the American Colonies, 1676–1703* (Chapel Hill: University of North Carolina Press, 1960); Stephen Saunders Webb, *Lord Churchill's Coup: The Anglo-American Empire and the Glorious Revolution Reconsidered* (Syracuse, N.Y.: Syracuse University Press, 1998).

22. See Yirush, *Settlers, Liberty, and Empire*, 64–65, 90–95, 186–87; Elizabeth Mancke, "Chartered Enterprises and the Evolution of the British Atlantic World," in *The Creation of the British Atlantic World*, ed. Mancke and Carole Shammas (Baltimore: Johns Hopkins University Press, 2005), 237–62.

23. The most detailed account of this event can be found in John Alexander Moore, "Royalizing South Carolina: The Revolution of 1719 and the Evolution of Early South Carolina Government" (Ph.D. diss., University of South Carolina, 1991).

24. Robert Ritchie, *Captain Kidd and the War against the Pirates* (Cambridge: Harvard University Press, 1989); Mark Gillies Hanna, "The Pirate Nest: The Impact

of Piracy on Newport, Rhode Island and Charles Town, South Carolina, 1670–1730" (Ph.D. diss., Harvard University, 2006).

25. Jack P. Greene, "Negotiated Authorities: The Problem of Governance in the Extended Polities of the Early Modern Atlantic World," in *Negotiated Authorities: Essays in Colonial Political and Constitutional History* (Charlottesville: University of Virginia Press, 1994), 1–24; Christine Daniels and Michael V. Kennedy, eds., *Negotiated Empires: Centers and Peripheries in the Americas, 1500–1820* (New York: Routledge, 2002).

26. Jack P. Greene, *The Quest for Power: The Lower Houses of Assembly in the Southern Royal Colonies, 1689–1776* (Chapel Hill: University of North Carolina Press, 1963).

27. Yirush, *Settlers, Liberty, and Empire,* 15–23, 51–112. Quotation on 16.

28. Gallay, *Indian Slave Trade;* Paul E. Hoffman, *Florida's Frontiers* (Bloomington: University of Indiana Press, 2002); Daniel H. Usner Jr., *Indians, Settlers, and Slaves in a Frontier Exchange Economy: The Lower Mississippi Valley before 1783* (Chapel Hill: University of North Carolina Press, 1992); David J. Weber, *The Spanish Frontier in North America* (New Haven: Yale University Press, 1992); Patricia Dillon Woods, *French-Indian Relations on the Southern Frontier, 1699–1762* (Ann Arbor, Mich.: UMI Research Press, 1980).

29. Maps provide contemporary perspectives on these imperial rivalries. See, for example, maps 13, 15, 17, 24, 27, and 36.

30. On the Spanish in Florida, their Indian relations, and the devastation wrought by the British, see: Amy Turner Bushnell, *Situado and Sabana: Spain's Support System for the Presidio and Mission Provinces of Florida* (Athens: University of Georgia Press, 1994); John H. Hann, *Apalachee: The Land Between the Rivers* (Gainesville: University Press of Florida, 1988), and *A History of the Timucua Indians and Missions* (Gainesville: University Press of Florida, 1996); John H. Hann and Bonnie McEwan, *The Apalachee Indians and Mission San Luis* (Tallahassee: University Press of Florida, 1998); Paul E. Hoffman, *Florida's Frontiers,* Bonnie McEwan, ed., *The Spanish Missions of La Florida* (Tallahassee: University Press of Florida, 1993); Weber, *Spanish Frontier in North America* (New Haven: Yale University Press); John E. Worth, *The Timucuan Chiefdoms of Spanish Florida,* 2 vols. (Gainesville: University Press of Florida, 1998).

31. Bowne, *Westo Indians;* Crane, *Southern Frontier;* Hahn, *Invention of the Creek Nation;* Tom Hatley, *The Dividing Paths: Cherokees and South Carolinians Through the Era of Revolution* (New York: Oxford University Press, 1993); James H. Merrell, *The Indians' New World: Catawbas and their Neighbors from European Contact through the Era of Removal* (New York: Norton, 1989); Gene Waddell, *Indians of the South Carolina Lowcountry, 1562–1751* (Columbia: University of South Carolina Press, 1980).

32. See Robert M. Weir, "'The Harmony We Were Famous For': An Interpretation of Pre-revolutionary South Carolina Politics," *WMQ* 26, no. 4 (October 1969): 473–501.

33. A. Roger Ekirch, *"Poor Carolina": Politics and Society in Colonial North Carolina, 1729–1776* (Chapel Hill: University of North Carolina Press, 1981); Wood, *This Remote Part of the World,* 145–73.

34. On wealth and gentility in early Charles Town, see Coclanis, *Shadow of a Dream;* Richard Waterhouse, *A New World Gentry: The Making of a Merchant and Planter Class in South Carolina, 1670–1770* (New York: Garland, 1989); Edward Pearson, "'Planters Full of Money': The Self-Fashioning of the Eighteenth-Century South Carolina Elite," in *Money, Trade, and Power,* 299–321; George C. Rogers Jr., *Charleston in the Age of the Pinckneys* (Norman: University of Oklahoma Press, 1969).

35. James Merrell, "Indians New World: The Catawba Experience," *WMQ* 41, no. 4 (October 1984): 537–65.

Part One
Backgrounds

Defining Carolina

Cartography and Colonization in the North American Southeast, 1657–1733

S. MAX EDELSON

As the English colonized Carolina, claiming and settling land within its changing boundaries, maps captured the transformation of a contested imperial borderland into one of British America's most populous and economically important regions. These images, produced over the course of eighty years that witnessed England's implantation of provincial societies around the rim of the western Atlantic, each offered a distinct view of Carolina as a settled place. Viewed in sequence, the maps render particular coastlines, mountain ranges, and rivers with increasing consistency, but they also show the space they called "Carolina" from a bewildering variety of visual perspectives. These images rotated the cardinal orientation from which the viewer beheld the land and ran the gamut of scale from the full breadth of the hemisphere to the high resolution of Charlestown's cityscape. Through them, one can see South Carolina and North Carolina take on familiar forms as clearly bounded territories, but the diversity within this collection of Carolina maps does not suggest progress toward a single, stable representation of geographic space.

Instead these maps reflect the aspirations, imaginations, and fears of English colonizers during moments of intense imperial competition and Anglo-Indian conflict in the early modern southeast. They record a process of imperial claims making in which cartographers articulated the extent of English (and, after the Act of Union of 1707, British) sovereignty on the continent and reinforced such assertions by documenting actual occupation. As Carolina's founders envisioned, established, and expanded the colony, these maps cleared a space for their ambitions and celebrated settlers' initial successes at taking possession of the land. The Yamasee War of 1715 reversed the colony's expansion to the south in a series of devastating Indian attacks on the plantation frontier. In addition to triggering the fall of the Proprietary government in 1719, the exposure of South Carolina's territorial vulnerability through this violent conflict undermined the idea of a continental range for English settlement and trade and posed a crisis of representation for the cartography of the colony. A new mode of mapmaking, guided by a vision of an integrated mainland advocated by the Board of Trade, sought to secure Carolina's borders against the strategic threats posed by Spanish Florida and French Louisiana after the war. This essay concludes with a brief analysis of some of the first of these new imperial maps, created in the 1720s to describe the defense of a reconstituted southern frontier at Fort King George on the Altamaha River in present-day Georgia. Together these images describe the spatial convergence of the new world *imperium* that Britain asserted through its explorations, charters, and relationships with Indian nations and the *dominium* that it maintained by ruling over discrete territories that had been transformed into civil spaces for English settlement, law, and production.

In the sixteenth century Gerardus Mercator mapped the spine of the Appalachian Mountains, and Abraham Ortelius labeled the whole of the North American southeast as Florida. French and Spanish attempts to settle the southeastern Atlantic coast produced cartographic artifacts of these failed colonization efforts (such as the short-lived sixteenth-century settlement at "Charles-Fort" at Port Royal), but there was no place known as "Carolina" before 1663 (map 1).[1] The first English Carolina grant, issued by Charles I to Sir Robert Heath in 1629, introduced the term, which drifted into European consciousness as a name for this particular part of the continent. Carolina came into being more than three decades later as a colonial outpost implanted during reign of its namesake sovereign, Charles II, at a particularly expansive moment of English engagement with the New World.

Carolina became more clearly defined as a place as the continent as a whole became more finely articulated into regions on European maps. In the late sixteenth and early seventeenth centuries, maps of eastern North America noted broad areas to which rival empires had staked their claims. Spanish Florida stretched well beyond the peninsula and Gulf Coast to encompass the entire southeast; English Virginia occupied the center of the seaboard; and English Norumbega and New France marked out prospective English and French territories at shifting positions along the northeastern Atlantic coast. Nicholas Comberford's manuscript map, titled "The South Part of Virginia[,] Now the North Part of Carolina" (1657), was the first to name Carolina, but its subtitle was inked in after the fact to register how the charters of 1663 and 1665 had rechristened the islands and inlets it depicts along the Outer Banks (map 2). At the close of the seventeenth century, England's most prolific cartographer, Herman Moll, still saw North America etched in three great divisions—Florida, New France, and Virginia—that endured as fundamental regions despite English (as well as Swedish and Dutch) efforts to lay claim to North American colonies. To Moll's categorical mind Carolina was a "part of Florida" in geographic fact, regardless of which kingdom flew a flag along its coast. Looking back from the early eighteenth century, William Byrd II still saw Carolina and other mainland colonies founded later in the seventeenth century occupying land "carved out of Virginia," once a "General Name" for English North America.[2]

"The South Part of Virginia" focuses on a discrete stretch of coastline featuring the mouths of rivers that vanish off the frame into an undefined interior. What had once been the heart of the Virginia colony during the English attempt to settle Roanoke Island some seventy years before was, by the 1650s, a marginal area written off as a "Swampy Wilderness" at the edge of the "Southern Virginia Sea." This first cartographic view of Carolina anticipated a place that had not yet been settled, yet the name adhered to the region around Albemarle Sound into the 1670s, when the Quaker evangelist George Fox referred to settlers near Roanoke as the "People of Carolina."[3]

Only after Charles II chartered Carolina in 1663 did a new body of maps emerge that featured a separate Carolina colony to the south. Promotional cartography was part of its conceptualization from the very beginning. The very first meeting of the Lords Proprietors included a resolution that "mapps be printed of the Province" to "invyte" prospective settlers with images of the land that was to be offered on generous terms to freeholder colonists. Joseph Moxon's *Americae Septentrionalis Pars* (1664) first inscribed the Carolina toponym—that is, the text "Carolina" situated in geographic space—on a published map (map 3). The colony took its place in print between Virginia and Florida, opening a new space in which to anticipate English colonial expansion.[4] The second published map to name Carolina, Robert Horne's "Carolina Described" (1666) was the first to picture it as a distinctive place that stretched well to the south of Albemarle Sound (map 4). Drawing its geographic information from William Hilton's exploratory voyages in 1662 and 1663, Horne's map was published with his *A Brief Description of the Province of Carolina* (1666) to promote the Lords Proprietors' new colony in images as well as words. The map depicts three coastal river systems viewed from the east. Colonizers sought inlets along the coast that promised safe anchorage as well as water routes pressing deep into the interior, and Horne marked soundings of the depths of coastal waters that identified safe passages into each of three potential harbor sites identified on the map. In addition to Albemarle, Horne mapped the Lower Cape Fear site of the first Proprietary settlement, the short-lived 1664 "Charles Town." To the south he located Port Royal, a long-standing object of interest for France and Spain and the intended destination of the English settlement expedition in 1670. Nowhere along this delineated coastline does Horne show what would become Charlestown Harbor or the rivers that form its peninsula. A similar manuscript chart in the Blathwayt atlas, a compendium of maps assembled for the Lords of Trade and Plantations around 1683, offers the same compressed, and to our eyes distorted, view of the coast between Roanoke River and Hilton Head.[5]

As Carolina colonists arrived in the 1660s and 1670s, they realized the English claim to the region by inhabiting it. European mapmakers re-etched their copperplates to insert "Carolina" between the dominant toponyms of Florida and Virginia that had defined southeastern North America for a century.[6]

With the Cape Fear settlement abandoned by 1667, the English reestablished Carolina in the Cusabo Indian country of Kiawah in 1670. Richard Blome's *A General Map of Carolina* (1673) conflates the first Charles Town, planted and abandoned in the 1660s at Cape Fear, with the new Charles Town on Ashley River, although this later, permanent settlement site was located more than one hundred miles further south along the coast (map 5). Such "errors" were signs that mapmakers were engaged in a process of synthesis as they struggled to place the names of reported sites in stable locations along southeastern edge of Atlantic North America. As mapmaking became part of the apparatus of provincial government, surveyors produced manuscript maps that located the Ashley and Cooper Rivers and the fortified tip of the peninsula, laid out the land for settlement, and provided source materials that shaped the post-exploration settlement phase of the colony's cartography.[7]

John Ogilby's *A New Discription of Carolina* (ca. 1672) was a landmark image that integrated the spatial knowledge generated by settlement with prevailing geographic views of the continent (map 6). When the writer and cartographer approached Peter Colleton for source materials, this influential Lord Proprietor volunteered to assemble existing maps of Cape Fear, Albemarle, and Port Royal drafted during the previous decade's explorations and "draw them into one." He asked Proprietary secretary John Locke to write a "discourse to bee added to this map" that might lure new settlers "without seeming to come from us."[8] Such texts enhanced the credibility of cartographic images derived from firsthand observation with landscape description steeped in humanistic learning. They promoted a campaign to populate Carolina and attempted to conceal the proprietors' interest in doing so by associating geographic description with the dispassionate inquiry of natural history.

Ogilby retraced the contour of the southern coastline between Port Royal and Cape Fear and, for the first time in a published map, situated Charles Town close to the spot where the Ashley and Cooper Rivers converge. An inset copied from manuscripts by the provincial surveyor, John Culpeper, reveals details about the new colonial capital, including soundings that mark out a passage over the bar to its harbor, coastal inlets to creeks that snake into the interior, and the location of the town at its original site on the southern bank of the Ashley River (map 7).[9] Carolina's vast coastal plain, more than one hundred square miles square, appears emblazoned with the coat of arms of Charles II. The *New Discription* explains how geography prepared this lush land to be planted, traversed, and defended. Although Carolina's extent reached across a full degree of latitude on the globe, this vast area could be drawn into the English Atlantic economy with its "five or six great Navigable Rivers, that empty themselves into the Sea," each of which connected an extensive new territory to maritime trade.

The map's graphic cartouche depicts industrious, civil Indians, including a figure that closely resembles the bow-wielding Susquehanna Indian wearing a wolf's-head necklace featured on John Smith's 1612 *Virginia* map. Settlers traveled "singly and unarm'd" through these woods, and the Indians they met along their paths stood "still till they are gone by, civilly Saluting them as they pass." Such gentle people posed no barrier to taking up the land the map pictured.[10] Its toponyms, however, make no reference to the presence of these Cusabo Indians in the lowcountry, although Spanish mission villages, copied from earlier maps by Willem Blaeu and Jocodos Hondius, populate the banks of the River May (an early name for the Savannah) all the way to the chimerical "Ashley Lake" in the interior. Anthony Ashley Cooper, Carolina's leading Lord Proprietor, gave Ogilby a new list of "nominations of the rivers" to insert in place of native names that the colonists were already in the habit of using. These new names celebrated individual proprietors and populated the countryside with English-sounding places. The renaming of Cusabo country was a priority for Ashley, who tersely corrected the governor when he referred to the colony by its indigenous name, "Kyawah."[11]

Joel Gascoyne's *A New Map of the Country of Carolina* (1682) pictured the English peopling of South Carolina twelve years after its first settlement (map 8).[12] Like Ogilby's *New Discription,* the map was published with a promotional tract that sang the praises of Carolina's temperate nature, and the proprietors paid Gascoyne for producing it. Like the text it illustrated, the map's lure for prospective immigrants was its depiction of available land within the colony's vast domain. The map located the site of "Olde Charles towne" that had appeared on the inset of the Ogilby map as well as that of the newly fortified city, replanted across the Ashley River on the tip of the peninsula. Gascoyne's *New Map* was the first to show the progress of European occupation by indicating where recently settled plantations were and who owned them. These amounted to just thirty-three sites, all along the Ashley and Cooper Rivers and their tributaries. Drawing on new geographic information conveyed through firsthand experience and deeper exploratory journeys into Indian country, Gascoyne's map depicted the colony's rivers with new precision. The emerging lowcountry was represented, for the first time, as nestled along the banks of a compact network of waterways that offered prospective planters good land and, because they converged on the harbor, easy water carriage to a thriving central town, port, and capital.

Carolina was a rough new American province, but in Gascoyne's map it had already taken on English characteristics of place that featured estates ruled by wealthy men and names that evoked English rather than Indian sovereignty. Divided into counties named for leading proprietors (Albemarle, Clarendon, Craven, Berkeley, and Colleton), the *New Map of the Country of Carolina* lacked signs of Indian inhabitants. It locates only the villages of the Westos and Combahees along with "Cafitaciqui," the powerful interior polity encountered by de Soto in the 1540s that soon disappeared from English maps as it had, many years before, from the landscape itself.[13] The Westos appear to live well beyond the compact pale of settled Carolina, far up the River May about one hundred miles from Charlestown, and more than fifty miles from the last English estate on the map. Such distance belied how tightly this Indian group was bound into a network of European trading and slave raiding. Nor does the map acknowledge the violence associated with the war that dispersed the Westos in 1680 as English trade shifted to the Savannah Indians. The modest but growing English presence in Carolina, by linking Indian groups into strategic alliances with colonists and to the Atlantic economy through trade, was having a broader impact into the interior than the map revealed.[14]

The most important map of the colony in Carolina's next decade—John Thornton and Robert Morden's *New Map of the Ch[ie]f Rivers, Bays, Creeks, Harbours, and Settlements, in South Carolina* (ca. 1695)—made good its claim to have been "Actually Surveyed" (map 10). It drew on an earlier manuscript map composed by Maurice Mathews, the colony's surveyor general and the official responsible for documenting the tracts of lands granted to aspiring planters. The Thornton-Morden map was among the first to change the shape of the Carolina settlement by abandoning the westward facing orientation of earlier images. Instead of putting the Albemarle region in the foreground and following a receding coast to Spanish St. Augustine, this new perspective put north at the top of the image and centered a view of the coastal plain squarely on Charlestown as the epicenter of the growing colony.

Thornton and Morden's *New Map* rendered South Carolina in terms of its waterways in its title's emphasis on "Rivers, Bays, Creeks, [and] Harbours" as well as its image of surging plantation agriculture along the Stono, Ashley, Cooper, and Wando Rivers. By 1695 plantations concentrated within a thirty-mile radius from Charlestown, an area defined by the watershed of this coastal river system. Even before the advent of commercial rice agriculture in the colony, the production of maize, lumber, livestock, and tar aimed at markets in the West Indies fueled significant territorial expansion. By the time this map was published in London, a handful of settlers had ventured beyond this radius, pointing the way to a new plantation frontier beyond this network of waterways linked by nature to Charlestown. To the south, along the Edisto River, the planned town of New London (later renamed Willtown) anchored a new plantation district. To the north, along the Santee River, recently arrived French Huguenots initiated another vector of colonization. South Carolina's plantation landscape expanded river to river, tracing a widening circle of colonization outward from the port.

The Thornton-Morden map showed, for the first time on a printed image, that Cusabo Indians still inhabited parts of the lowcountry some three decades after the establishment of English Carolina. Small surviving populations of independent "Settlement Indians" lived just beyond this plantation pale in the interior or clustered along coastal marshlands, leaving English settlers the higher spots of hardwood soils along navigable waterways that they prized.[15]

Conflicts over power in Proprietary South Carolina often focused on the spoils of an increasingly disruptive Indian trade. To avoid the bloody Anglo-Indian clashes that plagued seventeenth-century Virginia, the proprietors had sought to control the settlement system in ways that would avoid provoking Indian reprisals.[16] What they did not anticipate was that their own appointed officials, including resident proprietors, governors, and members of the governor's council, would figure among the chief "dealers in Indians" who sponsored an aggressive commerce for native captives as well as deerskins across the southeast. Lowcountry Indians, despite Proprietary injunctions to "suffer no Indians within 400 miles of Charlestown to be sent out of Carolina," fell victim to enslavement and exportation to the Caribbean.[17] Efforts to reform a trade that made a mockery of this benign vision for Indian affairs embroiled the colony in political conflicts during the 1690s. Where the roads and rivers of the settled colony end at the western edge of the map, the Santees built an "Indian Fort," possibly a palisaded encampment that offered secure shelter from the raids of Westo, Savannah, or Yamasee Indians from the south. Cusabo names —Edistow, Kayawah, Santee, and Sewee—appear as geographical descriptors on Thornton and Morden's map, but the peoples these names had once named struggled to survive as coherent groups. Naturalist John Lawson, North Carolina's surveyor general, pictured the vast Carolina proprietary in 1709 as an expanding network of counties arrayed across an increasingly well-rendered coastal landscape of rivers and creeks (map 11). The Tuscaroras still had a place on the map, at the headwaters of North Carolina's New River, but Lawson noted only "Indian Hutts" along the Santee River in South Carolina. No record survives to document that any Cusabo Indians lived independently in the lowcountry after 1751. This core plantation zone was fast becoming a place in which other Europeans (such as the Huguenots in the "French Settlem^t" along the Santee) assimilated to English culture and non-Europeans (especially Africans, but also some Indians) were subjugated as slaves under the rule of English masters.

The English settlement of the southeast changed the European categorization of regions and helped define an "English Empire" in the late seventeenth and early eighteenth centuries. As sustained colonization began in the colony in 1670, the idea of a separate geographic space between Florida and Virginia launched a new cartographic convention that put "Carolina" on maps of the continent. Between Cape Hatteras, which projects distinctively into the Atlantic Ocean, and the change of coastal orientation from the southwest to the south that marked the beginning of the Florida peninsula, more than one English mapmaker defined this broad stretch of the southeastern coast as Carolina.[18] The addition of Carolina narrowed English understandings of the spatial reach of Virginia. On such maps, "Virginia" was printed horizontally, west to east, and more clearly associated with the Chesapeake Bay than with the southeastern portion of the continent as a whole. Beginning in the late 1670s,

Virginia maps also changed to a more conventional orientation featuring north at the top of the image. Carolina's arrival possibly contributed to this shift and certainly recast the way English viewers in particular conceptualized North America. French and Dutch maps, by contrast, were much slower to register Carolina on their images of North America, preserving the Florida/Virginia division until English maps set a precedent that they followed a few decades later.[19]

By the end of the seventeenth century, the idea of Carolina as a generalized southeastern coastal region had spread from English maps to inform a general European conception of America, but its shape and extent was contested by mapmakers representing the overlapping sovereignty claims of imperial rivals. Vincenzo Maria Coronelli's influential synthesis of North American geography, "America Settentrionale" (1688), presented a Francophone division of colonial British America's mainland regions (map 12). Steeped in French surveys, accounts, and maps, Coronelli limited English settlements to coastal watersheds, according Virginia a substantial territory along the waters that flowed into the Chesapeake Bay but constricting Carolina to a coastal strip that corresponded with rivers that flowed from the mountains to the ocean. Neither of these provinces compared in size with the expansive "Nuova Francia," which extended from the banks of the Mississippi to an ocean that deserved the title "Mars Di Canada." Guillaume de Lisle echoed this view of an English North America hemmed between mountains and ocean in the first decade of the eighteenth century with his "Carte du Mexique et de la Floride" (map 13). This vision of a limited, coastal English mainland contrasted with more expansive claims made by English cartographers. In the same late-seventeenth-century moment, they advanced the idea of an "English Empire" that encompassed much of the eastern part of the continent north of Florida and south of the St. Lawrence River, including French-occupied areas of Acadia (renamed Nova Scotia) and the coastal fishing stations of Newfoundland.[20] Carolina's appearance as a coherent region within the hemisphere came about as English and French cartographers developed competing geographic visions of a North American empire.

In the years before the cataclysm of the Yamasee Indian War, English cartography focused attention on Carolina as place of surging settler populations whose presence shored up British claims to rule a contested territory. No map captured the extent of South Carolina's early eighteenth-century growth like Edward Crisp's *A Complete Description of the Province of Carolina* ([1711]) (map 14). Over ten thousand people inhabited the settled parts of South Carolina in 1710, slightly more than half of whom were African slaves. The turn of the century marked a moment of acceleration for the colony's export economy that helped make colonial South Carolina slave owners one of the wealthiest social groups in the early modern British world.[21] The image of four initial rivers of settlement converging at Charlestown in the upper right quadrant of the map is a close copy of Thornton and Morden's map, updated with new plantation sites that show the rise of rice as the province's staple commodity. Next to this revised image of early occupation, Crisp adds geographic coverage to show the reach of an expanding plantation landscape. His enlarged map of the lowcountry shows the sea islands and coastal tidelands from the Edisto River to the Savannah River. By stitching this image of the colony's eighteenth-century future to its seventeenth-century past, Crisp showcases the surge of speculation and settlement along the southern coast, South Carolina's most important new plantation frontier.

The map's two large insets picture Britain's expansive ambitions in the southeast and suggest the continental implications for plantation settlement along the coastal plain. One of these, "A Map of South Carolina Shewing the Settlements of the English, French, & Indian Nations from Charles Town to the River Missisipi," marks the path of Thomas Nairne's 1708 journey that aimed at alienating the Choctaws from their alliance with the French (map 15). Along his five-hundred mile route, South Carolina's Indian agent talked up the benefits of stronger English commercial alliances among the Talapoosas, Chickasaws, and other Indians who already made an enthusiastic practice of selling people living within the orbit of French influence as slaves to Charlestown traders. Narine's map conceives of Carolina's borders expanding to incorporate the territories of these Native American partners into a vast dominion of trade bounded by the Tennessee River to the north, the Mississippi to the west, and the Gulf Coast (and a much-constricted Spanish Florida) to the south. Although the map of colonial settlement featured in Crisp's main image suggests a regional space opened for new plantation development, Nairne's inset map pulls back to a continental scale to reveal larger configurations of roads, towns, coasts, and peoples that the English aspired to control.[22]

At the other corner of the Crisp's *Complete Description,* a second inset traces the length of the Atlantic coastline from the North Carolina–Virginia border at Cape Henry to the Florida Keys (map 16). It grants Spanish rule only over the native "Florideans" located south of Cape Canaveral as well as the southern Florida peninsula, understood in the early eighteenth century to be more of an archipelago of islands than an extension of the continental mainland. This image unifies the Atlantic coastal plain into a common geographic space characterized by rivers that flow from the interior and empty into the Atlantic Ocean to form a line of coastal islands. It situates St. Augustine as the southern terminus of an unbroken stretch of English coast, a view of North America that rendered England's expansionist goals as geographic facts. During Queen Anne's War (1702–13), Carolina and Creek Indian campaigns against St. Augustine and the allied Indian region of Apalache "entirely broke and ruined the Strength of the Spaniards in Florida."[23] Although the Spanish held their citadel at St. Augustine, they never recovered the network of Indian missions that had spread their influence across the region. This "New Chart of the Coast" pictured the southeastern coastal plain as space that no rival could inhabit "otherwise than as subjects to the Crown of Great Britain." It consolidated these Spanish losses into a claim of territorial sovereignty that pushed the limits of Carolina some seven hundred miles beyond Charlestown.[24] Together the images that compose Crisp's *Compleat Description of the Province of Carolina* envisioned a greater Carolina that stretched across eastern North America, pushing aside rival claims by France and Spain.

Territorial occupation—as an idea and a reality—shaped the production and reception of Herman Moll's *New and Exact Map of the Dominions of the King of Great Britain on the Continent of North America* (1715) and put Carolina's expansion in a wider geographic and imperial context (map 18). The map presents the British mainland as a fully occupied territory from Virginia to Nova Scotia. South Carolina was not included in this central image of the mainland, but four insets at the bottom of the map draw attention to the colony in relation to North American space at various scales. Unlike the more coherent and integrated populations to the north, this southern frontier was harder to present as a place of successful British occupation. Its dispersed population centers were surrounded by space left uncultivated, undefended, and unimproved—a wilderness traversed by Indians, as Europeans saw it.[25] Moll's map focused attention on how British planters and their slaves laid claim to the southeast and emphasized South Carolina's importance in the emerging contest with France over the North American interior.

Moll adapted Crisp's maps to create his Carolina insets. The enumerated list of Charlestown's churches and civil institutions demonstrated the implantation of ordered society at the center of this agricultural and commercial colony (map 19). The "improved Part of Carolina" emphasizes the method driving British colonization: liberal grants of land to aggressive, entrepreneurial settlers (map 20). By 1720 the proprietors had granted more than one million acres of lowcountry land, the first step in preparing a growing portion of the coastal plain to become a plantation landscape featuring fields of rice for export.[26] Two other inset maps put this process of colonization in an imperial context. Moll reworks Thomas Nairne's image of a greater Carolina to register growing British fears of French "encirclement" (maps 21 and 22). As French traders, soldiers, and settlers secured outposts from the Mississippi to the St. Lawrence, Britons monitored the new French capacity to assert control over the interior by commanding this network of rivers. It was with this integrated vision of space in mind that the Board of Trade urged a general program of North American colonization and defense in 1721, one that called for populating the "heads of your Majesty's Colonies north and south" and "building forts, as the French have done" on the "inland frontiers."[27] South Carolina had begun, like other colonial societies in British North America, as a seventeenth-century outpost that grew into an expanding regional society in the early eighteenth century. Moll imagined these separate colonies converging into a unified mainland territory, picturing its idealized form after the Treaty of Utrecht. His *New and Exact Map of the Dominions* carves out the Atlantic-facing portion of the seaboard and names it "the British Empire," a vast form that dominates the coast from Carolina to Newfoundland.

In the first phase of mapping Carolina, cartographers made two sorts of claims that defined the region as a colonial place. First, these maps imagined the spatial form of English imperium in the southeast by which the Crown asserted its sovereignty over territory. This aspirational mode of cartographic representation opened space for English settlement by erasing interfering European claims to possession, assigning Indian residents dependent status under the political authority of the Crown, and reshaping geography to show how nature affirmed the boundaries of royal charters. Second, the maps asserted dominium by showing how colonists had in fact extended the effective reach of British jurisdictions into new zones.[28] Such maps made demonstrative claims that settlers and provincial governments had taken possession of part of the land within this much larger area of sovereignty. As actual settlement grew from the fortified outpost at Charlestown in 1670, this enlarged dominium seemed to justify a vision of an ever-greater imperium.

This vision of South Carolina consolidating British control over its southern frontier in North America through agricultural expansion and an extensive Indian trade collapsed in 1715, just as Herman Moll's map appeared in print. Yamasee Indians and their confederates invaded the colony and "destroy'd great part of our Country with fire and Sword." These attacks left hundreds dead and shattered the trading network constructed by Carolina traders along the route of Thomas Nairne's journey to the Mississippi. The Yamasees began the attack on South Carolina by capturing and executing Nairne and other British traders in Pocotaligo, their town closest to the new Port Royal plantations, and continued it by launching an invasion into the heart of the colony from the south. Panicked colonists who had raised rice and cattle "to the Southward" retreated to the safety of fortified Charlestown and remained there, afraid to return to the exposed plantation countryside.[29]

The Yamasee War was the "greatest Calamity that ever befell" colonial South Carolina. As destabilizing as it was, however, historians have distorted its significance by speculating that the Indians "nearly destroyed the English colony." Rice exports declined far more modestly than would have been the case had they left "most of the colony's plantation districts in ruins." The war in fact did little to check the torrid growth of exports over the first quarter of the eighteenth century.[30] The idea that this invasion constricted the colony's "southern boundary to the outskirts of Charles Town" was a temporary effect: colonists soon reasserted control over their core territory, which extended thirty miles from town.[31] Yamasee attacks focused on South Carolina's southern coastal frontier between the "Combahee River & all the South Side of the Edisto River," areas in which observers considered "all the Settlements" lost.

Allied Indians descended on the Santee River, where they burned "all the English Settlements," a swath of destruction that presumably included the French settlement listed on maps from 1695 and 1711.[32] Indians penetrated the heart of the province to threaten the densely settled plantation districts around Charlestown. They crossed the Edisto River from the south and laid waste to plantations along the Stono River, burning "all before them as far as Mr. Farrs Plantation," a site noted on the Thornton-Morden and Crisp maps that puts the limit of this incursion at about fifteen miles from Charlestown. Another group sacked Bernard Shenkingh's fortified cow pen on Goose Creek (a site indicated on the maps by the toponym "Schernekingh" located just over ten miles from town). For a time during the summer of 1715, Indian fighters held positions at "Edistow River to the Southward, and at Goose Creek to the Northward, in the very midst of our Settlements." They fell back from these positions as colonists marshaled some fourteen hundred militiamen against them. A band of Yamasees attempted to cross the bridge to "Stono Island" (Wadmalaw Island) but were prevented by a "Garrison there."[33] Soon after the second wave of attacks in 1715, the provincial government deployed forces at the outer edges of this core settlement zone around Charlestown, a move that secured the heart of the colony, although the more sparsely settled countryside beyond the thirty-mile mark from town remained vulnerable to raids.

No place in South Carolina was safe from Indian violence at this moment when Anglo-Indian alliances collapsed, but this violence focused on the edges of the settled province and was most intense on its southern frontier. Colonists referenced the concentration of destruction in this new plantation district with the geographic language they used to sum up their losses. The Yamasees "destroyed most of the out settlements"—a term used to describe tracts settled more than fifty miles from town. Indians directed the worst of the violence against the "Inhabitants of Granville County," the colony's southernmost jurisdiction bordered by the Savannah and Combahee Rivers. They "ravaged the Country . . . doing all the Mischief they could, so that all the Southern Parts were broke up, to about the Distance of twenty Miles from Charles Town."[34]

The significance of the Yamasee War was not that it came close to wiping the colony off the map, although its English victims feared the worst while they struggled to comprehend the scale of the strategic threat it posed. The places destroyed by Indian attacks were disproportionately located in the large, sparsely settled area between the Savannah and Edisto Rivers, one that made up a comparatively small part of the productive plantation landscape. About half of all the land in the colony granted to 1715 was located in the core settlement zone, a relatively small area pictured on the Thornton-Morden map representing the colony's chief "Rivers, Bays, Creeks, Harbour, and Settlements." Landowners claimed about four times as much acreage here as they did along the Ashepoo, Chehaw, Combahee, Coosawhatchie, Port Royal, and Savannah Rivers, the places that bore the brunt of the attacks. Far more tracts in this core zone were granted before 1700 compared with the southern district, making them more likely to have been occupied, cleared, and planted.[35] Although colonists suffered some shocking losses, they managed to defend the heart of the settlements in which the plantation economy was concentrated and that was pictured on the Thornton-Morden, Crisp, and Moll maps. It took them much longer to regain possession of the devastated southern frontier.

Being precise about the geography of Indian attacks in 1715—and using contemporary spatial language and cartography to orient these events—helps us see them as part of a successful attempt to contain South Carolina's growth rather than as an all-out war of extermination that fell just short of the goal of dislodging the English from the southeast. The war cost Carolina the southern extension of this plantation landscape, precisely that territory that Crisp had added to his *Compleat Description of the Province*. Carolina planters and their slaves did not return to the southern frontier in large numbers until the 1740s. From this perspective, the Yamasee War resembles King Philip's War (1675–76) and the recently fought Tuscarora War (1711–15), in which alliances of aggrieved Indians living on an imperial borderland targeted a colonial frontier.[36] By destroying South Carolina's most important emerging plantation district, the Indians disrupted expectations that the colony's plantation system could reproduce itself outward in space within Carolina's vast Proprietary charter. Before they were driven out of the lowcountry by 1720, the Yamasees reduced South Carolina to the "narrow Compass" of long-settled lands and threw the southern limits of the colony into confusion.[37]

The postwar cartography of Carolina reflected new British efforts to define, defend, and populate a diminished dominion in the southeast. The war underscored Moll's vision of Carolina in his 1715 *Map of the Dominions of the King of Great Britain* as the "only Southern Frontier of British America," but it also erased that map's confidence that Carolinians were poised to inhabit the region fully and integrate it into an unbroken zone of seaboard settlement that Moll could name a "British Empire."[38] To shore up South Carolina's depopulated southern frontier after the war, the provincial government developed the Yamasees' Savannah River homeland, known thereafter as the "Indian Lands," as a strategically placed garrison community set aside for new settlers.[39] The proprietors granted Sir Robert Montgomery the land between the Savannah and Altamaha Rivers in present-day Georgia to be developed as the "Margravate of Azilia." Montgomery envisioned his new colony as "one continued Fortress" in which homes and fields would be secured by "Military Lines, impregnable against the Savages." He engraved a plan of Azilia along with a 1717 tract called that Carolina's southern wilds the "Most Delightful Country of the Universe," but also imagined it as an island of civilization besieged by encroaching barbarism (map 22). Resembling a vast planned city, Montgomery imagined Azilia as a militarized colonial countryside. In place of the practice of "settling without any form at all"—a legacy of the dispersion that had characterized past plantation settlement and had made the countryside so open to attack—he sought to impose a strict rectilinear shape on the occupied landscape. Azilia, although never planted, appeared on Herman Moll's map of the "north parts of America claimed by France" as if it were a full-fledged colony whose presence contested the reach of Louisiana and whose borders established British authority south of the Savannah River (map 23).[40]

The end of the Proprietary rule came in a bloodless revolution led by colonial elites in 1719, in part because the proprietors had failed to defend Carolina from Indian invasion and relieve it in the aftermath of the fighting. John Herbert's 1721 sketch of the "Ichnography or Plann of the Fortification of Charlestown" shows the scale of a defensive infrastructure undertaken by the province to defend the capital against the French, Spaniards, and Indians (map 25). Trenches, walls, and bastions bristling with artillery encompassed sixty-two acres at the heart of this Atlantic port, pictured as an island of security at the edge of a threatening continent. Two decades later, the creators of a new *Ichnography of Charles-Town* superimposed an image of this fortified line on a map of the expanding city as a historical curiosity. They explained that "after the signal Defeat of [th]e Indians in the Year 1717," parts of the wall were "dismantled & demolished to enlarge the Town" (map 26). From the vantage point of the 1720s, however, the new royal government did not take this capacity to expand safely across lowcountry space for granted.[41] British maps of Carolina in the 1720s reflected the shift in authority from the Lords Proprietors to the Crown. In place of the expansive vision promoted by the proprietors for drawing settlers to take up lands within the vast boundaries of their charter, new manuscript maps commissioned by the imperial state as it took control of the colony featured constrictive defensive boundaries, fortified strategic positions, and the clear delineation of jurisdictions.

Under the provisional government headed by Governor Francis Nicholson, Indian agent John Barnwell worked to create a new center from which to project British power into the interior. When the Lords Commissioners for Trade and Plantations (commonly known as the Board of Trade) asked Barnwell to describe South Carolina's "Reputed Boundaries" in 1720, he offered the commissioners an illustrated object lesson. If they followed the "Prict Line in Capt. Nairnes Mapp" they could see the dilated limits of an unsustainable greater South Carolina. The "Factories and Store Houses" by which Nairne had established Carolina's claim to Indian country before the war had now fallen into the hands of the French. The real "Bounds" of Carolina, argued Barnwell, extended only "as far as the Lands possessed by those Indians that Submitted to the English Government."[42] In place of the reckless history of predatory trade that had enlarged South Carolina's influence, Barnwell's program of fortified outposts, transparent diplomacy, and the recognition of indigenous sovereignty sought to secure a more modest geographic definition of South Carolina, but one that was more likely to endure in a hostile North American colonial world.[43]

A series of manuscript maps document this attempt to define a practical limit for South Carolina at the Altamaha River in the present-day state of Georgia, more than 120 miles to the south and west of Charlestown. Barnwell proposed to emulate the "method of the French," who built "forts on their frontiers, which it would be our interest to do likewise, not only to preserve our trade with the Indians and their dependence upon us, but to preserve our boundaries."[44] The maps show, with new geographic precision and at multiple scales, how Fort King George, which Barnwell led the effort to construct in 1721, reasserted British claims to the region. On his new map of the southeast from Virginia to the Mississippi, the fort was visible as a generic icon on the northern banks of the Altamaha, here renamed "St. George's River" for England's patron saint (map 27). This site marked a reconstituted a southern boundary for Britain's North American empire and put the whole in relation to a populated interior of established Indian towns as well as French Louisiana and Spanish Florida. This map brought together detailed information about routes, settlements, and populations that, for the first time, displayed the peoples and places of the southeast in ethnographic detail. Barnwell's map of the indigenous interior served as a foundational source for Britain's eighteenth-century knowledge of who Indians were and where they lived.[45] To better defend this new British frontier, large-scale maps of Fort King George pictured it within a well-defined network of waterways; imposed its footprint of barracks, palisades, and parapets on a well-rendered topography; and recorded the bearings, distances, and depths of the small tributary that provided water navigation between the fort and the large tidal river that emptied into the Atlantic Ocean (maps 29–33). Such precise images of this defensible frontier departed from the proprietors' earlier attempts to use maps to promote an idealized landscape for settlement. Instead they illustrated a new imperial vision for the continent, one that that rested on an empirical program for gathering geographic information and envisioned colonies as part of a larger mainland empire.

As Barnwell, Nicholson, and the Board of Trade worked to defend and reoccupy the southern frontier with the establishment of Fort King George, South Carolina's Indian allies created their own maps to describe how they saw themselves bound to the colony in a new continental order. The Catawbas and the Chickasaws each presented a painted deerskin map to South Carolina's governor in the early 1720s that pictured eastern North America as a network of circles (each of which represented an Indian nation or town) connected by lines that visualized relations of alliance, affiliation, and trade. The Chickasaws' node-and-spoke map put its nation at the western edge of an interconnected Anglophone southeast, where it appeared as the indispensible point of mediation between English Carolina and a complex world riddled with Francophone Indian groups along the Mississippi River and Gulf Coast (map 34). The Catawbas likewise drew a path that connected Nasaw, their most prestigious community, directly to English Carolina (map 35). As this line emerges from Catawba country and approaches the straight-edged maze of streets that stands for Charlestown, it widens into the Broad Path, the colonial roadway that crossed the narrows of the Charlestown peninsula and became King Street, this Atlantic port city's central artery. Seeing themselves standing between the source of the region's trade goods and the powerful presences of the Creeks and Cherokees further in the interior was part of a Catawba bid to maintain their autonomy as English society expanded around them.[46] In the wake of the diplomatic ruptures of the Yamasee War, these geographic images described how some Indians sought reconnection with colonial British America on their own terms.

South Carolina's transition from a Proprietary province to a royal colony was completed in 1729, when the king appointed Robert Johnson as its governor. This formal adoption of a new constitutional order for the colony was accompanied by attempts to define jurisdictions more precisely and shape the process of colonization on southeastern frontiers in the 1730s. The Board of Trade had long criticized the proprietors for putting their parochial interests over the common economic and strategic needs of the American empire as a whole, particularly as settlement began to spread into lands contested by French, Spanish, and Indian adversaries. It endorsed the idea that Britain's claims to sovereignty as well as its distinctive strength as an imperial power lay in planting populations of settlers and slaves on the land and improving it by clearing forests, raising goods for export, and establishing the rudiments of English society and the rule of law in new districts. At the close of the Proprietary era, the proprietors' undifferentiated claim on the continent in 1663 had become separate colonial jurisdictions clarified by new boundary surveys between North Carolina and Virginia (in 1728) and South Carolina (in 1735).[47]

South Carolina governor Robert Johnson's 1730 township scheme sought to define the interior edge of the province as a demographic buffer zone. The plan reserved large tracts of land around the slave-majority lowcountry for settlement by yeoman farmers who could protect the plantation districts from the dual threats of Indian war and slave uprising. Perhaps the most ambitious effort to populate these new townships focused on a plan to lead whole communities of Swiss Protestants to Purrysburg, strategically located on the Savannah River close to the former seat of the Yamasee nation.[48] The establishment of the Georgia colony in 1732 continued the logic of this township plan in its prohibition of slavery, a move designed to steer new colonial development of away from the twin strategic liabilities of dispersed plantation settlement and restive enslaved populations.

Georgia's founding also completed a process of geographic definition that brought South Carolina's position within the mainland into sharper focus. Henry Popple's *A Map of the British Empire in North America* (1733) included the new colony on a massive wall map that reasserted an aggressive vision of settler empire (map 36). Unlike Moll's broken picture of the continent in his *New and Exact Map of the Dominions of the King of Great Britain,* Popple envisioned British America as the dominant geographic presence within eastern North America and the Caribbean. The appearance of "Georgia" to the south of South Carolina was a small text addition to a map with hemispheric pretentions, but one that used new information to entrench the new colony in geographic reality and challenge Spanish claims to the area. Georgia's founder, James Oglethorpe, supplied the cartographer with descriptions of the three Atlantic rivers—the Savannah, Ogeeche, and Altamaha—that defined the colony's boundaries and promoted it to prospective settlers as a place of fertile riversides along bold, navigable waterways.[49] Although the Altamaha River marked the southernmost extent of British settlement efforts to date, Popple also marked the "Southward Boundary of CAROLINA by the last Charter" along the twenty-ninth degree of latitude. This line cut across the Florida peninsula south of St. Augustine from the Atlantic Ocean to the Gulf of Mexico. The gap between these two positions marked the distance between the actual reach of British colonizers and unrealized imperial aspirations for North American hegemony that had inspired Carolina's founding.

The cartography of early Carolina was particularly concerned with measuring the distance between the two scales at which land was claimed. At the scale of the continent, Carolina extended by charter across a band of North American latitude between Florida and Virginia "as far as the South-Seas." At the scale of occupation, it reached only as far as the last cleared field. For the better part of a century after "Carolina" first appeared on a map in 1657, mapmakers magnified their views of the settled landscape and put these images side-by-side with inset maps that showed the broader contexts of British claims within the hemisphere. The most ambitious maps of Carolina occasionally broke new ground as original depictions of geography. More often, cartographers repurposed older images, updating them with new evidence of intensive agriculture and extensive commerce to enable bolder claims to more land than was possible before.

Before 1715 cartographers served the interests of the Lords Proprietors, often as mapmakers-for-hire, and worked within the idiom of provincial aggrandizement as they created images of the region's boundaries, geography, and natural resources. The crisis of the Yamasee War not only dampened the prospects of Carolina's unlimited expansion past the Appalachian Mountains and into Spanish, French, and Indian territories to the south and west but also led to a change in the official audience for which maps were made. When the Crown assumed control over Carolina in the 1720s, it displaced the proprietors as patrons who were singularly interested in the province's independent expansion. Those who drafted maps under the direction or "Approbation" of the Lords Commissioners of Trade and Plantations, like John Barnwell and Henry Popple, catered to the more general imperial vision maintained by

Britain's agency charged with overseeing all the colonies. This view, put forward in the Board of Trade's report of 1721, rejected the idea of the colonies as separate places, each with its own independent program of expansion, and advocated instead a view of the entire mainland as a coherent domain, threatened as a whole by French and Spanish proximity and requiring a common, continental policy for defense, Indian affairs, and commerce. This new geographic vision of empire recognized Carolina's importance as a southern frontier of an integrated mainland empire.[50]

Notes

The author thanks Lee Wilson Bowden, Alexander Moore, and Bradford Wood for their comments and suggestions and Mike McNamara for sharing a draft version of his essay on North Carolina mapping. Two comprehensive cartobibliographies offer images and descriptions for most of these maps: William P. Cumming, *The Southeast in Early Maps*, 3rd ed., edited by Louis de Vorsey Jr. (Chapel Hill: University of North Carolina Press, 1998); Philip D. Burden, *The Mapping of North America: A List of Printed Maps, 1511–1670* (Rickmansworth, U.K.: Raleigh, 1996) (hereafter Burden I); and Philip D. Burden, *The Mapping of North America II: A List of Printed Maps, 1670–1700* (Rickmansworth, U.K.: Raleigh, 2007) (Burden II). Digital images of maps discussed in this essay, along with other visualizations, are available at http://www.mapscholar.org/carolina.

1. See also Jodocus Hondius, *Virginiae item et Floridae* ([Amsterdam, 1606]), University of South Florida Digital Collections, usf:http://digital.lib.usf.edu/?u15.9000 (accessed July 23, 2012); Willem Janszoon Bleau, *Virginiae partis australis, et Floridae partis orientalis*... ([Amsterdam: 1640]), USF Digital Collections, http://digital.lib.usf.edu/?u15.48-A (accessed July 23, 2012).

2. Herman Moll, *Thesaurus Geographicus. A New body of Geography: or, a Compleat Description of the Earth*... (London, 1695), 482; William Byrd, *William Byrd's Histories of the Dividing Line betwixt Virginia and North Carolina* (New York: Dover, 1967), 1, 7; Emerson W. Baker, ed., *American Beginnings: Explorations, Culture, and Cartography in the Land of Norumbega* (Lincoln: University of Nebraska Press, 1994).

3. Cumming, *Early Maps*, 11–14, 152–54, 178.

4. First Meeting of the Proprietors, May 23, 1663, in *Shaftesbury Papers*, 5; Cumming, *Early Maps*, 157; Burden I, 485.

5. Cumming, *Early Maps*, 156–58, 167–68; Burden I, 497–98; Janette D. Black, *The Blathwayt Atlas*, vol. 2, *Commentary* (Providence, R.I.: Brown University Press, 1975), 119–24.

6. See, for example, the third state of Richard Blome's *A New Mapp of America Septentrionale* (London, 1682); Robert Morden and William Berry, *A New Map of the English Plantations in America* (London, 1673); Burden I, 505; Burden II, 34–35.

7. Burden II, 12–15; Cumming, *Early Maps*, 158–63.

8. Sir Peter Colleton to John Locke, [1671?], in *Shaftesbury Papers*, 264–65.

9. Burden II, 41–43; Cumming, *Early Maps*, 163.

10. John Ogilby, *America* (London, 1671), 207–8, http://eebo.chadwyck.com/ (accessed July 24, 2012).

11. See Gene Waddell, "Cusabo," in *Handbook of North American Indians*, vol. 14, *Southeast*, ed. Raymond Fogelson and William Sturtevant (Washington, D.C.: Smithsonian Institution, 2004), 254–64. Colleton (1670) quoted in Burden II, 41. A derivative of Ogilby's map is John Speed, *A New Description of Carolina* (1676), Burden II, 457. S. Max Edelson, *Plantation Enterprise in Colonial South Carolina* (Cambridge: Harvard University Press, 2006), 33.

12. An important derivative of Gascoyne's map was John Thornton, Robert Morden, and Philip Lea, *A New Map of Carolina* (London, [ca. 1684]) (map 9).

13. Burden II, 193, 194–96; Gene Waddell, "Cofitachequie: A Distinctive Culture, Its Identity, and Its Location," *Ethnohistory* 52, no. 2 (Spring 2005): 333–69.

14. See Matthew Jennings, *New Worlds of Violence: Cultures and Conquests in the Early American Southeast* (Knoxville: University of Tennessee Press, 2011), chap. 6.

15. Stanley South and Michael Hartley, "Deep Water and High Ground: Seventeenth Century Low Country Settlement," Research Manuscript Series, South Carolina Institute of Archaeology and Anthropology, Book 159 (1980), http://scholarcommons.sc.edu/archanth_books/159 (accessed July 25, 2012).

16. Alan Gallay, *The Indian Slave Trade: The Rise of the English Empire in the American South, 1670–1717* (New Haven: Yale University Press, 2002), 43–45.

17. Ibid., 60–68; "Instructions to Governor Philip Ludwell, November 8, 1691," *Calendar of State Papers Colonial, America and the West Indies*, vol. 13, 1689–1692, British History Online, http://www.british-history.ac.uk/report.aspx?compid=70712 (accessed July 25, 2012).

18. See Burden II, 46–48, 117–18, 167–68.

19. The first published map to do so was John Thornton and Robert Greene, *A Mapp of Virginia Maryland, New-Jarsey, New-York, & New England* (London, ca. 1678), see Burden II, 144–45, 148. On non-English derivatives, see, for example, Burden II, 321, 323–24.

20. See, for example, Thornton, Morden, and Lea's untitled map of the Atlantic World from 1685, Burden II, 284–85.

21. Peter A. Coclanis, *The Shadow of a Dream: Economic Life and Death in the South Carolina Low Country* (New York: Oxford University Press, 1989), chap. 3.

22. See Thomas Nairne, *Nairne's Muskhogean Journals: The 1708 Expedition to the Mississippi River*, ed. Alexander Moore (Jackson: University Press of Mississippi, 1988). On important manuscript maps that seem to depict information from Nairne's journeys about Indian groups and their numbers, see Nairne, *Muskhogean Journals*, 22–24.

23. Nairne (1710) quoted in Gallay, *Indian Slave Trade*, 166.

24. Amy Turner Bushnell, *Situado and Sabana: Spain's Support System for the Presidio and Mission Provinces of Florida*, American Museum of Natural History, Anthropological Papers, No. 74 (Athens: University of Georgia Press, 1994), 190–95; Nairne (1710) quoted in Galley, *Indian Slave Trade*, 167.

25. Harry Roy Merrens, *Colonial North Carolina in the Eighteenth Century: A Study in Historical Geography* (Chapel Hill: University of North Carolina Press, 1964), chap. 2.

26. Coclanis, *Shadow of a Dream*, 68.

27. Quoted in Warren R. Hofstra, *The Planting of New Virginia: Settlement and Landscape in the Shenandoah Valley* (Baltimore: Johns Hopkins University Press, 2004), 79.

28. On the importance of this distinction see David Armitage, *The Ideological Origins of the British Empire* (Cambridge, U.K.: Cambridge University Press, 2000), chap 3; Christopher Tomlins, *Freedom Bound: Law, Labor, and Civic Identity in Colonizing English America, 1580–1856* (Cambridge, U.K.: Cambridge University Press, 2010), chap. 3.

29. "Address from the Assembly of Carolina to His Majesty," read June 12, 1716, *BPRO-SC* 6:167, South Carolina Department of Archives and History, Columbia, S.C.; Francis Yonge, *A View of the Trade of South Carolina with Proposals Humbly Offer'd for Improving the Same* ([London?], [1722?]), 6, Eighteenth-Century Collections Online, Gale (CW105744032).

30. "Calamity," J.H. Easterby, *The Journal of the Commons House of Assembly: November 10, 1736–June 7, 1739* (Columbia: Historical Commission of South Carolina, 1951) 306; Richard L. Haan, "The 'Trade Do's Not Flourish as Formerly': The Ecological Origins of the Yamassee War of 1715," *Ethnohistory* 28, no. 4 (Fall 1981): 341; William L. Ramsay, *The Yamasee War: A Study of Culture, Economy, and Conflict in the Colonial South* (Lincoln: University of Nebraska Press, 2008), 165. Although annual shipments dropped just below the three-million-pound mark in 1717 and 1718, they surpassed five million pounds in 1719 and never retreated below this during the colonial period. Over the five-year period 1718–22, average annual exports grew to 6.2 million pounds compared with the 1.8 million pounds produced in the period 1708–13. Figures for 1712 are missing. Coclanis, *Shadow of a Dream*, tables 3-13 and 1-14, 82–83.

31. Haan, "'Trade Do's Not Flourish,'" 341.

32. Robert Daniel, Ar[thur] Middleton, B. Goddin to Boon and Berresford, August 20, 1715, in *BPRO-SC*, 6:129.

33. Ibid.; Petition from Inhabitants of Carolina, July 18, 1715, *Colonial Records of North Carolina*, Documenting the American South, http://docsouth.unc.edu/csr/index.html/document/csr02-0098 (accessed July 25, 2012); Steven J. Oatis, *A Colonial Complex: South Carolina's Frontiers in the Era of the Yamasee War, 1680–1730* (Lincoln: University of Nebraska Press, 2004), 138.

34. "Out settlements": Minutes of the Commissioners for Trade and Plantations, July 28, 1715," in *BPRO-SC*, 6:140. For evidence that that the war's destruction halted at about the twenty-mile mark outside of town, see Gallay, *Indian Slave Trade*, 329n; see also J.H. Easterby, ed., *The Journal of the Commons House of Assembly, May 18, 1741-July 10, 1742* (Columbia: Historical Commission of South Carolina, 1953), 81.

35. The Memorials record series records 842 tracts of land granted before 1715 amounting to 390,031 acres. Of these, 429 tracts (51.0 percent) totaling 194,818

acres (49.9 percent) were located in the core settlement zone. One hundred and six tracts (12.6 percent) containing 52,844 acres (13.5 percent) were granted along the rivers and creeks of the southern coastal frontier. Only nineteen tracts totaling 15,746 acres were granted before 1700 in the southern coastal frontier zone compared with 165 tracts totaling 88,503 acres in the core zone. These records are a subset of the larger series that contain date information for the initial grant as well as geographic information about their location. Records of the Auditor General, Memorials of Land Titles (Copies), vols. 1–5, Microcopy Number 12, at SCDAH. See Edelson, *Plantation Enterprise*, 128–36, 271–75.

36. Edelson, *Plantation Enterprise*, 133–34.

37. "Address from the Assembly," in *BPRO-SC*, 6:167.

38. Memorial from Mr[.] Beresford, June 23, 1716, in *CRNC*, Documenting the American South, http://docsouth.unc.edu/csr/index.html/document/csr02-0116.

39. Gary L. Hewitt, "Expansion and Improvement: Land, People and Politics in South Carolina and Georgia, 1690–1745" (Ph.D. diss., Princeton University, 1996), 106–29.

40. Montgomery (1717) quoted in Cumming, *Early Maps*, 210.

41. "The Ichnograph of Charles-Town at High Water," Museum of Early Southern Decorative Arts, http://mesda.org/collections/paper_sprite/mesda_highwater_sprite.html (accessed July 26, 2012).

42. A Copy of the Queries relating to the Province of South Carolina prepounded by the Lords of Trade and Plantation[s] to Collo. Barnwell in London and his Answer to those Queres delivered in upon oath the 23d. day of August Anno Dni 1720, August 23, 1720, Records of the Board of Trade, Box 2, 80–81, Manuscript Division, Library of Congress, Washington, D.C.

43. On the 1721 report that outlines this approach to Indian relations on the part of the Board of Trade, see Craig Yirush, *Settlers, Liberty, and Empire: The Roots of Early American Political Theory, 1675–1775* (Cambridge, U.K.: Cambridge University Press, 2011), 185.

44. Journal, August 1720, *Journals of the Board of Trade and Plantations*, vol. 4, *November 1718–December 1722* (London: Public Record Office, 1925), 191–204, British History Online, http://www.british-history.ac.uk/ (accessed July 26, 2012).

45. Cumming, *Early Maps*, 216–19. See also Verner W. Crane, *The Southern Frontier, 1670–1732* (Ann Arbor: University of Michigan Press, 1964), 226–53. Map 28 is a copy of Barnwell's original map from the 1740s that includes details of subsequent settlements.

46. Gregory A. Waselkov, "Indian Maps of the Colonial Southeast," in *Powhatan's Mantle: Indians in the Colonial Southeast*, ed. Peter H. Wood, Gregory A. Waselkov, and M. Thomas Hatley (Lincoln: University of Nebraska Press, 1989), 296–306, 320–29. See also James Merrell, *The Indians' New Word: Catawbas and Their Neighbors from European Contact through the Era of Removal* (New York: Norton, 1989), 92–95.

47. Mike McNamara, "A New and Correct Map of the Province of North Carolina: The Discovery of a 1737 North Carolina Manuscript Map," *Journal of Early*

Southern Decorative Arts 33 (2012), http://www.mesdajournal.org/2012/correct-map-province-north-Carolina/ (accessed July 26, 2012).

48. Arlin C. Migliazzo, *To Make This Land Our Own: Community, Identity, and Cultural Adaptation in Purrysburg Township, South Carolina, 1732–1865* (Columbia: University of South Carolina Press, 2007).

49. Louis de Vorsey Jr., "Maps in Colonial Promotion: James Edward Oglethorpe's Use of Maps in 'Selling' the Georgia Scheme," *Imago Mundi* 38 (1986): 35–45.

50. See Hofstra, *The Planting of New Virginia*, 77–81.

Venturing Out

The Barbadian Diaspora and the Carolina Colony, 1650–1685

JUSTIN ROBERTS AND IAN BEAMISH

The Carolina colony was founded amidst a flurry of Barbadian expansion projects in the 1650s and 1660s. Nationalist approaches have situated the colony within the context of the area that eventually formed the United States. At its inception, however, South Carolina was part of a Caribbean world. Imperial rivalries and economic, demographic, and political forces in the early English Caribbean dictated the settlement of the Carolina colony. Most of its principal architects drew on their experiences in settling and cultivating the English Caribbean, envisioning the colony as a satellite to their Caribbean world. To better understand the impetus for the settlement of Carolina, its initial failures, and its ultimate survival, the story of early Carolina needs a broader Atlantic framework. The capital that fuelled the exploration and settlement of the Carolinas drew heavily on the fantastic wealth being generated in the sugar islands, and the leaders of the Carolina venture envisioned the colony as a satellite to their Caribbean world.

While Barbadian elites had a significant impact on the early settlement of Carolina, this colony was a secondary option for Barbadians, and they were a minority among settlers. The new colony initially struggled because of competing projects in St. Lucia, Surinam, and Jamaica. It nearly failed because much of the excess Barbadian population had already been siphoned off in other colonial projects. It survived, in part, because it was a peripheral area of the Caribbean world and because its competitor colonies for Barbadian expansion had collapsed or been conquered.

Several generations of early American historians and South Carolinian genealogists have emphasized the connections between Barbados and South Carolina. The standard narrative stresses that Barbados, overpopulated and starved for land, expanded to South Carolina, creating a "colony of a colony." Recent studies challenge both the numbers and influence of Barbadians and Caribbean in the Carolina colony.[1] The revisionist narratives correctly challenge the number of Barbadians in Carolina, but they fail to sufficiently explain why Barbadians did not populate the new colony in large numbers, glossing over the origins of Barbadian interest in the mainland and oversimplifying how Barbadians shaped the colony.

Only a few hundred Barbadians came to Carolina before 1700, but there were many elite planters and merchants among them, as well as many influential Barbadians who were deeply invested in the Carolina colony, without ever becoming resident.[2] This paper will explore the broader Atlantic forces that shaped the early settlement of Carolina, explain Barbadian motivations in the region, and suggest how Barbadians played a substantial role in the settlement and early shaping of the colony without supplying the majority of the migrants. It will also examine the areas in Carolina where Barbadians focused their settlement and how they sought to strengthen their claims as the principal architects of the colony.

The argument for South Carolina being the colony of a colony rests on a few key claims. The colonists at the first permanent settlement in Charles Towne in 1670 included a significant number of Barbadians. Barbadians and their relatives played a major role in the early political culture of Carolina, with a number of governors coming from the island, along with one of the Lords Proprietors. Most of all, however, Barbados has been credited with making Carolina in its image: Carolina's development as a plantation society dependent on slave labor, scholars have argued, was an extension of Barbadian slave culture. The first slave was brought to Carolina by a Barbadian. Carolina's slave code, like most slave codes in the British Atlantic, was modeled on a Barbadian predecessor. Barbadians owned the most slaves in Carolina, and most of the slaves came from Barbados. In the early years of the colony, the provision trade with Barbados was extensive, land ownership was disproportionately dominated by Barbadians, and Barbadians were omnipresent in the political life of the young colony. Armed with this extensive evidence of connections, historians have cast South Carolina's connections with Barbados as unique rather than as part of a series of seventeenth-century Barbadian expansion projects.[3]

Barbadians had many motives for venturing off-island in the mid-seventeenth century, and they had the capital necessary to plant other colonies. The sugar revolution swept quickly across the tiny island of Barbados in the 1640s.[4] A handful of wealthy sugar planters soon dominated the island, consolidating vast tracts of land and increasingly turning to slaves to cultivate a lucrative crop.[5] In 1666 Governor Francis Willoughby described the island as the "fair jewell" of the English empire in the Americas.[6] The "gentry bred here," he maintained "are all lively spirited men, very ingenious and industrious."[7] The value of Barbadian sugar exports by the end of the seventeenth century was far greater than the value of exports from Brazil's much larger sugar-producing Reconcavo of Bahia, suggesting not only the kinds of wealth elite Barbadian planters were developing, but also that the system of labor exploitation and sugar cultivation that had evolved in Barbados was even more productive than what had been brought from Brazil by the Dutch or from the Atlantic islands by the Portuguese before that.⁸ Barbados was deforested quickly for sugar and faced a growing ecological crisis as a result. The soils declined, and there was no timber to stoke the boiling-house fires, construct sugar containers, or build sugar works. Planters adapted. Some used more sustainable planting techniques; some searched for new sugar soils in the torrid zone; some began to seek settlements that would supply the resources that would allow Barbados to continue prospering.⁹ A rapacious and speculative capitalist ethos fostered schemes to extend the frontiers of the plantation complex or feed its needs; capital sought an outlet.

The sugar dons grew rich quickly, but there was a small window of opportunity before land became scarce.¹⁰ By 1647 no land remained in Barbados for new settlers or for servants who had survived their indentures. The rapid switch to sugar as a staple left the island packed with free landless men.¹¹ To colonial elites, embedded in ideologies that stressed hierarchy and dependency, landless and masterless men threatened political stability.¹² During the English Civil War, royalists fled to Barbados, many of them with significant capital for investment.¹³ Both during and after the war, rebels and convicts were banished to Barbados. Colonial administrators noted in the 1660s that Barbados was, in fact, "the best peopled spot in these parts of the world."¹⁴

Barbados needed outlets for expansion, and sugar profits helped mitigate the risks. Thomas Modyford, a Barbadian planter who would become governor of Jamaica, argued as early as 1652 that "a place must be thought upon where the great people [of Barbados] will find maintenance and employment."¹⁵ From 1650 through 1670, Barbadians spread outward. This period of outmigration peaked in the mid-1660s and fell sharply afterward.¹⁶ They moved to established colonies such as New England and Virginia and to newly budding colonies such as Antigua; they also became the chief actors in initiating colonial settlements in Surinam, St. Lucia, and Carolina, and they played a strong supporting role in settling Jamaica, transforming the island from a haven for buccaneers to a sugar-planting colony.¹⁷

The seventeenth-century Caribbean was unstable and heavily contested ground. The Spanish empire was weakening, and the English, French, and Dutch were making incursions, battling both the Spanish and each other to control trade to the Indies. Intense imperial rivalry, combined with rampant piracy and slow communication with the metropole, forced seventeenth-century Caribbean colonists to become self-reliant in their defenses. Barbados was a bulwark for the English Caribbean, and the Crown began to rely on them as a vanguard force in expansion. In the 1650s Modyford promised that any English expedition force against the western Caribbean or against the Spanish Main would be doubled in size if it stopped in Barbados.¹⁸ In 1652, during the Civil War, royalist Barbadians rose in rebellion and declared independence from Cromwell's Protectorate.¹⁹ After the Restoration the English initiated measures to gain more control over their empire, but Barbadians adamantly protested a 1663 act requiring a 4.5 percent duty on all produce exported from Barbados.[20] The planters' pleas failed to alter any imperial policies; the planters were sharply rebuked by imperial observers for not acknowledging that they were part of an empire.[21] The rebellions continued. Humphrey Walrond, a former royalist and a prominent planter, rode about the island after the passage of the act with a company of servants and slaves in open rebellion against the king, refusing to surrender the duties he owed.[22] An alienating critique of Barbadians, arguing that "men of any honour or innate courage do not leave their native country for servitude abroad," reinforced the development of a separate creole perspective.[23] Barbadians were conscious of their importance to the empire. Willoughby observed they had "merited much" and "expect[ed] much to be done for them."[24] Such a sense of distinctiveness led Barbadians to develop semiautonomous imperialist ambitions, outstripping even English imperial goals in the region.

In 1650, Surinam, on the coast of Guiana, became the first major Barbadian colonization project. The first English settlement grant in the Americas was a grant to settle Surinam in 1604, but the colony was not developed until the Barbadians became involved. It was a project begun in the midst of the English Civil War, shortly before the Barbadians declared independence. Willoughby sent a ship from Barbados to explore the coast of Guiana. Soon after, he sent a hundred men to settle the coast for sugar. In 1651 Modyford encouraged the Protectorate to fortify and protect Surinam, promising that it would prove as lucrative as Brazil. According to Modyford there were already 150 Barbadians on the coast, and many more would go if the colony was made safe.[25] Surinam grew rapidly. In 1654, after the suppression of the Barbadian royalists, Modyford informed the Protectorate that "we already have a colony" of six hundred men in Surinam.[26] He appears to have meant a *Barbadian* "colony." He was particularly enthusiastic about the prospect of a Surinam livestock trade, and he hoped that "the nearness of the colony to Barbados will be a good strengthening and countenance to each other."[27] Not only would the abundant land in mainland Surinam supply the resources Barbados sorely lacked, but sugar could easily expand to Surinam, offering an outlet for capital. It was the best of all possible new worlds for the land-hungry sugar barons.

Throughout the 1650s and early 1660s, more Barbadians migrated to Surinam than to any other region of the Caribbean. It was a mere three days' sail.[28] Willoughby, who remained a royalist sympathizer, fled to Surinam after the Protectorate unseated him. He personally invested £26,000 and looked to Barbados for settlers and supplies to keep the colony running, independent of Oliver Cromwell's Protectorate.[29] Surinam quickly became such a significant rival in sugar production that by the early 1660s some of the "Dons of Barbados" were discouraging outmigration, anxious that Surinam was competing for labor and driving down sugar prices.[30] In 1663 there were four thousand settlers in the region, most of them Barbadians.[31] When the Dutch conquered

Surinam in 1667 during the second Anglo-Dutch naval war, they sought to maintain the Barbadian settlers, concerned that they could not recruit colonists as adept at planting sugar.[32] Without Surinam, Barbadians lacked a mainland colony to provide the lumber, livestock, and provisions they needed.

As Surinam was developing in the early 1650s, prominent Barbadians encouraged the Protectorate to attack the Spanish Main and oust the Spanish from their hold on the western Caribbean.[33] The English took Jamaica in 1655 as part of this "Western Design." Until the 1660s, most Barbadian migrants chose Surinam over Jamaica.[34] Settlers were deterred from Jamaica by the high mortality from malnourishment and dehydration among the forces that had invaded the island. When buccaneers began to entrench themselves in Jamaica and enrich themselves by raiding the Spanish Main, landless men drifted from Barbados in search of wealth.[35] When Modyford was appointed governor of Jamaica in 1664, "scores" of Barbadian planters followed him to the island.[36] It was only after the surrender of Surinam in 1667 that the Jamaican population started increasing rapidly. Jamaica not only took Surinam's place as the destination for Barbadians interested in expanding the sugar frontier; it absorbed most of the Surinam refugees and their slaves.[37] The "best quality" of these Surinam refugees came, originally, from Barbados.[38]

From 1662 to 1667, Barbadian expansion projects escalated sharply. As hundreds of Barbadians continued to migrate to Surinam, Willoughby and Lewis Morris started to aggressively pursue settlements nearby in the Windward Islands.[39] In 1662 they sailed to Dominica, Nevis, St. Vincent, Grenada, and St. Lucia to explore expansion possibilities. St. Lucia was the closest island to Barbados, and Barbadian migrants were already drifting there from the late 1650s onward, independent from any specific colonization project or government directive. In 1663 the Barbadians purchased St. Lucia from Thomas Warner, the illegitimate half-Carib son of the governor of the Leeward Islands who claimed to be acting as a representative for the Caribs. Willoughby insisted that the Caribs had invited Barbadians to settle. He asked Charles II to discourage the settlement of St. Vincent by the Scots in order to maintain peaceful relations with the Caribs.[40] The purchase provided a legal pretext for settlement on an island also claimed by the French. It is significant that the island was sold not to the Crown but to a group of planters and merchants from "the island of Barbados."[41] In 1664 an army of approximately thirteen hundred Barbadians and Caribs drove a handful of French from St. Lucia in a largely bloodless battle.[42] But by 1665 disease had reduced the Barbadians in St. Lucia to less than a hundred, and tensions had erupted with the Caribs. In January 1666 the few survivors abandoned the island, burning the fort and fleeing on a passing pirate ship.[43] St. Lucia seemed a graveyard to Barbadians then, and they decided, drawing on theories of health and disease that stressed the intrinsic characteristics of a particular place, that it would always be such.[44]

In 1663, as one group of Barbadians purchased and planned to settle St. Lucia and others flocked to Surinam, another group (the Company of Barbadian Adventurers) sailed with William Hilton to explore the possibility of settling the coast of Florida—territory claimed by Spain on the mainland. The Adventurers' account of Carolina highlighted the quality of the soil, the easily available timber, and the potential for pasturage land.[45] They also observed that the Native Americans already kept cattle in Carolina.[46] The Adventurers stressed environmental factors that underscored the suitability of a Carolina as a resource satellite. They returned with a native from the region—"a Captain of the Nation named Shadoo"—and brought him back two years later to act as a liaison.[47] The principal investors in Carolina were aware, especially after the eruption of tensions in St. Lucia, that maintaining peaceful relations with the indigenous populations could be a key to success.

The Adventurers' expedition did not immediately result in a successful colony, but it did spur interest in settling Carolina. Of the eighty-five prominent Barbadians who formed the Adventurers, a large number were linked to the final successful settlement in Carolina: Charles Towne.[48] These men were the driving force behind Barbadian involvement in Carolina, obtaining land grants, sending agents and servants to work the plantations, and engineering the bustling trade between Barbados and Carolina. Initially however the Barbadians had to contend with rivals from New England determined to put a colony in Cape Fear, and in the their report on their initial exploration of the area, the Barbadians criticized the New England men's "scandalous" and disparaging reports of Carolina, which were probably designed to deter other settlers.[49] In 1663 the New Englanders, aware that the Barbadians had interests in the region, argued that New England was the most "fit" of any English colony for settling Carolina because, unlike Barbados at that point in time, New England had ample cattle and settlers; they should be the principal architects of the new settlement.[50]

Competing factions had emerged in Barbadian expansion projects by the time the Adventurers sailed, possibly divided along older political allegiances or networks. With the Restoration, Willoughby was returned to power in the English Caribbean. He was focused on the expansion of the sugar frontier in the Leeward Islands and in Surinam. Some of the Adventurers may have directed their efforts toward the Carolina colony to escape his sphere of influence.[51] Thomas Clutterboake, who owned a large plantation in the parish of St. Lucy in northern Barbados, appears to have been the only principal actor involved both in St. Lucia and with the Adventurers in Carolina. That he may be the only significant investor in both schemes suggests the extent to which the architects of these ventures differed.[52] Although he sailed with Hilton and received a warrant for 670 acres of land in Carolina, Clutterboake never migrated to Carolina. He did send two of his servants to Carolina to oversee his interests. Like many of the principal actors involved in Barbadian expansion projects, Clutterboake was already a large landowner; he was more interested in planting capital outside of Barbados than in leaving the island.[53]

In the early 1660s, there were several ambitious Barbadian expansion schemes, but a series of major setbacks in the mid-to-late 1660s curbed Barbadian expansion. These setbacks first discouraged and then ultimately helped foster the successful colonization of Carolina. In 1665 the collapse of the St. Lucia colony was exacerbated by the complete loss of the windward side of St. Kitts to the French, and the French invaded Antigua in 1666. Francis Willoughby—the great architect of expansion projects aimed at expanding the Barbadian sugar frontier—drowned in a hurricane while leading a party of Barbadians to protect St. Kitts. Thousands perished with him.[54] In 1667, with the support of Barbadians, the English managed to keep Nevis. Surinam, however, without its principal benefactor and devastated by an outbreak of the plague in 1666, was captured by the Dutch. The plague had also swept through England in 1665 to 1666, and a fire destroyed much of London in 1666. English concerns were increasingly focused internally. Finally in 1667 the Dutch raid on the Medway destroyed part of the English fleet and precipitated a crisis in English naval power. The Dutch were at the apex of their naval power by the end of the second Anglo-Dutch naval war in 1667, and the French took advantage of English weakness by strengthening their hold on the eastern Caribbean. The flow of servants from the British Isles began to slow significantly after the 1660s as wages improved in the metropole.[55]

By the end of the 1660s, the conditions were no longer ripe for settling new colonies. In 1668, with the English empire still reeling and the potential pool of settlers decimated by fire or plague or slowed by improving wages, the initial Carolinas settlement folded.[56] Led by an overly enthusiastic Barbadian vanguard, the English had spread themselves and their resources too thin in the Caribbean. Fears persisted that the French would use St. Kitts or Antigua as a base to launch an attack on Barbados.[57] Whereas there had been an abundance of potential migrants from Barbados and from England in the late 1650s and early 1660s when Hilton sailed for Carolina, by the end of the 1660s, planting sufficient men on the ground to defend and cultivate the new colony would be difficult.

Population management was a central issue in governance and in the maintenance of empire in the early circum-Caribbean. Tropical diseases, warfare, hurricanes, and brutal tropical labor conditions made death rates high, and predominantly male migration and the resulting unbalanced sex ratios had a deleterious effect on fertility rates and successful family formation. A plantation, in the seventeenth century use of the term, could denote a single operation for tropical cultivation on a large tract of land with a sufficient number of servants or slaves. "Plantation" could also denote a planned settlement in a new region—a planting of people. There were more planting projects than there were settlers in the early modern English Caribbean.

The notion of a zero-sum game in population management was widespread in the seventeenth-century Atlantic; it created significant population rivalries among imperial powers and among the leaders of colonial projects. Thomas Lynch, writing from Jamaica in 1672, stressed that movement from one colony to another would necessarily strengthen the colony receiving settlers and weaken the one losing them.[58] Willoughby used fears about depopulation as ammunition in his efforts to have the Navigation Acts repealed, arguing that the acts had led to thousands of people fleeing Barbados for French and Dutch colonies where they could still conduct free trade.[59] Losing colonists to another empire was an even greater geopolitical threat than losing them in failed settlement projects. In 1667 the Dutch, keen to retain the Surinam settlers and their knowledge of sugar production, gave them substantial capital loans and refused to allow them to leave until their debts had been paid.[60] The Carolina Proprietors petitioned the King to transport the remaining settlers out of Surinam after the Dutch captured the area. They hoped that the settlers would head for Carolina.[61] Most headed to Jamaica. Colonial leaders struggled to direct settlers toward what they felt would be the most appropriate colonies. In 1664 Modyford began to vigorously promote the settlement of Jamaica and the western Caribbean, and Willoughby, intent on spreading the Barbadian sugar complex through the Leeward Islands and Surinam, insisted that thus far Jamaica had been worthless to the empire, and that it had only "robbed" the other colonies of settlers.[62] To help foster population growth in Carolina, John Yeamans, in 1670, assured John Colleton that he had "by my dayly care and Industry withdrawn severall persons from their resolutions of other settlements" such as "Colonel Sharpe from New Yorke who intended a large settlement there."[63] New York, captured from the Dutch in 1664, offered yet another mainland destination for a scanty pool of migrants at the end of the 1660s.

To guarantee a successful settlement, sufficient settlers had to be transplanted voluntarily or through some measure of coercion, and they had to be encouraged to plant appropriately on the landscape. Desperate for sufficient bodies to establish Jamaica, Modyford, after becoming governor of Jamaica, encouraged wealthy men to settle plantations; he also requested that poor and delinquent English be forcefully transported there.[64] Settlers were needed to clear land, and they were needed to defend the settlement. Bodies were needed to guarantee that the settlement remain English both culturally and territorially. Many of the early plans for Carolina stressed that a critical mass of people was needed. The Lords Proprietors of the Carolina colony, in a 1665 letter to Barbadian John Yeamans, warned him not to take his six thousand acres of land grants too close to the main area of settlement because "it will thin the people and weaken that part to the indangering of the whole."[65] They hoped to attract many freeholders clustered in small farms close together. Population density could be achieved only if most of the settlers had small land grants alongside one another in strips stretching out from the river. In a letter to

William Berkeley of Virginia, the Lords Proprietors explained that they sought to plant people on closely bunched farms along the rivers "whereof there wilbe two hundred men armed and lodged within each myle and quarter square or thereabouts."[66] There was a balance to be maintained here, however: Settlers would not choose Carolina over other colonial options if the terms of settlement were less favorable. Large land grants were more likely to attract settlers, especially those with capital.

Whereas Surinam and St. Lucia had the advantage of being close to Barbados, Jamaica and Carolina did not; they both struggled to attract settlers at their inception. Distance was part of the issue, but ocean currents also played a role. The governor of Barbados explained in 1681 that because the island was "the Windwardmost of all the Caribbee Islands itt has little of Trade or Commerce with those that lye to Leeward of itt, it being difficult for theire Vessels to come up to us, or our own to get up again when sent to Leewrd."[67] Likewise whereas it took a few days to sail to Surinam or St. Lucia, the voyage from Carolina could take more than two months and captains were forced to navigate against the predominant currents to make the return voyage.[68]

Carolina, however, offered exactly what Barbados needed: timber, pasturage, and an almost limitless supply of land. The colony could serve the sugar industry in Barbados without glutting the sugar market or competing for workers. The Duke of Albemarle urged settlement of Carolina, predicting that it would "devirt many people that designe to plant from planting those commodyties your plantation abounds in (of which greater quantities being made will sinke the maker) and put them upon such . . . lands" that "will not I conceave produce" sugar.[69] Carolina, he believed, "will not injure nor overthrow the other plantations which may very well happen, if there be a very great increase of sugar workes."[70] The proprietors likewise argued that this was a strong selling point, insisting that the settlers would only plant cotton, tobacco, indigo and ginger. [71]

By the mid-1660s the outmigration from Barbados was troubling prominent men in the island. One contemporary source estimated that by 1667, at least twelve thousand free men had left over the past quarter century.[72] Few white men with vested interests remained to defend the island. By 1670 laws had been passed in Barbados to prevent further outmigration.[73] Laws were also passed to restrict land sales to large planters to help combat the consolidation of lands and encourage more white landholders in higher density.[74] The Carolina Proprietors were aware that they would have difficulty planting Barbadians in the new colony. As they established the first Carolina colony in 1665, they anticipated that "the greatest stocke of people will in probabillity come" to Carolina from New England because "our more southerne plantations" were "already much drayned" of people.[75] Barbadians would be the principal architects, but the people they would plant would need to come from elsewhere.

Contemporaries noted that a critical mass of settlers would be needed in Carolina to allow it to be "more strongly defended from the incursions of savages, and other enemies, pirates and robbers."[76] To encourage settlement in Carolina, John Locke suggested free passage for settlers from Barbados and the Leeward Islands.[77] Captain Henry Brayne, who was transporting the first loads of Carolinian timber to Barbados and returning with more Barbadians, suggested that he would stop at Antigua to try to find more settlers for Carolina. He was certain that the island (which lacks fresh water) was a "graveyard" and that "a great many soules . . . would willingly come off and transport farther from them terrible Hurry Caines that doth everie yeare distroye their Houses and crops."[78] By the time Brayne was sailing in 1670, English, and especially Barbadian, setbacks in the 1660s had made the mainland seem safer for settlement, especially given that the Spanish, Dutch, and French coveted more valuable prizes in the Caribbean Sea. Without Surinam or St. Lucia, Barbadians focused their efforts on Carolina. In fact it was only when these far more promising settlement projects failed that Barbadians—desperate for resources to fuel their sugar-based economy—were forced to revisit the far less attractive option of settling in Carolina.

In 1669 the proprietors assembled a fleet—composed of three ships, the *Carolina*, the *Port Royal*, and the *Albemarle*—in England to settle the Carolina coast. The *Carolina* and the *Port Royal* eventually made their way to the Carolina coast in 1670, after stopovers in Ireland, the Caribbean (including Barbados), and Bermuda, but the *Albemarle* wrecked off the coast of Barbados.[79] While not all the passengers were lost, the ship that was hired to replace the *Albemarle* in Barbados, John Colleton's sloop the *Three Brothers,* seems to have set sail for Carolina with a new set of passengers from the island. By May 1670 the three vessels had met at the mouth of the Ashley and Cooper Rivers to settle, after deciding that the intended location of Port Royal was too close to Spanish possessions. The colonists quickly laid out a town on the Ashley River and established plantations nearby. In February 1671 the *Carolina* returned to Carolina from Barbados, along with the *John and Thomas,* a sloop outfitted by Barbadian merchants John Strode and Thomas Colleton, with more migrants from Barbados.[80] The settlers were told in 1672 that the location was unsuitable; a new town was laid out at Oyster Point, the present location of Charleston. By 1680 Charles Towne was permanently established as the focal point of the colony.

The extent to which the Carolina project was part of a Barbadian narrative of expansion before 1670 is clear, but after Carolina was settled, Barbadians struggled to ensure that their project would serve their interests and conform to their expectations. There were simply not enough potential Barbadian settlers remaining. A comparison of migrants to Carolina with the names of landholders in Barbados shows that few Barbadian landholders traveled to Carolina.[81] Fewer than 120 of the twenty-five-hundred-plus migrants traveling to Carolina between 1670 and 1700 owned land in Barbados. Likewise only a handful of the landholders listed in a 1680 Barbadian census had traveled or would travel to the Carolina.[82] Wealthy Barbadians were not seeking to leave the island, but rather to expand the island's influence and grow their fortunes. It is more difficult to track landless men traveling from Barbados to Carolina, and some of the migrants to Carolina shared a last name with prominent Barbadian landholding families, raising the intriguing possibility that younger sons of these families migrated to Carolina, in search of land. Indeed some landless men probably did travel from Barbados to Carolina, but Barbadians were already complaining that their island's population was drained. The notion that early Carolina was physically settled by wealthy planters from Barbados is erroneous. Barbados played a central role in pushing for a Carolina colony, shaping the proprietorship that governed it, and providing the capital necessary for settlement; the island did not provide many migrants to Carolina. The broader context of the Barbadian diaspora helps explain the curious situation.

The relative scarcity of wealthy settlers from Barbados did not signal a lack of interest in the project. Many of the most prominent planters and merchants of Barbados invested considerable resources in the new colony and were keen to have it succeed, but on their terms. Years before the First Fleet reached Carolina, the 1665 Barbados Adventurers coaxed significant indulgences from the proprietors. They won the right to choose the site of their plantations, contrary to the wishes of the proprietors; they secured headrights for any slaves that they might import; and the planters who had invested in William Hilton's exploratory voyage and previous failed colonies were to get significant land considerations in the new proprietary colony.[83] Barbadians had taken great pains to shape the settlement patterns and productive activities in the prospective satellite. To invest in the prospect of a colony, Barbadians needed assurances that Carolina would encourage the institution of slavery. They demanded that migrants bringing slaves would receive the same headrights for their captives as those who brought servants.[84]

Although it is clear that the Carolina colony was part of a period of Barbadian expansion, scholars continue to debate the extent of the impact of Barbados on Carolina and who was actually "Barbadian," contesting what origins and identity meant in the seventeenth century, often establishing arbitrary standards. Some focus on lengthy, primary residence in Barbados, while others include those who stopped temporarily on the island.[85] The Barbadian influence in Carolina resulted from the influx of capital and from wealthy and well-situated individuals and their agents who had strong ties to the island. The wealth generated on Barbadian plantations was a catalyst for the settlement of Carolina. It is not necessary to talk about a "Barbadian identity" to show the influence of Barbados on Carolina.[86] The historiographical debate about who is "Barbadian" too often devolves into a simple correlation between the number of "Barbadian" migrants in Carolina and the influence that the island had on Carolina. A particularly Barbadian outlook and the development of Barbadian society influenced Carolina in ways that cannot be measured solely by the number of Barbadian immigrants.[87]

As they assess the impact of Barbados on South Carolina, most scholars seem to focus largely on the physical presence of Barbadian people—planted people—in Carolina, not being sufficiently attentive to other kinds of ties to and familiarity with Barbados or to the relative political and economic weight of certain people. James Moore, a governor of Carolina, is a useful example of an individual of complicated origins; a figure some characterize as Barbadian and others as Irish, Moore may or may not have lived in Barbados, but he married into a prominent Barbadian family and allied himself socially and politically with Barbadians in Carolina.[88] In fact he was part of the group that Joseph West identified as a "Barbadoes party," in 1671.[89] Regardless of the amount of time that Moore spent in Barbados, he was identified by contemporaries as someone who was furthering Barbadian goals in Carolina. Individuals like Moore are "Barbadians," with close ties to the island and with the potential to shape early Carolina far more than most migrants through their presence and capital investment.

Prominent Barbadians had particular goals for the colony, but their shared vision went beyond economic or political agendas. One of the most significant elements of a Barbadian outlook was likely its orientation toward a particular kind of geography. The landscapes and climates of the Caribbean were distinctly different from the British Isles, and part of becoming Barbadian was adapting to that environment. Environmental theories about health and character were so prevalent that white migrants to the Caribbean could expect a significant transformation in outlook. The absence of seasons, the nature of the tropical crops, the heat, the distance from the metropole, the ease with which the soil yielded riches, and hurricanes helped create a particular Barbadian set of experiences and perspectives that would have shaped their understanding of Carolina.

Barbadians were able to exercise significant influence on the culture and customs of the region. Indentured servants and slaves extended the culture of the Barbadian plantation complex to Carolina as much as free people did. Most recent studies of the Barbadian influence in Carolina have focused primarily on white migrants' influence in Carolina, but estimates of the enslaved proportion of the population of the colony before 1680 suggest that between a quarter and a third of the migrants were slaves, which increased to over 40 percent by 1700. Most historians agree that the majority of slaves in Carolina during these early years came from, or at least spent significant time in, Barbados.[90] Not all Barbadians envisioned Carolina as a slave colony because they were afraid of making a competitor for labor. The number of white laborers in Barbados had declined sharply by the late 1660s, and migrants were often forced to bring slaves to fill the labor needs of the new colony. Making Carolina a slave society was as much a demographic necessity as it was a determined choice.

Barbadian slaves are not often included in discussions of the impact of Barbadian plantation culture on Carolina. This omission is both glaring and unsurprising, given that records of slave migration and ownership are rare for this period, not just because of the paucity of documents in general, but because a majority of slaves were likely undocumented Africans for whom headrights could not be claimed.[91] Migrants to Carolina were granted headrights for each individual that they brought to the colony, ranging from fifty to 150 acres per person.[92] These warrants were issued only for documented individuals arriving legally, not for slaves who were illegally imported. Land warrants were commonly granted for importing indentured servants, but the few slaves who are claimed for headrights are recorded differently than indentured servants, with surnames rarely listed.[93] The lack of land warrants claiming headrights for importing slaves combined with the evidence of a large black population in the early years of the colony suggests that many undocumented Africans were brought to Carolina.

The few migrants who claimed headrights for slaves in the first decade of the Charles Towne settlement traveled to Carolina with their slaves. Each of the sixteen land warrants claiming land for importing slaves before 1681 also included a claim for a headright based on the immigration of the owner of the slaves. This suggests that during the first decade of settlement, prominent Barbadian planters did not send representatives with large numbers of slaves to establish a new plantation frontier based on staple crops. When Barbadian merchant Richard Dearsley received 310 acres of land for "five Negroes men & women" in December 1681, it marked the first time that a slave owner received headrights for slaves that arrived without their owner or another free migrant.[94]

The extent of the cultural influence of the slaves brought from Barbados to Carolina cannot be known, but the origins of many of the prominent white actors can be traced despite the sparse nature of the evidence. The difficulty in determining the exact origins even of elites is significant, but for most migrants to South Carolina before 1700, it is impossible with extant records.[95] Given this restriction, it is reasonable to make an argument based on the most likely origins suggested by the records and by the context of Barbadian expansion more broadly.

The arrivals in Charles Towne of ships that took on most, or all, of their passengers in Barbados can be used to determine which Carolinians departed from Barbados, unlike those colonists whose ships simply stopped at Barbados. The strong link between Barbados and Carolina was maintained by travel between the two colonies. In 1679, the one year for which thorough records survive, at least twenty ships sailed from Barbados to Carolina and Virginia and thirty-eight individuals departed for Carolina, with several making return trips. Many of these travelers were affluent Barbadians, and their agents traveling between the colonies to monitor their enterprises. They also dispatched family members in need of land to Carolina. Approximately half of the thirty-eight passengers headed to Carolina returned to Barbados in short order, while fifteen took out land grants in Carolina shortly after their arrival. Some of the most prominent men in Carolina, such as Arthur Middleton, were among those shuttling between Barbados and Carolina.[96]

While historians have attempted to detail the migration of Barbadians to Carolina and the political role of Barbadians in pushing the creation of a Carolina colony, the direct economic investment of Barbadians who never made their permanent residence in Carolina has not been well addressed. A significant number of prominent Barbadians who obtained large land grants in Carolina never migrated to the colony. Barbadians who remained resident in Barbados rather than Carolina often set up plantations in Carolina through agents or family but tended to be primarily concerned with trade and investment in the continental colony.[97] Many planters in Barbados began to trade on their own behalf, cutting out merchants after profits fell following 1660, resulting in merchants seizing many plantations to settle debts. When the merchants were cut out of trade with large planters in Barbados, they began to look for other avenues of investment in Carolina. While some merchants did migrate to Carolina and play a prominent role in the young colony, the major merchants conducted their business through agents and visits to the colony.[98] The most prominent Barbadians in South Carolina tended to be both merchants and planters.

The influence of Barbadians in shaping the landscape of early Carolina is clearly visible on early maps of Carolina that reflect the dominance of planters and merchants closely connected to Barbados in acquiring valuable, riverine plantation land. These maps represented both spatial distribution and social hierarchies. Surveyors and mapmakers made choices in selecting which individuals and plantations to place on maps based on how they viewed their status in society and the plantation economy.

The world that migrants to Carolina hewed out of the forested landscape was a constant arena of conflict and competition. Barbadians gained ownership of a large proportion of the desirable plantations near Charles Towne (map 7).[99] The success of Barbadians and their political allies in gaining the ability to choose their own land upon arrival in Carolina was important in establishing their prominence among planters. When land was first granted and surveyed in the 1670s, Barbadians planters were most capable of assessing what land had the greatest value. While all immigrants to Carolina likely prized riverside land, Barbadians and Caribbeans were much more familiar with a semitropical climate and with the type of land that could sustain agricultural production in that climate.[100] Captain Joseph West, an Englishman, had been told to plant in a "manner any planter of Barbados will show you."[101] As a future governor of the colony and the commander of the First Fleet, West was one of the most powerful and well situated settlers, yet he was being instructed to consult with the skillful planters of Barbadians on how best to farm in the Americas.

The valuable land fronting onto the Ashley and Cooper Rivers near the first site of Charles Towne was quickly seized by merchants and planters from Barbados. In the 1671 map, fourteen of the twenty-six plantations in the vicinity of Charles Towne were owned entirely, or in part, by Barbadians, totaling 1,393 of 2,614 acres, nearly half of the land (see map 7).[102] The land was owned by a small group of Barbadians, and most of these men came from prominent families in Barbados. In 1680, when the colonists moved Charles Towne across the Ashley River to the Oyster Point site at the behest of the Lords Proprietors, Barbadians were just as successful at obtaining riverside plantations near the town. Joel Gascoyne's 1682 "A Map of the Country of Carolina" (map 8) draws its material from the work of Maurice Mathews, who served as surveyor general from 1677 to 1684. The planters on the Gascoyne map are heavily Barbadian or like Mathews have strong ties to the island, especially those settled near Charles Towne along the Ashley and Cooper Rivers and their tributaries. In that region, 78 percent of the planters are of Barbadian origin.[103]

Goose Creek, the tributary of the Cooper River that lent its name to the infamous Goose Creek men, was known by contemporaries to be a particularly Barbadian enclave. Settlers loyal to the proprietors clashed with independently minded Barbadian planters and their allies; some of the Barbadian faction formed the Goose Creek men. This group was generally viewed as a key force opposing the Lords Proprietors and their distant rule. The Goose Creek men opposed many of the proprietors' attempts to reform Carolina in the 1680s, from linking quitrent payments and land grants to allowing Lord Cardross's Scottish settlement at Stuart Town. Their actions were often linked to their desire for autonomy and control over the Native American slave trade.[104] Many of these Native American slaves would be sent to labor in the Caribbean. In this sense Carolina was used by the English Caribbean for not just its timber and grazing land but for its labor resources. Although the historiographical emphasis has often been on the degree to which migrants left the English Caribbean to come to Carolina, it is important to acknowledge that if one includes Native Americans, there was probably a net out-migration of people from Carolina to the English Caribbean during the early years of the colony. In contesting the authority of the proprietors, the Goose Creek men were demonstrating the same rebellious autonomy at the heart of Barbadian imperialist and expansionist agendas in the Caribbean.

Given the prevalence of Barbadians in early land grants, many areas on the map look Barbadian, the Goose Creek region especially. Only one of the surnames tied to plantations along Goose Creek is not that of a prominent Barbadian planter or merchant. Historians have challenged the characterization of the Goose Creek men as a cohesive political group, but regardless of how unified the Goose Creek men were, the perception that resistance to the proprietors and agitation for slavery was emanating from this Barbadian enclave is significant. Even if the members of this loose coalition were not all from Goose Creek, they were identified with the place, presumably for its well-earned reputation as a Barbadian stronghold.[105] Aggressive, autonomous actions, independent of the proprietors and the metropole, were associated with the Goose Creek planters; the Goose Creek men were cast collectively in such terms whether they were Barbadian or from other areas of the British Atlantic. The label "Barbadian" came to stand for a certain political and economic agenda and stigmatized planters throughout the Goose Creek region.

John Thornton's 1685 "New Map of Carolina" (map 9) was modeled after his former apprentice, Joel Gascoyne's 1682 map, and the surnames and plantations listed on it were very similar.[106] The slightly more detailed Thornton map has 102 surnames, though a number are repetitions (multiple plantations owned by the same individual or family). Roughly 75 percent of the surnames whose origins can be confidently identified are of families who migrated from Barbados to Carolina, owned plantations in Carolina but lived in Barbados, or had married into Barbadian families.[107] Not only were there regions of concentrated Barbadian presence, like Goose Creek, as seen on Gascoyne's map, but the map shows a predominance of Barbadian landholding across the colony. It is no surprise that Anthony Ashley Cooper worried that Carolina would become "subservient . . . to the interests of Barbadoes."[108] While Cooper was referring to trade between the two colonies, these worries were linked to his larger worries about Barbados's relationship with Carolina. As early as 1671, the proprietors saw a shift in power, worrying that Peter Colleton "might have the advantage of [them] by his interest and mingling of trade with Barbados."[109]

Barbadians' economic and political influence in Carolina worried the Lords Proprietors, but individuals with close ties to Barbados were essential to creating and maintaining the mainland colony. It was a Barbadian venture at the outset, and the influence of this tiny sugar island on the new colony continued after 1670, if to a lesser to degree. Barbadian planters, merchants, and smallholders competed with other investors in the region and with new migrants to entrench their vision of what Carolina would become. The relatively small collection of Barbadians who did migrate to Carolina, coupled with the enormous investments made by Barbadians who did not migrate, allowed these island people to continue to exercise influence entirely out of proportion to their number. These Barbadians and their allies were able to identify and obtain the most desirable land, shape the practical governance of the colony, flaunt the directives of the proprietors, and direct its early economy. They shrewdly manipulated colonial politics; capitalized on the close proximity, compared to England, of Barbados to Carolina; fostering trade between the two colonies;

and filled the Carolina elite with leading wealthy Barbadians. In the wake of a series of dismal settlement failures in the Caribbean, Barbadians strove to retain control of the new mainland frontier.

Notes

1. Peter Wood, *Black Majority: Negroes in Colonial South Carolina from 1670 through the Stono Rebellion* (New York: Knopf, 1974), 13–34; Richard S. Dunn, "The English Sugar Islands and the Founding of South Carolina," *SCHM* 72, no. 2 (April 1971): 81–93; Jack P. Greene, "Colonial South Carolina and the Caribbean Connection," *SCHM* 88, no. 4 (October 1987): 192–210. John P. Thomas Jr., "The Barbadians in Early South Carolina," *SCHGM* 31, no. 2 (April 1930), 75–92; Adelaide Berta Helwig, "The Early History of Barbados and Her Influence upon the Development of South Carolina" (Ph.D. Dissertation, University of California, Berkeley, 1931); Alfred D. Chandler, "The Expansion of Barbados," *Journal of the Barbados Museum and Historical Society* 12 (May 1946): 106–36; Richard Waterhouse, "England, the Caribbean, and the Settlement of Carolina," *Journal of American Studies* 9, no. 4 (December 1975): 259–81; S. Max Edelson, *Plantation Enterprise in Colonial South Carolina*, (Cambridge: Harvard University Press, 2006). L. H. Roper, *Conceiving Carolina: Proprietors, Planters, and Plots, 1662–1729* (New York: Palgrave Macmillan, 2004), 45; Kinloch Bull, "Settlers in Early Carolina: Historiographical Notes," *SCHM* 96, no. 4 (October 1995): 329–39.

2. "Barbadian" here does not connote a shared Barbadian identity but rather includes residents of Barbados, and also those tied to the island who shared the Barbadian vision for the Carolina colony, even if their stay on the island was brief. This distinction is discussed in more detail later.

3. Wood, *Black Majority*, 13–34, 146–47; Peter Coclanis, *Shadow of a Dream: Economic Life and Death in the South Carolina Low Country, 1670–1920* (New York: Oxford University Press, 1989), 9–10; Helwig, "Early History of Barbados," 254. Thomas J. Little, "The South Carolina Slave Laws Reconsidered, 1670–1700," *SCHM* 94, no. 2 (April 1993): 86–101. Russell Menard, "Slave Demography in the Lowcountry, 1670–1740: From Frontier Society to Plantation Regime," *SCHM* 101, no. 3 (July 2000): 190–213.

4. Alison Games, *Migration and the Origins of the Atlantic World* (Cambridge: Harvard University Press, 1999), 102–31; Russell Menard, *Sweet Negotiations: Sugar, Slavery and Plantation Agriculture in Early Barbados* (Charlottesville: University of Virginia Press, 2006); Larry Gragg, *Englishmen Transplanted: The English Colonization of Barbados, 1627–1660* (Oxford: Oxford University Press, 2003).

5. B. W. Higman, "The Sugar Revolution," *Economic History Review* 53, no. 2 (May 2000): 213–36.

6. Lord Francis Willoughby to the King, May 12, 1666, in *CSPC*, vol. 2, no. 1204.

7. Willoughby to the King, May 12, 1666, in *CSPC*, vol. 2, no. 1204.

8. David Eltis, "New Estimates of Exports from Barbados and Jamaica, 1665–1701," *WMQ* 52, no. 4 (October 1995): 648.

9. David Watts, *The West Indies: Patterns of Development, Culture, and Environmental Change since 1492* (Cambridge, U.K.: Cambridge University Press, 1987), 382–447.

10. Menard, *Sweet Negotiations*.

11. Gragg, *Englishmen Transplanted*.

12. Linda Woodbridge, "The Neglected Soldier as Vagrant, Revenger, Tyrant Slayer in Early Modern England," in *Cast Out: Vagrancy and Homelessness in Global and Historical Perspective*, ed. A. L. Beier and Paul Ocobock (Athens: Ohio University Press, 2009), 64–87; A. L. Beier, "'A New Serfdom': Labour Laws, Vagrancy Statutes and Labor Discipline in England, 1350–1800," in *Cast Out*, ed. A. L. Beier and Paul Ocobock, 35–63.

13. Chandler, "The Expansion of Barbados," 106–36, and Gragg, *Englishmen Transplanted*.

14. Willoughby to the King, May 12, 1666, in *CSPC*, vol. 2, no. 1204.

15. Thomas Modyford to John Bradshaw, February 16, 1652, in *CSPC*, vol. 1, no. 41.

16. Chandler, "Expansion of Barbados," 106–36.

17. Cary Heylar to William Heylar, November 7, 1670, Heylar MS, Somerset Record Office, U.K.; Sarah Barber, "Power in the English Caribbean: The Proprietorship of Lord Willoughby of Parham," in *Constructing Early Modern Empires: Proprietary Ventures in the Atlantic World, 1500–1750*, ed. L. H. Roper and Bertrand Van Ruymbeke (Leiden, Netherlands: Brill, 2007), 197–98.

18. Thomas Modyford, "A paper of Col. Muddiford concerning the West Indies, December, 1654," in *A Collection of the State Papers of John Thurloe*, ed. Thomas Birch, (Burlington: Tanner Ritchie Publishing, 2006), 3:62–63; Thomas Gage, "Some briefe and true observations concerning the West-Indies, humbly presented to his highnesse, Oliver, lord protector of the commonwealth of England, Scotland and Ireland," in *State Papers of John Thurloe*, 3:59–61.

19. "An Account of the English Sugar Plantations [1668]," in *CSPC*, vol. 2, no. 1679; Thomas Modyford to John Bradshaw, February 16, 1652, in *CSPC*, vol. 1, no. 41.

20. Reverend C. Jesse, "Important Original Document Brought to Light in Trinidad: 7th June 1664 my Ld. Francis Willughbye instructions to the Governor of Sta. Lucia," *Journal of the Barbados Museum and Historical Society* 28, no. 4 (August 1961): 106.

21. An Account of the English Sugar Plantations [1668], in *CSPC*, vol. 2, no. 1679.

22. Proclamation by Lord Willoughby, November 4, 1663, in *CSPC*, vol. 2, no. 579.

23. Observations on the Barbadoes Petition, in *CSPC*, vol. 2, no. 1682.

24. Willoughby to the King, May 12, 1666, in *CSPC*, vol. 2, no. 1204.

25. Thomas Modyford to John Bradshaw, February 16, 1652, in *CSPC*, vol. 2, no. 41.

26. Thomas Modyford, "A paper of Col. Muddiford concerning the West Indies, December 1654," *State Papers of John Thurloe*, 3:62–63

27. Ibid.

28. Ibid.

29. Barber, "Power in the English Caribbean," 197; Jonathan Atkins to the Lords of Trade and Plantations, July 4/11, 1676, in *CSPC*, vol. 4, no. 973.

30. Renatus Enys to Henry Bennet, November 1, 1663, in *CSPC*, vol. 2, no. 577.

31. Ibid.

32. Petition of his Majesty's loyal subjects now residing in Surinam under the Government of the United Netherlands to the King, April 8, 1671, in *CSPC*, vol. 3, no. 485.1; "The Case of Andrew and Jeronimy Clifford, Planters, Surinam, 1698," Box 13, Item 1, Wilberforce House Museum, Hull, U.K.

33. Thomas Gage, "Some briefe and true observations concerning the West-Indies, humbly presented to his highnesse, Oliver, lord protector of the commonwealth of England, Scotland and Ireland," in *State Papers of John Thurloe*, 3:59–61.

34. Chandler, "Expansion of Barbados," 113.

35. Ibid., 127.

36. Thomas Modyford to Henry Bennet, May 10, 1664, in *CSPC*, vol. 2, no. 739.

37. Jas. Bannister to the King, April 8, 1671, in *CSPC*, vol. 3, no. 485; Thomas Lynch to Lord Arlington, June 7, 1671, in *CSPC*, vol. 3, no. 549.

38. Governor Lord Vaughan to Joseph Williamson, September 20, 1675, in *CSPC*, vol. 4, no. 673.

39. Reverend C. Jesse, "Barbadians buy St. Lucia from the Caribs: The Sale of St. Lucia by Indian Warner and Other Caribs to the Barbadians in A.D. 1693," *Journal of the Barbados Museum and Historical Society* 32, no. 4 (November 1968): 184.

40. Francis Willoughby to the King, November 4, 1663, in *CSPC*, vol. 2, no. 578.

41. As quoted in Jesse, "Barbadians buy St. Lucia from the Caribs," 181.

42. Jesse, "Barbadians buy St. Lucia from the Caribs," 186; Jesse, "Important Original Documents," 106.

43. Jesse, "Important Original Documents," 114.

44. William Willoughby to Lords of the Council, July 9, 1668, in *CSPC*, vol. 2, no. 1788; Andrew Wear, "Making Sense of Health and the Environment in Early Modern England," in *Medicine in Society: Historical Essays*, ed. Andrew Wear (Cambridge, U.K.: Cambridge University Press, 1992), 119–47.

45. *A True Relation of a Voyage upon Discovery of a Part of the Coast of Florida* (London, 1664), 9, 10, 12, 14, 21.

46. Ibid., 21.

47. Report by Robert Sandford concerning his voyage from Cape Fear to Port Royal, Jamaica from June 14 to July 12, 1666, in *CRNC*, 1:124.

48. Among the eighty-five names are some of the most prominent in the early history of Carolina: Dowden, Foster, Gibbes, Grey, Godfrey, Hall, Johnston, Merricke, Norvill, Thompson, Tothill, Yeamans, and many more. Articles of Agreement, January 16, 1664, in *Shaftesbury Papers*, 29–30.

49. Report by Anthony Long, William Hilton, and Peter Fabian concerning their voyage from Barbados to the Cape Fear River from September 29, 1663 to February 6, 1664 [Extract] Long, Anthony; Hilton, William; Fabian, Peter, fl. 17th cent. 1664, in *CRNC*, 1:67–71.

50. Letter from the Cape Fear Company to the Lords Proprietors of Carolina, August 6, 1663, in *CRNC*, 1:36–39.

51. Barber, "Power in the English Caribbean," 207–11.

52. Jesse, "Barbadians buy St. Lucia from the Caribs," 181; Articles of Agreement, January 16, 1664, in *Shaftesbury Papers*, 29–30; Hughes/Queree Name Books, Barbados Department of Archives, Black Rock, Barbados.

53. Clutterboake received a warrant for land in 1672: five hundred acres as his due from the Barbados Concessions and 170 acres for the importation of two servants, Robert Thomas and Mary Thomas. He did not receive a grant for his own migration. A. S. Salley, ed., *Warrants for Lands in South Carolina, 1672–1711* (Columbia: University of South Carolina Press, 1973), 15.

54. An Account of the English Sugar Plantations [1668], in *CSPC*, vol. 2, no. 1679.

55. Russell Menard, *Migrants, Servants and Slaves: Unfree Labor in Colonial America* (Burlington, Vt.: Ashgate, 2001).

56. William Willoughby to the King, July 1667, in *CSPC*, vol. 2, no. 1539.

57. William Willoughby to the King, December 8, 1666, in *CSPC*, vol. 2, no. 1347.

58. Thomas Lynch to the Council for Plantations, July 5, 1672, in *CSPC*, vol. 3, no. 886.

59. Francis Willoughby to the King, November 4, 1663, in *CSPC*, vol. 2, no. 578.

60. Petition of his Majesty's loyal subjects now residing in Surinam . . . , April 8, 1671; A Narrative of the Proceedings of Major Banister in the business of Surinam, November 15, 1670, to April 1671, in *CSPC*, vol., 3, no. 486.

61. Memorial of the Persons concerned in Carolina to the King, March 24, 1669, in *CSPC*, vol. 3, no. 41.

62. Francis Willoughby to the King, November 4, 1663, in *CSPC*, vol. 2, no. 578.

63. Sir John Yeamans to Sir John P. Colleton, November 15, 1670, in *Shaftesbury Papers*, 221–22.

64. Sir Thomas Modyford to Sir Henry Bennet (Lord Arlington), May 10, 1664, in *CSPC*, vol. 2, no. 739.

65. Letter from the Lords Proprietors of Carolina to John Yeamans, Carolina, January 11, 1665, in *CRNC*, 1:94.

66. Instructions from the Lords Proprietors to William Berkeley concerning the settlement of Carolina, 1663, in *CRNC*, 1:50–52.

67. Sir Richard Dutton's answers to the heads of enquiry respecting Barbados, June 11, 1681, CO 1/47, no. 7.

68. Report by Anthony Long, William Hilton, and Peter Fabian concerning their voyage from Barbados to the Cape Fear River from September 29, 1663 to February 6, 1664 [Extract] Long, Anthony; Hilton, William; Fabian, Peter, fl. 17th cent. 1664, in *CRNC*, 1:67–71.

69. Duke of Albemarle to Lord Francis Willoughby, August 3, 1663, in *CRNC*, 1:47.

70. Letter from George Monck, Duke of Albemarle to Thomas Modyford and Peter Colleton, August 30, 1663, in *CRNC*, 1:46–47.

71. Letter from the Lords Proprietors of Carolina to Thomas Modyford and Peter Colleton Carolina, September 9, 1663, in *CRNC*, 1:55–57.

72. Some Observations on the island of Barbados, in *CSPC*, vol. 2, no. 1657.

73. Sir John Yeamans to Sir Peter Colleton, in *Shaftesbury Papers*, 222.

74. Sir Peter Colleton and other planters in London to Christopher Codrington, Deputy Governor, the Council and Assembly of Barbadoes, December 14, 1670, in *CSPC*, vol. 3, no. 357.

75. Letter from the Lords Proprietors of Carolina to John Yeamans Carolina. Lords Proprietors, January 11, 1665, in *CRNC*, 1:93–94.

76. Charter granted by Charles II, King of England to the Lords Proprietors of Carolina Charles II, King of England, 1630–1685, June 30, 1665, in *CRNC*, 1:106.

77. Memoranda in the handwriting of John Locke [1670], *South Carolina Historical Society Collections* (Charleston: SCHS, 1897), 5:223–24.

78. Captain Brayne to the Proprietors, Barbadoes, November 20, 1670, *South Carolina Historical Society Collections* 5: 226–32.

79. Joseph West to Shaftesbury, November 8, 1669, in *Shaftesbury Papers*, 156–57.

80. All of the passengers aboard the *Carolina* on her return voyage to Charles Towne whose origins can be traced with any degree of confidence seem to be from Barbados, with a large number of prominent Barbadians on board. An additional forty-two people arrived aboard the *John and Thomas*. Joseph West to Peter Colleton, March 2, 1671, in *Shaftesbury Papers*, 271; Helwig, "Early History of Barbados," 226.

81. The authors compared the names of 2,541 white migrants to South Carolina between 1670 and 1700 with the names of landholders listed in the Barbadian archives. The authors found only 117 possible matches. The real number is likely much lower because several men probably shared the same name but were not the same person; see Queree/Hughes Name Books and Queree Hughes Plantation Books, Barbados Department of Archives, Black Rock; Agnes Leland Baldwin, *First Settlers of South Carolina, 1670–1700* (Easley, S.C.: Southern Historical Press, 1985).

82. Barbados census of 1680, CO 1/44, No. 47.

83. Each Adventurer who returned to Carolina was to get a grant of five hundred acres, though only Bartholomew Reese and Robert Sandford seem to have done so. Order on Sugar Receipts, December 24, 1670, in *Shaftesbury Papers*, 254–55.

84. Proposalls of Severall Gentlemen of Barbadoes, August 12, 1663, in *Shaftesbury Papers*, 10–12; Barbadoes Concessions, 1663, in *Shaftesbury Papers*, 29–49; Barbadoes Proclamation, November 4, 1670, in *Shaftesbury Papers*, 210–13.

85. Bull, "Barbadian Settlers," 333; Edward McCrady, *The History of the South Carolina Government under the Proprietary Government 1670–1719* (New York: Macmillan, 1897, reprint Russell and Russell, 1969), 327n–328n.

86. For the formation of a Barbadian identity, see Jack P. Greene, "Changing Identity in the British Caribbean: Barbados as a Case Study," in *Colonial Identity in the Atlantic World, 1500–1800*, ed. Nicholas Canny and Anthony Pagden (Princeton: Princeton University Press, 1987), 213–66. For the formation of new colonial identities and the existence of multiple, overlapping identities in the early colonies,

see John H. Elliot, "Introduction: Colonial Identity in the Atlantic World," in *Colonial Identity in the Atlantic World*, 3–14; Greg Dening, "Introduction: In Search of a Metaphor," in *Through a Glass Darkly: Reflections on Personal Identity in Early America*, ed. Ronald Hoffman, Mechal Sobel, and Frederika J. Teute (Chapel Hill: University of North Carolina Press, 1997), 1–6; James Horn and Philip D. Morgan, "Settlers and Slaves: European Migrations to Early Modern British America," in *The Creation of the British Atlantic World*, ed. Elizabeth Mancke and Carole Shammas (Baltimore: Johns Hopkins University Press, 2005), 38–44.

87. In order to determine which early Carolinians had strong ties to Barbados, the authors of this paper have cross-referenced individuals indexed in Baldwin and those mentioned in *Shaftesbury Papers*, with individuals in the 1680 census of Barbados, the Queree/Hughes Name Books, and wills and inventories and baptismal and parish records in Barbados. Baldwin, *First Settlers*, Hughes-Queree Books, Barbados Archives, Barbados census of 1680, CO 1/44, No. 47.

88. Estimates of the "Barbadian" population range from "almost half of the whites and considerably more than half of the blacks" coming in the first two years (Greene, "Caribbean Connection," 197), an estimate that is supplemented by data in Waterhouse ("Settlement of Carolina," 271) and Helwig ("Early History of Barbados," 227) arguing "at least two-thirds" of the white population in 1672. Richard Dunn suggests that while the number of Barbadians migrating to Carolina was low, those who did migrate were often planters and merchants of significant means. Dunn, "English Sugar Islands," 84. Bull makes a similar argument for the relative influence of a small number of Barbadians but challenges a number of the elites that Dunn discusses. (Bull, "Barbadian Settlers," 335). Bull (334) and Roper (7) deny that Moore can be considered Barbadian, while Helwig (273), Greene, *The Quest for Power: The Lower Houses of Assembly in the Southern Royal Colonies, 1689–1776* (Chapel Hill: University of North Carolina Press, 1963), 32, and others list Moore as of Barbados.

89. Joseph West to Shaftesbury, July, 1671, in *Shaftesbury Papers*, 349; Moore married the daughter of Benjamin Berringer, who was also the step-daughter of Sir John Yeamans. It is unclear where the marriage took place. The term "Barbadoes party" has been used to indicate a coherent, recognized political faction by scholars such as L. H. Roper, *Conceiving Carolina*, 45. West's usage, however, is ambiguous; he may be referring to a group of Barbadians immigrating to Carolina rather than to a political alliance.

90. Wood, *Black* Majority, 24, 25; Coclanis, *Shadow of a Dream*, 64; Richard S. Dunn, *Sugar and Slaves: The Rise of the Planter Class in the English West Indies, 1624–1713* (Chapel Hill: University of North Carolina Press, 1972), 115–16; Robert M. Weir, *Colonial South Carolina: A History* (Millwood, N.Y.: KTO Press, 1983), 63.

91. Gregory E. O'Malley, "Beyond the Middle Passage: Slave Migration from the Caribbean to North America, 1619–1807," *WMQ* 66, no. 1 (January 2009): 125–72.

92. Meaghan N. Duff, "Creating a Plantation Province: Proprietary Land Policies and Early Settlement Patterns," in *Money, Trade, and Power: The Evolution of Colonial South Carolina's Plantation Society*, ed. Jack P. Greene, Rosemary Brana-Shute,

and Randy J. Sparks (Columbia: University of South Carolina Press, 2001), 1–25; "Granting of Land in Colonial South Carolina," *SCHM* 77, no. 3 (July 1976): 208–12.

93. Salley, *Warrants for Lands*, 19–20, 379.

94. Salley, *Warrants for Lands*, 291.

95. The majority of the individuals in Baldwin's index for 1670–1700 do not have a place of origin listed, and Baldwin has made an exhaustive search of the South Carolina records and lists place of origin for anyone for whom even an educated guess can be made from the records. Baldwin, *First Settlers*. Richard Waterhouse calculates that a majority of the settlers before 1680 do not have a place of origin (403 out of 683 colonists), an estimate that is supported by the authors' calculations. Waterhouse, "Settlement of Carolina," 271n59.

96. Richard S. Dunn, "The Barbados Census of 1680: Profile of the Richest Colony in America," *WMQ* 26, no. 1 (January 1969), 6, 27–29; Barbados census of 1680.

97. Chandler, "Expansion of Barbados," 127–28.

98. Waterhouse, "Settlement of Carolina," 276–77.

99. *Culpeper's Draught of Ashley River, 1671, Collections of the South Carolina Historical Society*, vol. 5 (Charleston, S.C.: S. G. Courtney, 1987), front matter.

100. Edelson, *Plantation Enterprise*, 45–46.

101. Copy of Instruccons For Mr. West About O^r Plantation, July 27, 1669, in *Shaftesbury Papers*, 127.

102. These figures include only those individuals whose strong ties to Barbados could be confirmed in extant source material. For tracts of land owned by more than one person and not yet divided, the acreage was divided equally among all individuals named.

103. The plantations included in this calculation are the numbered locations near Charles Towne described in "A Table of the names of Such Settlements as are upon Ashley and Cooper Rivers & other adjacent places." Twenty-five of the thirty-two names for families with origins can be reasonably identified are Barbadian. This does not include colonists like Mathews who were politically linked to the "Barbadoes party" but came directly from England. Joel Gascoyne, "A New Map of the Country of Carolina. With it's Rivers, Harbors, Plantations, and other accommodations. Don from the latest Surveighs and best Informations, by order of the Lords Proprietors." Library of Congress, Geography and Map Division, American Memory.

104. Robert Weir, *Colonial South Carolina*, 64–67; Roper, *Conceiving Carolina*, 7–8; M. Eugene Sirmans, *Colonial South Carolina* (Chapel Hill: University of North Carolina Press, 1966), 41–43. Edgar, *South Carolina*, 84–85.

105. Clarence L. Ver Steeg, *Origins of a Southern Mosaic: Studies of Early Carolina and Georgia* (Athens: University of Georgia Press, 1975), 31n2. Roper identifies Job How, Ralph Izard, Sir Nathaniel Johnson, George Logan, Maurice Mathews, James Moore, and Robert Quarry as leading members of the Goose Creek faction. Of these only James Moore could be considered Barbadian, though Johnson was from the Caribbean. Roper argues that the Goose Creek men's lack of "direct experience with slavery" distances them from a connection to the Caribbean (6). See also L. H. Roper, "Conceiving an Anglo-American Proprietorship: Early South

Carolina History in Perspective," in *Constructing Early Modern Empires: Proprietary Ventures in the Atlantic World, 1500–1750*, ed. L. H. Roper and Bertrand Van Ruymbeke (Leiden, Netherlands: Brill, 2007), 399–401.

106. John Thornton, Robert Morden, Philip Lea, "A New Map of Carolina" (1685), in Cumming, *Early Maps*, map 104.

107. Fifty-six of the instances of surnames could be confidently identified; of these fifty-six, forty-two had strong Barbadian connections.

108. The Proprietors to the Governor and Council at Ashley River, May 18, 1674, in *Shaftesbury Papers*, 436.

109. Chandler, "Expansion of Barbados," 130–31; Shaftesbury to Joseph West, April 27, 1671, in *Shaftesbury Papers*, 317.

Dr. Henry Woodward's Role in Early Carolina Indian Relations

Eric E. Bowne

Dr. Henry Woodward played a little-known but crucial role in the success of the Carolina colony. As a go-between during the years 1666 through 1686, he was instrumental in obtaining food and intelligence from the native peoples of the region and in developing peaceful relations and commerce with several prominent nations, including the Westos, Yamasees, and Lower Creeks. Despite these activities, Woodward is only briefly discussed in most histories of South Carolina when he is mentioned at all.[1] He is likewise given little attention in scholarly works concerned with the development and expansion of Indian trade, most of which begin their studies about the time of Woodward's death.[2] The most extensive accounts of the doctor remain Verner Crane's *The Southern Frontier* and Herbert Bolton and Mary Ross's *The Debatable Land*, both published in the 1920s.[3] Recent scholars have begun to hint at the importance of Woodward, but none have fully explicated the source of his success or explored how his life can enrich our understanding of the nature of early Anglo-Indian relations.[4]

Although many others would eventually follow his path, Woodward, thanks in large part to his Indian wife, was the first Carolinian to immerse himself in the study of native language and culture and, more important, the first to gain a subtle understanding of native diplomatic principles and procedures. The uniqueness of his knowledge, the small-scale nature of the Indian trade, and its dependence on kinship ties and linguistic ability combined to give Woodward a tremendous advantage over other traders and made him indispensable to the colony. The doctor used these advantages to procure a position as one of the Lords Proprietors' principal agents and was given charge over their monopoly on the Indian trade, which placed Woodward at the center of the most contentious issue faced by the colony during its early years and put him in the vanguard of England's imperial struggle with Spain in the South. To the degree other Carolinians were able to gain some of his skills and experiences, Woodward's advantages were compromised, but this was slow in coming, and the doctor continued to have a profound effect on the development of the English deerskin and slave trade until his passing in the mid-1680s.

Henry Woodward's interactions with the native peoples of Carolina began in the summer of 1666, when he was a member of Robert Sanford's exploratory mission along the coast.[5] During late June and early July, the group encountered numerous Indian peoples and visited a number of native towns, including one that contained "a faire woodden Crosse of the Spaniards ereccon."[6] Shortly before the Englishmen departed the area for home, the cacique of Port Royal came aboard Sanford's ship with his nephew and, after some discussion, convinced the captain to accept the young man as an ambassador in exchange for one of his crew. Sanford already had someone in mind because "one of my Company Mr. Henry Woodward, a Chirurgeon, had before I sett out assured mee his resolucon to stay with the Indians if I should thinke convenient."[7] As part of a ceremony the following day, July 8, the "Cassique placed Woodward by him uppon the Throne, and after lead him forth and shewed him a large field of Maiz which hee told him should bee his, then hee brought him the Sister of the Indian that I [Sanford] had with mee telling him that shee should tend him and dresse his victualls and be careful of him."[8]

Henry Woodward had been left in disputed territory and would remain a central figure in the struggle between England and Spain for possession of "La Florida" over the next two decades. The key to usurping Spanish power lay in developing strong native allies, which was clearly what Sanford had in mind when he agreed to the exchange. On the other hand, what did the Indians of Port Royal seek to gain? As early as 1659, Indian slave raiders had invaded Spanish Florida in search of victims, and many outlying groups had fled to the missions seeking protection. The Spanish were unwilling to sell firearms to native peoples, however, and so the cacique of Port Royal was investigating other options. He hoped his nephew would gain some understanding of the English newcomers while his niece "trained" Woodward in native language and culture and at the same time bound him to the cacique as a kinsman.

The young doctor had entered a social world that was heavily influenced by women, and though it must have seemed extremely alien to him, Woodward proved to be an apt pupil. Most southeastern Indian societies, including the one into which he had married, were matrilineal.[9] Having married a daughter of the cacique's sister, Woodward effectively became a member of the society's leading family, which gave him an "international" status among neighboring native societies that later proved advantageous in establishing Carolina's Indian trade. Throughout the ensuing early colonial period, marriages such as this generally preceded exchange partnerships between Indians and Europeans, and both sides had much to gain from these relationships.[10] John Lawson, writing at the turn of the eighteenth century, found native wives "very serviceable to them on account of dressing their victuals and instructing 'em in the affairs and customs of the country. Moreover, such a man gets a great trade with the savages."[11] Thomas Nairne, a contemporary of Lawson, noted that by "taking a mistress . . . he [a trader] has at once relations in each Village . . . and if in travelling he acquaints them with what fameily he is incorporated into, those of that name treat, and wait on him as their kinsman."[12]

Over the next four years, Woodward became embroiled in the sorts of adventures generally found in Hollywood films, and his exploits became legend among the early Carolinians. Woodward lived among his native hosts for several months, but his presence eventually became known to the Spaniards, who captured him at Port Royal in 1667. The doctor remained prisoner of the Spanish until 1668, when he was rescued by the English privateer Robert Searle during the sacking of St. Augustine. After being dropped off on one of the Leeward Islands, Woodward joined another Caribbean privateer vessel, for which he served as surgeon. It seems Woodward intended to return to England, where he hoped to use his knowledge of Carolina to gain the favor of the Lords Proprietor. His ship, however, was lost in a hurricane near Nevis Island in August 1669, though Woodward managed to reach the shore. Before he had a chance to secure another passage, Woodward encountered the would-be colonists when they stopped at Nevis, and he volunteered to accompany them to Carolina.[13] Thus in December 1669, Woodward departed from Nevis Island aboard the ship *Carolina,* an official member of the colony of the same name, for which he would soon prove invaluable.

On March 15, 1670, after an arduous journey, Woodward arrived again in Carolina, and within weeks of the establishment of Charles Town, he set off to explore the interior, presumably with at least one Indian guide. It is not known whether or not the doctor suggested this mission or if the task was assigned to him by one of the leading men of the colony. In any case Woodward was gone for over a month, during which time he traveled "fourteene days journey [north] westward up into the Maine, as farr as the fruitfull Country of Chufytachyque," where he "contracted a league with ye Emperor & all those Petty Cassekas betwixt us & them."[14] Apparently Woodward also made a "very large discovery" during his explorations that he was willing to share with the proprietors only in person.[15] The doctor's first foray in international diplomacy on behalf of the Carolina colony was an unqualified success, and the natives of the region were "greatly affected towards him."[16] Woodward had clearly been an attentive student during his time among the Indians of Port Royal four years earlier and must have pleasantly surprised the people of Cofitachequi with his knowledge of native ways.

Although Europeans and Indians could agree on certain aspects of what made a good go-between—a well-known man with the right temperament and courage—they had fundamentally different ideas about the skill and position of negotiators. Native peoples did not care whether or not a go-between spoke European languages, and they did not commonly expect him to go to any great lengths to master the subtleties of European cultures. Native go-betweens were chosen from men of standing who possessed notable oratory skill and a nuanced understanding of native protocol.[17] Europeans, on the other hand, expected their go-betweens to be well versed in Indian languages and cultures. Learning native ways was hard, however, and did not appeal to many educated men, and consequently, most colonial go-betweens were of the meaner sort though officials longed for more educated negotiators.[18] Woodward—as a member of a cacique's family with an understanding of Indian protocol, and as an educated European with skill in native language and culture—lived up to both standards without the ambiguity of mixed-blood heritage. In fact the doctor was arguably as suited to the tasks of a go-between as anyone who played the role before or after him in Carolina.

When Woodward arrived back in Charles Town in July, the colonists were still waiting for the return of a ship that had been sent to Virginia in May to procure supplies, and the situation had become desperate. Using his newly developed influence with the neighboring Indians, Woodward obtained food enough for all the colonists. The Grand Council later reported to the proprietors, "The Doctor hath lately been exceeding useful to us in the time of scarcity of provision, in dealeing with the Indian for our supplyes."[19] Although he was English, Woodward had married into an important matrilineage and as a linguist and mediator between cultures occupied a prominent position in his own right. Woodward's request was thus a matter of international goodwill and because he had already established peaceful relations could be met only with a positive response.

In August, still awaiting word of the ship, Woodward received intelligence from Port Royal Indians that a combined force of Spaniards and mission Indians were lurking around the mouth of the Stono River in a Spanish vessel and as many as thirty dugouts.[20] He feared the Spanish knew of the scarcity of their provisions and intended to attack Charles Town or blockade the harbor to prevent resupply. Once again Woodward sought the assistance of natives, "& all the Indians about us came in with their full strength to our Ayde."[21] In the midst of the general alarm over the possibility of a Spanish assault, the supply ship finally arrived from Virginia, and the attack never materialized. Although hindsight obscures the fact, there was no guarantee that the colony of Carolina would be successful, and Woodward helped assure its sustenance and defense when the colony was in its weak, nascent state. Local native groups were forced to choose whether or not to ally themselves with the Spanish or the upstart English, and their choices had tremendous impact on the imperial struggle for the south. Woodward's skill and cultural acumen was an important part of the reason many native groups ultimately favored the Carolinians.

The Lords Proprietors of Carolina did not need to meet the good doctor to recognize what he had done for their fledgling colony, and in April 1671, Lord Ashley wrote to Woodward thanking him and assuring, "you shall have noe reason to repent the paynes you have taken, and the ventures you have run in Carolina in order to our settlement there."[22] He was given a hundred pounds credit by the proprietors, and Ashley added an extra twenty pounds "as a particular gratuity from my selfe."²³ Lord Ashley praised Woodward for keeping silent about his Cofitachequi discovery and gave him a code with which he could communicate about mineral resources in future correspondence without fear if the information fell into the wrong hands.²⁴ Woodward could hardly have envisioned such spectacular results when he volunteered to stay among the native peoples of Carolina five years before, but his "paynes" and "ventures" had truly paid off for both the colony and himself.

The doctor soon put his unique set of skills to further use, this time at the behest of John Yeamens, who asked him to undertake a secret overland journey to Virginia, a distance of several hundred arduous miles. On July 17, 1671, Woodward composed a will before he embarked on the trip and gave Yeamens the authority to handle his affairs while he was away.²⁵ It is likely Yeamens sent him to Virginia to learn about the nature of the Indian trade there and to discover the best way to compete in the business with their English neighbors to the north. The proprietors had always intended to develop native commerce, envisioning it as a means by which to fund the eventual development of plantations, and Woodward soon proved to be their most valuable agent in the trade. Sometime in late July or early August, Woodward, accompanied by an Englishman named James Needham and presumably one or more native guides, left for what would prove to be a journey of several months.²⁶

Although little evidence of their journey remains, Woodward and Needham undoubtedly learned a great deal about the southern Indian trade. During the seventeenth century, trade networks in the interior were in their nascent stage of development in the South, and Europeans, in addition to lacking the necessary linguistic experience, were not familiar with the "rules" of exchange. Native diplomacy involved a dizzying round of ceremonies, speeches, and feasts that seemed superfluous to most Europeans but were considered essential by Indians. Reciprocal gift giving, an old custom in establishing trade ties, took on new meaning and importance with the influx of European goods, and natives were likely to be offended when colonists refused their gifts or gave none in return.²⁷ When trade goods did change hands, native measuring systems were the only accounting methods used—beads came by the arm's length and rum by the mouthful.²⁸ Europeans, however, were able to incorporate some of their own practices (such as toasts and gun salutes) into the emerging Anglo-Indian forest diplomacy, and Woodward was part of the process of creating these new norms.²⁹

Much of Virginia's commerce with native peoples occurred in the Chesapeake Bay area until the powerful Powhatan Confederacy was destroyed in 1644, after which Fall Line forts were converted to trading posts, and a law was enacted that granted any free citizen of Virginia the right to trade with Indians.³⁰ By 1671 commerce was thriving in the Virginia backcountry. The stores of entrepreneurs such as Abraham Wood, Cadwallader Jones, and Thomas Stegge and his nephew William Byrd I were stocked with "Guns, Powder, Shot,

Hatchets (which the Indians call Tomahawks), Kettles, red and blue Plains, Duffields, Stroudwater blankets, and some Cutlery Wares, Brass Rings, and other Trinkets."[31] These goods were loaded onto packhorses, each of which could carry between 150 and two hundred pounds and could travel up to twenty miles a day.[32] Several packhorse trains left the Fall Line forts each year, generally traveling either south along the Occaneechee Path or west across the mountains to the New River and then north.[33]

Virginians lacked the experience and cartographic knowledge to take their goods directly to customers in the interior, however, and thus required native middlemen to help facilitate exchange. Paradoxically these brokers presented an obstacle to the expansion of interior trade by controlling access in both directions, creating a bottleneck of sorts with themselves in the preeminent position. In the Virginia backcountry, the most ambitious group of native middlemen was the Occaneechees, and the trade items they coveted the most were guns and ammunition. A small number of other groups in the area also had firearms at this time, including the Susquehanna around the Chesapeake Bay, the Tomahitans in the Appalachians, and the Westos on the northern frontier of Spanish Florida. As a result, Woodward and Needham discovered intense competition between native societies in the region, who were willing to violently protect their access to European goods. It was a fierce field of play, but Woodward soon proved he was as adept at economics as he was linguistics.

The astute doctor would have concluded that Carolina was in a position geographically to seriously challenge the Virginia market in Indian slaves since many of the captives were taken from the outskirts of the Spanish mission system in present-day Florida, Georgia, and Alabama, and Carolinians offered a closer source of arms and ammunition than their northern neighbors. Ultimately, although the Chesapeake remained an important port of entry for African slaves, Carolina was able to dominate the deerskin and Indian slave trade of the interior, and geography was not the only reason for their success. Diplomacy played a particularly important role in international affairs among the Indians of the Eastern Woodlands, and at this time, Woodward was the most accomplished English diplomat in the south. His counterparts in the Virginia trade, men such as Abraham Wood and William Byrd, though they may have had more business experience did not possess Woodward's skill set and were thus at a disadvantage in trade negotiations.

It was perhaps fortunate that Woodward had received an education in the Indian trade considering the task with which he was charged in 1674. In a letter dated May 23, Ashley instructed his trusted agent to "consider whether it be best to make a peace with the Westoes or the Cussitaws which are a more powerfull Nation . . . by whose Assistance the Westoes may be rooted out."[34] Once peace had been reached, Woodward was to manage a trade with the new native allies under the direction of Ashley's principal agent, Andrew Percival, for which the doctor was to receive one-fifth of the profit. In addition he was to negotiate with the Edisto Indians, among whom Woodward had spent his first night in a native village in 1666, for the purchase of part of their territory. Finally the doctor was instructed to write a letter, presumably in Spanish, to the governor at St. Augustine requesting a clandestine trade with the Lords Proprietors of Carolina. Woodward was assured that he would be well rewarded if his efforts were fruitful.[35] Ashley and his associates clearly trusted him to make important decisions and carry out politically sensitive tasks, and Woodward soon had a chance to prove their faith in him well founded.

Having received word from Andrew Percival that unfamiliar Indians had come to St. Giles plantation to trade, Woodward immediately traveled there by boat from Charles Town arriving on October 10, 1674.[36] He suspected the Indians were Westos, the group of slave raiders that so terrified the region's native societies, and his suspicions were correct. The Westos had been in the South for well over a decade, capturing prisoners, hunting deer, and trapping beaver, all of which they exchanged with Virginia traders.[37] Recently, however, the competition between native groups vying for trade opportunities in the Virginia backcountry had escalated, and as a result, the Westos were finding it increasingly difficult to maintain their economic and military advantages.[38] A partnership with Carolina made sense for the Westos, but they first had to negotiate a peace with the English newcomers whom they had been at odds with since the founding of the colony.

By this time Woodward had a widely known reputation among Indians as a linguistically gifted ambassador with regional kinship ties and the proper respect for native diplomacy. It is possible that the Westos sought Woodward out on purpose, but it may well have been a fortuitous coincidence. In any case, after they "bartered their truck," the Westos made it clear through signs that they wanted the Englishman to accompany them when they left, and Woodward quickly agreed.[39] Clearly wary of spending the night near the plantation, the ten Westo negotiators convinced their European counterpart to leave that very afternoon. As they proceeded on the eight-day journey to the Westo town, Woodward's companions reiterated their desires, having "drawne upon trees (the barke being hewed away) the effigies of a bever, a man on horseback and guns, Intimating thereby as I suppose, their desire for friendship, and comerse with us."[40]

On October 17, they reached the Westobau River, the present Savannah, where Woodward was greeted by a Westo leader who offered him "a good repast of those things they counte rarietys amonge them."[41] Following the meal Woodward was taken by dugout canoe a short way upstream to Hickahaugau, a palisaded town on the west bank, surrounded on three sides by a bend in the river. Upon landing, Woodward fired both his musket and pistol in the customary backcountry greeting and was promptly answered by a discharge of at least fifty firearms. Scores of young men painted for war, or as Woodward described them, "drest up in their anticke fighting garb," escorted the Englishmen past at least a hundred dugout canoes, up a steep bank, and through town to the residence of the leader.[42] Woodward understood what would have been a frightful sight to virtually all his contemporaries as simply a routine, if raucous, introduction to any important parlay. He knew what his hosts expected of him and acted accordingly as they "oyled my eyes and joynts with beares oyl, they presented mee divers deare skins, setting before me sufficient of their food to satisfy at least half a dozen of their owne appetites."[43]

After the preliminaries were out of the way, the "cheife of the Indians made long speeches intimateing their own strength (and as I judged their desire of friendship with us)."[44] Woodward did not have to be convinced of the strength of the Westos, and his letter to Lord Ashley in December 1674 suggests he had already spent a good deal of time gathering intelligence about them and their place in regional politics. He recounted in some detail the names and locations of the Westos' principal enemies, information that would have been difficult to obtain directly from them given the language barrier. Clearly Woodward was either well prepared for this initial meeting with the slave raiders, or he soon probed his native informants for intelligence. In any case, during the ten days he stayed at Hickahaugau, Woodward negotiated a trade deal with the Westos and expected them to return to St. Giles plantation the following spring with "deare skins, furrs and younge slaves," one of whom they presented to him as a token of their agreement.[45]

On October 25, two days before he returned to the colony, Woodward was party to the first meeting between the Savannahs, a group of Shawnee Indians, and the Westos. Although he could not understand the Shawnee language any better than that of his hosts, Woodward was able to discover they had journeyed nearly three weeks and "brought Spanish beads . . . makeing signes that they had comerce with white people like unto mee, whom were not good."[46] Apparently the Savannahs' dislike of Spanish trade policies, principally the ban on the exchange of arms and ammunition, had led them to seek another European trading partner. First, however, they had to establish peaceful relations with the most powerful native group in the region. Toward that end they warned the Westos of an impending assault on Hickahaugau, though the attack may have been a fabrication used to add weight to their claims of friendship. Either way, the two groups appear to have maintained an amicable relationship over the ensuing half dozen years.

Woodward's trip to Hickahaugau marked the beginning of a six-year trading partnership between Carolina and the Westos that would have ramifications for virtually every group, both Indian and European, that inhabited the American South. Their partnership protected the Westos' firearms advantage by giving them a monopoly on legally exchanged arms and ammunition originating from the Carolina colony and allowed them to bypass the difficulties in transporting slaves to Virginia. For their part the Carolinians gained a powerful Indian ally capable of "protecting" the colony from the incursions of the

Spanish and their native auxiliaries while also providing a lucrative source of income for the Lords Proprietors. The advantages of the partnership turned out to be short lived, but its effects were far reaching.

Westo aggression had already had a significant effect on the social geography of Spanish Florida during the early 1660s. The Westos first raided the Guale missions in 1661, and their depredations were directly responsible for the 1662 abandonment of the mission town of Talaje and probably for the relocation of the Satuache mission. The Westos perhaps also supplied the major impetus behind the formation of the Yamasees, a confederacy of diverse native peoples first recorded in 1662, the population of which was composed in large part of refugees from the chiefdoms of Altamaha, Ocute, and Ichisi, all of which were located along the mission frontier in present central Georgia. By 1667 the Westos were also attacking Indian settlements along the coast of present South Carolina, members of which sought aid from the English newcomers. The Westos may have sought a trade agreement with the Carolinians in 1674, before they began to slave in earnest the largest remaining Indian province in the region, Cofitachequi. They may also have desired an English alliance in order to keep other native groups from developing a similar partnership.[47]

At any rate news of the momentous agreement between the Westos and the Carolinians spread quickly throughout the region. In 1675 a Chisca Indian woman escaped from the English after having been sold by a Westo warrior for a shotgun and reported the new economic arrangement to the Spanish authorities in St. Augustine on May 23, claiming the Carolinians had established themselves just five days north of the Apalachee mission in present Tallahassee, Florida.[48] Historian Steven Hahn interprets the testimony as evidence of Woodward's first trip west to the Chattahoochee River valley, home of the Cussitas, Cowetas, and other groups that would later be known collectively as the Lower Creeks.[49] He further posits that the Indian boy given to Woodward the previous fall by the Westos may have been from the Chattahoochee valley and therefore able to serve him as a guide and source of intelligence about the area. In any event, the appearance of an Englishman deep in the interior seems unlikely at this time without the consent if not guidance of the Westos.

The Westos had good reason to lead Woodward to the Chattahoochee—the peoples of the valley had the potential to pose a significant threat to the preeminent position the Westos held in the Indian-European exchange system. The population of what the Spanish referred to as Apalachicola province was substantial enough to challenge the established slave raiders, and the Westos knew from experience that alliances could be broken if they weren't maintained by constant vigilance and regular maintenance. It is therefore possible that they took Woodward to the Chattahoochee valley hoping he would serve as an ambassador to help negotiate a peace with the Cussitas and their allies. It appears the Westos intended to serve as middlemen in the trade between the

English and the people of Apalachicola, allowing them to increase their supply of furs, skins, and slaves in response to the rapidly escalating demand from Carolina, while removing the threat of the Cussitas by becoming their supplier of European goods, and at the same time limiting their contact with the English. If the Westos indeed pursued such a strategy, it seems to have worked, because despite clear evidence of exchange between them, the Carolinians did not establish a direct trading partnership with the Cussitas until after the Westo were effectively dispersed nearly a decade later.

In 1677 the Lords Proprietors once again acknowledged the pivotal role Woodward played in Carolina's Indian relations by acknowledging that the "discovery of ye Country of ye Westoes & ye Cussatoes . . . hath bine made . . . by the Industry and hazard of Dr. Henry Woodward, and a strict peace & amity made Betweene those said Nations and our people in our province of Carolina."[50] Woodward's one-fifth share in the proprietary trade monopoly was reaffirmed, and he was made deputy of the Ashley River area in addition to receiving over two thousand acres of land from his patrons in England.[51] Woodward had used bold initiative to convert his standing among local native societies into profit and advancement in the colony. Predictably other Carolinians sought to procure the benefits of the Indian trade for themselves, and competition became fierce in the late 1670s. The power and leverage Woodward had derived from his linguistic and cultural knowledge during the early years of the colony decreased as other Englishmen gained experience in the region. The Westos inadvertently prolonged his advantage by blocking English access to interior native groups, but they could do so only as long as Woodward maintained their arms advantage by restricting the gun trade—a tenuous situation at best.

A group of planters known to history as the Goose Creek men, so named because many of them resided on the aforementioned creek near the head of the Cooper River, offered the greatest challenge to the Lords Proprietors and their agents. These antiproprietary Anglicans took advantage of the practice of enslaving prisoners captured in a "just war" as the "ancient soldier's pay" to force their way into the Indian slave trade, the most lucrative business in the colony.[52] Most Carolinians wished for an end to the trade monopoly of the proprietors, and the Goose Creek men used this sentiment to gain power in the Charles Town Grand Council, where their warmongering gained official sanction. Fomenting war among the natives of the region resulted in a dual advantage—it not only produced prisoners for sale but also created fear of Indian uprisings against the colony, which the Goose Creek men used to justify their commissions as captains with control over the colony's powder stores and the authority to raise fighting forces.[53] These planters, men such as James Moore, John Boone, and Maurice Mathews, had thus positioned themselves to remove the final obstacle to the trading empire they envisioned—the military presence of the Westos.

The Goose Creek men sought to undermine the advantage of the Westos by illegally exchanging firearms with other native groups. Once they received guns, these groups needed little prompting to seek war captives since it was the quickest means of obtaining the powder and shot they now relied on. The increased availability of firearms led to a rapid escalation in the volume of the Indian slave trade, and competition between native societies resulted in a number of fierce little wars. The Carolina backcountry was beginning to resemble that of Virginia, where the advances of the Occaneechee, Susquehanna, Tomahitan, and others had forced the Westos to seek out the Carolinians as alternative trading partners to the Virginians. This time however the Westos had nowhere to retreat and no new trading opportunities to exploit. They became simply one of several options for English traders and were hard-pressed to maintain the economic and military advantages that made them so feared an enemy for over twenty years.[54]

In late April 1680, a small number of Englishmen led a multinational force of Indians, including Westos, on a raid against the Guale mission province in present Georgia. There is evidence that suggests the Spanish believed Woodward led or at least prompted the attack, but English records do not indicate whether or not he even took part in the campaign.[55] Although the mission town of Santa Catalina de Guale was abandoned as a direct result of the assault, very few prisoners were taken in the raid, which was considered a financial failure by Charles Town traders.[56] The disappointment over the spring campaign created the opportune setting for the Goose Creek men to launch their plan to destroy the Westos; discredit their chief rival, Woodward; and destroy the proprietary monopoly on Indian trade. In June, at the behest of the planters from Goose Creek, the Grand Council made it illegal to trade arms and ammunition to the Westos and warned the native slave traders to stay away from Carolina "lest that they should fall among some of the people whose friends they had causeleslie killed for whose bloud noe Reperation hath yet been made."[57]

Following the council session, Moore and Boone traveled to Hickahaugau under the auspices of negotiating with the Westos, who may not yet have been aware that anything was amiss with their Carolina partnership. Woodward believed the Goose Creek men made the trip to the Westo town in order to scout their enemy and devise a plan by which they could capture the majority of Westos and sell them as slaves, and he apparently informed the group of his suspicions, perhaps even inciting them against his trade rivals. A Westo leader later testified that "Dr. Woodward did say that the people were bad and therefore they should knock Captain Moore and Mr. Boone on the head," a euphemism for murder.[58] The doctor's misgivings proved well founded when "ye heads of ye Westos [were] taken whilst they were in treaty with ye government and so under ye publiche faith for their safety, and put to death in Cold blood."[59]

The Westo response to the treacherous opening salvo of what would come to be known as the Westo War was a clear indicator that the balance of power in the region was shifting. The northern invaders, once so feared, desired only to negotiate a peace and sought out the Savannahs, erstwhile trading partners of the Goose Creek men, to plead their case to the Carolinians, but their onetime native allies sold the peace ambassadors into slavery.[60] The action taken by the Savannahs, who served as the principal combatants on the side of the colony during the war, was clearly an attempt to usurp the position of the Westos. The Savannahs, supplied by the Goose Creek men, had the advantage in the conflict after those same men convinced the Grand Council that Woodward had encouraged the Westos to enslave Indians allied to the colony, and he was stripped of his trade rights and fined.[61] The Westo War, which raged intermittently from 1680 to 1682, permanently shattered the preeminence the group had enjoyed since well before the founding of Carolina, though remnants of the nation remained in the region as late as the early eighteenth century.[62]

The proprietary monopoly had failed and would end officially in 1684. The volume of trade was expanding rapidly, and new strategies were required. Previously the Westos and the Lords Proprietors of Carolina had independently schemed to keep the traffic in Indian slaves flowing at a rate that they could control, but the rise to power of the Goose Creek men and the removal of the Westos as an obstacle to the expansion of Indian trade was like the bursting of a dam. The capture and exchange of slaves increased exponentially in the aftermath as Englishmen sought entrance into the trade and native groups sought the firearms necessary for protection against raiders. Eventually this "positive" feedback loop would spiral out of control and provide a major impetus for the native-initiated Yamasee War of 1715, but for now the Goose Creek men had gotten what they wanted.

Although they had successfully destroyed the Westos and temporarily hamstrung the trade efforts of Woodward, the Goose Creek men drew the wrath of the proprietors in the process. Lord Ashley and his associates were not informed about the Westo War until after it had begun and learned of the conflict from a ship's captain, not from any official correspondence from the Grand Council.[63] They could not ascertain "whether this warr was made upon a reall necessity for the preservation of the Colony, or to serve the ends of particular men by trade," but they strongly suspected the latter.[64] They feared war profiteers had induced the Savannahs "through Covetuousness of your gunns, Powder and shott and other European Comodities to make war upon your neighbors, to ravish the wife from the Husband, kill the father to get ye child and to burne and Destroy ye habitations of these poore people."[65] The accusations against Woodward could not be confirmed or denied by the proprietors, so for a time they considered him just as culpable as the Goose Creek men.

In February 1681 the proprietors instructed Andrew Percival to seek an end to the Westo War on terms agreeable not only to both parties but also to the relatives of Westo victims among the colony's other Indian allies—a nearly impossible task.[66] Percival was further instructed to "conceale all things from Dr. Woodward," and "take an exact account of all ye English goods by us sent to Carolina that remayne un-disposed of by Dr. Woodward: as allsoe an account of all skins Furrs slaves . . . [and] dispose of . . . ye Goods that shall remayne in ye hands of Dr. Woodward to our best advantage."[67] In March, still investigating Woodward's alleged involvement with the Westo War, the proprietors requested a copy of a letter in which the doctor had warned that "if Trade were not permitted to ye Westoes they would cut all yor throats," and a missive from the governor of St. Augustine accusing Woodward of inciting the Westos to raid the Spanish missions.[68]

The Goose Creek men had cleverly advanced their political and economic interests at the expense of their rivals—proprietors, Woodward, and Westos alike—but they may not have devised the scheme themselves. It is likely that Bacon's Rebellion in 1676 greatly influenced the strategies pursued by the Goose Creek men. Recent interpretations of the rebellion cast the conflict as a trade war between Virginians like Nathanial Bacon, who sought entrance to the Indian trade, and Governor Berkeley and his associates, who intended to keep the lion's share of the profits for themselves.[69] Bacon was reacting not only to the restrictive trade policies of Berkeley but also to the virtual stranglehold on native trade the Occaneechees enjoyed as partners of the governor. The parallels to the situation in Carolina are obvious and would have been clear to the Goose Creek men, who certainly kept abreast of the activities of their English rivals to the north.

Whereas Bacon seized control of the Virginia General Assembly from without, the Goose Creek men already had influence on the Grand Council in Charles Town, and thus their "rebellion" entailed less risk than Bacon's. Further, despite Bacon's audacity, he and his followers were not severely punished for their actions. In fact they essentially got what they wanted—the General Assembly legitimized Indian slavery with acts passed in 1677 and 1679 and loosened the restrictions that had so vexed Bacon and his supporters.[70] Bacon and his allies also effectively removed the Occaneechees, turning the primary slave raiders of the Virginia backcountry into slaves, and usurped their role as middlemen for the interior trade. The Goose Creek men likewise enslaved the majority of their Westo rivals and expanded their trade operations in the aftermath of the war. They, like their Virginian counterparts, escaped censure for their actions despite the anger of the proprietors, who noted in 1685 that the Goose Creek men could "With a bole of punch get who they would Chosen of ye parliament and afterwards who they would chosen of ye grand Councell, by which means they have heretofore gotten acts of parliament past that no man should sell armes to the Indians upon penalty of forfiture of all his estate and perpetual banishment, which by Reason of their power in ye grand Councell and parliament they caused to be observed by others but brook it themselves for their private advantage and escape ye penalty."[71]

Woodward was left with few options in the colony and departed for London in the fall of 1681 or the following spring. He gained an audience with Lord Ashley and three other proprietors in May 1682 and pled his case. The proprietors pardoned the doctor of the crimes with which he was charged, and perhaps at the behest of Woodward himself, Lord Ashley and his associates granted him an exploratory commission to search out "a passage over the Apalateans Mountains" and to "make discovery of those parts of our Province where you shall think any mines are . . . and how qualified [the country is] for Planting of Vines and Inhabitants."[72] Woodward was given the right to "Erect a house and reside in any part of our Province . . . and wee require all Governours Magistrates Millitary Officers and all other persons whatsoever not to molest or hinder you in your discovery."[73] While it is true the proprietors were interested in precious metals and discoveries that could facilitate the westward expansion of Carolina settlements, the true purpose of the commission was probably to give Woodward the authority to travel where he wished, interact with Indians (under the auspices they would be required as guides for his discoveries), and construct a blockhouse (which could be used to conduct trade) anywhere in the colony, regardless of any previous land claims. Armed with the commission and his high standing among native peoples of the region, Woodward was again ready to challenge the Goose Creek men on behalf of the proprietors.

Unfortunately virtually nothing is known of Woodward's activities from May 1682 to March 1685. He probably returned to Charles Town in the fall of 1682, but he may have delayed his departure until the spring of 1683. In any case, when he arrived in Carolina, Woodward found the Savannahs had literally taken the Westos' place, occupying a town near old Hickahaugau on the river that soon bore their name. The only way for Woodward and the proprietors to compete was to forge an alliance with a more powerful group than the Savannahs. The doctor naturally looked west to the Chattahoochee valley, though the area was officially claimed by Spain. The two European powers could no longer avoid the conflict that had been brewing between them since the founding of Carolina, and native groups were forced to choose sides. One such group was the Yamasee, an emergent society composed of remnants of several native peoples from central Georgia and the sea islands of Georgia and South Carolina, who abandoned their Spanish allies in 1683 and moved from the province of Guale to Port Royal in the hopes of establishing trade relations with the Carolinians.[74] It is not surprising that Woodward too sought to reestablish his place in the Indian trade in the Port Royal area considering his early interaction with the native peoples of the region. It is even possible that his original adoptive family had joined the growing Yamasee polity.

At some point during the spring of 1685, Woodward met a Yamasee headman named Niquisaya, who agreed to accompany the doctor to the towns on the Chattahoochee that summer.[75] The Goose Creek men had yet to establish a direct trade with the Cussitas, whose access to English goods had previously been controlled by the Westos. Woodward, who helped negotiate the peace between the two groups circa 1675, hoped to forge an alliance with the Cussitas before his English rivals. Taking Niquisaya insured that Woodward would be able to speak with leading men of the most important lineages, not only because Niquisaya was a cacique himself but also because the Yamasees had kinship ties with the peoples of the Chattahoochee valley.[76] Armed in addition with his own reputation as a linguist and negotiator, Woodward departed Charles Town in early summer 1685 with a handful of English companions, Niquisaya, and fifty Yamasee warriors.[77]

The group arrived at the town of Coweta sometime in June, having chosen their destination with an eye toward politics. Coweta and several other towns in the northern reaches of Apalachicola wanted access to English traders, but the Spanish had considerable influence in the province, particularly among the southern towns located closer to the Apalachee missions. The cacique of Coweta, whose influence was strong in all the pro-English towns in the valley, hoped to use an alliance with Woodward to strengthen his political position in the valley, and the doctor, for his part, knew what benefits might accrue to him as a result. Woodward also knew that native economics, like politics, was based on kinship, and his marriage that summer to the niece of the Coweta headman was thus a shrewd business move.[78] Without creating a position for himself within the town's leading lineage, it is unlikely that Woodward would have been able to begin construction on a palisade just north of the province or order the construction of a blockhouse near Coweta, the first English trading post in the interior south of Virginia.[79]

The Spanish were soon informed of the English activity in Apalachicola and dispatched a force of two hundred and fifty Apalachee Indians under the command of Antonio Matheos to investigate. The towns of the province were deserted by the time Matheos arrived; their inhabitants worried that the punishment for the Coweta mico's actions would be indiscriminate.[80] The cacique of Apalachicola Town, a man named Pentocolo, met with the Spanish commander in the hopes of protecting his and other towns that were not fully committed to welcoming English traders, but Matheos was determined to search for the Carolinians.[81] In Coweta, he found a note left by Woodward that read, "I am very sorry that I came with so small a following that I cannot await your arrival. Be informed that I came to get acquainted with the country, its mountains, the seacoast, and Apalache. I trust in God that I shall meet you gentlemen later when I have a larger following."[82] An infuriated Matheos failed to locate the English blockhouse near the town but did discover and destroy the partially completed palisade just north of the province.[83] After a month of fruitless searching, the army returned to Apalachee empty handed.

Once Matheos was gone, Woodward and his companions returned to Coweta and resumed trading. The doctor's letter had blatantly threatened the Spaniard's largest and most successful mission, and Woodward seemed ready to carry out his bold plans of English economic expansion. Up until this point, the English had been financing slave raids against Spanish-allied Indians, but Woodward's foray to Apalachicola was the first explicit attempt to persuade a group to forsake the Spanish in favor of an English alliance. The doctor's diplomatic skills no doubt played a part, but his overtures were accepted in large part because the people of Coweta sought the benefits that might accrue to them as a consequence of trade with the English, particularly the acquisition of firearms. Although neither the European nor native players in this drama could have foreseen the results of Coweta's decision, it turned out to have a tremendous impact on the geopolitical development of the entire region.

The Spanish were not about to let their old allies go so easily however. Matheos left spies in Apalachicola, and he returned with his army in January 1686 by a different route, but the inhabitants had spies of their own, and the valley's towns were again abandoned before the force arrived. This time the Spanish commander found Woodward's blockhouse about six miles from Coweta and confiscated the remaining goods and five hundred deerskins the English had already received in trade.[84] Using Pentocolo as a messenger, Matheos demanded to speak with the leaders of all twelve towns in Apalachicola, threatening to burn the villages of those who refused to comply. Eight caciques traveled to Coweta to meet with the Spaniard, but representatives from the four northern-most towns, including Coweta, were absent. Matheos did not punish those who willingly submitted to Spanish authority, but he made good on his threats and burned the towns of Coweta, Cussita, Colone, and Tasquiqui before he returned to Apalachee.[85]

Having lost their merchandise, the English traders returned to Charles Town for the winter, but Woodward, four additional traders, and a contingent of Yamasee arrived in the Chattahoochee valley with more goods in March 1686. It had become clear to Woodward that success in the province hinged on convincing the southern towns to join Coweta, Cussita, and their allies in welcoming English trade. Therefore the Carolinians sent one trader to accompany a delegation of forty-five Yamasees who were traveling to Apalachicola Town to speak about the advantages of an alliance with the English.[86] The identity of the trader does not appear in existing records; however there is a strong possibility it was Woodward. The Englishman brought twenty-six muskets and other trade goods as a gift and otherwise remained silent, letting the Yamasee, who had relatives among the Hitchiti-speaking Apalachicolas, take care of the negotiations.[87] Perhaps only Woodward (or someone carefully instructed by him) would have known the importance of gift giving in Indian diplomacy and had the sense to stay quiet while people with kinship ties served as mediators.

The proper etiquette and gifts of the English, along with the clear example of prosperity shown by the Yamasee ambassadors, who were well supplied with European arms and ammunition and had much influence with the English, swayed the Apalachicolas to accept the Carolinians' offer despite the objections of the Spanish. Woodward soon made arrangements for several important leaders and ambassadors along with 150 warriors carrying dressed deerskins to travel with him to Charles Town that summer to formalize their new relationship with the Carolinians. Although the records are not clear, Woodward apparently fell ill during his stay in the Chattahoochee valley, perhaps from snakebite, and had to be carried on a litter during his return trip to Charles Town in early August.[88] The doctor apparently died sometime soon after, and his name ceased to appear in the colonial records.

El Capitan Enrique, as the Spanish referred to Woodward, had landed the first real blow in the battle between England and Spain for control of the south. The conflict between the two nations pitted the old style of empire building—conquering nations and turning their people into vassals—against a newly developing one—incorporating the Indian nations of North America into the burgeoning world market. In other words, the native peoples of the region were choosing not just between Spanish and English allies but between imperial systems as well. The top-down system of the Spanish propped up the old native hierarchy and tried to keep new European goods in the hands of native leaders, while the economics-first model of the English allowed native commoners direct access to the kinds of prestige goods that in the past could be obtained only from their leaders.[89]

Woodward was in the vanguard of the latter model, and although it would take several years to reach fruition, his diplomacy in the Chattahoochee valley resulted in a lasting alliance between the English and the Cowetas, Cussitas, and other peoples who would soon be known collectively as the Lower Creeks. By 1690 most of the Creeks had abandoned the Chattahoochee valley and moved east to the Ocmulgee River and the newly constructed Macon trading house.[90] From there they launched dozens of English-sponsored raids on the Spanish missions in the coming years, culminating with James Moore's devastating expedition in 1704, which brought an end to Apalachee and effectively crippled the Spanish empire in the south.[91] Unfortunately, because of his untimely death in the winter of 1686 or the following spring, the doctor did not see the results of his bold exploits in the Chattahoochee valley.

Although he is little heralded in history texts, Dr. Henry Woodward was a vital part of the eventual success of the English-sponsored empire in the American south. He used his understanding of native languages and cultures, much of the knowledge of which he gained under the tutelage of his first Indian wife, and an astute application of native diplomacy to advance his own cause and that of the colony. Woodward was at the center of nearly every important interaction with Indian groups between 1666 and his death two decades later. His kinship ties with the native people of Port Royal helped insure the welcome received by the English upon their arrival in 1670, and his first forays into diplomacy resulted in sustenance for the colony at a critical early juncture. The information Woodward gathered from his native informants kept the Carolinians alert to the machinations of their enemies and gave them a measure of needed security. The doctor was also instrumental in the development of the Indian trade and negotiated alliances with two of Carolina's most important Indian allies, the Westos and the Lower Creeks. The colony's relationship with these two groups, perhaps more than any other single factor, gave the English an advantage over their Spanish (and later French) rivals in the region, an advantage that may never have developed without Woodward's ability to operate adeptly in a liminal state between English and Indian cultures.

Notes

1. Steven J. Oatis, *A Colonial Complex: South Carolina's Frontiers in the Era of the Yamasee War, 1680–1730* (Lincoln: University of Nebraska Press, 2004); Walter Edgar, *South Carolina: A History* (Columbia: University of South Carolina Press, 1998); David Duncan Wallace, *South Carolina: A Short History, 1520–1948* (Columbia: University of South Carolina Press, 1951).

2. Paul Kelton, *Epidemics and Enslavement: Biological Catastrophe in the Native Southeast, 1492–1715* (Lincoln: University of Nebraska Press, 2007); Tom Hatley, *The Dividing Paths: Cherokees and South Carolinians through the Revolutionary Era* (New York: Oxford University Press, 1995); Kathryn E. Holland Braund, *Deerskins and Duffels: Creek Indian Trade with Anglo-America, 1685–1815* (Lincoln: University of Nebraska Press, 1993); J. Leitch Wright, *The Only Land They Knew: The Tragic Story of the American Indian in the Old South* (New York: Free Press, 1981).

3. Verner W. Crane, *The Southern Frontier, 1670–1732* (Ann Arbor: University of Michigan Press, 1929); Herbert E. Bolton and Mary Ross, *The Debatable Land: A Sketch of the Anglo-Spanish Contest for the Georgia Country* (Berkeley: University of California Press, 1925).

4. Joseph M. Hall, *Zamumo's Gifts: Indian-European Exchange in the Colonial Southeast* (Philadelphia: University of Pennsylvania Press, 2009); Eric E. Bowne, *The Westo Indians: Slave Traders of the Early Colonial South* (Tuscaloosa: University of Alabama Press, 2005); Steven C. Hahn, *The Invention of the Creek Nation, 1670–1763* (Lincoln: University of Nebraska Press, 2004).

5. Robert Sanford, "A Relation of a Voyage on the Coast of the Province of Carolina, 1666," in Salley, *Narratives*, 86–88.

6. Ibid., 100.

7. Ibid., 104–5.

8. Ibid., 105.

9. For a discussion of matrilineal kinship systems, see Charles Hudson, *The Southeastern Indians* (Knoxville: University of Tennessee Press, 1976), 185–202.

10. For a concise explanation of these benefits, see Theda Perdue, "A Sprightly Lover Is the Most Prevailing Missionary: Intermarriage between Europeans and Indians in the Eighteenth-Century South," in *Light on the Path: The Anthropology and History of the Southeastern Indians*, ed. Thomas J. Pluckhahn and Robbie Ethridge (Tuscaloosa: University of Alabama Press, 2006), 165–78.

11. Lawson, *New Voyage*, 192.

12. Nairne, *Muskogean Journals*, 60–61.

13. Crane, *Southern Frontier*, 6–7; Joseph W. Barnwell, "Dr. Henry Woodward, the First English Settler in South Carolina," *SCHGM* 8 (1907): 29–41; Council to the Lords Proprietors, September 11, 1670, in *Shaftesbury Papers*, 190–91.

14. Council to the Lords Proprietors, September 11, 1670, in *Shaftesbury Papers*, 191; H. Woodward to Sir John Yeamans, September 10, 1670, in *Shaftesbury Papers*, 187.

15. From Sir Jno Yeomans, November 15, 1670, in *Shaftesbury Papers*, 220.

16. Council to Lords Proprietors, September 11, 1670, in *Shaftesbury Papers*, 191.

17. James H. Merrell, *Into the American Woods: Negotiators on the Pennsylvania Frontier* (New York: Norton, 1999), 57–59.

18. Merrell, *Into the American Woods*, 59–62.

19. Council to Lords Proprietors, September 11, 1670, in *Shaftesbury Papers*, 191.

20. H. Woodward to Yeamans, September 10, 1670, in *Shaftesbury Papers*, 187.

21. Stephen Bull to Lord Ashley, September 12, 1670, in *Shaftesbury Papers*, 194.

22. Lord Ashley to Henry Woodward, in *Shaftesbury Papers*, 315.

23. Ibid., 316.

24. Ibid., 316.

25. Alexander S. Salley, ed., *Records of the Secretary of the Province and the Register of the Province of South Carolina, 1671–1675* (Columbia: Historical Commission of South Carolina, 1944), 12–13.

26. Alan V. Briceland, *Westward from Virginia: The Exploration of the Virginia-Carolina Frontier, 1650–1710* (Charlottesville: University of Virginia Press, 1987), 147–70; Clarence W. Alford and Lee Bidgood, ed., *The First Explorations of the Trans-Alleghany Region by Virginians, 1650–1674* (Cleveland: Arthur H. Clark, 1912), 209–26.

27. James H. Merrell, *The Indians' New World: Catawbas and Their Neighbors from European Contact through the Era of Removal* (New York: Norton, 1989), 31.

28. Ibid., 61–62.

29. Nancy L. Hagedorn, "'A Friend to Go between Them': The Interpreter as Cultural Broker during the Anglo-Iroquois Councils, 1740–70," *Ethnohistory* 35, no. 1 (1988): 61.

30. Richard L. Morton, *Colonial Virginia* (Chapel Hill: University of North Carolina Press, 1960), 1:157–58; William Waller Hening, ed., *Statutes at Large: Being a Collection of all the Laws of Virginia from the First Session of the Legislature in the Year 1619* (Richmond, Virginia, 1809–1823), 1:326.

31. William Byrd, *Writings of Colonel William Byrd*, ed. J.S. Bassett, 2 vols. (New York: Harper Brothers, 1901), 1:234.

32. Ibid., 1:235.

33. Alvord and Bidgood, *The First Explorations of the Trans-Allegheny*, 32.

34. Instructions for Mr. Henry Woodward, in *Shaftesbury Papers*, 446.
35. Instructions for Mr. Andrew Percivall, in *Shaftesbury Papers*, 442–43.
36. Henry Woodward, "A Faithfull Relation of My Westoe Voyage," in Salley, *Narratives*, 130.
37. Ibid., 133.
38. Bowne, *Westo Indians*, 79–80.
39. Woodward, "My Westoe Voyage," in Salley, *Narratives*, 130.
40. Ibid., 130.
41. Ibid., 132.
42. Ibid., 132–33.
43. Ibid., 132.
44. Ibid., 132.
45. Ibid., 134.
46. Ibid., 133–34.
47. Eric E. Bowne, "'Caryinge awaye their Corne and Children': The Effects of Westo Slave Raids on the Indians of the Lower South," in *Mapping the Mississippian Shatter Zone: The Colonial Indian Slave Trade and Regional Instability in the American South*, ed. Robbie Ethridge and Sheri M. Shuck-Hall (Lincoln: University of Nebraska Press, 2009), 106–9.
48. John E. Worth, *The Struggle for the Georgia Coast: An Eighteenth Century Retrospective on Guale and Mocama* (New York: American Museum of Natural History, 1995), 27.
49. Hahn, *Invention of the Creek Nation*, 33.
50. William J. Rivers, *A Sketch of the History of South Carolina to the Close of the Proprietary Government by the Revolution of 1719* (Spartanburg, S.C.: Reprint Company, 1972), 388.
51. Alexander S. Salley, ed., *Warrants for Lands in South Carolina 1650–1674* (Columbia: Historical Commission of South Carolina, 1910), 148–49; Earl of Shaftesbury to Governor and Council, April 10, 1677, in *BPRO-SC*, 1:50.
52. Rivers, *South Carolina*, 106.
53. Bowne, *Westo Indians*, 94–95.
54. Ibid., 103–5.
55. Proprietors to Governor and Council, March 7, 1680/81, in *BPRO-SC*, 1:115–18.
56. Worth, *Struggle for the Georgia Coast*, 30–32.
57. Minutes, April 12, 1680, *JGC*, 1:84.
58. Ibid., 1:83.
59. Proprietors to Governor and Council, September 30, 1683, in *BPRO-SC*, 1:256.
60. Ibid., 1:257.
61. "Letters of Thomas Newe, 1682," in Salley, *Narratives*, 183–84.
62. Ibid., 182.
63. Proprietors to Governor and Council, February 21, 1680/81, in *BPRO-SC*, 1:104.
64. Proprietors to Governor and Council, March 7, 1680/1, in *BPRO-SC*, 1:115.
65. Proprietors to Governor and Council, September 30, 1683, in *BPRO-SC*, 1:258.

66. Instructions for Andrew Percivall [not sent], February 21, 1680/81, in *BPRO-SC*, 1:106.

67. Instructions for Andrew Percivall, March 9, 1680/81, in *BPRO-SC*, 1:113–14.

68. Proprietors to Governor and Council, March 7, 1680–81, in *BPRO-SC*, 1:115–16.

69. Robbie Ethridge, "Afterword," in *Mapping the Mississippian Shatter Zone*, ed. Ethridge and Shuck-Hall, 418–24; C. S. Everett, "'They shalbe slaves for their lives': Indian Slavery in Colonial Virginia," in *Indian Slavery in Colonial America*, ed. Alan Gallay (Lincoln: University of Nebraska Press, 2009), 67–108; Maureen Meyers, "From Refugees to Slave Traders: The Transformation of the Westo Indians," in *Mapping the Mississippian Shatter Zone*, ed. Ethridge and Shuck-Hall, 81–103.

70. Everett, "Indian Slavery in Colonial Virginia," 86–87.

71. Proprietors to Governor and Deputies, March 13, 1684/85, in *BPRO-SC*, 2:33–34.

72. Earl of Craven to Henry Woodward, May 18, 1682, in *BPRO-SC*, 1:159–60.

73. Ibid., 1:160.

74. Joseph M. Hall, "Anxious Alliances: Apalachicola Efforts to Survive the Slave Trade, 1638–1705," in *Indian Slavery in Colonial America*, ed. Gallay, 163.

75. Hahn, *Invention of the Creek Nation*, 42.

76. Hall, "Anxious Alliances," 164.

77. Hahn, *Invention of the Creek Nation*, 42; Mary Ross, *Papers*, at Georgia Department of Archives and History, Atlanta, folder 88, no. 27, 191.

78. Hahn, *Invention of the Creek Nation*, 43–44; Ross, *Papers*, folder 88, no. 27, 124.

79. Hahn, *Invention of the Creek Nation*, 43.

80. Ibid., 44.

81. Ibid., 44–45.

82. Bolton and Ross, *Debatable Land*, 50.

83. Ibid., 50.

84. Hall, "Anxious Alliances," 164; Bolton and Ross, *Debatable Land*, 51.

85. Hahn, *Invention of the Creek Nation*, 45; Ross, *Papers*, folder 88, no. 27, 228–34.

86. Hall, "Anxious Alliances," 166.

87. Hall, "Anxious Alliances," 166; Hahn, *Invention of the Creek Nation*, 46.

88. Hahn, *Invention of the Creek Nation*, 46.

89. John E. Worth, "Spanish Missions and the Persistence of Chiefly Power," in *The Transformation of the Southeastern Indians*, ed. Robbie Ethridge and Charles Hudson (Jackson: University Press of Mississippi, 2002), 39–64.

90. Bowne, *Westo Indians*, 108–9; Gregory Waselkov, "The Macon Trading House and Early European-Indian Contact in the Colonial Southeast," in *Ocmulgee Archaeology, 1936–1986*, ed. David J. Hally (Athens: University of Georgia Press, 1994), 190–95.

91. Bowne, *Westo Indians*, 112–13.

Part Two
Violence and Conflict

The Economic Philosophies of Indian Trade Regulation Policy in Early South Carolina

JESSICA STERN

Carolina was established during an unsettled time in England's economic history. The expansion of the market over unprecedented distances, and the emergence of a philosophy that posited that labor and not land created wealth, sparked debates about the role of government in economic affairs. Under scrutiny was the balance-of-trade theory, or mercantilism, which assumed that because global economic resources were based in land and thus finite, the sovereign needed to monopolize control over international trade to ensure that his country was retaining the greatest amount of wealth. In addition to limited resources, regulation of trade was necessary, many traditionally argued, because individuals who dealt primarily in moveable goods and owned minimal landed property were untrustworthy; unmanaged, they might harm a nation's security when dealing with foreign trading partners.[1]

The attack on the premises that underpinned the balance-of-trade theory, and the accompanying uncertainty of the place of the government in economic affairs, came into sharp relief in proprietary South Carolina during debates about the trade with Native Americans. Carolina's planners imagined their future colony as a plantation, operating according to a traditional economic model of landed property. True to the balance-of-trade goal of amassing global resources, Carolina would assist England in accumulating specie by supplying it, and its colonists in Barbados, with the agricultural goods they needed to become self-sufficient, so they could minimize their imports, and provide luxuries to England that they could sell to foreign countries.[2] Carolina's framers toed the line that the only true independent citizen was he who held land; mobile property, on the other hand, created artificial men whose appetites for power had to be governed.[3]

While a colony based in landed property served as the ideal model for Carolina, it soon became clear that slaves captured by and deerskins harvested by Native Americans, and not fruit from the land, were the only ready sources of revenue in the southeast.[4] Most of these skins and slaves were transacted between Native Americans and transient settlers. The economic realities of South

Carolina forced settlers and officials alike to assess the debates occurring in England and presents a microcosm of how a society dedicated to landed property would react to an economy based in goods that moved across international boundaries.[5] In analyzing how the colonists engaged with the ideologies of mercantilism, this essay adds to the chorus of scholars who argue that rather than originating from the center, economic policies were the product of negotiations between the metropole and peripheries.[6] As this essay shows, after an early period of very loosely regulated trade, the South Carolina proprietors and Commons House reacted to uncertainties in the Native American trade by moving away from a freer-trade model and instituting tight regulations on prices, trading locations, and trade partners, thereby reaffirming traditional economic mores. Historians who have discussed these regulations, and Native American conceptions of exchange more generally, argue that Native Americans, who traditionally exchanged goods as gifts, insisted on these policies because they were uncomfortable with market commodity exchanges.[7] By situating the Native American trade in early modern English economic debates, I show that the English were as uneasy as the Native Americans, and possibly even more so, about expanding markets and cross-cultural traders, and that they insisted on the regulations that historians mistakenly attribute solely to Native American pressure.

Though Carolina's planners did not intend for trade with Native Americans to hold a central place within their economy, as the first settlers' provisions dwindled they "were forced to live upon the Indians," creating a system in which casual trade with the Native Americans for food and deerskin clothing touched the lives of almost everyone during the first decades after South Carolina's founding.[8] For the settlers these exchanges were inextricably linked to social and diplomatic relationships. Peaceful neighbors were those who traded with them; menacing neighbors were those who refused to trade. In addition the settlers were surprised that these foreign nations, who they expected to use trade to fill their own coffers at their expense, as the English did, acted generously. Proprietor Lord Ashley's deputy Stephen Bull reported that they "sould vs Provisions att very reasonable rates & takeinge notice of our necessitys did almost daylie bringe one thing or another."[9] Similarly settler William Owen relayed that their indigenous neighbors supplied their "want of provisions without inhanceing the price upon our necessity."[10] By disregarding profit, the Native Americans were not behaving as the English expected competing nations to behave but were instead acting like their own countrymen. The proprietors seized on this climate of cooperation to speculate that Native Americans living within the patent boundaries would soon become members of the colony.[11]

South Carolinians were equally likely to read the refusal to trade as a hostile act. The Council concluded that the Cusabo Indians were plotting to destroy the colony because they had removed "a great quantity of Corne from time to time," thus choosing not to assist the Carolinians in subsisting, and had further withdrawn from "trading with our people."[12] Even more threatening were the Westo, who would barrel down "in the tyme of their cropp & destroye all."[13] The Westo represented a mercantilist's nightmare: a group who arbitrarily destroyed their livelihood, with seemingly little gain for themselves.

In assuming that the international competition for finite resources was a volatile affair, the settlers adopted a mercantilist mentality. Since one party became enriched while the other party was depleted, trading partners were yoked in a hostile relationship. A solution to this problem was to implement a monopoly, which, as mentioned earlier, not only had the benefit of appointing an expert who ensured that England was seizing the biggest piece of the pie, but also created a central authority that could marshal an army should the depleted party react violently.[14] Thus to contend with the Westo, the proprietors—despite their standing as Whigs, the party that usually opposed monopolies—instituted a monopoly over the inland trade beyond Port Royal. Trade relationships were unstable, and, the proprietors reasoned, "if quarrels should arise [it] might extreamly prejudice [the Indians]."[15] The frontier environment put the potential repercussions of these unstable trading relationships in sharp relief; weakening one's trading partner to the point of fury could pose an existential threat to South Carolina. Native Americans' material dependence, though a boon for profits, could harm the colony by creating a population that would do *anything* for European goods. The proprietors noted this danger when explaining that the 1683 war with their neighbors was sparked by the Savannah Indians' "Covetuousness of your [Carolinians'] guns Powder & shott & other Europian Comodities," which induced them "to make war upon their neighbours" in order to seize slaves to sell to the Carolinians.[16] Thus New World monopolies and trade in general walked a precarious line of attempting to exploit Native American trading partners while maintaining peace. As we'll see throughout the essay, the assumption that trade created contentious relationships would underlie various officials' suspicion of Indian traders and determine regulation throughout the colonial period.

Not only were their duel goals of profit and peace inherently in tension, but the legality of trade monopolies was increasingly contested in the latter half of the seventeenth century, and the settlers who opposed the proprietors' policies used this knowledge to their advantage. Defenders of royally sanctioned monopolies argued that companies that barred those who were not company members from trading within a designated territory were justifiable because the king had a right to control trade with foreign non-Christians, who could quickly become enemies and jeopardize the safety of the empire. Monopoly supporters also argued that only large companies had the economic power to orchestrate international trade for the benefit of England, an argument that the proprietors did not invoke. Opponents of royal monopolies doubted that company-run trade was safer than a freer-trade model and suggested that more individuals trading freely in moveable property would enhance England's wealth. Last they argued that only Parliament, as a representative body, had the right to regulate trade. The 1689 case *Nightingale v. Bridges* decided on behalf of the antimonopolists.[17] In 1699 the Board of Trade refused the right of proprietary monopolies to restrict English colonists from trading in an East New Jersey dispute. Savvy colonists used the anti-royal-monopoly turn in England to defend their rights to trade freely with Native Americans and repeatedly invoked English legal precedent.[18]

In 1679 the proprietors' justification for maintaining a monopoly for the sake of the colony's safety was shattered when a war with the Westo broke out under their watch. The Commons House, as a representative body, was able to seize control of the trade, and the proprietors were left with only the power of persuasion.[19] While some argue that 1707, the year the Commons House introduced its full regulatory system, marks a watershed moment when trade went from being free to regulated, compared to later policies it exerted limited control over the choices of Carolinian and Native American traders.[20] It demanded that traders take out licenses; appointed an Indian agent who spent ten months in Indian country resolving disputes; and created the Commissioners of the Indian Trade, composed of nine members of the Upper and Lower Houses of Assembly, to try egregious crimes. But it did not, as it would after the Yamasee War (1715–16), set prices, assign traders to specific Indian towns, or limit the goods that could be traded beyond alcohol and certain weapons. Nor did it monopolize the trade.

The years from 1707 to 1715 are thus best understood as a time when fears about foreign trade relationships receded and officials trusted Carolina and Native American traders to devise their own trading culture. Instead of top-down regulation, the Commons House relied on the same outlet available to traders in England and the English colonies: a judicial body, in this case the Commissioners of Indian Trade, that contained potentially hostile trading relationships by mediating disputes.[21] Though the proprietors had set the groundwork for this adjudication system to attend to disputes between settlers and Native Americans outside of their monopoly boundaries, the Commons House was unique in resting the colony's safety (for it too believed the trade and peace were interconnected) on the belief that mediation could dispel all trading disputes.[22] Realizing that "at this Distance" they would be unable to "restrane the Traders," the commissioners asked Native American leaders and communities to take the lead in regulating the trade.[23] Native Americans set the standard of conduct; the commissioners instructed the traders, simply, that "your Behaviour [should] be such towards the Indians that they may have no Reason or Grounds of Complaint."[24] They encouraged Native Americans to submit grievances to their local South Carolina agent, who they instructed "to hear all their Complaints and to doe right and impartial Justice between them an the Traders."[25] If the agent could not affect a resolution, he would alert the

Commissioners of the Indian Trade, and they would summon the disputants for a hearing.

The Commons House's faith that Carolinian and Native American traders could peacefully negotiate their business relationships, with the occasional help of a mediator, suggests that it had abandoned the fears of international trade of its English counterparts. Instead of seeing economic culture as differing across societies and religions, it believed in the commensurability, if not universality, of trading norms. It is significant that neither the proprietors nor the Commons House officials differentiated between Native American and British property rights, and stipulated that an exchange was legally binding only if both parties consciously and willingly agreed to its terms.[26] Accordingly most of the cases the commissioners decided hinged on scrutinizing a transaction for evidence that both the Carolinian and Native American traders consented to the exchange. Common disagreements involved questions surrounding which items could be bought and sold (including slaves), at what price, and the time at which ownership would transfer hands. Instead of codifying rules of exchange, as they would do later, the commissioners simply voided disputed transactions. While not as critical of slavery as the proprietors, they regularly deferred to indigenous categorizations of slavery and spent much of their time freeing the wrongly enslaved.[27] Oftentimes instead of attempting to compel the disputing parties to understand each other's positions, they dipped into public funds and gave restitution to both parties, allowing everyone to walk away feeling that justice had been served.[28]

While the commissioners granted Carolinian traders a great deal of freedom, their choice in words reveals that they were quick to blame white trader malfeasance for conflicts instead of cultural difference. The commissioners' use of "force" when invalidating commercial transactions underlines this predisposition. For instance when Captain John Musgrove complained that the Creek Indians still owed him skins for powder and bullets, the commissioners released the Creek of their obligation to pay this debt, ruling that he "forced the said powder and bullets upon the Indians."[29] Unlike theft, in a forced trade the initiator foisted goods on the reluctant individual and seized other goods in exchange, usually according to the standard rates of exchange. Indian Forster, a leader of the Tuscarora Indians, complained, "Daniel Callihaun had violently seized and taken a canoe from him, on pretence that he had sold it to him, the said Callihaun, for twenty shillings, current money, because Forster said he was willing to sell his canoe for money."[30] Twenty shillings was a standard price for a used canoe, suggesting that instead of Callihaun being a cheat, this dispute arose from a different conception of the nature of a verbal contract or the time at which traded goods should change hands.[31] Although it never reached final verdict because Indian Forster chose not to reappear before the commissioners, based on past decisions it is likely that the commissioners would have determined that because Forster and Callihaun did not agree about the specific terms of the exchange, the verbal contract was not legally binding. Further, instead of merely reading this case as a contract dispute, or cultural misunderstanding, the commissioners would have insisted that Callihaun had acted unethically by forcing the sale on Forster. Ultimately interpreting cases through a balance-of-trade lens, the commissioners were guided by the belief it was likely that one party was walking away from the exchange with a less valuable object, and thus they were prone to trust the account of the aggrieved Native American party.

Like Indian Forster, Carolinian and Native Americans traders alike seldom called on the commissioners to negotiate their disputes, leaving the commissioners at the periphery of the emerging trading culture. In spaces far from colonial oversight, they developed a commodity exchange system that, when viewed by colonial officials, smacked of anarchy. While colonial officials equated trade with social and political relationships, there is ample evidence that southeastern Native American individuals (though perhaps not their leaders) and Carolina traders were more than comfortable with asocial exchange, a fact that frustrated and confused some officials. In his 1708 report, the first Indian agent, Thomas Nairne, complained that the Chickasaw Indians had "not a right notion of Allegiance" to those from whom they purchased commodities. "They're apt to believe themselves at Liberty, when they please to turn to those who sell them the best pennyworths," Nairne continued.[32] A South Carolina committee reported that the southeastern Indians "indiscriminately visited and traded with the *French, Spaniards* and *English,* as they judged it most for their Advantage."[33] Though officials took "pains to instruct them" otherwise, the Native Americans held to the "erroneous doctrine" that one could trade with whomever he or she wanted.[34] Carolinian traders likewise believed that they were free to choose their trading partners.[35] They did not always share their government's political allegiances and formed partnerships with individuals from rival European nations and sold goods to enemy Indian groups.[36] Their disrespect for the commissioners was palpable. Agent John Wright reported that traders contemptuously tore up the commissioners' warrants right in front of him.[37] The commissioners put as much tooth in their orders as they could, but they recognized their limited ability to enforce some areas of trade, such as insisting that traders obtain licenses. As the commissioners informed the agents, "You must be cautious how you deal with the Indian traders about paying their arrears of license money. You may threaten them with Warrants, and probably that way may persuade them into compliance, but upon considering the Act of Parliament we do not think we have sufficient power to prosecute the same."[38] The increasing openness of trade in Britain left colonial officials with few tools to restrain the traders, who were adopting a modern market exchange mentality faster than governmental officials.

The May 1714 case of trader Alexander Long fully convinced the commissioners that the supposition of the proprietors, that international trade was too risky to leave unregulated, was correct. The commissioners, who previously held that "headstrong, unruly traders" could *unwittingly* cause hostilities between British American and Native American communities, found Long guilty of using the influence he garnered through trade with the Cherokees to *intentionally* incite them to go to war against the Yuchis of Chestowa, against whom he harbored a grudge.[39] On hearing rumors that the Yuchi and Cherokee Indians were on the brink of war, the commissioners summoned traders to explain the situation. In retrospect it appears that the dispute arose when a Chestowa Yuchi man murdered a Cherokee, touching off a cycle of retribution. Long's involvement, by all reliable accounts, stopped with him selling the Cherokee powder and bullets. But rumors ran rampant that Long had played a more instrumental role in the war. "Mr. Long had some Difference with a Yuchi Indian who had pulled some of his Hair" and another who had left a debt unpaid a few years ago, traders recounted. To avenge these wrongs, Long fabricated a "Governor's Order for cutting off Chestowee," thereby prompting the Cherokee to go to war. Most of the traders agreed that the "Cherokees would not have cut off the Yuchis if they had been expressly ordered to the Contrary." Despite the fact that the Cherokee Skiacasea claimed that Long did not know about their plan to attack the Yuchi, the commissioners ruled that "Mr. Long was instrumentall in encouraging the Cherokee Indians to cut off the Yuchis." They stripped Long of his license and recommended that the governor prosecute him.[40]

The amount of hearsay evidence in this case suggests that the accusation that Long started a war was a rumor that fed on the settlers' predisposition to be wary of merchants in general, and peddlers in particular, for they held a precarious position in the expanding early modern market and were at the forefront of the drive to help Britain amass global resources.[41] International traders served as a locus of the anxieties Britons had about the exploitative and potentially hostile trade relationships that the balance-of-trade philosophy engendered. This fear of explosive trading relationships dovetailed with a wariness of individuals who relied on mobile, rather than real landed, property. Traditionally landholders, who held a stake in a community and were required to take up arms to protect it, were considered reliable community members. Merchants, on the other hand, were so greedy that their lust for money overshadowed any concern they might have for the welfare of their community or their trading partners.[42] The fears of moveable property were most clearly directed at peddlers, who were not only landless but peripatetic, and thus accused of being so disconnected from their home community that they had turned into foreigners.[43] In the play *The Royal Merchant: or, Beggars Bush*, performed widely in the eighteenth century, a newly returned merchant declares, "My five year's absence hath kept me a Stranger/So much to all the Occurrens of My Country."[44] Instead of categorizing them as hard-working individuals, early modern legislation, in the mainland and the colonies, "stigmatized peddlers and itinerant tradesmen as inveterate rogues" and useless vagabonds.[45] In Britain anxiety invoked by traveling salesmen rose sharply from the mid-1670s onward, coinciding with the settlement of South Carolina.[46]

Of all the occupations in Britain, early southeastern Indian traders most resembled peddlers. They were highly mobile, splitting their time between the colonies and Indian territory and traveling up to twenty-five days at a time; operated primarily out of doors; and connected distant people in an international trade.[47] Therefore it is not surprising that settlers imported English derogations and suspicions against peddlers and hurled them at Indian traders. Many assumed that Indian traders, like peddlers, had no sense of allegiance to anyone but themselves and, as shown in the Long case and later their interpretation of the Yamasee War, would go to any length to protect their economic interests. Settlers often referred to foreigners and traders in the same breath as enemies of the British colonies.[48] Well before the commissioners and the traders acquainted with Long grabbed onto the vengeful trader as an explanatory devise, the proprietors, who wholeheartedly adopted the ideal of landed property, looked suspiciously at traders. When they first learned about the Westo War, they assumed that "particular men by trade"[49] had promoted the war and had thus jeopardized the "Interest of the Planters."[50] They even wondered if their trusted agent of the monopoly, Henry Woodward, was applying "himself to war also."[51] In their schema planters were men of peace whereas traders were men of war. The fact that these traders were supplying slaves to the plantation owners did not complicate this equation.[52] The Long case demonstrates how, when push came to shove, members of the Commons House had the same fear that trade was inherently unequal and traders potentially exploitative.

Their untrustworthiness was in part linked to their trade in moveable property. Indian traders were "people of loose disorderly lives" with "no kind of property or visible way of living or supporting themselves."[53] They had to be regulated, officials argued, because they "generally lead loose, vicious lives, to the scandal of the Christian religion, and do likewise oppress the people among whom they live, by their unjust and illegal actions."[54] These untrustworthy Indian traders were particularly dangerous when they assumed a governmental role, a position traditionally reserved for disinterested, independent property owners.[55] Three years prior to the Long case the commissioners added a provision to their instructions to the Indian traders that stipulated that those given a government post must "not abuse itt by making Use therof to promote your perticular Interest with the Indians."[56] Long's rumored invocation of a governor's order played into this anxiety. In the next draft of the instructions they ordered that traders were "not to promise or engage the word of the government or of the commissioners, or any Indian whatsoever, without a particular Order for the same."[57]

That Indian traders were trading with foreigners aroused even more suspicion. In medieval and early modern England, trading with foreigners sparked such anxiety that transactions had to take place in public view. Although traders found ways to circumvent these strictures as buying and selling between locals and outsiders became more common, exchanges conducted away from the authoritarian eye continued to evoke suspicion within English communities.[58] Well into the eighteenth century, British communities created commercially controlled spaces to ensure that exchanges were visible and easily regulated. In Britain sales had to occur "in a place that is overt and open; not in a back-room, warehouse, nor behind hangings or cupboards in a shop, so that those who stand or pass by the shop cannot see it."[59] South Carolina officials similarly strove to ensure that trade was conducted transparently. Trading on unregistered ships in the harbor, for instance, was strictly forbidden.[60] Most trade occurred in public markets where trading times, items, and terms were regulated and weights and measures were standardized.[61] Through these measures that kept trade under the watchful eyes of the government and other community members, colonial officials strove to protect consumers from the "scheming merchant," which "was a stock figure in the early modern world."[62]

Native American consumers also needed to be protected from Indian traders. Though settlers feared that Indian traders would act contrary to the interests of British communities, they rarely, if ever, accused traders of exchanging their British loyalty for a Native American identity. This stood at odds with the realities on the ground, where traders formed intimate relationships with Native Americans. But although traders to the Native Americans spent at least half of the year living in Native American communities, were fluent in Native American languages, and formed families with Native American women, they escaped the label "White Indian" and the precarious position of cultural boundary crossers in the British Atlantic World.[63] That the members of the settler community who scorned Indian traders did not add accusations of cultural ubiquity to the list of attributes that compromised the fidelity of the traders is striking. In fact, in the southeast, intermarriage with Native Americans increased, rather than detracted from, a trader's status.[64] Colonists, who viewed merchants within their own community cynically, did not tar Indian traders as "White Indians" because they assumed that Native Americans were wise enough to keep merchants at arm's length as well. Though they were certain that buyers and sellers formed at least a rudimentary relationship, the British suspected that both parties hid their motives and personalities to gain a strategic bargaining advantage.[65] Consistent with the balance-of-trade mindset, settlers believed that trade encompassed two conflicting expectations: buyer and seller were bound by the common and complementary act of exchange while, at the same time, concerned solely with their own interests and not those of the other party.[66] Colonists did not fear that Native American communities would wholly absorb white traders because they believed that white traders were able to form only tenuous ties with their Native American trading partners.

Yet as the Long episode demonstrated with chilling clarity, traders were able to finesse commercial alliances to convince Native Americans to complete their dirty work. Settlers and officials referred to Indian traders who weaseled their way into Indian communities as "rogues" who used disguises to infiltrate a community with which they were, in fact, at odds.[67] Indian traders impersonated well-meaning, honest friends and merchants while, in fact, conspiring against the best interests of the Native American communities in which they lived.[68] Acting neither for the benefit of Native American or British settler communities, the Long episode made one thing clear: traders would do anything to pad their pocketbooks, and they used the unregulated frontiers for cover.

It took one major war to cement the suspicion that trade across boundaries was volatile and that interested Indian traders were deceitful. One year after the Long incident, the Yamasee, in conjunction with surrounding indigenous groups, waged a serious assault against the young colony, killing nearly four hundred settlers. To make sense of the calamity, settlers and colonial officials immediately blamed the "extortion and knavery of ye traders," accusing them of inciting the hostility of the surrounding Native Americans through unethical commercial practices.[69] A group of planters suggested that "the want of good government among the Indian traders might have given provocation. That trade being at present under no good regulation."[70] Mr. Crawley, who lived on the outskirts of the settlement, reported that he had seen the Carolina traders "frequently take from them their hogs, poultry, corn and other provisions, as they wanted it, and had only paid the Indian for it, what they thought fit." Crawley further claimed that the traders forced the Native Americans to "carry their burthens, thro' the woods for little or nothing, and beat and abuse them when they scrupled it."[71] William Byrd of Virginia explained that South Carolina "traders have so abused and so imposed upon the Indians in selling them goods at exorbitant prices, and receiving their peltry at very low rates, that they have been thereby very much disgusted."[72] In other words, the traders were abiding by balance-of-trade principles on an individual instead of a national scale, which the English had long acknowledged created volcanic relationships. All strata of society, from powerful planters to colonial officials to small farmers and traders, pointed accusatory fingers in one direction: the Indian traders.[73]

Unsurprisingly, after the Yamasee War, the General Assembly, acting on the same suppositions as the proprietors, resurrected a monopoly and settled the trade by relocating all trading activities to three forts.[74] As a representative governing body, the assembly was safe from the legal criticisms that royal monopolies faced, though Carolina merchants still vociferously objected to being shut out of the trade.[75] The assembly paid employees a salary to exchange public goods for skins and strictly forbade them from selling any personal property or keeping any of the deerskins they obtained.[76] Prices for skins and all European trade goods were standardized, and negotiations strictly forbidden.[77]

Their goal was to deprive Indian traders of any profit incentive for lying or cheating.

The revolt against the Proprietary government in 1719 led to the dissolution of the public monopoly, which was fully dismantled by 1721, barely five years after the Yamasee War. The royal governor (who had more regulatory power over the Indian trade than the proprietors had had) and the Lower House ensured, however, that the Indian trade was tightly regulated. Traders could purchase and sell their own goods, but their locations and trading partners were predetermined through licenses that restricted their movement to a few towns; they could not privately negotiate the prices of their goods, which remained standardized; and they could not decide how much credit to extend to their trading partners. Throughout the colonial period these regulations remained stable, even when the structure of governing the Indian trade changed.[78]

The regulations on private trade, location, price, and debt all sprang from the traditional assumption that sedentary people who operated within stable economic networks had to be trustworthy. In 1725 Indian Trade commissioner Colonel George Chicken, who suggested that the South Carolina legislature pass a law requiring "that the traders be confined to trade in any one or two towns of their own choice," explained that such regulation would tame these "loose vagabond sort of people" and reduce competition between these traders who would "say or do anything among the Indians for the lure of a few skins."[79] He invoked the same suspicion of peddlers that his predecessors deployed and determined that the solution was to take the traveling out of the Indian trade. Domestic trade was less exploitative than international trade.

Traders embraced regulations that determined where they could trade, even when they ignored price and debt restrictions. Instead of being unmoored and relishing the opportunities afforded by being far from the imperial eye, as officials feared, surviving journals suggests that Indian traders were as eager to add structure to the frontier as the officials were. Case in point is John Evans, a resident of southern Virginia who participated in the South Carolina Indian trade during the Proprietary period.[80] Evans, who marked his starting point in Virginia as "home," assiduously recorded the number of miles he traveled daily and where those travels led him. A typical selection of his journal reads:

> I went from home to Stony Creek. From thence y 11: to Magtoyim. Got at Nottoway skins. Thence to Meherrin river to Arthrr—Rananah y: 12: to y Sappones from thence to the Oconees at Roanoke y: 13: down y same river to weekcoano crossing y same going : 8: miles to sappony swamp . . .[81]

Sometimes, at the end of the day, he computed the distances he traveled in a row, rather than in his usual narrative form:

> Tiacoro: 30: miles to
> Routa: 12 miles to
> Noreanten to Co___ha to
> Nuhanied 8 to Yoahamina: 8
> to Conmery 6: to Cottann: 10:
> Connorock = Nonoreaneack
> 6: thence to Tiacoro: 16
> Juonoach: and three villages in miles of the country

Underneath this row of computation, he rewrote the distances in a paragraph, at times using variable Native American and English place names:

> Tiacoro ye first town, and from thence to Rourta 30 miles from thence to Nonhuna. 12 from thence to Kenhay, from thence to Worsuckca 8 from thence to Yoahawuney 8 from thence to Connewcartho, 6 from thence to Cottanaw 10 ffom thence to Cunnoryounh. 30 to Tiacoro and three villages in the middle and Juneiwach.[82]

Evans's journal demonstrates that Indian traders studiously pondered the question of how to traverse space, sometimes more than they did the items they traded. In form his journal bears a striking resemblance to colonial surveyors' records.[83] Despite his existence at the edge of the empire, Evans wholly embraced (whether intentionally or not) European methods of conquering land. He also shows how the Tory conception of an empire of land, and the Whig conception of an empire of trade, often intersected in the minds of colonial traders. His connection to the space he traversed was so strong that he eventually purchased land that he surveyed in his journal.[84] If Evans is representative of other Indian traders, it is not surprising that they welcomed an excuse to forgo the hardships involved in being a traveling merchant and thus did not resist the new regulations that limited their movements and domesticated the trade.

As historians have shown, Native American leaders, whose traditional control over trade was jeopardized when their community members had the freedom to trade beyond their oversight, welcomed and encouraged the settled trade.[85] But by focusing solely on Native American desires to contain commodity exchange, scholars have ignored how Indian trade regulations grew out of early modern British debates about dangerous and safe economies. Reared on the balance-of-trade philosophy and the belief that landholding determined citizenship, Carolinians were prone to view cross-cultural trade as potentially exploitative and volcanic, and landless, traveling traders as self-interested and devious. Although these suppositions fell into the background from 1707 to 1715, when the Commons House relied on mediation more than regulation, the Long episode and the Yamasee War snapped these suspicions about trade back to the forefront of trade philosophy and policy. After the Yamasee War, the South Carolina officials came full circle, focusing on the social threat of trade and instituting a monopoly. When the monopoly disintegrated under the royal government, they restricted the Indian trade to designated forts and Indian towns, thereby removing from Indian-white exchanges the potentially harmful elements introduced by traveling traders who operated according to a profit motive. Rather than embracing the changes in economic philosophies developing in England in the late seventeenth and eighteenth centuries, South Carolina's Indian trade regulations demonstrate the hesitancy to adopt a free-market model.

Notes

1. Lars Magnusson, *Mercantilism: The Shaping of an Economic Language* (London: Routledge, 1994), 9; Andrea Finkelstein, *Harmony and the Balance: An Intellectual History of Seventeenth-Century English Economic Thought* (Ann Arbor: University of Michigan Press, 2000), 179, 247–53; Keith Wrightson, *Earthly Necessities: Economic Lives in Early Modern Britain* (New Haven: Yale University Press, 2000), 249–55; Steve Pincus, "Rethinking Mercantilism: Political Economy, the British Empire, and the Atlantic World in the Seventeenth and Eighteenth Centuries," *WMQ* 69, no. 1 (January 2012): 12–14, 17–23.

2. Thomas Nairne, "A Description of Carolina," [1710?], Manuscript of published edition, Codex Eng. 10, at John Carter Brown Library, Providence, Rhode Island, unnumbered pages between 12 and 13; The Port Royall Discovery, July 14, 1666 and Proposealls of Several Gentlemen of Barbadoes, August 12, 1663, in *Shaftesbury Papers*, 11, 82. See also Max Edelson, *Plantation Enterprise in Colonial South Carolina* (Boston: Harvard University Press, 2006), 13–16; Robert M. Weir, "'Shaftesbury's Darling': British Settlement in the Carolinas at the Close of the Seventeenth Century," in *The Oxford History of the British Empire: The Origins of Empire: British Overseas Empires to the Close of the Seventeenth Century*, ed. Nicholas Canny (Oxford: Oxford University Press, 1998), 376–81, 392; Justin Roberts and Ian Beamish's essay in this compilation; Joseph M. Hall Jr., *Zamumo's Gifts: Indian-European Exchange in the Colonial Southeast* (Philadelphia: University of Pennsylvania Press, 2009), 84. That the proprietors based their dominion over Carolina on an agriculturist argument, see David Armitage, "John Locke, Carolina, and the 'Two Treatises of Government,'" *Political Theory* 32, no. 5 (October 2004): 617–18.

3. Weir, "'Shaftesbury's Darling,'" 381; William James Rivers, *A Sketch of the History of South Carolina to the Close of the Proprietary Government by the Revolution of 1719* (Charleston, S.C.: McCarter, 1856), 119. For the historiography of early modern property, see David Lieberman, "Property, Commerce, and the Common Law: Attitudes to Legal Change in the Eighteenth Century," in *Early Modern Conceptions of Property*, ed. John Brewer and Susan Staves (London: Routledge, 1995), 145–47. For the landed-property argument, see J. G. A. Pocock, *Virtue, Commerce, and History* (Cambridge, U.K.: Cambridge University Press, 1985), 68. For the growing importance of commerce and debates about landed and mobile property in the late seventeenth century, see Steve Pincus, *1688: The First Modern*

Revolution (New Haven: Yale University Press, 2009), 370–85; Ralph Davis, "English Foreign Trade, 1660–1700," *Economic History Review* 7, no. 2 (1954): 162; Natasha Glaisyer, *The Culture of Commerce in England, 1600–1720* (Woodbridge, U.K.: Boydell Press, 2006), 1–2; Magnusson, *Mercantilism*, 10.

4. For slave and deerskin export numbers, see Alan Gallay, *The Indian Slave Trade: The Rise of the English Empire in the American South, 1670–1717* (New Haven: Yale University Press, 2002), 294–308; Peter Mancall, Joshua Rosenbloom, and Thomas Weiss, "Indians and the Economy of Eighteenth-Century Carolina," in *The Atlantic Economy during the Seventeenth and Eighteenth Centuries*, ed. Peter Coclanis (Columbia: University of South Carolina Press, 2005), 312.

5. The immigrants to Carolina, including those who first lived in Barbados, New England, and Virginia, were primarily of English ancestry: Weir, "'Shaftesbury's Darling,'" 392.

6. Christian J. Koot, "Balancing Center and Periphery," *WMQ* 69, no. 1 (January 2012): 41–46.

7. For historians who argue that Native Americans were unfamiliar with commodity exchange, see Christina Snyder, *Slavery in Indian Country: The Changing Face of Captivity in Early America* (Boston: Harvard University Press, 2010), 55–56; Tom Hatley, *The Dividing Paths: Cherokees and South Carolinians through the Revolutionary Era* (Oxford: Oxford University Press, 1995), 48; Joshua Piker, *Okfuskee: A Creek Indian Town in Colonial America* (Boston: Harvard University Press, 2004), 159; Claudio Saunt, *A New Order of Things: Property, Power, and the Transformation of the Creek Indians, 1733–1816* (Cambridge, U.K.: Cambridge University Press, 1999), 40; Richard White, *The Roots of Dependency: Subsistence, Environment, and Social Change among the Choctaws, Pawnees, and Navajo* (Lincoln: University of Nebraska Press, 1983), 59. Kathryn Braund stands contrary to this trend: *Deerskins and Duffels: Creek Indian Trade with Anglo-America, 1685–1815* (Lincoln: University of Nebraska Press, 1993), 27, 63.

8. F. O'Sullivan to Lord Ashley, September 10, 1670, in *Shaftesbury Papers*, 189. See also Stuart Owen Stumpf, "The Merchants of Colonial Charlestown, 1680–1756" (Ph.D. diss., Michigan State University, 1971), 13–18; Thomas Ashe, "Carolina, or a Description of the Present State of that Country (1682)," in Salley, *Narratives*, 150; Eirlys Mair Barker, "'Much Blood and Treasure': South Carolina's Indian Traders, 1670–1755" (Ph.D. diss., College of William and Mary, 1993), 204.

9. Stephen Bull to Lord Ashley, September 12, 1670, in *Shaftesbury Papers*, 104.

10. Memoranda, Wm. Owen, September 15, 1670, in *Shaftesbury Papers*, 224.

11. Rivers, *Sketch*, 90; Instructions for Joseph Morton Esq., May 10, 1682, in BPRO-SC, 1:141–42; September 27, 1671, Records of the Grand Council and Proprietors' Council, John S. Green Transcripts of Journals, 1671–1721 (hereafter Green Transcripts), at SCDAH, 8.

12. September 27, 1671, Green Transcripts, 8.

13. Stephen Bull to Lord Ashley, September 12, 1670, in *Shaftesbury Papers*, 104.

14. Thomas Leng, "Commercial Conflict and Regulation in the Discourse of Trade in Seventeenth-Century England," *Historical Journal* 48, no. 4 (December 2005): 933, 954; Finkelstein, *Harmony and the Balance*, 22–25, 89–97; Pincus, "Rethinking Mercantilism," 18–19.

15. Shaftesbury, Craven, and Colleton to [unknown], October 22, 1677, in *BPRO-SC*, 1:60.

16. Proprietors to the Governor, Grand Council, and Parliament, September 30, 1683, in *BPRO-SC*, 1:258.

17. Perry Gauci, *The Politics of Trade: The Overseas Merchant in State and Society, 1660–1720* (Oxford: Oxford University Press, 2001), 112–15; Pincus, *1688*, 376–77, 385; Ludwell H. Johnson III, "The Business of War: Trading with the Enemy in English and Early American Law," *Proceedings of the American Philosophical Society* 118, no. 5 (1974): 460; W. Derrell Stump, "An Economic Consequence of 1688," *Albion* 6, no. 1 (1974): 28–35; March 15, 1632/4, Leo Francis Stock ed., *Proceedings and Debates of the British Parliaments respecting North America* (Washington, D.C.: Carnegie Institution of Washington, 1924), 58. That trade could be regulated to benefit the public good; see Finkelstein, *Harmony and the Balance*, 66–67; Tim Keirn, "Monopoly, Economic Thought, and the Royal African Company," in *Early Modern Conceptions of Property*, 427–66. For late seventeenth-century debates about the East Indian Company, see James Vaughn, "The Politics of Empire: Metropolitan Socio-Political Development and the Imperial Transformation of the British East Indian Company, 1675–1775" (Ph.D. diss., University of Chicago, 2009), 131–35, 162–64.

18. Ian K. Steele, *Politics of Colonial Policy: The Board of Trade in Colonial Administration, 1696–1720* (Oxford: Oxford University Press, 1968), 67; South Carolina General Assembly, *Report of the committee appointed to examine into the proceedings of the people of Georgia, with respect to the province of South-Carolina* (Charles-Town, SC: Timothy Lewis, 1736), 16. See also Virginia's antimonopoly argument against South Carolina: Steven Oatis, *Colonial Complex: South Carolina's Frontiers in the Era of the Yamasee War, 1680–1730* (Lincoln: University of Nebraska Press, 2008), 76.

19. Earl of Shaftesbury and P. Colleton to Andrew Percivall and Maur. Mathews, March 9, 1680/1, in *BPRO-SC*, 1:112; Proprietors to Gov. Joseph Blake and Council, December 20, 1697, in *BPRO-SC*, 3:234; Instructions for Nicholas Trott, March 8, 1697/8, in *BPRO-SC*, 4:13; Mr. Amy to James Moore, August 28, 1698, in *BPRO-SC*, 4:71; M. Eugene Sirmans, "Politics in Colonial South Carolina: The Failure of Proprietary Reform, 1682–1694," *WMQ* 23, no. 1 (January 1966): 33–55; Gallay, *Indian Slave Trade*, 57–69, 215–16.

20. For the process of establishing trade regulations see Minutes, February 3, 4, 10, and 12, 1702/3, in *JCHA 1703*, 32, 35, 38, 41; Minutes, September 20, 1710, in *JCIT*, 3; Oatis, *Colonial Complex*, 46, 53–54; Crane, *Southern Frontier*, 142–44. For the historiography about free versus regulated trade, see William Ramsey, *The Yamasee War: A Study of Culture, Economy, and Conflict in the Colonial South* (Lincoln: University of Nebraska Press, 2008), 81.

21. An Act Appointing a Special Court for the Speedy Deciding of Controversies between Merchant and Merchant, or Mariner and Mariner, or Merchants and Mariners, about freight, damage, and other maritime Cases, 1661, *Acts of Assembly, Passed in the Island of Barbadoes, from 1648, to 1718* (London: John Baskett, 1732), 12–13. On the increasing use of judicial outlets to resolve trading disputes in the early modern period, see Craig Muldrew, *Economy of Obligations: The Culture*

of Credit and Social Relations in Early Modern England (New York: Palgrave, 1998), 199–271.

22. For the proprietors' use of the Grand Council to resolve trading disputes, see Minutes, February 24, 1672/73, March 4, 1672/73, and February 2, 1673, in *JGC*, 1:54, 55, 66–67; Proprietors to Joseph West and others, May 17, 1680, in *BPRO-SC*, 1:97–102; see also Instructions for Joseph Morton Esq., May 10, 1682, in *BPRO-SC*, 1:142.

23. Minutes, July 27, 1711, in *JCIT*, 11.

24. Minutes, August 3, 1711, in *JCIT*, 14.

25. Minutes, July 9, 1712, in *JCIT*, 31.

26. Lieberman, "Property, Commerce, and the Common Law," 144–45; "A Bill of Complaint in Chancery, 1700," *SCHM* 21, no. 4 (1920): 139–43; Pocock, *Virtue, Commerce, and History*, 56. The proprietors defended Native American ownership of land as well as of personal property; see Proprietors to the Governor, Grand Council, and Parliament, September 30, 1683, in *BPRO-SC*, 1:258.

27. Minutes, September 21, 1710, in *JCIT*, 4; Minutes, March 9, 1711, in *JCIT*, 6; Minutes, July 28, 1711, in *JCIT*, 11; Minutes, August 2, 1711, in *JCIT*, 13; Minutes, March 21, 1712, in *JCIT*, 20; Minutes, April 17, 1712, in *JCIT*, 23; Minutes, April 18, 1712, in *JCIT*, 23. On differing categorizations of slaves, see Theda Perdue, *Slavery and the Evolution of Cherokee Society, 1540–1866* (Knoxville: University of Tennessee Press, 1979), 4–18.

28. Minutes, March 9, 1711, in *JCIT*, 6; Minutes, August 3, 1711, in *JCIT*, 14; Minutes, June 10, 1712, in *JCIT*, 27.

29. Minutes, October 28, 1710, in *JCIT*, 5. See also Minutes, April 17–18, 1712, in *JCIT*, 23.

30. Minutes, March 2, 1716, in *JCIT*, 262.

31. Jonathan Whilden, Lieutenant Thomas Ferrington, Thomas Stone, Inventories of Estates, 1736–1739, vol. 68, microfilm ST0467, at SCDAH; Hugh Campbell, Inventories of Estates, 1744, microfilm ST0446, at SCDAH.

32. Nairne, *Muskogean Journals*, 56.

33. South Carolina General Assembly, *Report of the committee appointed to examine into the proceedings of the people of Georgia*, 8.

34. Nairne, *Muskhogean Journals*, 56.

35. See for instance the dispute between Henry Woodward and the third Baron Cadross: Crane, *Southern Frontier*, 29–30.

36. The South Carolina Indian traders' license agreements specified they were allowed to trade only with "Indians in amity with this Government"; see Commissioners to Theophilus Hastings, July 24, 1716, in *JCIT*, 85; Instructions to Theophilus Hastings, July 19, 1718, in *JCIT*, 310. For traders forming partnerships with individuals of other nations, see Cherokee Traders before the Governor and Council, July 6, 1753, in *Documents Relating to Indian Affairs*, 2 vols., ed. William L. McDowell Jr. (1970; reprint, Columbia: South Carolina Department of Archives and History, 1992) (hereafter *DRIA*), 1:446; Affidavit of David Dowey, May 25, 1751, in *DRIA* 1:57; Governor Henry Ellis to John Rae, Lachlan McGillivray, Francis McCartan Esquires, December 7, 1759, document GLC05228.02, at Gilder Lehrman Institute of American History, New York, New York.

37. Minutes, March 9, 1711, in *JCIT,* 6.
38. Minutes, July 17, 1713, in *JCIT,* 47.
39. Commissioners to John Wright, May 30, 1711, in *JCIT,* 8.
40. Minutes, May 4, 1714, in *JCIT,* 53–56.
41. Jean-Christophe Agnew, *Worlds Apart: The Market and the Theater in Anglo-American Thought, 1550–1750* (New York: Cambridge University Press, 1986), 40–42; David Sacks, *The Widening Gate: Bristol and the Atlantic Economy, 1450–1700* (Berkeley: University of California Press, 1991), 78; Nuala Zahedieh, "Overseas Expansion and Trade in the Seventeenth Century," in *Oxford History of the British Empire: The Origins of Empire,* 398–99.
42. T. H. Breen, *The Marketplace of Revolution: How Consumer Politics Shaped American Independence* (New York: Oxford University Press, 2004), 137–40; Daniel Defoe, *The Complete English Tradesman* (London, 1726), 25; Agnew, *Worlds Apart,* 3.
43. Linda Woodbridge, "The Peddler and the Pawn: Why Did Tudor England Consider Peddlers to Be Rogues?," in *Rogues and Early Modern English Culture,* ed. Craig Dionne and Steve Mentz (Ann Arbor: University of Michigan Press, 2004), 143–70, esp. 164.
44. Francis Beaumont, *The Royal Merchant: Or, Beggars Bush. A Comedy. As It Is Acted at the Theatre-Royal in Smock-Alley . . . Written by Beaumont and Fletcher* (Dublin, 1736), 6.
45. Woodbridge, "The Peddler and the Pawn," 144; Theodore Barlow, *The justice of peace: a treatise containing the power and duty of that magistrate, . . . Together with a table . . . By Theodore Barlow, . . . To which is added an appendix, . . .* (London, 1745): 7–9, 726. For South Carolina punishment of rogues and vagabonds, see Minutes, in *Journals of the Commons House of Assembly, November 8, 1734–June 7, 1735,* ed. A. S. Salley (Columbia: Historical Commission of South Carolina, 1947), 55, 159, 61, 79. For Barbadian vagrant legislation, see *An Act to Prevent the Prejudice that may happen to this Island by loose and vagrant Persons in and about the same, n.d.,* in *Acts of Assembly, Passed in the Island of Barbadoes, from 1648, to 1718* (London: Printed by order of the Lords Commissioners of Trade and Plantations, by John Baskett, 1732–39), 37. Barbados outlawed travelling merchants in 1668: *An Act prohibiting wandering Persons from carrying goods and Wares in Packs, or otherwise, from House to House in this Island,* in *Acts of Assembly, Passed in the Island of Barbadoes* (London: Printed by order of the Lords Commissioners of Trade and Plantations, by John Baskett, 1732–39), 64.
46. Margaret Spufford, *The Great Reclothing of Rural England: Petty Chapmen and Their Wares in the Seventeenth Century* (London: Hambledon Press, 1984), 10. J. G. A. Pocock argues that the debates regarding virtue and moveable/landed property began in earnest in the 1690s, twenty years after the first settlement in South Carolina, in *Virture, Commerce, and History,* 65–66. See also Ronald Berger, *The Most Necessary Luxuries: The Mercers' Company of Coventry, 1550–1680* (University Park: Pennsylvania State University Press, 1993), 32.
47. Woodbridge, "The Peddler and the Pawn," 145, 52, 63; Spufford, *The Great Reclothing of Rural England,* 21–31; Eirlys Mair Barker, "Indian Traders, Charles Town, and London's Vital Links to the Interior of North America, 1717–1755," in

Money, Trade, and Power: The Evolution of Colonial South Carolina's Plantation Society, ed. Jack P. Greene, Rosemary Brana-Shute, and Randy J. Sparks (Columbia: University of South Carolina Press, 2001), 133–34, 141.

48. Minutes, in *JCHA* June 2, 1724–June 16, 1724, 4; May 16, 1751, in "Proceedings of the President and Assistants in Council of Georgia, 1749–1751, Part II," ed. Lilla Mills Hawes, *GHQ* 36, no. 1 (1952): 50.

49. Proprietors to Governor and Council, March 7, 1680/1, in *BPRO-SC*, 1:115.

50. Proprietors to Governor and Council, February 21, 1680/1, in *BPRO-SC*, 1:104.

51. Proprietors to Governor and Council, March 7, 1680/1, in *BPRO-SC*, 1:116.

52. By 1708 Indian slaves made up twenty-five percent of South Carolina's slave population: Ramsey, *Yamasee War*, 37.

53. Act Against Vagabonds, February 29, 1764, in *The Colonial Records of the State of Georgia*, ed. Allen Daniel Candler et al. (Atlanta: Franklin Printing, 1904), 18:588.

54. Act 269, *Statutes at Large*, 2:309.

55. Bernard Bailyn, *The Origins of American Politics* (New York: Vintage, 1965), 86–87; Richard Beeman, *The Varieties of Political Experience in Eighteenth-Century America* (Philadelphia: University of Pennsylvania Press, 2006).

56. Minutes, August 3, 1711, in *JCIT*, 16. See also Minutes, March 25, 1713, in *JCIT*, 42.

57. Colonel Mackey to Theopilus Hastings, July 24, 1716, in *JCIT*, 86. William Ramsey argues that this episode underlines the dangers posed in the southeast by having two competing discourses in the southeast, trade talk and treaty talk: *Yamasee War*, 79–97.

58. Agnew, *Worlds Apart*, 44–49; Muldrew, *The Economy of Obligation*, 63; Sacks, *The Widening Gate*, 77–79; T. H. Lloyd, *Alien Merchants in England in the High Middle Ages* (Sussex, U.K.: Harvester Press, 1982), 2–3.

59. Barlow, *The Justice of Peace*, 206.

60. Minutes, April 13, 1692, in *JGC*, 2:5.

61. An Act to prevent Abuses by false Weights and Measures, 1710, in Nicholas Trott, *The Laws of the Province of South-Carolina, in Two Parts* (Charles-Town S.C.: Printed by Lewis Timothy, 1736), 59, 168. See also An Act for Settling a Fair and Markets, 1723, in Trott, *The Laws of the Province of South-Carolina*, 409–11. Similar laws were passed in Barbados: An Act for Weights and Measures, 1652, in *Acts of Assembly, Passed in the Island of Barbadoes*, 6; An Act for Establishing Market Days, 1661, repeal in 1668, in *Acts of Assembly*, 58; An Act concerning Forestallers and Ingrossers of Provisions, 1672, in *Acts of Assembly*, 83–84; An Act to prevent the Inconveniencies upon the Inhabitants of this Island by Forestallers, Ingrossers and Regulators, 1676, in *Acts of Assembly*, 96–98; An Act for the better regulating of Outcries in Open Market, 1688, in *Acts of Assembly*, 128–29.

62. Toby L. Ditz, "Secret Selves, Credible Personas: The Problematics of Trust and Public Display in the Writing of Eighteenth-Century Philadelphia Merchants," in *Possible Pasts: Becoming Colonial in Early America*, ed. Robert Blair St. George (Ithaca: Cornell University Press, 2000), 219. See also Finkelstein, *Harmony and the Balance*, 15–16, 22–25.

63. "White Indian" is a term used by James Axtell to describe Europeans who chose to join Native American communities: *The Invasion Within: The Contest of Cultures in Colonial North America* (Oxford: Oxford University Press, 1985), 302–27. For a general historiographical essay on cultural brokerage, see Eric Hinderaker, "Translation and Cultural Brokerage," in *A Companion to American Indian History*, ed. Philip Deloria and Neal Salisbury (Malden, Mass.: Blackwell, 2002), 357–75. For the uneasy position of people who spanned two cultures in colonial America, see Karen Kupperman, *Indians and English: Facing Off in Early America* (Ithaca: Cornell University Press, 2000), 212–40; Jill Lepore, *The Name of War: King Philip's War and the Origin of American Identity* (New York: Vintage Books, 1998), 21–47; James Merrell, "'The Cast of His Countenance': Reading Andrew Montour," in *Through a Glass Darkly: Reflections on Personal Identity in Early America*, ed. Ronald Hoffman et al. (Chapel Hill: University of North Carolina Press, 1997); James H. Merrell, *Into the American Woods: Negotiators on the Pennsylvania Frontier* (New York: Norton, 1999), 37–38, 64–65, 94–95, 289–94. For relationships between Native American women and British Indian trader men, see Barker, "Much Blood and Treasure," 149–67; Braund, *Deerskins and Duffels*: 36, 78, 83–86; Hatley, *Dividing Paths*, 52–63; Theda Perdue, "'A Sprightly Lover Is the Most Prevailing Missionary': Intermarriage between Europeans and Indians in the Eighteenth-Century South," in *Light on the Path: The Anthropology and History of the Southeastern Indians*, ed. Thomas J. Pluckhahn and Robbie Franklyn Ethridge (Tuscaloosa: University of Alabama Press, 2006), 165–78; Piker, *Okfuskee*: 166–76.

64. Barker, "Indian Traders, Charles Town, and London's Vital Links to the Interior of North America," 142.

65. Woodbridge, "The Peddler and the Pawn," 160; Muldrew, *Economy of Obligation*, 148.

66. Agnew, *Worlds Apart*, 68.

67. Craig Dionne and Steve Mentz, "Introduction: Rogues and Early Modern English Culture," in *Rogues and Early Modern English Culture*, ed. Craig Dionne and Steve Mentz (Ann Arbor: University of Michigan Press, 2004), 1–2; Colonel John Barnwell, "The Tuscarora Expedition: Letters of Colonel John Barnwell," *SCHM* 9, no. 1 (1908): 43; Deposition of James Francis, June 1, 1751, in *DRIA*, 1:24; Governor James Glen Talk, November 14, 1751, in *DRIA*, 1:197; T. F. Brewer and J. Baillie, "The Journal of George Pawley's 1746 Agency to the Cherokee," *Journal of Cherokee Studies* 16, no. 1 (1991): 18.

68. For the disguises of itinerant workers, see Patricia Fumerton, "Making Vagrancy (In)Visible: The Economics of Disguise in Early Modern Rogue Pamphlets," in *Rogues and Early Modern English Culture*, 193–210.

69. Rev. William Tredwell Bull, "Letter to the Society for the Propagation of the Gospel, August 10, 1715," *SCHM* 32, no. 4 (1931): 254.

70. Minutes, July 16, 1715, in *JCIT*, 56–57.

71. Oral Report to the Commissioners of Trade, July 26, 1715, in *JCIT*, 62.

72. Oral Report to the Commissioners of Trade, July 15, 1715, Great Britain, Board of Trade, in *Journal of the Commissioners for Trade and Plantations*, 14 vols. (London: H. M. Stationery Off., 1920), 2:54.

73. This trope persisted long after South Carolina became a royal colony; see Tyler Boulware, "'Traders, Pedlars, and idle Fellows': Community Boundaries and Collective Identity in the Southeastern Deerskin Trade," in *Global Economies, Cultural Currencies of the Eighteenth Century*, ed. Michael Rotenberg-Schwartz (New York: AMS Press, forthcoming); Minutes, in *JCHA November 8, 1734–June 7, 1735*, 20; Minutes, May 16, 1751, in *DRIA*, 1:50–51; January 8–January 12, 1760, in *South Carolina Newspapers: The South-Carolina Gazette 1760*, ed. Mary Bondurant Warren and Robert S. Lowery (Danielsville, Ga.: Heritage Papers, 1988). It used to be standard for historians to accept the colonists' interpretation of the causes of the Yamasee War; see James Axtell, *The Indians' New South: Cultural Change in the Colonial Southeast* (Baton Rouge: Louisiana State University Press, 1997), 49; Bradley Scott Schrager, "Yamasee Indians and the Challenge of Spanish and English Colonialism in the North American Southeast, 1660–1715" (Ph.D. diss., Northwestern University, 2001), 173. For a synopsis of the Yamasee War historiography, see Ramsey, "'Something Cloudy in Their Looks,'" 44–49. Recently a handful of historians have worked against this trend of blaming Indian traders for the strife in the southeast; see Ramsey, *Yamasee War*, 13–53; Richard L. Hahn, "The 'Trade Do's Not Flourish as Formerly': The Ecological Origins of the Yamassee War of 1715," *Ethnohistory* 28, no. 4 (1981): 341–58; Hall, *Zamumo's Gift*, 117–44.

74. Minutes, July 17, 1716, in *JCIT*, 81.

75. Crane, *Southern Frontier*, 197–98.

76. Samuell Muckleroy and Joseph Thompson to Eleazer Wiggan, July 6, 1716, in *JCIT*, 71; Minutes, July 10, 1716, in *JCIT*, 73–4; An Act for the Better Regulation of the Indian Trade [no date], in *JCIT*, 327.

77. Instructions to the Storekeeper, &c., July 6, 1716, in *JCIT*, 72; An Account of Prices of Goods negotiated on April 30, 1716, in *JCIT*, 89.

78. Crane, *Southern Frontier*, 200.

79. Records of His Majesty's Council in South Carolina, July 17, 1725, at SCDAH, 63–64.

80. On March 22, 1711, South Carolina licensed John Evans of Virginia; in *JCIT*, 7. The Evans journal (1700–1715) is split between the Library of Congress (hereafter LOC) and the South Caroliniana Library in Columbia, South Carolina. On the Evans journal as a personal, rather than diplomatic, journal, see James H. Merrell, *The Indians; New World: Catawbas and Their Neighbors from European Contact through the Era of Removal* (New York: Norton, 1989), 73.

81. Evans journal, at LOC, 18.

82. The distances match up perfectly in these two examples, suggesting that Evans was giving the alternate English and Native American place names, Evans journal, at LOC, 14.

83. For a surveying example, see "Journal of the Proceedings of the Commissioners Appointed to Ascertain and Mark the Boundary Lines Agreeably to Treaties between the Indian Nations and the United States," in *The Collected Works of Benjamin Hawkins, 1796–1810*, ed. Thomas Foster (Tuscaloosa: University of Alabama Press, 2003), 144, 149–51. Evans did not use surveying instruments but rather estimated distances based on the time it took to travel: Linda Marie Pett-Conklin,

"Cadastral Surveying in Colonial South Carolina: A Historical Geography" (Ph.D. diss., Louisiana State University, 1986), 4, 69–104.

84. According to Evans's journal, he traveled through much of the land he would later purchase. Evans purchased 1,001 acres in Prince George County on Stony Creek, December 23, 1714. On November 13, 1721, he bought land that spanned Sappone Creek at the Trading Branch. He bought two hundred acres on the south side of Nottoway River and the Little Swamp, which is probably the swamp he referred to as "Small Swamp" in his journal. Nell Marion Nugent, *Cavaliers and Pioneers: Abstracts of Virginia Land Patents and Grants,* vol. 3, 1695–1732 (Richmond: Virginia State Library, 1979), 166, 231, 303. For a later example of an Indian trader journal that is also attentive to movement and space, see Anonymous, "Gurnal of my Traveling to the Indian Cuntray, 1767," at Georgia Historical Society, Savannah.

85. Minutes, July 10, 1716, in *JCIT,* 73; For traditional southeastern Native American leader control over trade see Hall, *Zamumo's Gifts,* 2–7, 67, 87; Snyder, *Slavery in Indian Country,* 26–27, 35, 41; White, *The Roots of Dependency,* 52–53, 74–75, 80; Ramsey, *Yamasee War,* 79–97; Piker, *Okfuskee,* 138–40; Brewer, ed., "The Journal of George Pawley's 1746 Agency to the Cherokee," 18; Lower Creek to Governor Reynolds, October 13, 1756, in *DRIA,* 2:239; Talk between James Glen and Cherokee of Hiwasee, Stecoe, Tuccoigia, Toxoway, November 14, 1752, in *DRIA,* 1:191.

"Cutting one anothers Throats"

British, Native, and African Violence in Early Carolina

MATTHEW JENNINGS

As the British, various native peoples, and enslaved Africans came into contact with one another in late-seventeenth-century Carolina, they exchanged a wide array of goods, diseases, and ideas. Some of these exchanges are relatively well understood: the Indian slave trade, the Muskogee-English deerskin trade, and the role of African expertise in European planters' choice of rice as their colony's staple have been the subject of important book-length studies.[1] Less well known is the fact that British, African, and Native American cultures of violence collided with one another, and that all were reshaped by the force of the collision.[2] To make matters more complicated, the world into which the English colony of Carolina was born had already been remade by violence many times over. Before the advent of the Europeans, indigenous towns clashed over resources, captives, tribute, and prestige. As the Spanish, French, and English entered the Americas, they brought new sorts of violence to bear on their indigenous enemies, and occasionally each other. The violence that took place along Carolina's frontier was neither wholly native nor English nor African in its nature, and it was a microcosm of what happened when European violence met Native American violence.

Violence and the Birth of Carolina

The British conquered the southeast through a combination of shrewd diplomacy, exploitative trade, and warfare. They recruited armies of indigenous allies to debilitate the Spanish missions of Florida. They expanded their dominion with the forced assistance of thousands of Native American and later African American slaves, and they extended a violent slave labor regime based on precedents from the Chesapeake and the Caribbean. After some initial thoughts on English charters and violence, this chapter features several case studies of the burgeoning British (really Anglo-American) culture of violence: the Westo War; late-seventeenth- and early-eighteenth-century mission raids; and early slavery. These case studies illuminate two themes. First, the British conquest remained frustratingly incomplete from an imperial perspective, as "subject" peoples such as interior Indian nations and enslaved Africans continued to express their independence well into the eighteenth century. Second, at the imperial level the British did not believe their mode of colonization to be particularly violent. They saw "planting" as a more peaceful mode of claiming American territory than Spanish conquest. Carl Jacoby, writing about a nineteenth-century massacre, has argued that violence "often ends as a contest over meaning, as the participants struggle to articulate what has happened to them."[3] This contest is ongoing, and the perils of taking eighteenth-century Britons at their word regarding colonial violence are quite real. If we fail to recognize the violence associated with British colonization, we risk buying into a sanitized version of early American history.

When the Lords Proprietors heard about their fledgling colony's war against the Westos, they were disappointed. Accounts they received indicated that the war had begun under questionable circumstances, may have involved what they judged to be excessive cruelty, and threatened to wreck what the proprietors perceived to be a profitable peace. The distance between the proprietors and the planters was considerable—both in nautical miles and worldview—and the proprietors' only recourse was to a series of strongly worded letters. One of these included a telling phrase: the proprietors in London reminded the colonists around Charles Town that "Peace is in the Interest of Planters."[4]

The events surrounding the establishment and expansion of Carolina would seem to indicate that the opposite was true. Slave raiding, exploitative trade, and plantation violence made early Carolina a volatile, dangerous place. Yet individual colonists, if they had sufficient capital or credit to start plantations or if they could enter the Indian trade, could turn striking profits. Peace might eventually come to Carolina, but only after the consolidation of English rule on the coast, which would presumably entail violence or the threat of violence. Even then the plantation regime that took hold as the colony grew rested on the violent subjugation of African and indigenous slaves. From some perspectives, a "planters' peace" was no peace at all.

English documents do not usually emphasize the violence of colonization, even as they set the stage for imperial contests and conflict between native communities and colonists. The key documents of English Carolina's earliest years often mention violence, at the very least. In 1665 Charles II granted the proprietors title to land extending from Daytona Beach (south of St. Augustine) to Virginia's southern border. That the grant was a colonial fantasy—or long-term goal?—of the highest order is indicated by the western border, placed modestly at the Pacific Ocean.[5]

The 1665 charter granted the proprietors the right of "taking away member or life" if necessary to enforce the laws of the colony, recognizing that state-sponsored violence might be appropriate.[6] The Crown was not naïve enough to believe that everyone in the southeast would welcome the English presence: the charter mentioned that the proprietors had the right to procure "ordnance, powder, shot, armour, and all other weapons, ammunition, and habiliments of war, both defensive and offensive."⁷ The proprietors had wide latitude when it came to prosecuting wars on behalf of the colony "because that in so remote a country, and situate among so many barbarous nations, the invasions of savages and other enemies, pirates and robbers, may probably be feared." The proprietors could raise men "to make war, and pursue the enemies aforesaid, as well by sea, as by land; yea, even without the limits of the said province, and, by God's assistance, to vanquish, and take them; and being taken, to put them to death, by the law of war, and to save them at their pleasure."⁸ This is a rare admission on the part of the highest-ranking official in the English empire that colonization was a violent undertaking. Not only are the proprietors charged with defending the colony's perimeters, the charter grants them permission to pursue the colony's enemies beyond its borders, to "vanquish" said enemies and to put them to death according to the laws of war. At first glance, this appears to be in keeping with the culture of international conflict present in earlier times, such as the Spanish promise to make "war of fire and blood" (*a fuego y a sangre*) against enemies of God and the Spanish state in the 1500s. On closer inspection, the 1665 charter looks to occupy a middle ground between the crusading, all-encompassing violence of past epochs and conflicts that heed some limiting rules of war, no matter how nebulous the rules may be, and how flexibly they might be applied to situations far from European capitals.

The charters provided the legal basis for English Carolina to exist, while the Concessions and Agreements of the Lords Proprietors, also from 1665, and the more widely known Fundamental Constitutions, drafted and issued in the late 1660s, addressed colonial governance.⁹ The Concessions and Agreements do not treat violence in great detail. When the Fundamental Constitutions do treat the subject of violence, they are most concerned with the chain of command.¹⁰ The grand council had the power to "make peace and war, leagues, treaties &c., with any of the neighbour Indians" and had the authority to raise and disband forces.¹¹ These are the sole utterances of the Fundamental Constitutions on the subject of violence. Lacking specific guidance, and probably not caring particularly, colonists were free to forge their own culture of violence.

Westo War

The proprietors sought to eliminate intercultural violence, which they perceived as backward and debilitating, and viewed colonization as a positive undertaking for everybody involved. Anthony Ashley Cooper and others discounted conquest and religious conversion as part of the colonization and touted English agriculture and trade as avenues to wealth and social stability. Two problems are immediately apparent. First, the settlers of Carolina may not have shared the enlightened perspective of the proprietors. Second, trading and plantation agriculture were rarely peaceful in the charged atmosphere of the southeast. The type of agriculture that developed in Carolina relied on violence against Africans, and its expansion put pressure on native communities. The type of trade—in firearms, alcohol, slaves, and deerskins—that spread from Charles Town throughout the region could easily spark violence between native peoples and the English. Metropolitan dreams of peace and trade conflicted with the ideas of the settlers, but the proprietors' vision was also at odds with itself when it apportioned land to English people that was still populated by native communities.

Three decades separated the Westo and Yamasee Wars, and they differ in their particulars: in the later conflict, Yamasees attacked, and when they did, they went against a more established coastal enclave, featuring some characteristics of a dynamic plantation regime. Still the two conflicts are analogous to an extent. In both instances, the English fought against indigenous peoples who were already fairly familiar with Europeans, merchant capitalism, and colonial violence. Westos had learned these lessons in Iroquois Country, while Yamasees had learned them in the southeast. Each group moved into Carolina's orbit for trade. English behavior was comparable in both cases. Planters and policymakers preferred to use proxies to distance themselves from the hazards of combat. The British fancied themselves as rather above the fray in the southeast and exploited existing rivalries and tension to bring about their desired ends.

The English were not above the fray, of course, and they were also tardy in the extreme among the participants in the fight for the region. The first English people to settle in Carolina entered a world that was in the process of being remade through violence, though the Carolinians were probably only dimly aware of this fact. Nicholas Carteret, one of the first white settlers of Carolina, noted the coastal peoples' willingness to entertain the English and invite them to settle. According to Carteret, they were greeted with cries of "Hiddy doddy Comorado Angles Westoe Skorrye (which is as much as to say) English very good friends Westoes are nought, they hoped by our Arrivall to be protected from ye Westoes."[12] The warm invitation might seem at first to be a figment of the colonial imagination. However tracing the Westos' story through eastern North America adds weight to the colonists' claims about being invited and welcomed.

In the wake of increased Five Nations Iroquois attacks, one community of Eries, known as the Riquerhonnons, moved to the falls of the James River by 1656. The English called them "Rickahockans" or "Richahecrians" and, after an initial confrontation, engaged in a profitable trade with the newcomers.[13] Within a couple of years, the Richahecrians were undertaking long-distance journeys for slaves and furs; the Spanish called them "Chichimecos," a term applied to many groups outside of the Spanish sphere of influence. Westos attacked the Spanish mission province of Guale in 1661, forcing colonial officials to rethink their policies and previewing the raids of the early eighteenth century.[14]

Westos combined the mentality of the mourning war with the mindset of the market to great effect.[15] In other words, the Westos' culture of violence was a potent mixture of previously existing Iroquoian ideas about violence and the dictates of the Atlantic market. As disease took a toll on the native northeast, and as native people sought European goods, mourning wars increased in size and expanded in meaning to include economic motives. The Eries arrived in Virginia armed and well aware of the skills necessary to thrive in the world between the native interior and the colonial market. Their Virginia experience prepared the Westos to become the premier Indian slavers of the southeast.[16] Dr. Henry Woodward, a trader and interpreter, wrote in 1674 that Westos traded "drest deare skins furrs and young Indian Slaves" for "arms, ammunition [and] trading cloath . . . from the northward [Virginia]."[17] Woodward also observed that the Westos were "at continuall wars" with other western peoples.

The Westos' skill at raiding was enhanced by the fact that they were the only firearm-equipped indigenous group in the area. Stephen Bull, Anthony Ashley Cooper's deputy, reported that they "war agt all Indians . . . & doe strike a great feare in these Indians havinge gunns & powder & shott & doe come upon these Indians heere in the tyme of their cropp & destroy all by killinge Caryinge away their Corne & Children & eat them."[18] The Westos were terrifying enough that by 1670 coastal peoples welcomed English settlement.[19]

After 1670 the Westos sold their captives exclusively to the English, reorienting the entire Indian slave trade to Carolina. The type of violence unleashed by the Westos could only have existed within the specific historical circumstances of the early southeast.[20] These outsiders came into a region previously rocked by violent competition between Mississippian towns; Soto's rampage; and finally the establishment of European colonies looking for allies and anything that could be sold, including human beings. Westo exploitation of the prevailing conditions likely served as an example to others, specifically Shawnees (known to white Carolinians as Savannahs) and the Yamasees.

Ten years after the founding of the colony at Charles Town, the English were in a position to assert their dominance over the Westos, who had apparently outlived their usefulness as slave raiders and trading partners. The causes of the Westo War are tied up in the politics of English Carolina: essentially Woodward and the proprietors intended to regulate trade with Indians, while a planter faction known as the Goose Creek men desired to expand the trade as far inland as possible.[21] To achieve this goal, the Goose Creek men armed the Savannahs. The Savannahs proceeded to defeat and enslave much of the Westo population. Here is an early example of one of the key features of the developing British culture of violence. The colonizers relied on Native American allies, arming one community against another. It shouldn't be assumed, however, that native communities were simply pawns in a British game. Over time the balance of power favored Europeans, but indigenous communities might reap short-term rewards in trade. They also ensured, at least temporarily, that they would not fall victim to the slave trade.

Hostilities began in the winter of 1679–80 and flared sporadically afterward. Hundreds of captured Westos were brought to Charles Town and sold into West Indian slavery.[22] The war may have begun with some treachery on the part of white Carolinians. A 1683 letter from the proprietors chided the colonists for the "heads of the Westohs being taken whilst they were in treaty with that Government . . . & put to death in Cold blood & the rest Driven from their country."[23] No firsthand accounts of the actual combat survive, so it's unclear if the reference to heads being taken is literal.[24] The Westo War dispersed the Westos as a people. Splinter groups moved north to Iroquoia and west to what would become Creek Country.[25] The Savannahs became one of Carolina's main Indian trading partners, with all the advantages and disadvantages thereof.

The Westo War demonstrates an instance of the "Americanization" of the English culture of violence. European theories that put all Native Americans on one side of a vast cultural divide between savagery and civilization were of little use when it came to dealing with diverse indigenous communities. The English in other parts of North America had recognized something of the complexity of Native American politics and alliances or competition between native communities, and the planters of Carolina were no exception. North American realities forced English colonizers to adapt to the politics of the indigenous southeast, in part by exploiting existing Native American rivalries. The benefits to Carolina were great, but the behavior carried risk, too, since violence could beget violence and move in unpredictable directions.

The proprietors found out about the Westo War far too late to affect its prosecution or outcome, voiced strong disapproval, and blamed the violence on the white Carolinians: "If friendships had been preserved with ye Westos it would have kept all the neighbouring Indians from dareing to offend you; and if you had protected them from being injured by the Westoes, that protection would have made them love as well as feare you." The letter goes on to note, as mentioned above, that "Peace is in the Interest of Planters."[26] In South Carolina's lowcountry, it would be more accurate to say that war was in the interest of planters. Planters benefited from lands vacated by fleeing Indians, and if two neighboring groups went to war, Carolina's traders could expect an influx of slaves. The proprietors also suspected that the Westo War was undertaken for inappropriate reasons. They despaired that they "could not well judg whether this war was made upon a reall necessity for the preservation of the Collony, or to serve the ends of particular men by trade."[27] The difference between "reall necessity" and "the ends of particular men" was not a distinction that Carolina's colonizers were willing to recognize or accept.

Mission Raids

When Yamasees attacked Spanish missions, their motives and tactics blended old and new worlds of violence. The Yamasees arrived in the sea islands at about the same time Lord Henry Cardross of Scotland was planting Stuart's Town. In the heady world of long-term colonial goals, the Scots intended to find a Southwest Passage of sorts—a route from Port Royal to New Mexico.[28] More short-term, pragmatic motives lay behind the effort to befriend the Yamasees: "we have consented to them that they remaine here during their good behaviour, and the truth is they are so considerable and warlike that we would not doe utherwayes."[29] Cardross also averred that it was in the interest of the Scots and English to keep the large number of Yamasees "effectionit," since they were "Inveterat enemies to the Spainzard."[30] At a time when the Scots' population hovered in the fifties and the numbers of English and Africans were about fourteen hundred and five hundred respectively, the English slave trader Caleb Westbrooke wrote from Port Royal and estimated the number of Yamasees at "a thousand or more" and expected that figure to rise daily.[31]

Soon after their withdrawal from the Spanish sphere of influence, a force of Yamasees carried out a devastating raid on a mission in Timucua. A party of Yamasees under Altamaha attacked Santa Catalina de Afuyca (Ajoyca) in 1685 in a fashion that bespoke a mix of old enmity, anti-Catholic feeling, and new economic motives provided by the Scots and Westbrooke of Stuart's Town. Niquisalla, a cacique from Guale with prior knowledge of the attack, cited long-standing Yamasee-Timucua hatred as a motivating factor.[32]

When several Yamasees appeared before colonial officials months later in Charles Town, they described a horrific scene: the raiders "burnt severall Townes and in particuler the said Chappell and the Fryers house."[33] The Yamasees, who had rejected Christianity, struck forcefully at the symbols of mission life. The dawn raid resulted in the destruction or theft of religious articles and texts. Yamasee actions that morning seem to have moved beyond the quest for immediate profit. Their destruction of the chapel and friary indicate a forceful rejection of Spanish missionization. The cost in human lives was also dear: fifty Timucuans perished, and twenty-two were carried off as slaves.[34]

Enmity between the Timucuas and Yamasees and Yamasee mistrust of Catholic intentions could have developed without any external persuasion. But the looming presence of Carolina's slave market and the actions of Lord Cardross and Caleb Westbrooke also played some role. Native Americans had taken and held captives before the arrival of Europeans but hadn't jettisoned them onto Atlantic markets. Native cultures of violence reflected the influence of new ideas and opportunities. Prior to the attack, John Chaplin reported to Henry Woodward that he saw "armes and other things delivered to the Yamases."[35] Woodward reminded the colony's deputy governor that this would inflame tensions between the Spanish and English unnecessarily. It seemed unlikely that the Spanish, should they choose to retaliate, would distinguish between Scottish and English plantations.[36] Yamasee testimony given after the raid also mentioned that it was carried out at Westbrooke's suggestion, but this may have been an easy way for the Yamasees to deflect blame. The trader and the Scots had armed the Yamasees with muskets and swords, and Lord Cardross had paid the Yamasees for the slaves and other booty taken during the assault.[37] Retaliation came in 1686, as a Spanish force fell on the recently abandoned Stuart's Town and burned it. The soldiers also attacked English plantations, carrying off slaves, silver, and a robe taken during the Santa Catalina raid.[38] The attack slowed English expansion along the coast of Georgia and put a temporary halt to Yamasee raids.

Recent scholarship has shed much-needed light on the meaning of captivity in eastern Native America.[39] For many groups captivity stopped serving a social purpose and began to serve an economic one in an emerging system of merchant capitalism. Of course social and economic motivations cannot be so easily separated. Economics alone is probably not enough to explain why adoption of captives slowed, and the sale of captives to slave traders picked up. The answer is likely related to the uncertainties of Native American life in the colonial world: some groups saw advantages in remaining mobile, not getting attached to their present surroundings. Other groups, most notably the large interior nations, while nominally slave raiders, saw the benefits of remaining rooted and letting refugees from smaller, collapsing polities swell their ranks. Slavery was widespread in the indigenous southeast, but the practice of traveling long distances to secure slaves for eventual sale as forms of chattel property did not exist before extensive contact with Europeans. In the early years of Carolina's white settlement, indigenous communities in the southeast had to choose between being enslaved by people working for Carolina planters and traders, or trading for arms and enslaving their neighbors. This was a poor choice, but it was the kind of poor choice that English violence forced on indigenous people.

By the late seventeenth century, the French had joined the European contest for the southeast, and the outlook was ominous for imperially minded Carolinians: Florida and Louisiana could combine to thwart Carolina's expansion and dominance. Carolina could suffer, in the words of the legislature's petition for arms, since it was "a Frontier to the Spanish and French who have threatned to attack us and have lately attempted by their Spies to withdraw the Yamasee Indians from us to them and so to invite the other Indyans to make Warr upon us."[40] The petition failed to mention that the English had been meddling in the native southeast for decades, or that Native Americans might choose for themselves when to forge alliances or "make Warr."

Carolina's slave raiders took advantage of the international conflict to escalate their assaults on the missions of Florida. Between 1701 and 1706, joint Muskogee-Yamasee-English attacks, the most devastating of which were led by Governor James Moore and Deputy Governor Robert Daniel of South Carolina, annihilated the mission provinces of Apalachee and Timucua but fell short of capturing the fortified Castillo de San Marcos of St. Augustine. This war was a windfall for those engaged in the Indian slave trade, including the Yamasees, but its failure to destroy St. Augustine completely and expel the Spanish struck a nerve with some English, who accused Moore of putting personal profit ahead of the good of the colony.[41] One critic called it a "Project of Freebooting under the specious Name of War."[42]

For the Spanish and the mission Indians, the devastation could hardly have been more traumatic.[43] A joint English-Indian army of about nine hundred men left Charles Town over land and by boat in the fall of 1702 and burned several coastal installations on its way to lay siege to St. Augustine. In 1703 James Moore returned at the head of a private army made up almost entirely of Muskogean-speakers to attack the mission province of Apalachee. The proceedings near the town of Ayubale in January 1704 were particularly grisly. Muskogee soldiers burned sixteen prisoners and cut out their eyes, tongues, and ears.[44]

This kind of violence was not undertaken lightly, and Creek torture had deep roots. The method chosen for these captives' execution obviously inflamed Spanish passions and could be used to further the Spanish argument that Native Americans were in need of continued religious instruction to tame their allegedly savage nature (interestingly, this appears to apply primarily to indigenous groups allied with the English). The event was probably not so simple from a Muskogee perspective. The practice of torture was widespread in the southeast, and both early modern Native Americans and Europeans took trophies from their defeated enemies: disembodied heads and headless scalps seem to have transmitted messages across cultural lines in Ireland, on Roanoke, in the interior southeast, and in the Carolina lowcountry. These trophies demonstrated mastery of a defeated enemy and in some cases served to warn others of the might of those who had taken the trophies. Torture fulfilled a different role in Native American communities, though. Torture, far from being a dehumanizing act, could be the exact opposite. The fact that such great care was taken in dispatching victims might even be seen as a way of recognizing a common humanity. For many groups, this was a "considered, rational, and necessary act."[45] Among the Creeks torture served a crucial function: it allowed aggrieved parties to grieve publically the wrongs done them, and it allowed for "the brave to exit this world in a manly fashion."[46] For many groups, the ritual death was a way of bringing episodes of violence to a close, of "killing the war itself."[47] The killings at Ayubale also demonstrate a Muskogee culture of violence in flux. If the Muskogees had bought into the English, market-driven culture of violence fully, then killing captives rather than selling them does not make sense. But if older Muskogee ways of looking at violence persisted, then it would make perfect sense, and might even be necessary, to torture some captives while the bulk were sold on the Anglo-American slave market.

English involvement in the southeast raised the stakes of indigenous violence considerably. Thomas Nairne, who would die by torture at the outset of the Yamasee War, described the English strategy in 1705 when he noted, "We have these two . . . past years been intirely kniving all the Indian Towns in Florida which were subject to the Spaniards and have even accomplished it."[48] Native Americans went to war, but their goals in warfare rarely involved "intirely kniving" whole towns before the English arrived. Even during the longer campaigns, involving higher-risk battles that the English preferred, native ideas about violence were not entirely absent. From the Creek perspective, careful, ritually performed torture might have been the proper way to take the lives of Florida mission Indians, while the English would have probably preferred that they stayed alive to be sacrificed to sugar plantations on Barbados or elsewhere.[49]

South Carolina's frontier defenses relied on the combination of native and English fighters. Twice during Queen Anne's War, Charles Town came under military threat. The first assault came over land from the Spanish mission provinces in 1701. A handful of Spanish soldiers, along with more than eight hundred Apalachees, were turned away by a smaller but more heavily armed force of Muskogees. In 1706 Charles Town repelled a seaborne invasion by the French and Spanish with the assistance of Santee Indians from the lowcountry. The smaller nations of "Settlement Indians" were crucial partners in Carolina's defense on numerous occasions.[50]

The Yamasees and English had not taken the heavily fortified heart of St. Augustine, but they had burned the town and weakened Spanish religious and civil authority nearly everywhere else. This era marked the height of Yamasee power and Yamasee-English interdependence. Yamasees, other native groups, and English, though they conceived of violence in different ways, could work together toward common goals. The English had combined diverse native people into large multiethnic war parties. This included Muskogees from different towns, who may have recognized that they had important goals or historical experiences in common. English imperialism may have played a crucial role in Creek nation building in this instance.[51] The violence of Queen Anne's War also could be chaotic and have unintended consequences. Even groups that were allied with the English were not guaranteed immunity from enslavement in such violent times. Steven Oatis has recently brought to light two incidents in which Carolina traders paid Cherokees to take slaves from Creek towns whose contributions were essential to Carolina's war efforts.[52]

The fighting of the early eighteenth century represents an awakening of sorts on the part of the English at Carolina. The colony's government began to perceive Carolina as a leading edge of empire in the southeast. Raids in the 1700s served a number of functions. In addition to enriching the men who led them and drawing more slaves to sale at Charles Town, they also sought to establish English dominance over a territory contested by multiple European empires. This imperial perspective underlay the criticism directed at James Moore for his inability to vanquish the Spanish completely, even though his mission was a success from a financial standpoint. Moore himself had warned the Commons

House of Assembly in August of 1701 that French liberality could turn former native allies into enemies. Moore also explicitly compared the situation in South Carolina to the violent border between French Canada and New England.[53] The Yamasee War made it clear that while the perspective of white Carolinians may have expanded, their ability to project imperial power into the interior was limited.

The cases of the Westos, Savannahs, and Yamasees are indicative of the kind of violence associated with the early phases of white settlement in Carolina, trade and adaptation to the emerging Atlantic market, and colonial realities. Trade itself need not be violent, but the type of trade fomented by Carolina all but precluded long-term peaceful, mutually beneficial relations between the peoples of the southeast. As William Ramsey has recently shown in the case of the Yamasee War, the very nature of the trade between the English and Native Americans could itself breed violence.[54] In the shattered southeast, indigenous violence reoriented itself to deal with the realities of the plantation and the trading house and was eventually circumscribed by these institutions. The English conquered the southeast by subverting forms of violence they perceived as savage; the plantation and trading house were violent institutions, but English planters did not seem to mind the type of violence they could control.

Early Slavery

The rise of rice agriculture transformed Carolina around the close of the seventeenth century with profound implications for English profits, African labor, and violence in the region. Rice exports began in the 1690s and by 1709 had surpassed the one-million-pound mark. It is no coincidence that 1708 or 1709 is the year that the colony's African population first surpassed that of the English. In 1731 over twenty million pounds of rice were exported, and exports would drop below this level only for a handful of years before the War for Independence. At the end of the 1730s and the beginning of the 1740s, rice exports rocketed past thirty and forty million pounds per year.[55] The emergence of a plantation economy had ripple effects on all aspects of South Carolina society. It made planters hunger for land in regions suited to rice production. If they were able to obtain land, they turned their thoughts to labor. From the 1690s, when rice production began, to the 1730s, vast new tracts of land fell under the control of Carolina.[56]

The expansion of rice agriculture marked a new chapter in early Carolina's violent history as English planters imported large numbers of African women and men to work rice plantations. The era in which coastal native communities welcomed English arrivals in small numbers had passed. The period that saw Indians relocate to be close to Carolina and its burgeoning Indian slave trade was gone as well. In the 1720s large interior nations like the Creek and Cherokees faced off against a Carolina that barely resembled its colonial roots.

English-owned plantations worked by Africans spread out from Charles Town. The English also now actively promoted violence between native peoples with an eye toward expansion, not simply the slaves that might result from such a conflict. The trick, as stated by Joseph Boone, a member of South Carolina's legislature, became trying to "hold both [Creeks and Cherokees] as our friends, and assist them in Cutting one anothers throats with out offending Either."[57] English colonists had long perceived themselves to be "absolute Masters over the *Indians,*" in the words of John Lawson, but the period after the Yamasee War saw the English come to dominate Indian territory and trade in ways that approached mastery.[58] The aftermath of the Yamasee War witnessed the end of proprietary rule in South Carolina and put the colony's planters in a position to spread South Carolina's regional influence on their own violent terms. James Moore Jr., the leader of South Carolina's militia and son of the former governor and slave raider, was elected provisional governor as the House of Commons seized control.[59] In the years following the Yamasee War, the English put the brakes on an Indian slave trade that had led to regional instability and violence.[60] Of course several decades of the trade had created deep fault lines in the Native American southeast, and had opened up swaths of territory between the "Settlement Indians" of the coast and the large nations of the interior. The trade had never been unprofitable, but it had outlived its usefulness, and English agents could still turn a profit in Native America, at the same time as their cousins took tentative steps to establish plantations further inland. The English hold on the Atlantic coast was secure, and they could turn their attention to developing a full-blown plantation economy, which rested on its own violent Anglo-American labor regime.

English plantations were the sites of violence, not only when under attack, but also in labor relations between African slaves and English masters. The violence of slavery was multifarious. When masters disciplined their slaves, they could be enacting violence of a domestic nature. White men in South Carolina could bring down violence on any number of people, including their wives, children, and social inferiors. But since the violence of slavery crossed racial lines, it had some of the characteristics of intercultural violence as well. African slavery was an integral part of the Anglo-American culture of violence that was taking shape in South Carolina around the turn of the eighteenth century.

The Fundamental Constitutions were nearly silent on slavery, and Carolina's slave laws were a mix of Barbadian influences and trial and error on the part of slaveholders.[61] Carolina's earliest slave codes came from Barbados and regulated the behavior of slaves and established guidelines for the appropriate use of violence on the part of masters. These acts were revised several times in the late seventeenth and early eighteenth centuries. The slave codes were based on the assumption that Africans were naturally violent. One slave law from 1712 explained that "negroes and other slaves . . . are of barbarous, wild, savage natures" and are "naturally prone" to "disorders, rapines, and inhumanity."[62]

The slave codes, then, were to have a taming effect on allegedly savage African and Native American violence. Nonviolent resistance, such as running away out of Carolina, carried a violent penalty: death. For inciting others to run away, slaves were to be whipped and branded. Later codes softened these penalties somewhat. Perpetual short-term runaways, assumed *not* to be running away out of Carolina, faced punishments of increasing violence: a public whipping for the first offense, a branding for the second, an ear cut off for the third—and castration for male slaves. Running away five times resulted in the Achilles tendon being severed or death, at which point the loss of slave property would be compensated by public funds.[63]

Slavery was based on coercion and violence, but in order for it to work as a system of labor and remain profitable, negotiation (obviously not between equals in power) had to be present as well. For this reason, slave codes reined in English violence. The 1712 slave code provided for a fine when a master killed a slave out of "wantoness, or only of bloody-mindedness."[64] White servants who killed slaves could be imprisoned under this law, and masters could be fined. The 1735 slave code increased the maximum penalty from £50 to £500. Slave codes enacted in 1722 and 1735 also noted a form of violence that might be overlooked. If slave owners were not providing their slaves with enough food, they could be fined.[65]

Some of the earliest incidents of slavery-related violence in South Carolina were public. Francis Le Jau recounted one example: "a poor Slavewoman was burnt alive near my door without any positive proof of the Crime she was accused of . . . [she] protested her innocence even to my self to the last."[66] Punishments for slaves in the early 1700s were swift, severe, and corporal. Maiming by "castration, nose-slitting, or chopping off such extremities as ears, hands, or toes" was not uncommon.[67]

Slaves who committed egregious violations of the established order were put to death in public. Many were decapitated afterward, and severed African heads were not an uncommon site in early Carolina. The idea behind such displays was to discourage other slaves from engaging in similar practices. In one 1732 case, a white man robbed by a runaway slave was ordered by a justice of the peace to behead his assailant. The severed head was then "fix[ed] upon a Pole, and set . . . up in a Cross-Road."[68] When Quash, a fugitive slave who managed to remain at large for seven years, was hanged in 1734, his head was severed and attached to the gallows.[69] The more spectacular the resistance, the more spectacular the grisly display; as the Stono rebels were apprehended and killed, according to one source, "Planters . . . Cutt off their heads and set them up at every Mile Post they came to."[70]

Most violence directed at slaves, while it had the sanction of the state, was not administered by the state. The threat of the lash was universal in Carolina's variant of slavery, and the most common physical form of violence that accompanied slavery was whipping. Robert Olwell, author of *Masters, Slaves, and Subjects* notes that "because whipping was considered such a routine part of slave management, it was seldom thought worthy of mention by either overseers or masters."[71] This type of intercultural violence was so commonplace and considered so legitimate that the people employing it felt little need to describe it or account for it. The violence of slavery was intercultural and interracial, but it was also highly personal. According to one eighteenth-century observer, "the common Method is to tie [slaves] up by the Hands to the branch of a Tree, so that their Toes can hardly touch the ground." The same observer noted that there was "hardly a Negro but bears the marks of Punishment in large Scars on his Back and Sides."[72] If early Carolina functioned like every other slave society, it is safe to assume that slave owners forced their slaves to have sex with them. That such coerced sex does not appear too often in records is not surprising: planters assumed that rape was one of their rights, though they were not proud enough of this intimate violence to record it.[73]

The Stono Rebellion falls outside the chronology of this book, but several of the factors that led to the 1739 uprising were already present during the proprietary period of Carolina. In the historical literature, the Stono Rebellion has been used to prove a lot of different things over the centuries since it took place, from the survival of African traits in America to the Marxist leanings of black slaves. Stono draws such scrutiny because it is so rare.

On September 9, 1739, a handful of slaves gathered at the Stono River, a few miles west of Charles Town. The rebels stormed Hutchinson's store, arming themselves and killing the men who were minding the shop. The white men at the store were beheaded and their heads were left on display. The slave army—whose core consisted of literate, Catholic, BaKongo men from the kingdom of Kongo—then marched south, killing whites (though selectively, it must be added) and burning plantations. The rebels signaled their presence with drums and banners and shouted "Liberty!" as they marched. The black army eventually included between sixty and one hundred people. In a pitched battle, the slaves engaged South Carolina's militia under the command of Lieutenant Governor William Bull and were dispersed. A week later, Carolina militia caught up with a group of rebels thirty miles to the south of the original engagement and won a second battle.[74]

Some scholars have traced the motivation and behavior of the Stono rebels to Africa. In recreating an African American culture of violence, this line of questioning is most provocative. John Thornton, in particular, has looked to Africa for the origins of the rebellion. Thornton acknowledges that poor treatment on Carolina plantations was the immediate cause of hostilities but sees deeper roots are in the kingdom of Kongo, a region marked by Catholicism and the speaking of Portuguese, and wracked by violence from the 1500s onward. Each of these characteristics played some role in the events of 1739. The initial conspirators spoke the same language, which combined Portuguese and African languages, and the behavior of the rebels on the battlefield indicates some level of organization beyond what would be associated with a simple desire to kill some white people and escape slavery. Thornton remains cautious when it comes to drawing a direct line from Kongo military practice to Carolina slave military practice, but he does note that "a military revolution was altering war in Kongo . . . increasing the size of armies, and replacing the hand-to-hand combat of lances, swords, and axes with the missile combat of muskets."[75] Stephen Williams, author of one of the few primary accounts of the rebellion, noted that the rebels "furnished themselves with Arms and Ammunition," while another firsthand account stated that the slaves "behaved boldly" and "fought stoutly."[76]

The timing of the Stono Rebellion and the behavior of the rebels at various points in the rebellion indicate the persistence of a BaKongo culture of violence in the colonial southeast. Though the alarm was raised on Sunday, September 9, 1739, and the Carolina militia rushed out of church to counter the growing threat, the rebels had actually begun their struggle on a Saturday that coincided with the nativity of the Virgin Mary, who was a central figure in the BaKongo-Catholic hybrid religion so cherished by many BaKongo men and women.[77] One scholar has argued that the people "regarded the Virgin Mary as Christ's female co-chief." Another interpretation links her to the Kongolese conception of the "feminine embodiment of the earth." The army also stopped on the shores of the Edisto River, which didn't make sense from a tactical perspective, but was clearly important from a cultural perspective. Perhaps thanks had to be given for prior success, and rituals needed to be performed before continuing. One unknown English writer recalled that they "halted in a field, and set to dancing, Singing and beating Drums."[78] The BaKongo army was dispersed shortly thereafter but resorted to a skirmishing style of warfare for weeks afterward and added a psychological benefit of keeping whites in constant fear of renewed hostilities.[79] BaKongo soldiers put their trust in Mary as they put the skills they honed on African battlefields to use against the English in Carolina.

In the aftermath of the Stono Rebellion, South Carolina passed a new slave code. The "Act for the better ordering and governing of Negroes and other Slaves" built on earlier slave codes by limiting already limited black freedoms and went further to curtail the kinds of abuses some white men felt had led to Stono in the first place. Masters were forbidden to force their slaves to work on Sunday and could be fined for such offense. Masters also had to provide "sufficient cloathing, covering or food" for their slaves. The 1740 act set limits on the amount of work that slaves could legally be expected to perform, with some seasonal variances.[80]

It should not be assumed from the previous paragraphs that most African violence in Carolina was channeled into large-scale revolt. Indeed Stono is a remarkable exception to the kind of violence normally associated with slaves in North America. Most slaves were not BaKongo rebels trained in a particular style of intercultural violence, but Africans did resist slavery violently, and in the process, African cultures of violence became an African American culture of violence. Throughout the eighteenth century, there were very few murders of white masters or overseers by black slaves. Spectacular acts like this were usually suicidal, and their rarity attests to the level of mastery achieved by Carolina's master class. An African American culture of violence took shape in other arenas: violence against property, and, more rarely, poisoning.

For slaves to damage the bodies of their masters carried a death sentence, whether immediate or delayed by some legal proceeding. Violence against property could take many forms, including sabotage of plantation equipment and arson. The fact that African American violence was more often directed at things rather than people indicates how thoroughly the English culture of violence had reshaped African cultures of violence. Planters' houses may have been the highest value targets for arsonists—the Anglican missionary Francis Le Jau witnessed a woman burned to death after she was accused of just such a crime—but barns were more likely to be burned. Peter Wood has noticed that as rice production increased, the number of barn fires increased in the months when the heaviest labor was required to clean and barrel rice. Slave codes dealt harshly with even minor incidents of fire-related crime, assigning the death penalty to any slave who burned "rice, corn, or other grain."[81] A cautionary letter to the *South Carolina Gazette* in 1732 warned that "Mr. James Grey work'd his Negroes late in his Barn at Night, and the next Morning before Day, hurried them out again, and when they came to it, found it burnt down to the Ground, and all that was in it."[82] It may have been too difficult or dangerous to strike out directly against slave owners in most cases, but attacking the source of the planters' agricultural wealth could hurt the planter's pocketbook and carry symbolic meaning as well.

Slave poisonings were rare, so it is not entirely appropriate to treat them on the same level as more everyday forms of violence. Slaves poisoned other slaves as well as white masters, and the practice of conjuring did not always relate to violence or intend to harm. As slaves practiced magic and conjured, they drew on a wide array of spiritual sources.[83] In the 1750s white physician Alexander Garden noted "that the Negroes bring their knowledge of the Poisonous Plants, which they use here, with them from their own Country."[84] Poisoning drew on diverse African origins but developed along similar lines throughout English colonies and continued after slaves converted to Christianity. South Carolina's master class feared slave magic, exaggerated the threat it posed, and sought to legislate it out of existence in 1751. The assembly made it a capital crime for a slave to "teach or instruct another slave in the knowledge of any poisonous root, plant, herb or other sort of poison whatever."[85] The ways the slaves fought against slavery in the early eighteenth-century southeast demonstrate the lingering presence of African cultures of violence and the very beginning of an African American culture of violence.

Conclusion

Violence was not an exception in an otherwise peaceful planting of English Carolina. Rather it was part of the project from the start. Even as colonial lords dreamt of peace and profits, reality intruded. The English did not introduce violence into the southeast, of course. Centuries before their arrival, native towns had gone to war against one another. More immediately prior to the advent of the English, Spanish entradas had remade the southeast through violence once again. English violence, driven by the Atlantic World's trade and plantation slavery, was the latest sort of violence to make its appearance in what had long been a volatile region. Through eliminating and enslaving slaving societies such as the Westos, through sponsoring devastating raids on Spanish missions and reaping the benefits, and finally through establishing English rice plantations, the English established a pattern that would play out in later years. It should not be assumed that this was a complete conquest, in which other peoples, other worldviews, and other cultures of violence were totally eliminated or silenced. Though indigenous towns along the coast were subject to English authority, interior nations such as the Creeks and Cherokees were not, at least until much later, and even that conquest was incomplete. Though individual Africans were severely limited in their ability to resist English domination, evidence indicates that violent resistance to enslavement was one avenue that Africans and their descendants would continue to explore, collectively, as they forged an identity that would allow them to cope with the horrors of their condition. It is becoming difficult, if not impossible, to tell the story of early Carolina as a peaceful undertaking. Rather the establishment of English Carolina itself carried the potential for great violence, and the colony reached its potential, with only minimal periods of peace gracing its first few decades.

Notes

The author thanks the staffs at the Washington Memorial Library in Macon, Georgia; the South Carolina Department of Archives and History in Columbia, South Carolina; and the Georgia State Archives in Morrow, Georgia. S. Max Edelson, James Carson, Michelle LeMaster, Brad Wood, and Alan Gallay gave helpful comments.

1. See Alan Gallay, *The Indian Slave Trade: The Rise of the English Empire in the American South, 1670–1717* (New Haven: Yale University Press, 2002); Kathryn E. Holland Braund, *Deerskins and Duffels: Creek Indian Trade With Anglo-America, 1685–1815* (Lincoln: University of Nebraska Press, 1993); Judith Carney, *Black Rice: The African Origins of Rice Cultivation in the Americas* (Cambridge: Harvard University Press, 2001); and S. Max Edelson, "Beyond 'Black Rice': Reconstructing Material and Cultural Contexts for Early Plantation Agriculture," *AHR* 115, no. 1 (February 2010): 125–35.

2. "Culture of violence" in this usage refers to a group's ideas about when it is appropriate to use violence, and which sort of violence is appropriate to a given

situation. See Evan Haefeli, "Kieft's War and the Cultures of Violence in Colonial America," in *Lethal Imagination: Violence and Brutality in American History*, ed. Michael A. Bellesiles (New York: New York University Press, 1999), 17–40, esp. 18. See also Matthew Jennings, *New Worlds of Violence: Cultures and Conquests in the Early American Southeast* (Knoxville: University of Tennessee Press, 2011), xv–xxxiv, esp. xx–xxi.

3. Carl Jacoby, *Shadows at Dawn: A Borderlands Massacre and the Violence of History* (New York: Penguin, 2008), 4.

4. Craven, Albemarle, Shaftesbury and P. Colleton to the Governor and Council att Ashley River, February 21, 1680/1, in *BPRO-SC*, 1:104–5.

5. "The Second Charter Granted by King Charles the Second, to the Proprietors of Carolina," in *CRNC*, 1:102–14.

6. Ibid., 1:105.

7. Ibid., 1:111. This nearly replicates the language of the 1663 charter. See "The First Charter Granted by King Charles the Second, to the Proprietors of Carolina," in *CRNC*, 1:20–33.

8. "The Second Charter Granted by King Charles the Second, to the Proprietors of Carolina," in *CRNC*, 1:112.

9. "Concessions and agreement between the Lords Proprietors of Carolina and William Yeamans et al," in *CRNC*, 1:75–93; and "The Fundamental Constitutions of Carolina," in *CRNC*, 1:187–206.

10. "The Fundamental Constitutions of Carolina," in *CRNC*, 1:194.

11. Ibid., 1:196.

12. "Mr. Carteret's Relation," in *Shaftesbury Papers*, 165–71, quotation on 168–69.

13. Eric Bowne, *The Westo Indians: Slave Traders of the Early Colonial South* (Tuscaloosa: University of Alabama Press, 2005), esp. 37–53; John T. Juricek, "The Westo Indians," *Ethnohistory* 11, no. 2 (Spring 1964): 134–73; Marvin T. Smith, *Archaeology of Aboriginal Culture Change* (Gainesville: University Press of Florida, 1987), 131–32; and Gallay, *Indian Slave Trade*, 41–42.

14. Amy Turner Bushnell, *Situado and Sabana: Spain's Support System for the Presidio and Mission Provinces of Florida*, American Museum of Natural History, Anthropological Papers, No. 74 (Athens: University of Georgia Press, 1994), 134–35.

15. Daniel Richter, *The Ordeal of the Longhouse: The Peoples of the Iroquois League in the Era of European Colonization* (Chapel Hill: University of North Carolina Press, 1992), 32–38; and Richter, "War and Culture: The Iroquois Experience," *WMQ* 40, no. 4 (October 1983): 528–59.

16. Richter, *Ordeal of the Longhouse*, 62; Smith, *Archaeology*, 132; and Bowne, *Westo Indians*, 39–41 and 49–52. See Gallay, *Indian Slave Trade*, 41–43; Bowne, *Westo Indians*, 72–75; John Worth, *The Struggle for the Georgia Coast: An Eighteenth-Century Spanish Retrospective on Guale and Mocama*, American Museum of Natural History, Anthropological Papers, No. 75 (New York: American Museum of Natural History, 1995), 17; and Maureen Meyers, "From Refugees to Slave Traders: The Transformation of the Westo Indians," in *Mapping the Mississippian Shatter Zone: The Colonial Indian Slave Trade and Regional Instability in the American South*, ed. Robbie Ethridge and Sheri M. Shuck-Hall (Lincoln: University of Nebraska Press, 2009), 81–103.

17. Woodward's "Faithfull Relation of My Westoe Voiage" appears in Salley, *Narratives*, 125–34; and as "Woodwards Westo Discovery," in *Shaftesbury Papers*, 456–62. Quotation from Salley, *Narratives*, 133.

18. Stephen Bull to Lord Ashley, September 12, 1670, in *Shaftesbury Papers*, 192–96, quotation on 194.

19. Bowne, *Westo Indians*, 79; and Verner W. Crane, *The Southern Frontier, 1670–1732* (1928; reprint, New York: Norton, 1981), 6.

20. Eric Bowne, "'Caryinge awaye their Corne and Children': The Effects of Westo Slave Raids on the Indians of the Lower South," in *Mapping the Mississippian Shatter Zone*, ed. Ethridge and Shuck-Hall, 104–14; and Jennings, "Violence in a Shattered World."

21. Gallay, *Indian Slave Trade*, 60–61.

22. Bowne, *Westo Indians*, 100; and J. Leitch Wright, *The Only Land They Knew: American Indians in the Old South* (1981; reprint, Lincoln: University of Nebraska Press, 1999), 107.

23. Proprietors to Government and Council in Charles Town, September 30, 1683, in *BPRO-SC*, 1:256.

24. Accounts of the war can be found in Chapman Milling, *Red Carolinians* (Chapel Hill: University of North Carolina Press, 1940), 82–83; Verner Crane, *Southern Frontier*, 18–21; and Gallay, *Indian Slave Trade*, 57–58.

25. Bowne, *Westo Indians*, 106–7.

26. Craven, Albemarle, Shaftesbury and P. Colleton to the Governor and Council att Ashley River, February 21, 1680/1, in *BPRO-SC*, 1:104–5.

27. Craven, Shaftesbury, and P. Colleton to the Governor and Council att Ashley River in Carolina, March 7, 1680/1, in *BPRO-SC*, 1:115–20, quotations on 115.

28. Lord Henry Cardross and William Dunlop to Peter Colleton, March 27, 1685, quoted in George Pratt Insh, "Arrival of the Cardross Settlers," *SCHGM* 30, no. 2 (April 1929): 69–80; quotation on 75. See also Insh, "The *Carolina Merchant*: Advice of Arrival," *Scottish Historical Review* 25 (1928): 99–108.

29. Cardross and Dunlop to Colleton, quoted in Insh, "Arrival of the Cardross Settlers," 76.

30. Ibid.

31. Peter Wood, "The Changing Population of the Colonial South," in *Powhatan's Mantle: Indians in the Colonial Southeast*, ed. Peter Wood, Gregory Waselkov, and M. Thomas Hatley (Lincoln: University of Nebraska Press, 1989), 46. Westbrooke's letter, February 21, 1685, in *BPRO-SC*, 2:8–9.

32. Amy Turner Bushnell, *Situado and Sabana*, 166–67.

33. "The Examination of Severall Yamasse Indians," in *BPRO-SC*, 2:66.

34. Ibid.

35. Henry Woodward to John Godfrey (Deputy Governor), March 21, 1685, in *BPRO-SC*, 2:49.

36. Worth, *Struggle for the Georgia Coast*, 46.

37. "The Examination of Severall Yamasee Indians," in *BPRO-SC*, 2:66; see also Bushnell, *Situado and Sabana*, 166–67, and Worth, *Struggle for the Georgia Coast*, 45–46.

38. Worth, *Struggle for the Georgia Coast*, 146–71.

39. Christina Snyder, *Slavery in Indian Country: The Changing Face of Captivity in Early America* (Cambridge: Harvard University Press, 2010); and Alan Gallay, ed., *Indian Slavery in Colonial America* (Lincoln: University of Nebraska Press, 2009).

40. Legislature to John Earl of Bath and the rest of the true and Absolute Lords and Proprietors of the Province of Carolina, in *BPRO-SC*, 5:35. The document's date can be found in Milling, *Red Carolinians*, 105.

41. Gallay, *Indian Slave Trade*, 135–48.

42. John Ash, "The Present State of Affairs in Carolina," (1706), in Salley, *Narratives*, 267–76. Ash and Moore were on opposite sides of a bitter factional struggle.

43. See *Firestorm and Ashes: The Siege of 1702, El Escribano* 39 (2002) 1–131; Gallay, *Indian Slave Trade*, 135–48; Mark Boyd, Hale Smith, and John Griffin, *Here They Once Stood: The Tragic End of the Apalachee Missions* (Gainesville: University of Florida Press, 1951); Crane, *Southern Frontier*, 71–107; John H. Hann, *A History of the Timucua Indians and Missions* (Gainesville: University Press of Florida, 1996), 268–95; John Worth, *The Timucuan Chiefdoms of Spanish Florida*, 140–46; Charles W. Arnade, *The Siege of St. Augustine in 1702* (Gainesville: University of Florida Press, 1959); and Steven Oatis, "'To Eat Up a Village of White Men': Anglo-Indian Designs on Mobile and Pensacola, 1705–1715," *Gulf South Historical Review* 14, no. 1 (Fall 1998): 104–19. Overviews of mission life appear in Jerald T. Milanich, *Florida Indians and the Invasion from Europe* (Gainesville: University Press of Florida, 1995); Bonnie G. McEwan, ed., *The Spanish Missions of La Florida* (Gainesville: University Press of Florida, 1993); and John Hann and Bonnie McEwan, *The Apalachee Indians and Mission San Luis* (Gainesville: University Press of Florida, 1998).

44. See Mark Boyd, Hale Smith, and John Griffin, *Here They Once Stood*, 11–13. Torture testimony comes from a July 8, 1704, letter by Manuel Solana to Governor Zùñiga at San Luis, in *Here They Once Stood*, 50–55. See also John E. Worth, "Razing Florida: The Indian Slave Trade and the Devastation of Spanish Florida, 1659–1715," in Ethridge and Shuck-Hall, *Mapping the Mississippian Shatter Zone*, 295–311.

45. Georges Sioui and Sheila Fischman, *For an Amerindian Autohistory: An Essay on the Foundations of a Social Ethic* (1992; reprint Montreal: McGill-Queen's University Press, 1995), 54–56, quotation from 55.

46. Kathryn E. Holland Braund, "The Creek Indians, Blacks, and Slavery," *JSH* 57, no. 4 (November 1991): 601–36, quotation from 602. See also Joel Martin, *Sacred Revolt: The Muscogee's Struggle for a New World* (Boston: Beacon Press, 1991), 19, 27–28.

47. Sioui, *For an Amerindian Autohistory*, 54.

48. Nairne quoted in Crane, *Southern Frontier*, 81.

49. Wayne Lee, "Peace Chiefs and Blood Revenge: Patterns of Restraint in Native American Warfare, 1500–1800," *Journal of Military History* 71, no. 3 (July 2007): 701–41.

50. Oatis, *A Colonial Complex*, 51–52; and Crane, *Southern Frontier*, 86–87.

51. Steven C. Hahn describes the nation as a colonial-era phenomenon. Hahn, *The Invention of the Creek Nation, 1670–1763* (Lincoln: University of Nebraska Press, 2004).

52. Oatis, *A Colonial Complex*, 53; Minutes, April 29, 1703, in *JCHA 1703*, 75–78.

53. Minutes, August 13, 1701, in *JCHA 1701*, 4.

54. Ramsey, *Yamasee War;* William L. Ramsey, "'Something Cloudy in Their Looks': The Origins of the Yamasee War Reconsidered," *JAH* 90, no. 1 (June 2003), 44–75, esp. n. 5. On trade, see Joel Martin, "Southeastern Indians and the English Trade in Skins and Slaves," in *The Forgotten Centuries: Indians and Europeans in the American South, 1521–1704*, ed. Charles Hudson and Carmen Tesser (Athens: University of Georgia Press, 1994), 304–24; James Merrell, "'Our Bond of Peace': Patterns of Intercultural Exchange in the Carolina Piedmont, 1650–1750," in Wood et al., *Powhatan's Mantle*, 196–222; and Braund, *Deerskins and Duffels*.

55. Carney, "Rice Milling, Gender, and Slave Labour," *Past and Present* 153 (November 1996), 108–34.

56. S. Max Edelson, *Plantation Enterprise in Colonial South Carolina* (Cambridge: Harvard University Press, 2006), 135.

57. Joseph Boone to Proprietors, April 25, 1717, in *BPRO-SC*, 7:75.

58. Lawson, *New Voyage*, 10. Lawson spoke too soon in his own case; he was put to death by Tuscaroras in 1710.

59. Robert M. Weir, *Colonial South Carolina: A History*, 2nd ed. (1983; reprint, Columbia: University of South Carolina Press, 1997), 101.

60. Gallay, *Indian Slave Trade*, 345–51.

61. The Fundamental Constitutions did contain the instruction that "Every Freeman of Carolina shall have absolute power and authority over Negro slaves, of what opinion or Religion soever." See A. Leon Higginbotham Jr., *In the Matter of Color: Race and the American Legal Process*, vol. 1, *The Colonial Period* (Oxford: Oxford University Press, 1980), 163.

62. Higginbotham, *In the Matter of Color*, 167. *Statutes at Large*, 7:352.

63. Higginbotham, *In the Matter of Color*, 167. *Statutes at Large*, 7:352.

64. Higginbotham, *In the Matter of Color*, 189. *Statutes at Large*, 7:353–54.

65. Higginbotham, *In the Matter of Color*, 191.

66. Peter Wood, *Black Majority: Negroes in Colonial South Carolina from 1670 through the Stono Rebellion* (New York: Norton, 1975), 135; Francis Le Jau, *The Carolina Chronicle of Dr. Francis Le Jau, 1706–1717* (Berkeley: University of California Press, 1956), 55.

67. Wood, *Black Majority*, 278.

68. Ibid., 283.

69. Ibid., 284.

70. Mark M. Smith, *Stono: Documenting and Interpreting a Southern Slave Revolt* (Columbia: University of South Carolina Press, 2005), 8.

71. Robert Olwell, *Masters, Slaves, and Subjects: The Culture of Power in the South Carolina Low Country, 1740–1790* (Ithaca: Cornell University Press, 1998), 189.

72. Wood, *Black Majority*, 279.

73. See Sharon Block, *Rape and Sexual Power in Early America* (Chapel Hill: University of North Carolina Press, 2006), 64–73; and Jennings, *New Worlds of Violence*, 160–61, 232n15.

74. Smith, *Stono*, xiii; James Carson, *Making an Atlantic World: Circles, Paths and Stories from the Colonial South* (Knoxville: University of Tennessee Press, 2007), 112–15; and Peter Wood, *Black Majority*, 308–26.

75. John Thornton, "African Dimensions of the Stono Rebellion," *AHR* 96, no. 4 (October 1991): 1101–13. Quotation appears on 1109.

76. Smith, *Stono*, 15.

77. Smith notes that the rebels were slightly off, having timed their rebellion by the Julian, rather than the Gregorian, calendar. See *Stono*, 117.

78. "Account of the Negroe Insurrection in South Carolina," in Smith, *Stono*, 13–15, quotation on 15.

79. Smith, *Stono*; James Carson, *Making an Atlantic World*, 112–15; and Peter Wood, *Black Majority*, 308–26.

80. Smith, *Stono*, 20–27.

81. Wood, *Black Majority*, 293; and *Statutes at Large*, 7:402.

82. *South Carolina Gazette*, October 14, 1732, quoted in Wood, *Black Majority*, 293.

83. Philip D. Morgan, *Slave Counterpoint: Black Culture in the Eighteenth-Century Chesapeake and Lowcountry* (Chapel Hill: University of North Carolina Press, 1998), 612.

84. Morgan, *Slave Counterpoint*, 617.

85. *Statutes at Large*, 7:423.

"Before long to be good friends"

Diplomatic Perspectives of the Tuscarora War

STEPHEN FEELEY

Understandably the Tuscarora War has been approached principally as an episode of violence.[1] Beginning in September 1711 and lasting for approximately two years, a loose coalition of eastern North Carolina Indians, chief among them Tuscaroras, launched devastating attacks that wrecked European settlements along North Carolina's Neuse and Pamlico Rivers. North Carolina settlers, relying on neighboring colonies and allied Indians, eventually launched retaliatory expeditions of their own, ransacking communities, and enslaving perhaps as many as two thousand Tuscaroras. These assaults culminated in the fiery destruction of the Tuscaroras' stronghold at Neoheroka.[2] Many Tuscaroras evacuated north, eventually joining the Haudenosaunee as the Sixth Nation of the Iroquois Confederacy. In terms of casualties, the mass enslavement of Indians, the reshaping of the native political landscape, and far-reaching repercussions on colonial society and governance, the war bears comparison with better known conflicts such as the closely related Yamasee War in South Carolina, the 1622 Powhatan uprising and Bacon's Rebellion in Virginia, and the Pequot War and King Philip's War in New England.

An emphasis on the violence, however, obscures other facets, in particular the Tuscaroras' perceptions and goals. During a pause in the fighting, Tuscarora warriors called from the riverbanks to canoes carrying wounded colonists, speaking "kindly to them, and . . . [saying] they hoped before long to be good friends."[3] What sort of settlement did Tuscaroras and other Indians hope to achieve? What sort of existence did they envision for themselves and their colonial neighbors?

Before, during, and after the conflict there were multiple attempts at negotiation. Even when they failed, the resulting treaties represent one of the best opportunities to hear native voices—but only when approached carefully. Self-serving Europeans exerting authorial control penned the documents. Moreover, unlike many grand conferences of the mid-eighteenth century where scribes carefully recorded native speeches seeking to capture their eloquence, these meetings generated only the barest of records. And yet these documents were the product of negotiation. Colonists were never confident enough of their strength that they could blithely dictate the treaties' contents. By exploring the boundary of what the colonists thought they could gain and what they thought the Tuscaroras would accept, we can hear traces of native voices. At other times, when Tuscaroras dictated treaty terms to a terrified captive, or stormed out of negotiations, their authorial role came even more to the fore. Therefore rather than seeing treaties simply as a tool of colonial control, we should seek to understand the ways that Indians took advantage of treaties as a means of shaping colonists' behavior.

Complicating analysis is the fact that neither natives nor colonists ever negotiated with a single unified voice. Internal divisions in North Carolina that had culminated in Cary's Rebellion persisted into the Tuscarora War. When Virginia and South Carolina entered the war, their agents negotiated separately. Likewise there was no single Tuscarora polity. Instead members of that Iroquoian-speaking cultural group inhabited approximately fifteen communities, each with their own councils headed by headmen or *teethas*.[4] Europeans often referred to teethas as kings, but typically teethas and their councils aspired for consensus within and between communities and lacked the authority to impose decisions.[5] During the war years, several factions emerged, most prominently an assortment of Tuscaroras and neighboring Mattamuskeets, Neuses, and Corees (referred to here as the Catechna Alliance), who took an aggressive stance, and the Upper Towns, who aspired toward neutrality. Interactions and alliances with other Indian communities added to the babble.

As a result different negotiations and meetings reshuffled the deck, bringing together fresh configurations of colonists and Indians. Nonetheless within the broad spectrum of perspectives emerged common themes. Rather than seeking outright destruction or expulsion of Europeans, Tuscaroras viewed fighting and negotiations as a means to establish the terms of future contact. Negotiations repeatedly returned to the same issues. Participants argued about the disposition of land: where native and colonial settlements would be located and how land would be disposed of or sold. They debated movement: where Indians and colonists could travel or hunt and what activities they could engage in during these travels. They debated trade: what constituted fair exchanges and how to deal with matters of debt. Perhaps most important, treaties repeatedly returned to establishing frameworks for future conciliation. Even in the darkest days of war, treaties recognized that contacts between natives and colonists would continue. The key would be establishing a structure whereby leaders from both sides could rectify any future disputes. How would they react to violence? Who would have authority and whose system of justice would prevail? How would leaders of each side cooperate or relate to one another? An approach that focuses on diplomacy reveals that the war began in part as an effort to force Europeans to negotiate these issues. Likewise, although military victories and defeats played a key role, the war ended not on the battlefield but through hard-wrangling diplomacy in which Tuscaroras took an active part.

There is no shortage of potential causes for the Tuscarora War. Yet the prewar litany of complaints over cheating, thefts, and violence also reveals how intertwined colonists' and Indians' lives had become.[6] Before becoming the war's first victim, the surveyor John Lawson had gained prominence by publishing a cheerful account of his travels through the heart of Carolina Indian Country.[7] Natives likewise ventured among colonists vending furs, meat, and finely woven mats and baskets.[8] For several decades native strength and numbers paired with colonists' weakness and isolation fostered in North Carolina the sort of freewheeling flexibility described by historian Ira Berlin as characterizing creole communities around the rim of the early Atlantic World.[9]

Within such flexibility could exist opportunity, but more often this mixture of amity and animosity resulted in vexing uncertainty. In 1703 an Indian named Wehuna approached Samuel Slockum to "ask him whether the English did intend to make war or no." No, insisted the shaken settler; but Wehuna pressed him, saying that the Indians believed otherwise.[10] For nearly a decade, Indians and settlers reenacted the same scene: seeking out reassurance, listening to each other's pledges, and then walking away in doubt and fear.

One cause of this bewildered frustration was North Carolina's contradictory approach to Indian diplomacy. On several occasions, Indians and North Carolina officials negotiated treaties or formal agreements. Despite impositions, Carolina Indians valued treaties and the official support they represented. In 1702 settlers complained to the governor that Chowans were engaged in "destroying . . . [settlers'] Stocks burning their houses and other hostilities under pretense they are under yor Honrs protection and no Englishman ought to Seate within four miles of their Towne."[11] Tuscaroras may have made some sort of similar accord with North Carolina as early as 1672.[12]

But unsettling to the Indians, officials often backed away from their agreements, instead aiming at "the more speedy peopling" of the colony so that the "Inhabitants of this Government by reason of their fewness" would no longer owe "their Lives and safety's to the courtesy of the Heathen rather than their own strength."[13] To attract settlers the assembly made a Faustian bargain, passing laws making settlers immune to past debts, offering guarantees of religious freedom, and easing enforcement of vestry acts beckoning a minor flood of debtors, runaway servants, pirates, Quakers, and other dissenters.[14] In such an environment, even when North Carolina did sign agreements with Indians, officials either could not or would not enforce provisions. Governor Alexander Spotswood of Virginia warned that officials needed to "restrain" settlers or "consider [that] there are a great many . . . tribes that will take the alarm when they find the English have broke their faith with them and there is no dependence on our Treaties."[15]

Natives did take alarm, but rather than abandoning such agreements, in their quest to make sense of the confused swirl around them, they grasped onto their treaties even more tightly. In 1701 several shipwrecked Englishmen got into a fracas with five Machapunga Indians who claimed to be rescuing them. Later when John Lawson investigated, the Machapunga leader waved a paper in his face—a copy of a treaty concluded two years earlier. Among its provisions was the requirement that the Machapungas assist shipwrecked Englishmen. Lawson reported that the chief "always (told me) they might not ... [suffer?] any breach of their articles from the English."[16] But in this remote corner of the colony, the government could not even prevent its own settlers from sacking stranded ships, much less dictate settlers' behaviors toward the Indians.[17]

Similar frustrations played out at New Bern, a settlement of German and Swiss Palatines established by Baron von Graffenried in 1710 at the confluence of the Trent and Neuse Rivers and on the site of a Coree Indian community called Chatouka. Graffenried's effort to purchase the land typified the frustration natives felt trying to decode colonial leaders' willingness and capacity to govern. The meeting began well, with mutual displays of authority. But then one of Graffenried's business partners, Franz Ludwig Michel, who had been drinking stormed into the circle, knocked off the Indian leader's headdress, and began beating one of the councilors. The spell was broken. The native king complained that "if the Christians made peace and their alliances after that fashion he did not want to have anything to do with them."[18] It was not the treaty process itself that frustrated as much as the sense that Europeans did not take the measures seriously. As if to prove Graffenried's impotence, the next night Michel hit the bottle again, and then sneaked into the Indian camp, found the poor orator, and repeated the drubbing.

Efforts on a larger scale followed the same muddled contours. Rumors spread in late 1703 that several Tuscarora towns, influenced by frustrated coastal tribes, were considering war. Still, pleaded local settlers, "sum of the Cheifs of the Indians would come in" to make an agreement if only Governor Daniel would "speedily please to send a good Interpreter here with orders what to doe."[19]

An undated rough draft of a treaty mandating peace "so long as Sun and Moon endure" may be the only surviving record of the subsequent agreement. Not surprisingly many provisions favored its North Carolina amanuensis: Tuscaroras should repay their debts in a timely fashion, retrieve runaway servants and slaves, and refrain from fire hunting or locating towns within "half a days travell of any English plantation." Disobedience could lead to facing English courts and suffering death, banishment, or the lash.[20]

Despite highhanded language, North Carolina was in no position to dictate terms outright. Threats of Tuscarora violence, after all, had spurred the meeting, and the Indians' concerns likely shaped aspects of the agreement. Above all the treaty relied on Tuscarora and colonial leaders cooperating, so "that if any occasione should fall out that there may be as soon as conveniently be a meeting of the greatt men appointed to settle it friendly and amicably." Tuscaroras facing trial were guaranteed the benefit of having present "some of the great men of the Tuscaroroes . . . to see that no prejudice may come to him." Moreover aggrieved Tuscaroras could themselves bring suit against "any Englishman of this Government [who] shall injure or wrong any of the Tuscaroroe Indians." Much rested on the premise that "the Great Men of this government the English" could fairly administer English law and effectively wield authority over colonists.[21]

But establishing exactly who were "the Great Men of this government the English" and how much authority they had were *the* central questions of early North Carolina politics. It is unclear whether the treaty was ever signed, especially since Tuscaroras may have balked at its harshest stipulations.[22] Even if it had been, it is almost unimaginable that its terms would have been adhered to in the ensuing years of internal division that culminated in Cary's Rebellion. Government in the southern half of the colony virtually ceased to function. Colonist fought colonist. Formal Indian diplomacy gave way to rumors, informal meetings, and perhaps secret efforts—never proven—to entice Tuscaroras into the fray.[23] If Tuscaroras wished to strike when the colony was at its weakest, this would have been the time.

Instead, in their search for order, Tuscaroras sought to circumvent the mire in North Carolina. In 1710 representatives journeyed to Conestoga on the Susquehanna River to meet Pennsylvania officials and Iroquois diplomats. There they began the process of reconciliation with the Iroquois, whose raids had terrorized Tuscarora towns in the previous decade. The Tuscarora spokesmen also discussed the possibility of relocating, asking that Pennsylvania "take them by the hand and lead them." Pennsylvania's officials were sympathetic. Nonetheless they demanded that the Tuscaroras obtain a certificate of good behavior from North Carolina's government—an almost impossible request during that turbulent period. Escape north might eventually be an option for some, but in the meanwhile Tuscaroras had to seek solutions closer to home.[24]

Ironically North Carolina Indians' preference for negotiation over bloodshed fostered dangerous complacency among colonists. In September 1711, as Cary's Rebellion receded, Lawson set out in high spirits with Graffenried and several slaves and native guides to survey a route toward Virginia. Instead Tuscaroras at Catechna (on a tributary of the Neuse River) captured the party (Catechna appears as "Hancock's Town" on map 17). Joined by Corees and other coastal Indians, these Tuscaroras tortured and executed Lawson. While Graffenried remained hostage, a native coalition launched surprise raids on colonial settlements. Thus began the Tuscarora War.

Obscured beneath this violent story line, however, resides a more revelatory narrative—one centered on efforts at coalition building and diplomacy. Tuscaroras initially transformed the encounter into something akin to an impromptu treaty conference. King Hancock, the teetha of Catechna, treated the captives "very politely," personally fed them, and granted them the "liberty of walking about the village." When a "great number of Indians with the neighboring kings" assembled in a council, Tuscaroras seated their captive guests on wicker mats specially laid out as "a sign of great deference and honor." For hours Lawson and Graffenried scrambled to answer "general complaints" about colonial abuses. Finally, after conversing long into the night, the council decided to release the captives.[25]

What if the episode had ended here? At last native leaders had gained the ears of two of the most influential colonists, even if it required taking them captive to do so. Lawson and Graffenried had offered apologies and assurances. Problems remained, but a path to goodwill had been cleared.

And then something went terribly wrong. The next morning, as the captives prepared to depart, Lawson got into a shouting match with a leader named Coree Tom. Earlier Lawson had "excused himself the best he could," but now all decorum was gone. Carolina Indians keenly distrusted Europeans given to "Heats and Passions," as "mad Wolves, and no more Men," who ought to be avoided, Lawson had once written.[26] And now with his roaring threats Lawson himself embodied the diplomatic uncertainty and frustration that the Tuscaroras had sought to cure, undercutting any promise of peace.[27]

Only after this outburst did the Indians at Catechna inaugurate ceremonies that concluded with Lawson's torture and execution. But rather than negating diplomacy, violence punctuated the Indians' concerns in a way that words could not. Moreover Graffenried described an intricate ritual, in the middle of which stood a chanting conjurer carefully laying out rings of grain.[28] The core elements intriguingly echo a similar ceremony that took place a century earlier in Virginia among the Powhatans during the well-known captivity of Captain John Smith. Anthropologists have described that earlier Powhatan ceremony as a "ritual of redefinition," in which the rings of grain served as a sort of symbolic remapping used to establish the "forms of the relationship between the colony and the Powhatans."[29]

In the case of the Powhatans, Smith famously endured a mock execution only to be "saved" at the last moment by Pocahontas. Afterward Smith was reborn as a *werowance,* or local chief, over the Jamestown settlers owing fealty and tribute to Powhatan. No such salvation awaited the mad wolf Lawson, whose execution was real. A terrified Graffenried, however, played his part perfectly, offering his "services and all sorts of favors" and promising to "live on good terms with them." Hancock's Indians spared Graffenried and led him to a joyous feast. Afterward Graffenried promised coats, powder, and rum to native leaders—goods the Indians probably viewed as tribute. In effect the Catechna Indians created a new diplomatic covenant that recast Graffenried in a subordinate position as headman of Chatouka, the old native name for New Bern, which they promised to spare in the impending war.[30] Rather than casting out Europeans, Indians at Catechna imagined that violence could begin the process of bringing some settlements *in*.

As Graffenried's captivity continued, the cadences of native ceremonies were reinscribed into the formal language of a treaty text. Dictated by Indians to a captive audience, the agreement repeats some themes from the earlier "Sun and Moon" treaty, but with a more clearly native perspective. The first point asserted that "both parties shall forget the past and henceforth be good friends." Other points continued this theme: conflict would be resolved via appeals to "the authorities of both sides"; colonial expansion would be limited without Indian approval. Indians asserted their right to hunt near settlers' farms but promised not to interfere with cattle or to set uncontrolled fires. The Indians gained a pledge that "wares and provisions shall be allowed to come at a reasonable and just price"—an important provision for a culture that viewed fair dealing as synonymous with peaceful intent. Here was an image of an orderly frontier emphasizing consensus, candor, and fairness.[31]

But just as Lawson's death had accompanied the treaty with Graffenried, bloodshed might serve to awaken other colonial leaders from diplomatic complacency. The Catechna Alliance of Tuscaroras, Corees, Mattamuskeets, and other Indians attacked North Carolina settlements on September 22, killing as many as 130 settlers in the initial attack and capturing many more.[32] In the short run, Tuscaroras probably hoped their treaty with Graffenried's New Bern would further divide and militarily weaken the colony. Afterward the treaty could serve as the kernel of a broader peace.[33]

If this was the plan, several problems intervened. Warring Indians had difficulties distinguishing between Graffenried's people and other settlers and soon found themselves fighting all.[34] Hancock released Graffenried, but the baron's suspicious survival left him persona non grata and his treaty a dead letter. More broadly put, native attacks were *too* successful. North Carolina's government, already weakened from the divisions of Cary's Rebellion, staggered helplessly.[35] Unable to wage war, unable or unwilling to negotiate, North Carolina's government looked afield, pleading for military assistance from Virginia and South Carolina. Any chance of a speedy war followed by a broader peace gave way as Tuscaroras soon found themselves enmeshed in a much larger conflict.

In late October South Carolina's legislature voted to raise a relief expedition to be headed by Colonel John Barnwell. South Carolina had a history of engaging Indian trading partners accompanied by agents and traders to raid for slaves among natives associated with the Spanish and French.[36] Now it was Tuscaroras who endured a fortnight of terror in January 1712 as Barnwell led thirty-three whites and 530 Yamasees and Siouan Indians into North Carolina, killing and enslaving as they went (for Barnwell's route, see maps 17 and 28).[37] After laying waste to 374 houses and approximately two thousand bushels of corn, Barnwell sought to end the war in a "stroke" through an attack against the "principle murderers"—Hancock's allies who had taken refuge at a sturdy fort at Catechna.[38] However after a lengthy, violent siege that saw desperate hand-to-hand fighting in rain-soaked trenches, exhausted warriors on both sides laid aside their weapons and negotiated a treaty.

The ensuing treaty raised immediate howls of betrayal from officials like Governor Spotswood of Virginia, who considered the agreement too lenient, likely to "render . . . [the Tuscaroras] more insolent," and perhaps even part of a plot to undercut North Carolina's government.[39] The real answer was simpler: Barnwell estimated that continued assaults on the fort would have required "a good many [of his own men to] . . . be killed before it could be taken."[40] Therefore if some of the provisions were "very odd and unaccountable," it was because Tuscarora tenacity set limits and ensured they still had an implicit voice.[41]

It is worth noting that the treaty included no provisions for widespread punishment. Barnwell demanded only that Hancock and three "notorious murderers" be handed over. But they had fled. Tuscaroras did return twenty-four white children held as captives, along with two black slaves (one, "a notorious Rogue," was "cutt to pieces immediately").[42]

Key portions of the agreement returned to the theme of orderly relations. One provision required Indians "to make complaints regularly to Magistrates upon any quarrel between them and whites." Another required yearly meetings with the governor at which the Indians would offer symbolic tribute. Moreover it was agreed that in twenty days they would have another council to reaffirm this treaty and "such other articles as shall be agreed upon." Further articles demanded land concessions and limited Indians' hunting, planting, and fishing to the upper Neuse and its tributaries. Restrictive as this was, the Tuscarora signatories retained the bulk of their lands and may have even interpreted the provision to mean that lands inside these bounds would be protected. To be sure, compared to the agreement with Graffenried, the balance of authority shifted markedly toward colonial officials and was given greater weight when Barnwell took several hostages. Nonetheless Barnwell reported that certain points were "Intirely agreed to by ye Tsucaruro Indians."[43]

But arrangements agreed to by Tuscaroras were "grunttéd at by the Coves [Corees]," who would have lost the bulk of their lands, "upon which they quarreled." Barnwell speculated that if only he had a few days more provisions, he could split the Catechna Alliance and contrive "the matter so well that in that time I could oblige the Tuscaroras to have delivered all the Corees for slaves."[44] Indeed somebody—North and South Carolinians each blamed the other—used the fiction of further talks to lure a "goodly number" of Corees, Bear River, Neuse, and Machapunga Indians. Nearly two hundred women and children were seized for transport to South Carolina as "living plunder," in addition to forty or fifty who were killed.[45] Regardless of the perpetrator, Indians learned the exact lesson that Barnwell had hoped to avoid, namely that "there could be no dependence in our promises."[46] The war resumed.

As these battles were fought, diplomacy continued on other fronts. In some ways the Tuscarora War is a misnomer since much of the fighting was done by non-Tuscarora members of the Catechna Alliance such as the Corees, Mattamuskeets, and Neuse Indians. Likewise only a fraction of Tuscaroras actively participated in the fighting, while many—perhaps more than half—attempted to remain neutral or at peace with Europeans. The outward behavior of these neutral communities, often referred to as the Upper Towns, and described by Graffenried as "seven villages . . . somewhat farther distant, more beyond [that is, closer to] Virginia," differed radically from that of those who made war.[47] As storm clouds gathered and burst in North Carolina, the Upper Towns sought shelter by reaching out to the government of Virginia, in hopes of achieving some sort of settlement. It is significant that despite their different approaches, both factions shared similar underlying goals of creating a framework for orderly frontier relations while maintaining much of their own autonomy.

Trade with Virginia and cultural ties to Indians residing there—notably the linguistically related Nottoways and Meherrins—partially explain the Upper Towns' diplomatic direction. Compared to North Carolina, Virginia had adopted nearly a mirror opposite approach to Indian affairs. Decades earlier Virginia had had its own brush with rowdy unscripted Indian relations, which had sparked Bacon's Rebellion. Never again, swore officials. Thereafter Virginia's policies actively aimed to prevent a recurrence of "the mutual discontents, Complaints, jealousies, and feare of English and Indians."[48] Thereafter the two colonies' Indian relations fit within the diverging spectrum of social and political patterns described by historians: whereas early-eighteenth-century North Carolina experienced chaos and tumults, Virginia saw consolidation under an established planter class.[49] Treaties placed serious limitations on Virginia's so-called native tributaries. Native leaders submitted to the Virginia courts, paid annual tribute, and found their freedom of movement and ability to trade curtailed; they were obligated to police against enemy Indians or runaway slaves.[50] Nonetheless tributaries partially offset restrictions by taking advantage of the letter of the law and appealing to the paternalistic ethos of officials wary of disorderly white settlers and willing to step in on behalf of "loyal" Indians.[51]

Tuscaroras had never fully embraced Virginia's tributary system, despite efforts by the colony to use threats, trade embargoes, and the courts to draw them under control.⁵² Instead, despite being a frequent presence in the colony and having "a constant trade with our Inhabitants for the like commodities as our own Indians," according to Spotswood, Tuscaroras always hovered just outside the limits of Virginia's authority, enjoying many of the benefits of Virginia's efforts to impose order, but also maintaining their own autonomy.⁵³

The Upper Towns continued this careful dance during the war years. In October 1711, early in the conflict, five delegates from the Upper Towns came to the Nottoway village where they met Spotswood drilling sixteen hundred militiamen in a display of force. "I could not hope for a more favourable Conjecture," bragged Spotswood, "than now when they are under great apprehension of our Resentments for the late Barbaritys committed in Carolina, and the impressions made on them by the appearance of so great a force as I then show'd them."⁵⁴ Rather than sending armies crashing toward North Carolina, Spotswood focused closer to home, taking steps toward establishing a "new project for securing our frontiers," a greatly expanded version of Virginia's tributary model. Indians would be relocated alongside strategically placed forts. There trade would be monopolized, movement would be monitored, and schoolmasters and missionaries would oversee cultural and religious reeducation. These policies, effused Spotswood, "will create in them a liking to our Laws and Governm't . . . secure a necessary dependence on this colony . . . banish their present savage customs" and in "a generation or two," "bind them . . . to be good subjects and useful neighbours."⁵⁵ Some tributary groups, most notably the Saponis and Nansemonds, eventually did cluster near the massive five-sided palisade of Fort Christanna.⁵⁶ Others, including the Nottoways and Meherrins, resisted.⁵⁷

It was the Tuscaroras, as most powerful group in the region, who were to be central to this plan. However continuing previous practices, they sought to align with Virginia without fully subordinating themselves. Spotswood reported the Upper Town delegates as "very desirous to continue in peace." He tried to push the Upper Towns to take up arms against the Catechna Alliance, offering six striped blankets "for the head of each man," and "the usual price of Slaves" for each woman and child captured.⁵⁸ Spotswood also demanded two hostages from each town "for the better assuring us of their future good behavior."⁵⁹ To all this, Spotswood optimistically opined, the diplomats were "well enough inclined."⁶⁰ But their actions spoke otherwise. In a pattern repeated throughout the war, the Tuscarora spokesmen agreed with the plan, promised to consult with their people, and then departed, only to disappear into a fog of delays.

These patterns repeated for months. Spotswood eventually suspected that Tuscaroras were merely toying with him, offering only "some trifling excuses" in a never-ending delaying tactic.⁶¹ Postponements probably also reflected the difficulties divided towns faced in achieving consensus around agreements their delegates brought home.⁶² Most of all, perhaps, the relative order that Virginia offered came with too high a price—the virtual surrender of the Upper Towns' political and cultural autonomy. Negotiations ended in spring 1712 with Virginia's executive council concluding that "the Tuscaroro Indians have failed in the performance of every Article of their Treaty."[63] The Tuscaroras' inaction voiced their decision—Spotswood had asked too much.

In early 1713 Tuscaroras faced another invasion by an army of South Carolina and its native allies, this time led by Colonel James Moore—son of a former governor. As they had done previously against Barnwell, members of the Catechna Alliance took shelter in a carefully constructed fort, this one called Neoheroka (map 17). But whereas Tuscaroras had fought Barnwell's army to a stalemate, this time Tuscaroras faced overwhelming military defeat. By Moore's estimate, approximately 950 Tuscaroras and other Indians were captured or killed.[64] Thus ended the last major battle of the war.

But military defeat for the Catechna Alliance did not translate into a clear victory for the colonists. Survivors retreated to impenetrable swamps and began a series of guerrilla raids terrifying in their unpredictability. North Carolina's clumsy militia proved helpless. And wary of native allies they could neither feed nor pay, the colony turned back a third army en route from South Carolina. War was not an option. Therefore the "best expedient to free you from yr troubles, and in all probability to quiet the Tuscoruroes for a long time," advised Spotswood, would be an "honorable peace."[65] But how?

Colonial leaders thought the answer lay with a Tuscarora leader named Tom Blount, whose appearance marks a new phase of Tuscarora diplomacy. Beginning in late summer of 1712—the second year of the war and months before the final assault on Neoheroka—Blount had begun intermittent negotiations with North Carolina. At first glance, these dealings seem to be a mere extension of earlier talks between the Upper Towns and Virginia, in which Blount's town, Ucouhnerunt, had taken part.[66] However deeper changes were afoot. For the first time Blount shifted the focus of diplomacy to the government of North Carolina itself, which now after Governor Hyde's death was under newly forceful leadership by the council president, Thomas Pollock.

Moreover, while delegations from other Tuscarora towns dithered, Blount acted, sometimes as part of a group, but more often on his own prerogative. As early as October 1712, Blount leaked crucial intelligence. Blount further ratified the shift by seizing Hancock while the two were hunting together, and then turning him over to Pollock. The North Carolinians promptly executed Catechna's leader, pausing only long enough to inflict "exquisite tortures."[67]

Shortly afterward Blount and an Upper Town delegation signed a treaty with Pollock, in November 1712. Almost before the ink dried this treaty was rendered a dead letter by the arrival of Moore's South Carolina army and the final assault on Neoheroka—nonetheless it bears analysis. Much echoed earlier agreements put forward by colonists, including limitations on where Tuscaroras could hunt and plant, demands for the return of prisoners and booty, and a requirement for towns to hand over hostages and pay a symbolic yearly tribute. In return there would be peace, "a free and open trade . . . as existed formerly," and a commission to investigate future complaints.[68]

But the treaty marked significant new ground in other ways. First, Blount and the other signatories took the furthest steps yet toward separating themselves from other Tuscaroras and the rest of the Catechna Alliance in their bid for peace. Hancock had been the first sacrifice. Now they agreed to capture nine Catechna Alliance leaders and deliver them with "three hoops" under a white flag of peace. They pledged to war on the "towns or nations of Catchny, Cores, Nuse, Bare River and Pamptico," giving no quarter to men and enslaving boys under the age of fourteen. (Virginia had made similar demands, but Tuscarora negotiators had always deferred, claiming a need to consult with their people). Second, the treaty secured Blount's novel position. Although there were several signatories on behalf of nine towns, Blount alone gained special privileges: no hostages would come from Blount's town; no boundaries dictated where Blount's people could travel and hunt. These immunities, Pollock explained, stemmed from "the trust that we put in him."[69] As far as Blount's people were concerned, war with kinsmen would purchase colonists' good will and a framework for future trust.

But this supposed trust lasted only days until Moore's South Carolina army arrived in the region and threatened Blount's community, Ucouhnerunt. Storming off, Blount upbraided Pollock "for giving him nothing for all he is done only words."[70]

Despite their earlier parting, when the question of how to arrange a peace reasserted itself after the destruction of Neoheroka, officials again thought of Blount. Their plan exaggerated patterns evident in the earlier treaty. "Talk high" to Blount, explained Spotswood in a letter. "Stir up his ambition. . . . [Tell him, you are willing to] conclude a peace with him and all the other Indians of the Tuscaroro . . . [and neighboring tribes], that will put themselves under his Government. . . . [Tell him] you will make him King of all those Indians under the protection of North Carolina." This would be the way to "oblige him to be faithful to the English for the future."[71] Blount had his community to protect. Moreover he had already been moving toward circumventing slow-moving councils and the past teethas' reliance on consensus in favor of personal power. Therefore it was no great step in April 1713 when Blount signed articles that acknowledged him "King and Commander in Chief" of Indians in the region.[72]

Colonial authorities imagined Blount as a puppet, but the cagey Tuscarora leader proved equally capable of pulling strings. Pollock privately admitted a want of "men, provisions, and ammunition; sufficiency of neither of which is to be raised or had in this government."[73] If Blount chose to "fly back with the rest of the Tuscaroras," admitted the North Carolina leader, "we shall lie open to the insults of all of them, and of all other straggling Indians, and by that means know no end of the war."[74] Blount held the key to peace.

Another card in Blount's hand was tension between North Carolina and Virginia. The two colonies had long squabbled over their shared border, and both imagined that claiming Tuscaroras specifically as *their* tributaries would strengthen their bid to the region. The colonies made a show of coordinating, but Blount witnessed strains firsthand when the two governors fought over Hancock's dead body, whom both considered their honor and privilege to execute. Later when the colonies jostled over access to Blount, Spotswood and Pollock accused each other of being "highly prejudicial," "very disrespectful," "ill deserving," "unjust," and "destructive to her Majesty's subjects."[75]

These factors gave Blount choices and leverage. Blount eventually made peace with both colonies but steered clear of Virginia's stringent tributary requirements.[76] No massive fort stocked with soldiers, missionaries, and agents would watch over them. Instead Blount and his followers chose to remain in North Carolina. Although the exact text of the treaty he negotiated with North Carolina is missing, much of its content can be divined from other documents and circumstances. North Carolina promised "a firm and lasting peace with him [Blount] and all the Indians that acknowledge him as sachem."[77] As part of their "articles of agreement," Blount's Tuscaroras promised to police the frontier and capture runaway slaves.[78] They retained a tract between the Pamlico and Neuse Rivers as a reservation. Tuscaroras could likely travel to hunt or trade abroad, but only in limited numbers. Several years later when Blount petitioned to relocate to the north shore of the Roanoke River, North Carolina agreed, citing that "the said Blount and his Indyans have been very Serviceable to this Government."[79]

Perhaps most important, Blount was able to deal with a chastened North Carolina government newly ready to take its diplomatic obligations seriously. This spirit was captured in a 1715 law enacted to remedy previous patterns of "daily and grievous" depredations by settlers and "for Cultivating a better Understanding with ye said Indyans the want of which has been so Injurious to the Government." The law emphasized the settling of disputes over trade, land, or poaching by commissions composed of a magistrate acting jointly with the "ruler or headman" of the Indian community—namely, Blount.[80] Likewise unregulated settlement on Indian land was outlawed. In many of its basic objectives, this law hearkened back to the treaty Hancock and other members of the Catechna Alliance had put forward during Graffenried's captivity.

And for once these were not merely empty words. The following decades reveal Tuscaroras availing themselves of new avenues for conflict resolution along with officials concerned over the "many inconveniences . . . to be feared to the tranquility and peace of this government."[81] When one settler unleashed his dog on a Tuscarora hunter, rather than blankly accepting excuses that the Indian was trespassing, officials listened to both sides, took the settler into custody, and then scheduled a hearing on the Tuscarora reservation.[82] After another similar assault, the injured Indian "said he would goo and tell King Blount for King Blount he said would go to Capt. West" (a North Carolina Indian agent)—a nearly perfect example of the pattern for resolution envisioned by the 1715 law.[83] A jury trial attended by tribal leaders acquitted another Tuscarora of breaking and entering—this despite the fact that he was caught red-handed in a Pollock's bedroom![84] Another Tuscarora blasted shots into a settler's cabin and wounded several children. Arguing that he had been drunk, he miraculously escaped with no more punishment than reimbursing medical expenses.[85] In the mid-1730s the Tuscaroras complained of "several abuses committed by the white people living near them" whereas the settlers complained that Indians "burnt upon their lands, and kill and disturb their cattle."[86] Making a show of neutrality, the governor shuttled between Tuscaroras and settlers, trying to appease both. Violent disputes, often fueled by alcohol, flared just as they had before the war. The difference was in the way that the government reacted.

It is ironic that Blount, who had opposed the war, reaped the benefits—if they can be called that—and Hancock, who had fought, did not live to see the transformations he had wrought. The Tuscarora War, and the implied threat that if pushed hard enough Tuscaroras could rise again, had brought changes.[87] These changes, moreover, had come at terrible, overwhelming cost. Whatever offerings of stability that the government could offer, and whatever gestures were made toward giving Blount a voice in relations, were a hollow simulacrum of earlier aspirations. They could not hide the fact that Blount and the Tuscaroras under him had become dependents, unable to act on their own, limited in their ability to move about or dispose of their lands. Protection in the courts came tempered with the knowledge that the legal system was not their own, and depended on judicial paternalism.

For most of the war, Tuscaroras had avoided open arms against one another, despite the efforts of colonial officials. Blount crossed that line. As part of his agreement, Blount had agreed to police the frontiers against the remaining members of the Catechna Alliance—a duty in which one settler judged Blount "indefatigable."[88] In June 1713 Blount delivered eight Catechna Alliance combatants to Pollock (who promptly loaded them as slaves on the first ship bound for the Caribbean).[89] By November Blount's people had brought in thirty scalps.[90]

Over the next two decades, Blount worked with colonial officials to subvert old political practices among the Tuscaroras that had depended on town councils and consensus. He consolidated his position as a "king" unlike any teetha.

He was not shy about calling in the government to assist against Tuscaroras who protested his choices: Indians he labeled "Pirates and Robbers" and men "formerly of the Tuskarooroe Nation."[91] This was the price of peace.

Nonetheless it is important to point out that while it was Blount who negotiated with officials, none of his decisions would have carried weight unless other Tuscaroras chose to follow him. The decision was difficult, and for many Tuscaroras, the costs were too great.

Emphasizing the existence of such choices—and their difficulty—was the appearance in Virginia's piedmont and mountains of about fifteen hundred half-starved Tuscarora refugees from at least five towns.[92] At least some hailed from the neutral Upper Towns. Their spokesmen claimed that once their communities and Blount's had been "all together." But they had grown uncomfortable with Blount's exclusive authority. Preserving older patterns, they assembled councils of as many as 160 men headed by several teethas.[93] In early 1714 three of their deputies signed a treaty with Virginia, finally fulfilling, it seemed, Spotswood's long-held hopes for Tuscarora tributaries.[94] But ultimately they could not stomach the controls over trade, movement, religion, and education that Spotswood's reconstruction plans entailed. The treaty went ignored. Some of these Tuscaroras probably integrated quietly with the Nottoways; some may have joined a short-lived community in South Carolina; others swallowed their frustration and returned to Blount in North Carolina.

Still others decided to join the ranks of those who eventually journeyed north to resettle among the Iroquois along the Susquehanna River and near Oneida Lake. Between fifteen hundred and two thousand made the choice. In doing so they abandoned more than their homeland, they also abandoned earlier aspirations of using a mixture of warfare and diplomacy to reshape colonial encounters in North Carolina. Thereafter when these emigrants engaged diplomatically with Europeans, they would not do so by themselves, but instead as the newly adopted "Sixth Nation" of the powerful Iroquois Confederacy. Thus, beyond its violence and casualties, the Tuscarora War also fostered the beginnings of a new political and cultural landscape. Thereafter different Tuscarora groups—some among the Iroquois, some still in North Carolina—took separate paths while traversing an increasingly English-dominated eighteenth-century world.

Notes

1. The most complete account of the Tuscarora War remains Herbert Richard Paschal, "The Tuscarora Indians in North Carolina" (master's thesis, University of North Carolina, Chapel Hill, 1953). Also see Thomas C. Parramore, "With Tuscarora Jack on the Back Path to Bath," *NCHR* 64, no. 2 (1987): 115–38; and Thomas C. Parramore, "The Tuscarora Ascendancy," *NCHR* 59, no. 4 (1982): 307–26. Alan Gallay emphasizes the role of the slave trade in *The Indian Slave Trade: The Rise of the English Empire in the American South, 1670–1717* (New Haven: Yale University

Press, 2002). For an account that emphasizes the political and economic consequences, see Christine A. Styrna, "The Winds of War and Change: The Impact of the Tuscarora War on Proprietary North Carolina, 1690–1729" (Ph.D. diss., College of William and Mary, 1990). For a fuller account of the issues described in this essay, see Stephen Feeley, "Tuscarora Trails: Indian Migrations, War, and Constructions of Colonial Frontiers" (Ph.D. diss., College of William and Mary, 2007), esp. chaps. 2–6.

2. Gallay estimates a low range of one thousand to twelve hundred and a high range of eighteen hundred to two thousand Tuscaroras and allies enslaved. Gallay, *Indian Slave Trade*, 298–99.

3. John Barnwell, "Journal of John Barnwell," *VMHB* 5, no. 4 (April 1898): 391-402, and 6, no. 1 (July 1898): 42-55, quotation from 6:47.

4. Lawson, *New Voyage*, 236. Literally this term translates roughly as one "exempted from work." Blair A. Rudes, *Tuscarora-English/English-Tuscarora Dictionary* (Toronto: University of Toronto Press, 1999), 232. Many communities of the Tuscaroras and other eastern North Carolina Indians can be seen on John Barnwell's maps of southeastern North America (map 27 and map 28). Since these maps were born of military expeditions against the Catechna Alliance, many Upper Town communities are omitted.

5. For political structures, see Douglas W. Boyce, "Did a Tuscarora Confederacy Exist?," *Indian Historian* 6, no. 3 (1973): 34–40; Douglas W. Boyce, "Notes on Tuscarora Political Organization, 1650–1713" (master's thesis, University of North Carolina, Chapel Hill, 1971); Douglas W. Boyce, "Tuscarora Political Organization, Ethnic Identity, and Sociohistorical Demography, 1711–1825" (Ph.D. diss., University of North Carolina at Chapel Hill, 1973). Also see Alexander Spotswood, *The Official Letters of Alexander Spotswood*, ed. R. A. Brock, 2 vols. (Richmond: Virginia Historical Society, 1857), 2:200. Europeans occasionally claimed to spot a Tuscarora "Emperor," but it seems likely that such individuals were merely a particularly persuasive or influential teetha or other spokesperson.

6. For tensions, see Christoph von Graffenried, *Christoph von Graffenried's Account of the Founding of New Bern*, ed. and trans. Vincent H. Todd (Raleigh: North Carolina Historical Commission, 1920), 234; Barnwell, "Journal," 3:397; Minutes, January 26, 1691, in *EJCCV*, 1:147; Minutes, February 18–19, 1691, in *EJCCV*, 1:157–58; "Letter from Chrisoph von Graffenried to Edward Hyde, 1711," in *CRNC*, 1:991.

7. Lawson, *New Voyage*. Also see map 11.

8. Lawson, *New Voyage*, 192, 195–96, 212, 224; Graffenried, *Account*, 316–17.

9. Ira Berlin, "From Creole to African: Atlantic Creoles and the Origins of African-American Society in Mainland North America," *WMQ* 53 (1996): 251–88.

10. *NCHGR*, 2:194.

11. March 28, 1702, Petition, in "Indians: Treaties, Petitions, Agreements, and Court Cases (1698–1736)," Colonial Court Records, Box 192, at NCSA. Also see *NCHGR*, 3:242 and "Minutes of the General Court of North Carolina, November 26–30, 1694," in *CRNC*, 1:432. For similar treatment of the Yawpin Indians

(another small native group in the coastal swamps), see Record of Council Held at the House of John Hecklefield, April 12, 1704, in "Indians: Treaties, Petitions, Agreements, and Court Cases (1698–1736)," Colonial Court Records, Box 192, at NCSA; *NCHGR*, 3:73.

12. Parramore, "Tuscarora Ascendancy," 313; Paschal, "Tuscarora Indians," 28.

13. "Act of the North Carolina General Assembly Concerning Settlement, 1707," in *CRNC*, 1:674–75.

14. Styrna, "Winds of War," 47. Two contemporary estimates in 1708 and 1709 put the percentage of Quakers at between one-seventh and one-tenth of the total population. William S. Price, Introduction, in *CRNC* (2nd ser.), 4:xv; "Description by John Blair Concerning his Journey to North Carolina, 1704," in *CRNC*, 1:600–603; "Letter from James Adams to John Chamberlain, Sept. 18, 1708," in *CRNC*, 1:686–87;" Letter from William Gordon to John Chamberlain, May 13, 1709," in *CRNC*, 1:708–15. For pirates being "kindly entertained in Carolina," see "Letter from the Board of Trade of England to the Lords Proprietors of Carolina, February 9, 1697," in *CRNC*, 1:475.

15. Spotswood, *Letters*, 2:48; Boyce, "Tuscarora Political Organization," 7. In the contest for the uncertain borderlands between the two colonies, North Carolina used lax laws to win settlers; Virginia on the other hand often supported tributary Indians as a way of exerting influence. For an account that emphasizes the role of the Meherrins, a group linguistically and culturally close to the Tuscaroras, in these border struggles, see Shannon Lee Dawdy, "The Meherrins' Secret History of the Dividing Line," *NCHR* 72, no. 4 (October 1995): 386–415.

16. "Order from Gov. Henderson Walker Relating to Bay River Indians, May 14, 1701," in *NCHGR*, 1:597–98; "Letter from John Lawson to Gov. Walker Relating to the Bay River Indians, June 23, 1701," in *NCHGR*, 1:598; "Articles of Agreement with the Bay River Indians, September 23, 1699," in *NCHGR*, 1:598–99. Originals are in "Indians: Treaties, Petitions, Agreements, and Court Cases (1698–1736)," Colonial Court Records, Box 192, at NCSA.

17. North Carolina settlers fired upon and plundered a beached vessel. "Report by Edward Randolph concerning illegal trade in North Carolina [Extract], March 24, 1700," in *CRNC*, 1:527.

18. Graffenried, *Account*, 374–75.

19. "Relating to the Indians, 1703," in *NCHGR*, 2:193–94. Also see Lawson, *New Voyage*, 211–12.

20. "Sun and Moon Treaty," reprinted in appendix A of Paschal, "Tuscarora Indians," 160–62, and "Articles of Peace with the Tuscarora Indians," in *NCHGR*, 2:218–19. Some accounts posit that this treaty is a draft of an earlier agreement made in the 1670s. The placement of an image of this treaty in Parramore's article implies that it was signed in 1672, but he makes no explicit claim. Parramore, "Tuscarora Ascendancy," 314. The editors of *NCHGR*, however, speculate that it was a draft for a later treaty, at the conclusion of the Tuscarora War. George Stevenson of the North Carolina State Archives proposes that handwriting and other internal evidence suggests a date very early in the eighteenth century, a date that fits the chronology presented here. Personal communication, July 2001.

21. "Sun and Moon Treaty," in appendix A of Paschal, "Tuscarora Indians," 160–62; "Articles of Peace with the Tuscarora Indians," in *NCHGR*, 2:218–19.

22. Lawson suggests that some young men among the Tuscaroras may have rejected the treaty because it placed new regulations on the rum trade. Lawson, *New Voyage*, 212. There is no explicit mention of the rum trade in the draft of the Sun and Moon treaty. However clause 9 restricts a practice in which Tuscaroras would leave a "paun or pledge" with English traders in return for trade goods.

23. "Letter from Edward Hyde to the [Lords Proprietors of Carolina], August 22, 1711," in *CRNC*, 1:802; "Letter from Alexander Spotswood to the Board of Trade of Great Britain, October 15, 1711," in *CRNC*, 1:810–11. Other rumors focused on the possible role of Virginia traders spurring the Tuscaroras to war but upon investigation proved unsubstantiated. Barnwell, "Journal," 5:398. See also, Alonzo T. Dill, "Eighteenth Century New Bern," *NCHR* 22, nos. 1–4 (January, April, July, and October 1945), 305. For earlier accusations of provocation by Virginia traders, see Minutes, August 9, 1704, in *EJCCV*, 2:381–82; Minutes, September 28, 1704, in *EJCCV*, 2:390; Minutes, October 26, 1704, in *EJCCV*, 2:402; Minutes, December 4, 1704, in *EJCCV*, 2:405; Minutes, October 26, 1708, in *EJCCV*, 3:199–200.

24. Samuel Hazard, ed., *Minutes of the Provincial Council of Pennsylvania*, 16 vols. (Harrisburg, Penn.: Theophilus Fenn, 1838–53), 2:511. Also see "Minutes, 31 July," in William Penn Papers, Indian Affairs, Historical Society of Pennsylvania, Philadelphia. Shared linguistic and cultural roots may have made Iroquoian-speaking Tuscaroras particularly attractive targets for Iroquois war parties seeking captives for adoption. For examples of Iroquois raids, see Minutes, July 4, 1703, in *EJCCV*, 2:331; Lawson, *New Voyage*, 207. For Tuscarora-Iroquois relations, see Douglas W. Boyce, "'As the Wind Scatters the Smoke': The Tuscaroras in the Eighteenth Century," in *Beyond the Covenant Chain: The Iroquois and their Neighbors in Indian North America, 1600–1800*, ed. Daniel Richter and James H. Merrell (Syracuse, N.Y.: Syracuse University Press, 1987), 151–63. Peace with the Iroquois may have freed Tuscaroras to consider war against colonists. Despite frequent colonists' fears of direct Iroquois intervention, their actual role in the Tuscarora War was ambiguous, perhaps reflecting internal divisions. They offered and in at least one case gave military aid; they attempted to spur New York officials to help broker a peace; finally they used the war to coerce Tuscaroras towards joining them. See Feeley, "Tuscarora Trails," chap. 7.

25. Unless otherwise noted, quotations and description in this section are from Graffenried's "Copy of the Account Written Mr. Edward Hyde, Governor of North Carolina, the 23rd October, 1711, With Reference to My Miraculous Deliverance from the Savages," in Graffenried, *Account*, 261–82. Graffenried describes these events as a trial for his life rather than as a council, but his perception was shaped in hindsight by Lawson's death. Much of his account is structured to exonerate himself.

26. Lawson, *New Voyage*, 97.

27. William Ramsey describes a similar start of the Yamasee War, four years later. Again natives were frustrated by a lack of diplomatic attention to problems related to the deerskin trade. Two officials who had both held the post of Indian

commissioner traveled to the principle Yamasee town to address concerns. However one official immediately undermined the agreement by issuing threats that same night. Indians, feeling betrayed by the contradictory messages, killed the two South Carolinians the next day and afterwards went to war. See William L. Ramsey, "'Something Cloudy in Their Looks': The Origins of the Yamasee War Reconsidered," *JAH* 90, no. 1 (June 2003): 44–76.

28. Graffenried, *Account*, 267–69.

29. Frederic W. Gleach, *Powhatan's World and Colonial Virginia: A Conflict of Cultures* (Lincoln: University of Nebraska Press, 1997), 114–15. These rings may have resembled the sort of symbolic maps among southeastern Indians described in Gregory A. Waselkov, "Indian Maps of the Colonial Southeast," in *Powhatan's Mantle: Indians in the Colonial Southeast*, ed. Gregory A. Waselkov, Peter H. Wood, and M. Thomas Hatley (Lincoln: University of Nebraska Press, 1989), 292–343.

30. Graffenried, *Account*, 269–71.

31. The text of this treaty is contained in Graffenried, *Account*, 281–82.

32. "Letter from Christopher Gale to [his sibling], November 2, 1711," in *CRNC*, 1:827.

33. Graffenried himself initially hoped to eventually incorporate the entire colony within the treaty negotiated with the Catechna Alliance. Graffenried, *Account*, 238.

34. For an example of this confusion, see Graffenried, *Account*, 273. Adding to the difficulty of analysis and probably reflecting confusion all around, John Barnwell recorded that Tuscarora prisoners thought "the people Massacred were outlandish [that is, foreigners—the Swiss and Palatines] and not English, and so they doubted not but soon to make peace with the English and that they were then about it." Barnwell, "Journal," 5:398. Either way, it seems clear that the Catechna Alliance believed they were fighting a limited war and could soon make peace.

35. For descriptions of North Carolina's divided and disorderly condition, see "Letter from Alexander Spotswood to William Legge, Earl of Dartmouth, October 15, 1711," in *CRNC*, 1:814; "Minutes of a meeting of the Lords Proprietors of Carolina, January 24, 1712–January 29, 1712," in *CRNC*, 1:832–33; "Pollock's Letter Book, September 9, 1712," in *CRNC*, 1:869; "Letter from Thomas Pollock to the Lords Proprietors of Carolina, September 20, 1712," in *CRNC*, 1:873–74; "Letter from Thomas Pollock to John Carteret, Earl Granville, September 20, 1712," in *CRNC*, 1:877; "Alexander Spotswood to the Board of Trade, February 8, 1712," in Spotswood, *Letters*, 1:142; "Alexander Spotswood to the Lords Commissioners of Trade, February 11, 1713," in Spotswood, *Letters*, 2:12; Graffenried, *Account*, 241, 263; Barnwell, "Journal," 6:49.

36. Gallay, *Indian Slave Trade*, esp. 127–54; Steven J. Oatis, *A Colonial Complex: South Carolina's Frontiers in the Era of the Yamasee War* (Lincoln: University of Nebraska Press, 2005), esp. 42–111.

37. For arrangement of the army, see Barnwell, "Journal," 5:393–94; Gallay, *Indian Slave Trade*, 267–68. Indians had their own reasons for participation, particularly to seek captives to repay trade debts. Siouan-speaking Saras and Saxapahaws were further motivated by revenge after Tuscaroras killed several for refusing to join the uprising. Barnwell, "Journal," 5:394; April 9, 1712, in *CHJ*, 4:19. For relations

with the Esaws and Wacksaws, see April 4, 1712, in CHJ, 4:8. For figures on destruction see Barnwell, "Journal," 5:396.

38. Quotation from Barnwell, "Journal," 6:44–45. For figures on destruction, see Barnwell, "Journal," 5:396. For a discussion of the Tuscaroras' adaptation and use of fortifications against Europeans, see Wayne E. Lee, "Fortify, Fight, or Flee: Tuscarora and Cherokee Defensive Warfare and Military Culture Adaptation," *Journal of Military History* 68, no. 3 (2004): 713–70; Charles L. Heath and David S. Phelps, "Architecture of a Tuscarora Fortress: Neoheroka Fort and the Tuscarora War" (paper presented at the 63rd Annual Meeting of the Society for American Archaeology, Seattle, Wash., January 1998).

39. "Alexander Spotswood to the Council of Trade, July 26, 1712," in Spotswood, *Letters*, 1:169–71; "Letter from Thomas Pollock to Charles Craven, February 20, 1713," in *CRNC*, 2:20; "Letter from Thomas Pollock to Charles Craven, May 25, 1713," in *CRNC*, 2:46. Adding to the ill will, both Governor Hyde and Barnwell aspired to the same tract of land on the former site of Coree Town (which Graffenried also openly coveted). "Letter from Thomas Pollock to John Carteret, Earl Granville, September 20, 1712," in *CRNC*, 1:878.

40. Barnwell, "Journal," 6:54.

41. "Alexander Spotswood to the Council of Trade, May 8, 1712," in Spotswood, *Letters*, 1:150.

42. Barnwell gives a lengthy description of the treaty in Barnwell, "Journal," 6:52–54.

43. Barnwell, "Journal," 6:52–54.

44. Barnwell, "Journal," 6:54.

45. Graffenried, *Account*, 244–45; "Letter from Thomas Pollock to the Lords Proprietors of Carolina, September 20, 1712," in *CRNC*, 1:875; "Minutes of the South Carolina Commons House of Assembly, June 1712," in *CRNC*, 1:900–901; Spotswood, *Letters*, 1:170–71; "Minutes of the North Carolina Governor's Council, May 09, 1712–May 10, 1712," in *CRNC*, 1:843; Parramore, "With Tuscarora Jack," 134. Gallay, *Indian Slave Trade*, 274–75. Barnwell never admitted to the act and instead blamed greedy North Carolinians. Another possibility is that South Carolina Indians acted on their own, perhaps feeling cheated out of captives they felt they had been promised. Graffenried, who blamed Barnwell, admitted that the South Carolina Indians were "entirely inclined because they hoped to get a considerable sum from each prisoner." Graffenried, *Account*, 244–45.

46. Barnwell, "Journal," 6:54.

47. Graffenried, *Account*, 276. In other cases eight towns are mentioned. For a list of North Carolina Tuscarora villages, see appendix A of Boyce, "Tuscarora Political Organization," 257–58. There were also differences within towns, although these were less visible to Europeans. See, for example, Barnwell, "Journal," 5:397.

48. The Treaty of Middle Plantation is reprinted as "Treaty between Virginia and Indians, 1677" in *VMHB* 14, no. 3 (January 1907): 289–96, quotation page 291. This treaty also appears in W. Stitt Robinson, ed., *Virginia Treaties, 1607–1722*, vol. 4 of *Early American Indian Documents: Treaties and Laws, 1607–1789* (Frederick, Md.: University Publications of America, 1983), 82–88.

49. There is an extensive literature on increased order and control by Virginia's planter class. See, for example, Jack P. Greene, *Pursuits of Happiness: The Social Development of Early Modern British Colonies and the Formation of American Culture* (Chapel Hill: University of North Carolina Press, 1988), 81–100.

50. For tributaries, see W. Stitt Robinson, "The Tributary Indians in Colonial Virginia," *VMHB* 67, no. 1 (January 1959): 49–64; James H. Merrell, *The Indians' New World: Catawbas and their Neighbors from European Contact through the Era of Removal* (New York: Norton, 1989); Helen C. Rountree, *Pocahontas's People: The Powhatan Indians of Virginia through Four Centuries* (Norman: University of Oklahoma Press, 1996). For the basis of this status see the 1646 treaty, in Robinson, ed., *Virginia Treaties*, 67–71 and "Treaty between Virginia and Indians, 1677."

51. "Letter of Benjamin Harrison, July 14, 1709," in *CVSP*, 1:131–32; Minutes, October 24, 1690 in *EJCCV*, 1:136; Minutes, April 24, 1703, in *EJCCV*, 2:315, 316; Minutes, June 17, 1703, in *EJCCV*, 2:322–23; Minutes, April 23, 1708, in *EJCCV*, 3:172.

52. Minutes, October 16, 1693, in *JHBV, 1659–1693*, 454; Minutes, May 10, 1699, in *JHBV, 1696–1702*, 156; William Waller Hening, *The Statutes at Large: Being a Collection of All the Laws of Virginia, from the First Session of the Legislature in the Year 1619*, 13 vols. (Richmond, Va.: 1809–23), 3:343–44. Particularly emblematic were Virginia's failed efforts to use courts and embargos to bring to justice several Tuscaroras accused of killing a settler named Jeremiah Pate of New Kent County in October 1707. See Minutes, October 25, 1707, in *EJCCV*, 3:158; Minutes, October 29, 1707, in *EJCCV*, 3:159, 161; Minutes, October 31, 1707–April 22, 1708, in *EJCCV*, 3:163–74; Minutes, June 4, 1708, in *EJCCV*, 3:182; Minutes, June 10, 1708, in *EJCCV*, 3:185; Minutes, September 20, in *EJCCV*, 3:191; Minutes, October 26, 1708, in *EJCCV*, 3:200; Minutes, March 1, 1708/9, in *EJCCV*, 3:211; "Letter by Nathaniel Harrison, October 29, 1707," in *CVSP*, 1:117; "Letter to the Earl of Sunderland, 1708," in *CVSP*, 1:123; "Council of Trade and Plantations to Col. Jenings, January 12, 1709," in *CSPC*, item 295, vol. 24 (1709): 198–99; "Col. Jenings to the Council of Trade and Plantations, June 24, 1708," in *CSPC*, item 1573, vol. 23 (1707–8): 763–67. For the resulting failed trade embargo, see Minutes, October 26, 1708, in *EJCCV*, 3:199; Minutes, February 10, 1709, in *EJCCV*, 3:204–5; Minutes, February 18, 1708, in *EJCCV*, 3:207; Minutes, April 26, 1709, in *EJCCV*, 3:214; William Byrd, *The Secret Diary of William Byrd of Westover, 1709–1712*, ed. Louis B. Wright and Marion Tinling (Richmond, Va.: Dietz Press, 1941), 25.

53. "Alexander Spotswood to the Council of Trade, July 26, 1712," in Spotswood, *Letters*, 1:167. Also see a complaint by the Nottoway Indians regarding the Tuscaroras' status in "Complaints of Severall Indians to his Excellency reported by B. Harrison, May 2, 1699," in *CVSP*, 1:65.

54. "Letter from Alexander Spotswood to the Board of Trade of Great Britain, November 7, 1711," in *CRNC*, 1:816–17.

55. "Alexander Spotswood to the Lords Commissioners of Trade, March 9, 1713," in Spotswood, *Letters*, 2:57. See also "Alexander Spotswood to the Council of Trade, November 17, 1711," in Spotswood, *Letters*, 1:121–23.

56. Journal, April 13–15, 1716, in Edward P. Alexander, ed., *The Journal of John Fontaine* (Charlottesville: University of Virginia Press, 1972), 90–94.

57. Minutes, February 23, 1714/15, in *EJCCV*, 3:396; "Alexander Spotswood to Lords Commissioners of Trade and Plantations, February 7, 1716," in Spotswood, *Letters*, 2:197.

58. Minutes, October 15, 1711, in *EJCCV*, 3:287–88.

59. "Alexander Spotswood to the Council of Trade, November 17, 1711," in Spotswood, *Letters*, 1:121.

60. Minutes, October 15, 1711, in *EJCCV*, 3:287.

61. Byrd, *Secret Diary*, 516; "Alexander Spotswood to the Council of Trade, May 8, 1712," in Spotswood, *Letters*, 1:149.

62. "Alexander Spotswood to Lord Dartmouth, October 15, 1711," in Spotswood, *Letters*, 1:121; Minutes, August 18, 1712, in *EJCCV*, 3:320.

63. Minutes, February 1711/12, in *EJCCV*, 3:301; Minutes, April 1, 1712, in *EJCCV*, 3:302–3. Byrd, *Secret Diary*, 516; "Alexander Spotswood to the Council of Trade, May 8, 1712," in Spotswood, *Letters*, 1:149.

64. "Letter from James Moore, March 27, 1713," in *CRNC*, 2:27.

65. "Letter from Alexander Spotswood to Thomas Pollock, April 1713," in *CRNC*, 2:31; "Letter from Alexander Spotswood to Thomas Pollock, March 1713," in *CVSP*, 1:164.

66. See Minutes, June 10, 1708, in *EJCCV*, 3:185; Minutes, August 18, 1712, in *EJCCV*, 3:320–21; "Letter from Thomas Pollock to Alexander Spotswood, October 05, 1712," in *CRNC*, 1:880–81; "Letter from Thomas Pollock to [Alexander Spotswood], 1712," in *CRNC*, 1:883–84.

67. "Letter from Alexander Spotswood to Thomas Pollock, May 1713," in *CVSP*, 1:166–67; "Letter from Alexander Spotswood to Thomas Pollock, December 13, 1712," in *CRNC*, 1:890–91. Although often considered leader of the Catechna Alliance, Hancock survived only the first year of the war.

68. "Preliminary Articles, 25 November, 1712," in Thomas Pollock Papers, at NCSA. Also transcribed in appendix B of Paschal, "Tuscarora Indians." Another copy of the treaty appears in the John Devereux Papers, Land Records 1712–1872, at NCSA. Also see "Letter from Thomas Pollock to Charles Craven, February 20, 1713," in *CRNC*, 2:19.

69. "Letter from Thomas Pollock to Alexander Spotswood, October 05, 1712," in *CRNC*, 1:880–84.

70. Quotation from "Letter from Thomas Pollock to [Alexander Spotswood], December 23, 1712," in *CRNC*, 1:894. Blount was also angered at the captivity of his brother and cousin, who were held by Virginia.

71. "Letter from Alexander Spotswood to Thomas Pollock, April 1713," in *CRNC*, 2:32; "Letter from Alexander Spotswood to Thomas Pollock, March 1713," in *CVSP*, 1:164.

72. "Letter from Thomas Pollock to Alexander Spotswood, April 25, 1713," in *CRNC*, 2:38.

73. "Letter from Thomas Pollock to Alexander Spotswood, April 2, 1713," in *CRNC*, 2:29–31.

74. "Letter from Thomas Pollock to Charles Craven, May 25, 1713," in *CRNC*, 2:46.

75. Minutes, August 12, 1713, in *EJCCV*, 3:347; "Letter from Thomas Pollock to Alexander Spotswood, December 28, 1712," in *CRNC*, 1:896; "Minutes of the Virginia Governor's Council, August 12, 1713," in *CRNC*, 2:57; "Letter from Thomas Pollock to Alexander Spotswood, November 16, 1713," in *CRNC*, 2:73–75; "Letter from Alexander Spotswood to Thomas Pollock, December 1713," in *CVSP*, 1:172.

76. Minutes, February 1714/15, in *EJCCV*, 3:395–97; Minutes, April 25, 1715, in *EJCCV*, 3:397.

77. In particular see Pollock's description of preliminary agreements. There was talk of seeking punishment for several Tuscaroras who subjected themselves to Blount, but it is unclear to what extent this was acted on. Colonial leaders were wary of weakening Blount's position. "Letter from Thomas Pollock to Alexander Spotswood, April 25, 1713," in *CRNC*, 2:38; "Alexander Spotswood to Thomas Pollock, May 1713," in *CVSP*, 1:166–67.

78. "Minutes of the North Carolina Governor's Council, July 31, 1724," in *CRNC*, 2:534. Tuscaroras also expected captives to be the chief reward for patrolling the frontiers against Indians. "Letter from Thomas Pollock to Charles Eden, May 03, 1718," in *CRNC*, 2:304–5.

79. "Minutes of the North Carolina Governor's Council, June 04, 1717–June 05, 1717," in *CRNC*, 2:283. The location of Ucouhnerunt, labeled "K. Blount's Town," and the site where his people later relocated, labeled "Remnant of the Tuskeroroos settled here," are depicted on map 28.

80. "Acts of the North Carolina General Assembly, November 17, 1715–January 19, 1716," in *CRNC*, 23:87–88.

81. Quotation from Arrest Warrant for Christopher Dudly, March 13, 1722, box 192, Colonial Court Records, Miscellaneous Papers, 1677–1775, at NCSA.

82. "Minutes of the North Carolina Governor's Council, June 14, 1722," in *CRNC*, 2:458.

83. Quotation from Deposition of Richard Nixon, box 192, Colonial Court Records, Miscellaneous Papers, 1677–1775, at NCSA. Also see Arrest Warrant for Christopher Dudly, March 13, 1722, box 192, Colonial Court Records, Miscellaneous Papers, 1677–1775, at NCSA. Several other depositions and subpoenas related to this case are in the same collection. It is interesting that settlers were willing to testify on behalf of the wounded Tuscarora against their white neighbor and may have even intervened during the scuffle.

84. "Minutes of the North Carolina Governor's Council, August 8, 1722," in *CRNC*, 2:459. See "Examination of John Cope Christian Indian belonging to King Blount's Town," "Deposition of Thomas Pollock," "Deposition of Cullon Pollock," and "Jury's Verdict," in box 192, Colonial Court Records, Miscellaneous Papers, 1677–1775, at NCSA.

85. "Minutes of the North Carolina Governor's Council, May 28, 1725–May 29, 1725," in *CRNC*, 2:565.

86. "Minutes of the North Carolina Governor's Council, March 01, 1735–March 23, 1735," in *CRNC*, 4:45; "Minutes of the Upper House of the North Carolina General Assembly, September 21, 1736–October 12, 1736," in *CRNC*, 4:237–39.

The settlers blamed the Tuscaroras' behavior explicitly on the governor's apparent support for the Indians.

87. The fear that militarily powerful Iroquois might aid the Tuscaroras gave such considerations greater force.

88. "Letter from Giles Rainsford to John Chamberlain, July 18, 1713," in *CRNC*, 2:54, "Letter from Thomas Pollock to Hart, September 1, 1713," in *CRNC*, 2:62.

89. "Minutes of the North Carolina Governor's Council, June 25, 1713," in *CRNC*, 2:52.

90. "Letter from Thomas Pollock to Alexander Spotswood, November 16, 1713," in *CRNC*, 2:74.

91. See, for example, "Minutes of the North Carolina Governor's Council, April 4, 1727," in *CVSP*, 1:210–11; "Minutes of the North Carolina Governor's Council, August 02, 1723–August 03, 1723," in *CRNC*, 2:496; "Minutes of the North Carolina Governor's Council, August 03, 1725–August 24, 1725," in *CRNC*, 2:570–73.

92. "Alexander Spotswood to the Lords Commissioners of Trade, November 16, 1713," in Spotswood, *Letters*, 2:42; Alexander Spotswood [?], "Examination of Indians, 1713 [?]," *VMHB* 19, no. 3 (July 1911): 273; "Memorandum, December 19, 1713," in *CVSP*, 1:173; "Spotswood's Treaty with Tuscaroras," in Robinson, *Virginia Treaties*, 212.

93. Spotswood [?], "Examination of Indians," 273–74; Minutes, January 27, 1713/14, in *EJCCV*, 3:363–64; Minutes, February 26, 1713/14, in *EJCCV*, 3:365; Minutes, February 27, 1713/14, in *EJCCV*, 3:365–67.

94. Minutes, February 26, 1713/14, in *EJCCV*, 3:365; "Spotswood's Treaty with Tuscaroras," in Robinson, *Virginia Treaties*, 211–16. See also "Treaty between Virginia and Tuscarora Nation, February 27, 1713," in Fulham Palace Papers Relating to the American Colonies (microfilm), reel 4, vol. 11.

War, Masculinity, and Alliances on the Carolina Frontiers

MICHELLE LEMASTER

In August 1702 Governor James Moore of South Carolina led an expedition of about five hundred white men and 370 Indians in fourteen boats south from Charles Town to attack St. Augustine, Florida. Moore sent his deputy governor, Robert Daniel, with a small party of settlers and a much larger contingent of Indians to raid coastal mission villages. Meanwhile a smaller group of Yamasee, accompanied by the Scottish trader (and later agent) Thomas Nairne, attacked the Timucua along the St. Johns River. Although Moore's army succeeded in destroying the town of St. Augustine itself and did substantial damage to surrounding Indian settlements, it failed to take the fortified Castillo de San Marcos. The arrival of a Spanish fleet from Havana forced Moore to burn several of his own boats and retreat to Charles Town. The English considered the invasion a failure because it did not completely rout the Spanish, and Moore lost his position of governor as a result. Moore and his Indian allies had, however, decimated the area surrounding the Spanish fort and taken numerous captives, which the natives deemed a tremendous success.[1]

Less than two years later, Moore led a second force of about fifty white men and more than a thousand Indians (largely Ochese) against the province of Apalachee. His allies raided mission villages, taking many captives and destroying churches and homes. Many more Apalachee chose to join Moore's force, resettling along the Carolina frontier. The invasion shattered the Florida missions, and the Spanish in the region never really recovered from the losses inflicted. The cost to Spain's Indian allies was even higher. The power of the Apalachee was broken, and remnants would be absorbed by other surrounding groups.[2]

The tactics Moore employed against the Spanish and especially against their Indian allies were nothing new in the colonial southeast, although his invasion force was unprecedented in size. Over the previous three decades, the English in the Carolinas had developed a military system that relied on both white recruits and Indian allies for both defensive and offensive operations. Still relatively few in number, the English depended on native warriors to protect their settlements, man defensive outposts, provide intelligence, and when necessary defeat troublesome native neighbors or erstwhile former allies. More dangerous, perhaps, English traders had long accompanied Indian raiding parties when they attacked enemy villages in order to take captives for the slave trade. In short, over the years Englishmen and native warriors had created a series of practices that facilitated joint military expeditions and on which Moore was able to draw for his two invasions.

Moore's expeditions are now familiar to most students of the colonial southeast. An explosion of scholarship (some by contributors to this volume) in the last few years on Anglo-Indian relations in the southeast during the first few decades of English settlement has greatly expanded our knowledge of this long-neglected era. This work has helped us to understand the international implications of Anglo-Indian alliances, especially relating to the slave trade. It explains why Indians sought English friendship in spite of the threats it often posed. The desire for guns and other trade goods, a need for assistance against long-standing enemies, and internal political wrangling all shaped how Indian peoples pursued interactions with Europeans (French, Spanish, and English alike). Indian choices shaped the fates of empires and reconfigured the geopolitical landscape of the region.[3] Further, military histories in other regions have investigated the significance of Indian warfare for the development of Anglo-American military tactics.[4] Little attention has yet been paid, though, to the impact of joint military ventures on the formation and maintenance of alliances in colonial America. Although scholars acknowledge English reliance on native allies, most discussions of military culture focus either on tactics or on negative English evaluations of native practices, especially those derived from outraged statements regarding "atrocities" committed by native enemies. Yet the English went to war together with Indian allies as often as they fought against Indian enemies. English soldiers and native warriors, for all their differences, learned to work together toward a common goal, building relationships of mutual reliance that grew out of the necessity of trusting one another for their very lives. Fighting together promoted a kind of masculine comradery and personal friendships that served to strengthen alliances. Although misunderstandings could and did arise and each might blame the other for wartime failures, the experience of fighting alongside one another created bonds that cannot and should not be overlooked. Furthermore joint military ventures led to the exchange of both tactics and values regarding warfare. It would be going too far to say that the English and southeastern Indians developed a shared martial culture, but the martial cultures of each increasingly overlapped and were influenced by encounters with the other.

Military collaboration served to create relationships, not necessarily between "nations" but rather between individual men, in a way that scholars have yet to fully recognize. When talking about personal ties that were the keys to creating cross-cultural alliances, the focus has largely been on male-female relationships, particularly those forged through intermarriage. Such ties were of course indispensable, largely because native peoples recognized only two categories of people: kin and enemies. Intermarriage turned strangers into family and allowed native societies to integrate newcomers.[5] Less well known is the significance of male-male friendships, particularly those produced when men joined together on the field of battle, for solidifying diplomatic relationships. Men trusted and esteemed other men whose mettle they had tested and who had proven that they were willing to put their lives on the line for their friends. Military collaboration, in turn, was facilitated by some surprising commonalities in notions of masculinity and martial honor. Both the English and southeastern Indians had developed gendered ideals that associated manhood with warfare. Each had institutionalized methods of recognizing martial prowess and courage under fire, and each linked military success to both personal and national (or at least communal) prestige. Each expected that alliances would be not only economic but military in nature and hoped to be able to count on the wartime support of their "friends" when facing enemy opposition. Joint military ventures allowed each side the opportunity to demonstrate their martial abilities, manhood, and character to the other (although conversely failure in such expeditions threatened to prove weakness and undermine respect). For both, convincing their allies of their power increased their own value as a "friend," while the right kind of military assistance created obligations that helped to cement relationships.

From the very beginning, Anglo-Indian military collaboration was crucial to the establishment of the Carolina colonies. The southern settlements, which were much closer to the Spanish and to larger, more powerful Indian nations, were particularly vulnerable. The area around Albemarle Sound that would form the core of North Carolina had fewer concerns about defense and therefore relied on native people less. For South Carolina, however, issues of defense were paramount.[6] Shortly after founding an outpost along the Ashley River, settlers noted the arrival of a contingent of Spanish-allied Indians, followed by three Spanish ships. The English first received word of the attack "from the Indians y^t are our friends." Desiring to know if and where the Spanish had come ashore, the English "sent out a p'ty of our Indians with two of our people to discouer their Camp." They found only Indians, who promptly retreated "as ur Indians informe us at the noise of our great Gunns."[7] Settler William Owen later noted that if necessary, they could count on additional Indian support. "I am persuaded y^t in 10 dayes time we might haue muster'd neere 100 bowemen they seemed verie zelous in our behalfe." Owen only trusted his new allies so far, however, noting that "we onlye made us of them as scouts wch they would performe with care, and as we did not depend vpon their courage."[8] Indian support was probably more important than Owen was willing to admit, however, because, as Governor West later noted, "wee cannot yet make in the Collony 150 men, y^t are fit to beare Armes."[9]

The English would continue to depend on the assistance of native allies for exactly that reason. The early settlements along the Carolina coast were very weak, and settlers few in number and often suffering the effects of seasoning. In the early years, they were also short of provisions and forced to depend on the Indians for their supply of food as well.[10] Although the settlers quickly organized themselves militarily, constructing fortifications and forming militia companies to facilitate training, they were aware that such methods would not be enough.[11] Facing a war with the aggressive Westo in 1673, the council voted to send several leading settlers to raise Indian support, noting that "the present warr of the Westoes will be most effectually accomplished by the assistants of the Esaugh Indians who are well accquainted with the Westoe habitacons, and have promised all the helpe they can afford."[12] When war broke out against the Westo again in 1679–80, the proprietors did not hesitate to recommend that if the Westo refused to make peace, the governor should "send to the Cofitaciquis, Esaus, and all other nations and unite with them."[13] The reliance on Indian allies to manage Carolinians' wars became regularized over the first decade or so of settlement, and thereafter officials immediately sent emissaries to neighboring tribes at the first rumor of alarm in order to secure their support.[14]

By the first decade of the eighteenth century, if not before, English settlers also began to draft plans to staff regular defensive posts with Indians, as well as to hire Indian warriors to serve as scouts. In 1701 the Commons House voted to fund a "Look out on ye north Poynt of ye Savana River [to] be mannaged by 2 white men & Six Indjans, to Cary ye allarum To Capt Nearnes, who is to allaram all the Adjacent inhabitants."[15] Six years later, in the wake of a Spanish invasion (made in retaliation for Moore's earlier raids), the Commons created a more elaborate system of "watches" placed at various strategic locations "to alarm the province." Each watch was to be staffed by a white man and a varying number of Indians and was to answer to a leading colonist. In some cases the Commons specified the tribes from whom they expected to derive the watchmen, while in others it seems any willing warrior would do. For the outpost on "Ottoe Island," for example, the Commons recommended calling up "any Indians living on the North side of Combahee River," but if this failed the commander was "to hire a St Helena Indian by the year." For the outpost on "Notche Island," the assembly suggested employing "five Indans Yamasees" to serve as "a scout watch."[16] For the most part (with the exception of the Yamasee), the Commons expected that they would hire native men from neighboring "settlement Indian" tribes. Settlement Indians were generally small, relatively weak groups that lived near (or surrounded by) English plantations. They often performed hired labor for the English, hunting or fishing for pay or performing agricultural work.[17] Military service, therefore, was simply an additional form of wage labor. The hiring of Indians to serve at lookout posts or as scouts, however, demonstrates the extent to which Indian allies had become an institutionalized part of Carolina's regular defensive plans. Further, no one voiced any opposition to these plans, indicating that this kind of reliance on neighboring Indians was relatively uncontroversial, if not expected.

Over time a set of mutually accepted practices for joint military engagements developed. Ordinarily the English supplied native allies with firearms and ammunition, while warriors were expected to provide their own food and other supplies. Although Indians allied to the English also procured weapons through the trade (and the arms trade appears to have been a primary motivator leading Indians to form alliances with the English), the legislature voted to supply guns, powder, and shot for military expeditions in exchange for the Indians' service. As early as 1687, Captain William Dunlop began to follow this kind of policy. He gathered a force of thirty-seven Englishmen, sixty Yamasee, and three Wimbee to attack the Florida frontier. Nearing a Spanish outpost at "Amaira," he "drew up all the Indians armed 10 of them w^t. Guns . . . powder & shott . . . the rest of them were armed w^t. swords, some pistols & Bowes."[18] The promise of guns and ammunition was an attractive incentive for native warriors, as was the opportunity to gain martial honors and take captives.

Beyond providing arms, however, the English were shamefully stingy, rarely supplying wages or other goods. In the case of the 1707 plan for "watches," the assembly agreed to pay wages for the white men to be staffing the outposts, but not for the Indians. An estimate of annual expenses for the watches set aside £20 for each of seven white men, funds for powder and bullets, and extra money for start-up expenses including the supplying of boats, materials for building beacons, and the like. Only the Cusabo Indians were to receive provisions while on the watch, the presumption seeming to be that the other Indians would supply their own by hunting.[19] For the Commons the fact that Indian warriors could be enlisted with far less expense than white planters made them particularly attractive as a part of Carolina's defensive scheme. When larger forces were raised for short-term offensive engagements, the system was much the same, except that allies were lured with promises that they could keep any plunder or captives that they might take during the expedition. In some cases, as in Moore's two expeditions, the promises remained unspecified and warriors probably dealt privately with traders to set the price for such captives. In others, government officials might try to quantify how much compensation Indians could expect. For example, the Virginia Council, hoping to motivate those Tuscarora that remained neutral during the Tuscarora War in North Carolina in 1711 to join on the English side, offered "a reward of six blankets for the head of each man of the said Indians killed by the Tuscaruros, and the usual price of slaves for each woman and Child delivered captives."[20] A policy of rewarding captive taking and plundering could be problematic, though. Colonel John Barnwell of South Carolina led an expedition of thirty white men and nearly five hundred Indians against the Tuscarora. They succeeded in taking the fort at the Tuscarora town of Narhantes. After this battle, however, Barnwell accused his Indian allies of "loading themselves with English plunder of which these Towns are full, and running away from me, nothing left for the white men but their horses tired & their wounds to comfort them."[21] It isn't clear whether Barnwell objected more to the Indians' "desertion" before he had completed his campaign against the Tuscarora, or to their taking all the good loot. The disappearance of Barnwell's allies, however, seems to indicate the flaw in the system. While wages might have motivated warriors to remain with the expedition, plunder was often quickly acquired, leaving Indian men few reasons to continue risking their lives. Barnwell, finding his forces reduced, had no choice but to make peace with the Tuscarora.

A second South Carolina expedition against the Tuscarora a few months later revealed another problem with Carolina policy. Colonel James Moore Jr. (the son of the former Governor Moore) led a second force of allied Indians north in late 1712. Because neither the North nor South Carolina governments supplied provisions for the expedition, the Indians were forced to forage for themselves. Settlers complained that the warriors had committed "such ravages among the stocks of y'r People, where they were quarter'd" that it had "more exasperated the Inhabitants ag't these Auxiliarys than against the Tuscaroros, their Enemys."[22] While this method had not inconvenienced the elder Moore, who raided in hostile territory, fighting a war on one's own turf on such terms was clearly less advantageous. For all the settlers' complaints, however, the benefits of employing native allies far outweighed the costs. North Carolina, as weak and conflict-ridden as it was, was utterly unable to defend itself and desperately needed Indian assistance. North Carolina representative Christopher Gale told the South Carolina government that his colony was unable to mount a counterattack, the population having withdrawn into defensive garrisons and showing a decided reluctance to venture out. Furthermore, he added, it was "impracticable to attempt such a body of men, flushed with their first success, without Indians who are acquainted with their manner of fighting." Indian manpower and expertise was indispensable in this situation. Carolinian need for Indian auxiliaries was so strong that even in those cases in which settlers grew frustrated with Indian behavior, they did not dare complain too strenuously. Governor Craven of South Carolina questioned the Sewee, Winiaw, and Saxapahaws about why they had left Barnwell before he had defeated the Tuscarora, but although he found their answer very "dark," he resolved nevertheless to "give them all proper encouragement," requesting that the Commons pay them appropriately for the scalps they had brought in.[23]

In addition to standardized methods of recruiting and compensating Indian warriors, the English also developed plans for organizing joint expeditions. At least in theory, each fighting force was to have an English commander. Thomas Nairne confidently asserted that "*English* Officers are appointed over the *Indians* with whom we are in Friendship."[24] In an expedition like Barnwell's, provincial or militia officers might serve this function.[25] At other times the government expected that traders who accompanied raiding parties would be the "leaders." In 1707, hoping to raise a force to attack the French outpost at Mobile, the South Carolina Commons agreed to enlist the Creek Indians, "to be Encouraged & Lead on by what Indian Traders will be willing thereto."[26] Such structuring reflected English ideas that their Indian allies had agreed to be the king's subjects when they created alliances with the colonists. John Lawson claimed that the Carolinians were "absolute Masters over the Indians, and carry strict a Hand over such as are within the Circle of their Trade."[27] In reality, though, the selection of English "commanders" reflected little more than wishful thinking. Officers had little ability to control the behavior of warriors, who pursued their own agendas and paid little heed to outside direction. When the Spanish complained that Moore Sr.'s native allies tortured mission Indians during his 1704 raid into Apalachee, he was forced to admit that "he could not prevent it."[28] The son had little more success in controlling his allies. When Yamasee warriors stole livestock from North Carolina settlers, even "Colo. Moore's presence and authority Could not restrain them."[29]

The English also quickly discovered that Indian allies performed best when allowed to pursue their own tactics. Grossly outnumbered by the warriors during his raid of Apalachee, Moore Sr. had little choice but to allow the natives to design their own attacks. The outcome, by both English and Indian standards, could be deemed a success, as the warriors took large numbers of captives and devastated Apalachee settlements. When the English tried to force Indians to conform to English methods of waging war, however, the results were generally unsuccessful. In some cases Indians simply refused to comply with English orders. In 1687 William Dunlop tried to enlist a party of Yamasee to set up beacons along the coast. He found them willing to accompany him on raids against the Spanish, "but no[t] so forward for the Beacons."[30] At other times warriors might go along with English plans, but reluctantly or with limited success. Barnwell made plans to lay siege to Fort Narhantes but found that his Yamasee allies had other ideas. While Barnwell thought that he had plans to "do the same orderly," the Yamasee "were so mettlesome as to advise to force it by Assault." The long delay that Barnwell planned probably was less than popular among warriors, who wished to take captives and return home. Barnwell agreed but soon found that although the Yamasee were quick to rush in, "they soon began to cool," leaving the burden on the white troops.[31] Barnwell later concluded that "Indians will never of themselves attempt the taking of any fort, without they be led by a considerable number of White men."[32] Moore Jr. concurred, noting that he was hampered in his efforts, "his indians not being very ready in attacking Forts wthout Englifh."[33]

The English often complained about their frustrations in dealing with Indian warriors and regularly maligned Indian tactics. Such kvetching, however, disguises the cultural similarities that allowed colonists and natives to work together over and over again. The military orientation of each culture, the association of warfare with masculinity, and notions of honor all provided a set of overlapping assumptions and institutions that facilitated wartime collaboration.[34] English delusions that they could command allied Indians to fight for them also mask the very important role that joint warfare played, at least as far as natives were concerned, in constructing and maintaining diplomatic relationships on the southern frontier. For Indians personal relationships played a pivotal role in diplomacy, and the ties that villages could form with traders (in a variety of ways) and with leading colonists during the dangerous exigencies of warfare were at times almost as important as the trade itself in shaping decisions regarding alliances. Joint warfare also provided a venue in which men could assert their masculinity in front of other men. Alliances often could hinge on assessments of the martial ability of one's potential allies; no one wanted to conclude a treaty with a weaker partner when a stronger was available.

Both the English in the Carolinas and southeastern Indians came from military societies. Warfare was a regular occurrence on both sides of the Atlantic, and military organization was institutionalized. Each had an established military hierarchy and awarded titles to deserving men. Each recognized outstanding performance and valued courage under fire and other displays of personal valor.[35] England during Carolina's proprietary period fought two major wars in Europe (the War of the League of Augsburg and the War of the Spanish Succession) and employed a variety of regular fighting forces, ranging from cavalry to navy, as well as irregular militia troops. Regular forces were gradually coming to replace militia by the late seventeenth century, but both continued to play a significant role. Military forces were hierarchically organized and officers were generally appointed out of the nobility. Those who wished to rise through the ranks needed to purchase commissions in order to gain military titles.[36] In the colonies standing armies were generally lacking, and militia played a much more important part. Although the colonies generally lacked a nobility, militia officers were usually drawn from among leading colonists, and colonial governments were able to use military titles as a form of patronage. In a frontier society, military success could provide an avenue of advancement (although failure could have detrimental effects for a man's political ambitions, as Moore Sr. learned the hard way).[37]

Because of the precarious frontier status of the Carolina colonies, the military orientation of Carolina settlements far exceeded anything found in the mother country. From the beginning proprietors and settlers alike expected that their settlements would be managed as military ventures, and the settlers began building forts and training the militia as soon as they arrived.[38] Early governors like Nathaniel Johnson and James Moore also served as military leaders. Military service was widespread, with most men taking part in the colony's defensive forces. In 1710 Thomas Nairne reported that:

> For Defence of the Colony, our Laws oblige every Male Person from 16 to 60 Years of Age, to bear Arms. . . . It is not here as in *England*, where an ordinary Mechanic thinks himself too good to be a Soldier. Every one among us is versed in Arms, from the Governour to the

meanest Servant, and are all so far from thinking it below them, that most People take Delight in military Affairs, and think no body so fit to defend their Properties as themselves.[39]

The Carolinas fought frequent wars against both the Indians and Spanish and French during the proprietary period, further spurring the exaggerated emphasis on the military that characterized the era.

In Indian society military service was even more widespread and war a more important factor in shaping social organization. Most men were expected to take part in warlike endeavors. Although referring to a group living to the west of the Carolinas, the observations of an anonymous French traveler among the Choctaws seem to reflect general southeastern values. The Choctaw clearly distinguished between what they called "tasca" (warriors) and "atac emittla" (those who had not yet "struck blows or who have killed only a woman or a child.") The latter group, he reported, made up the lowest order of men in the nation.[40] In contrast to the English, southeastern Indians awarded war names and titles to those who had demonstrated the greatest ability.[41] Thomas Nairne noted that among the Chickasaw, the military leaders "arrived to this Honor by the greatness of their Actions, and the respect which all the soldiery bear to them."[42] It is not clear how much the Indians understood about English methods of determining military leadership, nor whether they doubted the command abilities of officers who had purchased their commissions. Although they do not seem to have recognized English officers' authority over them in the ways that the English might have liked, they do appear to have respected individual commanders. Military success (reckoned according to native rather than English values) could help an English officer like James Moore Sr. to gain support for future ventures as well as considerable diplomatic clout. Although the English may have considered Moore's 1702 expedition a failure, his Indian allies did not, and he had little difficulty enlisting a large force for his 1704 expedition into Apalachee.

Colonization also increased the importance of warfare for native men. The breakdown of larger chiefdoms into smaller communities during the protohistoric period meant that there were fewer avenues to advancement for men outside of military service. As hereditary chiefs lost influence, particularly as commoners gained access to prestige goods through European trade, warfare came to play a larger role in determining male status.[43] The rise and expansion of the English slave trade from roughly 1660 to about 1720 led to a significant increase in conflict in the region, with devastating results for most tribes. Robbie Ethridge has referred to the southeast in this era as a "shatter zone," destabilized by the collapse of Mississippian-era chiefdoms, disease, and the introduction of capitalism (especially the slave trade). The result, she writes, was the emergence of "militaristic Native slaving societies."[44] The slave trade led to an exaggeration in the military orientation of Indian societies that coincided with that observed among the English.

Both the English and Indians also associated military activity closely with manhood. (Although occasional exceptions certainly can be found, for the most part women did not actively participate in warfare.)[45] Consequently, military prowess was an integral part of masculine identity, both in the colonies and in southeastern Indian society. In fact, because of the unusual expansion in warfare produced by the slave trade and the imperial rivalry between European nations in the region, participation in warfare took on a greatly expanded importance for both English and native notions of manhood. All the societies of the southeast, European and Indian alike, had well-established standards for military behavior that recognized success and penalized failure, while defining what tactics were deemed honorable and manly. As noted above, both had recognized military hierarchies in which leadership was almost exclusively male, creating parallel systems of masculine hierarchies that then had to work together during joint engagements. Both sides also engaged in a well-established language of insult that stigmatized men who were deemed to have failed militarily or to have not displayed sufficient courage. Such insults, which most often denigrated such men by likening them to women, highlight the importance of military success to masculine identity and status.[46] Although the various behaviors and outcomes that qualified as manly and honorable might differ from society to society, the parallel structures of evaluating manhood based on military accomplishment facilitated relationships between English and native war leaders and created a military framework that at least appeared familiar to both sides.

The exaggerated military masculinity that developed on the southern frontier had devastating consequences for native societies (and less often for English societies). The military culture of the southeast during the proprietary period was particularly aggressive, with warfare waged not to meet defensive ends or to maintain a balance of power, but to enslave and destroy. Alan Gallay has estimated that somewhere between thirty thousand and fifty thousand people were enslaved in the Lower South during the years of the Indian slave trade.[47] How many people were killed in the process isn't entirely clear, but the numbers were probably equally appalling. The slave trade and the endemic warfare it produced, combined with the devastation of disease, produced a radical reorganization of the surviving populations of the southern interior. Many groups ceased to exist as separate nations, while new nations arose out of remnants of older communities.[48] The trauma experienced by survivors of the slave trade is only beginning to be understood by scholars, and academic studies can never fully recapture the range of human suffering that accompanied the upheaval of those years. This devastation was in part the product of masculine military cultures run amok. Such a situation could not be sustained indefinitely, and it produced its own destruction when it erupted into the Tuscarora and Yamasee Wars. While it survived, though, the exaggerated military ethos of the southeast yielded an avenue of intercultural interaction and cooperation.

Because of the strong emphasis on military accomplishment and strength in both societies, the warlike abilities of both individuals and communities had a significant influence on diplomatic relations in the colonial southeast. Certainly English ability and willingness to supply trade goods at reasonable prices (especially guns and ammunition) was the primary motivator leading native groups to seek out an English alliance. There was more to it than this, however. As Thomas Nairne noted, "nothing but a much better trade *and the reputation of far greater Courage then the French* could have kept this Tribe [the Chickasaw] in any tolerable subjection."[49] Although the English were weak enough to need Indian military support and relied on native warriors for their own defense, they still demonstrated greater strength than either the Spanish or the French. In the early years, many tribes sought out the English in hopes that the new colonists would be able to assist them against aggressive enemies. Nicholas Carteret reported that several Indian nations he met welcomed the newcomers because "they hoped by our Arrivall to be protected from ye Westoes."[50] How useful this tactic was, however, is questionable. The proprietors later faulted South Carolinians for failing to protect neighboring Indians "from being injured by the Westoes," whereas defending these allies "would have made them love as well as feare you."[51] The English could be powerful friends or dangerous enemies, a factor that seems to have had at least some influence on how native groups made decisions regarding which alliances to pursue.

While the military might of an ally was an important consideration in deciding to establish friendly relations, going to war together created personal ties between English commanders, traders, and soldiers on the one hand, and Indian war leaders and warriors on the other. An incident that occurred a few years after the collapse of the proprietorship demonstrates the important role that native people believed joint military action played in maintaining alliances. In February 1727 Carolina commissioner of Indian affairs Colonel John Herbert sought to convince the Cherokee of the town of Great Tellico to help avenge several "murders" the Creek (the Cherokees' traditional enemies) had committed against Englishmen. Headman Choateehee agreed to send some warriors but then asked Herbert to accompany him. Choateehee told Herbert that "he was never at Warr with me & that he wanted me to go to Warr with him." Herbert refused but offered as an excuse: "I should be glad to go with him but that I would not go without Orders from the Govern[r] about it." Disgusted, Choateehee replied that "he beleiv'd the English were afraid of the Creeks."[52] Choateehee's request demonstrates how important the personal ties created when men fought together were for Indian diplomacy. The chief wanted to have the opportunity to observe Herbert in action, to judge whether he was a good warrior and therefore a trustworthy ally. He may also have resented the fact that the English were willing to pressure the Cherokee to go to war against the Creek but were unwilling to risk their own lives in the venture. When Herbert refused to go with him, he concluded that both Herbert and the people he represented were cowards.

In contrast English officers (or traders) who met Indian expectations for military courage and success gained native respect. Individual English or Scottish men could achieve a degree of personal influence that they could then use to advance their own (and sometimes the colony's) interests in native villages. The Moores (father and son) had a long history in the Indian trade. Although Moore Sr.'s aggressive pursuit of profit (especially in the form of slaves) was known and recognized by his native allies, they also appear to have respected his military successes in Florida, and many warriors had gained both war honors and captives as a part of those earlier invasions. Moore Jr. seems to have enjoyed a similar level of respect among many of South Carolina's allies. Traders, well known to the people among whom they lived, had the opportunity to establish deep personal ties within the nations. Their willingness to accompany warriors into battle (even if the traders were doing so for their own self-serving purposes) also helped solidify these relationships. Many years later James Adair would remember that in these early years "the traders . . . kept them [the Indians] in proper awe."[53]

For Indian nations, alliances were intensely personal, more than they were national. Ties were often to individual traders or diplomats, rather than to the English as a nation. The degree to which the Indians identified the English as a unified group is unclear. The dispersed nature of English settlements probably made them appear more like the relatively autonomous native villages than representatives of a cohesive empire.[54] The fact that traders often advanced their own interests at the expense of national ones likely proved confusing. South Carolina officials complained that the Yamasee and their allies had launched their war against the southern colony because "Virginia Traders encouraged our Indians to do what they have done and promised to supply them at a much easier rate than our Indian Traders did and that they would give them much better treatment."[55] As a result of such divisions, alliances were local rather than national in nature, making personal relationships all that much more important. Relying on personal loyalties, however, could render such diplomatic relationships precarious. Warriors might be willing to follow respected individuals into battle but were just as likely to leave if faced with a less-respected commander. Alexander Spotswood warned the Board of Trade that the allegiance of South Carolina's Indian allies was not to be relied on. Colonel Moore Jr.'s force was "made up of a great many different nations and kept together by the sole Authority of that single person." He feared that "if he [Moore] should fall or receive any considerable disadvantage in his attempt upon the Tuscaruros all these Indians would imediately disperse and leave their friends in a much worse condition than they found 'em."⁵⁶ Carolina officials recognized the importance of having leaders with experience working with the Indians when they selected leaders for joint military ventures. The South Carolina Commons objected to appointing Captain Lorey to lead a part of the second expedition against the Tuscarora. The assemblymen did not doubt Lorey's "courage or conduct" but found that he was not "acquainted with the way & manner of Indian War" and therefore concluded "a more proper officer maybe thought of for his occasion."⁵⁷ Lorey's lack of experience was a concern for two reasons. He did not know how to work with native tactics, and therefore probably could not make the best use of his allies. He also, perhaps more important, did not have the reputation among the Indians to command their respect or loyalty.

The scarcity of records that survive from the proprietary period in the Carolinas does not allow us to reconstruct the kinds of personal relationships that individuals formed when fighting side by side in these early wars. Commons House records detail plans to create lookout posts and watches staffed by white men and Indians but do not tell us what happened during the long hours that these men would have spent together. Two accounts of expeditions, by William Dunlop and John Barnwell, survive but mostly report distances traveled or the outcome of engagements. Hints of the personal ties can be found, though. When reporting his losses, for example, Barnwell mostly listed the number of allied Indians killed, but a few gained special mention. Following the attack on Narhantes Fort, the casualties included the Peterba King, the Wateree King, a King Robin, and a man named Cunaba Tom. The leaders of each war party, at least, were known to Barnwell.⁵⁸ A few days later, Barnwell reported that a Seneca ally named Tom Gils had been badly wounded and was expected to die.⁵⁹ Again Gils appears to have been personally known to Barnwell. The nature of their relationship, however, will probably never be recaptured.

Because the ties of alliance were so personal, the rupture of alliances was too. The Tuscarora War demonstrates the extent to which the repudiation of former friendships came to center on certain individuals. John Lawson, long-time trader and sometime agent, was tortured to death by the Tuscarora at the beginning of the war; the women "stuck him full of fine small splinters of torchwood like hogs' bristles, and so set them gradually on fire."⁶⁰ Enraged warriors then fell on settlements along the Neuse River. One hundred and thirty settlers of all ages and sexes were killed. Christopher Gale told the South Carolina Council that the people were "butchered after the most barbarous manner that can be expressed, and their dead bodies used with all the scorn and indignity imaginable.... And what makes it the more surprising," he added, was "that nefarious villainy was committed by such Indians as were esteemed as members of the several families where the mischiefs were done."⁶¹ Many of the dead had previously traded with their killers. The Tuscarora clearly had not chosen their victims at random but instead were sending a very strong message that the alliance had failed on a very intimate level.

Claudio Saunt has referred to European and Indian conflicts in the eighteenth century as "proxy warfare," in which "European empires exported their conflicts to other nations." He notes the contemptuous attitudes of European officials toward the native peoples that they enlisted to do their dirty work, as well as the devastating effects that the influx of guns and other goods had on native societies.[62] This description applies well to the kinds of warfare the English employed in the Carolinas during the proprietary period. In many ways English use of Indian allies to fight their wars for them was grossly exploitative. Growing native dependence on English goods, especially firearms, put pressure on native warriors to comply with English demands for allies. Debt helped to spur the slave raiding that destabilized the region (demonstrated perhaps most clearly in Moore Sr.'s Florida expeditions). However, had joint warfare only been exploitative, it wouldn't have worked. Indians sought out English allies for a number of reasons that were all their own. They desired English trade goods, support against their own enemies, war honors for young men that could be gained through the slave trade, revenge for the loss of loved ones, and a myriad of other things. The alliances they built with the English, though, were not only mechanistically designed to meet these needs. They were also intensely personal, based on intermarriage and the creation of close friendships and the ties that men created when they fought together toward a common aim. Native loyalties were always first and foremost to their own communities, of course, and villages could create complex ties with multiple outsiders. We lose something in our view of alliances, though, if we ignore the importance of the relationships created between individuals. Investigating those areas of intercultural cooperation, even in a violent arena like warfare, reminds us of those areas of cultural overlap and commonality that allowed the English and Indians to construct functioning alliances that lasted for decades. Further, English weakness and need for Indian support during these decades must not be forgotten or overlooked in favor of later developments.

In some ways, the post–Yamasee War diplomatic world of the southeast was less destructive than that which had characterized the Proprietary Period.[63] The kind of pathological warfare that had ripped apart the region declined, returning to more "normal" levels. Warfare did not cease, of course, and it continued to be shaped and driven by European imperial rivalries and native dependence on manufactured goods, but it was less devastating than it had been during the slave trade era. Military collaboration continued, but on a different level. In the years that followed the collapse of the proprietorship, the British would persist in enlisting native allies for military ventures. General Oglethorpe's 1739–40 invasion of Spanish Florida would especially rely on native warriors for a considerable part of the British manpower.[64] Even as late as Andrew Jackson's expedition against the Red Stick Creeks, Indian warriors would come to the aid of Anglo-American soldiers.[65] The level of dependence declined, however. The size of the English population grew exponentially over the years, while native peoples experienced demographic losses and increasing dependency on European goods. Furthermore as the Indian slave trade declined after the Yamasee War, the English entered a period of relative peace with their native neighbors. Although the English continued to encourage hostilities between traditional enemies like the Creek and Cherokee and a few border skirmishes might temporarily create panic in isolated regions, there were no major Anglo-Indian wars on the southern frontier for more than forty years between the end of the Yamasee War and the Cherokee War of 1759–61.[66] The importance of notions of martial masculinity for cross-cultural interaction and diplomacy did not decrease appreciably, however. British officials and native headmen continued to meet one another as leaders of military societies. They referred to one another using military titles, and they regularly discussed matters of war even during times of peace. In fact in the years after the Yamasee War, an elaborate rhetoric linking manhood and warfare developed and figured prominently in southeastern diplomacy.[67] It was somewhat less personal and more abstract than what had existed before, however. Although there are some exceptions—most notably James Oglethorpe and Andrew Jackson—few later governors or army officers created the kinds of personal ties with native warriors that the two Moores or Barnwell had experienced. Formal diplomacy, although still drawing on military imagery and ceremony, increasingly came to replace more immediate military collaboration as a way to maintain alliances. The change was gradual and incremental, rather than absolute, and military collaboration continued for another century, but the shift had begun with the Yamasee War. Nevertheless as long as the British (or later Americans) needed native military support, the military would be a venue for the construction of personal bonds. Although not always healthy or constructive, military friendships were crucial to the maintenance of alliances.

Notes

1. For primary accounts of the St. Augustine expedition, see John Ash, "The Present State of Affairs in Carolina, by John Ash, 1706," in Salley, *Narratives,* 269–76, esp. 272–73; John Oldmixon, "From the History of the British Empire, by John Oldmixon, 1708," in Salley, *Narratives,* 317–73, esp. 341–44; Mark F. Boyd, "The Siege of Saint Augustine by Governor Moore of South Carolina in 1702 as Reported to the King of Spain by Don Joseph De Zuniga Y Zerda, Governor of Florida," *Florida Historical Quarterly* 26, no. 4 (April 1948): 345–52. The Commons House minutes from 1702–3 make numerous mentions of the St. Augustine expedition (although they are disappointingly vague). See Minutes, August 20 through September 10, 1702, in *JCHA 1702,* 64–102; Minutes, January 15–September 17, 1703, in *JCHA 1703,* 6–128. For secondary accounts, see Charles W. Arnade, *The Siege of St. Augustine in 1702* (Gainesville: University of Florida Press, 1959); Verner Crane, *The Southern Frontier, 1670–1732* (1929; reprint, Tuscaloosa: University of

Alabama Press, 2004), 75–77; Alan Gallay, *The Indian Slave Trade: The Rise of the English Empire in the American South, 1670–1717* (New Haven: Yale University Press, 2002), 135–37; John H. Hann, *A History of the Timucua Indians and Missions* (Gainesville: University of Florida Press, 1996), 293–95; Steven Oatis, *A Colonial Complex: South Carolina's Frontiers in the Era of the Yamasee War, 1680–1730* (Lincoln: University of Nebraska Press, 2004), 47–50.

2. Mark F. Boyd, Hale G. Smith, and John W. Griffin, *Here They Once Stood: The Tragic End of the Apalachee Missions* (Gainesville: University of Florida Press, 1951); Boyd, "Further Considerations of the Apalachee Missions," *The Americas* 9, no. 4 (April 1953): 459–80; Minutes, September 15 and 16, 1703, in *JCHA 1703*, 121, 125–26. See also Crane, *Southern Frontier*, 79–81; Steven C. Hahn, *The Invention of the Creek Nation, 1670–1763* (Lincoln: University of Nebraska Press, 2004), 63–65; John H. Hann, *Apalachee: The Land between the Rivers* (Gainesville: University Press of Florida, 1988), 264–83; Gallay, *Indian Slave Trade*, 144–49; Oatis, *Colonial Complex*, 50–51.

3. Eric E. Bowne, *The Westo Indians: Slave Traders of the Early Colonial South* (Tuscaloosa: University of Alabama Press, 2005); Robbie Ethridge and Sheri M. Shuck-Hall, eds., *Mapping the Mississippian Shatter Zone: Colonial Indian Slave Trade and Regional Instability in the American South* (Lincoln: University of Nebraska Press, 2010); Gallay, *Indian Slave Trade*, and *Indian Slavery in Colonial America* (Lincoln: University of Nebraska Press, 2010); Steven C. Hahn, *The Invention of the Creek Nation, 1670–1763* (Lincoln: University of Nebraska Press, 2004); Joseph M. Hall Jr., *Zamumo's Gifts: Indian-European Exchange in the Colonial Southeast* (Philadelphia: University of Pennsylvania Press, 2009); Oatis, *Colonial Complex*; William L. Ramsey, *The Yamasee War: A Study of Culture, Economy, and Conflict in the Colonial South* (Lincoln: University of Nebraska Press, 2008).

4. John Ferling, *A Wilderness of Miseries: War and Warriors in Early America* (Westport, Conn.: Greenwood Press, 1980), esp. 60–61; John Grenier, *The First Way of War: American War Making on the Frontier, 1607–1814* (New York: Cambridge University Press, 2005); Wayne E. Lee, "The Military Revolution of Native North America: Firearms, Forts, and Polities," in *Empires and Indigenes: Intercultural Alliance, Imperial Expansion, and Warfare in the Early Modern World*, ed. Wayne E. Lee (New York: New York University Press, 2011), 49–80; Patrick Malone, *The Skulking Way of War: Technology and Tactics in New England Indian Warfare* (Baltimore: Johns Hopkins University Press, 1993); Peter Way, "The Cutting Edge of Culture: British Soldiers Encounter Native Americans in the French and Indian War," in *Empire and Others: British Encounters with Indigenous Peoples, 1600–1850*, ed. Martin Daunton and Rick Halpern (Philadelphia: University of Pennsylvania Press, 1999), 123–48.

5. The scholarship on intermarriage is extensive, and I am citing only a few examples here. See Kathryn E. Holland Braund, *Deerskins and Duffels: The Creek Indian Trade with Anglo-America, 1685–1815* (Lincoln: University of Nebraska Press, 1993); Kirsten Fischer, *Suspect Relations: Sex, Race, and Resistance in Colonial North Carolina* (Ithaca: Cornell University Press, 2002); Andrew K. Frank, *Creeks and Southerners: Biculturalism on the Early American Frontier* (Lincoln: University of Nebraska Press, 2005); Tom Hatley, *Dividing Paths: Cherokees and South*

Carolinians through the Era of Revolution (New York: Oxford University Press, 1995); Michelle LeMaster, *Brothers Born of One Mother: British–Native American Relations in the Colonial Southeast* (Charlottesville: University of Virginia Press, 2012), 149–84; Theda Perdue, *Cherokee Women: Gender and Culture Change, 1700–1835* (Lincoln: University of Nebraska Press, 1998), and *"Mixed-Blood" Indians: Racial Construction in the Early South* (Athens: University of Georgia Press, 2003).

6. North Carolina records do not indicate a substantial dependence on Indian allies for defense before the Tuscarora War. Therefore this portion of the essay draws on South Carolina records.

7. Council to the Proprietors, September 9, 1670, in *Shaftesbury Papers*, 178–79. See also Sir John Yeamans to the Proprietors, November 15, 1670, in *Shaftesbury Papers*, 217–20; Capt. H. Brayne to the Proprietors, November 20, 1670, in *Shaftesbury Papers*, 226–32; Memoranda (in Locke's hand), September and November 1670, in *Shaftesbury Papers*, 256–64.

8. William Owen to Lord Ashley, October 15, 1670, in *Shaftesbury Papers*, 196–202. Owen identified Carolina's allies as "Wando, Ituan, seweh and sehey."

9. Governor West to Lord Ashley, March 21, 1670/71, in *Shaftesbury Papers*, 296–300.

10. Council to the Proprietors, September 9, 1670, in *Shaftesbury Papers*, 178.

11. Council to the Proprietors, September 9, 1670, in *Shaftesbury Papers*, 178–79; and Governor West to Lord Ashley, March 21, 1670/71, in *Shaftesbury Papers*, 296–300. On South Carolina fortifications, see: Larry Ivers, *Colonial Forts of South Carolina, 1670–1775* (Columbia: University of South Carolina Press, 1970).

12. Minutes, October 7, 1673, in *JGC*, 1:64. On the Westo, see Bowne, *Westo Indians*; and "'A Bold and Warlike People: The Basis of Westo Power," in *Light on the Path: The Anthropology and History of the Southeastern Indians*, ed. Thomas J. Pluckhahn and Robbie Ethridge (Tuscaloosa: University of Alabama Press, 2006), 123–32.

13. Instructions to Andrew Percivall, February 21, 1680/81, in *BPRO-SC*, 1:106–7.

14. For example, in 1709, fearing an attack on Charles Town (presumably by the Spanish), the Commons resolved to send for three hundred Indian allies, asking them to come to the settlements to supply additional military force. Minutes, April 21, 1709, in *CHJ*, 3:415–18.

15. Minutes, August 15, 1701, in *JCHA 1701*, 6.

16. Minutes, April 11, 1707, in *CHJ*, 3:149–50. For a similar example, see Minutes, June 17, 1707, in *JCHA 1707*, 36.

17. Michelle LeMaster, "In the 'Scolding Houses': Indians and the Law in Eastern North Carolina, 1684–1760," *NCHR* 83, no. 2 (April 2006): 193–232; Daniel H. Usner Jr., *Indians, Settlers, and Slaves in a Frontier Exchange Economy: The Lower Mississippi Valley before 1783* (Chapel Hill: University of North Carolina Press, 1992); Gene Waddell, *Indians of the South Carolina Lowcountry, 1562–1751* (Columbia: University of South Carolina Press, 1980).

18. "Capt. Dunlop's Voyage to the Southward, 1687," *SCHGM* 30, no. 3 (July 1929): 127–33.

19. Minutes, April 11, 1707, in *CHJ*, 3:149–50.

20. Virginia Council Minutes, October 24, 1711, in *CRNC*, 1:815.

21. John Barnwell to [unknown], February 4, 1711/12, in "The Tuscarora Expedition: Letters of Colonel John Barnwell," *SCHGM* 9, no. 1 (January 1908): 28–54, quote from 33. On the Tuscarora War, see Stephen D. Feeley, "Tuscarora Trails: Indian Migrations, War, and Constructions of Colonial Frontiers" (Ph.D. diss., College of William and Mary, 2007); Gallay, *Indian Slave Trade*, 259–87; Oatis, *Colonial Complex*, 84–91; Thomas C. Parramore, "With Tuscarora Jack on the Back Path to Bath," *NCHR* 64, no. 2 (1987): 115–38; and the essays by Feeley and James Taylor Carson in this volume.

22. Alexander Spotswood to Carolina Proprietors, February 11, 1712/13, in *CRNC*, 2:14–16.

23. Minutes, April 9, 1712, in CHJ, 4:18–19.

24. Thomas Nairne, "A Letter from South Carolina [1710]," in *Selling a New World: Two Colonial South Carolina Promotional Pamphlets*, ed. Jack P. Greene (Columbia: University of South Carolina Press, 1989), 52.

25. Barnwell divided his force into four different companies, which he designated as Captain Steel's Troops, the Yamasee Company, Essaw Captain Jack's Company, and Captain Bull's Company. Barnwell to [unknown], February 4, 1711/12, in "Tuscarora Expedition," 30–31.

26. Minutes, November 22, 1707, in *JCHA 1707–8*, 48–49.

27. Lawson, *New Voyage*, 4.

28. Testimony of Juan de la Cruz, June 1705, in Boyd et al., *Here They Once Stood*, 74–77, quote from 76.

29. Alexander Spotswood to Carolina Proprietors, February 11, 1712/13, in *CRNC*, 2:14–16.

30. "Capt. Dunlop's Voyage," 129.

31. Barnwell to [unknown], February 4, 1711/12, in "Tuscarora Expedition," 32.

32. Minutes, August 7, 1712, in CHJ, 4:98.

33. Governor Pollock [N.C.] to [unknown], December 23, 1712, in *CRNC*, 1:892–94.

34. For a more extensive analysis of the meeting of British and native notions of masculinity in the colonial southeast, see LeMaster, *Brothers Born of One Mother*.

35. On prehistoric native warfare in the southeast, see: Patricia S. Bridges, et al., "Warfare-Related Trauma in the Late Prehistory of Alabama," in *Bioarchaeological Studies of Life in the Age of Agriculture: A View from the Southeast*, ed. Patricia Lambert (Tuscaloosa: University of Alabama Press, 1999), 35–62; David E. Jones, *Native North American Armor, Shields, and Fortifications* (Austin: University of Texas Press, 2004); Lewis H. Larson Jr., "Functional Considerations of Warfare in the Southeast during the Mississippi Period," *American Antiquity* 37 (1972): 383–92; Maria O. Smith, "Beyond Palisades: The Nature and Frequency of Late Prehistoric Deliberate Violent Trauma in the Chickamauga Reservoir of East Tennessee," *American Journal of Physical Anthropology* 121 (2003): 303–18; Karl T. Steinen, "Ambushes, Raids, and Palisades: Mississippian Warfare in the Interior Southeast," *Southeastern Archaeology* 11(1992): 132–39; Joseph O. Vogel and Jean Allen, "Mississippian Fortifications at Moundville," *Archaeology* 38, no. 5 (1985): 62–63. On Indian warfare in the protohistoric era, see David H. Dye, "Warfare in the

Sixteenth-Century Southeast: The de Soto Expedition in the Interior," in *Columbian Consequences*, vol. 2, *Archaeological and Historical Perspectives on the Spanish Borderlands*, ed. David Hurst Thomas (Washington D.C.: Smithsonian Institution Press, 1990), 211–22, and "Warfare in the Protohistoric Southeast, 1500–1700," in *Between Contacts and Colonies: Archaeological Perspectives on the Protohistoric Southeast*, ed. Cameron B. Wesson and Mark A. Rees (Tuscaloosa: University of Alabama Press, 2002), 126–41. On early modern European warfare, see Jeremy Black, *European Warfare, 1660–1815* (New Haven: Yale University Press, 1994); George Clark, *War and Society in the Seventeenth Century* (Cambridge, U.K.: Cambridge University Press, 1958); Frank Tallett, *War and Society in Early-Modern Europe, 1495–1715* (New York: Routledge, 1992), 232–45. On Anglo-American warfare during the colonial period, see John Ferling, *A Wilderness of Miseries: War and Warriors in Early America* (Westport, Conn.: Greenwood Press, 1980); John Grenier, *The First Way of War: American War Making on the Frontier, 1607–1814* (New York: Cambridge University Press, 2005).

36. Jeremy Black, *A Military Revolution? Military Change and European Society 1550–1800* (Atlantic Highlands, N.J.: Humanities Press International, 1991), 77–82; Robert A. Doughty et al., *Warfare in the Western World*, vol. 1, *Military Operations from 1600 to 1871* (Lexington, Miss.: D. C. Heath, 1996), 33; Walter Millis, *Arms and Men: A Study of American Military History* (New York: G. P. Putnam and Sons, 1956), 18.

37. On militias during the colonial period, see John Grenier, *The First Way of War: American War Making on the Frontier, 1607–1814* (New York: Cambridge University Press, 2005); Larry Ivers, *British Drums on the Southern Frontier: The Military Colonization of Georgia* (Chapel Hill: University of North Carolina Press, 1974); James M. Johnson, *Militiamen, Rangers, and Redcoats: The Military in Georgia, 1754–1776* (Macon, Ga.: Mercer University Press, 1992).

38. Council to the Proprietors, September 9, 1670, in *Shaftesbury Papers*, 178–79; Memoranda (in Locke's hand), September and November 1670, in *Shaftesbury Papers*, 256–64; Governor West to Lord Ashley, March 21, 1670/71, in *Shaftesbury Papers*, 296–300.

39. Thomas Nairne, "A Letter from South Carolina [London, 1710]," in *Selling a New World: Two Colonial South Carolina Promotional Pamphlets*, ed. Jack P. Greene (Columbia: University of South Carolina Press, 1989), 51.

40. Swanton, "An Early Account of the Choctaw Indians," *Memoirs of the American Anthropological Association* 5, no. 3 (April–June 1918): 53–72, esp. 54–55.

41. Greg O'Brien has suggested that military success represented mastery of spiritual forces, which in turn qualified a man for leadership. Greg O'Brien, *Choctaws in a Revolutionary Age, 1750–1830* (Lincoln: University of Nebraska Press, 2002), esp. 27.

42. Nairne, *Muskogean Journals*, 41.

43. John Worth, "Spanish Missions and the Persistence of Chiefly Power," in *The Transformation of the Southeastern Indians, 1540–1760*, ed. Robbie Ethridge and Charles M. Hudson (Jackson: University Press of Mississippi, 2002), 39–64.

44. Robbie Ethridge, "Creating the Shatter Zone: Indian Slave Traders and the Collapse of the Southeastern Chiefdoms," in *Light on the Path: The Anthropology*

and History of the Southeastern Indians, ed. Thomas J. Pluckhahn and Robbie Ethridge (Tuscaloosa: University of Alabama Press, 2006), 207–18; and "Introduction," in Ethridge and Shuck-Hall, *Mapping the Mississippian Shatter Zone*, quote from 2.

45. I have discussed women's involvement in warfare at greater length elsewhere. See LeMaster, *Brothers Born of One Mother*, 85–91.

46. For scholarship on the use of the trope of "woman" to insult men, see Gunlög Fur, *Nation of Women: Gender and Colonial Encounters among the Delaware Indians* (Philadelphia: University of Pennsylvania Press, 2009), 160–98; LeMaster, *Brothers Born of One Mother*, 68–74; Jane T. Merritt, "Metaphor, Meaning, and Misunderstanding," in *Contact Points: American Frontiers from the Mohawk Valley to the Mississippi, 1750–1830*, ed. Andrew R. L. Cayton and Fredrika J. Teute (Chapel Hill: University of North Carolina Press, 1998), 77–81; O'Brien, "Trying to Look Like Men: Changing Notions of Masculinity among Choctaw Elites in the Early Republic," in *Southern Manhood: Perspectives on Masculinity in the Old South*, ed. Craig Thompson Friend and Lorri Glover (Athens: University of Georgia Press, 2004), 49–70, esp. 52–55; Saunt, "'Domestick . . . Quiet Being Broke': Gender Conflict among the Creek Indians in the Eighteenth Century," in Cayton and Teute, *Contact Points*, 151–74, esp. 154–55; Nancy Shoemaker, *A Strange Likeness: Becoming Red and White in Eighteenth-Century North America* (New York: Oxford University Press, 2004), 105–24, and "An Alliance between Men: Gender Metaphors in Eighteenth-Century American Indian Diplomacy East of the Mississippi," *Ethnohistory* 46, no. 2 (Spring 1999): 239–63; Richard C. Trexler, *Sex and Conquest: Gendered Violence, Political Order, and the European Conquest of the Americas* (Ithaca: Cornell University Press, 1995), 71–81.

47. Gallay, *Indian Slave Trade*, 299.

48. On the responses of native peoples to the devastation of the slave trade, including the very complex process of ethnogenesis that reshaped the human landscape of the region, see Boyd, *Here They Once Stood*; Ethridge and Shuck-Hall, eds., *Mapping the Mississippian Shatter Zone*; Gallay, *Indian Slave Trade*, and *Indian Slavery in Colonial America*; Hahn, *Invention of the Creek Nation*; James Merrell, *The Indians' New World: Catawbas and their Neighbors from European Contact through the Era of Removal* (New York: Norton, 1989).

49. Thomas Nairne to Robert Fenwick, April 13, 1708, in Nairne, *Muskogean Journals*, 56 (emphasis added).

50. Relation of Nicholas Carteret, [1670], in *Shaftesbury Papers*, 168.

51. Proprietors to Governor and Council, February 21, 1680/81, in *BPRO-SC*, 1:104–5.

52. Alexander S. Salley, ed., *Journal of Colonel John Herbert, Commissioner of Indian Affairs for the Province of South Carolina* (Columbia: Historical Commission of South Carolina, 1936), 25.

53. James Adair, *Adair's History of the American Indians*, ed. Samuel Cole Williams (Johnson City, Tenn.: Watauga Press, 1930), 151.

54. On the persistence of village independence and the intense localism of Indian "nations" throughout the eighteenth century, see Tyler Boulware, "The Effect of the Seven Years' War on the Cherokee Nation," *Early American Studies* 5, no. 2 (Fall

2007): 395–426; Duane Champagne, *Social Order and Political Change: Constitutional Governments among the Cherokee, the Choctaw, the Chickasaw, and the Creek* (Stanford: Stanford University Press, 1992); Patricia Galloway, "'So Many Little Republics': British Negotiations with the Choctaw Confederacy, 1765," *Ethnohistory* 41, no. 4 (Fall 1994): 513–37; Hahn, *Invention of the Creek Nation*; Merrell, *Indians' New World*; Joshua A. Piker, "'White and Clean' and Contested: Creek Towns and Trading Paths in the Aftermath of the Seven Years' War," *Ethnohistory* 50, no. 2 (Spring 2003): 315–47, and *Okfuskee: A Creek Indian Town in Colonial America* (Cambridge: Harvard University Press, 2004).

55. Extracts of Letters from Carolina, June 19, 1715, in *CRNC*, 2:251.

56. Alexander Spotswood to Board of Trade, February 11, 1712/13, in *CRNC*, 2:12–14.

57. South Carolina Commons House Journal, August 8, 1712, in Joseph Barnwell, "The Second Tuscarora Expedition," *SCHGM* 10, no. 1 (January 1909): 33–48, quote from 44.

58. John Barnwell to [unknown], February 4, 1711/12, in "Tuscarora Expedition," 33.

59. John Barnwell to [unknown], February 12, 1711/12, in "Tuscarora Expedition," 36.

60. Christopher Gale to [unknown], November 2, 1711, in *CRNC*, 1:825–27, quote from 826.

61. Christopher Gale to Governor Gibbes of South Carolina and Council, [1711], in *CRNC*, 1:827–29.

62. Claudio Saunt, "'Our Indians': European Empires and the History of the Native American South," in *The Atlantic in Global History, 1500–2000*, ed. Jorge Cañizares-Esguerra and Erik R. Seeman (New York: Prentice-Hall, 2006), 61–76.

63. Scholarship on the post–Yamasee War period has been far more extensive than that for earlier periods. For examples, see Braund, *Deerskins and Duffels*; James Taylor Carson, *Searching for the Bright Path: The Mississippi Choctaws from Prehistory to Removal* (Lincoln: University of Nebraska Press, 1993); Hatley, *Dividing Paths*; Merrell, *Indians' New World*; Greg O'Brien, *Choctaws in a Revolutionary Age*; Perdue, *Cherokee Women*; Piker, *Okfuskee*.

64. On Oglethorpe's invasion of Florida, see Rodney M. Baine, "General Oglethorpe and the Expedition against St. Augustine," *GHQ* 84, no. 2 (Summer 2000): 197–229; Alan Gallay, *The Formation of a Planter Elite: Jonathan Bryan and the Southern Colonial Frontier* (Athens: University of Georgia Press, 1989); Larry Ivers, *British Drums on the Southern Frontier: The Military Colonization of Georgia, 1733–1749* (Chapel Hill: University of North Carolina Press, 1974); LeMaster, *Brothers Born of One Mother*, 64–66; Julie Anne Sweet, *Negotiating for Georgia: British-Creek Relations in the Trustee Era, 1733–1752* (Athens: University of Georgia Press, 2005).

65. On the Red Stick War, see Joel W. Martin, *Sacred Revolt: The Muskogees' Struggle for a New World* (Boston: Beacon Press, 1991); Claudio Saunt, *A New Order of Things: Property, Power, and the Transformation of the Creek Indians, 1733–1816* (New York: Cambridge University Press, 2003); J. Leitch Wright Jr., *Creeks and Seminoles* (Lincoln: University of Nebraska Press, 1986).

66. On the Anglo-Cherokee War, see Fred Anderson, *Crucible of War: The Seven Years' War and the Fate of Empire in British North America, 1754-1766* (New York: Knopf, 2000); Boulware, "Effects of the Seven Years' War in the Cherokee Nation"; David Corkran, *The Cherokee Frontier: Conflict and Survival, 1740-62* (Norman: University of Oklahoma Press, 1962); Hatley, *Dividing Paths*; John Oliphant, *Peace and War on the Anglo-Cherokee Frontier, 1756-63* (Baton Rouge: Louisiana State University Press, 2001); Perdue, *Cherokee Women;* Matthew C. Ward, *Breaking the Backcountry: The Seven Years' War in Virginia and Pennsylvania, 1754-1765* (Pittsburgh: University of Pittsburgh Press, 2003).

67. LeMaster, *Brothers Born of One Mother,* 66-83.

Histories of the "Tuscarora War"

JAMES TAYLOR CARSON

Any effort to come to grips with this thing we have for so long called the Tuscarora War is bound to end in confusion, a confusion, mind you, that first enveloped those events of the winters of 1712 and 1713 and that only gets more refined as generations of scholars try to locate the war's causes and consequences. But confusion nonetheless because it can also be said that there was no Tuscarora War. In its conventional telling, the Tuscarora War pitted two peoples against one another in nothing less than a struggle for survival. That label, however, has for too long covered a complicated and overlapping series of aggressions and bloodsheds fought by different people for different reasons. The reduction of all this into one war, named after one blamed nation, relies wholly on an elemental colonial spirit that once postulated inevitable war between European civilization and native savagery and that today proposes somewhat more flatly an ineffable conflict between humans whom we still divide into "whites" and "Indians." That spirit seems to constitute one of the most basic truths of our continental profession and remains both the story we write and the one we flee.[1]

Those of us who are descended either in part or in whole from the European invasion that populated the continent have inherited an idea from Christopher Columbus that frames how we think and write about the past that made us possible. A line he drew that never came up for discussion in the negotiations for the Treaty of Tordesillas has raced shadow-like across time, harried us before it, pressed us to give it breath, self-consciously and unthinkingly, over and over and over. It is the line that classical, medieval, and renaissance Europeans used to divide the "savage" from the "civilized," a longitude that has made the imagination, creation, and destruction of the people that Columbus named "Indian" possible both in thought and in deed. And so long as we remain devoted to what might be fairly described as an essentially Columbian view of ourselves, we shall be doomed to reproduce in our words and in our deeds that first fateful seashore apprehension of otherness that ever since has locked us into a way of thinking that cannot be called anything other than colonial.

The first source one confronts in any investigation of the events we remember as the Tuscarora War is the journal Colonel John Barnwell recorded while waging war in the winter of 1712 at the head of some thirty South Carolinians.

By his count, just fewer than five hundred men from various nations threw in with the men from Charles Town in the hopes of taking plunder, scalps, and captives back to their homes, back to their families, back to their creditors. His journal narrated revenge for a series of attacks by men from a number of indigenous towns the preceding fall on the outlying farms of North Carolina, just after their families had harvested their corn but before they had scattered to begin their winter hunts. He waged a war that sought either the "reduction" or "extirpation," as he put it, of that people he and his side called Tuscaroras when they were feeling charitable, other things when they were not.[2]

Barnwell's journal, though, is tricky because he could be frustratingly unclear about what happened to whom when and where. And also because it is both a primary source in the narrowest sense of being a record of what he said happened as well as a work of history, the war's first, because days lapsed between the events he experienced and the narrative he wrote. As a source, Barnwell's journal complicates the war that it, as history, narrated because he makes clear that there were no easy lines to be drawn between friends and foes. If we return to his journal and weigh the narrative carefully and, even at times, it must be admitted, speculatively, we can perhaps reframe our understanding of the subsequent histories that have come to be laid atop it like those inert strata we see all around us that tell of whole geological eras gone past and that yield up only fossils when asked for the once living stories they might tell.[3]

Invaders like Barnwell almost invariably invoked God to sanction their operations. In late January 1712 when he faced the broad, flat, chilly waters of what he called then and we call today the Neuse River, he saw on the other side a kind of oblivion where lay a land and people neither he nor the men who accompanied him knew, save for a handful of Saxapahaws who had refused to run the red path with their "Tuscaroro" neighbors. Nonetheless he leapt like those of his kind whose horoscopes had in store for them grim adventure and terrible violence, "relying on the justice of war, and the blessing of God upon our arms." God blessed more than the guns, swords, and arrows that pricked the air around his force, however, for in the service of civilization against savagery God took the side of the righteous and moved his hand, Barnwell swore, "to grant us the finest weather that could be devised."[4]

That longitude between civility and savagery that Columbus mapped for this place that came to be called America grounded Barnwell's narrative in spite of the bewildering turns of events he confronted at the head of that babel of men who were always on the verge of melting away into the countryside, leaving him and his cutlass to carry on alone. Against his "Brittains" stood a foe to whom he referred variously as "skulking dogs," "cowardly miscreants," "desperate villains," and "ye most barbarous enemy." Even those scores of Yamasees and others on whom the success of the mission with which he was charged depended, because thirty meanly armed Carolinians were not going to pull it off, rated only as "our own heathen friend."[5] What Barnwell did, just as

John Smith and Cotton Mather had done in different places and at other times, was to craft a basic conquest myth, this time on behalf of South Carolina, that put in place a virgin land, beastly savages, divine sanction, and, finally, a recurrent and ordained conquest that, when practiced in later times as history, stretched a kind of "we" across the centuries that rooted our identity in pasts that may have not been ours and that was founded at the most basic level on the same denial of humanity that emboldened Barnwell to rage against those "dogs" who so befuddled his war. In such conflicts and attitudes we find the first steps taken in the formation of those singular ideologies—the Monroe Doctrine, Manifest Destiny, the Domino Theory, and the War on Terror—that have been but momentary iterations of the English colonists' and their descendants' underlying belief in themselves as a chosen people doomed to live in an endless state of impending siege.[6]

At the same time, as a source, Barnwell's narrative punctures such colonial verities. Look no further than his scathing characterizations of the North Carolinians who backed to his banner after he liberated New Bern and asked for food. For the Palatine Germans who produced those artful fascines that protected the men who besieged King Hancock's town, Barnwell had nothing but scorn when they turned tail and fled once lead balls started plopping into their wickerwork bundles. Maybe it was the same God who had stilled the winds and cleared the sky that day on the Neuse who also saw to it that, as Barnwell observed, those "base, cowardly people" were "deservedly shott . . . in their arses" when they dropped their weapons and ran for a nearby swamp. He heaped abuse on other North Carolinians as well, both common and gentry folk, naming them all as "the most impertinent, imperious, cowardly Blockheads that ever God created." Even worse, such dolts, he complained, "must be used like negros if you expect any good of them." He never had a good word to say about Virginians either.[7]

In castigating the cast of losers that surrounded his "brave South Carolina men," Barnwell gave the lie to one of the most basic truths that his journals have, in part, sustained since they were written, that lie of whiteness on which the Columbian binary has come to depend for its truth.[8] At the start Barnwell knew he was not embroiled in a war that pitted "whites" against "Indians" though at the end it appears he had come to believe as much such was his fatigue and disillusionment. Even his army belied any such conclusions, and they marched not on a nation called Tuscarora but rather on a handful of towns, some we might call Tuscarora and others we might not, that had allied with one another to resist the loss of their land and to protest their dignity. He did not fight a Tuscarora War because there was no Tuscarora War to be fought. No more than the dawn parties of men who sortied out one early autumn morning to bloody the farms and bodies of those North Carolinians who had crept too far up the Neuse and Pamlico River plains fought a Tuscarora War. Instead they waged concurrent and conflicting fights that through both convention and belief Barnwell had to narrate as a cogent war even though at the same time we find that time and again it was not.

Nonetheless historians' earliest verdicts about the war noted its great success. One such conclusion found its way into the standard textbook on which generations of North Carolina undergraduates have been reared, Hugh Lefler and Albert Newsome's *The History of a Southern State*. "[T]he removal of the Indian menace," they judged, speeded the "growth and expansion of the colony." More recent interpretations of the war have stepped away from such triumphalism to restore a kind of balance to our appraisal of what caused the conflict and what it meant for all involved, although the land's original inhabitants still tend to be cast as the aggressors.[9] If we can agree, however, that the most basic points Barnwell made in his journal have endured to the present to shape and, at times, to valorize the standard account of that thing that has been called the Tuscarora War—that it happened, that they started it, that it pitted "whites" against "Indians," we can also see the reproduction, in a very basic and deeply structural sense, of Barnwell's colonial gaze at three centuries' remove. Other stories, however, can fundamentally change the questions we ask and conclusions we reach, stories that, if we allow them to be heard, take us away from the primordial clash of civilization and savagery to the possibilities of finding a different way of thinking about the past, a way that can allow histories to stand where history has held the ground for so long.[10]

Not to posit one version as truth and the other as fable but the perspective of the people we have for so long referred to as Tuscaroras has never really figured into scholarly accounts of the so-called war. If we recognize that in recalling the awful consequences of invasion and conquest different interpretations need not fight to the death but can stand together all the while challenging one another, reviling one another even, but more importantly demanding we meet them and grant them their place, then we can next wonder what their coincidence can say about us and the past we seek to explain.

Elias Johnson grew up within a community that in the nineteenth century identified itself as Tuscarora under the piney boughs of the Great Tree of Peace and Power that then as now spanned the boundary between Canada and the United States. Even though Johnson had learned to mistrust the English language during his training for the ministry, he nonetheless gathered for publication stories that generation had handed down to generation ever since those bloody winters of 1712 and 1713. Back then, his elders remembered, colonial agents had called his ancestors to assemble at a place where they would receive their annual allotment of gifts. Once there they were instructed to grasp with their right hands, the hand farthest from the heart and therefore less true than the left, a cord that stretched taut for more than a mile once everyone had lined up one behind the other and taken hold. Those in the front could see that the cord was attached to a large bundle covered in cloth, what they thought were the goods—kettles, axes, knives, guns, ammunition, cloth—owed them as due tribute by the invaders of their land. But when the English removed the cloth they uncovered a primed cannon, the single shot of which traveled the length of the line leaving the ground, the tellers told, "strewn with the meats of the Tuscarora."[11]

If we can allow Johnson's story, another kind of history, to speak in one way or another, then perhaps we can agree that its exclusion from the extant historiography of this thing called the Tuscarora War calls all previous conclusions into question. Indeed allowing the survivors to speak through even one memory of what happened exposes the varying degrees to which the standard literature is premised on a denial of their full humanity that his story, if accounted, will simply not allow.

Because they were people, and, at some point in the past, thousands of years ago, for reasons unknown, their ancestors, a people to whom archaeologists refer as proto-Iroquoians on account of shared specific cultural practices inferred from evidence recovered from archaeological sites, moved out of the mountains. Most of those who left followed the valleys north and east where they huddled in fortified towns and, after a time, founded the Great League of Peace and Power in an effort to stop killing one another. Another group headed south and east, arriving on what we call the coastal plain of North Carolina and what they knew more colloquially as "the wooded swampy land."[12]

At this time all across the land societies sought power through control of the flow of goods and the relationships that travelled with them—shells from the Atlantic and Gulf coasts, chert from the Blue Ridge mountains, copper from the Great Lakes, maize from those who farmed, venison from those who hunted, ceremonial items from the craftsmen of Adena, Hopewell, and Cahokia, ideas and iconography from the Valley of Mexico. Within this sprawling world humming with energy, at times violent and at others amicable, no more and no less than any other place and time where people have done what they do, the people whom the Iroquois would one day welcome as their sixth nation stopped their journey out of the mountains at a river mouth in a place they called Catechna, "pine in water."[13]

Monsters plagued them from the start. At first, great bearded heads covered in fire flew through the sky and terrorized the people. Then a nation of stone giants, people gone wrong who had turned to eating other people, came to drive them away from their homes and into the swamps. Only the intercession of the "Holder of the Heavens" lifted the scourge and restored to them the towns they had encircled with upright logs on bluffs overlooking rivers so that when invaders threatened they could withdraw within and still retain access to the creeks and rivers that gave them the water they needed and that carried their news across the land.[14]

The arrival of the English in Virginia challenged Catechna's place in its world too. In an effort to compete with Powhatan's confederacy, Jamestown began drawing in captives, maize, and deerskins and sending out glass beads, cloth, metal tools, and copper to secure indulgences for its expanding tobacco farms. Rivalries formed among towns jockeying for access to the newcomers and their goods, either through or around Powhatan, and in the loose clusters of towns that shared what archaeologists might call a proto-Tuscaroran culture, leaders would have risen and fallen depending on their ability to tap into exchanges of the new and exotic items. The people who inhabited the northern towns remained safe in their palisades from the fighting that followed the arrival of the English while those to the south relaxed their guard, perhaps because St. Augustine was so far away and feeble and because microbes deposited by Soto and those who had followed him had sickened those lands that carried the slow moving rivers of the coastal plain on their dreary paths to the sea.[15]

When the government in Jamestown sought in a 1677 treaty to set up its own paramountcy in the aftermath of the complete destruction of the one that Powhatan had built, the nations that had made up his confederacy struggled to maintain their hold on what land remained to them while the people who were coming to be called Tuscaroras were far enough away and secure enough in their own right to stand their swampy ground. Bacon's Rebellion, however, shattered the buffers between them and Virginia and thrust them into a rivalry with the Occaneechees who, on their river-bound island, tried to control the slave and skin trade that knitted Virginia and the first stirrings of the colony of North Carolina into relationships with peoples who lived farther to the west.[16]

For the moment let us set aside that word *Tuscarora*, though, because it prejudges, closes the gap between now and then, puts in place a linear history where none ought to be found, and collapses different things into that sincere and exasperated narrative that Barnwell put on paper. It is also not what they called themselves then, as far as can be determined. In fact Johnson argued that the word stood not for what we might call an ethnicity but rather was the title of the league or an alliance his people had forged with the neighboring Corees, Mattamuskeets, Machapungas, Neuses, and Bear Rivers who all resented the invaders' encroachments on their land. In one Tuscarora dictionary, compiled from modern speakers and historical documents, we find two terms that they used to describe themselves. "Ongwehonwa," "a real people," was the name given them by the Good Twin who had made them from the earth, who had given to them the corn, beans, squashes they grew, and who had filled the forests with the deer they hunted.[17]

Another term seems to have grown out of the contact experience, for it is paired with the name they gave the imperial invaders of their land. The people we know today as Tuscarora once called themselves the "people who gather hemp" in contradistinction to those other "people who gather wool," placing the ones we call today "white" firmly on the other side of a stark line, their own longitude, between peoples in ways that had nothing to do with skin color or Columbus but rather with their different relationships to the land and to "civility." Hemp, for one, sprouted from earth that the Good Twin had heaped onto Turtle's back. Wool, on the other hand, was not even a true product of the land but instead sprouted on animals that the Good Twin would have never made, animals that lacked hoofs and antlers and useful hides, were not swift but rather stupid. Such creatures hailed from the other side of the waters that surrounded Turtle that the people had always known was home to the Bad Twin who labored constantly to thwart the Good Twin's designs. Wool's utility could not be doubted but its origins, like those of its gatherers, were dubious and foretold disaster.[18]

At the end of the seventeenth century, the people from the other side of the water, in this case a sickly gang of French Huguenots who had failed in an attempt to settle in Virginia, took up residence along the Pamlico River. Just a few years later the colony's surveyor, John Lawson, laid out for them the town of Bath, and, by 1710, forty to fifty people called its muddy streets home. Lawson drafted a second town in the shape of a cross on the former site of a Coree town called Chatookas that as New Bern would become home to four hundred Palatine Germans and Swiss under the always reasonable leadership, if he is to be believed, of Baron Christoph von Graffenried.[19]

In response Machapungos, Corees, Bear Rivers, Mattamuskeets, and others began talking with their neighbors about different ways to safeguard their homes and towns against the newcomers. Among the northern towns, a man whom the wool gatherers named King Blount (not knowing that it was considered impolite by those people to refer to them by individual names) sought to strike a neutral balance with his counterpart in Virginia, Governor Alexander Spotswood, while in the southern towns a man called King Hancock endeavored to rebuff colonial advances up the Neuse River by drawing together a number of peoples and towns in common cause. It would be a mistake, however, to fall for such talk of kings because in such societies at this time individuals rarely held what we might call the power to command. Instead authority was premised on the ability to persuade others to cooperate. Such efforts, not surprisingly, were often fragile if not fickle, for the slightest disagreement or the appearance of an ill omen would be all one man or one woman or one group would need to justify going in a different direction altogether. Naming individuals and investing them with powers by analogy helped the invaders to make sense of the people they faced but also fundamentally distorted how politics, leadership, and diplomacy worked in that wooded swampy land.[20]

As an outgrowth of the contacts that came with colonization, each side formed opinions of the other that gave fuller human shape to the abstractions that had been formed through rumor and contact over long-distant trade routes. One local man, for example, informed Lawson that the hemp gatherers thought that the wool gatherers were a "very Wicked people," and they diagnosed among the invaders a keen anxiety. "They say," Lawson learned, "the *Europeans* are always rangling and uneasy, and wonder [why] they do not go out of this World, since they are so uneasy and discontented in it." From the side of the wool gatherers, Lawson too made generalizations. "They are a very craving people," he wrote, "and if a man give them any thing of a present, they think it obliges him to give them another; and so on, till he has given them all he has." At least one Palatine, however, disagreed. "The so-called wild and naked Indians," he remarked, "[were] not wild, for they come to us often and like to get clothes of us."[21]

The incidents that brought so many of the real people and the wool gatherers to violence were no different than any of the other miserable rosters of slights that occurred everywhere else. Encroachment on land, infringement on persons, unruly behavior, bad manners, disrespect, arrogance, hubris. But if names must be named John Barnwell had heard that some "white men" had punished an "Indian" over an insult given and received after a drink, which, in those days, might be better described as a drunk. In the background too, he feared, lurked a party of Seneca warriors just arrived from the north who were reported to have thrashed their distant kin for having become "slaves" to the "white people." Graffenried, however, believed that internal colonial dissent had given some hemp gatherers the impression that the divided colony was ripe for a toppling. Indeed there was something to this for while former governor Thomas Cary agitated against Governor Edward Hyde, Cary sent an agent to enlist the hemp gatherers to cut off and surround Hyde's supporters. Rumor had it that young warriors champed at the plan but that their elders had counseled restraint. Forces supporting the rival governors clashed at arms on June 30, 1711, and the battle ended with Cary's flight to Virginia.[22]

Graffenried also admitted that his enemies had spread word among the hemp gatherers that he and Lawson were plotting to gather up land now that New Bern was firmly seated. Such rumors were undoubtedly true because as fall approached Graffenried and Lawson set out on a surveying expedition up the Neuse, accompanied by two enslaved men who presumably carried their belongings and cooked their meals and two guides who knew the creeks and pathways well. On the second day out Lawson sent one of the guides to scout the route ahead, only instead of reporting back which way they should go he went to Cautechna and informed Hancock of Lawson's approach. Everyone knew of Lawson's work as a surveyor, and, believing that Graffenried was actually Governor Hyde, a party of young men returned, seized the travelers, and brought them back to the town where Hancock fed them cornbread and boiled venison out of a mangy skin cap. If a woman had fed them they would have been sanctioned as friends and thereby gained entry into the town as guests rather than as the prisoners they found themselves to be at Hancock's feet picking fur out of their cold food.[23]

For two days representatives of the hemp gatherers who resented the encroachments on their land and other people known to us today as Corees, Pamlicos, and Neuses considered Hancock's charge that he had given neither man permission to survey the land. Upon the arrival of a Coree leader who bore Lawson a special grievance, and in light of Lawson's own refusal to behave in a penitent manner, the council stripped the back-talking Lawson and the quaking Graffenried of their hats and wigs, leaving them, for the time being, as unmade men, and then deprived them of the mats on which they had sat and which had given them some tiny place in the town, leaving them on the bare ground with the two trembling, no doubt, enslaved men. A man of great spiritual and intuitive power then circled the sacred fire around which the interrogators sat with two lines of ground maize and in so doing surveyed in his own way the clear and unbroken paths that compassed their place and that bound the different towns by a plant given by the Good Twin to the women of their land for the sustenance and support of all. Within the circle, however, sat the intruders, who, bareheaded and slumped by the fire, were the reasons that on that day the league of Tuscarora had chosen, after years of deliberation, to punish the invaders of their land for all that they had endured. In the end Lawson and one of the enslaved men met the kind of death that Lawson himself had witnessed less than a decade before. Women and children would have impregnated his and the other man's skin with countless pitch pine splinters, lit them, and forced them to dance around a fire while onlookers beat and taunted them. Whether or not Lawson and the enslaved man sang their life's songs is unknown, as is the duration of their ordeals, but it all would have ended with, as Graffenried heard, Lawson's throat being cut with his straight razor and then the dismemberment of the two men at the hands of those who had lost kinfolk to the violence that was such an important part of just about every colonial world. Graffenried, who, unlike Lawson, had no problem showing contrition, meanwhile brokered a deal that would, in exchange for Swiss and German neutrality, spare New Bern from attack and save the life of the other enslaved man.[24]

It all happened under a moon that the Good Twin had made of his dead mother's body and placed in the sky to drive away those monsters from across the water that had haunted the real people for so long. The coup they launched, however, was not intended to ruin the colony nor was it aimed at driving the newcomers back across the sea over which they had come. They were too important to life there now, and so the five hundred or so young men, hemp gatherers and their allies, who broke camps under liquid silver light in the small hours of a day their victims would count as September 22, intended to teach them a lesson—a lesson that would confront the invaders with their vulnerability, confine them to their original habitations, and remonstrate them for their refusal to live properly. Cattle and pigs fell dead in the forests. Barking dogs too. Torches tossed into corn cribs and barns saw them to ruin while terrified wool gatherers found themselves hauled out of bed and into their yards, where they learned their proper manners at the butt ends of guns, yielded their spirits to scalpers' knives, and their lives to the men who hoped to teach them to behave as proper guests on Turtle's back. The several hundred wool gatherers who had survived fled to Bath and New Bern, where they found safety among fellow invaders who lacked the means to either avenge or feed them.[25]

The coup outraged Governor Spotswood of Virginia because, according to him, no fair warning had been given. He quickly mustered six hundred militia men, all of whom were equally outraged at the bloodshed, to punish those people they called Tuscaroras, and he hoped to join with the Tuscarora "king" Blount to crush Hancock's men. The House of Burgesses, however, opted in their deliberations to kill any and every "Indian" on which they could get their hands. It costs to kill, though, and when faced with the necessary appropriations bill to fund the murderous adventure, the Burgesses balked and no force ever took to the field from Virginia. Instead Spotswood satisfied himself with a treaty to secure Blount's neutrality while in return Blount gained protection for the traders, who would supply Hancock with the powder and lead he needed as well as for the children and elderly who had dispersed into the countryside to gather acorns and hickory nuts to put away against what everyone knew would be a lean winter. Meantime, Bath and New Bern starved in quiet panic.[26]

For the frightened inhabitants of the two towns word had no doubt preceded Barnwell's march up from Carolina and the hemp gatherers no doubt watched him cross the Neuse on that late January day when the colonel thanked God for the good weather. On the river's other side, he embarked on what one historian has called "extirpative" warfare, a kind of war that had been in the making for more than a century of English colonization in Barnwell's natal home, Ireland, and later in America. The goals of such warfare set aside the traditional encounter between armies in the field and valued instead the burning of towns and fields and the killing or enslaving of men, women, and children. The first town, Narhantes, which had not even participated in the uprising, fell on January 30, 1712, when the hemp gatherers retreated from the palisade they had built into two strong houses, where women who had sung songs to the men who defended them picked up the bows and arrows of the dead and returned fire as well as they could until the barricaded doors gave way. Most of them, Barnwell wrote, "were put to the sword." It took half an hour.[27]

For such a short fight the toll on Barnwell's allies was terrible too. The Yamasee leader Peterba King fell as did the Wateree King, a leader named Cunaba Tom and another King Robin. Leaders were not supposed to die in battle, and when they did men went home because everything in their world happened for a reason and none of this boded well. All thirty-two who fell wounded that day hailed from the nations that had accompanied Barnwell's march while only one of the seven dead traced his family tree to the other side of the Atlantic. The fifty-two scalps and thirty slaves taken, however, pointed to the lopsided loss of life in the battle but still left the colonel "concerned at my loss with no greater Execution of the enemy." Turning his mind toward the next task, "the word," Barnwell said, "was revenge," and four hundred homes and two thousand bushels of maize—358,403 cubic feet—went up in smoke. His allies were appalled, and we can wonder if any survivors saw his bearded head against the flames and cinders whirling in their idiosyncratic ways atop invisible and rushing columns of furnace air and remembered those stories of their beginning that had become as much their prophecy as their history.[28]

Word of the debacle stirred the nearby town of Kenta to action. Now that the conflict had been fully engaged the real people crafted a grand strategy that can be found in Barnwell's journal if we read closely. The utter destruction that motivated Barnwell's war was never part of theirs. Instead they sought to contact the enemy, inflict damage, acquire scalps and captives, and convince the invaders to withdraw from their land, all the while conserving their limited quantities of men, powder, and balls—an approach to war that Barnwell called "extremely cowardly." The warriors of Kenta put the plan into motion by keeping to the fringes of the invaders' fields of fire to draw them on and on in a running attempt by each to encircle the other. In the end nine men of Kenta fell without their hair while two others caught by the men under the command of Esaw Captain Jack were later burned alive at the Carolinians' camp, probably to compensate Jack's men for the two Waterees in his company that had died during the previous day's assault on Narahontes.[29]

After the destruction of Narahontes and Kenta, a Yamassee party caught a man and interrogated him to find out the strength and disposition of their enemy. Let's linger over this unfortunate man for a moment because Barnwell does not. After the man's capture some of the most tumultuous events that faced Barnwell occurred, so this moment deserves our attention because of the interpretive opening it allows. Barnwell deemed the man an "acceptable present" from his Yamassee allies, and, given that the Yamasees tortured other men they captured during the invasion in order to procure information, it is reasonable to assume the same here, even though Barnwell makes only cryptic mention of it taking so long that it delayed his crossing of a river.[30]

If the Yamasees tortured the man, he would have made powerful boasts during his ordeal, as any such man would have done, and his words, probably in the form of a song, would have been audible to all. And sing he must have because during the following night all hundred or so men who served under Captain William Bull, men who have been forgotten as Waterees, Peedees, Winiaws, Hoopengs, and Waraperes and whose descendants would become known as Catawbas, plus the Saxapahaws who, presumably, had avenged their people enough, fled Barnwell's camp trailing scalps, buckles, clothes, and captives behind them. Many who belonged to Esaw Jack's company also used the occasion to desert, leaving only twenty-three Esaws of the original one hundred fifty-five men in his company. Several of the Yamasees, who were the force's most renowned slavers, also refused to continue further and held Barnwell off by promising to return with more warriors. They might have also told him, the man whom South Carolina would lionize as "Tuscarora Jack," that the ten bags of spare musket balls they took with them would be put to good use in outfitting their new recruits. Barnwell was powerless to stop them, and in this one evening, when the disappearance of most of the gunmen who had accompanied him left only a motley force of what he described as "Bowmen and boys," the colonel could do little more than lament that "the Confusion was so great."[31]

When the morning of February 5 dawned on Barnwell's quiet camp, the Yamasees who had remained did not awaken, for it appears they never went to sleep. Instead they had talked and talked and talked about the situation in which they found themselves. Barnwell met with their leader and implored him to stay, and he relayed the message to his men, who, in spite of the dissent Barnwell could hear, agreed that they would stay on the condition that Barnwell promise to undertake no offensive action. They feared that with so many wounded men in such an unknown country they would be easy pickings against an enemy they had come to believe was both overwhelming and everywhere. Such must have been the impact of that man they had cut, burned, and questioned that Barnwell further assured them the captive had pledged him his life and had promised to guide the group to Hancock's town. To a man they cried "Whough!" and so Barnwell ordered his Carolinians to mount the wounded on the horses and to start walking with sodden feet the thirty or so miles he had ahead of him.[32]

The captive man, no matter the wounds he had suffered at the hands of the Yamasees, remained a quiet combatant. He offered Barnwell two routes: a short one through the leafless forests and black swamps or a "round about way" through several of the towns that had provided the league with men and supplies but that had, for the most part, been abandoned after the burning of Narhantes. Though we cannot be sure, it is reasonable to assume that he hoped Barnwell would opt for the shorter way, which would have exposed his force to unremitting ambushes. But Barnwell knew how his foes wanted to fight, so he avoided the close forests and chose instead to travel through the towns, where he knew open ground would afford room for his horses to be used in battle and where he expected to find the provisions his force needed so desperately. Equally important, he wanted to "carry on the terrore" in open view while at the same time hiding that singular emotion that was, he admitted both to his journal and to us, "our fear." At this point he could count 178 Yamasees, Apalachees, Esaws, and perhaps others while twenty of his remaining twenty-five Carolinians were in various states of injury. The first town they entered, Innennits, was empty, but they did find fourteen fair-haired scalps and piles of goods taken from those who had fallen back on September 22. Barnwell refused to allow the Carolinians to rummage through the stuff but gestured to the Yamassees, Apalachees, and Esaws to help themselves. After two hours he had the town burned and continued his march through the fields of washed out corn stalks, yellowed squash and pumpkin leaves, and tangles of lifeless bean stalks that had marked his way since leaving Narhantes.[33]

At last they reached the Pamlico River, one of the league's principal lines of defense. On its banks the Yamasees took two scalps and six slaves and, at night, scouted up the Tar River in search of the town Ucouhnerunt, which was home to King Blount, only to find it abandoned and bereft of the canoes they had hoped to find. Stuck, Barnwell ordered thirty men, Yamasees most likely because so few of his men were fit for anything, to swim the river to establish a beachhead with the rest following on a bridge fashioned from those enormous ancient trees that could be seen wherever European axes had not yet had occasion to declare their own kind of war. The horses swam the wounded over without the party's hearing a shot, but until his men could fell the trees they needed for the crossing, Barnwell's force remained spread out across a wide river and its banks. Almost on cue came the attack he had expected. The fifty or so men who had sprung the ambush were not enough to crush Barnwell's column, but they inflicted wounds, nattered spirits, and showed the ease with which they came and went, fired and hid. The Yamasees, however, knew this art and launched an encirclement of their own, but two scalps and some clothing and guns were all they could show for their efforts. A second attack on the rearguard failed to draw blood, but the Yamasees spent the better part of the rest of the day chasing footfalls for nearly two miles before giving up the chase. The sun set with Barnwell's allies exhausted from the pursuit and his Carolinians tired from chopping trees and being hurt. They forlornly encamped on either side of the river and awaited dawn.[34]

The league's warriors allowed Barnwell to break camp the next day and to complete the crossing. His men marched for the better part of the day until another flooded creek blocked their way just as the sun set. Those eyes that had never lost sight of their foes struck when the sentries switched at what Barnwell's pocket watch told him was five a.m. They unleashed a volley at some inscrutable signal and took special aim at him, having seen and perhaps even heard how his indefatigable will and cutlass had kept the invasion going. Balls ripped through his camping gear and smashed into the tree against which he was leaning, having himself awoken at four to begin preparing for the day. Barnwell's men responded with two volleys into the dark, but their attackers were already gone, saving their lives and ammunition for another day and another opportunity because for them there was no shame in retreat. No breakfast was eaten till dawn, while the men clutched their guns beside dampened fires waiting for the sun to chase away the shadows and the cold.[35]

They began to pass burned-out barns with such regularity that Barnwell knew he was nearing Bath and New Bern, and three boats from Bath arrived to ferry the wounded to town. The awful appearance of the men from Bath and the pitiful stories they told, however, brought Barnwell's men to tears and offset whatever relief came from knowing that his wounded would be safe. Still

Barnwell mustered sixty-seven new men, though most of them lacked ammunition, and no one could provide him with enough food to feed them. Rather than wait, though, he struck for Catechna, Hancock's Town, the league's seat, where he hoped the cribs would be full of corn.[36]

The month of March opened with ninety-four "white men" and 148 "Indians"—Barnwell had stopped using his allies' town or national names and now more or less only spoke of "whites" and "Indians"—marching in water that was at times up to their waists. Another day and twelve miles brought them to Catechna, and though the people had fled to the opposite riverbank, their maize remained, much to Barnwell's "great joy." Across the river swarmed enough men to convince Barnwell to set up camp and await what the morning would bring, but what it brought was the disappointment of finding only disabled canoes on his side of the river; flashes of light, sharp reports, and puffs of smoke on the other side that gave away the snipers' ever-changing positions; and roiling brown waters in between. Those few shooters whom the Yamasees captured sang under torture of the strong fort and prime warriors who were poised to welcome them.[37]

The men who observed Barnwell's movements the following day saw him divide his force before dawn and place a party of about seventy men under a captain they did not know was named Brice. And as we have learned, they would never have called him, had they known him, by his surname, preferring, as was their custom, something more indirect like "that man over there who wants to burn our houses and seize our children" or "that man who thinks he is going to fool us." Barnwell told Brice to march up the river and have his men to blare away on trumpets and clang forest trees with their axes to give the impression of something big happening. Meanwhile Barnwell took another group down the river and attempted to build a raft to ferry a handful of men at a time across the water. Brice signaled as planned but then pulled out and rejoined Barnwell, bringing with him both those men on the other side of the river who had been listening to his noisy efforts and concentrated gunfire on Barnwell's rafters. Rather than pitch battle and slug it out on the shore where they would be vulnerable to Yamassee encirclement, however, the league's men allowed two of Barnwell's to cross the river and made a production of appearing to flee before them, perhaps hoping to lure them and anyone who might follow into a trap. Once news of their flight crossed over to Barnwell's side, the Yamasees, who at this point had refused to climb aboard his raft, plunged in and swam across in desperate pursuit of slaves while the North Carolinians, with their handful of musket balls each, refused to budge.[38]

On the fifth, after the invaders finally crossed the river, the league had little choice but to allow Barnwell's force to surround their fort. It would have risked too much to stand and fight on the ground around it that they had cleared in order to give them open fields of fire. At the same time, there were no skulking dogs to be found either, at least as far as Barnwell could see through his spyglass. He surveyed the long approach strewn with broken limbs and sharpened canes to impede any progress he might want to make and spotted the flickering shadows of the young men who had come to pick off the invaders one by one through the two rows of loopholes that let light through the log walls here and there.[39]

The fort he faced was a marvel of Iroqouian and European military engineering. Not circular like the palisades that the real people had built for so long to protect them from the giant bears, cats, and mosquitoes that harried their land, but squarish with each corner crowned by a bastion, a fortified projection that enabled defenders to fire into the sides and rear of any soldiers who might make it to the walls. Barnwell was stunned, and the many questions that must have come to mind were answered in the various taunts the defenders lobbed his way. What he learned was that an enslaved man named Harry, a person who in those days was called a "negro" but today would just be called "black," had somehow made his way to Catechna and convinced the league to listen to what he knew about forts. Whether or not this is true just as where or how he might have learned to build European-style forts is impossible to say, but Barnwell had known Harry's former owner, Dove Williamson, back in South Carolina and that Harry had committed enough "rogueries" there to warrant his deportation to the Virginia plantation from which he had escaped. Harry too no doubt peered through a loophole and must have marveled at the degree to which so many others had invested in his own fight against enslavement.[40]

A steady rain played havoc with the invaders' flash pans and footing as they advanced on the fort. The first volley of return fire hit at twelve yards, and though it caused little loss of life, the Palatines, who had only reluctantly crossed over the Pamlico, fled for the swamp behind their original positions. Without them there were not enough men of courage to continue the assault, and so those who remained on the field slung the fascines over their backs to cover their retreat. Barnwell asked the Yamasees, Apalachees, and Esaws to make a feint on the opposite side of the fort, and it is hard to tell if he was being sarcastic or complimentary when he reported that "they did [it] with such caution that they had not a man hurt." That night Barnwell rallied only sixteen men for a second charge and decided to call an end to the action.[41]

The next day Barnwell somehow had wooden shovels made and instructed his men to dig in. That night, after surveying the scene, he hatched a plan to entrench on a small rise that would afford his force a clear field of fire at the river landing where the defenders kept their canoes and drew their water. He also lodged a small group on the opposite bank to suppress any activity by the river. The defenders knew Barnwell's move threatened the tenability of their position, and so they tried to flee the fort that had become a trap, but Barnwell's careful positioning of his men foreclosed any escape. Instead captives were sent to fetch the water.[42]

It is obvious to say but bears mentioning, this was not a quiet place. Sporadic shots punctuated the Carolinians' shouts of encouragement to the captives bearing buckets, urging them to hold on just a little longer. But the men inside decided to use sound to their advantage as well, so they seized Mr. Taylor's eight-year-old daughter. If they did to her the kinds of things done to other captives doomed to death, small wonder that her screams moved the North Carolinians in Barnwell's force to beg him to call off the siege. Hearing their pleas, the men and women inside the fort too yelled to their liberators to quit the scene and spare their lives.[43]

In the midst of this madness, Barnwell called for a parley, and a woman whose husband's last name was Perce and whose five children were being held in the fort, appeared at its gate to inform the besiegers that the league would not negotiate until the siege was lifted. After consulting his officers, Barnwell approached the door calmly and saw inside elaborate trenches and fortifications that gave cover to scores of well-armed men. He reported, however, that Hancock and his adjutants were trembling "exceedingly," most likely from fear he thought, but it has been said of Iroquoian men that they would show neither pain nor fear in such circumstances.[44]

If Barnwell consoled himself with the certainty that his foes were afraid, he also concluded that "in case I broke in, I should have hard work against a parcel of desperate villains who would do all the mischief they could before their death." He knew his allies would refuse to storm the palisade and that his "whites" left capable of bearing arms could not bring his campaign to the conclusion for which he had so hoped. Short of ammunition and food, without any prospect of victory, and having endured weeks of arduous, exhausting, and nerve-wracking campaigning, he gave credence to the shouts coming from within the fort that well-armed allies and terrifying Senecas were marching to their relief. So he quit. But before leaving, Barnwell insisted that the men inside deliver twelve of their captives plus two canoes that he sorely needed, not knowing himself how to make them. He also convinced the league's leaders to agree to free at a later date another twenty-two captives and twenty-four "negros" that were hiding in the swamps nearby. For their part, the defenders surrendered none of their principal leaders, retained their arms and ammunition, and forced the invaders from their land. To ensure an easy separation, the league's leaders dispatched men on foot and by canoe to call off those who had moved into the woods between Barnwell and New Bern.[45]

Insults must have followed Barnwell's retreat to New Bern, and the shaky truce he had concluded allowed the defenders time to improve on their works in anticipation of the hero's return. When he came it was at the head of "153 white men & 128 Indians," though Graffenried claimed that some two hundred English North Carolinians, fifty Palatines and Swiss, and "some few of our Indians" had also joined Barnwell's force to carry through the second assault. What Barnwell and his troops found before them, however, was a new fort that had grown to encompass lines formerly held by his men, including the entrenched position that had interdicted the river landing, installations of bomb-proof shelters, and a protected approach to the nearby creek for more secure access to drinking water should the siege go that far. Graffenried, whom Barnwell fails to note was present but who claims he was, noted that the defenders included men from Weetox, Bay River, Neuse, Pamlico, and Coree towns while only a portion of the force were men he called Tuscaroras.[46]

Events never arrived, however, at that final conclusive test that so often defines what has happened and what will follow. After ten days of siege, a lack of food and his men's refusal to leave their trenches persuaded Barnwell to quit again and once and for all. Graffenried, who had insisted that they bring with them two small cannons he had seen in Bath rusting and full of sand, claimed that two shots from them had so frightened the forces within the fort that they called for a truce. Barnwell makes no mention of this but instead worried that he only had enough powder for ten shots. Still, if we are to go back and listen again to Johnson's story, those cannons made a difference, for one of them survived the centuries in the memories of the survivors to play a central role in mediating their total destruction. But at the same time, no elders seem to have recalled for Johnson the Yamasees, Apalachees, and Esaws who had done so much damage over the course of the campaign but who, during the ten-day siege, did so little to risk their lives.[47]

In the end, another uneasy truce saw several captive children handed over to Barnwell as well as two "negros," one of whom was a "notorious Rogue," most likely Harry, whom Barnwell had "cut to pieces immediately." The fort's occupants also dismantled a bastion and allowed Barnwell's men to march two by two through the breach to the sounds of trumpets and drums. Once inside he marveled both at the "subtill contrivances" that had made the fort so formidable and at the horrible conditions in which the defenders had lived and fought. Breathing through his mouth, he had his men raise their colors and fire the cannons before telling the defenders that he would "not take this advantage to murder them." On the one hand, he wanted to impress his allies that he was a man of his word. On the other, he did not want to antagonize the seventy or so warriors he knew still lurked in the countryside, poised to menace Bath and New Bern. At that he abandoned the field and the colony just ahead of rumors of treachery, accusations of incompetence, and a coffle of some two hundred men, women, and children he had managed to enslave.[48]

After Barnwell's campaign ended, the colonial government positioned King Blount as Bath's most crucial ally. In exchange for his investiture with colonial authority, Blount agreed to apprehend Hancock, which he did, and, after a round of torture, the governor ordered that man's final execution. Blount's abrogation of the Tuscarora league unleashed another round of coups that struck the isolated farmsteads that remained between the hemp and wool gatherers and that also pitted the real people against one another as well. But just as

Blount's men were about to descend on the Lower Towns, Corees, and Neuses who had resisted Barnwell, South Carolina undertook a second war of extirpation and enslavement led by Colonel James Moore Jr., whose father, in 1704, had led a mixed force of Carolinians and fifteen hundred Yamasees, Talapoosas, and Cherokees on an attack against the Apalachee missions of La Florida. Many of the two thousand captives the force seized filled the holds of slave ships while South Carolina relocated thirteen hundred of the surviving Apalachees to its southern border and saw several hundred more find refuge at La Mobile. Junior rode this time at the head of an army of thirty-three "white men" and nine hundred "Indians," and arrived at the Neuse in March 1713. After waiting for deep snows to melt, his force invested a new fort at Catechna called Neoheroka, whose defenders had improved on the basic principles of defense Harry had taught. Nearly one thousand men and some scores of women hoped to rebuff the second invasion and the enslavement they knew would follow if their power proved insufficient. After a bloody back and forth siege in which artillery played a signal role, Neoheroka finally fell to flames on March 23.[49]

Moore lost twenty-two "white men" while another twenty-four fell wounded. Of the Yamassees and Cherokees that had accompanied him, people he just called "Indians," thirty-five died and fifty-eight were wounded. For the league's defenders two hundred or so congealed pools of grease and blackened bones marked the spots where flames had claimed lives, and another 166 defenders fell outside of the fort to be disemboweled or dismembered by the Yamassees and Cherokees or simply eaten by the feral pigs that were always so quick to appear once the shooting stopped. Another two hundred scalps were passed in whole or in part amongst those who knew that possession of such things would herald their own bravery and skill, while the people who were able to walk out of Neoheroka alive were clapped in chains for transport to Charles Town and thence to the sugar plantations of the West Indies or to the prosperous households of New England, where they would die enslaved. Those few who were not caught at Neoheroka raced to rejoin their kin to prepare for the long walk north through Virginia and Pennsylvania to find sanctuary under the boughs of the Great League of Peace and Power. Sporadic attacks, however, continued in North Carolina as Corees, Coves, Catechnans, and others struggled to remain afloat in the destruction that had followed Moore's invasion until a peace treaty in 1715 left Blount as the titular king of those who had survived and remained. It was almost as if the stone giants had returned to eat everyone, but Blount was no "Holder of the Heavens."[50]

Can we continue to name these events, as has been our custom, the Tuscarora War? A war begun by "Indians" against "whites" that was a tragic part of a grander colonial story about the extension of British hegemony and the founding of the United States? Not if we read across, behind, and between the pages of Barnwell's journal. Not if we listen to what Johnson's elders had learned from their elders.

Clearly Johnson's story of the shot that felled his people so challenges conventional conclusions about the war's place in colonial history that we need to reconsider our understanding of what happened in order to get out from under Columbus's shadow, to leave the cant of conquest, even in its attenuated twenty-first-century form, and to find another means by which we might be able to articulate a different kind of story about the past and those events. And to do this, we need to begin to rethink the central place race holds in the histories we write and to see if we can put the art of history on an altogether different premise.

Much of the writing of the history of colonial America, a field of which the so-called Tuscarora War was but one small episode, is prefigured on the existence and opposition of races. If "black," "white," and "Indian" were the very structures on which colonial control came to rest, they also work today as scholarly conventions. Such categories born of the colonizing mind and worked out in colonial practice have yielded a particular kind of history that, for the Americas at least, privileges a priori identities rooted in race over other kinds of perceptions, categories, and behaviors that might challenge and circumvent race's closed system of thought. The interconnectedness of historical and historiographical race languages that is so prevalent, however, makes it difficult for scholars to break out of what we might call "the strict rules of historiography."

When we use such constructions of race to narrate the past, however, we substitute the illusory simplicity of a phenotypically and behaviorally bounded and ordered society for the variety and complexity of the human relationships that actually constituted the colonial societies of the Americas.[51]

Any substantial revision to the way we currently write colonial history must, therefore, confront the fundamental importance of race in the writing of American history but also push beyond to attempt to understand and convey the disparate behaviors and beliefs that constituted individuals' and cultures' basic ways of living and remembering. We can, in this way, look to an approach that makes room for multiple perspectives, multiple histories, to vie over the past's terrain in ways that cannot be seen, even in their barest outline, so long as we insist on naming everyone "white," "black," or "Indian." Such an approach can, as well, decenter agency and demand not one narrative but many, each of which can challenge the power of the other and force us to confront the limits of what we can say ever happened.[52]

Anthropologist Irene Silverblatt once argued that colonialism involved "contests over social selves, over potential ways of being human," and so too does the practice of colonial history. While it is important for historians to take into account the specific historical power of categories like "Indian" and "white," relying on the same terms as historiographical givens highlights the close proximity between modern interpretive assumptions and conclusions and colonial forms of knowledge, dehumanization, and triumphalism. We must then at least consider abandoning such colonial polemics in order to articulate a more open understanding of the past that recognizes that, in a place as complicated as colonial Catechna, old historical and historiographical verities have no safe place.[53]

To unhitch historiography from its colonial moorings is not, however, to lapse into idle political correctness, "an attribute," David Hackett Fischer has written recently, that is known for its "revulsion against great white men, especially empire-builders, colonial founders, and discoverers." An approach he dismissed as "delusions" of "multiculturalism," however, can also be seen as one that challenges the ways we remember people and their pasts that do not simply reify the worlds built by those great men, of whom it is unclear whether or not Barnwell ought to be counted.[54] None of this will be possible, however, if we allow a Tuscarora War born of the minds of an "empire-builder" like Barnwell to define our sense of that past at the expense of other histories involving the real people, the Good Twin, hemp gatherers and wool gatherers, coups, wars of extirpation, vengeful Saxapahaws, valiant Carolinians, blockheaded Palatines, skinflint Burgesses, runaway slaves, and Yamassees in the red. It took all of them and their disparate stories to smash into oblivion a world whose roots reached back centuries and over continents and that existed for two generations in that place hardly anyone anymore remembers had been the land of pines in the water for the better part of a millennium.

But Johnson's parents and their parents and their parents remembered, for in the story he had heard and then written down, he knew that those like him who had learned it as children had to confront a dilemma about themselves and the world they inhabited. If all their people had fallen at the shot of that cannon, how were they who sat and listened or how were they who told it even there? If the descendants of the "whites" see in what they have called the "Tuscarora War" for so long now a story of colonial struggle and national birth, those born of the people who for so long have been effaced as "Indians" know too that in spite of that act of treachery that ended in that one cannon shot, they live still and that in their living resides a history that for three centuries now has contested everything that Barnwell did and wrote.

Notes

The author would like to thank Brad Wood and Michelle LeMaster for their encouragement and support as well as Catherine Dhavernas and Alan Gallay for their comments and criticisms.

1. Jill Lepore, *Name of War: King Philip's War and the Origins of American Identity* (New York: Knopf, 1998), xv.

2. John Barnwell, "Journal of John Barnwell," *VMHB* 5, no. 4 (April 1898): 391–402, and 6, no. 1 (July 1898): 42-55, quote from 5:397

3. Lepore, *Name of War*, x; James D. Drake, *King Philip's War: Civil War in New England, 1675–1676* (Amherst: University of Massachusetts Press, 1999), 6.

4. Barnwell, "Journal," 5:394.

5. Barnwell, "Journal," 5:395, 398, 400; 6:47.

6. Drake, *King Philip's War*, 5; Tzvetan Todorov, *Conquest of America: The Question of the Other* (New York: Harper and Row, 1984), 49; Jean-Philippe Mathy, "The Atlantic as Metaphor," *Atlantic Studies* 1 (2004): 110.

7. Barnwell, "Journal," 6:45, 51.

8. Barnwell, "Journal," 6:45.

9. Hugh T. Lefler and Albert R. Newsome, *History of a Southern State: North Carolina*, 3rd ed. (Chapel Hill: University of North Carolina Press, 1973), 71; Alan Gallay, *The Indian Slave Trade: The Rise of the English Empire in the American South* (New Haven: Yale University Press, 2002), 264.

10. Neil Whitehead, "Introduction," in *Histories and Historicities in Amazonia*, ed. Neil Whitehead (Lincoln: University of Nebraska Press, 2003), x–xiii.

11. Elias Johnson, *Legends, Traditions, and Laws of the Iroquois* (Lockport, N.Y.: Union Printing and Publishing, 1881), 6–7, 67.

12. Stephen D. Feeley, "Tuscarora Trails: Indian Migrations, War, and Constructions of Colonial Frontiers" (Ph.D. diss., College of William and Mary, 2007), 325–36.

13. James T. Carson, *Making an Atlantic World: Circles, Paths, and Stories from the Colonial South* (Knoxville: University of Tennessee Press, 2007), 6–11; John E. Byrd and Charles L. Heath, "'The Country Here Is Very Thicke of Indian Towns and Plantations': Tuscarora Settlement Patterns as Revealed by the Contentrea Creek Survey," in *Indian and European Contact in Context: The Mid-Atlantic Region*, ed. Dennis B. Blanton and Julia A. King (Gainesville: University Press of Florida, 2004), 99; Wayne E. Lee, "Fortify, Fight, or Flee: Tuscarora and Cherokee Defensive Warfare and Military Culture Adaptation," *Journal of Military History* 68 (July 2004): 724–27; David Cusik, *Sketches of Ancient History of the Six Nations* (Lewiston, N.Y., 1828), 21–34.

14. Johnson, *Legends*, 54–58.

15. Feeley, "Tuscarora Trails," 87; Lee, "Fortify," 726–27; Byrd and Heath, "'The Country Here,'" 101–6.

16. Feeley, "Tuscarora Trails," 21–25, 37, 44, 48, 70–79; Michelle LeMaster, "In the 'Scolding Houses': Indians and the Law in Eastern North Carolina, 1684–1760," *NCHR* 83 (April 2006): 198.

17. Johnson, *Legends*, 40–41, 61–62.

18. Johnson, *Legends*, 40–41; Blair A. Rudes, *Tuscarora-English/English-Tuscarora Dictionary* (Toronto: University of Toronto Press, 1999), 301–2.

19. Feeley, "Tuscarora Trails," 46–47; Lefler and Newsome, *History of a Southern State*, 55–56; Christoph von Graffenried, *Christoph von Graffenried's Account of the Founding of New Bern*, ed. Vincent H. Todd (Raleigh: Edwards and Broughton, 1920), 63; Steven J. Oatis, *A Colonial Complex: South Carolina's Frontiers in the Era of the Yamassee War, 1680–1730* (Lincoln: University of Nebraska Press, 2004), 84–85; Noeleen McIlvenna, *A Very Mutinous People: The Struggle for North Carolina, 1660–1713* (Chapel Hill: University of North Carolina Press, 2009), 17, 110, 113–14, 118–19.

20. Byrd and Heath, "'The Country Here,'" 99; Lee, "Fortify," 732; McIlvenna, *Very Mutinous People*, 114–17.

21. Lawson, *New Voyage*, 64; 184, emphasis in original; 240.

22. Barnwell, "Journal," 5:397; Oatis, *Colonial Complex*, 85; Graffenried, *Account*, 234; Johnson, *Legends*, 64; Alexander Spotswood to Lord Dartmouth, July 15, 1711, in *The Official Letters of Alexander Spotswood*, ed. R. A. Brock, 2 vols. (Richmond: Virginia Historical Society, 1882–87), 1:85; Spotswood to Lord Dartmouth, 28 July 1711, in *Official Letters of Alexander Spotswood*, 1:106; Lefler and Newsome, *History of a Southern State*, 60–61.

23. Oatis, *Colonial Complex*, 85; Graffenried, *Account*, 234, 265; McIlvenna, *Very Mutinous People*, 148–49.

24. Graffenried, *Account*, 266–70, 281; Christina Snyder, *Slavery in Indian Country: The Changing Face of Captivity in Early America* (Cambridge: Harvard University Press, 2010), 95; McIlvenna, *Very Mutinous People*, 149.

25. Oatis, *Colonial Complex*, 86; Byrd and Heath, "'The Country Here,'" 102; Lee, "Fortify," 732; Graffenried, *Account*, 238; Johnson, *Legends*, 41; Feeley, "Tuscarora Trails," 136, 146; Frederic Gleach, *Powhatan's World and Colonial Virginia* (Lincoln: University of Nebraska Press, 1997), 43–54, 154–58.

26. Oatis, *Colonial Complex*, 86; Byrd and Heath, "'The Country Here,'" 104; Spotswood to the Council of Trade, December 28, 1711, in Spotswood, *Official Letters*, 1:130; Spotswood to Council of Trade, October 15, 1711, in *Official Letters*, 1:116; Spotswood to the Council of Trade, November 7, 1711, in *Official Letters*, 1:121–22; Spotswood to Lord Dartmouth, December 28, 1711, in *Official Letters*, 1:135.

27. John Grenier, *The First Way of War: American War Making on the Frontier, 1607–1814* (Cambridge, U.K.: Cambridge University Press, 2005), 43–44; Armstrong Starkey, *European and Native American Warfare, 1675–1815* (London: Routledge, 1998), 41–42; Barnwell, "Journal," 5:395; McIlvenna, *Very Mutinous People*, 151.

28. Grenier, *First Way of War*, 44; David H. Fischer, *Champlain's Dream* (Toronto: Knopf Canada, 2008), 328; Barnwell, "Journal," 5:395–96.

29. Starkey, *European and Native American Warfare*, 18–22; Patrick M. Malone, *Skulking Way of War: Technology and Tactics among the New England Indians* (Baltimore: Johns Hopkins University Press, 1993), 26–29; Gleach, *Powhatan's World*, 43–54; Barnwell, "Journal," 5:396–97.

30. Barnwell, "Journal," 5:399.

31. James Merrell, *The Indians' New World: Catawbas and Their Neighbors from European Contact through the Era of Removal* (New York: Norton, 1991), 106; Snyder, *Slavery*, 96; Barnwell, "Journal," 5:399.

32. Barnwell, "Journal," 5:399.

33. Barnwell, "Journal," 5:399–400.

34. Feeley, "Tuscarora Trails," 275; Barnwell, "Journal," 5:402.

35. Barnwell, "Journal," 5:402.

36. Barnwell, "Journal," 5:402, 6:43.

37. Barnwell, "Journal," 6:43.

38. Barnwell, "Journal," 6:44.
39. Graffenried, *Account*, 244; Barnwell, "Journal," 5:400 and 6:43–45, 50.
40. Barnwell, "Journal," 6:45; Lee, "Fortify," 736.
41. Barnwell, "Journal," 6:45.
42. Barnwell, "Journal," 6:46.
43. Barnwell, "Journal," 6:46.
44. Barnwell, "Journal," 6:47; and Peter N. Moogk, *La Nouvelle France: A Cultural History* (East Lansing: Michigan State University Press, 2001), 26.
45. Barnwell, "Journal," 6:47.
46. Lee, "Fortify," 736–40; Graffenried, *Account*, 244; Barnwell, "Journal," 6:48–54.
47. Graffenried, *Account*, 244; Barnwell, "Journal," 6:48–54.
48. Barnwell, "Journal," 54.
49. Feeley, "Tuscarora Trails," 276–78; Graffenried, *Account*, 244; Joseph W. Barnwell, "The Second Tuscarora Expedition," *SCHGM* 10 (January 1909): 35–36; Lee, "Fortify," 713–14, 743; M. Thomas Hatley, *The Dividing Paths: Cherokees and South Carolinians through the Era of Revolution* (New York: Oxford University Press, 1995), 25.
50. Graffenried, *Account*, 244; Barnwell, "Second Tuscarora Expedition," 10:35–36, 39; Oatis, *Colonial Complex*, 47–51; Gallay, *Indian Slave Trade*, 278, 285; Margaret Ellen Newell, "Indian Slavery in Colonial New England," in *Indian Slavery in Colonial America*, ed. Alan Gallay (Lincoln: University of Nebraska Press, 2009), 50–51; Feeley, "Tuscarora Trails," 285.
51. Barbara Fields, "Ideology and Race in American History," in *Region, Race, and Reconstruction: Essays in Honor of C. Vann Woodward*, ed. J. Morgan Kousser and James MacPherson (New York: Oxford University Press, 1982), 144; Henry Louis Gates, "Editor's Introduction: Writing 'Race' and the Difference It Makes," *Critical Inquiry* 12 (Autumn 1985): 4–5; Mina Bay, *White Image in the Black Mind: African-American Ideas about White People, 1830–1925* (New York: Oxford University Press, 2000), 225; Ian Hacking, *Social Construction of What?* (Cambridge: Harvard University Press, 1996), 165–68, quoted in Ashis Nandy, "History's Forgotten Doubles," *History and Theory* 34 (May 1995): 50.
52. Jack P. Greene and Philip D. Morgan, "Introduction: The Present State of Atlantic History," in *Atlantic History: A Critical Appraisal*, ed. Jack P. Greene and Philip D. Morgan (New York: Oxford University Press, 2009), 10.
53. Irene Silverblatt, "Becoming Indian in the Central Andes of Seventeenth Century Peru," in *After Colonialism: Imperial Histories and Postcolonial Displacements*, ed. Gyan Prakesh (Princeton: Princeton University Press, 1995), 291.
54. Fischer, *Champlain's Dream*, 8, 10.

Part Three
Building Plantations, Challenging Authority

Thomas Pollock and the Making of an Albemarle Plantation World

BRADFORD J. WOOD

In the morning hours before daybreak during a summer day in 1711, Thomas Pollock watched cannons from a brigantine in the Chowan River launch two balls toward his house. They were aimed too high and did little damage. Pollock and his allies—the governor and council of North Carolina and about sixty others—responded by firing their own cannon, also to little effect, and the attackers in the brig dispatched two boats toward the land. As the intruders approached land, a blow to one boat from continued cannon fire, and perhaps the sight of a servant dressed in yellow livery, convinced them to make a confused retreat. The yellow-clad servant accompanied the Baron Christoph von Graffenried, and, according to Graffenried, his appearance might have led the attackers to believe that they were facing large numbers of German-speaking immigrants under his leadership. In any case the assault on Pollock's plantation, Belgra, and on the leadership of North Carolina had failed, and now Pollock's enemies became the pursued.[1]

Pollock must have felt a sense of relief. Less than a year before, when Edward Hyde arrived from England to become the colony's governor, Pollock wrote him that, amid its "distractions and disorders," North Carolina was "in danger to be insulted and trodden down by Quakers, Atheists and Deists, and other evil disposed persons."[2] Pollock considered the men on the brigantine and their leader, Thomas Cary, to be among these "evil disposed persons," and their support among North Carolina's largest and most outspoken religious dissenters, the Quakers, intensified his concern. Some of the men around Pollock shared his sense of crisis and described it with even greater hyperbole, such as when Governor Hyde characterized the Albemarle as "the most distracted Country in the Queen's Dominion" and its people as "poor Subjects that are under such a Lawless Usurpation and Oppression." Hyde believed that it was "very evident that neither mercy can engage or justice awe or Controule these Rebells."[3] John Urmston, an Anglican clergyman, accused the Cary rebels of ruining settlers through ravaging and plundering, of driving recent immigrants to the brink of starvation, and of planning violent attacks in conjunction with Native Americans.[4]

But Hyde and Urmston were relative newcomers to North Carolina, and it was Pollock's home that had been attacked. Pollock should not have been surprised that Belgra became a target. The North Carolina governor and executive council met at Pollock's house on this occasion and on many others.[5] So did the vestry of St. Paul's Anglican Church. In an Albemarle region without a notable town, Belgra had become one of the most important locations, and though Pollock—unlike Hyde—had not yet claimed the office of governor, he had become the dominant figure in a North Carolina government that seemed devoid of stable and consistent leadership.[6] For three decades by this time, and for eleven more years until Pollock's death, Pollock's life was intertwined with the history of the Albemarle, and he had been so influential that he might have imagined that he had shaped it almost as much as it had shaped him. So it seemed fitting that the last offensive of the Cary rebels failed before Belgra, which he had proudly named for the Pollocks' ancestral home in Renfrewshire. He had little time to enjoy this reprieve. A little more than two months later, a group of Tuscaroras and other Native Americans attacked hundreds of settlers on the Neuse and Pamlico Rivers, plunging North Carolina into an unusually brutal war. When Hyde died in 1712, Pollock reluctantly became acting governor of North Carolina, during the worst crisis in the colony's history, connecting Pollock's life and the history of the colony even more completely.[7] Pollock and the early North Carolina settlements both faced destruction enough times that both metropolitan authorities and modern day historians have been tempted to forget that they ever existed at all, but somehow both persevered.[8]

While Pollock believed that Belgra belonged to him, however, it also belonged to an early modern Atlantic plantation system that thrived, in one form or another, in most British American colonies and accounted for much of British America's wealth and population. In the late seventeenth and early eighteenth centuries, slavery and the plantation system underwent a dramatic expansion in the British Empire, reaching its limits in Barbados, spreading like wildfire through the British Caribbean, taking firm root in the Chesapeake and South Carolina, and becoming surprisingly important in places such as the Pennsylvania iron industry or the dairy farms of the Narragansett River valley. By the early eighteenth century, a plantation model associated with commercial agriculture and exploiting bound labor had become a goal throughout British America, even if it was a goal that was much easier to achieve in some places than in others.

For Thomas Pollock, and other ambitious men of means in a relatively remote and poor corner of the British Atlantic World such as the Albemarle, the plantation system provided both a route to greater prosperity and a set of organizing principles. Ultimately the plantation system came to dominate the North Carolina tidewater, and Thomas Pollock owned and managed a number of plantations, but neither of these outcomes came as easily or as completely as they might have in other plantation societies that have received more scholarly attention. North Carolina's treacherous coastline proved to be the biggest obstacle, because it made transatlantic trade seem impossible at times and expensive and difficult even in the best conditions. Thus the story of Thomas Pollock's career, and of the experiences of other Albemarle elites, is a story of efforts to make a plantation society on the margins, and it is, therefore, a story of mixed results.

However, the history of the Atlantic plantation system cannot be reduced to a teleological balance sheet. While planters showed as much economic acumen and interest in maximizing profits as other early modern colonists, the plantation system also sometimes depended on seemingly irrational power dynamics and required levels of organization that extended beyond economics into more political, social, and ideological concerns. While some colonies developed full-fledged slave societies and others remained merely societies with slaves, often the differences between these groups remained unpredictable to contemporaries and may have had as much to do with geographies, credit networks, and the length of growing seasons as with colonists' decision making, cultural values, or factor allocations. Thus partly successful Albemarle planters shared many of the same ideas and cultural imperatives as wealthier planters in the Chesapeake, the South Carolina lowcountry, and the British West Indies. Within this context, Thomas Pollock's experiences reveal a different glimpse at the world of more studied plantation elites. His aspirations for a place such as the Albemarle show the power of their shared vision; his failures show the precariousness of all their efforts; and his successes show the flexibility and pervasiveness of the plantation system. To Pollock, all these concerns were at stake in the summer of 1711, when the cannonballs flew at Belgra, and the following year, when the Tuscarora and their allies attacked. In this context Pollock's career as planter and leader, and with it the broader history of the early Albemarle, can be readily understood as an expansion of the ideas and impulses that made the early modern plantation system.

The following essay focuses on attempts to make the Albemarle more like other British plantation societies, and it explores them by describing Thomas Pollock's experiences. Pollock and his peers recognized a number of prerequisites for successful plantation enterprises. The most obvious of these, a ready supply of bound labor and a valuable export staple, largely eluded Albemarle planters, with significant consequences for the economic development of North Carolina. At the same time, planters such as Pollock recognized that a plantation society required more than slaves and staples, and they tried to shape the Albemarle accordingly. They sought to create a unified settler society that would make it easier to maintain order on plantations; they worked to solidify a system of racial hierarchy that would rationalize and support the subordination of both Africans and Native Americans; and they aimed to integrate North Carolina into Atlantic and imperial networks of communication and trade. While North Carolina remained on the margins of the plantation system, Pollock's generation of Albemarle elites did create a more unified and stable political order, established a clear and rigid racial hierarchy, and made the Albemarle less isolated from the rest of the British world.

Elite individuals can never be fully representative, and sources for the early Albemarle are very limited, but there is no reason to think that Pollock's attitudes toward the plantation system were anomalous. The pursuit of landed property, the use of bound and nonwhite labor, and the practice of commercial agriculture all functioned as cultural norms in British America. North Carolina's higher court records, the largest single collection of records surviving from the colony in the seventeenth century, reveal considerable attention to, pursuit of, and dispute over property, much of it in either land or labor, and no North Carolinians in this generation, including the colony's significant population of outspoken and politically active Quakers, expressed open opposition to slavery.[9] Pollock and some of his peers in the Albemarle worked to build plantations with a single-minded determination that suggests a strong cultural imperative. Indeed their efforts resemble those by contemporaries in a number of other British colonies. Pollock's efforts also show that residence in a relatively poor colony did not preclude plantation agriculture. The most comprehensive analysis of Proprietary-era North Carolina property records found clear evidence that "a fair number of settlers in the whole population were capable of commercial farming" and concluded that "their numbers force us to revise markedly the view that North Carolina was predominantly a subsistence farm region."[10]

The first permanent colonial residences in the Albemarle cannot be dated precisely but probably began within a few years of Pollock's 1654 birth in Glasgow.[11] While small numbers of settlers gradually straggled out of Virginia past the Dismal Swamp and built homes in the unpromising wilderness north of Albemarle Sound, Pollock came of age in a dynamic if provincial Scottish culture turning increasingly outward toward the wider world. When he left Scotland in the later decades of the seventeenth century, Pollock moved in the early waves of Scottish sojourners, immigrants, officials, and opportunists who would play a key role in the making of the British Atlantic. He began a career in trade after an apprenticeship with Dover merchant Thomas Cullen.[12] The details of his activities are sketchy, but he later remarked on his losses during his first seven or eight years of commerce because of his "often trading from one place to another" while he was still unacquainted with colonial trading.[13] According to Pollock, he arrived on the Piscataqua River in New England and shortly thereafter went to Boston, then to New London, Connecticut, where an unsuccessful venture in a ketch forced him to return to Boston with few resources. After this, he relocated again to North Carolina, but his fortunes failed again when he lost another shipload of goods, which he had consigned to a prominent merchant in New Providence in the Bahamas immediately before the island was taken by the Spanish in 1684. One more unprofitable relocation, this time to Barbados, drove Pollock back to the Albemarle again, where he faced "severall disappointments ther for some years for want of suit and some times no porke nor pay to be had of the people."[14] Pollock settled into the Albemarle for over two decades, but years later he revealed a long-held desire to return to Scotland, and he arrived in North Carolina with a broad view of a transatlantic British empire.[15]

By 1691 Pollock had been in North Carolina long enough to earn the enmity of the widely unpopular and contentious Governor Seth Sothell.[16] Pollock had also clearly arrived with important connections. About this time he was named a deputy for one of the proprietors, Lord Carteret, and Pollock's business activities and later correspondence reveal acquaintances with well-placed merchants in both Great Britain and in other colonies, as well as an especially well-developed network of commercial connections in Boston.[17] Moreover Pollock entered the Albemarle as part of a new generation of opportunistic newcomers who aimed to fill a power vacuum left by the passing of North Carolina's tenuous first generation of leaders.[18]

Thomas Pollock also left no account of his motives for coming to North Carolina, but the availability of land gave the Albemarle whatever allure it may have held for settlers in the late seventeenth century. The notoriously difficult coastline along the Outer Banks put severe constraints on commercial opportunities in the Albemarle, and anyone who made a profit from North Carolina's trade during these decades was more likely to do so from New England or elsewhere than from the colony itself. Pollock did remain quite active in trade after settling in the Albemarle, but ultimately he turned much of his attention to the acquisition and use of land.[19]

Pollock accumulated much larger landholdings than any other North Carolina colonist during his lifetime. Tax lists, patents, deeds, and other sources make it clear that Pollock probably owned well over fifty thousand acres across several North Carolina counties. With Pollock's sons' patents, the Pollock family also patented close to ninety thousand acres between 1706 and 1729, even while large patents of over a thousand acres proved less common in the Albemarle than in Virginia.[20] Most of Thomas Pollock's documented landholdings came through patents, primarily after 1712, but he also purchased large amounts of land and held thousands of acres by the early 1690s.[21] This vast acreage of land could not all be cleared and put into use, and much of it may have been unsuitable for agriculture, but Pollock clearly pursued land with more than merely speculative intentions. Belgra and at least a half dozen of the pieces of land mentioned in his will were named, and the will makes reference to a variety of uses for these lands, noting tracts suited for gathering lightwood; to the locations of mills; to which lands were still being cleared by slaves; and to the allocation of profits that Pollock expected from crops that had already been planted and for tar and pitch yet to be made.[22] Pollock and other Albemarle settlers had obviously learned plantation management techniques from Virginia, the British West Indies, and elsewhere.

In addition to significant amounts of useful land, successful plantations usually required access to markets, marketable commodities, and sufficient labor. Unfortunately for Pollock and his peers, the geography of eastern North Carolina imposed serious limitations on the development of the plantation system. The inaccessible coastline made shipping dangerous, more expensive, and necessarily small scale, while poor soils made crop cultivation precarious and often unrewarding. In the late seventeenth and very early eighteenth centuries, plantation agriculture on the North American mainland proved challenging even where it was well established, so the prospects for building plantations in the Albemarle must have been daunting.[23] Tobacco, which proved to be so important in nearby Virginia, dominated the Albemarle economy in its earliest decades, but by the start of the eighteenth century most North Carolina farmers had given up on growing large amounts of tobacco in the face of declining markets, increasing competition, and continued opposition from Virginians who sought to prevent Albemarle tobacco planters from using their more convenient port facilities.[24] Most of the records relating to Pollock's plantations postdate this decline in Albemarle tobacco cultivation, and there is no indication that Pollock grew much tobacco, instead devoting his resources to cultivating maize, making naval stores, and selling pork and other provisions. South Carolinians developed a profitable rice economy in these decades, but neither rice, so successful in South Carolina, nor the sugar of the West Indies could be grown successfully in the Albemarle. When faced with too much adversity to imitate plantations in Virginia and Barbados, Pollock and others in the Albemarle crafted their own more diversified if less profitable plantation model. Rather than producing one major staple, Albemarle plantations made the most efficient use of limited labor resources by balancing the production requirements of multiple crops with forest industries and other activities.[25] Pollock's apparent success with this entrepreneurial strategy indicates that it held some promise, even if it could not compare to profits from tobacco, rice, or sugar.[26]

Pollock's efforts to implement a plantation system in North Carolina faced their biggest obstacle in the limited supply of bound labor. While the transatlantic slave trade expanded during these years and brought slaves to almost every corner of the British colonial world, traders overlooked the Albemarle because of the dangers of its coast and because its markets offered nothing to make the sale of slaves sufficiently profitable.[27] Pollock's letters provide ample testimony to the limited slave trade to the early Albemarle. In twenty-six out of Pollock's eighty-nine surviving letters related to trade, he expressed interest in buying slaves. Pollock's inquiries followed a clear and almost unvarying pattern from 1715 to 1719, indicating that he wished to obtain slaves more than any other commodity, that he would forego any other opportunities for them, and that he would pay for them by any means available to him. Pollock always specified a preference for "young lykely" slaves and sometimes also asked that they be "sound or "new." He also wanted slaves in an age range from twelve to the early twenties, and, while he was content to buy about as many women as men, he expected to pay more for men. But Pollock clearly could not be selective, and the letters do not indicate that he actually purchased many slaves as a result of these inquiries, probably because he lacked connections to merchants involved in the African trade or even in other ports with substantial numbers of slaves. New England merchants dominated both the Albemarle's coastal trade and Pollock's trade networks, so Pollock could buy only small numbers of slaves, who would become available in the marginal Boston slave market.[28] Because of these obstacles, African slaves in North Carolina numbered in the hundreds and not the thousands during Pollock's lifetime. In this context it is not surprising that Pollock would pay slave traders "as much as I believe any will," because, when it came to slaves, he was "much in want of having some of them for[,] having a considerable quantity of land[,] I want hands to settle it."[29]

Some North Carolinians, like European colonists in a variety of other settings, enslaved Native Americans to meet labor shortages, but this too remained a limited solution.[30] Pollock's letters reveal that he could not count on buying enslaved Native Americans in the Albemarle. For example, in 1716 he wrote a correspondent specifically to buy an "Indian slave" in another location.[31] Other sources indicate that on at least a few occasions Pollock bought Narragansetts from merchants in Boston.[32] By contrast South Carolinians exported many thousands of bound Native Americans during Pollock's career, so it is not entirely clear why a similar trade could not be accessed in the Albemarle. South Carolina's emphasis on enslaved native labor may not have been much greater than North Carolina's prior to the South Carolina expedition against Spanish St. Augustine and native groups to the south starting in 1702, but in any case North Carolinians had smaller numbers of both African and native slaves.[33] Native Americans remained a formidable presence in eastern North Carolina, but no specific native group emerged to provide slaves to colonists as the Westos, Savannahs, and Yamasees did further south.[34] Competition from Virginians and South Carolinians may have combined with geographic factors to limit the scale of Native American slavery in the early Albemarle. While significant numbers of Native Americans labored on Albemarle plantations during these years, they never compared to the numbers of enslaved Africans. Indentured servants might have been another, cheaper alternative, but they also remained few in number, often depended on transatlantic migration patterns, and were fading in importance even in the Chesapeake by this time.[35] Ultimately Pollock turned partly to each of these alternatives to build the largest labor force in the region, but he never acquired as many laborers as he needed to implement a plantation system comparable to those operated by some elites elsewhere.

Headright claims, lists of taxables, and Pollock's will all provide some evidence about his ownership of bound labor. For example, from 1693 to 1712, Pollock claimed thirty-seven headrights that were identified by race in the surviving records. Thirty-two were African, and five were Native American, and all these individuals were probably enslaved. Pollock seems to have been typical in his labor choices, as other colonists' headright claims during this period shared a similar ratio of Africans to Native Americans.[36] Lists of taxables and other sources indicate that he had over thirty laborers in the 1710s, though conceivably these could have been slaves or servants, European, African, or Native American; but in 1709 he had already given his children over twenty other slaves in a series of deeds.[37] Pollock's will distributed over seventy additional slaves between his three sons and made no references to servants. The lists of slave names in Pollock's will and similar documents offer little clarity about the origins of his slaves, but names such as "Manuel," "Mingo," "Cajo," and "Diego" suggest their varied backgrounds and heterogeneity.[38] In sum the evidence about Pollock's property strongly suggests that Pollock had to acquire his work force gradually, in small groups, from different locations, and from indentured servants, African slaves, and Native American slaves. If his persistent search for laborers seems frenetic and ineffectual compared to the efforts of planters in some other colonies, in the context of the early Albemarle even the lowest number given for his slaveholdings, thirty-one in 1717, substantially exceeds any other single slaveholding on the surviving lists of taxables for North Carolina during his lifetime.[39] In the Albemarle, Pollock and Pollock alone acquired a slave labor force comparable to the some of the largest in South Carolina lowcountry rice parishes around the time of his death.[40] Yet nothing in Pollock's letters or the other surviving sources indicates that he relented in his drive to acquire more slaves, and both the frequency of his references to the slave trade and the size of his slaveholdings seem to have increased later in his life. Thus Pollock's experience suggests that Albemarle planters failed to develop a more fully fledged plantation system first and foremost because of an insufficient supply of exploitable labor. Land ownership in North Carolina was unusually widespread, and a diversified combination of commodities could make plantations profitable, but few North Carolinians could marshal a larger labor force than that of a large family farm.[41] Still, by the start of the eighteenth century, Pollock and other Albemarle setters worked hard to make North Carolina into a slave society in order to reap the economic benefits of the Atlantic plantation system, even if their efforts yielded limited results.

As Pollock and other planters discovered, however, the plantation system required as much attention to power dynamics as to profit and loss. Bound laborers resisted exploitation, and the survival of the plantation system depended on a social and cultural order that supported planters' idea of their own mastery. In thinly settled regions with relatively few slaves such as the Albemarle, authority seemed tenuous, order often proved elusive, and planters sometimes found recalcitrant laborers to be even more formidable.⁴² Ultimately, making the Albemarle into a slave society required both more slaves and a social order that supported masters in exploiting their slaves.

Little is known about Pollock's earliest experiences with slave labor, but by 1697 he had learned that slavery depended on force and could make other aspects of the social order more vulnerable. When contentious North Carolina colonists and strong-willed slaves came together in disputes surrounding the estate of John Lear, Pollock, as an estate executor, ended up in the middle. He complained to a court about his efforts "keeping peace on the plantations between Mr Hawkins Mr Stephens and Negro Mannuell" while they were "threatning one anothers life." Because of these potentially violent disputes between two free men and a slave, Pollock found that he was "forced to goe many tymes over myself and sometimes to cary men in arms alonge with me." Consequently his "Trouble and care" over the Lear estate became "so greatt that I solemly protest I would nott undertake to goe through the lyke again for a greatt deallmore then whatt I charge."⁴³ The court records do not indicate why these three men had so much difficulty getting along, but they do make it clear that, Manuel, one of the slaves in Pollock's care, was involved in a very tense and dangerous situation and that at times only considerable force could maintain order on Albemarle plantations. Pollock believed that he could use slave labor profitably in the Albemarle, but he could not have indulged in any illusions about the potential for violence in this system after repeatedly bringing armed men to prevent Manuel and others from committing murder on Lear's plantation.

Pollock's anxieties about controlling bound labor became even more apparent a few years later. In a petition Pollock explained to the North Carolina Court of Chancery that he could not attend the court "having twoe slaves newly runaway." Pollock felt that if he failed to catch the runaway slaves, the consequences would be greater than merely the loss of two slaves. He "had great reason to suspect" that they might "gather to a greater head and doe mischief on this shore." Moreover he explained that the court should excuse him, because the escape of these two slaves threatened his "own interest," the "safty" of his family, and "the peace of the place." He also argued that his absence would encourage more slaves to flee and would therefore multiply the problem.⁴⁴ This document testifies to both Pollock's determination to maintain order on his plantations and his failure to do so. If two runaway slaves could pose such a serious threat to Pollock's authority or, even more tellingly, to his peace of mind, then one wonders how he functioned as the master of dozens, and later scores, of bound laborers.

Pollock's experiences as a slave owner can be traced further in evidence about his relationship with his slave Manuel, who is mentioned in two court cases in 1697 and in a few scattered property records afterward. Thomas

Pollock acquired Manuel, and his wife, Frank, while serving as an estate executor.[45] When the court asked Pollock to list goods in his possession, he included that "Negro Manuel and Franck had their bed and bed cloaths and Manuell one gunn or barrell of a Gun at Isaac Rowdens."[46] The location of this property at the residence of Isaac Rowden, a free white colonist, suggests that Manuel was allowed significant mobility. Manuel's ownership of firearms may also help to explain the death threats between Manuel and Hawkins and Stephens, and it underscores the difficulty Pollock faced if he tried to curb Manuel's autonomy.[47] In 1697 Manuel gave a group of white fugitives refuge on one of Pollock's plantation. When the fugitives gave depositions in an adultery case, their narratives mentioned that they "were up at Colonel Polickes house" where they "had sum tobaco and Rosting yeares of Corne of Colonel Pollickes negro Manuell" and also gave another slave a gun to serve as their pilot. This passing reference to Manuel reveals his complicity in various forms of social disorder and crime, and he seems to have been able to act with impunity and without supervision.[48] Yet even if he might have stood out as one of Pollock's most potentially troublesome and recalcitrant slaves, he might also have exercised so much autonomy because of the confidence Pollock placed in him. Pollock referred to one of his plantations as "ye plantation where manuel lived," which may have indicated that Manuel ran the plantation for Pollock, and the plantation continued to be referred to as "Manuells" by another generation of Pollocks.[49] Perhaps Pollock felt that he could trust Manuel, because by 1709 Manuel and Frank had at least five enslaved children in the Pollock estate.[50] Plantation owners often put slaves in positions of authority over each other and sometimes allocated them substantial autonomy in the Atlantic plantation system. Still, while Manuel himself remains an enigma, the flexibility of Manuel's situation must have still been unsettling to Pollock, who feared that two runaways could threaten the safety of his family and the general peace. Yet Pollock continually worked to amass larger slaveholdings for another twenty years after these incidents.

If Pollock could scarcely feel at ease with African slaves, even when he could obtain them, his other prominent labor alternative, enslaved Native Americans, presented equally daunting problems. While virtually all early modern British colonists considered Native Americans to be culturally inferior savages, they often disagreed about the appropriate direction for relations between natives and colonists. Many colonial leaders preferred to maintain peace and keep trade open with native groups as long as it suited their interests. Pollock made his position clear in 1707 by leading an apparently unprovoked attack against a group of Meherrins. The Meherrins complained to the Virginia Council that Pollock and other armed men "sett upon" their settlement and "having taken 36 of the said Indians prisoners kept them two full days in a fort till with the excessive heat and for want of water they were almost destroyed." Pollock and his allies also "broke down their cabins and committed several other outrages" including "threatening to cut off their corn and to turn them off their land." These actions seemed especially controversial because the government of Virginia maintained a relatively peaceful trading relationship with the Meherrins, whom they considered their tributary subjects. By contrast, North Carolinians denied the authority of the Virginians over the Meherrins and considered them both more of a threat and an obstacle to expansion. The 1707 attack cast Pollock as a leader among Albemarle colonists who believed in using more aggressive means against Native Americans. According to the Virginians, Pollock claimed his actions had the authority of the British Crown, but in fact he acted for "some few insatiable people who aim at the Indian land." [51] For Pollock, and others who shared his views, however, the civilizing project of the British Empire in North Carolina could not readily be reconciled with the presence of "savages" such as the Meherrin, and the desire to dispossess them could be rationalized as "improvement" instead of mere greed. In this context, Pollock's hostility toward and mistrust of the Meherrins and other native peoples made it difficult for him to accept the widespread use of indigenous slaves on his plantations, because Native Americans were too numerous, and the threat was too great if natives and colonists could not coexist peacefully.

By the time Pollock launched his attack on the Meherrins, he had resolved to put almost as much energy into improving and developing Albemarle society, culture, and government as he had put into his own plantations. In doing so, he pursued many of the same goals as aspiring plantation owners in other British colonies. If plantation owners in a slave society, or even a society with slaves, were to marshal the resources required for large profits and maintain control over their labor forces, they needed stability, social and political order, and a well-established hierarchy.

Thomas Pollock relied on the Anglican church as one of the bulwarks of a British social order, and contemporaries recognized him as one of the staunchest supporters of an established church in North Carolina. Along these lines he supported two controversial processes in the Albemarle, the implementation of a formal Anglican church structure through several vestry acts and the marginalization of Quakers and other dissenters that many Anglicans perceived as threatening. For Pollock these religious efforts blended with broader concerns about authority, civility, and morality. Along these lines, when Anglican minister William Gordon left North Carolina, Pollock praised the "religion and Charity" Gordon had for the colonists and hoped Gordon would help them to once again "injoy the Sunshine of religion; justice and order." By contrast, in Gordon's absence North Carolina disintegrated into "confusion and order," and the absence of an established Anglican church transcended solely religious concerns and enabled "darke clouds of quakarisme, Envy, and ignorance."[52] Pollock must have been acutely aware that North Carolina had existed for almost half a century before British assistance made it possible for Anglican religious services to be conducted on a regular basis, and the sizeable and politically active Quaker minority in the Albemarle seemed to be a threat to much that he valued. Pollock and other Albemarle Anglicans considered their religious differences with the Quakers to have broad moral and political implications, even though many of the Quaker leaders resembled the Anglicans in their property holdings and slave ownership.

Tensions between North Carolina's Anglicans and Quakers contributed to a period of political instability culminating in an event known as Cary's Rebellion. Complicated political maneuvering, shifting allegiances, and limited sources make the events around Cary's Rebellion hard to summarize or fully explain, but the key issues, and Pollock's relationship to them, seem clear. Quakers found political allies among religiously tolerant Anglicans, especially those with interests in North Carolina's recently settled Bath County, and together they challenged the authority of the colony's predominantly Anglican leadership, which was anchored in the Albemarle and especially in Chowan County. Thomas Cary was a wealthy merchant sent from South Carolina to govern North Carolina, and when he became embroiled in several challenges to his political authority, Cary used force to try to seize power.[53] Pollock took a predictable stance in favor of the established Chowan County Anglicans, but his writings make it clear that he was driven by a deep sense of anxiety about both religious dissent and political disorder.

Consequently Pollock positioned himself on the side of the Chowan Anglicans but repeatedly sought to contain the disturbance and reinforce what he perceived to be legitimate authority. During election proceedings in 1708 violence appeared imminent between the voters for and against the Cary faction, but Pollock intervened. As William Glover described the situation, "if Col Pollock (being on a plantation of his that joined on the election field) had not hindered and persuaded the people to keep the peace, [the quarrels] would have ended in blows."[54] As a series of complicated events unfolded, however, the Chowan Anglicans achieved greater political legitimacy, partly through the leadership of Edward Hyde, and the Cary faction proved more willing to use violence and disorder as means to their ends. Ultimately Pollock's loyalties and desire for stability reinforced each other, and he became a staunch opponent of the Cary rebels. When Cary gained control of the government, Pollock fled to Virginia for a time because he was not "willing to live under a government I knew was altogether illegal."[55] His religious concerns, quest for political stability, vast property holdings in land and labor, and even Belgra itself hung in the balance by the time the Cary Rebels had armed their brig in the summer of 1711.

Pollock and others also viewed the disruptions of Cary's Rebellion in the context of the British Empire. On one level, most of the participants in the political events surrounding Cary's Rebellion acknowledged or, in some cases exploited, the Carolina Proprietors' neglect of North Carolina, which clearly contributed to the chaotic situation.[56] In addition to this obvious problem with transatlantic authority and communication, however, British elites, even in a remote place such as the Albemarle, readily drew on a well-known imperial discourse about instability and challenges to hierarchy. At the time of Cary's Rebellion, many British officials were fixated on the murder of Leeward Islands governor Daniel Parke in 1710, which came to symbolize the threat of antiauthoritarian colonial violence. It is not surprising that this comparison entered into conversations about the Cary rebels, as Virginia's Governor Spotswood wrote that Cary "had the madness to insinuate" that Edward Hyde "might expect the same fate Collo Park had in Antegoa."[57] Anglican clergyman John Urmston, in his characteristically dramatic fashion, drew on an older and more religiously oriented but equally potent image of disorder in British elite culture. According to Urmston, North Carolina during these years resembled the Cromwellian Protectorate, or "Olivers days come again" because "people did and said what they list."[58] To men such as Spotswood, Hyde, Urmston, and Pollock, the ascent of the Cary rebels heralded the destruction of a hierarchy that protected their position and enabled the development of British colonial plantations.

If Cary's Rebellion reminded Pollock and his peers of the weakness of authority in some British societies, the onset of the Tuscarora War showed them the vulnerability of all British American colonies.[59] When Tuscaroras and their allies attacked the North Carolina settlements on the Neuse and Pamlico in September, 1711, the colonists reeled from the shock, groped unsuccessfully to gather enough provisions, ammunition, and even clothing for warfare, and struggled to organize a military response. Settlers across the colony sought protection, while the attackers killed over 150, took captives, harassed livestock, and destroyed farms, and consequently Bath County was "totally wasted and ruined" by the end of the war.[60] Even in the Albemarle region, trade slowed to a halt, and families clustered in forts. Partly due to poor growing seasons during the war years, food shortages and war-related economic problems would continue for years. Low morale, apathy, and disorganization made it difficult to find soldiers. When Edward Hyde died in a 1712 yellow fever epidemic, Pollock, as acting governor, wrote that Hyde left North Carolina "in a most deplorable condition: a barbarous enemy to deal with; a scarcity of provisions, being scarce able to supply our garrisons and what small forces have out; and, the worst of all, a divided ungovernable people."[61] Even allowing for some exaggeration in the surviving accounts, the Tuscarora War in North Carolina may have caused as much desperation and anxiety as any similar crisis in the history of any British colony in America.

The dire situation persuaded Hyde, Pollock, and others to turn to neighboring colonies for assistance. It became clear as early as 1711 that North Carolina could not defend itself, when a planned militia counterattack under Pollock's leadership was abandoned. At about the same time, North Carolina sought assistance from Virginia and South Carolina. South Carolina provided an army, primarily of Yamasees and Catawbas with some colonists, under the leadership of John Barnwell. Barnwell's force had considerable success against the Tuscarora in 1712 before Barnwell signed a highly controversial truce, probably because he had been insufficiently supplied for a longer expedition. When the truce failed after a few months, South Carolinians were persuaded to send a larger expedition, this time led by James Moore. Moore's forces dealt a shattering blow to the Tuscarora at Fort Neoheroka in March 1713. The enormous cost of supplying Moore's expedition and the adverse conditions of the war in general persuaded Pollock to turn to negotiation. In spring 1713 he made a truce with Tom Blount, who emerged as a leader among Tuscaroras and other Native Americans in northeastern North Carolina during the war. Blount's authority among the Tuscarora seems to have been a recent construction and clearly had limits. Blount rose in the northern Tuscaroras towns, whose residents preferred peaceful relations and had not attacked the colonists, but with the support of Pollock and other colonists he claimed leadership of all the Tuscaroras.[62] Despite lingering hostilities with dissident natives, by this time the worst of the storm had passed. The Tuscaroras began an exodus from North Carolina, and their allies found themselves increasingly marginalized.

As William S. Price has noted, during the Tuscarora War, Pollock led with skill and decisiveness. In a colony facing a scarcity of food, he organized the collection and transportation of thousands of bushels of corn and other provisions to supply Moore's expedition. He also strengthened the colony's government with innovative measures, including the first emission of currency in its history and new taxes.[63] None of Pollock's decisions during this period of crisis, however, marked a serious departure from his outlook on the Albemarle or from his determination to make it into a place suited for plantations. He remained at least as concerned about social stability as about new problems, refused to trust Native Americans even when they supported his cause, and increasingly considered the Albemarle part of a larger British imperial system.

Pollock, like many contemporaries and many historians since, drew a connection between Cary's Rebellion and the outbreak of the Tuscarora War. In fact some of his political allies and a few scholars have gone so far as to argue that the Cary rebels encouraged the Native American attack on the Bath County settlements.[64] It was claimed that, for their "rebellious purposes" Edmond Porter, Thomas Cary, and others "endeavoured by promises of reward to draw into their conspiracy the neighbouring Indians" in order to "cut off all such of her majesty's subjects as should oppose their lawless proceedings."[65] Despite his deep resentment of the Cary rebels, Pollock offered a different interpretation of the relationship between these events. In his view the Tuscaroras chose to strike when they did because they were aware that disunity among the colonists made their settlements more vulnerable, and he continued to lament that the Quakers and others failed to support the war effort. Pollock summed up his interpretation by writing that "Our own divisions (chiefly occasioned by the Quakers and some other evil disposed persons) hath been the cause of all our troubles."[66] He continued to see issues of internal instability and conflict as the fundamental problem in North Carolina, even as external enemies threatened to destroy much of the colony.

While Pollock blamed Quakers and other colonists for North Carolina's problems, the Tuscarora War did little to change his negative view of Native Americans. As before 1711, he considered them a threat to the spread of British civilization in North Carolina, as well as a possible source of plantation labor. Regardless of this attitude, however, Native American allies proved necessary for North Carolina's survival, and it was they, rather than colonists, who did most of the fighting against the Tuscaroras, both as part of the expeditions from South Carolina and after the truce with Tom Blount. While in the heat of war Pollock referred to enemy warriors as "vermin," he also expressed continual suspicion of Blount and other allies. When "forced at present to bear with" Blount, he wrote, of Native Americans, that "there is no dependence on their promises, they being bound by no ties of religion, honor, nor honesty."[67] When peace was finally achieved, he feared that hostilities would break out again, "there being but little trust to be put in Indians."[68] Given these sentiments, it is not a surprise that Pollock also saw the conflict as a means of acquiring slave labor, and the Tuscarora War is inexplicable without the region's slave trade. Slave trading may well have provoked the Tuscarora attack that began the war; both the Barnwell and the Moore South Carolina expeditions depended on the capture of slaves as an incentive for the colonists and their Native American allies; and the government of North Carolina itself sold captured warriors into slavery.[69] In at least one instance during the war, Pollock, an experienced slave buyer and seller, used his own money to buy captured Native Americans and arranged for their sale in the British West Indies.[70]

Pollock's continued hostility, even toward Native Americans fighting on his side, underscores his focus on British solidarity, even across colonial lines. As Stephen Feeley has noted, the Tuscarora War combined characteristics of more localized seventeenth-century conflicts between colonists and natives and broader and transregional frontier wars of the nineteenth century.[71] No one played a more instrumental role in expanding the scope of the Tuscarora War than Pollock, who worked diligently to find allies from across the southeast. His repeated requests for assistance from the colony's "guardian angel," South Carolina's Governor Craven, led not only to two successful military expeditions against the Tuscaroras but also to South Carolina's substantial and decisive involvement in the Tuscarora War.[72] While similar overtures to Governor Spotswood did not result in military aid or comparable involvement from Virginians, they did ensure that Spotswood's government provided resources, organizational assistance, and encouragement to the North Carolina war effort.[73] Both the Native Americans in the South Carolina expeditions and the alliance supporting the Tuscarora War efforts drew on far-flung native networks of interaction and diplomacy. Pollock recognized this dynamic and corresponded with authorities in colonial New York, attempting to assess and limit the chances of the Tuscaroras receiving military assistance from the Five Nations Iroquois to the north.[74] By the end of the Tuscarora War, new experiences and connections had much more fully integrated the Albemarle into both Native American and colonial networks of communication and diplomacy.

In the years after the peace agreement in 1713, open conflict between North Carolina colonists and Native Americans gradually faded. Both sides had experienced considerable suffering during the war, and many colonists had "quitted their plantations," but the cost to the Tuscaroras had clearly been much greater, leading most of them to leave the Carolinas and reconstitute themselves among the Iroquois to the north.[75] From Pollock's perspective, the indigenous peoples of the tidewater no longer posed as formidable a threat or offered a viable labor force. Still, they did not vanish, with new reports of violence against colonists for at least five years after the war ended, and Pollock remained anxious, knowing that some of his enemies fled to the swamps "where it is impossible for white men to follow them."[76] In fact one of the last references to Pollock in the surviving records before his death in 1722 underscores his continued sense of vulnerability years after Cary and the Tuscaroras had been defeated, indicating that John Cope, "a Christian Indian belonging to King Blounts Towne" broke into Pollock's bedroom at Belgra during the night and assaulted him.[77]

Still, despite the war's costs and lingering concerns and insecurities that might often remain hidden from the documentary record, the end of the Tuscarora War brought considerable and tangible benefits to Pollock and his peers in the Albemarle elite. Not only were Native Americans in the region far more marginalized, but the political power of the Quakers remained diminished after Cary's Rebellion, and even though they initially showed little support for the war effort, Quakers began to work together with Pollock and other Anglicans. While under Glover's and Hyde's governorships, they had been "refractory and ungovernable"; Pollock felt that he "must needs acknowledge" that they had been "as ready (especially in supplying provision for the forces) as any others in the Government."[78] The decline of Quaker opposition marked part of a broader process in which the Albemarle elite consolidated their political power, and their dominance would remain largely unchallenged until after the settlement of Cape Fear a decade later.[79] Concerns about white solidarity in the colony must have also been assuaged by the passage of North Carolina's first comprehensive slave code in 1715. While these laws may have merely codified existing practices, they demonstrated a white consensus in support of race-based slavery and gave the institution additional trappings of legitimacy.[80]

Some of the economic setbacks caused by the Tuscarora War also seemed surprisingly short lived. Shipping records indicate that North Carolina's intercolonial trade increased after the end of the Tuscarora War, probably partly because of peace between European powers.[81] Pollock's own letters suggest at least as extensive trading activities after the war as before. The Albemarle's elite-dominated government also issued far more land patents after the Tuscarora War, and most of Pollock's patents came during the period after 1712.[82] Even in the midst of the Tuscarora crisis, he remained attentive to opportunities to acquire land, writing Lord Carteret regarding a large tract of land on the Neuse River.[83] The expanding colony also became increasingly connected to the rest of the British Atlantic World, a process that would only accelerate after the opening of the Cape Fear. When Yamasees attacked colonists in South Carolina a few years after the Tuscarora War, North Carolina sent help this time. If North Carolina and its neighbors continued to bicker and compete, they were also less isolated from each other.

The development of the Albemarle enabled the formation of a Pollock family dynasty, as Thomas Pollock became acting governor a second time upon the death of Governor Eden in 1722 and arranged for one of his sons, Thomas Pollock Jr., to replace him on the North Carolina Council. The Pollocks continued to be among the most important families in North Carolina politics throughout the colonial period. After taking advantage of these and other opportunities, Pollock accepted life in the Albemarle on its own terms, spending his remaining years as the wealthiest and most prominent man in a colony that seemed far more promising than it had a few years before. He wrote a relative in Scotland that "now being old, and not able to endure the fatigues of such a long passage, and being (praised be God) indifferent well settled here and having three hopeful sons," he did not expect to see his "beloved native country" again.[84]

Pollock died in 1722, leaving an Albemarle that had been changed in profound ways by its greatest crisis but which also faced some of the same challenges as when Pollock arrived. Partly through Pollock's leadership, North Carolina had become more politically stable, Native Americans had ceased to undermine the colony's racial hierarchy, and Albemarle elites had obtained greater access to imperial and Atlantic World connections. While Pollock may have considered these developments to be prerequisites for a successful plantation economy, however, they did not guarantee successful plantations. North Carolina continued to lack a profitable staple, though Pollock and some others could combine naval stores and other commodities with limited success. More significant is that North Carolina planters could not achieve access to the Atlantic slave trade and could not obtain the bound labor force they considered necessary. Under these circumstances, North Carolina elites considered themselves planters and embraced plantation culture, but they remained on the economic margins of the Atlantic plantation system, in a place contemporaries considered "Poor Carolina."

Notes

The author would like to acknowledge helpful comments and suggestions from Michelle LeMaster, Robert Olwell, William S. Price, the members of the Kentucky Early American Research Seminar, and, as always, Susan Kroeg.

1. This description is based on several accounts of this incident. See *CRNC*, 1:762–63; Rev. John Urmstone to Secretary, S.P.G., 1711 July 17, in *CRNC* (2nd ser.), 10:122–24; Vincent H. Todd, ed., *Christophe von Graffenried's Account of the Founding of New Bern* (Raleigh: North Carolina Historical Commission, 1920), 231.

2. A Copy of a Letter Sent by Mr Maule for Ed Hyde Esqr Deputy Governor Newly Come Out of England, in *CRNC*, 1:731.

3. Letter from President and Council to Governor of Virginia, June 29, 1711, in *CRNC* (2nd ser.), 7:438–39.

4. Rev. Urmston to Secretary, S.P.G., 1711 July 17, in *CRNC* (2nd ser.), 10:122–24.

5. Belgra appears on contemporary maps as early as 1709 but is referred to as "Colonel Pollock's." See map 11.

6. Pollock's career has not received sustained attention in any scholarly study. Most of his surviving letters can be found in *CRNC*, 1–2. The rest of his letters are in Thomas Pollock Letterbook, Pollock Family Collection, at NCSA. Some of the surviving information about Pollock's life comes from nineteenth-century genealogies and can no longer be verified with primary sources. I relied on a summary of this material in William Richard Cutter, ed., *New England Families: Genealogical and Memorial* (New York: Lewis Historical Publishing, 1913), 3:1204–5. Because of the obvious problems with these genealogical sources, I have used them with caution.

7. See A True Copy of A Letter to the Lords Proprietors Dated Sept 20th 1712, in *CRNC*, 1:873–76.

8. While North Carolina remains one of the least studied and understood of the thirteen British mainland colonies that declared independence, the early Albemarle is now probably less studied and understood than the eighteenth-century settlements in the Cape Fear River valley or in the Piedmont. For one recently published narrative of North Carolina history until 1713, see McIlvenna, *A Very Mutinous People: The Struggle for North Carolina, 1660–1713* (Chapel Hill: University of North Carolina Press, 2009). For this author's view of this narrative, see "Struggling to Find Proprietary North Carolina," *Reviews in American History* 38, no. 4 (December 2010): 601–6.

9. Jack Greene notes that perhaps 80 or 90 percent of all actions in the early higher court records involved civil litigation or other matters related to property. See Greene, "Courts and Society in Proprietary North Carolina: A Review Essay," *NCHR* 60, no. 1 (January, 1983): 100–105. On the lack of opposition to slavery, see Charles B. Lowry, "Class, Politics, Rebellion and Regional Development in Proprietary North Carolina (1697–1720)" (Ph.D. diss., University of Florida), 1979,

78–80, 123–24, 167–68; Susan H. Brinn, "Blacks in Colonial North Carolina, 1660–1723" (M.A. thesis, University of North Carolina, 1978), 43.

10. Lowry, "Class, Politics, Rebellion," 131.

11. See map 2 for evidence of these earliest settlers.

12. Cutter, *New England Families*, 1204.

13. Copy of A Letter Sent to Sir Robert Pollock by Capt Henderson's Kinsman, April 3, 1717, in *CRNC*, 2:277.

14. Thomas Pollock to unidentified, January 29, 1717, Thomas Pollock Letterbook.

15. Copy of A Letter Sent to Sir Robert Pollock by Capt Henderson's Kinsman, April 3, 1717, in *CRNC*, 2:276.

16. Lords Proprietors to Gov. Sothel, May 12, 1691, in *CRNC*, 1:367–71.

17. On Pollock's relationship to the Carterets, see Letter to Lord Carteret, September 20, 1712, in *CRNC*, 1:876–78. There are references to Pollock's trade connections outside of North Carolina and especially in New England interspersed throughout the Higher Court Records for these years in *CRNC* (2nd ser.) as well as in Pollock's Letterbook.

18. See Styrna, "Winds of War and Change," 42–46.

19. For the dominance of New England merchant in early North Carolina and for some of Pollock's trading activities, see Robert Earle Moody, ed., "Massachusetts Trade with Carolina, 1686–1709," *NCHR* 20, no. 1 (January 1943): 43–53.

20. Several other North Carolina families accumulated comparable holdings by the end of the Proprietary Period, but these included large acreages from the Cape Fear settlements that began shortly after Pollock's death. See Jacquelyn H.Wolf, "Patents and Tithables in Proprietary North Carolina, 1663–1729," *NCHR* 57, no. 3 (July 1979): 263–77. On patents in South Carolina, see Meaghan N. Duff, "Creating a Plantation Province: Proprietary Land Policies and Early Settlement Patterns," in *Money, Trade, and Power: The Evolution of South Carolina's Plantation Society*, ed. Jack P. Greene, Rosemary Brana-Shute, and Randy J. Sparks (Columbia: University of South Carolina Press, 2001), 1–25.

21. For land patent information, see Margaret Hofmann, ed., *Province of North Carolina: Abstracts of Land Patents, 1663–1729* (Weldon, N.C.: Roanoke News Company, 1979). The definitive study of these records has been done by Jacquelyn H. Wolf. See her "Patents and Tithables" and "The Proud and the Poor: The Social Organization of Leadership in Proprietary North Carolina, 1663–1729" (Ph.D. diss., University of Pennsylvania, 1977). For headrights, see Carolina B. Whitley, *North Carolina Headrights: A List of Names* (Raleigh: North Carolina Office of Archives and History, 2008). Pollock's will can be found in Bryan J. Grimes, ed., *North Carolina Wills and Inventories, Copied from the Original and Recorded Wills and Inventories in the Office of the Secretary of State* (Raleigh: Edwards and Broughton Printing, 1912), 342–47. Other relevant sources include Chowan County Tax Lists, at NCSA; and Weynette Haun, ed., *Old Albemarle County North Carolina Miscellaneous Records, 1678–1737* (Durham, N.C.: Weynette Haun, 1982), 122–38.

22. Grimes, *Wills*, 342–47.

23. On the challenges facing tobacco planters in the Chesapeake during these years, see especially Lorena S. Walsh, *Motives of Honor, Pleasure, and Profit:*

Plantation Management in the Colonial Chesapeake, 1607–1763 (Chapel Hill: University of North Carolina Press, 2010), 194–393.

24. The decision to abandon tobacco was also made by a number of planters in Maryland and Virginia during this period. See Walsh, *Motives of Honor, Pleasure, and Profit*, 293–393.

25. For a similar plantation system elsewhere in North Carolina, see Bradford J. Wood, *This Remote Part of the World: Regional Formation in Lower Cape Fear, North Carolina, 1725–1775* (Columbia: University of South Carolina Press, 2004), 174–216.

26. Scholarship on early North Carolina often makes much of the colony's undeniable economic limitations, but the handful of studies that have devoted sustained attention to North Carolina's early economic development have found somewhat more prosperity and commercial sophistication than other interpretations might suggest. The most comprehensive treatment of this line of interpretation can be found in Christopher C. Crittenden, *The Commerce of North Carolina, 1763–1789* (New Haven: Yale University Press, 1936), but it has been supported by H. R. Merrens, *Colonial North Carolina in the Eighteenth Century: A Study in Historical Geography* (Chapel Hill: University of North Carolina Press, 1964); Wood, *This Remote Part of the World*; and various articles by Alan D. Watson.

27. On the slave trade to early North Carolina, see Marvin L. Michael Kay and Lorin Lee Cary, *Slavery in North Carolina, 1748–1775* (Chapel Hill: University of North Carolina Press, 1995), especially 19–22, 307–8; Walter E. Minchinton, "The Seabourne Slave Trade of North Carolina," *NCHR* 71, no. 1 (January, 1994): 1–61; Wood, *This Remote Part of the World*, 38–40; Gregory E. O'Malley, "Beyond the Middle Passage: Slave Migration from the Caribbean to North America, 1619–1807," *WMQ* 57, no. 1 (January, 2009): 125–72.

28. This analysis is based on Pollock's letters in *CRNC* and the Thomas Pollock Letterbook. Many of the letters do not provide the name of the recipient, but it is clear that almost all the letters about buying slaves went to a small group of merchants in Boston.

29. Thomas Pollock to [unknown], July 5, 1716; Thomas Pollock to [unknown], May 23, 1718; both in Thomas Pollock Letterbook.

30. Alan Gallay, ed., *Indian Slavery in Colonial America* (Lincoln: University of Nebraska Press, 2010); Alan Gallay, *The Indian Slave Trade: The Rise of the English Empire in the American South* (New Haven: Yale University Press, 2003).

31. Thomas Pollock to unidentified, July 5, 1716, Thomas Pollock Letterbook.

32. Cutter, *New England Families*, 3:1204.

33. See William L. Ramsey, "'All and Singular Slaves': A Demographic Profile of Indian Slavery in Colonial South Carolina," in *Money, Trade, and Power*, 168.

34. On the population of slaves in eastern North Carolina, see Wood, "The Changing Population of the Colonial South: An Overview by Race and Region, 1685–1790," in *Powhatan's Mantle: Indians in the Colonial Southeast*, revised and expanded edition, eds., Gregory A. Waselkov, Peter H. Wood, and Tom Hatley (Lincoln: University of Nebraska Press, 2006), 57–70. The author thanks Stephen Feeley for his helpful comments on this subject.

35. For a discussion of indentured servitude and slavery in the Chesapeake during this period, see Walsh, *Motives of Honor, Pleasure, and Profit*, 373–86.

36. Whitley, *North Carolina Headrights*; CRNC (2nd ser.), 2–3. In comparison, Native Americans constituted fifty-six out 491 nonwhite headright claims in the surviving records of the Proprietary Period. Therefore Native Americans made up about 13 percent of Pollock's nonwhite headrights and about 11 percent of all nonwhite Proprietary Period headrights. While it is difficult to be precise about the absolute numbers involved in these headright claims, the ratio is the most important issue for this point.

37. Wolf, "Patents and Tithables," 273 ; Chowan County Tax Lists, at NCSA; Haun, *Old Albemarle County North Carolina Miscellaneous Records*, 122–38; Secretary of States Records, Probate, 41, pp. 1–4, 49–52, at NCSA.

38. Grimes, *Wills*, 342–47. For evidence of other estates in North Carolina during Pollock's lifetime that had a similarly mixed bound labor force, see Grimes, *Wills*, 13–15, 273–76, 357–60, 472–74, 560–61.

39. It should be noted that not many of these lists survive for this period and they generally only list tithables in one county. See Wolf, "Patents and Tithables," 272–74.

40. See Peter H. Wood, *Black Majority: Negroes in Colonial South Carolina from 1670 through the Stono Rebellion* (Chapel Hill: University of North Carolina Press, 1975), 156–66.

41. The evidence on land ownership and labor forces is surveyed in Wolf, "Patents and Tithables," and Lowry, "Class, Politics, Rebellion."

42. On this point, see especially Brinn, "Blacks in Colonial North Carolina."

43. General Court Minutes, April–June, 1697, in *CRNC* (2nd ser.), 3:61–63.

44. Records of the Court of Chancery, date undetermined, in *CRNC* (2nd ser.), 3:513–14.

45. Records of the General Court, April–June, 1697, in *CRNC* (2nd ser.), 3:23–24, 38–40; Brinn, "Blacks in North Carolina," 32–35. The foregoing account of the relationship between Pollock and Manuel owes a significant debt to Brinn.

46. Records of the Court of Chancery, May, 1697, in *CRNC* (2nd ser.), 3:490.

47. Brinn, "Blacks in North Carolina," 33–34.

48. Records of the General Court, October–November, 1697, in *CRNC* (2nd ser.), 3:90, 126–27; Brinn, "Blacks in North Carolina," 34; Fischer, *Suspect Relations*, 13–15.

49. Brinn, "Blacks in North Carolina," 35.

50. Ibid.

51. Journal of the Virginia Council, September 2, 1707, in *CRNC*, 1:667–71. See also Stephen D. Feeley, "Tuscarora Trails: Indian Migrations, War, and Constructions of Colonial Frontiers" (Ph.D. diss., College of William and Mary, 2007), 66–133.

52. Thomas Pollock to Rev. William Gordon, ca. 1709, in *CRNC* (2nd ser.), 10:75.

53. Perhaps the best narrative account of Cary's Rebellion has been written by William S. Price and can be found in *CRNC* (2nd ser.), 4:xxiv–xxx, 5:xxi–xxv.

For other interpretations, see Lefler and Powell, *Colonial North Carolina*, 195–97; Lowry, "Class, Politics, Rebellion," 150–202; and McIlvenna, *A Very Mutinous People*, 127–47.

54. William Glover to unidentified, [1708], Pollock Letterbook, in *CRNC*, 1:696–99.

55. A Copy of A Letter to Mr John Lawson, by Mr Maule, to be Left for Him at President Glover's, May 27, 1710, Pollock Letterbook, in *CRNC*, 1:727–28.

56. See, for example, "A Copy of A Letter to Mr. Chenin and Mr Boyds, April 16, 1710," Pollock Letterbook, in *CRNC*, 1:723–24.

57. Spotswood to the Lords Proprietors of Carolina, July 28, 1711, in *CRNC*, 1:794–96; Journal of the Virginia Council, July 5, 1711, in *CRNC*, 1:762–63.

58. John Urmston to Secretary, S.P.G, July 7, 1711, in *CRNC* (2nd ser.), 10:115–21.

59. Feeley, "Tuscarora Trails," 134–16, now offers the most complete analysis of the Tuscarora War. See also McIlvenna, *A Very Mutinous People*, 148–60; Gallay, *Indian Slave Trade*, 259–87; in *CRNC* (2nd ser.), 5:xxv–xxxii; Lefler and Powell, *Colonial North Carolina*, 65–80. On the consequences of the war and its political dimensions within North Carolina, see Styrna, "The Winds of War and Change."

60. President Pollock to Governor of South Carolina, Pollock Letterbook, in *CRNC*, 1:882.

61. Pollock to the Lords Proprietors, September 9, 1712, in *CRNC*, 1:869.

62. See Feeley, "Tuscarora Trails," 273–85.

63. *CRNC* (2nd ser.), 5:xxviii.

64. See Colonel Spotswood to the Board of Trade, July 25, 1711, in *CRNC*, 1:779–83; Colonel Spotswood to Lord Dartmouth, July 28, 1711, in *CRNC*, 1:796–97; Letter from Governor Hyde, August 22, 1711, in *CRNC*, 1:801–3; President and Council of North Carolina to the Board of Trade, in *CRNC*, 1:806–7. Most modern historians have followed William L. Saunders in dismissing this claim. See *CRNC*, 1:xxix. Recently the question has been revived by Noeleen McIlvenna, who asserts that the Cary Rebels and the Tuscaroras both conspired to destroy the authority of the Albemarle elites. McIlvenna, *A Very Mutinous People*, 143–49, 189–90. The surviving evidence may not be sufficient to determine whether these charges against the Cary Rebels were accurate, but it would be highly unusual and surprising for a group of British colonists to encourage Native Americans to attack other British colonists.

65. President and Council of North Carolina to the Board of Trade, in *CRNC*, 1:806.

66. Pollock to Governor Craven, Pollock Letterbook, April 30, 1713, in *CRNC*, 2:40.

67. Pollock to Governor Craven, Pollock Letterbook, October, 1712, in *CRNC*, 2:883.

68. Pollock to Governor Craven, September 1, 1713, Pollock Letterbook, in *CRNC*, 2:60.

69. See Gallay, *Indian Slave Trade*, for the larger context for these issues.

70. Records of the Executive Council, Minutes, June 25, 1713, in *CRNC* (2nd ser.), 7:39.

71. Feeley, "Tuscarora Trails," 547–48.

72. Thomas Pollock to Governor Craven, September 1, 1713, Pollock Letterbook, in *CRNC*, 2:60.

73. See, for example, Thomas Pollock to Governor Spotswood, January 15, 1712/13, Pollock Letterbook, in *CRNC*, 2:4–5.

74. Thomas Pollock to Governor Hunter, March 6, 1712/13, Pollock Letterbook, in *CRNC*, 2:23–25.

75. Rev. Giles Ransford to Secretary, S.P.G., February 17, 1712/13, in *CRNC* (2nd ser.), 10:158. The Tuscarora situation is described in some detail in Feeley, "Tuscarora Trails," especially 270–404.

76. Thomas Pollock to Governor Craven, May 25, 1713, in *CRNC*, 2:45. On the persistence of Native Americans in eastern North Carolina, see Michelle LeMaster, "In the 'Scolding Houses': Indians before the Colonial Courts in North Carolina, 1684–1760," *NCHR* 82, no. 2 (April 2006): 193–232.

77. General Court Minutes, October, 1722, in *CRNC* (2nd ser.), 5:320.

78. Pollock to the Proprietors, October 20, 1714, Pollock Letterbook, in *CRNC*, 2:145.

79. This is one of the central themes of Styrna, "Winds of War and Change."

80. "An Act Concerning Servants and Slaves," in *CRNC*, 23:62–66.

81. Styrna, "Winds of War," 255–56, 259–60.

82. Styrna, "Winds of War," 285–86, 309–11, 319, 324–26.

83. A True Copy of A Letter to My Lord Carteret, dated September 20, 1712, Pollock Letterbook, in *CRNC*, 1:877–88.

84. Copy of A Letter Sent to Sir Robert Pollock by Capt Henderson's Kinsman, April 3, 1717, Pollock Letterbook, in *CRNC*, 2:276.

Diversity in the Slave Trade to the Colonial Carolinas

GREGORY E. O'MALLEY

"We think there is a chance of making Money on a parcel of Slaves.... There must not be a Callabar amongst them. Gold Coast or Gambias are best; next to them the Windward Coast are prefer'd to Angolas."

Henry Laurens, Charleston, 1755

When Henry Laurens scribbled his rankings of preferred African backgrounds for the South Carolina slave market, his list of alternates captured an important truth about the Atlantic slave trade.[1] With high demand for labor throughout the Americas, buyers' specific requests were mere wish lists. Plantation owners had preferences among African peoples, but they could not count on their preferences being met by slave traders. That even a prominent merchant like Laurens, in the biggest slave market in British North America, recognized that he might have to settle for third, fourth, or fifth choices, even during the heyday of the transatlantic slave trade, illustrates the extent to which it was almost always a sellers' market for slaves in colonial America. This inability to dictate the terms of trade was only more apparent for American ports that were not major hubs of the slave trade, and in the early decades of settlement in the Carolinas, neither Charleston nor any other Carolina port held that dubious distinction. In other words, by the time Henry Laurens penned his list of "ethnic" preferences, South Carolina planters had long settled for whatever enslaved Africans they could get, giving rise to a multiethnic slave community.[2] In fact, despite the hierarchy of Laurens's list and his threat to refuse certain types of people, this list of preferred ethnicities implies familiarity with a wide range of African peoples by the 1750s. How could South Carolina planters know they preferred captives from the Windward Coast to those from the Angola, or that they did not like slaves from the Bight of Biafra (that is, "Callabars"), unless they had experience exploiting workers from even these regions that were low on their list of favorites? In fact, despite his emphatic rejection of "Callabars" as unsuitable for the South Carolina market, Laurens himself repeatedly managed to sell Africans of just that description to labor-hungry planters. They paid only slightly lower rates than was typical for the preferred captives from the Gold Coast or Gambia.³

In recent years scholars of slavery have increasingly based interpretations of early African American culture on patterns in the slave trade, capitalizing on slave trade historians' steadily increasing knowledge of the numbers of enslaved Africans forced across the Atlantic and the proportion of those captives hailing from various African regions. A unified African American culture was not developing, we are told, but rather myriad African American cultures in various American regions; patterns in the slave trade, as well as varied local labor regimes, created regional diversity.

While this more nuanced understanding of varied African American experiences across space is undoubtedly useful, many such studies oversimplify the slave trade, despite their sensitivity to complex regional diversity in the Americas. Recent studies depict Igbos shaping slave culture in Virginia, Gambians in South Carolina, and so on.⁴ There is a kernel of truth in such interpretations. Data on the Atlantic slave trade does show the Chesapeake importing disproportionate numbers of people from the Bight of Biafra (as did most of North America), where Igbo people predominated among captives. Likewise Gambians were indeed somewhat overrepresented in South Carolina (though Virginia actually received an even higher proportion of Gambians than South Carolina did). But a closer look at patterns in the slave trade, including changes over time and considering branches of the slave trade that linked American colonies indirectly with Africa, reveals that nowhere in North America did a single African culture dominate. Diversity was the rule.⁵

This essay uses South Carolina as a case study for a more nuanced interpretation of the slave trade's role in shaping African American populations and cultures. Recent studies of slave trading within Africa, reinterpretation of the latest data on the transatlantic trade, and my own research on the thriving intercolonial trade within the Americas all suggest that many recent studies of North American slave cultures oversimplify the slave trade in all three phases—intra-African, transatlantic, and intra-American. The tendency to draw linear connections between single African regions and specific American destinations overlooks convoluted lines of migration and minimizes change over time, tending to overemphasize the dominance of particular African ethnicities in shaping slave cultures in various parts of America.

This assertion is not meant to challenge the notion that enslaved Africans carried vibrant cultures and ideologies to the Americas. Resilient survivors of the slave trade surely carried religious beliefs, foodways, artistic sensibilities, and understandings of the world with them through the forced migration. But the complex, overlapping patterns of the slave trade suggest a thrusting together of a wide range of African traditions and beliefs in varying combinations in various American regions. This African diversity within American regions calls for scholars to give greater attention to the acculturative processes of diverse Africans (and African Americans) adapting to one another—in addition to adjusting to Europeans, to varied chattel slavery regimes, and to new American environments.[6]

It is well known that enslaved Africans arrived with England's first Carolina settlers, and that the Carolina colony—unlike other North American settlements—embraced slave labor from its earliest days, but little definitive information survives about the backgrounds of Carolina's black founders. We can only speculate about their origins circumstantially through examination of how the slave trade delivered African captives to the region. Unfortunately the early slave trade to South Carolina is also difficult to document. Carolina import records do not survive for the first several decades of European and African settlement in the region. Furthermore much slave trade scholarship of recent years focuses exclusively on transatlantic slave movements, but the first known arrivals in South Carolina directly from Africa did not occur until 1710. By that time the colony's African population already topped four thousand individuals, leaving the first forty years of slave arrivals in Carolina minimally examined and poorly understood.[7]

In the first forty years of the Carolina colony's history, with direct trade with Africa not yet established, slaveholders relied on two main sources for African laborers: other English colonies, on one hand, and pirates and privateers, on the other. The first and more substantial of these streams, the intercolonial trade, brought slaves primarily from the English Caribbean. The origins of South Carolina are tied intimately to Barbados, since so many early Carolina settlers hailed from that island, and the early slave trade was part of the connection between these two colonies. So close were these ties that Peter Wood famously dubbed South Carolina, "the colony of a colony."[8] By 1670 slavery had been well established as the dominant labor regime in Barbados, so not surprisingly, many Carolina settlers from Barbados brought African slaves from the island when they migrated. In addition, after settling in Carolina, colonists from Barbados continued to use connections on the island to request transshipments of slaves for their fledgling colony on the mainland since Barbados received more slaves from Africa than did any other English colony in the seventeenth century. Accordingly, in 1709, the governor and council of South Carolina reported that in addition to occasional direct African shipments, "Wee are allso often furnished with negros from the American Islands, chiefly from Barbados and Jamaica."[9]

Before 1700 Barbados surely supplied the majority of these Africans transshipped "from the American Islands," given Barbados's central role in the early English slave trade and its extensive links with South Carolina. For instance at least twenty ships sailed from Barbados to South Carolina in 1679 alone. Many Barbadians owned land in Carolina, and many Carolina settlers maintained family ties in the Caribbean colony. Carolina also exported substantially to Barbados, making enslaved Africans a convenient return for the timber products, livestock, and enslaved Native Americans that Carolina settlers sent to the island.[10] By the early eighteenth century, Jamaica outpaced Barbados as a recipient of captives from Africa and began to transship several dozen African people to South Carolina annually.[11]

These intercolonial links between Barbados, Jamaica, and Carolina reveal something of the sources of Carolina's early slaves, but knowing the location of these migrants immediately prior to Carolina is not the same as knowing their background. Just who were the African immigrants aboard these Caribbean shipments? One might assume they were so-called seasoned slaves—individuals who had spent significant time in Barbados or elsewhere in the Caribbean, adapting to an American environment and the English colonial regime—but there is cause for skepticism. Barbadian planters had little incentive to whisk African workers away from their sugar plantations, especially since any skills acquired for cultivating or processing sugar would be useless in Carolina. Depriving Barbados plantations of slaves to provide labor to fledgling Carolina was especially unlikely given that most Barbadians envisioned the Carolina project as a means to supply Barbados with various necessities, not the other way around. Instead those Barbadians migrating to or investing in Carolina likely used their commercial ties in Barbados to purchase Africans for Carolina upon their arrival in the Caribbean from the Middle Passage. As such, the time most Africans spent in Barbados before their forced migration to Carolina was more likely to be measured in weeks than years. To be sure, some wealthy planters (and especially younger sons of wealthy planters) in Barbados opted for Carolina and likely brought some seasoned slaves to their new colony. But even in such cases these Carolina settlers likely purchased additional African laborers to supplement the Barbadian slaves they brought with them at the moment of initial settlement. At least after the very first years of Carolina's founding, most slaves arriving from the islands had spent only a brief layover in the Caribbean en route from Africa.[12]

Regardless of how long these first African settlers had spent in the Caribbean before moving to the mainland, the patterns in the transatlantic slave trade to Barbados in the years prior to 1670 offer the best evidence for speculating on their African backgrounds. Most were probably Igbo or other people hailing from the Bight of Biafra's hinterland because, in the five-year period before 1670, about half of the Africans reaching Barbados arrived on ships from that African region (table 1). Another third of Barbadian immigrants from 1666 to 1670 were likely Akan peoples since they left Africa from the Gold Coast. Colonists often referred to such people as "Coromantees," after the port city of Koromantin on the Gold Coast, where European slave traders acquired many of their captives. The remaining one-sixth of Africans reaching Barbados in this period came from the Bight of Benin, where Aja captives predominated.

If indeed English emigrants from Barbados purchased slaves in preparation for their move to Carolina, the first African settlers of the lowcountry likely reflected these source populations. If more of the Africans settling Carolina had spent several years in Barbados, then patterns in the transatlantic trade to Barbados over a longer period leading up to 1670 are relevant, and the likely predominance of Igbos only increases. In the three decades before 1670, vessels from the Bight of Biafra delivered roughly 60 percent of Barbados's African colonists. Most of the remaining peoples hailed from the Gold Coast, Senegambia, and the Bight if Benin (in descending order of significance).

Table 1: Estimated African Migrants to Barbados by African Region, 1641–1670

	Bight of Biafra	Gold Coast	Senegambia	Bight of Benin	Other
1641–45	5,160	741	4,625	0	1,118
1646–50	13,576	657	0	0	0
1651–55	3,033	0	1,596	375	0
1656–60	6,844	0	3,169	0	1,195
1661–65	5,995	6,443	0	3,862	451
1666–70	7,772	5,481	0	2,492	0
Totals	42,379	13,322	9,390	6,729	2,764
%	57%	18%	13%	9%	4%

Source: *Voyages* (http://slavevoyages.org/tast/assessment/estimates.faces?yearFrom=1641&yearTo=1670&disembarkation=302; accessed August 30, 2010.)

After Carolina's founding moment, trends in the background of African migrants transshipped from Barbados and other English Caribbean colonies would have altered as the transatlantic slave trade acquired captives from different parts of Africa. Most notable, the relative importance of the Bight of Biafra as a source for the English Caribbean's slaves declined dramatically after 1675, with transatlantic traders buying captives in a wider variety of African regions (table 2). As a result, from 1671 to 1710, no one African ethnicity contributed the majority of African immigrants to Barbados. In fact only people from the Bight of Benin accounted for more than one-third of the arrivals in Barbados, while the Gold Coast contributed about a fourth. Five other broad regions contributed the other 40 percent of African immigrants. In addition to this array of African departure areas, one should bear in mind that regions such as the Bight of Benin and the Gold Coast spanned hundreds of miles of coastline and drew their slaves from vast hinterlands. As a result, the diversity of the African population reaching Barbados in this period must have been considerable. Presumably the transshipment trade from Barbados to South Carolina reflected this amalgam.[13]

Table 2: Estimated African Migrants to Barbados by African Region, 1671–1710

	Bight of Biafra	Gold Coast	Senegambia	Bight of Benin	West Central Africa	Sierra Leone and Windward Coast	Southeast Africa
1671–75	9,768	2,923	0	1,243	0	0	0
1676–80	2,729	4,309	340	4,909	2,399	0	1,212
1681–85	2,145	3,440	3,196	8,974	3,634	344	4,659
1686–90	1,456	830	263	8,230	2,783	135	208
1691–95	1,176	2,831	1,445	7,638	145	0	0
1696–1700	2,062	9,873	1,482	9,014	715	433	63
1701–5	2,438	9,049	0	7,596	6,090	541	0
1706–10	0	4,618	123	3,814	0	98	0
Totals	21,775	37,873	6,850	51,416	15,765	1,550	6,141
%	15%	27%	5%	36%	11%	1%	4%

Source: *Voyages* (http://slavevoyages.org/tast/assessment/estimates.faces?yearFrom=1501&yearTo=1710&disembarkation=302; accessed August 30, 2010.)

The addition of Jamaica as an important source of slaves for South Carolina around the turn of the eighteenth century did not change this pattern considerably. Jamaica imported enslaved people from the various African regions in similar proportions to Barbados, excepting only that Jamaica relied more extensively on west central Africa (that is, the greater Kongo and Angola region)—drawing nearly one-quarter of its Africans from there (table 3). The reason for this discrepancy, however, suggests that few of these Congolese and Angolan people would have ended up in South Carolina. Transatlantic traders bound for the English Caribbean tended to send west central Africans to Jamaica because such people were highly sought after for the lucrative contraband trade to Spanish America, which operated largely out of Jamaica. As a result of this Spanish trade siphoning off the Angolan and Congolese people from the island, Jamaica probably shipped no higher a proportion of west central Africans to Carolina than did Barbados.[14]

Intercolonial trade from Barbados and Jamaica was not the only source of Carolina's slaves before 1710, however, and the other main source likely added to the polyglot nature of the African population. The first half century of the Carolina colony coincides with the so-called golden age of piracy in the Atlantic, and Carolina developed a reputation for harboring sea bandits fencing prizes. These stolen "goods" of pirates often included enslaved African people. That pirates plundered slaves from merchant ships comes as little surprise when one considers that commoditized African workers fetched higher

Table 3: Estimated African Migrants to Jamaica by African Region, 1671–1710

	Bight of Biafra	Gold Coast	Senegambia	Bight of Benin	West Central Africa	Sierra Leone and Windward Coast	Southeast Africa
1671–75	1,091	711	0	1,876	0	0	1,947
1676–80	2,225	2,647	273	1,969	1,437	0	315
1681–85	2,131	734	942	8,021	4,225	177	0
1686–90	2,568	0	448	4,562	4,652	0	199
1691–95	1,968	184	2,780	5,030	7,829	279	0
1696–1700	5,443	3,415	3,034	2,817	2,426	418	0
1701–5	1,087	6,429	1,889	10,364	7,226	0	0
1706–10	182	14,577	1,045	7,473	3,101	576	0
Totals	16,695	28,696	10,410	42,112	30,896	1,449	2,461
%	12%	22%	8%	32%	23%	1%	2%

Source: *Voyages* (http://slavevoyages.org/tast/assessment/estimates.faces?yearFrom=1501&yearTo=1710&disembarkation=302; accessed September 2, 2010.)

prices per shipload than nearly anything traded in the English Atlantic; pirates were nothing if not opportunistic.[15]

Of course black market activities do not lend themselves to documentation, so the scale of pirates' slave deliveries to early Carolina is impossible to calculate. The anecdotal record, however, suggests a considerable contribution. Many merchants reported losses of slaves to pirates in Caribbean waters and—less frequently—off the North American coast. Sometimes pirates stole entire ships full of African captives, but more typically they plundered slaves out of ships in smaller numbers. These smaller groups of captives could be more easily controlled (and fed) aboard the pirates' ships. Small groups were also more easily fenced without attracting attention. For instance, in 1716 a pirate vessel under a Captain Kennedy attacked the *Greyhound Galley* as it sailed through the Lesser Antilles en route from the Gold Coast to Jamaica. When the *Greyhound* surrendered, the pirates stole forty captives (and all the gold on board) before allowing the slaver to continue to Jamaica.[16] This was far from a unique event. Famous pirates documented stealing slaves include William Kidd, Stede Bonnet, Edward Teach (better known as Blackbeard), Charles Vane, and John Rackam (whose crew included the famous women pirates Anne Bonny and Mary Read). In fact the infamous Blackbeard's ship, *Queen Anne's Revenge*, was a captured, converted slaver, as was the wrecked pirate ship *Whydah*, which was recently discovered and excavated on the ocean floor near Cape Cod.[17]

Where pirates sold the slaves they plundered was rarely documented (for the obvious reason that those who acquired slaves *from* pirates were less likely to record the act than those who lost slaves *to* pirates), but Carolina offered one promising destination. The colony offered a logical market for pirates selling African captives because, prior to 1710, transatlantic slave traders rarely (if ever) met the region's demand for enslaved laborers. (North Carolina would struggle to attract shipments directly from Africa throughout the colonial period and perhaps not coincidentally would be accused of harboring pirates even after South Carolina shook off that stigma.)[18] In addition South Carolina was notorious for harboring pirates. In 1684, for example, Jamaican governor Thomas Lynch complained of Carolina's open door to pirates, resulting in an order from the Crown for South Carolina to pass an antipiracy statute. The colony assented, but complaints continued.[19] Most slave deliveries by pirates were probably small, but documentation survives of at least one large delivery of captive Africans to South Carolina. In 1683 a multinational fleet of pirates, aboard at least thirteen ships, staged one of the boldest pirate attacks of the "golden age," laying siege to Vera Cruz, plundering all manner of goods, and "carrying also with them about a thousand Negroes and Mulatos." The pirates then scattered to Dutch, French, and English settlements, with South Carolina reportedly receiving about two hundred of the human prizes.[20]

The enslaved Africans delivered to the Carolinas by pirates likely added to the colonies' diversity, because pirates opportunistically preyed on traders of almost any background. For this reason, while intercolonial shipments from the English Caribbean reflected the parts of Africa where English traders were active, the ethnic composition of the African population aboard pirate vessels likely reflected the full diversity of the transatlantic slave trade in the period. This does not mark an enormous change, with the notable exception that pirates were far more likely to ferry west central Africans to Carolina than were traders from the English Caribbean (table 4). Portuguese slave traders—the most prolific of the seventeenth century—were far more active in west central Africa than the English, so any of their vessels bound for Brazil or Spanish America that fell prey to pirates likely redirected west central Africans to other parts of the Americas, including the Carolinas.[21]

After the first decade of the eighteenth century patterns in the supply of African laborers to South Carolina shifted significantly. The year 1710 saw the first documented delivery of enslaved people directly from Africa to the colony. Occasional earlier African voyages may have occurred, but without question, it was in the 1710s that direct trade between Africa and South Carolina became routine. Eighteen known transatlantic shipments delivered slaves directly to the colony in the decade, carrying perhaps two thousand people. This direct African trade altered the ethnic composition of South Carolina's black population because these transatlantic shipments to Carolina did not hail from the

Table 4: Estimated African Migrants to the Americas by African Region, 1671–1710

	Bight of Biafra	Gold Coast	Senegambia	Bight of Benin	West Central Africa	Sierra Leone and Windward Coast	Southeast Africa
1671–80	26,003	23,133	10,788	23,902	93,479	0	5,435
1681–90	14,938	12,532	17,744	63,499	96,177	1,585	6,560
1691–1700	21,912	32,609	18,828	89,315	115,487	3,255	1,835
1701–10	17,516	67,253	13,372	115,083	118,050	3,737	96
Totals	80,009	135,528	60,731	291,800	423,193	8,577	13,927
%	8%	13%	6%	29%	42%	<1%	1%

Source: *Voyages* (http://slavevoyages.org/tast/assessment/estimates.faces?yearFrom=1671&yearTo=1710; accessed September 10, 2010.)

Table 5: Estimated African Migrants Directly to South Carolina by African Region, 1711–1725

	Bight of Biafra	Gold Coast	Senegambia
1711–15	0	161	764
1716–20	609	931	260
1721–25	0	1,102	2,665
Totals	609	2,194	3,689
%	9%	34%	57%

Source: *Voyages* (http://slavevoyages.org/tast/assessment/estimates.faces?yearFrom=1711&yearTo=1725&disembarkation=203; accessed September 10, 2010.)

wide range of African regions that supplied the English slave trade in general. Instead the African trade to South Carolina in the 1710s was dominated by deliveries from Senegambia, with the Gold Coast and the Bight of Biafra in supplementary roles (table 5). While it is tempting to think that this pattern in the African origins of captive migrants to Carolina reflected planter preferences, it is unlikely. Even with transatlantic deliveries becoming frequent, buyers could rarely dictate terms in the slave trade. What concerned transatlantic traders most was matching slave shipments of various sizes to American markets of an appropriate size to handle them. Numbers of captives and seasonal cycles, not ethnicities, determined the transatlantic trade routes. As a relatively young colony, South Carolina offered transatlantic slave traders a fairly small market, and coincidentally vessels purchasing slaves in Senegambia tended to be relatively small due to conditions of supply in the region. European slave traders in Senegambia needed to make numerous small transactions at a variety of locations, so to load with reasonable speed they kept their vessels small. It was this fit for the transatlantic merchants, of small markets of supply and demand, that determined the linkage of Senegambia and South Carolina in the first ten or twenty years of the transatlantic slave trade to the lowcountry. (The same dynamic explains why Maryland—which grew no rice—received more enslaved people from Senegambia than from any other region before 1730.)[22]

Virtually all such transatlantic slaving ventures to Carolina delivered Africans to Charleston specifically, raising the question of ethnic patterns in the dispersal of captives from Charleston to its hinterland—both within South Carolina, and in North Carolina. Little evidence exists on ethnic patterns in this distribution, and educated guesswork points in competing directions. If rice planters preferred Gambian slaves, then such people may have tended to remain in greater proximity to Charleston since local rice planters enjoyed access to the entrepôt, giving them greater opportunity to purchase the most-coveted slaves. On the other hand, selling agents for transatlantic slavers relied on drawing large crowds to sell the large groups of arriving Africans from transatlantic vessels. As a result, they tended to spread word of upcoming slave sales far and wide. Likewise remote planters seeking slaves ventured (or sent agents) to Charleston when they knew large numbers of Africans would be available for sale. As Henry Laurens put it, "When such a [large] Number are for Sale it draws down the People from every part of the Province." Given these competing lines of reasoning, there is little reason to suspect strong ethnic patterning in the dispersal of Africans outward from Charleston. More likely, merchants and planters headed from Charleston to North Carolina or outlying regions of South Carolina acquired slaves opportunistically when their business took them. This opportunism would lead the dispersal trade to roughly mirror the overall slave trade to Charleston. North Carolina might have seen even greater diversity since that "remote part of the world" looked not only to Charleston as an entrepôt for enslaved Africans, but also to the Chesapeake and colonies further afield.[23]

Even as transatlantic slave deliveries to South Carolina were on the rise after 1710, the Caribbean slave trade to South Carolina was still growing. This intercolonial trade drew captives from a broader range of British Caribbean territories than in prior decades, reflecting the British transatlantic slave trade's growth in the era after the Crown rescinded the Royal African Company's monopoly. As the transatlantic trade grew, Carolina was both one of the new markets served and also a recipient of intercolonial shipments from a number of new Caribbean entrepôts—most notably Antigua and St. Kitts—in addition to Barbados and Jamaica. Overall this intercolonial trade from the Caribbean probably delivered nearly as many Africans to the Carolinas as the transatlantic trade did in the decade. (Piracy, by contrast, was on the wane, with the British Crown cracking down on piracy in Caribbean waters in the 1710s.)[24]

The ethnic composition of these intercolonial deliveries to South Carolina shifted after 1710, reflecting changes in the transatlantic trade. As the British transatlantic slave trade to the Caribbean grew dramatically in this period, the merchants involved developed increasingly strong trade relationships with specific African rulers and regions, decreasing somewhat the diversity in African migration to the British Caribbean. Nearly half of the approximately 175,000 African captives delivered to the British Caribbean between 1711 and 1725 came from the Gold Coast, with another quarter hailing from the Bight of Benin. The remaining 25 percent of African immigrants drew from a smattering of other regions (table 6). As a result, while African immigration to the British Caribbean grew less diverse, the transshipment of such people to Carolina increased diversity there. Apart from the importance of peoples from the Gold Coast to South Carolina's direct African and Caribbean trades, the cultural background of the Africans reaching South Carolina via Caribbean transshipment contrasted markedly to Senegambian predominance among those Africans who arrived directly, continuing a trend toward a pluralistic slave community in the lowcountry between 1711 and 1725.

Table 6: Estimated African Migrants to the British Caribbean by African Region, 1711–1725

	Bight of Biafra	Gold Coast	Senegambia	Bight of Benin	West Central Africa	Sierra Leone and Windward Coast	Southeast Africa
1711–15	4,300	28,325	4,917	14,728	2,409	481	0
1716–20	2,827	33,007	2,582	15,462	1,479	1,449	4,435
1721–25	1,090	23,708	6,182	16,807	7,448	1,702	0
Totals	8,217	85,040	13,680	46,997	11,335	3,632	4,435
%	5%	49%	8%	27%	6%	2%	3%

Source: *Voyages* (http://slavevoyages.org/tast/assessment/estimates.faces?yearFrom=1711&yearTo=1725&disembarkation=305.304.307.306.309.308.311.310.301.302.303) Accessed 10 September, 2010.

The early 1720s saw another significant transition in the slave trade to South Carolina, reflecting the stabilization and maturation of the South Carolina settlement and plantation regime after the Yamasee War that so many essays in this volume highlight. Beginning in 1724, direct arrivals from Africa spiked; transshipments from the Caribbean correspondingly plummeted as intercolonial traders struggled to compete with abundant African trade. The intercolonial trade from the Caribbean never dried up altogether, with merchants occasionally capitalizing on price imbalances between American regions, but from 1724 to the Revolution, shipments from the Caribbean dropped to only about 5 percent of African arrivals in South Carolina. North Carolina, on the other hand, increased its Caribbean trade in the mid-eighteenth century, exporting provisions and naval stores, especially to Jamaica, and importing sugar, rum, limes, British manufactures, and African laborers in return.[25]

This shift in the Carolinas' sources of African workers brought further change and diversity to the colony's black population. Unlike in prior decades, no one (or two) African regions predominated in the transatlantic supply of enslaved people to South Carolina. In these peak years, the lowcountry drew laborers from nearly all African exporting regions in considerable numbers. About one-quarter of the captive migrants embarked from Senegambia; another quarter hailed from west central Africa; about one-fifth came from Sierra Leone and the Windward Coast; one in ten came from each the Bight of Biafra and the Gold Coast. Among the major exporting regions in the Atlantic slave trade, only the Bight of Benin and southeast Africa failed to send significant numbers of captives to South Carolina (table 7). In other words, the Africans arriving in South Carolina were astonishingly diverse, especially when one considers that each of these exporting African regions was vast and drew its captives from a deep hinterland and that the Gold Coast had contributed a much higher proportion of Carolina's Africans in earlier periods.

Table 7: Estimated African Migrants Directly to the Carolinas and Georgia by African Region, 1724–1780

	Bight of Biafra	Gold Coast	Senegambia	Bight of Benin	West Central Africa	Sierra Leone and Windward Coast	Southeast Africa
1724–30	498	866	4,373	0	306	1,013	0
1731–40	5,582	447	3,469	0	18,362	0	0
1741–50	1,378	219	769	0	287	330	0
1751–60	4,724	2,655	7,369	529	3,183	4,084	311
1761–70	1,476	3,368	7,367	698	5,754	9,380	0
1771–80	150	4,877	7,889	1,117	2,638	8,234	0
Totals	13,808	12,432	31,236	2,344	30,530	23,042	311
%	12%	11%	27%	2%	27%	20%	<1%

Note: These figure include African arrivals in North Carolina and Georgia because the *Voyages* database provides estimates of the total migration by region rather than colony. Nonetheless, these figures largely represent the migration to South Carolina, since transatlantic deliveries to South Carolina were nearly twenty times greater than to either of her neighbors.

Source: *Voyages* (http://slavevoyages.org/tast/assessment/estimates.faces?yearFrom=1724&yearTo=1780&disembarkation=203.)

While much attention is paid to numbers in this essay, the quantification should not dehumanize the people subjected to the human trafficking of the slave trade. On the contrary estimates of the routes and scale of the slave trade facilitate historians' grappling with some very human questions (a point too often missed or ignored by critics of quantitative studies): What were the likely backgrounds of the forced African immigrants to the Carolinas? What are the implications of their cultural heritage for the development of the culture and economy of the lowcountry? Without a solid understanding of the scale and patterns of the forced migration, scholars cannot adequately address these fundamental questions about the African diaspora.

The most striking conclusion to emerge from the numeric analysis of African arrivals in colonial South Carolina is a picture of enormous cultural diversity. African people's many routes to South Carolina strongly support Max Edelson's suggestion that, "as communities peopled by the transatlantic slave trade," South Carolina's communities of enslaved people inhabited "societies defined by ethnic pluralism."[26] This diversity is rendered even more striking when one bears in mind that the African regions that scholars typically use to impose order on quantitative studies of the slave trade do not correspond to neatly monolithic African cultures. All people who embarked on the Middle Passage from Senegambia, for example, did not share a language or a religion. Some were Bambara; others were Wolof. Some practiced Islam; others embraced animist faiths. Some cultivated rice; others herded cattle. Similar diversity reigned in other African regions, and most of those regions contributed significant numbers of unwilling settlers to South Carolina.[27]

Given that enormous diversity, the claim that "principal groups [of Africans] . . . tended to be concentrated in respective locations" in North America is severely undermined by a detailed look at South Carolina's importations of enslaved people. This is especially striking because South Carolina, of all British mainland colonies, was most likely to develop a strong tie to a particular African region. After all, South Carolina and Virginia were the only North American colonies to draw the vast majority of their slaves from direct African shipments; other colonies relied on a smattering of direct and intercolonial sources. Furthermore South Carolina was unique in its devotion to a cash crop that was also a staple in a particular African region. If any colony should have drawn a majority of slaves from a particular part of Africa or a single ethnic group, it was South Carolina, yet the colony rarely saw even a slim majority of arriving slaves hail from one broad African region for a decade—and virtually every decade saw the dominant African region of origin change. If diversity was the rule for South Carolina, it was only more likely to reign elsewhere in North America.[28]

Among the most hotly contested questions about early African culture in the lowcountry focuses on what knowledge Africans contributed to the development of the region's rice cultivation regime, and on this question the implications of the data on slave arrivals are ambiguous.[29] On one hand, rice arrived in the colony within just a few years of the colony's founding, while the evidence suggests that very few people from rice-producing parts of Africa (primarily Senegambia, Sierra Leone, and southeast Africa) arrived in these earliest years (tables 1, 2, and 3). On the other hand, by the 1680s and 1690s people from Senegambia appeared in fairly significant numbers (though still very much in the minority) in the slave trade to Barbados and Jamaica, from whence Carolina received most slaves. These were precisely the years in which rice was taking hold as a staple crop in the lowcountry, so the question becomes: how many people with experience cultivating rice in Africa would it take to impact the organization of labor and style of cultivation in South Carolina? Might a small minority of Gambian slaves with experience cultivating rice have risen to positions of influence on various plantations or contributed key insights that allowed cultivation of the crop to flourish? The questions are vexing, but tantalizing.

The surge in arrivals of Senegambian peoples in South Carolina once a direct trade with Africa emerged after 1710 might lead one to conclude that Carolina planters had indeed come to appreciate the rice expertise of some people from that region, but several lines of reasoning urge caution on that point. First, as noted above, slave traders' logistical concerns likely had more to do with the brief surge in Senegambian deliveries to Carolina than planter preferences did. Regardless of South Carolinians' preferences, there is little reason to expect that their desires shaped the intercolonial slave trade. Given the high demand for exploitable labor throughout the Americas, the slave trade was almost always a sellers' market. Buyers surely had their preferences—be they ethnic, gender, age, skill, or other concerns—but rarely did buyers succeed in pressuring slave traders to cater to their whims. (Spanish American buyers, with their ability to pay in specie, offered the most notable exception to this, as slave traders often sought Spanish buyers above all others.) European slave traders in Africa typically failed to dictate the specific composition of the groups of people they purchased from African rulers and merchants; since most American ports similarly struggled to attract as many slaves as local planters desired, there was little hope of dictating terms with regard to ethnicity, age, or gender.[30] As a result colonial planters and merchants often grumbled that arriving Africans did not meet their specifications, but almost invariably they laid their money down anyway. To colonial planters any slaves were better than no slaves, and this was especially true for those planters on the margins of the colonial world rarely targeted by transatlantic slave traders coming directly from Africa. Prior to the 1720s, South Carolina certainly qualified as just such a marginal place.

In fact throughout the colonial period Carolinians complained that merchants ignored their preferences for slaves. This was especially true of North Carolina. As former governor George Burrington complained in the 1730s, "the planters are obliged to go into Virginia and South Carolina [to buy slaves] . . . where they pay a Duty on each Negroe, or buy the refuse, distemper'd or refractory Negroes brought into the Country from New England and the Islands, which are sold at excessive rates." North Carolina was in a particularly disadvantaged position for the slave trade, but even merchants and planters in Charleston had little luck dictating the terms of trade. Henry Laurens routinely groused about the steady stream of enslaved people from the Bight of Biafra that slave traders sent him for sale, despite his repeated instructions that "there must not be a Callabar amongst them." For instance, in April 1764, while describing the current market in Charleston for slaves, Laurens reported that "I sold as wretched a fifty Ebo [Igbo] Slaves this week as ever I saw here at £34.6/ [each] Sterling round. They were sent to me by a friend in the West Indies contrary to my will as well as expectation. Had they been tolerable they would have yeilded £8 or £10 more." What is striking for an understanding of the ethnic makeup of the lowcountry is that, despite all his protestations and complaints, Laurens not only received people from the Bight of Biafra but routinely sold them to area planters with reasonable success, albeit at lower prices than he obtained for people from other parts of Africa. As a result of this deaf ear that traders turned to Carolinians' ethnic preferences in the peak years of the slave trade to colonial Charleston, there is little reason to believe that Carolinians in the 1710s had better luck dictating which Africans they received.[31]

Along the same lines, if planter preferences forged the link between Senegambia and Carolina between 1710 and 1724, why did it not persist? Rice remained the lowcountry's staple throughout the colonial period, yet Senegambians' predominance in the African migration to the region declined after those initial years. Merchants, such as Henry Laurens, continued to request Senegambian captives in the mid-eighteenth century, but there is reason to question how important skill with rice was in that preference. After all, the other African region that Carolinians preferred was the Gold Coast—where no rice cultivation existed. One striking trait that these two regions did share, however, was predominance in the early transatlantic slave trade to South Carolina. In the first decade and a half of direct slave deliveries to South Carolina from Africa, the Gold Coast and Senegambia combined to account for 90 percent of the captives (table 5). Perhaps when later Carolina planters expressed a preference for people from these regions their predilections derived from familiarity as much as anything. This is not to suggest that forced Senegambian settlers in early Carolina did not contribute knowledge to rice cultivation. A critical mass of people would not be required to introduce key innovations. The impact of such knowledge on patterns in the transatlantic slave trade, however, was probably minimal.

Beyond the issue of rice cultivation, the implications of the data on African arrivals in South Carolina are clearer. Understanding the development of African American culture in the lowcountry must emphasize adaptations. In addition to adjusting to a new American environment; to chattel slavery, American style; and to English language and customs, the Africans who settled Carolina had to adapt to one another. Despite black majorities in many parishes and on many plantations, Africans of any particular ethnicity were unlikely to find themselves in the majority anywhere. Even those sharing roots in a particular African region might be separated by years (or generations) in their arrival in and adaptation to America. To preserve elements of their varied African pasts, survivors of the Atlantic slave trade needed to share with one another, seek common ground where possible, and embrace adaptation. Charles Joyner's arguments about the formation of the Gullah language as the means by which "Africans from various backgrounds not only communicated with and entertained one another but also linked themselves into a community" thus offer one example of how scholars can reckon with the tremendous diversity of Africans reaching South Carolina while still acknowledging the flowering of African culture in the Americas. Gullah, as Joyner notes, was no one African language transplanted but had roots in Wolof, Ibo, Ga, Yoruba, Ewe, Fante, Kikongo, Kimbundu, Mandinka, and Twi. Nonetheless Gullah did inject America with African culture and helped give enslaved people a social and cultural sphere that colonists of European descent could not readily penetrate.[32]

Where enslaved Africans failed to adapt to one another, the results could be disastrous. John Thornton has argued that the core rebels in the Stono Rebellion hailed from the kingdom of Kongo (in modern Angola), where by the early eighteenth century many men learned to use muskets. This skill with firearms explains the Stono rebels' immediate seizure of a cache of arms and their initial success using them. But as other enslaved people—presumably of more diverse backgrounds—flocked to these rebels, their movement failed to last. In the first pitched battle with a colonial militia, most of insurgents fled back to their plantations, leaving a small group of armed Africans to fight, whom Thornton plausibly surmises were those same Kongolese rebels that started the uprising. Given that such men from Kongo composed a small minority of South Carolina's population, perhaps the failure of the Stono Rebellion to grow or persist more than it did can be attributed to the enslaved populations' great diversity. The Kongolese rebels and Africans of other backgrounds failed to bridge their differences and capitalize on the black majority of the region.[33]

This emphasis on diversity is not to suggest that African practices and traditions could not be preserved—far from it—but adaptation, negotiation, and hybridization must have been vital parts of the transfer of African folkways to Carolina's slave quarters. With the diversity of African people arriving in the colony it could not have been otherwise. That such accommodation was difficult, painful, and perhaps not always successful only makes the flowering of a vibrant African American culture in the lowcountry all the more astonishing and triumphant.

Notes

I would like to thank the participants at the Crisis and Conflict in the Early Carolinas conference for their insightful questions and suggestions on my essay, as well as all I learned from their papers. I also thank Philip D. Morgan for reading and critiquing my essay.

1. *The Papers of Henry Laurens*, 15 vols., ed. Philip M. Hamer, George C. Rogers, David R. Chesnutt, and C. James Taylor (Columbia: University of South Carolina Press, 1968–2003); epigraph is from 1:294–95.

2. I place *ethnic* in quotation marks here because what Laurens refers to in the quoted passage are not actually ethnic groups or specific cultures, even though planters and merchants routinely referred to people from these regions as sharing ethnic, racial, or cultural traits.

3. For examples, see *Laurens Papers*, 1:257–58; 2:493; 4:246–47, 320–21.

4. For example, Michael A. Gomez argues, "A number of principal groups comprised the African presence in America," and "they tended to be concentrated in respective locations": *Exchanging Our Country Marks: The Transformation of African Identities in the Colonial and Antebellum South* (Chapel Hill: University of North Carolina Press, 1998), 13; see also Douglas B. Chambers, "Ethnicity in the Diaspora: The Slave-Trade and the Creation of African 'Nations' in the Americas," *Slavery and Abolition* 22, no. 3 (December 2001): 25–39; Judith Carney, *Black Rice: The African Origins of Rice Cultivation in the Americas* (Cambridge: Harvard University Press, 2001), esp. 89–90; Gwendolyn Midlo Hall, *Africans in Colonial Louisiana: The Development of Afro-Creole Culture in the Eighteenth Century* (Baton Rouge: Louisiana State University Press, 1992).

5. Overall, about 12.5 percent of Africans forced across the Atlantic in the slave trade departed from the Bight of Biafra; another 6 percent of captives embarked from the Senegambia region. For the Chesapeake, however, people from the Bight of Biafra made up 35 percent of arriving slaves, and those from Senegambia accounted for another 25 percent. Likewise for the lowcountry, captives from Senegambia accounted for about 21 percent of African immigrants; see *Voyages* estimates for the total slave trade and for the Chesapeake and lowcountry: http://slavevoyages.org/tast/assessment/estimates.faces?yearFrom=1501&yearTo=1866; http://slavevoyages.org/tast/assessment/estimates.faces?yearFrom=1501&yearTo=1866&disembarkation=202; http://slavevoyages.org/tast/assessment/estimates.faces?yearFrom=1501&yearTo=1866&disembarkation=203 (accessed September 20, 2010). See also Lorena S. Walsh, "The Chesapeake Slave Trade: Regional Patterns, African Origins, and Some Implications," *WMQ* 58, no. 1 (January 2001): 145, 166. David Eltis, Philip Morgan, and David Richardson, "Agency and Diaspora in Atlantic History: Reassessing the African Contribution to Rice Cultivation in the Americas," *AHR* 112, no. 5 (December 2007): 1335.

6. For a nice discussion of this complex of acculturations, see Gomez, *Exchanging Our Country Marks*, 8–11. But as this essay should make clear, I am less comfortable with Gomez's argument that patterns in the slave trade resulted in distinct "African ethnic enclaves" in various parts of North America; see 11, 38, 150.

7. On the growth of the African population in South Carolina to 1710, see Peter H. Wood, *Black Majority: Negroes in Colonial South Carolina from 1670 through the Stono Rebellion* (New York: Knopf, 1974), 131, 143–45; Russell R. Menard, "Slave Demography in the Lowcountry, 1670–1740: From Frontier Society to Plantation Regime," *SCHM* 101, no. 3 (July 2000): 193. Peter Coclanis estimates an even larger population of African descent by 1710, putting the figure at 5,768: *Shadow of a Dream: Economic Life and Death in the South Carolina Low Country, 1670–1920* (New York: Oxford University Press, 1989), 64.

8. Wood, *Black Majority,* chap. 1; see also the essay by Justin Roberts and Ian Beamish in this volume; Richard S. Dunn, *Sugar and Slaves: The Rise of the Planter Class in the English West Indies, 1624–1713* (Chapel Hill: University of North Carolina Press, 1972), 112–16; Jack P. Greene, "Colonial South Carolina and the Caribbean Connection," in *Imperatives, Behaviors, and Identities: Essays in Early American Cultural History* (Charlottesville: University Press of Virginia, 1992), 68–86; S. Max Edelson, *Plantation Enterprise in Colonial South Carolina* (Cambridge: Harvard University Press, 2006), 43–45, 50.

9. Governor and Council of South Carolina to the Board of Trade, September 17, 1709, in Elizabeth Donnan, ed., *Documents Illustrative of the History of the Slave Trade to America,* 4 vols. (Washington D.C.: Carnegie Institution of Washington, 1930), 4:256.

10. On the maintenance of shipping and family ties between early South Carolina and Barbados, see Roberts and Beamish in this volume; see also Dunn, *Sugar and Slaves,* 114–15. On South Carolina exporting enslaved Indians to the Caribbean, see Greene, "Caribbean Connection," 74; Alan Gallay, *The Indian Slave Trade: The Rise of the English Empire in the American South, 1670–1717* (New Haven: Yale University Press, 2002), 299–301, 313. Gallay also notes a planned 1686 venture to Barbados to acquire African slaves for South Carolina's new Stuart Town settlement, 80–81.

11. Jamaican export records from mid-1709 to mid-1711 show fifteen vessels (carrying 237 slaves) departing for South Carolina in the two-year period. Naval Office Shipping Lists for Jamaica, CO 142/14. Records for most prior years do not survive, but significant exports from Jamaica to South Carolina likely did not begin much before 1700 because it was only after 1700 that Jamaica began to import more slaves from Africa than Barbados did. To compare arrivals from Africa for Barbados and Jamaica, see *Voyages:* http://slavevoyages.org/tast/database/search.faces?yearFrom=1514&yearTo=1866&mjslptimp=34200.35100 (accessed August 30, 2010). Barbados shipping lists survive for much of this early period, but unfortunately they document only the exports of "enumerated goods" from the British Navigation Acts; slaves were not so "enumerated." Thus a detailed accounting of this trade (and migration) is impossible. For a sample shipment from Barbados, see the sloop *Turtle* carrying an unspecified number of slaves from Barbados to South Carolina in 1697: Donnan, *Documents,* 4:249. Anecdotal reports do note occasional Carolina planters venturing to more established mainland colonies for slaves in the earliest years, as well, most notably Virginia and New York: see Wood, *Black Majority,* 24.

12. For an example of the assumption that slaves arriving in South Carolina from the Caribbean were so-called seasoned slaves, who had spent enough time in the islands to acculturate, see Charles Joyner, *Down by the Riverside: A South Carolina Slave Community* (Urbana: University of Illinois Press, 1984), 205. Russell Menard cautions scholars not "to jump to the conclusion that most [Africans from the Caribbean] were therefore partly Anglicized, seasoned, and experienced plantation workers," but nonetheless refers to such people as "island blacks" and "West Indian blacks," implying that they had indeed acculturated to life in the islands. By contrast, Jack Greene argues that high slave mortality in Barbados (and other islands) prevented significant emigration of acculturated slaves to South Carolina: "Caribbean Connection," 76. For the predominance of recently-arrived Africans in the intercolonial slave trade between the Caribbean and North America more generally, see Gregory E. O'Malley, "Beyond the Middle Passage: Slave Migration from the Caribbean to North America, 1619–1807," *WMQ* 66, no. 1 (January 2009): 135–37; Darold D. Wax, "Preferences for Slaves in Colonial America," *Journal of Negro History* 58, no. 4 (1973): 371–401; John C. Coombs, "Building 'the Machine': The Development of Slavery and Slave Society in Early Colonial Virginia" (Ph.D. diss., College of William and Mary, 2003), 103–4. Wood, *Black Majority*, presents examples of Barbadian planters and slave owners migrating to South Carolina, but also notes such individuals quickly seeking additional laborers from Barbados and other colonies after their moves, 19–24.

13. Philip D. Curtin notes that Europeans' use of African port names or region names to refer to various African peoples they enslaved led to much imprecision with regard to identifying actual African ethnicities or cultures: *The Atlantic Slave Trade: A Census* (Madison: University of Wisconsin Press, 1969), especially, 184–90. Furthermore, Alexander X. Byrd argues that violence between Africans of varied backgrounds was common aboard slave trading vessels as captives struggled to create a social hierarchy within a diverse community: "Captives and Voyagers: Black Migrants Across the Eighteenth-Century World of Olaudah Equiano" (Ph.D. diss., Duke University, 2001), 100–106. Byrd also emphasizes the diversity of peoples entering the slave trade from the Bight of Biafra, specifically, stressing that there was no one monolithic Igbo culture, 24–27. See also Jerome S. Handler, "Survivors of the Middle Passage: Life Histories of Enslaved Africans in British America," *Slavery and Abolition* 23, no. 1 (April 2002): 37–38; Philip D. Morgan, "The Cultural Implications of the Atlantic Slave Trade: African Regional Origins, American Destinations and New World Developments," in *Routes to Slavery: Direction, Ethnicity and Mortality in the Transatlantic Slave Trade*, ed. David Eltis and David Richardson (London: Frank Cass, 1997), 122–45; Patrick Manning, *Slavery, Colonialism, and Economic Growth in Dahomey, 1640-1960* (New York: Cambridge University Press, 1982), 30

14. On the Spanish preference for Africans from Angola influencing the slave trade to Jamaica, see the owners' "Instructions [to Captain Thomas Brownbill] for the *Blessing*, bound for Africa, 10 October 1700," Liverpool Record Office, Norris Papers, vol. 2, f.179; see also the letters of Tyndall & Assheton, who were Jamaican merchants involved in the slave trade to Spanish America in the 1720s, Bristol, England, Bristol Central Library, Jeffries Collection, vol. 13, for example, 103, 113.

15. On the high price of slaves, see Eltis, *Rise of African Slavery*, 151–53; Herbert S. Klein, *The Atlantic Slave Trade* (New York: Cambridge University Press, 1999), 100–101.

16. J. Evans, [captain of the *Greyhound Galley*] to Captain Johnson, printed in Daniel Defoe [Captain Charles Johnson], *A General History of the Pyrates* (Mineola, N.Y.: Dover Publications, 1999 [1724]), 6770. Records in *Voyages* lend credibility to this letter. The database lists a John Evans as captain of a vessel called *Greyhound* that delivered captives from the Gold Coast to Jamaica in late 1716 or early 1717 [Voyage ID #78305], and again from an unknown African port to Jamaica in 1718 [#76593]. According to *Voyages* the *Greyhound* left Africa in 1716 with 273 captives, but delivered only 236 to Kingston. While losing 37 captives to disease on the Middle Passage was by no means unheard of, losing them to pirates remains a distinct possibility and meshes quite well with Johnson and Evans's estimate that the pirates stole 40 captives. For another example of pirates stealing some slaves from a vessel before allowing it to continue, see David Cordingly, *Under the Black Flag: The Romance and the Reality of Life Among the Pirates* (San Diego: Harcourt Brace, 1997), 104–5.

17. Kidd: Edgar J. McManus, *Black Bondage in the North* (Syracuse, N.Y.: Syracuse University Press, 1973), 20; Bonnet: *The Tryals of Major Stede Bonnet*, reprinted in *British Piracy in the Golden Age: History and Interpretation, 1660–1730*, Joel H. Baer, ed. (London: Pickering & Chatto, 2007), 2:327; Teach/Blackbeard: Defoe/Johnson, *General History of the Pyrates*, 71–74, and Alexander Spotswood to Charles Eden, 7 November 1718, Richmond, Virginia Historical Society, Lee family papers, 1638–1867, section 76, folder 1, Mss1L51f109; Vane: Shirley Carter Hughson, *The Carolina Pirates and Colonial Commerce, 1670–1740* (New York: Johnson Reprint Corporation, 1973 [1894]), 91–93; Rackam: Baer, *British Piracy*, 3:21–26; Whydah: http://www.nationalgeographic.com/whydah/story.html (accessed September 1, 2010).

18. On North Carolina's minimal direct importation, see Marvin L. Michael Kay and Lorin Lee Cary, *Slavery in North Carolina, 1748–1775* (Chapel Hill: University of North Carolina Press, 1995), 15–21; Bradford J. Wood, *This Remote Part of the World: Regional Formation in Lower Cape Fear, North Carolina, 1725–1775* (Columbia: University of South Carolina Press, 2004), 38–40; see also *Voyages:* http://slavevoyages.org/tast/database/search.faces?yearFrom=1514&yearTo=1866&mjslptimp=21200 (accessed September 1, 2010).

19. On South Carolina's harboring of pirates: Mark Gillies Hanna, "The Pirate Nest: The Impact of Piracy on Newport, Rhode Island and Charles Town, South Carolina, 1670–1730" (Ph.D. diss., Harvard University, 2006), esp. 114–16; Hughson, *Carolina Pirates*, esp. 13–21.

20. Quotation from Governor Thomas Lynch of Jamaica's account of the Vera Cruz raid, see Baer, *British Piracy*, 1:228. On the arrivals in South Carolina: Wood, *Black Majority*, 44.

21. Because the line separating pirates from privateers was often blurry some pirates refused to prey upon merchant shipping of their own nation, viewing themselves more as privateers even if they lacked a commission from their government; most pirate crews, however, comprised "villains of all nations" and displayed little

preferential treatment for ships flying one flag or another; Marcus Rediker, *Villains of All Nations: Atlantic Pirates in the Golden Age* (Boston: Beacon Press, 2004). Linda Heywood and John Thornton have demonstrated that privateers in the first decades of North American slavery delivered primarily Angolan captives to the region (because they preyed primarily on Portuguese slavers), but they focus on the period before the founding of Carolina, so the pirates and privateers who delivered slaves to early Carolina likely drew their captives from the broader range of transatlantic slave traders active at that time: Linda M. Heywood and John K. Thornton, *Central Africans, Atlantic Creoles, and the Foundation of the Americas, 1585–1660* (Cambridge, U.K.: Cambridge University Press, 2007), ix, 8–48.

22. For direct African arrivals in South Carolina in the 1710s, see *Voyages* (accessed September 10, 2010): http://slavevoyages.org/tast/database/search.faces?yearFrom=1710&yearTo=1719&mjslptimp=21200.21300. Steven D. Behrendt demonstrates that complementary seasonal cycles of supply and demand determined many routes of the transatlantic slave trade, but for the South Carolina-Gambia link in the early eighteenth century, market size was the more important factor: "Markets, Transaction Cycles, and Profits: Merchant Decision Making in the British Slave Trade," *WMQ* 58, no. 1 (January 2001): 171–204, esp. 188–94. For other examples of slave traders matching vessel sizes to market sizes, see Walsh, "Chesapeake Slave Trade," 155. For direct African voyages to Maryland before 1730, see *Voyages* (accessed December 7, 2011): http://slavevoyages.org/tast/database/search.faces?yearFrom=1660&yearTo=1730&mjslptimp=21000.

23. Austin & Laurens to Law, Satterthwaite, & Jones, January 12, 1756: *Laurens Papers*, 2:65–66. Wood, *This Remote Part of the World*, 38–40; Kay and Cary, *Slavery in North Carolina*, 15–21.

24. For estimates of Caribbean shipments to South Carolina, see O'Malley, "Beyond the Middle Passage," 142. For the crackdown on piracy, see Rediker, *Villains of All Nations*, chap. 7; Robert C. Ritchie, *Captain Kidd and the War against the Pirates* (Cambridge: Harvard University Press, 1986).

25. Walter E. Minchinton, "The Seaborne Slave Trade of North Carolina," *NCHR* 71, no. 1 (January 1994): 7; O'Malley, "Beyond the Middle Passage," 147–49.

26. Edelson, *Plantation Enterprise in South Carolina*, 4.

27. For the diverse peoples of the Senegambia region, see Gomez, *Exchanging Our Country Marks*, chaps. 3 and 4. Stephanie Smallwood argues powerfully for the diversity of captives aboard ships leaving Africa from the Gold Coast, noting—for example—that in the late seventeenth century European traders often purchased some captives at the Bight of Benin before completing their slave purchasing at the Gold Coast. Likewise, she notes a rebellion on a vessel from Gambia being undermined by internal divisions among the captives: Stephanie E. Smallwood, *Saltwater Slavery: A Middle Passage from Africa to American Diaspora* (Cambridge: Harvard University Press, 2007), 86–87, 102–9, 188–89.

28. Quotation: Gomez, *Exchanging Our Country Marks*, 13; on the proportion of slaves that North American colonies obtained directly from Africa, see O'Malley, "Beyond the Middle Passage," 166.

29. For the argument for the importance of Africans with experience cultivating rice for the development of the Lowcountry's rice cultivation and labor regime,

see Carney, *Black Rice*; Daniel C. Littlefield, *Rice and Slaves: Ethnicity and the Slave Trade in Colonial South Carolina* (Baton Rouge: Louisiana State University Press, 1981). For a critique of these arguments, see Eltis, Morgan, and Richardson, "Agency and Diaspora in Atlantic History." For a discussion of this debate, see the *AHR*'s forum on the issue: "AHR Exchange: The Question of 'Black Rice,'" *AHR* 115, no. 1 (February 2010): 123–71.

30. On African sellers' concerns shaping the slave trade in Africa, see David Eltis, *The Rise of African Slavery in the Americas* (New York: Cambridge University Press, 2000), chap. 7. Likewise, Lorena S. Walsh has powerfully demonstrated that the Lower James River in Virginia received disproportionate numbers of people from the Bight of Biafra, despite the fact that "No Chesapeake planter is known to have expressed a preference for laborers originating in the Bight of Biafra;" "Chesapeake Slave Trade," 153.

31. George Burrington's report on the ports of North Carolina, July 27, 1736, CO 5/295, f.32–33; Laurens to John Knight [Liverpool], April 14, 1764, *Laurens Papers*, 4:246–47. If, as Judith Carney argues, "by 1712 conventions between slave and master were already in place over permissible norms regulating work in the rice economy," the minimal number of enslaved people from rice-producing regions in Africa to reach South Carolina by that date is problematic for the argument that expertise with rice gave enslaved people in the lowcountry negotiating power: Carney, *Black Rice*, 82.

32. Charles Joyner, *Down by the Riverside*, chap. 7; quotation from 197.

33. John K. Thornton, "African Dimensions of the Stono Rebellion," *AHR* 96, no. 4 (October 1991): 1101–13.

Marooned

Politics and Revolution in the Bahamas Islands and Carolina

ALEXANDER MOORE

In the last weeks of 1719, a sizeable cabal—perhaps a majority—of influential South Carolinians executed a coup d'état, repudiating Governor Robert Johnson and the rule of the Lords Proprietors of Carolina. They immediately sought British Crown recognition of their actions and petitioned the Crown to take the government of the province under direct royal authority. The rebels took this action as a Convention of the People, modeling their political rationale and course of proceedings on the Convention Parliament of 1689. They even crafted a document stating their reasons for revolution that bore elements comparable to the Declaration of Right. The Revolution of 1719 was an act of desperation lest the colony be destroyed by internal and external enemies. For twenty years the proprietors had been unwilling or unable to govern their province and had in the few years before 1719 obstructed local leaders' efforts to govern themselves.[1] Desperation mingled with self-interest; fear of extermination by Native Americans or rival imperial powers complemented opportunism; republican principles gave color to local economic main chances.

The Revolution of 1719 simultaneously aimed to give the government to the queen in Parliament and to assert clearly expressed principles of local self-rule under the umbrella of distant Crown oversight. The British Crown recognized the revolutionary government and soon thereafter assumed sovereignty over South Carolina when it appointed Francis Nicholson the first royal governor of the new royal colony. The fact that Robert Johnson, ousted in 1719 for his loyalty to the proprietors, was appointed the colony's second royal governor in 1729 suggested some amicability, if not collusion, in 1719 between Carolina rebels, Crown officials, and even Robert Johnson. In the same year that Johnson was appointed royal governor, the British Crown purchased the title to the lands of South Carolina for the sum of £22,500, thereby extinguishing Proprietary rule and ownership of South Carolina.[2]

While the Carolina revolutionists marshaled complicated political principles and skillfully made their case for Crown governance, they had some beforehand confidence of success, for they had a precedent—nearly a road map—to successful overthrow of Proprietary rule. That precedent was found in the recent history of the Proprietary Bahamas Islands. This essay explores the political connections between the Bahamas Islands and the Carolina province during the fifty years in which both were the property of Lords Proprietors, with particular attention to how both provinces overthrew proprietary rule and became royal colonies. The troubled history of Proprietary South Carolina had a comparative "troubled history" of the Bahamas. The course of events in the Bahamas from 1670 to 1717 foretold—if such a verb might be used in modern history writing—the Revolution of 1719.

Among many Carolina and Caribbean connections, that between South Carolina and Barbados is best known. English Barbadians explored the Carolina coast and the Company of Barbadian Adventurers projected settlements in the Cape Fear region in the 1660s. A look at the proprietors' 1665 Concessions and Agreements with the Barbadian Adventurers reveals that the Concessions were a prototype of the Fundamental Constitutions of Carolina.[3] Barbadian surnames abounded on the mainland province. The Yeamans, Gibbes, Colleton, and Quintyne families had branches in both provinces. Seven of the ten Church of England parishes established in South Carolina by 1716 had Barbadian predecessors. Indeed generations of scholars have successfully traced Carolina political and economic institutions, architecture, and even patterns of vice and virtue to Barbados.[4]

Ties between Proprietary Carolina and the Bahamas Islands were less well known, but they extended as far back into the seventeenth century as the Carolina-Barbados connection. Unlike those with Barbados, the Carolina's Bahamas ties had distinctive characteristics of being nonconformist in faith and republican in political principles. Carolina and Barbados shared Anglicanism and a taste for wealth; Carolina and the Bahamas shared dissenter values and a political economy that might be called buccaneer enterprise. Certainly the Carolina-Bahamian links were more tenuous than Carolina's links with Barbados because the Bahamas colony was small, impoverished, and neglected. It is ironic that the Bahamas' troubled history made the islands' experience pertinent to South Carolina.[5] An examination of the course of events that led the English Crown to assume the government of the Bahamas in 1718 provided insights and a rationale for the haste with which the Crown recognized the success of the South Carolina Revolution of 1719.

The first connection to be emphasized was the fact that in 1670 six of the founding Carolina Proprietors obtained a royal charter that expanded their colonial domain to the Bahamas. The six were Christopher, Duke of Albemarle; William, Earl Craven; John, Lord Berkeley; Anthony Ashley Cooper; Sir George Carteret; and Sir Peter Colleton. After years of complaint by Bahamians and a few successful local ousters of governors, the government of that "woeful" province was resumed by the British Crown in 1718 for the same reasons that two years later the Crown reclaimed Carolina.[6]

The two provinces' ties had in fact begun forty years earlier in 1629 when Sir Robert Heath, Charles I's attorney general, secured a vast grant of territory on the North American continent and in the Caribbean Ocean. Called Carolana, the territory of Heath's grant encompassed the portion of North America between 31 and 36 degrees north latitude (hypothetically from coast to coast), the Bahamas, and other Caribbean islands.[7] Not only was the geographical scope of Carolana and Carolina similar, but also many terms of the Heath grant anticipated terms of the 1663 and 1665 Carolina grants. Among those specific terms was the Bishop of Durham clause, which gave the proprietors independence from some specific Crown prerogatives exercised in royal colonies, remissions of certain customs duties, and indeed some war-making license in their overseas empires.[8]

English settlers first landed on the Bahamas during the 1640s. They were Bermudians impelled by the twin spirits of the era—religious enthusiasm and fractious republicanism.[9] William Sayle and his coreligionists had settled Bermuda in the 1630s under a grant from the old Somers Island Company, which had founded the Bermuda colonies in 1612.[10] Sayle, who later became Carolina's first proprietary governor, and a group of Bermudian Independent Congregationalists projected a Bahamian settlement as a haven for the exercise of their particular brand of Protestant religion and republican-minded politics.[11] Satellite settlements would also alleviate serious overcrowding in Bermuda, which could support only a small population. Sayle visited England in 1647, where he formed the Company of Eleutherian Adventurers and sought a charter for the Bahamas or Eleutherian Islands.[12] The company advertised for settlers and financial backing for a colony founded on independent, republican principles. The Adventurers found support among English Puritans and republicans and in the Massachusetts Bay Colony but failed to secure a charter from the revolutionary government of the Long Parliament.[13] With the collapse of the Protectorate of Oliver Cromwell and his son Richard Cromwell and restoration of Charles II and the Stuart dynasty in 1660, the Eleutherian Adventurers lost all hope of a grant. However initial lack of a charter did not deter the Adventurers. In 1648 they placed a squatter colony on Eleuthera. This small outpost survived under the direct leadership of Sayle and his family. In 1666 a settlement called Charles Town was founded on Sayle's Island. Charles Town became Nassau, and Sayle's Island was renamed New Providence. Within three years there were nearly eleven hundred whites and African slaves on the islands of Eleuthera, Abaco, and New Providence, but the government of the islands was still in the hands of the Somers Island Company.[14]

Charles II voided the 1629 Heath patent in August 1663 to grant Carolana to a new group of investors, the Lords Proprietors of Carolina. Edward Hyde, Earl of Clarendon, and George Monck, Duke of Albemarle, had been allies of Charles when he reclaimed the British Crown in 1660. Clarendon, Albemarle, Anthony Ashley Cooper, and the seven other Lords Proprietors of Carolina were powerful politicians and assiduous businessmen. They sought rewards from Charles for their loyalty to him during the interregnum and aimed to make that reward a lucrative New World investment. William Sayle tried again to obtain a Bahamas charter but again failed. Too closely attached by politics and dissenter faith to the Protectorate, he and the other Bahamian Adventurers had little expectations of favor from the restored Stuart monarch.[15] However, he knew that Ashley Cooper and the Proprietary secretary John Locke were sympathetic to religious liberty and local authority because they had introduced those principles in their Barbadian Concessions and Agreements.[16] If Sayle could not obtain his own charter to the Bahamas the proprietors might succeed and aid him to achieve his intention. To that end he and other Eleutherian Adventurers suggested to the proprietors the wisdom of acquiring the Bahamas.[17]

The death in December 1669 of proprietary Palatine Duke of Albemarle brought Anthony Ashley Cooper to leadership of the proprietors. A member of Charles's Privy Council and the Council for Trade and Plantations (forerunner of the Crown Board of Trade), Ashley Cooper was an energetic promoter of overseas expansion. In addition he was the chief spokesman in England for nonconformity and was also influenced by republican notions.[18] For all these reasons, the Bahamas appealed to him. The islands were strategically located, unencumbered by earlier grants, and already a haven for dissenters and political outsiders—his kind of people. To demonstrate further the interconnections of the Bahamas, Carolina, and Bermuda, it is well to understand that Ashley Cooper was also a principal shareholder in the Bermudian Somers Island Company. In 1671 Ashley Cooper became governor of that company, uniting in his own convoluted, brilliant person the fortunes of all three provinces.[19]

Two Eleutherian Adventurers, John Dorrell and Hugh Wentworth, met the Carolina fleet when it stopped in Bermuda in February 1670. They wrote to Ashley Cooper urging that the Bahamas would be a good acquisition per se and would complement the infant Carolina colony. Bermuda was overcrowded, and many of the inhabitants (particularly nonconformists) looked to settle in the Bahamas. The islands produced good cotton and "gallant Tobacco" and had a sufficiency of locally grown provisions. The two men argued primarily for the Bahamas' strategic importance. A strong military presence there would be the first line of defense for the Carolina colony. If the Spanish of La Florida and Cuba sought to conquer the southern mainland colonies, they must first secure the Bahamas.[20] The Bahamas would be a strong dissenter "marcher colony" from which tough-minded anti-Catholic seamen would defend Carolina and the profits arising from buccaneer enterprise against threats from the New World colonies of Spain and France.

Ashley Cooper replied to Dorrell and Wentworth on October 29, 1670, informing them that as of July 1670 he and five other of the Carolina Proprietors had acquired a warrant for a Bahamas grant precisely for the reasons the two men had given.²¹ Ashley Cooper had proven prescient in his thinking about the Bahamas, and the Adventurers had been wise in their patron seeking. The date of the Bahamas grant was November 1, 1670.²² By 1670 Edward Hyde, Earl of Clarendon, was already in exile in Holland, and Sir William Berkeley was governor of Virginia. Neither man had a share in the Bahamas grant. Ashley Cooper also informed Wentworth that the proprietors had elected him governor of New Providence. They had resolved to govern the Bahamas according to the Fundamental Constitutions of March 1, 1670, and to offer headright grants there on the same terms as those in Carolina. Finally, Wentworth's commission and instructions were similar to those sent to William Sayle and Joseph West, the first governors of Carolina.²³ In nearly every aspect, the Bahamas appeared in the proprietors' vision to have a place equal to that of Carolina.

By creating an interlocking directorate of charter holders, the proprietors hoped that the two colonies would be mutually beneficial. Ashley Cooper, John Locke, Dorrell, Wentworth, William Kiffin, and others founded a company to exploit the resources of the Bahamas, but the company eventually faltered as the dismal history of the Bahamas province unfolded in the ensuing decades.²⁴ The Bahamas would provide safe harbors and strategic security for travelers between England and North America. New Providence would produce Brazilwood for international markets and raise provisions, including livestock, for Carolina. With the Bahamas managing to serve the specific needs of Carolina, the latter province could devote itself single-mindedly to developing a profitable staple crop in the manner of Barbados and Jamaica.²⁵

Whatever hopes the proprietors had for the Bahamas, they were dashed even sooner than their grander hopes for Carolina. Starting in 1670 foreign and internal threats, local political dissention, and ineffectual Proprietary governance that kindled the Revolution of 1719 were also at work in the Bahamas. Indeed in the islands these elements were more accelerated and destructive than they were in Carolina. Misgovernment, an unruly populace holding republican dissenter values, pirates, and international conflict kept the islands in a state of anarchy and led to the downfall of Proprietary rule. Royal initiatives to reclaim charter colonies after the Restoration, driven by recently strengthened Navigation Acts, James II's "attack on the charters," and the emerging power of the first British Empire kept unrelenting pressure on the proprietors at Whitehall and Westminster. By 1718 the proprietors were grateful to find a way to escape their obligations to the struggling Bahamas province. The Bahamians' "overthrow" of Proprietary rule in that year was a narrow escape for both the Bahamian settlers and the proprietors. It was soon followed by the Revolution of 1719, a more traumatic event—but another narrow escape—for South Carolinians and proprietors alike.

John Dorrell and Hugh Wentworth had accurately stated the strategic importance of the Bahamas. Because of the influence of prevailing currents and winds, any seaborne threat to the mainland colonies would first be met in the Bahamas.[26] Indeed the Bahamas were the first target of any attack on Carolina. The proof of that assertion was seen in the frequent devastation of the islands. That situation had dire consequences for the small, isolated province. For the next fifty years the Bahamas were the first target of nearly every French and Spanish campaign against the British in the Caribbean and on the southern mainland. The strategic importance of the Bahamas and their terrible vulnerability loomed large in the imperial thinking of the Council of Trade, its successor Board of Trade and Plantations, and other Crown officials responsible for colonial administration. If the Bahamas had seemed a good acquisition for the proprietors in 1670, within twenty years it became a millstone around their necks: unprofitable, tumultuous, and troublesome.

Such were the contradictions of proprietary, imperial, and local policies that Bahamians imperiled the proprietors' charter when they tried to defend themselves from England's enemies in the region. In addition, by the first decade of the eighteenth century, any initiatives by the proprietors (if they chose to make any) only worsened their situation vis-á-vis colonists and imperial authorities. In 1682—even before James II became king—Governor Robert Clarke issued letters of marque to John Coxon, "a pirate turned privateer." News of Clarke's actions reached Whitehall and triggered the Crown's first of several attempts to extinguish the Bahamian charter. During January 1683 the Lords of Trade investigated Clarke's action and instructed the attorney general to render an opinion whether Clarke's action had been an act of lèse-majesté by the proprietors of the king's power to wage war. The lords were poised to institute a scire facias warrant against the Bahamas Proprietors when Peter Colleton convinced them not to proceed. Quo warranto writs were royal writs in which Crown officials demanded to know from a charter holder "by what authority" he exercised his charter rights. Scire facias was a writ in which Crown authorities demanded to know from a charter holder why their charter rights and authority should not be resumed to the Crown or abolished outright. Colleton argued that the Bahamas charter authorized the proprietors to wage war, but the Crown sensibly replied that this authority was commonly understood to apply to warfare against noncivilized native populations, not against the nations of Europe. Colleton had better success when he reported that the proprietors had already grasped that diplomatic principle and had issued arrest warrants for Clarke and had instructed the Bahamian governor to cease issuing letters of marque. This episode proved a minor irritant to the proprietors, who, through Colleton's adroit presentation, turned aside this first threat to their charter.[27] But this was only the beginning of colonial and Crown campaigns to strike down the proprietors' charters in the Bahamas and Carolina.

The first Spanish military campaign against the Bahamas occurred in January 1684. Governor Richard Lilburne fled into the woods when the Spanish landed at Charles Town, New Providence. The attackers pillaged the town but did not burn it. However, when they returned in October they burned the town, kidnapped settlers for ransom, and carried off most of the African slaves. Charles Town was desolated and took several years to recover the semblance of permanent habitation.[28] The physical desolation was compounded by another political threat when, on May 30, 1686, James II ordered his attorney general to initiate quo warranto proceedings against the charter of the Lords Proprietors of the Bahamas.[29]

It must have seemed to the proprietors of the Bahamas and Carolina that the year 1686 would never end, for, having destroyed New Providence and cleared the way for a larger campaign, the Spanish turned their military forces against Carolina. In August and December 1686 they attacked and laid waste Stuart Town, the Scottish settlement at Port Royal south of Charles Town. In the second attack Spanish forces reached Edisto Island and burned Governor Joseph Morton's plantation but did not have the strength to mount an attack against the metropolis at Charles Town.[30] Carolinians fortuitously escaped destruction, but Stuart Town, established at Port Royal to defend the southern frontier, and New Providence, the first line of Carolina's sea defenses, had both been effaced by the Spanish.

Weak government at home, indifferent oversight, and threats from international rivals taught some Carolina and Bahamas settlers that their best hopes of survival—not to mention success—lay with direct rule by the British Crown. The exigencies of self-preservation led colonists to collaborate to overthrow Proprietary governance in Carolina and the Bahamas. Their most effective tools for that end proved to be petitions and appeals for redress from settlers and local assemblies to the Board of Trade, the Crown, and Parliament. They were especially effective when their petitions complemented emergent British imperialist aims.

In 1694 Thomas Bulkley stated the Bahamians' case for Crown resumption of the Bahamas government in a long, rambling memorial to the proprietors that also found its way to Whitehall. Bulkley's catalog of grievances offered an alarming portrait of local corruption, anarchy, and oppression. According to Bulkley, governors Nicholas Trott of Bermuda and Joseph Blake of Carolina were conspiring with Bahamas governor Cadwallader Jones to despoil the petitioner and all the inhabitants of the southern colonies—island and mainland. Bulkley traveled to England to seek redress but never received a hearing from the proprietors or Crown officials[31] John Graves, a disaffected Proprietary secretary and enterprising royal customs collector in the Bahamas, made another strong case against Proprietary rule.[32] Graves petitioned the House of Lords in March 1706 "in behalf of himself and all others her Majesty's distressed subjects" in the Bahamas. He called on the Crown to take the province under royal governance to save it from the proprietors' negligence. The chief argument of Graves's memorial was that "the whole trade, welfare, and safety of Carolina depends upon the security of the Bahamas Islands."[33]

Whether by design or coincidence, Graves's memorial arrived in the House of Lords just as the lords were investigating the legality of the Carolina Exclusion and Establishment Acts of 1704 and 1705. The well-orchestrated groans of Carolina dissenters suffering under the proprietors' High Church tyranny complemented those of Bahamians suffering under anarchy, pirate infestation, and fear of the Spanish. On March 12, the House of Lords informed Queen Anne that the Carolina Church Acts were repugnant to British law and requested her "to use the most effectual methods to deliver the said province from the arbitrary oppressions under which it now lies." They recommended that the Crown should void the proprietors' charter and take Carolina "under your royal care."[34]

A week later another Lords committee read Graves's memorial and interviewed him and other Bahamians at the bar. That committee made an even stronger report to the queen beseeching that "in compassion to your Majesty's distressed subjects in those parts, as for the security of the trade in general, you will be pleased to use such methods . . . fit, for taking the said islands into your hands."[35]

Queen Anne ordered issuance of both scire facias and quo warranto writs against the proprietors. However, these proceedings were squelched in the House of Lords on a technicality that most of the proprietors were peers not subject to these writs.[36] That technicality also blunted the threat to the Bahamas charter. During Queen Anne's War (1702–13) both Nassau and Charles Town were targets of the allied French and Spanish forces. In October 1703 the Spanish captured Nassau and occupied the city for two weeks.[37] These charter attacks were contemporaneous with Queen Anne's War (War of Spanish Succession) so they had a military dimension that proceeded contemporaneously with the political ones. The August 1706 joint French and Spanish attack on Charles Town was another dramatic campaign of the Caribbean theater of that war.[38] Repulsed at Charles Town by Carolinians led by Governor Nathaniel Johnson, the attackers found easier pickings in the Bahamas, where the fleet commander captured a few English prizes on the way back to Havana.[39] Two months after the Charles Town campaign, the Spanish returned to Nassau. Again they methodically burned the town and kidnapped inhabitants.[40] For the third time in twenty-five years, the colony was nearly depopulated.

The Treaty of Utrecht, signed in 1713, ended Queen Anne's War, but that event brought little peace to the Caribbean and the southern mainland. Piracy took the place of privateering on the high seas and plunged the maritime region into a condition worse than that of a declared war. On the continent French, Spanish, and English settlers subsidized their Indian allies to raid rival colonies. The Yamasee War of 1715–17 was an example of the kinds of conflicts that took place during this time of "peace" between the European powers. That conflict came closer to destroying South Carolina than any conflict before or since.[41]

The Yamasee War quickened the pace of royalization in Carolina and the pirate crises of the decades between 1700 and 1720 hastened royalization of the Bahamas. The war afforded colonial malcontents and Board of Trade officers ample opportunity to renew their pressure on Crown, Parliament, and Proprietors. In fact the Board of Trade tried to use the Carolina crisis to resume all Proprietary charters in America. On August 10, 1715, the board instructed a House of Commons committee to introduce a comprehensive "bill for the better regulation of the Charter and Proprietary governments in America." The bill had its first reading on August 13 and its second on August 15.[42] The committee that wrote the bill was inundated with petitions, memorials, and remonstrances from the Carolina and Bahamas Proprietors, representatives of other proprietary colonies in America, and colonial agents of the New England colonies.[43] Among those who argued against the bill was Jeremiah Dummer of Massachusetts, who claimed that Carolina's problems were self-inflicted and should not be used to attack better governed provinces in New England.[44] The opposition prevailed, and the bill died without a third reading when the Parliamentary session adjourned.[45]

Although the general resumption plan had failed, it generated another publication that linked the fates of Carolina and the Bahamas in the manner of Graves's memorial of 1706. The anonymous author of the broadside *Presumptive Reasons why the Government of South and North Carolina and the Bahamas—should (more especially) be Reassumed into the Hands of the Crown of Great Britain* enumerated ten familiar points in favor of resumption. He reiterated the threats to the empire; described the proprietors' High Church bigotry in ratifying the Church Acts; and denounced their reluctance to spend their private fortunes to defend Carolina and the Bahamas.[46] The bill failed, as has been stated, but the broadside and the House of Commons proceedings demonstrated that by 1715 the plights of South Carolina and the Bahamas had become one and the same in the minds of Parliament and royal officials.

Judging from the destructiveness of the Yamasee War and pirate depredations it was fortunate for Carolina and the Bahamas that the era of European peace was short lived. In December 1718, Great Britain, France, Holland, and Austria jointly declared war on Spain to force that nation to adhere to the provisions of the Treaty of Utrecht. In Europe the War of the Quadruple Alliance was an affair of diplomatic maneuvering with little actual combat. But in the Caribbean and on the southern frontier, the declaration of war simply gave a name to the unbroken, violent state of affairs that had been underway since 1702.[47]

Although the Bahamas escaped the terrors of Indian warfare between 1713 and 1718, it suffered another scourge—piracy—that accomplished what the Yamasee War had done in South Carolina. Piracy brought the Proprietary government of the Bahamas to an ignominious end and foreshadowed its end in Carolina. South Carolina was a revolution; Bahamas was an administrative coup d'état. Piracy and privateering were contemporaneous with European settlements in the New World. Sir Francis Drake, John Hawkins, and other Elizabethan "sea dogs" invented a New World enterprise that linked adventure, profit, and chauvinism in the 1580s when they began to capture and despoil the shipping of Spanish America.[48] They also engaged in the African slave trade and enterprises that made them cautiously welcome in some of the places they harried. They traded mostly in hard currency and bullion, always welcome in the English regions of the New World. From that time until nearly the mid-eighteenth century, both English adventurers and French Huguenot mariners acquired ships and gathered crews to venture against the flotas and carracks of Spain and Portugal in the Caribbean Sea and the Pacific Ocean. The brief, violent history of the French settlement of Charlesfort was part of the story of New World piracy and privateering.

Violent sea fights and coastal raids were only part of the pirate and privateer business. More important was the creation of pirate commerce—political economies that included not only the captains, crews, and vessels of war, but also support facilities and logistical supply. To conduct their enterprises, pirates and privateers required provisions, ship repair, refreshment, and safe havens. Privateers needed letters of marque and reprisal issued by legitimate governments to distinguish their actions from those of pirates. Most of all, both legitimate and outlaw sea raiders required means to dispose of their booty and prizes. Pirates could pay well in scarce hard currency for supplies and services. For these reasons, in the Carolinas and especially in the Bahamas, the self-interest of colonists, local officials, and pirates led to frequent collusion. According to royal authorities and residents excluded from the profits, the Bahamian and Carolina governments were hand in glove with their pirate clients.[49]

While the pirate business was a ready source of cash for prominent colonists, it was a constant headache for the proprietors. The stream of complaints from local law-abiding or excluded inhabitants was augmented by numerous inquiries, reports, and visitations by Crown officials that condemned the proprietors' governance. The proprietors abhorred and discouraged pirate trade, but they were unable to halt it. The 1696 Navigation Act extended royal Admiralty jurisdiction to all the English colonies in North America and the Caribbean and obligated proprietors to appoint governors sworn to uphold the acts. Those governors had to post large performance bonds. The act was the essential element in the extension of royal authority into hitherto unregulated regions of the British Empire.[50]

Had it not been for Queen Anne's War, piracy and pirate economies in America likely would have withered away in the face of the 1696 Navigation Act. That long maritime war extended piracy's lease on life. It created a whole new class of privateers who preyed successfully on French and Spanish shipping under letters of marque. Privateering proved too lucrative for many to stop at the war's end. This period from 1713 through the 1720s has been called the golden age of piracy, but in reality it was the last gasp of an anachronistic economic activity.[51] Stede Bonnet, Edward Teach, Charles Vane, and Benjamin Hornigold had been privateers who passed over into outlawry. However, times had changed in the American colonies. If a few individuals willingly risked hanging to enjoy the fruits of piracy, fewer colonial governments were willing to collude with them. The economies of the southern colonies had begun to outgrow their dependence upon pirate commerce. Carolina in particular found a position in the world market—through its rice, deerskin, and naval stores production—in which piracy was inimical rather than helpful.[52] The capture of Stede Bonnet in 1718 by William Rhett and Governor Robert Johnson and the fatal battle between Edward "Blackbeard" Teach and Captain James Maynard of Virginia signaled the beginning of the end of pirate commerce in the Caribbean and southern mainland.[53]

Another great change in the Caribbean occurred on July 27, 1718, when Governor Woodes Rogers sailed into Nassau Harbor and proclaimed his commission as the first Crown-appointed governor of the Bahamas. With his arrival the Bahamas entered the modern British Empire.[54] His arrival was the culmination of the Crown's resumption of the Bahamas government. The Bahamas Proprietors had voluntarily surrendered the civil government to the Crown—voided that portion of their charter giving them the governance of the islands—and also leased for twenty-one years their rights to the rents, produce, and profits of the islands to a group of merchants called the "Co-Partners."[55]

The appointment of Woodes Rogers governor of the Bahamas culminated a skillful campaign by Rogers and his co-partners. Well aware of Crown pressures for resumption, Rogers approached the proprietors in early summer 1716 with a proposal that he and his group of London merchants would finance an expedition "to rid the islands of pirates and re-settle them" in exchange for which services the proprietors were "to assign their claims on the Bahamas to them to cover their expenses, or, alternatively, to grant them a lease of their lands and royalties for twenty-one years."[56] Rogers also suggested that the proprietors surrender the government of the Bahamas to the Crown to rid themselves of the headaches and expenses of government. They could then leisurely enjoy a share of the profits of land tenure without suffering the burdensome duties of governing and defending the islands.

In May 1717 Lord Carteret testified before the Board of Trade that he and his fellow proprietors were willing to surrender their Bahamas charter. They had received several proposals in addition to that of Rogers, but none had been acceptable.[57] Finding the proprietors slow to respond, Rogers approached his friend Joseph Addison, editor of the *Spectator*, who also happened to be secretary of state. Through Addison's sponsorship, Rogers's plan received a favorable hearing by the Board of Trade and the Privy Council.[58] The co-partners' proposal was sure to please the board. Rogers recited the Bahamas' strategic importance, their desperate condition, and looming Spanish threat to the whole region. He also enclosed petitions from London and Bristol merchants to the same effect, wanting to trade in the Bahamas but fearful to do so under present conditions.[59] The Board of Trade endorsed Rogers's proposal on July 26, 1717. It affirmed that the proposal was "of great advantage [not only] to the publick, but also to the Lords Proprietors," and called on them to surrender voluntarily "their right of Government." If they refused the board prepared immediately to recommend that the Crown initiate quo warranto and scire facias proceedings to recover the Bahamas charter—an offer the proprietors could not refuse.[60] During August 1717 the terms of surrender were worked out. On September 2, secretary of state Addison reported that the king had appointed Rogers governor and captain-general of the Bahamas. In addition to his command of the co-partners' vessels, Rogers also secured a royal commission to command a flotilla of warships that would accompany him to his post.[61]

The formal surrender of the Proprietary government took place on October 28, 1717, clearing the way for King George to issue Rogers's commissions. In November the board sent the Privy Council a draft commission and instructions for Rogers, which the king signed on January 16, 1718. Royal instructions were issued on February 6, and the expedition assembled over the next few months.[62] When Rogers sailed out of the Thames on April 11, 1718, he was royal governor, chairman of the board of the co-partners, and commodore of a war fleet.[63] Rogers and his flotilla arrived at Nassau in late July.[64] After forming his government, Rogers quelled the pirates. He captured and hanged many over the next three years and also proclaimed the royal amnesty of September 1717 to pirates who voluntarily struck their black flags.[65]

With the December 1718 declaration of the War of the Quadruple Alliance, invasion rumors reached a fever pitch. Rogers was in place to defend the Bahamas. But in Carolina, where the proprietors still misgoverned, the populace was in terror. By November 1719 the fear was so great and discontent so pervasive that the Carolinians staged a rebellion to "remove themselves" from the proprietors' authority and place themselves under Crown protection.[66] The Spanish broke the tension in late February 1720 when they launched a major seaborne assault against the Bahamas. Until British and Spanish forces actually met it was not known whether Carolina or New Providence was to be the first Spanish target. Another measure of Rogers's transformation of the Bahamas was his successful defense of the islands against this attack.[67] His victory was a first for the English settlement. It consolidated royal authority and popularity to a greater extent than any other action could have done.

South Carolina was fortunate that the Spanish chose to attack the Bahamas at that immediate moment. Preoccupied with consolidating revolutionary authority, revolutionary governor James Moore and his compatriots may have been unable simultaneously to repulse the invaders and preserve the revolution. In attacking New Providence, the Spanish faced a royal governor armed with extensive authority, a good store of weapons, and for the first time a united populace. Rogers and the Bahamians threw back the Spanish attack, saving both themselves and also—it must be believed—the South Carolina Revolution of 1719.

Notes

1. See John Alexander Moore, "Royalizing South Carolina: The Revolution of 1719 and the Evolution of Early South Carolina Government" (Ph.D. diss., University of South Carolina, 1991); "Revolution of 1719," in *South Carolina Encyclopedia*, ed. Walter Edgar (Columbia: University of South Carolina Press, 2006), 786–87.

2. Richard P. Sherman, *Robert Johnson: Proprietary and Royal Governor of South Carolina* (Columbia: University of South Carolina Press, 1966); "Robert Johnson," *South Carolina Encyclopedia*, 506–7. Lord Carteret retained his one-eighth share by accepting a land grant in North Carolina, which he retained until the 1740s. The other Proprietors accepted £2,500 for each of seven shares and £5,000 for arrears of quitrents.

3. "Concessions and Agreements between the Lords Proprietors and Major William Yeamans and Others, January 7, 1665," in *CRNC* (2nd ser.), 1:107–27.

4. John P. Thomas, "The Barbadians in Early South Carolina," *SCHM* 31, no. 2 (April 1930): 75–92; Adeline Helwig, "The Early History of Barbados and Its Influence upon the Development of South Carolina" (Ph.D. diss., University of California, 1931); Richard S. Dunn, "The English Sugar Islands and the Founding of South Carolina," *SCHM* 72, no. 2 (April 1971): 81–93; Richard Waterhouse, "England, the Caribbean, and the Settlement of Carolina," *Journal of American Studies* 9, no. 4 (December 1975): 259–81; Warren Alleyne and Henry Fraser, *The Barbados-Carolina Connection* (London: Macmillan Caribbean, 1988); Justin Roberts and Ian Beamish, "Venturing Out: The Barbadian Diaspora and the Carolina Colony, 1650–1685," in this volume.

5. Harcourt Malcolm, *Historical Documents Relating to the Bahama Islands* compiled by Harcourt Malcolm, Deputy Speaker of the House of Assembly (Nassau, Bahamas: Nassau Guardian, 1910), no. 10.

6. Ibid., no. 2.

7. William S. Powell, "Carolana and the Incomparable Roanoke: Explorations and Attempted Settlements, 1620–1663," *NCHR* 51, no. 1 (January 1974): 1–21; Paul E. Koppman, "Profile of a Failure: The Carolana Project, 1629–1640," *NCHR* 59, no. 1 (January 1982): 1–23; Daniel W. Fagg Jr., "Carolina, 1663–1683: The Founding of a Proprietary" (Ph.D. diss., Emory University, 1970), 253–61.

8. Charter to Sir Robert Heath, October 30, 1629," in *CRNC* (2nd ser.), 1:62–73.

9. Michael Craton, *A History of the Bahamas* (London: Collins, 1962), 56–64; Henry C. Wilkinson, *The Adventurers of Bermuda. A History of the Island from Its Discovery until the Dissolution of the Somers Island Company in 1684* (London: Oxford University Press, 1958), 278–80; A. Talbot Bethell, *The Early Settlers of the Bahamas and Colonists of North America*, 3rd rev. ed. (Holt, U.K.: Rounce and Wortley, 1937), provided genealogical data linking Bahamas and Carolina families.

10. Craton, *History of the Bahamas*, 56–64; Wilkinson, *Adventurers of Bermuda*, 272.

11. Articles and Orders of the Company of Eleutherian Adventurers, July 9, 1647, in Malcolm, *Historical Documents*, no. 1; [William Sayle,] *A Broadside Advertising Eleutheria and the Bahama Islands* (London: n.p., 1647). The Articles and Orders granted wide religious liberties and referred to the proposed government of the Bahamas as a "republike."

12. Craton, *History of the Bahamas*, 56–64; "Articles and Orders," Malcolm, *Historical Documents*, no. 1. See also Robert Brenner, *Merchants and Revolution: Commercial Change, Political Conflict, and London's Overseas Traders, 1550–1653* (Princeton: Princeton University Press, 1993), 523–25.

13. [William Sayle,] *A Broadside*, in *Shaftesbury Papers*, 3–4.

14. "William Sayle," in *Oxford Dictionary of National Biography: In Association with the British Academy: From the Earliest Times to the Year 2000*, ed. H. G. C. Matthew and Brian Harrison (Oxford: Oxford University Press, 2004), 49:172; W. Hubert Miller, "The Colonization of the Bahamas, 1647–1670," *WMQ* 2, no. 1(January 1945): 36.

15. Cheves, *Shaftesbury Papers*, 8–9.

16. Concessions and Agreement between the Lords Proprietors and Major William Yeamans and Others, January 7, 1665," in *CRNC* (2nd ser.), 1:107–27.

17. Cheves, *Shaftesbury Papers*, 160–61.

18. K. H. D. Haley, *The First Earl of Shaftesbury* (Oxford: Clarendon Press, 1968), chap. 12, 227–65, "Trade and Plantations," elaborates Shaftesbury's role in overseas expansion, including his membership in the Somers Island Company, Hudson's Bay Company, and Royal African Company.

19. Wilkinson, *Adventurers of Bermudas*, 337–39; Haley, *First Earl of Shaftesbury*, 233.

20. Cheves, *Shaftesbury Papers*, 160–61.

21. Ibid., 207–8; Fagg, "Carolina, 1663–1683," 253–61; Wilkinson, *Adventurers of Bermudas*, 339; Warrant to Attorney and Solicitor General, July 11, 1670, to prepare a grant of the Bahamas, Eleuthera, commonly called the Bahamas or Lucayos, between 22 degrees and 27 degrees N. Latitude under the same terms as the Carolina Charter of June 3, 1665, in *CSPC*, vol. 9, *1675–1676*, no. 384.

22. Royal Grant of Islands to Lords Proprietors, 1st November 1670, Malcolm, *Historical Documents*, no. 2.

23. Ibid., nos. 3, 4.

24. Haley, *First Earl of Shaftesbury*, 234.

25. Grand Council to Lords Proprietors, September 9, 1670, in Cheves, *Shaftesbury Papers*, 180.

26. Cheves, *Shaftesbury Papers*, 160.

27. Lords of Trade Journal, January 18, 1683, in *CSPC, 1681–1685*, no. 895; Thomas Lynch to the Lords of Trade, June 12, 1682, in *CSPC, 1681–1685*, no. 552; Lords of Trade Journal, January 25, 1683, in *CSPC, 1681–1685*, no. 912.

28. [Unknown] to Thomas Lynch, April 22, 1684, in *CSPC, 1681–1685*, no. 1644; Narrative of Occurrences at New Providence, in *CSPC, 1681–1685*, no. 1927; Affidavit of Richard Lilburne, November 17, 1684, in *CSPC, 1681–1685*, no. 1944.

29. W. L. Grant and James Munro, *Acts of the Privy Council of England, Colonial Series*, vol. 2, *1680–1720* (London: His Majesty's Stationers' Office, 1908), 92–93.

30. Crane, *Southern Frontier*, 31; J. G. Dunlop, "Spanish Depredations, 1686," *SCHM* 30, no. 2 (April 1929), 81–89.

31. [Thomas Bulkley,] *To the Right Honourable William, Earl of Craven; John, Earl of Bath; John, Lord Berkley; George, Lord Carteret; Anthony, Lord Ashley; Sir John Colleton, Baronet: Being Proprietors of Carolina and the Bahama Islands* (London, 1694). In this memorial Bulkley accused Governor Joseph Blake of Carolina of conspiring with Bulkley's enemies at New Providence. See Craton, *History*, 81–83.

32. John Graves, *A Memorial: Or, A Short Account of the Bahamas Islands . . . Deliver'd to the Lords, Proprietors of the said Islands, and the Honourable Commissioners of Her Majesty's Customs . . . And now Humbly Presented to both Houses of Parliament* (London: n.p., 1706; repr., 1708).

33. Leo Francis Stock, ed., Proceedings and Debates of the British Parliaments respecting North America (Washington, D.C.: Carnegie Institution of Washington, 1930), 3:125–26; Petition of John Graves to the House of Lords, March 12, 1706, enclosing "A Brief Memorial . . . Relating to the Bahamas," in American Papers in the House of Lords Record Office: A Microform Edition with a Printed Calendar and Index, ed. Walter Minchinton (East Ardsley, U.K.: Microform Limited, 1983), reel 5:1706.2c.

34. Stock, *Proceedings and Debates*, 3:124–25.

35. Ibid., 3:127.

36. Great Britain, Privy Council, *Acts of the Privy Council, Colonial Series, 1613–1783* (London: His Majesty's Stationery Office, 1908–12), 2:507.

37. Craton, *History*, 93.

38. An Impartial Narrative of the Late Invasion of So. Carolina by the French and Spaniards, in the Month August 1706, in *CSPC, 1702–1706*, nos. 517, 517i; Kenneth R. Jones, "A 'Full and Particular Account' of the Assault on Charleston in 1706," *SCHM* 83, no. 1 (January 1982): 1–11. Jones's edition lists other contemporaneous reports of the attack upon Charles Town.

39. Thomas Gower to John Graves (September 22, 1706), in *CSPC, 1706–1708*, no. 553.

40. Craton, *History*, 93–94.

41. "David Lee Johnson, "The Yamasee War" (M.A. thesis, University of South Carolina, 1980); Crane, *Southern Frontier*, 162–87. Recent scholarship on the Yamasee War includes William L. Ramsey, *The Yamasee War: A Study of the Culture, Economy, and Conflict in the Colonial South* (Lincoln: University of Nebraska Press, 2008); and Stephen J. Oatis, *A Colonial Complex: South Carolina's Frontiers in the Era of the Yamasee War, 1680–1730* (Lincoln: University of Nebraska Press, 2004).

42. Stock, *Proceedings and Debates*, 3:361–62.

43. Ibid., 3:363–66.

44. Jeremiah Dummer, *A Defense of the New England Charter* (London: W. Wilkins, 1721), 19.

45. Stock, *Proceedings and Debates*, 3:366.

46. *Presumptive Reasons Why the Government of South and North Carolina, and the Bahama or Lucaios Islands being Proprietary Governments in America, should (more Especially) be Reassumed into the Hands of the Crown of Great Britain: Humbly offer'd to the Consideration of the Committee of the Honourable House of Commons; To whom a Bill, for the better Regulating of the Charter and Proprietary Governments in America, and of his Majesties Plantations, is Committed* (London: n.p., 1715). The writer's main argument was the Proprietors' failure to defend their provinces.

47. Crane, *Southern Frontier*, 227, 262. Wolfgang Michael, *England under George I: The Quadruple Alliance* (London: Macmillan, 1939) is a study of the domestic politics and international diplomacy of the Quadruple Alliance (1718–21) and makes no mention of the New World.

48. Shirley G. Hughson, *The Carolina Pirates and Colonial Commerce, 1670–1740*, in *Johns Hopkins University Studies in Historical and Political Science*, 12th ser., no. 5–7 (Baltimore: Johns Hopkins University Press, 1894; repr., New York: Johnson Reprint, 1973), 9–10; Craton, *History*, chap. 9, "Pirates," 83–99. See Daniel Defoe, *General History of the Robberies and Murders of the Most Notorious Pyrates*, ed. Manuel Schonhorn (Columbia: University of South Carolina Press, 1972), for biographies of Bonnet, Hornigold, and others. See also Henry L. Osgood, *American Colonies in the Eighteenth Century* (New York: Columbia University Press, 1924), vol. 1, chap. 16, "Piracy during the Early Colonial Wars," 525–52.

49. Edward Randolph to the Board of Trade on the State of the Bahamas, March 11, 1699, in *Edward Randolph; including His Letters and Official Papers from the New England, Middle, and Southern Colonies in America, with other Documents relating chiefly to the vacating of the Royal Charter of the Colony of Massachusetts Bay, 1673–1703*, ed. Alfred T. S. Goodrick (Boston: Prince Society, 1898; repr., New York: Burt Franklin, 1967), 7:617–18. See also Mark Hanna, "Protecting the Rights of Englishmen: The Rise and Fall of Carolina's Piratical State," in this volume.

50. Thomas C. Barrow, *Trade and Empire: The British Customs Service in Colonial America* (Cambridge: Harvard University Press, 1967), chap. 3, "A New Policy Defined," and chap. 4, "The System Takes Shape," describe the new order imposed by the Navigation Acts. See also Osgood, *American Colonies in the Eighteenth Century*, vol. 1, chap. 6, "Administrative Changes Consequent to the Trade Act of 1696," 185–227.

51. Robert C. Ritchie, *Captain Kidd and the War against the Pirates* (Cambridge: Harvard University Press, 1986), 29–30.

52. Hughson, *Carolina Pirates*, 42–45; Converse D. Clowse, *Economic Beginnings in Colonial South Carolina, 1670–1730* (Columbia: University of South Carolina Press, 1971), 87–90, 146. William Gilmore Simms's *The Cassique of Kiawah: A Colonial Romance* (New York: Redfield, 1859; repr., Gainesville, Ga.: Magnolia Press, 1989) is a historical novel set in Charles Town in 1684. It describes in fiction the ambiguous relationship between colonial authorities and West Indian pirates.

53. Richard P. Sherman, *Robert Johnson Proprietary and Royal Governor of South Carolina* (Columbia: University of South Carolina Press, 1966), 33–34, 37; Osgood, *American Colonies in the Eighteenth Century*, 1:546–49.

54. *Dictionary of National Biography*, s.v. "Rogers, Woodes," by John Knox Laughton; Bethell, *Early Settlers of the Bahamas*, 64–67; Malcolm, *Historical Documents*, no. 9.

55. Malcolm, *Historical Documents*, nos. 7, 8, are respectively the texts of the Proprietors' October 28, 1717, surrender of the Bahamian civil government to the Crown and the lease, of the same date, of the Bahamas to the "Co-Partners." See Craton, History, 102.

56. Woodes Rogers to Bahama Proprietors, July, 1716, in *CSPC, 1716–1717*, no. 657ii.

57. Great Britain, Board of Trade, *Journal of the Commissioners for Trade and Plantations . . . from 1704 to 1782 . . . preserved in the Public Record Office* (London: HMSO, 1920–38), 3:237.

58. Petition of Woodes Rogers to the King, July 19, 1717, in *CSPC, 1716–1717*, no. 657i.

59. Ibid.

60. Extract from Letter from the Board of Trade to His Majesty the King. Dated, Whitehall, July 26th 1717, in Malcolm, *Historical Documents*, no. 7.

61. Malcolm, *Historical Documents*, no. 9.

62. Surrender to King of Civil and Military Government by Lords Proprietors, October 28, 1717, in Malcolm, *Historical Documents*, no. 7, abstracted in *CSPC, 1716–1717*, no. 176; Draft Commission for Woodes Rogers, January 16, 1718, in *CSPC, 1716–1717*, nos. 220i, 220ii; Royal Instructions to Woodes Rogers, February 6, 1718, in Malcolm, *Historical Documents*, no. 10, abstracted in *CSPC*, vol. 30, *1717–1718*, no. 220ii; Rogers, Brief Remarks of the Most Material Transactions relating to the Bahama Islands, in Papers Relating to the Bahama Islands, 5 ms. vols., John Carter Brown Library, Providence, R.I.

63. Malcolm, *Historical Documents*, no. 6.

64. Craton, *History*, 103; Riley, *Homeward Bound*, 69.

65. Royal Proclamation for the Suppressing of Pirates, September 5, 1717, in "Royal Proclamations," *Transactions and Collections of the American Antiquarian Society* 12 (1911): 176–77; Bethell, *Early Settlers of the Bahamas*, 91–97.

66. Extracts of Sundry Letters from Carolina and the Island of Providence, Giving an Acct. of the Spaniards Designs On Carolina & the Isle of [Providence], Public Record Office, Records of the Privy Council, PC1/58/B2. The extracts are from letters of Christopher Gale, Chief Justice of Providence, to Governor Robert Johnson, October 29, 1719; correspondence from John Parris at Havana to his father Alexander Parris at Charles Town, September 16, 1719; and from Alexander Parris to an unknown correspondent, October 27, 30, 1719.

67. Craton, *History*, 105–6.

"The Proprietors Can't Undertake for What They Will Do"

A Political Interpretation of the South Carolina Revolution of 1719

Hanno T. Scheerer

In December 1719 the South Carolina Commons House of Assembly called itself a "Convention of the People," resolved that it would "pay no further duty or obedience to the Lords Proprietors," and petitioned the king to "extend [his] most Gracious Goodness" to his subjects in South Carolina. In other words, the assembly effectively ended proprietary rule in South Carolina and boldly declared that the colony would now operate under the immediate control of the British monarch, George I.[1]

The "Revolution of 1719" has often been attributed to the proprietors' failure to provide their colonists with military security. According to this view, the spark that ignited the revolutionary movement was a rumor about a Spanish plan to attack Charleston. The people of South Carolina, already discontented with the proprietors' refusal of military support during the Yamasee War of 1715–16, renounced allegiance to them and claimed control of the colony in the name of the British king, whom they perceived to be the sole power able to protect them.[2]

Robert M. Weir neatly sums up this dominant interpretation of the revolt: "Constitutional issues played only a minor role, and tyranny was not the focal point of the dispute; rather it was the failure of proprietary government to do what governments were supposed to do—that is, provide protection."[3] Certainly South Carolina was a frontier colony in constant danger of attacks from Native Americans, other European colonial powers, and pirates. The proprietors' limited financial means were inadequate to address these problems, and South Carolinians often pleaded for royal military assistance. Yet a narrow view of the Charleston 1719 Revolution as a provincial protest against a neglectful imperial administration misses the conflict's full transatlantic dimensions. Indeed there is much evidence to suggest that constitutional issues rather than questions of defense lay at the core of the quarrels between the Carolina proprietors and their settlers. While the proprietors' inability to protect their colony provided the backdrop for widespread popular sentiment against them, the revolution itself was not a popular uprising against a neglectful government, but rather the breaking point in a constitutional conflict between the Lords Proprietors and the South Carolina Commons House of Assembly.

The constitutional issues at the core of the proprietors-assembly conflict strikingly resemble those that have been identified by imperial historians and neo-imperial historians (most notably Jack P. Greene) as one of the main causes of the American Revolution: Local governments in the thirteen colonies believed they had developed their own constitutions, which diverged drastically from the British authorities' interpretation of an imperial constitutional setup. In a process that Jack P. Greene has called the "negotiation of authorities," local government bodies had grown into confident political institutions that would hardly accept imperial challenges to their political autonomy, especially after 1763.[4] In line with recent interpretations of proprietary and charter ventures not as abnormalities, but rather as integral parts of early modern European Empires, I argue that much of what was at stake in the American Revolution had already crystallized in the South Carolina Revolution of 1719.[5] The South Carolina revolt centered around three key questions, which continued to trouble British authorities and settlers alike throughout the eighteenth century: First, how far did the imperial authorities' prerogative reach into the colony? Second, to what extent was colonial legislation exempt from imperial control? Third, did the colonies' constitutions exist at the will of their Lords in England, or had precedence, custom, and key documents such as colonial charters, built individual colonial constitutions? In the course of the eighteenth century, the settlers would argue that both natural right and the common law entitled them to a high degree of political autonomy.[6] Yet in 1719 the conflict was just beginning to unfold, and South Carolinians discussed them primarily on a pragmatic level.

This essay is divided into two larger parts to uncover the conflict in South Carolina. First, it provides evidence for the proposition that the conflict was constitutional, scrutinizing the constitutional issues at stake. Second, it examines the underlying causes of the constitutional conflict. Constitutional conflicts never exist in a vacuum but are usually triggered by political issues vital to both parties. I will argue that South Carolina's increasing interconnectedness with the British trade empire triggered the conflict, causing transatlantic clashes between imperial merchants and local planters.

Closer scrutiny of the events preceding the revolt provides evidence that it resulted from a constitutional conflict between the proprietors and the assembly. Unfortunately, what would be the two most important records of the political scene immediately before the revolt are nonexistent: almost no Commons House journals and no legislative Grand Council journals have survived for the period between December 11, 1717, and February 3, 1720.[7] Luckily, however, several contemporary accounts have survived, the most comprehensive among them being a 1726 pamphlet written by Francis Yonge, a South Carolinian immediately involved in the revolt.[8] Although Yonge had a distinct objective—he wrote his pamphlet to justify a coup d'état against a legally constituted government—his pamphlet provides an indispensible insight into the events preceding the Revolution of 1719.

Yonge's pamphlet combined with other source materials reveals the following narrative: The Yamasee War was the revolution's catalyst. Yet, although the war triggered "in the Inhabitants in general, an Opinion of their being very unhappy in living under a Government that could not protect them,"[9] the war's major significance for the revolt of 1719 was not that it exposed the military deficiencies of proprietary government, but that it caused the South Carolina assembly to adopt several measures that came under close scrutiny of the Lords Proprietors in England.

The colonists had identified abuses in the Indian trade as the main cause of the Yamasee War.[10] Accordingly one of the first measures they adopted was to place the Indian trade under a public monopoly.[11] In addition the assembly opened the so-called Yamasee Lands for settlement and passed a law to encourage the immigration of prospective settlers from Great Britain and Ireland.[12] Since both the proprietors and the Crown had refused to send considerable military support to South Carolina, the cost of war was left almost exclusively to the colonists. To pay for these costs, the South Carolina assembly adopted three measures: it issued paper money (which quickly depreciated), imposed high duties on goods imported from England, and levied a tax on estates (plantation land and town lots in Charleston) and slaves.[13]

Although considerable distress existed in the colony during and immediately after the Yamasee War, there is no sign of particular discontent with the proprietary government after the worst of the Yamasee War was over. On the contrary, at the end of 1717, the assembly had never before been "observ'd to be in so good a Disposition towards the *Proprietors,* [and was] doing every thing that could be ask'd of."[14]

The assembly's good attitude toward the proprietors came to an abrupt end in the fall of 1718, when proprietary orders repealing seven laws arrived in the colony. Four were directly related to the Yamasee War: the Indian Trade Act, the Import Duty Act, the Yamasee Land Act, and the Act to Encourage the Settlement of the Yamasee Lands. The three other repealed laws were acts that had extended or consolidated the power of the South Carolina assembly: two had shifted assembly elections from Charleston to the parishes, and a third had given the assembly authority to nominate the public receiver. In addition the proprietors, in accordance with their repeal of the election law, dissolved the assembly and called for new elections following the pre-1716 method.[15]

When the assembly learned of the disallowances, "prodigious Heats and Debates about the *Proprietors* Right of Repeal, or of their Authority to allow of or disallow any of the Laws pass'd in that Province" immediately began.[16] The assembly presumed that the proprietors already enjoyed a direct voice in the legislative process through their council deputies, and regarded the proprietors' "second" veto to be illegal and not warranted by their charter.[17] It should be noted that at this point the revolution had tacitly begun. The assembly was questioning the proprietors' most important instrument in the governance process of the colony: their right to review colonial laws. By questioning the proprietors' right, the assembly effectively changed the constitutional setup of the colony and declared it semi-independent from proprietary control in England. That the assembly did not overtly revolt in 1718 was not because the issue lacked importance, but simply because they still hoped to maintain their legislative independence through negotiation rather than rebellion.

In the past direct negotiation had often helped diffuse political tensions between the proprietors and their settlers. In 1694 proprietor John Archdale had personally traveled to the colony to solve the disputed question of land titles and quitrents.[18] In 1715 the assembly had sent to England John Boone and Richard Beresford, who successfully campaigned with the proprietors against the legislative veto power recently assigned to the colony's chief justice and proprietary councilor, Nicholas Trott. In an address to the Lords Proprietors, the assembly elaborated on the importance of direct negotiations: "The sad experience of the great misery we labour under in being so vastly distant from you [the proprietors] is daily renewed, by the injuries done your Lordships Province by crafty and designing men. They have too great an opportunity of misrepresenting persons and things to you. But we are positive that by such artifices we may suffer for a time, yet as soon as your Lordships have received a true information and an impartial account of affairs here you will perceive the varnish and disguise of such wicked Practices who when detected can't fail of being the object of your just displeasure."[19] The assembly also attributed the 1718 decisions of the proprietors to the designs of "crafty men"—Nicholas Trott and William Rhett (a Carolina merchant and proprietary creature), who had allegedly used their contacts with the proprietary secretary, Richard Shelton, and their influence with the proprietors to push through their interests.[20] If these men could be bypassed by direct communication between the settlers and the proprietors, it was assumed that the political conflict of 1718 could be solved.

The council (with the exception of Trott), aware of the deplorable state of the colony, conspired with the assembly and, for the time being, ignored proprietary orders. Aside from the Import Duty Law that had received not only the proprietors' but also the king's veto, all laws repealed by the proprietors remained in force, and the assembly continued to sit.[21] Both houses and the governor agreed to send council member Francis Yonge to England to negotiate with the proprietors. Equipped with a memorandum and three laws (one law regulating the proprietors' quitrents and revised versions of the Election Law and the Import Duty Act), Yonge departed for London, where he arrived in May 1719.[22] In London Yonge learned that the proprietors were not in the mood to negotiate. They regarded the governor's failure to enforce their repeals and dissolve the assembly as an infringement on their powers, reprimanded him for his neglect of duty, called a new council with twelve members instead of seven, and removed three disobedient councilors. Confirming each repeal and again declaring the assembly dissolved, the proprietors firmly declared that they would never recede from their privilege of repealing colonial laws.[23]

When Yonge returned with these orders to the colony in late September or early October, the situation exploded. Fears of a Spanish attack were strong at this time, but the assembly's disregard for the proprietors' veto was even stronger. When Governor Johnson suggested raising private money to rebuild the damaged Charleston fortifications, the former assembly members answered that it was unnecessary to raise funds as the money provided for by the Import Duty Act sufficed. Johnson reminded the assembly members that the Import Duty Act had been repealed, but they answered that they "would not look on *their* [the proprietors'] repeal as any thing," even though Chief Justice Nicholas Trott had declared that he would not prosecute persons who refused to pay the duties.[24]

The assembly's contempt rose to open rebellion after Governor Johnson called elections according to the old law. Assembly members formed a secret "association," whose goal it was to "get rid of the Oppression and Arbitrary Dealings of the *Lords Proprietors.*"[25] Although the original association quickly dissolved, it returned as a "Convention of the People" on the date the newly elected assembly was scheduled to sit. The convention renounced allegiance from the proprietors and proclaimed James Moore Jr. temporary governor in the name of the king.[26]

Two documents reveal clues regarding the convention's incentives, and complaints about the proprietors' neglect to defend the colony are conspicuously absent from both. The question of defense arises, but with a certain twist. In their address to the king, the convention complained that they found themselves in an "Impossibility . . . of defending ourselves from our Enemies under a Proprietary Government," and in a list of grievances and resolutions, the convention criticized that through the proprietors' repeals they had been unable to put themselves "in a posture of defense."[27] The proprietors' unwillingness to provide for the colony's protection appears to have been an unpleasant yet well-known fact to colonists in 1719—a fact that they had learned to cope with by taking matters into their own hands. They had fortified Charleston, had averted Spanish attacks by sea, had beaten the Yamasee Indians in a destructive war, and had survived a pirate blockade of the port of Charleston in 1718.

The proprietors' orders prevented the colonists from continuing to "protect themselves," that is, from handling the situation by appropriating public money through legislative action. It was these proprietary orders, and not the lack of military assistance, that eventually convinced the assembly that they were not secure under a proprietary government. When Governor Johnson had called on the assembly to subscribe private money for the improvement of the fortifications, according to Yonge, "hot arguments arose among them, and they broke up without doing anything, chusing rather to hazard the loss of the Country to the *Spaniards,* than submit to acknowledge a right in the *Proprietors* of Repealing their laws."[28] It is astonishing that the assembly seems to have valued their constitutional rights more than the immediate security of the colony.

The vehemence with which the assembly defended its rights had already become apparent when pirates attacked the colony in October 1718. In a coup de main, Governor Johnson had outfitted two sloops and, under the command of William Rhett, had managed to capture one of the most notorious pirates, Stede Bonnet.[29] The planter-dominated assembly applauded Johnson for removing this threat to trade, but at the same time it harshly reminded him of the unconstitutionality of his actions: "we do hereby accquaint yor Hon^r that we expect for the future to be consulted with by yor Hon^{rs} on such likes, or any other emergent occasion that may happen [and] may call for ye disbursement of Publick Money, before ye same shall be undertaken, otherwise this House will make any Provisions to defray the charge of an Affair wherein we are not advised nor which we do not give our consent to."[30]

Given the assembly's fierce attack on Johnson's disregard for its supremacy in questions of public moneys even when he had acted for the good of the whole colony, it comes as no surprise that the assembly seethed with anger when the proprietors vetoed its laws. Accordingly, the convention's list of grievances and resolutions begins with the accusation that the proprietors had "taken upon themselves to repeal Several Laws made for the Support of this Government," thereby "exceeding the Powers granted to them by their Charter,"[31] and the convention's first measure was to declare five acts still in force: The Import Duty Act, the Public Receiver Act, the two Election Laws, and an act encouraging Protestants to move to South Carolina.[32]

In February 1720 the revolutionary assembly again addressed King George in an extended list of grievances. Here, the crucial argument of what Craig Yirush has called the "settler political theory" already unfolded:[33] "the Lords Proprietors having but small regard to the Royal reserve of your Majesties Soveraignty over this Province have assumed a despotick authority exceeding the regal power in Great Britain in repealing and abrogating by themselves alone several beneficial laws . . . for the good Government and safety of this Province after a most arbitrary manner trampling upon the rights and liberties of your Matyes. subjects who have as Englishmen a incontestable right of being governed by noe laws made here but what are consented to by them."[34]

The political conflict that ended in the revolution of 1719 revolved around the question of who had authority to legislate for the colony: the local governing bodies, or the Lords Proprietors in England. The settlers ultimately answered this question by invoking their "incontestable rights" as Englishmen, but as Craig Yirush has rightly pointed out, such arguments did not appear suddenly.[35] Rather they were the result of long-term political processes and intense debate.

In South Carolina the proprietors' insistence on a direct voice in the colonial legislative process had been a source of discontent for the settlers as early as 1693, but it had not provoked open conflict.[36] While it would go too far to assume that there had been a proprietary period of "salutary neglect" before 1718, it is symbolic of the proprietors' disinterest in their colony that the only two letters they dispatched for Carolina in 1717 were Governor Johnson's commission and instructions.[37] With regard to the review of colonial legislation, the proprietors had remained remarkably inactive in the twenty-one years between 1697 and 1718. With the exception of the 1706 veto to the Establishment and Exclusion Acts, the proprietors had not made use of their veto power on colonial laws after 1697.[38] Only three times did the proprietors interfere with South Carolina legislation between the 1697 and 1718: in March 1713 they ordered Governor Craven to introduce a quitrent law drawn up by their chief justice, Nicholas Trott; in September 1714 the proprietors consented to a bill regulating the fees of public officers; and in 1714 they suggested an amendment to the 1712 Bank Bill, which had caused discontent among merchants in England.[39] Yet the proprietors never formally repealed a South Carolina law between 1697 and 1718, with the exception of the 1706 veto, which had really been more the queen's than the proprietors'. Why had the proprietors declined to make use of their veto power? While a certain general proprietary neglect cannot be denied, a more practical reason might have prevented the proprietors from issuing disallowances: in their 1697 repeal, the proprietors complained that their governor and council deputies had failed to send all acts to England for their review, and that those laws that had been transferred expired so quickly that a veto was useless.[40] How were the proprietors to repeal laws they had never seen?

In any case this nonuse led to what Jack P. Greene has called a "growing divergence between imperial theory and colonial practice."[41] The Lords Proprietors in England and the colonists in South Carolina had developed entirely different assumptions about the constitutional nature of colonial governance. The proprietors presumed that they were at the colony's constitutional center, and that they enjoyed not only a direct voice in the colony's legislative process, but also the final word. Despite the nonuse of their veto power, the proprietors, in each set of instructions to their governors, insisted that all laws passed in the colony be sent to them for confirmation or disallowance at their discretion.[42] Yet although the proprietors had always insisted on this right, they had failed to make active use of it after 1697—establishing a new dangerous precedent, especially in the British legal environment so fond of precedent and custom.

By not using their veto power, the proprietors had unwillingly nourished the assembly's notion that it was at the constitutional center of the colony.

Left alone in situations of extreme danger, the assembly had grown into a confident governmental institution, working on the assumption that matters of local governance had to be left to local governing bodies. In fact it seemed that the proprietors had tacitly accepted the limitation of their influence on the assembly. When the merchants Stephen Godin and William Rhett petitioned the Lords Proprietors regarding a scheme to import poor Palatines into South Carolina, the proprietors replied that they would be pleased to support this proposal, but that they could not guarantee that the assembly would do the same: "the assembly of Carolina being a free Representative of the People of that part of the Province, the Propriet$^{rs.}$ can't undertake for what they will Do."[43]

The two conflicting assumptions about the nature of colonial governance could coexist as long as they were not put to the test. Yet in 1718, when the proprietors tried again to enforce their reputed veto power after twenty-one years of nonuse, imperial theory violently clashed with colonial practice in a constitutional conflict that eventually ended with the Revolution of 1719.

In qualifying the South Carolina Revolution of 1719 as a constitutional conflict, it is crucial to dig deeper, to examine the concrete and abstract factors at stake for each of the parties involved. By taking a closer look at the motivations of both the assemblymen and the Lords Proprietors, it becomes apparent that the constitutional questions that dominated the revolt had grave consequences for the social realities of both the proprietors and the settlers.

The political impasse between the proprietors and the assembly was closely related to South Carolina's increasing interconnectedness with the British trade empire. South Carolina's growing economic prosperity had helped create an environment in which governing the colony had become increasingly difficult for the proprietors, and in which their interests were often at odds with those of South Carolina's political elite.[44]

By 1719 South Carolina had developed from a peripheral pocket of the British Empire largely subsisting on the Indian trade and cattle farming, into a small but thriving plantation colony and producer of two staples: rice and naval stores. Both were major catalysts for the colony's development into a plantation economy, and these two commodities already dominated the trade in the 1710s.[45] Although South Carolina's development into a plantation economy was still at a very early stage by the end of proprietary rule, the way had been paved, and the colony's increasing economic prosperity (which suffered a severe blow from the Yamasee War) had decisive consequences for the revolt of 1719. In England it had put South Carolina on the map of both Crown officials and merchants. While there is only scant record of British overseas merchants engaging in South Carolina politics before 1716, merchants actively sought to influence policy making after 1716 and vigorously pursued their interests with the proprietary board. In the colony South Carolina's economic growth had facilitated the formation of a self-assured planter elite, who strove for local control and had transformed the representative assembly from a subordinate legislative body into the dominant element of South Carolina politics.[46]

The Revolution of 1719 was a planters' revolt. Richard Waterhouse has pointed out that South Carolina's assembly was largely dominated by planters before 1719. In the period from 1711 to 1719, Waterhouse has identified 75 percent of the assemblymen as planters.[47] The 1719 revolt was a revolution in the English tradition whose nucleus was the elected assembly. Given the dominance of planters in the assembly, it comes as no surprise that planters also dominated the revolutionary Convention of the People. Of the twenty-eight men who were immediately involved in the proceedings of 1719, twenty (more than 70 percent) can clearly be identified as planters. Only three members, Colonel John Fenwick, Captain William Dry, and Andrew Allen, were large-scale Charleston merchants. Several other members were planters with some trading interests, such as George Logan, who was part owner of a trading sloop, or George Chicken, who was a planter with stakes in the Indian trade. All merchants or planter-merchants in the Convention of the People held conspicuously strong ties with the colony, often invested in land, and supported a limited issuance of paper money.[48]

The initiative for the revolt came from this elite circle of planter-politicians, and not from an unruly mob on the streets, dissatisfied with proprietary rule. An unidentified observer told the Board of Trade on November 14 that the proprietors' repeals had made "all or most of the landed men very uneasy," and he further reported that "the Country Gentlemen" were about to meet, "from which great speculations are made."[49] When Governor Johnson acquainted the Board of Trade with the events that had taken place in the colony, he suggested that "severall of the richest inhabitants . . . have put it in the heads of the Commonallity, that neither they nor their posterity can be secure in their persons or estates, and that the Province cannot long subsist, without the immediate protection and assistance of the Crown."[50] William Rhett, one of the few South Carolinians who opposed the revolt, even depicted it as a cunning plan of the planters to eliminate their outstanding quitrent payments.[51] Although the proprietors' lack of military assistance had created widespread sentiment against proprietary rule, it was the planter elite who consciously kicked off the revolt after it had become certain that the proprietors would not revoke their repeals.

Having qualified the revolt as a planters' revolt, it becomes necessary to take a closer look at the planters' incentives. The planters' main goal was to retain political power in local hands. The question that remains is: political power *for what?* First, it is plausible to regard political power *as such* as a main goal of the planters. South Carolina's settlers had always been unruly and partial to quarreling—either amongst themselves or with the proprietors—about political power. Personal animosities often played a powerful role, and this might have been the case in the 1719 revolt with men like Alexander Skene, a former proprietary deputy, who turned on the proprietors when they ousted him from their council.

Aside from political and personal quarrels, economic interests were paramount in fostering the rebellion. Gary L. Hewitt has suggested that South Carolina's transformation into a plantation colony was not a "natural" development, but a planned scheme pushed through by a planter-dominated assembly at the cost of the economic interests of traders.[52] Hewitt shows how two key measures, the issuance of paper money and the regulation of the Indian trade, facilitated the establishment of a plantation economy in South Carolina. Building on Hewitt's foundation, it may be argued that even more measures served to tighten planter control in the 1710s. The 1716 election law that shifted elections from Charleston to the parishes aimed at securing the election of planters to the assembly. The import duty law reduced tax burdens, thereby shifting payment for the debts of the Yamasee War onto merchants. The law that had given the assembly the sole power to nominate a public receiver can be seen as part of an effort to consolidate the assembly's control over the colony's finance. With such control, the planter-dominated assembly could influence all matters of local governance that required the disbursement of public moneys, especially costly military operations.

All these measures came under proprietary attack beginning in 1718. By vetoing their laws, the proprietors challenged the planters' political and economic supremacy. Viewed in light of Hewitt's argument, the proprietors threatened the planters' plot to complete the transformation of South Carolina into a plantation colony. This plot had been phenomenally successful on a local level, as Hewitt has pointed out. After 1715 the planters had managed to elevate the "interests of planters into a 'public' interest," thereby repressing the interests of local Indian traders.[53] Yet during the crisis of 1718–19 the planters were up against a more vocal enemy: merchants in the City of London.

The political conflict of 1718–19 can be understood only when viewed as a transatlantic conflict between South Carolina's planter elite and overseas merchants in London (who sided with some Charleston-based merchants)—a conflict fought through middlemen, the Lords Proprietors. Most likely the proprietors could have prevented the revolt had they conceded to the assembly's demands in the summer of 1719. But they stuck to their heavy-handed policy and ceded to severe pressure from British overseas merchants, who were seconded by the two highest British authorities, Parliament and the king.

Between 1715 and 1719, the Lords Proprietors found themselves in difficult circumstances. British colonial administration in the early eighteenth century did not function as a centralized modern state but rather operated as a network of different governance agencies.[54] The proprietors, although technically at the head of government in South Carolina, were only one part of this network and worked under severe pressure by interest groups and agencies who believed that they had a word in the governance of the colony. Although the Carolina charter had few stipulations for direct Crown interference, the Crown had massively enlarged its influence over the colony between 1696 and 1719: it had established Courts of Vice-Admiralty, it had ordered the proprietors to veto Carolina laws, and, together with Parliament, it had tried to revoke the Carolina charter three times.[55] The proprietors were able to curb efforts to have their charter revoked, but it is evident that, especially after the Yamasee War, which had demonstrated the shortcomings of proprietary government, the proprietors tried hard to convince Crown officials that they were properly running their colony. In addition, since many of the proprietors had political aspirations, they tried to avoid any controversies with Crown officials.

Just how cautious the proprietors were to avoid trouble with higher authorities became evident in March 1719, when Sir Robert Thornhill appeared before the proprietary board. Thornhill, a rich attorney,[56] held the legal title to a debt that Sir Nathaniel Johnson, former governor of South Carolina, owed in the West Indies and threatened to bring the matter before Parliament. Eager to prevent this trouble, the proprietors wrote to Governor Robert Johnson, the son of the late Sir Nathaniel: "S^r·Robert [Thornhill] informed us that he did design to apply to the House of Commons here in order to procure a short Bill for the speedy Relief of Creditors against persons indebted in the West Indies, upon your acco^t·, which we are apprehensive may be very expensive and troublesome to you, and may reflect upon Us the Proprietors."[57]

If the proprietors feared the consequences that even a small debt matter might have on their reputations, it can easily be imagined how they reacted when more grave matters, such as colonial laws that could be interpreted as "repugnant to the laws of England," came before their board. Since the government of the colony and therefore the review of colonial legislation lay in the hands of the Lords Proprietors, the Board of Trade and the Privy Council expected that they would not consent to such laws. Stephen Godin, a London merchant, expressed this view before the Board of Trade in July 1716: "the Proprietors by ratifying such acts of their assembly do *ipso facto* forfeit their Charters elce they may truely be termed Independents of the Crown and Laws of Great Britain, as is often asserted in those Assemblies."[58] In 1718 the king's solicitor general supported the view that proceedings against the Carolina charter could be started if the proprietors consented to laws that were repugnant to the laws of England.[59]

The group of people who benefited from the proprietors' fear of trouble with higher authorities were London merchants who traded with Carolina. Rebecca Starr has pointed out that a small Carolina trade lobby already existed in London before 1719.[60] These London merchants actively and significantly influenced Carolina politics between 1716 and 1719, and they were jointly responsible for triggering the revolt of 1719.

A Charleston port clearings book for the period of 1717 to 1721 suggests that a well-defined group of traders who specialized in the trade from

Charleston to London had not yet been fully established, since shareholders of vessels who left Charleston for London varied considerably during this period. Yet there are some merchants who conducted trade between South Carolina and London on a regular basis, even at this early stage of South Carolina's economic development. Several long-term trading partnerships and single individuals stand out, who held shares in more than one vessel or who traded between Charleston and London more than once with the same vessel. Among the close trading partnerships, two Charleston-based companies rank most prominent before 1719: the partnership of Allen and Gibbon, and the partnership of Godin and de la Conseillere. Andrew Allen and William Gibbon were, as Converse Clowse has put it, very "Charleston oriented" and mostly operated with Charleston-built boats and Charleston-based partners.[61] This was different from the Huguenot partnership of Benjamin Godin and Benjamin de la Conseillere. They operated their trade with Britain in joint partnerships with London-based merchants, either Richard Shubrick or John Loyd, and Benjamin Godin's brother, Stephen Godin, probably acted as the company's London contact person.[62] Stephen Godin himself regularly participated in the London-Charleston trade in joint partnerships with other British merchants, as did other London merchants such as Samuel Baron, James Crane, and James Deane.[63]

Stephen Godin and Samuel Baron were at the core of a London lobbying network that vigorously pursued its interests with the proprietary board. Both maintained contacts with persons residing in South Carolina. Baron had joined in a trading partnership with William Rhett.[64] In addition to connections with his Carolina brother, Benjamin, and his partner, Benjamin de la Conseillere (two of the fiercest paper money opponents in Charleston), Stephen Godin seems to have been a personal friend—or at least a good business acquaintance—of Rhett's, for both had filed a petition regarding the transportation of poor Palatines to South Carolina in 1709.[65] Godin and Baron are two names that frequently appear on petitions to Parliament and the Board of Trade regarding the Carolina trade.[66]

The London-Carolina trading lobby operated on four fronts. First, they petitioned the British Parliament and the Board of Trade for beneficial trading laws in England. Second, they supported South Carolinians in their pleas for royal military aid.[67] Third, they agitated before the Board of Trade for their political interests in South Carolina, and fourth, they petitioned the proprietors for assistance whenever they saw their trade affected by Carolina laws.

Of these the latter two are of prime significance for the development of the 1719 revolt. London merchants opposed many of the measures taken by South Carolinians before and especially after the Yamasee War: they opposed depreciating paper money because they usually sold manufactured goods from Britain and slaves to planters on credit;[68] they opposed any locally levied import duties because they reduced their profit; and some of them feared a public monopoly of the Indian trade, because a government-owned trading company could dictate prices for British trading goods.[69]

The lobby easily managed to solve this last problem. Stephen Godin and Samuel Baron were at the center of the efforts to have the Indian Trade Act repealed. On August 19, 1718, Godin presented a letter from an unidentified South Carolinian (probably Stephen's brother Benjamin) to the Board of Trade. The correspondent complained that the Indian Trade Act was "not thought to be for the advantage of the country," and that most of the trade would be lost to the Spanish and French if the monopoly was carried on. He then suggested that the act be repealed in England, as the Privy Council had done with a similar Virginia law on July 31, 1717.[70] The proprietors had already been confronted with the situation by Joseph Boone, Samuel Baron, and, unsurprisingly, Stephen Godin, on July 10, 1718.[71] As a direct consequence of Godin's and Baron's lobbying, the proprietors declared, in an order of July 22, 1718, that "H.M. having been graciously pleas'd upon application made to him by the merchants of London, to repeal the Laws made in Virginia to the same effect, we the Lord Palatin and the rest of the Lords Proprietors of the Province of South Carolina do think it proper to repeal and make void the said Indian Trade Act."[72]

The lobbyists were equally successful with the issuance of paper money. As early as September 1714, before the Yamasee War broke out, the proprietors reported to their governor and council that they had received "complaints from several hands" against the colony's Bank Act, which had issued bills of credit as governmental loans secured by mortgages on slaves and land. The proprietors warned Governor Craven to "consider of some expedient to prevent the mischiefs of that Act," or they would be forced to repeal it, as "our London Merchants" believed it was "very prejudicial to trade."[73] Aware that the Bank Act Bills were still circulating, and afraid that the Bank Act was "an Infringement & Violation of the Laws of Great Britain," the proprietors repeated their warnings in the instructions to Governor Robert Johnson in April 1717. Johnson complied with the proprietors' wishes and managed to convince the assembly to sink the bills of credit by levying a tax on land and on real estate in Charleston.[74] On August 29, 1718, the London lobbyists sent word to the proprietors that the assembly might be planning to elude the tax law.[75] The proprietary minute book mentions only unnamed "London Merchants," but Stephen Godin was most likely the driving force once more, using the same letter he had laid before the Board of Trade on August 19 with regard to the Indian trade. In this letter the correspondent had also explained that the assembly had levied a tax to sink outstanding bills of credit, at the same time suggesting that the assembly might "think fitt to break again thro' their Act and forfeit their publick faith."[76] Godin's mission with the proprietors proved phenomenally successful: "Ocassioned upon a Pet.[ition] from the London Merchants to the Board," the proprietors drew up a letter to their governor in which they "strictly enjoined & commanded" him not to "stamp any more Bills of Credit nor to consent to any act of assembly whereby the Tax act may be eluded."[77] They also ordered Johnson not to consent to any law that would make goods legal tender to discharge debts. With these orders, the proprietors had deprived the colony of their most important instrument to cope with their debts acquired during the costly military expeditions of the Yamasee War.

Import duties equally attracted the lobby's attention. In July 1716 Stephen Godin, conscious of the Board of Trade's hostility toward proprietary colonies, informed the board that a law had been passed in South Carolina putting British merchants at a disadvantage to local merchants. He specifically mentioned import duties levied on British merchandise as well as a clause in the colonial acts that had exempted locally built vessels from paying the duties.[78]

There is no evidence that the Board of Trade reacted to Godin's petition, but the matter produced dramatic consequences in March 1718, when William Rhett, the Carolina acquaintance of Stephen Godin and Samuel Baron, notified the Commissioners of Customs of a general import duty of 10 percent levied on all British goods imported into the colony—a measure the assembly had taken to pay for the debts of the Indian war and, in the words of Rhett, to "exempt themselves from paying taxes."[79] Rhett's information triggered official action by the King-in-Council, who, on May 14, ruled that the act was "illegal" and ordered the proprietors to declare it "null and void."[80] The proprietors did as they were told and repealed the act, but the matter was not closed, for the South Carolina assembly continued to experiment with different import duties. On February 13, 1719, Samuel Baron "and other Merchants" petitioned before the proprietors against an import duty of £40 levied on each slave imported into the colony, but the proprietors, mindful that the high number of slaves was a "matter of great consequence" to the stability of the colony, refused to veto the law.[81] On February 27 "the London Merchants" (probably again Baron and Godin) delivered a petition to the proprietary board against an additional import duty act that had again exempted South Carolina–owned vessels from paying duties, and an "act for the better ordering of Negroes & all other Slaves." The proprietors repealed the first but, for the same reasons that they had left the slave import duty act in force, declined to repeal the latter. Yet the lobbyists' persistence obviously alerted the proprietors. For fear of more "illegal" trade laws, the proprietors ordered their South Carolina secretary, Charles Hart, to transfer all laws passed in the colony to them. In addition they ordered their governor and council not to pass any acts that might "affect the Trade or Shipping of this Kingdom" without a "suspending clause."[82]

Between February 1719 and the revolt, there are no more records of merchant lobbying before the proprietors or the Board of Trade. The London merchants had succeeded in implementing their political and economic interests. This came at the expense of the planter-dominated colonial assembly in South Carolina, which was left with a heavy debt but lacked the instruments to tackle it: the assembly could neither issue more paper money nor levy more import duties. The cost of the war was left to the citizens of South Carolina, who had to pay for it with their taxes on land and property in Charleston.

To ensure that the assembly would not again pass laws that "may reflect on them," the proprietors further curtailed its power. They repealed the act that had given the assembly the right to nominate the public receiver,[83] and they strengthened representation from Charleston (where merchants were over-represented) by revoking the Election Act. Realizing that their council had collaborated with the assembly, they changed its composition and nominated six merchants or planter-merchants, two proprietary officials, and only four planters, some of whom were faithful proprietary supporters like William Bull.[84]

Not only did the proprietors' orders degrade the colonial assembly to a dependent governing body, but they also seriously challenged the planters' hegemony in the colony: putting their scheme for complete planter domination in jeopardy, the planters could not accept the proprietors' measures and revolted.

The constitutional conflict between the proprietors in England and the assembly in South Carolina was nourished by three entangled processes. The first was the development of South Carolina into a staple-producing economy, which made it interesting for British merchants and promoted the formation of a merchant lobby group in London. The second was the development of a confident planter class in South Carolina, which established strong local political institutions and increasingly challenged imperial authorities. The third was the transformation of Great Britain into what John Brewer has called the "fiscal-military state."[85] This emergent state considered proprietary colonies counterproductive to its mercantilist visions.[86] These three processes created increasing tensions and pressures that the Carolina proprietors could not adequately address. They found themselves trapped between the interests of the planters in their colony and the merchants in England, backed by British colonial offices. The Lords Proprietors eventually opted to side with the merchants in 1718, because they feared that noncompliance with their wishes could mean trouble with Crown authorities. It is ironic that this attempt to save their charter from revocation ended in the total elimination of proprietary government in South Carolina with the Revolution of 1719.

Notes

This work would not have been possible without the generous funding of the German Research Foundation (DFG), distributed through the Research Center on Governance in Areas of Limited Statehood (SFB 700) at the Free University of Berlin. I would like to thank Ursula Lehmkuhl, Dominik Nagl, and Marion Stange for their comments on my work, and Jack P. Greene for his thought-provoking discussions. I am also heavily indebted to Chuck Lesser and the staff at the SCDAH for granting me easy access to their materials.

1. Address to King, December 1719, Document 11, South Carolina General Assembly, Commons House Sessional Papers, 1718–1725, SCDAH.

2. Steven J. Oatis, *A Colonial Complex: South Carolina's Frontiers in the Era of the Yamasee War, 1680–1730* (Lincoln: University of Nebraska Press, 2004), 165; Marion Eugene Sirmans, *Colonial South Carolina: A Political History, 1663–1763* (Chapel Hill: University of North Carolina Press, 1966), 125–28; Robert M. Weir, *Colonial South Carolina: A History,* 2nd ed. (Columbia: University of South Carolina Press, 1997), 101–3. This interpretation is also dominant in general surveys of American colonial history: Brendan McConville, *The King's Three Faces: The Rise and Fall of Royal America, 1688–1776* (Chapel Hill: University of North Carolina Press, 2006), 47; Richard Middleton, *Colonial America: A History, 1565–1776,* 3rd ed. (Oxford: Blackwell, 2002), 184–87; Alan Taylor, *American Colonies: The Settling of North America* (New York: Penguin, 2001), 226. For interpretations with a different emphasis, see Converse D. Clowse, *Economic Beginnings in Colonial South Carolina, 1670–1730* (Columbia: University of South Carolina Press, 1971), 191–94; Walter B. Edgar, *South Carolina: A History* (Columbia: University of South Carolina Press, 1998), 82–108; L. H. Roper, *Conceiving Carolina: Proprietors, Planters, and Plots, 1662–1729* (New York: Palgrave Macmillan, 2004), 143–57. The most complete survey of the revolt is an unpublished Ph.D. dissertation: John Alexander Moore, "Royalizing South Carolina: The Revolution of 1719 and the Evolution of Early South Carolina Government" (Ph.D. diss., University of South Carolina, 1991).

3. Weir, *Colonial South Carolina,* 102. For a similar comment, see: Sirmans, *Political History,* 128.

4. Charles McLean Andrews, *The Colonial Period of American History,* 4 vols. (New Haven: Yale University Press, 1934–37); Oliver Morton Dickerson, *American Colonial Government, 1696–1765: A Study of the British Board of Trade in Its Relation to the American Colonies, Political, Industrial, Administrative* (1912; repr., New York: Russel and Russel, 1962); Jack P. Greene, *The Constitutional Origins of the American Revolution* (New York: Cambridge University Press, 2011); Jack P. Greene, *Peripheries and Center: Constitutional Development in the Extended Polities of the British Empire and the United States, 1607–1788* (Athens: University of Georgia Press, 1986); Jack P. Greene, *The Quest for Power: The Lower Houses of Assembly in the Southern Royal Colonies. 1689–1776* (Chapel Hill: University of North Carolina Press, 1963); A. Berriedale Keith, *Constitutional History of the First British Empire* (Oxford: Clarendon Press, 1930).

5. Ursula Lehmkuhl, "Regieren im kolonialen Amerika: Colonial Governance und koloniale Gouvernmentalité in französischen und englischen Siedlungskolonien," in *Regieren ohne Staat? Governance in Räumen begrenzter Staatlichkeit,* ed. Ursula Lehmkuhl and Thomas Risse (Baden-Baden, Germany: Nomos, 2007), 111–33; Elizabeth Mancke, "Chartered Enterprises and the Evolution of the British Atlantic World," in *The Creation of the British Atlantic World,* ed. Elizabeth Mancke and Carole Shammas (Baltimore: Johns Hopkins University Press, 2005), 237–68; L. H. Roper and Bertrand Van Ruymbeke eds., *Constructing Early Modern Empires: Proprietary Ventures in the Atlantic World, 1500–1750* (Leiden, Netherlands: Brill, 2007).

6. Craig Yirush, *Settlers, Liberty, and Empire: The Roots of Early American Political Theory, 1675-1775* (New York: Cambridge University Press, 2011).

7. Charles E. Lee and Ruth S. Green, "A Guide to South Carolina Council Journals, 1671-1775," *SCHM* 68, no. 1 (January 1967): 1-13; Charles E. Lee and Ruth S. Green, "A Guide to the Commons House Journals of the South Carolina General Assembly 1692-1721," *SCHM* 68, no. 2 (April 1967): 85-96.

8. Francis Yonge, "A Narrative of the Proceedings of the People of South-Carolina in the Year 1719," in *Historical Collections of South Carolina*, ed. B. R. Carroll (New York: Harper and Brothers, 1836), 2:141-92.

9. Yonge, "Narrative," 146.

10. Ibid., 145; Act No. 367 of 1716, *Statutes at Large*, 2:692; Act No. 401 of 1719, *Statutes at Large*, 3:91. William L. Ramsey has recently suggested that the war was caused by diplomatic mismanagement. However, contemporaries attributed the coming of the war to a fraudulently conducted Indian trade. William L. Ramsey, "'Something Cloudy in Their Looks:' The Origins of the Yamasee War Reconsidered," *JAH* 90, no. 3 (June 2003): 44-75.

11. Act No. 360 of 1716, *Statutes at Large*, 2:677-80.

12. Act No. 357 of 1716, *Statutes at Large*, 2:641-46; Act No. 372 of 1717, *Statutes at Large*, 3:2.

13. On paper money, see Gary L. Hewitt, "The State in the Planters' Service: Politics and the Emergence of a Plantation Economy in South Carolina," in *Money, Trade, and Power: The Evolution of Colonial South Carolina's Plantation Society*, ed. Jack P. Greene, Rosemary Brana-Shute, and Randy J. Sparks (Columbia: University of South Carolina Press, 2001), 64; Richard M. Jellison, "Paper Money in Colonial South Carolina: A Reappraisal," *SCHM* 62, no. 3 (July 1961): 134-47. For the laws adopted, see Acts Nos. 355 of 1716, 359 of 1716, 364 of 1716, *Statutes at Large*, 2:627-41, 649-76, 682-83; Acts Nos. 386 of 1717, 395 of 1719, 398 of 1719, *Statutes at Large*, 3:32-38, 56-68, 69-84.

14. Yonge, "Narrative," 150, emphasis in original.

15. Proprietors to Governor and Council, July 22, 1718, Proprietors' Entry Book, 1710-1726, 115-17. The text of the public receiver act is not printed in the *Statutes at Large* but may be found in Nicholas Trott, "Manuscript Code of Laws," 1719, Codes and Session Laws, at SCDAH, 311-12. June 20, 1707–July 5, 1707, 3:223-65, 1692-1724, in CHJ; November 28, 1717–December 11, 1717, 5:380-410. For the election laws, see Act No. 365 of 1716, *Statutes at Large*, 2:683-89; Act No. 373 of 1717, *Statutes at Large*, 3:2-4.

16. Yonge, "Narrative," 151, emphasis in original.

17. Ibid.

18. From a proprietary letter to their former governor, "Landgrave" Thomas Smith, it appears that Smith had asked the board to send over one of the proprietors, "fully impowered with their authorities" to settle matters in the colony. Proprietors to Thomas Smith, August 31, 1694, Proprietors' Entry Book, 1693-1710, CO 5/289. Microfilm copy at the SCDAH, 10. On Archdale, see Sirmans, *Political History*, 61-67.

19. February 23, 1715, in CHJ, 4:376.

20. Yonge, "Narrative," 162.

21. Ibid., 150–51.

22. Ibid., 152.

23. Proprietors to Governor Johnson, June 19, 1719; Proprietors to Governor Johnson and Council, July 24, 1719, Proprietors' Entry Book, 1710–1726, 142–43; 154–55.

24. Yonge, "Narrative," 163, emphasis in original.

25. Yonge, "Narrative," 165–66, emphasis in original.

26. Ibid., 168–70; Mabel L. Webber, "The First Governor Moore and His Children," *SCHGM* 37, no. 1 (January 1936): 1–23.

27. Address to King, December 1719; List of Grievances and Resolutions, December 1719, Documents 11, 18, Sessional Papers.

28. Yonge, "Narrative," 163–64, emphasis in original.

29. Richard P. Sherman, *Robert Johnson: Proprietary and Royal Governor of South Carolina* (Columbia: University of South Carolina Press, 1966), 31–42.

30. This quote comes from the single surviving house document for the year 1718. It is among the collection of Sessional Papers of the South Carolina Commons House of Assembly at the Department of Archives and History, Columbia, South Carolina. The papers were discovered by John Alexander Moore in late 1984 at the SCHS in Charleston. Draft Message to Governor Johnson, October 17, 1718, Document 1, Sessional Papers.

31. List of Grievances and Resolutions, December 1719, Document 18, Sessional Papers.

32. Titles of Acts, December 1719, Document 19, Sessional Papers. It should be noted that three of the laws (the two election acts and the act encouraging settlement in South Carolina) are crossed out.

33. Yirush, *Settlers*.

34. Petition of the Council and Assembly of the Settlements in South Carolina to the King, February 3, 1720, in *BPRO-SC*, 7:271–99.

35. Yirush, *Settlers*, 263–65.

36. September 20, 1693, in CHJ, 1:65.

37. Proprietors' Entry Books, 1710–1726, 103–13.

38. On these acts, see Edward McCrady, *The History of South Carolina under the Proprietary Government, 1670–1719* (New York: Macmillan, 1897), 402–51; Sirmans, *Political History,* 75–93; Dorothy Louise Brown, "Who Has Authority? The Struggle for Power in Colonial South Carolina" (Ph.D. diss., University of South Carolina, 2002). The proprietors did veto laws of North Carolina after 1706; see Lesser, *South Carolina Begins,* 260; Minutes of Meeting of the Lords Proprietors, April 24, 1708, Proprietary Minute Books, 1708–1727, 2–3; Board of Trade to the Queen, November 12, 1707, in *CSPC,* 23:597–99. For the 1697 repeal, see Nicholas Trott, *The Laws of the Province of South Carolina* (Charleston: Lewis Timothy, 1736), 60; Trott, "Manuscript Code of Laws," 101–2; Act No. 151 of 1697, *Statutes at Large,* 2:130; Proprietors to Governor Blake and Council, August 30, 1697, Proprietors' Entry Book, 1682–1698, 18b, Proprietors' Entry Book, 1682–1698, 117–18, CO 5/290. Microfilm copy at the SCDAH; Governor and Council to Lords Proprietors, March 12, 1698 in A. S. Salley, ed., *Commissions and Instructions from the Lords Proprietors of Carolina to Public Officials of South*

Carolina, 1685–1715 (Columbia: Historical Commission of South Carolina, 1916), 103.

39. Proprietors to Charles Craven, March 27, 1713; Proprietors to Nicholas Trott, March 27, 1713; Proprietors' Confirmation of An Act for Ascertaining Publick Officers Fees, September 1714; Proprietors to Governor and Council, September 1714, Proprietors' Entry Book, 1710–1726, 65–66; 78; 82.

40. Proprietors to Governor Blake and Council, August 30, 1697, Proprietors' Entry Book, 1682–1698, 18b.

41. Greene, *Quest for Power*, 363.

42. Instructions for Robert Johnson, April 30, 1717, Proprietors' Entry Book, 1710–1726, 108–13. For similar instructions to Philip Ludwell, Nathaniel Johnson, Edward Tynte, and Charles Craven, see Instructions for Coll. Philipp Ludwell, November 8, 1691, Proprietors' Entry Book, 1682–1698, 94b–97; Instructions for Sir Nathaniel Johnson, June 18, 1702; Instructions for Colonel Edward Tynte, March 24, 1709, Proprietors' Entry Book, 1693–1710, 47–47b; 81b–92b; Instructions for Charles Craven, 1711, Proprietors' Entry Book, 1710–1726, 17–40.

43. Minutes of Meeting of the Lords Proprietors, September 3, 1709, Proprietors' Minute Book, 1708–1727, 24–26.

44. This article employs a "realist" approach, assuming that subjects acted rationally according to their "interests." Other incentives on a more emotional level such as fear, anger, disappointment, and personal animosities might have played a key role in the revolt, but they are difficult to reconstruct.

45. Clarence Ver Steeg, *Origins of a Southern Mosaic: Studies of Early Carolina and Georgia* (Athens: University of Georgia Press, 1975), 117–30. Naval stores in particular dominated the trade between 1713 and 1725. See Converse D. Clowse, "The Charleston Export Trade, 1717–1730" (Ph.D. diss., University of South Carolina, 1963).

46. Green, *Quest for Power;* Newton B. Jones, "The Role of the Commons House of Assembly in Proprietary South Carolina," *Proceedings of the South Carolina Historical Association* (1976): 5–13.

47. Richard Waterhouse, *A New World Gentry: The Making of a Merchant and Planter Class in South Carolina, 1670–1770* (New York: Garland, 1973), 41. The proprietary council was more evenly cast with four planters, four merchants, one Indian trader, and one placeman between 1711 and 1719; Waterhouse, *A New World Gentry*, 37.

48. These numbers are based on the signatures on the convention's petition to the king and are reconciled with Walter B. Edgar and N. Louise Bailey, eds., *Biographical Directory of the South Carolina House of Representatives*, vol. 2, *The Commons House of Assembly, 1692–1775* (Columbia: University of South Carolina Press, 1977); A .S. Salley, ed., *Warrants for Lands in South Carolina, 1672–1711*, rev. and ed. R. Nicholas Olsberg (Columbia: University of South Carolina Press, 1973). For the signatures, see Address to King, December 1719, Document 11, Sessional Papers.

49. Extracts of Letter from Charleston in South Carolina, November 14, 1719, in *BPRO-SC*, 7:218.

50. Governor Johnson to Board of Trade, December 27, 1719, in *BPRO-SC*, 7:227–29.

51. William Rhett to Board of Trade, December 21, 1719. Privy Council Records, PC 1/58/2A. I would like to thank Alex Moore for making copies of this and other Privy Council Records available to me.

52. Hewitt, "Planters' Service."

53. Ibid., 66.

54. Lehmkuhl, "Regieren"; Dominik Nagl and Marion Stange, *Staatlichkeit und Governance im Zeitalter der europäischen Expansion. Verwaltungsstrukturen und Herrschaftsinstitutionen in den britischen und französischen Kolonialimperien* (Berlin: SFB-Governance Working Paper Series, 2008).

55. Moore, "Royalizing."

56. James Waylen, *The House of Cromwell: A Genealogical History of the Descendants of the Protector*, rev. and ed. John Gabriel Cromwell (London: Elliot Stock, 1897), 57.

57. Proprietors to Governor Johnson, March 24, 1719, Proprietors' Entry Book, 1710–1726, 135–36.

58. Stephen Godin to Board of Trade, July 25, 1716, in *BPRO-SC*, 6:227–29.

59. Mr. Solicitor General to Mr. Popple, April 5, 1718, in *BPRO-SC*, 7:116–17.

60. Rebecca Starr, *A School for Politics: Commercial Lobbying and Political Culture in Early Carolina* (Baltimore: Johns Hopkins University Press, 1998), 27.

61. Clowse, "Charleston Export Trade," 121. Note that Clowse's calculations cover the period 1717–37 and are therefore of only limited applicability to this study.

62. Ibid., 119–20. It is interesting that the two brothers, Benjamin and Stephen, never operated vessels together between 1717 and 1719. However, Stephen Godin must have had good contacts to South Carolina, for he acted as the council's agent in 1728. Stephen Godin's connection with his brother is suggested by Arthur Hirsch, but without proper evidence. Arthur Hirsch, *The Huguenots of Colonial South Carolina*, ed. Bertrand Van Ruymbeke (1928; repr., Columbia: University of South Carolina Press, 1999), 145.

63. Naval Officer, Records of Clearings, 1717–1721; Clowse, "Charleston Export Trade," appendix, 58.

64. Naval Officer, Records of Clearings, 1717–1721.

65. Minutes of Meeting of the Lords Proprietors, September 3, 1709, Proprietors' Minute Book, 1708–1727, 24–26.

66. Memorial of Joseph Boone and Richard Beresford, February 22, 1717; Memorial of Joseph Boone and Richard Beresford, March 4, 1717, in *BPRO-SC*, 7:5–8, 13–14; Leo Francis Stock, ed., *Proceedings and Debates of the British Parliaments Respecting North America* (Washington, D.C.: Carnegie Institution, 1930), 3:266–67, 413–14.

67. Leo Francis Stock, ed., *Proceedings and Debates of the British Parliaments Respecting North America* (Washington, D.C.: Carnegie Institution, 1930), 3:266–67, 413–14.

68. Unfortunately the wordings of the merchants' petitions against paper money for the period before 1719 are lost. In a petition of May 22, 1723, the merchants explained that they opposed paper money because "the British merchants and traders who had given the planters large credits to stock themselves with negroes etc., lost

immediately full half of their debts" due to paper money depreciation. Merchants and Traders to South Carolina to the Council of Trade and Plantations, May 22, 1723, in *BPRO-SC*, 10:87–91. On the merchants' opposition to paper money, see Stuart O. Stumpf, "The Merchants of Colonial Charleston, 1680–1756" (Ph.D. diss., University of South Carolina, 1971), 113–25.

69. The Godin–de la Conseillere partnership especially suffered from the Indian Trade Act, because the Indian Trade Commission declined to pay their "excessively high prices." Stumpf, "Merchants," 104.

70. Extracts of several letters from Carolina, August 19, 1718, in *BPRO-SC*, 7:71–73; William Lawson Grant, ed., *Acts of the Privy Council of England: Colonial Series* (London: British Public Record Office, 1910), 2:721.

71. Minutes of Meeting of the Lords Proprietors, July 10, 1718, Proprietors' Minute Book, 1708–1727, 97–99.

72. Proprietors to Governor and Council, July 22, 1718, Proprietors' Entry Book, 1710–1726, 115–17.

73. Proprietors to Governor and Council, September 8, 1714, Proprietors' Entry Book, 1710–1726, 82.

74. Instructions to Robert Johnson, April 30, 1717, Proprietors' Entry Book, 1710–1726, 108–13; October 30, 1717, in *CHJ*, 5:340.

75. Minutes of Meeting of the Lords Proprietors, August 29, 1718, Proprietors' Minute Book, 1708–1727, 102.

76. Extracts of Several Letters from Carolina, August 19, 1718, in *BPRO-SC*, 7:71–73.

77. Proprietors to Governor Johnson and Council, September 4, 1718, Proprietors' Entry Book, 1710–1726, 155–57; Minutes of Meeting of the Lords Proprietors, September 5, 1718, Proprietors' Minute Book, 1708–1727, 103.

78. Stephen Godin to Board of Trade, July 25, 1716 in *BPRO-SC*, 6:227–29.

79. Extract of Letter from William Rhett to the Commissioners of Customs, March 20, 1718, in *BPRO-SC*, 7:104–6. It is rather odd that Rhett, who was the Proprietors' Receiver of Quitrents, should chose to inform the Customs Commissioners (whom he served as collector of the King's Customs in Charleston), rather than his proprietary patrons—a clear breach of trust that testifies to the sagging proprietary authority. Rhett's letter also indicates that his influence with the proprietors was much less substantial than his Carolina opponents claimed, for if he had indeed controlled proprietary decision making through their secretary, he would not have needed to resort to a royal agency for eliminating the duty act.

80. Order of King in Council, May 14, 1718, in *BPRO-SC*, 7:131–33.

81. Minutes of Meeting of the Lords Proprietors, February 13, 1719; February 20, 1719, Proprietors' Minute Book, 1708–1727, 113–15.

82. Proprietors to Governor, Council and Assembly of South Carolina, February 27, 1719, Proprietors' Entry Book, 1710–1726, 132–35.

83. This act was repealed because of the interference of Governor Johnson and his council. Minutes of Meeting of the Lords Proprietors, July 10, 1718, Proprietors' Minute Book, 1708–1727, 97–99.

84. Samuel Wragg, William Gibbon, Benjamin de la Conseillere, Francis Yonge, and Jacob Satur can clearly be identified as merchants. Hugh Butler was a planter

with strong interests in the Indian trade. Nicholas Trott was the proprietors' chief justice, and Charles Hart was the proprietors' secretary. William Bull, Ralph Izard, and Peter St. Julien were planters. Jonathan Skrine lived in Charleston before 1719 and became a planter when he married Elizabeth Gaillard in 1719. There is a schism between the proprietary minute and entry books concerning the nomination of Jonathan Skrine. He was not mentioned on the list entered into the minute book for the proprietary board's session on June 19, 1719. However, he replaced John Kinloch on the list that was eventually prepared for transmittal to Governor Johnson on the same date. Kinloch was probably dropped because he had sympathized with the antiproprietary movement; Edgar and Bailey, *Biographical Directory*, 2:120–22, 131, 163–64, 276–77, 358–60, 379, 584–85, 623–24, 681–84, 729–30. Proprietors to Governor Johnson, June 19, 1719, Proprietors' Entry Book, 1710–1726, 142–43; Minutes of Meeting of the Lords Proprietors, June 19, 1719, Proprietors' Minute Books, 1708–1727, 124–26.

85. John Brewer, *The Sinews of Power: War, Money, and the English State, 1688–1783* (New York: Knopf, 1989).

86. I am greatly indebted to Dominik Nagl for calling my attention to the connection between the Revolution of 1719 and the process of state building. He deals more fully with this question in "Governance im kolonialen Nordamerika—Rechtstransfer, Staatsbildung und Praktiken der Disziplinierung in Massachusetts und South Carolina, 1630–1769" (Ph.D. diss., Free University of Berlin, 2011).

Protecting the Rights of Englishmen

The Rise and Fall of Carolina's Piratical State

MARK G. HANNA

During the late seventeenth century Charles Town was one of the most infamous pirate nests in the Atlantic World. The roots of Carolina's piratical state can be traced back well before the colony's foundation to Port Royal, Jamaica, during the decades following its acquisition by the English in 1655. Sea marauders of all nations fit out their vessels in its deep harbor and spent their hard-fought Spanish pieces of eight on liquor and prostitutes in its many taverns. Without a thriving sugar plantation economy built on slave labor like that in Barbados, early Jamaicans relied on the plunder of largely independent crews emphatically deemed "privateers" despite their obvious transgressions against international treaties of peace.[1] By the mid-1670s a rapidly expanding slave population began to produce stable profits from sugar exports. Wealthy planters could no longer allow bloodthirsty pirates to destabilize international affairs, which might lead to a Spanish invasion or even a bloody slave revolt foreshadowing similar developments in the Carolina colony a few decades later. By the 1680s Jamaican authorities not only banned English pirates; they tried and executed scores of them and hung them in gibbets at the entrance of the port. Even Henry Morgan, a man once considered a pirate by the Spanish and a supporter of "privateering" as deputy governor during the 1670s, became one of the wealthiest planters on the island who, as vice admiral, personally hunted pirates by the 1680s.

The closing of Port Royal certainly did not compel all former pirates to abandon a life before the mast to work as laborers on plantations. As fewer men owned more and more land in Jamaica, opportunities to join the landed gentry in the West Indies diminished. Some crews sailed to the Bay of Campeche to illegally cut logwood used for dyeing cloth. These roving bands periodically united with international armadas to raid along the Spanish Main. Their most infamous attack was the sack of the Spanish entrepôt port of Vera Cruz in 1683. Many of these men crossed over the Isthmus of Darien (today Panama) to prey on the Spanish in their most vulnerable ports on the southern Pacific coast known as the "South Sea." Bent on maintaining peace with Spain, Jamaica's governor, Sir Thomas Lynch, passed what would be known as the

Jamaica Act in 1684, forbidding trade with pirates and establishing procedures for the prosecution their of aiders and abettors on land.

Carolina's Lords Proprietors initiated their settlement amid this transformation of the English West Indies settling in its present location on Oyster Point in earnest in 1680. Hoping to begin plantations of their own on cheaper and more readily available land, colonists arrived with dreams of establishing a new Barbados, a successful commodity producing plantation economy based on slave labor. Instead Carolinians produced no staple crop during the first two decades and survived primarily on selling provisions in the West Indies or participating in the unscrupulous Indian trade.[2] Many pirates of the West Indies soon learned that if they could not return to Port Royal they could follow the Gulf Stream north through the Florida Straights to Charles Town to refit and careen their vessels and purchase a wide variety of victuals. Charles Town was in a perfect position to gain the pirate market, close to the major sites of West Indian plunder but far enough away to escape those who might seek retribution. The treacherous coastline that separated Charles Town and Virginia also isolated the colony from the prying scrutiny of its northern neighbors and their Crown-appointed governors.

However much they might have wanted to replicate Barbados, Carolinians instead established a community in Charles Town that resembled more closely the Port Royal of the 1670s in its willingness to welcome vessels that had quite clearly performed acts of piracy.[3] Some pirates, like Captain Jacob Hall, were based primarily in Carolina.[4] Other pirates, like the Frenchman Captain Grammont, simply anchored off the sand bar in Charles Town harbor letting Carolinians come to him while some even joined his crew.[5] As Alex Moore notes in his essay in this volume, early Carolina shared more with its actually pirate-supporting political sister colony in the Bahamas than say Virginia to the north. The same proprietors controlled both colonies, and Carolina governors often settled political disputes that arose in the capital town of New Providence. The settlements had in common similar daily threats from the wrath of the Spanish empire, and neither produced a reliable staple crop.

Following the outbreak of war sparked by the 1688 Glorious Revolution, some English captains began to seek greater riches in the East India Company's territory by preying on Muslim pilgrimage vessels in the Indian Ocean. One of the first of these "Red Sea men" originated in Charles Town, and their vessels sailed in and out of the harbor for over a decade. Witnesses claimed pirates "came to Charleston with a vast quantity of gold from the Red Sea," where "they were entertained, and had liberty to stay or go to any other place."[6] The Virginian William Byrd II, always wary of his southern neighbors, blamed this proliferation of piracy on Carolinians who, "by their frequent harbouring of Pyrates, by their receiving and furnishing them with Provisions and other necessarys," have supported these rogues "in Carrying on their Villany." Without these accessories to global crime, it would be "impossible for those

Free booters to subsist."[7] Francis Nicholson, lieutenant governor of Virginia, estimated Red Sea pirates brought to Charles Town a hundred-man crew with £2,000 apiece. Other witnesses described thousands of gold and silver coins as well as jewels. Nicholson feared that like Jamaica in the 1670s, "if such people be encouraged they will debauch the inhabitants and make them leave planting to follow the same trade."[8] Although the numbers were likely embellished, they are still staggering considering a common sailor who was fully employed (not a guarantee) made roughly £16 a year.[9]

Historians of early Carolina's relationship with global piracy have traditionally blamed it simply on the corrupt and lawless conditions on marchland peripheries.[10] Even some contemporaries like Governor John Archdale described Carolina's first setters as men of "most desperate Fortunes" and "ill Livers," led by a council made up of "loose principled Men."[11] The proprietors' aggressive efforts to populate the colony using religious toleration and political liberalism as bait did indeed attract a diverse population of disenfranchised individuals. One visitor to Charles Town in 1708 described the populace as "a perfect Medley or Hotch potch made up of Bank[r]upts, pirates, decayed Libertines, Sectaries and Enthusiasts of all sorts" and "the most factious and Seditious people in the whole World."[12]

Such sweeping generalizations about the dissipation of moral values on the imperial periphery, however, could be made in other colonies that did not openly support piracy. Barbados was infamous for its debauched planter class, yet we find few pirates in Bridgetown. The same could be said about Virginia, where by the late seventeenth century the rare pirates unfortunate enough to enter the Chesapeake were most likely to lose their lives. While economic motives obviously went a long way toward explaining the presence of pirates in Carolina, I will argue here that it had as much to do with a complex three-way struggle over power on both sides of the Atlantic, between the Crown, Carolina's Lords Proprietors, and the local ruling gentry, where pirates were really pawns in an elaborate political chess match. The Carolina gentry openly supported piracy to demonstrate local autonomy and their defense of the basic political rights of Englishmen, like the right of property owners to vote or to sit on the jury of a criminal trial. The Lords Proprietors wanted to eradicate piracy largely for fear Crown officials might use criminal behavior as grounds for taking away their charter and their property rights. The Crown would use the piracy problem to implement imperial policies, like the construction of vice-admiralty courts, to undermine the power of both the local gentry and the Lords Proprietors. In turn the Carolina gentry's attempts to negotiate the encroachment of power by both entities across the Atlantic fueled political divisions within the colony that would eventually lead to rebellion.

Recent scholarship on piracy has established a sort of class division between the oppressed labor on board ships and the merchant gentry who exploited them.[13] The opposite was true in seventeenth century Charles Town, where the common seamen were not the ones voicing rebellious radical political ideologies. Instead the merchant traders, elected members of the council, and the governors who controlled the port of Charles Town were the ones actively supporting pirates to protest the encroachment of power against the rights ascribed by their charter. For example, although the English Crown and therefore her subjects were nominally at peace with the Spanish, Charles Town and St. Augustine waged a decades-long undeclared war fought by independent sea marauders. Beginning in the early 1680s, governors in both Carolina and the Bahamas issued commissions to men who at one point or another had committed acts of piracy.[14] Carolina's leaders argued that since their charter provided them the right to wage war, sea marauders were "privateers" not "pirates." This same rationale for autonomous military engagement helped the colony in other moments of crisis, especially with native peoples. Taking a middle ground between the Crown and her colonists, the proprietors admitted that their charter permitted Carolinians to pursue the Spanish "in heat of a victory" but not to grant commissions for a deliberate peacetime invasion. Certainly "no rational man can suppose that the subjects of any prince can be permitted to make war upon any of his allies for the reparation of their private injuries, or for any other cause whatever, or that any such power was granted by our patent."[15]

In the late seventeenth century Carolinians rarely used the word *pirate* to describe sea marauders, so it was reserved primarily for their political enemies. Francis Nicholson, lieutenant governor of the royal colonies of Virginia and then Maryland, feared the dangers of this flexible legal culture in proprietary Carolina, where "these sort of privateers, or rather pirates, when they have lavishly spent what they unjustly get, are ready to make a disturbance."[16] If captains did not hold a Carolina commission they could purchase one from the Danes in St. Thomas or the French in Petit Guavre. Many South Sea pirates claimed they were mercenaries serving under the Indian king of Darien, ally of Charles II and longtime enemy of the Spanish. These commissions were considered illegal to Parliament or Crown officials but were acceptable in most charter colonies.[17] Others justified their attacks on religious grounds, like the pirates based in Charles Town who attacked Florida missions, mutilating religious images by cutting off their heads, hands, and feet.[18] Governor Seth Sothell had been captured by "Turkish" pirates and enslaved in Algiers on his way to the colony. When he finally did arrive in Carolina, he was inundated with rumors of the torture and captivity of Protestant Carolinians in St. Augustine that likely reminded him of his own harrowing experience. In 1691 the proprietors accused Sothell of granting "commissions to pyrats, for wch wee conceive you had no authority."[19]

The Lords Proprietors genuinely feared the support of piracy would give the Crown grounds for quo warranto proceedings that would lead to nullification of their charter and property rights. Alex Moore notes how a commission given to the notorious pirate John Coxon nearly cost them the Bahamas. They were adamant about protecting their charter primarily out of financial, and too often short-term, interests. They wanted returns on their investments in their own lifetimes despite the difficulty of settlement and the time necessary to establish a staple commodity. There were in fact tangible financial consequences between the semantic divide between privateering and piracy. While a privateer would have to purchase commissions from colonial governors and pay them fees and duties out of their prizes, the booty stolen by "pirates" never changed ownership according to law so those goods could be sued for by the original owner, or they would revert to the Crown or Lord Admiral. This explains why there was no incentive for colonial officials to hunt pirates. The proprietors did not want to relinquish "pirate" booty to the Crown nor "privateer" prizes to their governors so they used the words interchangeably depending on their financial interests. The proprietors ordered financially strapped Carolina governors, surrounded by enemies against whom they were in constant need of fortifications, to not only condemn illicit "privateers" but also to take care that their booty "be kept for our use."[20]

The main force behind Carolina's foundation was Anthony Ashley Cooper, the Earl of Shaftesbury, and his secretary, John Locke, who produced the first Fundamental Constitutions of Carolina in 1669. Shaftesbury expected his governors to protect Proprietary financial interests but became frustrated as early as 1675 when there were few signs of future profits.[21] Although they focused on the bottom line, they constructed a remarkably liberal political and legal regime in the hope of enticing potential colonists from places where they had lived under political oppression. They also understood that a flexible system was necessary because they could not anticipate the many contingencies of frontier society. The proprietors as well as Crown observers blamed this flexible and liberal system on the rampant support of piracy. More specifically they argued that a strong local council, a weak executive power, liberal enfranchisement policies, and a remarkably independent jury system fostered piracy in the colony.

Although the governor was initially provided wide legislative and judicial powers, local resistance compelled the Lords Proprietors to diminish this authority when they issued their second (1681) and third (1682) sets of fundamental constitutions.[22] These limitations on executive power were meant to woo potential Scottish settlers and continued to prove a strong selling point three decades later, when one observer noted how Carolina governors were "obliged to know their bounds, so far as they may go and not farther."[23] Governors were supposed to be nominated by the Lords Proprietors, usually resident in England, but in reality locals chose most of them during the first decades from among the residents of the colony. They were typically allied with local merchants even before they took their positions, unlike in royal colonies where the Crown appointed and paid for their governors.[24]

The merchants in the colony council found pirates especially welcome in Charles Town because the community struggled to establish a local medium of exchange. To entice pirates the South Carolina assembly voted to overvalue specie in 1685, so that for decades it maintained the highest extrinsic value in the colonies bolstering the pirates' spending powers.[25] By 1690 the proprietors conceded that because "English money is scarce in Carolina, so you may receive our rents in Spanish money" as long as the "money be Mexico or Pilar pieces and of good weight" knowing full well its nefarious origins.[26] The first treatise printed in Charles Town in 1732 was *An Essay on Currency*, which recalled how "formerly Silver was very plenty" because the "Privateers brought in great Quantities of Spanish Silver."[27]

The planters in the council also benefited from the pirate market when they brought slaves, especially because the Royal African Company monopoly severely limited the supply of slaves to colonies outside of Barbados and Jamaica in the late seventeenth century. The depositions of a number of runaway English servants at St. Augustine claimed that Carolina obtained nearly two hundred black slaves from the raid on Vera Cruz alone.[28] They also kidnapped local "Indians" enslaved by the Spanish in Cuba and Florida to sell in Carolina and the Bahamas.[29] Some pirates also brought slaves and "negroes' gold" to Carolina directly from the coast of west Africa.[30]

The most active participants in the pirate market were a powerful faction of Anglican Barbadians, experienced colonists who adamantly challenged proprietary policies, known the "Goose Creek men." Many of them combined their support of piracy with the illicit Indian slave trade. In 1684 the Carolina Council appointed Robert Quary, the colony's secretary and a "Goose Creek man," governor without the proprietors' consent. The proprietors removed Quary from office after only two months because of his flagrant encouragement of pirates. This offense did little to tarnish his reputation in the community, and he was then elected to the Carolina Council and appointed sheriff of Berkeley County in 1691, a position made available when locals removed the previous sheriff for attempting to halt the pirate trade.[31]

The Admiralty instructed all colonial governors to pass antipiracy statutes modeled on the Jamaica Act in 1684.[32] Carolina's Lords Proprietors made a similar request, but the Carolina Council created a statute so purposely filled with caveats and loopholes it was completely ineffectual.[33] They followed this token gesture by actually reinforcing their right to commission privateers and to condemn Spanish prizes.[34] Since the governor was ultimately responsible for controlling who entered and left Carolina ports, the proprietors ordered Governor Joseph Morton in 1686 to "do your best to seize and try" pirates under this act along with "any people in Carolina that hold correspondence with them" with little success. The proprietors were unsurprisingly furious then when a pirate named Morgan (not Sir Henry) was openly welcomed after a popular parliamentary vote.[35] They feared the Council's behavior would further antagonize the Spanish, who did indeed attack in 1686, a nominal time of peace, looting and stealing slaves. The proprietors blamed the invasion on the fact that "the people of Carolina have received the pirates who have unjustly burned and robbed the houses of the Spaniards." They asked: "could any rational man doubt that the Spaniards would seek revenge[?]"[36]

Governor Morton planned retaliation but was halted upon the arrival of his successor James Colleton in the fall of 1686.[37] Son of colony Proprietor Sir Peter Colleton, James was the first governor of Carolina (and the only one during the late seventeenth century) to make a concerted effort to wean the colony from its dependence on the pirate market and stem the subsequent escalating private war with Spain. Bitter Carolinians alleged he must have had a treasonous financial arrangement with the new governor of St. Augustine.[38] The proprietors ordered Colleton to "secure" Joseph Morton and to investigate Quary's alleged crimes.[39] James Colleton's zeal for eradicating piracy in the proprietors' interest made him so unpopular he refused to call the parliament into session again, and he was eventually banished from the colony.[40] This was not an anomalous incident since the people rose up against governors who would not support piracy in both the Bahamas and Bermuda.[41]

Francis Nicholson, the lieutenant governor of the royal colony of Virginia and later Maryland complained that the governors of proprietary colonies "have power only (like civil magistrates in petty corporations in England) to make municipal laws with the consent of the people."[42] He complained that the Carolina Council thought no English laws "Ought to be in force, and binding to them; without their own consent."[43] Indeed Carolina legislatures repeatedly prevented the proprietors as well as the Crown from obtaining copies of their laws and records.[44] It was true that the Crown possessed practically no power in nonroyal colonies to compel governors to enforce piracy laws or to punish governors who clearly acted against the Crown's interests.[45] Some even questioned whether royal proclamations, one of the primary instruments used to attack piracy, had any authority in proprietary colonies.[46] "Private" colonies, meaning both proprietary and charter, did not hold the king's commission and did not correspond directly with the Lords of Trade. One witness deposed before the Board of Trade said that it was well known that the pirates themselves actually believed that because private colonies were not "immediately under the King, they cannot be seized and punished there, which contributes not a little to their boldness."[47] This political independence meant the kind of intracolonial policies that would be necessary to close the pirate market throughout the empire were impossible to enforce. If pirates arrived from the South Sea or Indian Ocean to find that one colony had shut its ports, they needed only to continue on to another.

This relatively democratic balance of power was compounded by wide enfranchisement. A 1693 act passed to regulate elections to the assembly considered all persons worth £10 eligible for election to the General Assembly. The proprietors believed the council purposefully omitted length of residency as a constraint so that "by this act all the pyrats that were in the shipp that had been Plundring in the Redd Sea: had been Quallified to vote for Representatives in Carolina."[48] They previously complained that John Boone had been expelled from the Carolina Council because he supplied two known pirates with food and supplies and "concealed part of their stolen goods," but he was soon reelected. The proprietors harangued: "This must not be. Men convicted of such misdemeanours must not be chosen again and restored."[49]

Even with antipiracy laws on the books and an informal "admiralty court" system in place, Carolina's juries generally acquitted the unlucky few men actually charged with piracy. This was such a commonly notorious practice in the private colonies that James II issued a royal proclamation to enforce piracy laws because of "a practice having grown up of bringing pirates to trial before the evidence was ready, and of using other evasions to insure their acquittal."[50] The Lords Proprietors complained that the juries on these courts were packed with bad apples and ordered Colleton in 1687 to clear them out "and put honest men in their place" who were "unstained by any commerce with privateers."[51] They hoped "the accession of more Morall People to our Province" might lessen the power of the Barbadian faction so that pirates might not "receive any Refreshment." They begged Colleton to make at least one pirate face trial "for we find it necessary to make some Examples thereby to stop this Ruinous Practice of receiving of Pyrates."[52]

Carolinians bristled at the thought of tampering with the independence of their juries. Christopher Hill argues that the English Civil War raised the stature of trial by jury to a quasi-religious status.[53] Just as maritime communities began to support piracy, the faith in juries reached its apex in England and was carried over to the colonies. William Penn's 1670 trial for fomenting riot in England (known as "Bushel's Case") solidified the sanctity of independent juries in England and America. Before this famous trial, juries could be fined or imprisoned for finding a defendant not guilty against the advice of a judge. The jury's refusal to condemn Penn, despite their imprisonment, led Chief Justice Sir John Vaughan to declare that a judge "may try to open the eyes of the jurors, but not to lead them by the nose."[54]

One of the major revisions made in 1682 to Locke's original 1669 Carolina constitution was to create the colony's unique system of selecting juries.[55] The sheriff wrote the name of each eligible juryman on an individual piece of paper, and a child drew the jury members' names from a box. A majority of the jury could make a decision without unanimity. Colonial juries could ignore the recommendation of judges, especially when they felt a distant monarch had imposed law on them.[56] Since such a large percentage of Carolinians participated in the pirate market, it was quite difficult to convince juries that dealing in goods forcibly seized, especially from the Spanish, was a crime.

In his history of the colony, John Oldmixon extolled Carolina's "Manner of impanelling Juries" arguing it "is so much preferable to that of England and all other Colonies."[57] The Lords Proprietors were not so supportive. In 1693, a year after Red Sea pirates allegedly brought thousands of pounds worth of riches to Charles Town, the Lords Proprietors directly correlated the liberal jury system to the proliferation of piracy. They declared that the provisions of an act designed to provide "indifferent jurymen" were "unreasonable and dangerous, and likely to leave the most enormous crimes, especially piracy, unpunished." It was too easy for the sheriff "to insert the name of some notorious favourer of pirates in every list" of possible jurymen. Jurymen embroiled in the pirate trade could then "be able to Constraine the Rest of the Jury to Consent to what verdict they please." The proprietors requested a nullification of this act to no avail.[58] The qualifications of jurors remained a hotly contested issue for years while outsiders took for granted Carolina's propensity for acquitting pirates.[59] In 1697 the governor of Pennsylvania alleged that a French privateer attacked vessels off the coast of Pennsylvania with the help of "an Englishman by name Cross on board, who had been tried for piracy at Carolina and acquitted" without any tangible proof of his claims.[60]

While the Goose Creek men fought with the Proprietary interests into the 1690s, men appointed by the Crown, like Francis Nicholson along with many of the inhabitants of royal colonies, argued the piracy problem was the natural consequence of proprietary regimes in general. In his 1698 memorial to the House of Lords, customs collector Edward Randolph claimed it would be "impossible to suppress piracy" as long as proprietors expected great profits but refused to provide adequate financial support for their governors.[61] Virginian William Byrd II agreed and placed the blame on the excessive power of Carolina's merchant gentry, which allowed them to welcome "their old friends the Pyrates." Likely referring to James Colleton, Byrd noted of governors who even attempted to crack down on the pirate market, "they have been either clappt up into the Logg-house, or else forc't to run for their lives" to safety in the royal colonies. Even a diligent governor possessed too little authority "being onely the Deputy of their fellow Subjects." So beholden to local interests, governors paid no attention to the laws of the mother country and were "in a fair way of shakeing off their Dependence upon England."[62] Some royal officials called for Crown appointment of all governors or to revert all the colonies under Crown control.[63]

Parliament began paying close attention to antiproprietary rhetoric as it became increasingly aware of and enraged by the blatant support of global piracy in the colonies. They became particularly enraged when one of the most notorious Red Sea pirates in the world, Captain Every, was allegedly welcomed with open arms in the Bahamas by Governor Nicholas Trott. Every's notoriety stemmed from his having captured a vessel belonging to the Great Mughal of

India himself with his own granddaughter on board. Trott's vast haul "made so great a noise in the world," one royal governor called him "the greatest pirate-broker that ever was in America."[64] Captain Every was never brought to justice, but dozens of his former crewmates settled in the American colonies, and several of his men faced trial in London in 1696. Their depositions exposed just how widespread the active support of piracy was in "private" colonies, and the Crown put the Lords Proprietors on notice.[65]

Parliament passed a number of sweeping acts from 1696 to 1701 meant to not only rein in piracy but to control and administer justice over the governors in private colonies.[66] Perhaps most threatening was the decision to implement formal vice-admiralty courts in the colonies with officers appointed by the Crown through the Admiralty in London. Although documents refer to Carolina's maritime tribunals as "admiralty courts," they did not have any tangible connection to the Lord High Admiral and Admiralty at all but were instead local modified versions of a common law criminal trial. Instead of the common law, these courts were supposed to be administered by the civil law. This was a codified law meant to assist international trade since foreigners could pursue cases without needing to know local common law traditions. Admiralty law was taught in Doctor's Commons away from the Inns of Court and was relatively unfamiliar to even the best-trained English lawyers. Worst of all, these courts administered justice without the use of a jury of one's peers, which was meant to speed the process in a transitory maritime world and to make justice fair for foreign merchants. By eliminating juries packed with the accessories to piracy, Parliament hoped justice could finally be served. Many members of the Carolina gentry feared the eradication of traditional rights of Englishmen in one fell swoop and suspected their proprietors were complicit.

At this critical juncture in the history of early South Carolina, Nicholas Trott the younger arrived on the scene, nephew of the disgraced governor of the Bahamas. Admitted to the Inner Temple in 1695, Trott was one of the first English-trained lawyers in America.[67] He was also experienced in the regulation of privateers and the abuses of piracy, having practiced law in Bermuda in the 1680s, where he had been the colony secretary and attorney general. The younger Trott paid for his uncle's reputation because many contemporaries, and even some modern historians, conflated the two men.[68] Trott was appointed in 1698 by the Lords Proprietors to be attorney general, advocate general of the admiralty court, and naval officer on the recommendation of customs official Edward Randolph.[69] When he arrived in May 1699, Trott quickly realized that the struggle for power between the proprietors and the Crown not only threatened local autonomy; it divided the colonial gentry. The Crown claimed control over admiralty court appointments, and Jonathan Amory already held the office of advocate general. When Amory died soon after, Trott took both positions at the behest of Governor Blake. The Admiralty subsequently appointed its own advocate general, former governor Joseph Morton.[70]

Not only was Nicholas Trott angry that Joseph Morton usurped his appointment; more important, he feared the new court would challenge the sanctity of the common law and trial by jury. His training at the Inner Temple made Trott well versed in the nearly century-long battle between advocates of the common and civil law that sometimes masked a deeper conflict over the rights of the people (based in specific local precedents) versus the royal prerogative (exemplified by royal proclamations). With the help of Trott's expansive legal knowledge, the Carolina General Assembly, where Trott was elected Speaker, essentially ignored Parliament by establishing an admiralty court of its own making that used the common law and local juries. The assembly also curtailed the power of this court by limiting the fees taken by court officers and opened those officers to fines and countersuits, which hamstrung their ability to pursue cases. References to fourteenth-century precedent in these statutes reveal Trott's fingerprints.[71] As a Crown appointee, Morton feared the acts not only ignored the Crown's explicit commands, but also assured the protection of illicit trade since most jury members were personally complicit.[72]

Realizing their actions directly challenged both Proprietary and royal authority in Carolina, colonial authorities held a show trial to feign loyalty. In 1700 Captain John Breholt arrived in Charles Town in the *Carlisle* frigate. Breholt had allegedly committed a number of acts of piracy with an international crew. The English members of his crew abandoned him and when they arrived in town pretended to be the victims of piracy rather than its perpetrators. This turned out to be a poor decision because one of their victims was Trott's brother-in-law, Captain William Rhett, one of the most powerful merchants in Carolina, and they arrived in Charles Town when customs official Edward Randolph happened to be in town. They were seized and tried, but in a public show of defiance, not in a "vice-admiralty" court but before a jury in "a Sessions of Oyer & Terminer & Goal Delivery for the Jurisdiction of ye Admiralty," where eight men were convicted and later executed. Breholt on the other hand was acquitted.

Despite the conviction, Governor Blake feared the obvious irregularities of the court proceedings (particularly Trott's unwillingness to refer to the tribunal as a "vice-admiralty court") might give Randolph even more ammunition against proprietary regimes. Trott's enemies claimed Breholt was acquitted because he was the judge's friend. Immediately after, the captain allegedly gathered a new crew of local debtors and pirates he helped escape from the Charles Town jail. He then fitted out a vessel "and made it his business to make it known everywhere that he was bound to ye redd Seas."[73] One royal official wrote to the secretary of state that he heard "there were abt half a dousin Pyrats lately hang'd in Carolina, but it was because they were poor" while "the rich ones appear'd publickly and were not molested in the least."[74] In 1709 a former Red Sea pirate testified that Breholt did in fact sail out of Charles Town harbor in the ship *Carlisle* in 1700 with the "intention to go to

Madagascar a pyrating."[75] As in many accusations of piracy, it is difficult to surmise which parts of this story were true and which parts were merely accusations against political rivals. Governor Blake removed Trott from his office as naval officer. Edward Randolph defended Trott, believing that it was actually his zeal in condemning the pirates that offended the governor, especially because at least Carolinians were no longer pretending these men were merely "privateers."[76] The members of the General Assembly were clearly pleased with Trott's attempts to steer a middle ground that protected their autonomy, so they restored him to his former positions.

When Blake died in September 1700, Joseph Morton was next in succession as determined by the charter. The Carolina Council blocked his appointment by voting him "incapable of the Government" in retaliation for accepting the Admiralty's commission as judge of the detested vice-admiralty court.[77] The Council elected their own governor, James Moore, a Goose Creek man and notorious pirate supporter. Despite the controversy, the Admiralty issued Moore a commission to try pirates in the summer of 1701.[78] Accepting such a commission, in Trott's eyes, was just as criminal by Moore as it had been by Morton. After Trott voiced his displeasure, Moore had him arrested on charges of sedition.[79] These simmering confrontations rose to a boil when a locally owned vessel, the *Cole and Bean,* charged with illegal trade, was brought before the vice-admiralty court. In his position as attorney general, chosen by the proprietors, Trott protested the Admiralty's jurisdiction in Carolina by refusing to prosecute the vessel. Joseph Morton claimed that Trott, as prosecutor, actually "espoused the cause of the defendant, and, in the open street and among a crowd of people, fell upon the Informer, and struck him several times, crying out, this is the Informer, this is he that will ruin the country."[80] A riot ensued.

While Carolinians battled over who controlled the port of Charles Town, former governor Robert Quary, a man once deposed by the proprietors for supporting piracy, returned to the colony. During his absence, Quary was paradoxically appointed vice-admiralty judge of Pennsylvania in 1697, where he battled the local Quaker dignitaries who controlled William Penn's proprietary colony. He was rewarded for his service to the Crown when he was appointed to replace Edward Randolph as surveyor general of his majesty's customs upon his death. When the prodigal son returned to Charles Town, he focused his venom on Carolina's "irregularities," recognizing that the statutes passed against piracy were really designed to thwart the power of the Admiralty. Quary reported to the Board of Trade that Carolinians continued to "entertain and encourage pirates," and through these "disloyal and unjust actions grow rich and get estates." Carolina would soon become like the Bahamas under these proprietors, where "by the corruption, rapine, and extortion of the late Governors, they seemed only to shelter, receive and harbour Pirates, and encourage all manner of illegal trade." In Carolina there was "nothing but anarchy and confusion," while Virginia was a model governments led by "experienced and vigilant Generals." This anarchy stemmed from what he considered radical and "licentious Commonwealth principles." The Carolina gentry considered the inhabitants of royal colonies "slaves and miserable in comparison of themselves."[81]

Despite these direct challenges to their charter, Carolinians continued to believe that the colony's fragile position on the border of the Spanish Empire required extralegal measures. This belief compelled Governor Moore to launch a preemptive strike on St. Augustine in 1702, a year of peace, with the assistance of military intelligence provided by pirates.[82] The general failure of the siege led Moore's enemies to claim that the preemptive strike was really "a Project of Freebooting under the specious Name of War."[83] In response the French and Spanish decimated New Providence in the Bahamas. Quary warned the Board of Trade that the cycle of violence would end only with a strong royal governor paid for by the Crown and not beholden to plunder profits.[84]

The Lords Proprietors appointed Nicholas Trott chief justice in 1703, from which post he gauged how many Carolinians feared royal officials like Quary were using the "piracy problem" to eliminate the trial by jury, implement a "foreign" law, remove the charter that protected their liberal form of government as well as religious toleration among other rights, and replace governors beholden to merchant interests with one answerable only to the Crown. This was exactly what happened in Boston in 1704 when Captain John Quelch was tried before a vice-admiralty court presided over by men appointed by the Crown without a jury of his peers leading to a popular uproar.[85] We know Nicholas Trott and his brother-in-law William Rhett paid attention to the controversial Quelch trial because Rhett later criticized the legal sophistries of the proceedings in a letter to the commissioner of customs.[86] Clearly Trott and Rhett agreed such an injustice should never happen in Charles Town. Was it really worth losing fundamental rights to preserve an informal legal culture designed to protect the short-term financial rewards of the pirate market?

Trott began to plot a middle ground by gradually formalizing the colony's legal culture while also aggressively protecting what he considered inalienable rights. Over the next few years, he wrote down his own speeches given to Charles Town juries. With the fervent zeal of a missionary, he lectured Carolinians on the history of the common law, warned about the evils of jury corruption, and waxed poetic about the sanctity of oaths. The acquittal of pirates in Charles Town threatened these institutions. One visitor complained in 1709 that Carolina still would accept English laws only if they were passed by the local assembly, making the legal system "a strange sort of Proteus capable of putting on all shapes and figures as occasion requires."[87] Over the next decade, Trott molded this Proteus into a formal body by assembling Carolina's first written body of laws in 1712.[88] That year the General Assembly passed another act further limiting the authority of vice-admiralty courts. Trott referred to fourteenth- and fifteenth-century legal precedent to delineate exactly with

"What things the Admiral and his Deputy shall meddle." Soon after, the assembly passed another act against piracy in direct confrontation with the Parliamentary Act of 1700 by assuring that accused pirates would receive a trial by jury composed of twelve men who "inhabited in the shire." Rewriting Charles Town's recent history and instead referring to legal debates under Henry VIII, the act bluntly stated that pirates had gone unpunished *because* they had been tried in admiralty courts "after the course of the civil laws."[89] The Lords Proprietors were so pleased with Trott's formalization of the colony's laws when he visited London in 1714 that they extended his authority so that no laws could be passed without his approval, a power revoked by a perturbed assembly in 1716.[90] He even acquired a Proprietary right.[91]

Like Jamaica decades before, Carolina transformed into a slave society that produced a staple crop (rice) that actually benefited from the protection of global shipping lanes during the first decade of the eighteenth century. The elimination of the Royal African Company's monopoly in 1698 helped independent traders to rapidly expand the legal supply of slaves, especially in colonies north of the West Indies. After the Treaty of Utrecht (1713), England's involvement in the slave trade rose dramatically. Peter Wood has shown how slaves made up roughly a quarter of the population of Carolina before 1695, which boomed to a majority over the course of less than two decades.[92] No longer suppliers of slaves, pirates now directly threatened their importation to Charles Town. For example, in 1718 the pirate Charles Vane took a slave ship from Guinea on its way to Carolina. A crew of primarily Spanish and French pirates attacked merchant captain Nicholas Webb on his way to Charles Town with 155 slaves.[93] As in Jamaica, these attacks heightened the anxiety over the specter of slave revolt exacerbated by Spanish offers of freedom to Carolina slaves in order to disrupt its economy.[94]

Charles Town's reputation as a pirate nest was difficult to shake. In 1716 James Fellows, an officer of the royal ship *Shoreham*, used to hunt pirates, was arrested for declaring "that all the Inhabitants of this Province were pirates."[95] Determined to display the colony's transformation, Trott tried pirates in June 1717, leading to the execution of four men. In June 1718, Blackbeard laid siege to Charles Town, capturing two eminent Carolinians, one of whom, Samuel Wragg, was a member of the Council. Blackbeard threatened to kill the men and burn their vessel if he was not provided with a chest of medicine. While Charles Town led the assault on piracy, the Lords Proprietors' more peripheral holdings either passively accepted the sea marauders or succumbed to their superior power. In 1717 pirates descended on New Providence, making Carolina's sister colony their stronghold. Governor Eden in North Carolina was either coerced or bribed by Blackbeard when he arrived in the town of Bath. Soon after, a crew of Virginians captained by a royal navy officer captured Blackbeard and decapitated him.[96]

The Carolina gentry once so welcoming to global pirates now launched their own attacks. Governor Robert Johnson personally took command of a squadron to combat pirates sited off the harbor. According to one eyewitness, after a brutal struggle Johnson's men took the pirates "within Sight of Charles-Town: The People seeing the Action from the Tops of their Houses, and the Masts of the Ships in the Harbour, where they had placed themselves for that Purpose." The pirates' booty consisted of both male and female transported convicts. The pirates had planned to take the "virtuous Ladies" to one of the Bahamas Islands, where they would have founded "a most hopeful Colony."[97]

William Rhett with a crew of Carolinians captured Stede Bonnet and his crew after a brutal four-hour engagement leaving twenty-nine of Rhett's own men dead or wounded.[98] Bonnet had actually owned an estate in Barbados, where he lived with his wife and children and had business relations and sympathizers in Charles Town. One account claimed this "Gentleman Pirate" turned to sea marauding after he went insane "occasioned by some Discomforts he found in a married State."[99] While his crew was held in the Guard House, Bonnet stayed in the house of a local merchant, under guard at night. Because the colony did not possess a royal commission to try pirates two weeks after Bonnet was brought to Charles Town, the General Assembly voted itself permission by passing another act "for the more speedy and regular trial of pirates." This time, the assembly eliminated many of the loopholes of previous acts but maintained the use of a jury. Unlike its predecessors, the act referred to pirates as not only "enemies to his Majesty and his subjects, but to all of mankind."[100]

Evidently not everyone in Charles Town had changed their stance on piracy, and Bonnet and his skipper escaped with local assistance.[101] Concerned the rest of his crew might do the same, Nicholas Trott quickly tried all thirty-four in custody on October 28, 1718. Trott insisted on using a jury the way pirates would have been tried in England. He opened the trial with a four-hundred-line legal dissertation on the history and jurisdiction of the court of admiralty from its medieval origins to its present manifestation in Carolina. The treatise quoted extensively from some of the greatest luminaries of common and civil law: Godolphin, Selden, Grotius, Coke, Spelman, Ridley, and many others. Trott even displayed his keen grasp of Greek, Latin, and Hebrew in order to provide adequate translations of ancient definitions of piracy from their original texts, including the legal precedents of ancient Rome and the Old Testament, one of his particular realms of expertise. His arguments in favor of a guilty verdict were so convincing and persuasive, the local jury found twenty-nine men guilty. The indomitable William Rhett recaptured Bonnet the following day, just in time to witness the largest mass hanging on the American mainland at Chalk Point.

Bonnet was finally put on trial on November 10 and convicted after a long speech by Trott that resembled an execution sermon citing the Bible twenty-two times. Despite his success in prolonging the case, Bonnet was executed on December 10, 1718. The Bonnet trial did more than simply put to rest Charles Town's reputation as a pirate nest. The trial was printed, along with Trott's speech, in London in 1719, and both were again reprinted in Captain Charles Johnson's widely popular *General History of the Pirates* (1724).[102] Nicholas Trott transformed a place synonymous with informality into the standard bearer of piracy law, and his treatise provided precedent into the twentieth century, making it arguably one of English America's first great contributions to the "law of nations."[103]

For decades Trott helped protect Carolina from the encroaching power of the Crown and the Admiralty. As a show of gratitude, Trott was made a proprietor in his own right. Unfortunately for him the rising planter class had become increasingly frustrated with proprietors' inability to protect their property and interests. Envisioning the long-term benefits of becoming an important part of an integrated empire where piracy did more harm than good, they became determined that as long their natural rights were safe they were better off under a royal regime.[104] When word spread that the Spanish were planning a massive assault in 1719, Carolinians rose up in rebellion against the Lords Proprietors, ousted Trott from office, and begged for royal protection. The Admiralty sent the *Flamborough* to protect Charles Town's harbor.[105] Trott returned to London, where he presented a printed copy of the trial to the Society for the Propagation of the Gospel in 1720. He later published *The Laws of the British Plantations* (1721) and was awarded a doctorate in civil law from Oxford in 1720 and doctor of laws degree from the University of Aberdeen in 1726. In 1736 he completed *The Laws of the Province of South Carolina*, codifying the colony's statutes up to 1719.

To bring order to the colony, the Crown appointed none other than royalist pirate hunter Francis Nicholson in 1721. After 1725 a sloop protected the coast that ranged as far north as the Chesapeake. That summer the Carolina Council feared that if the Bahamas continued to be "a nest of Pyrates," they would "render us in a manner tributary to the latter."[106] Working with Virginia's Governor Spotswood, Nicholson aggressively attacked the last vestiges of the pirate market between New Providence and Charles Town, only this time with wide local support.[107] When Carolina Captain James Sutherland captured a pirate vessel with thirty-five men off the bar of Charles Town in May 1725, he issued a petition to the Crown for a reward signed by "135 of the principal inhabitants."[108]

In 1729 the Crown officially purchased North and South Carolina, appointing Robert Johnson royal governor of the latter. When Johnson finally arrived in Charles Town in 1731, his speech to the General Assembly proclaimed that royal government would finally provide the "Security we have been long praying for, the good Effects of which we only experience by the Safety we enjoy, as well in our Trade by the Protection of our Ships" from the insolence of pirates.[109] Now both Charles Town merchants and planters were formally part of an integrally connected British Empire.

Notes

The majority of this essay originated in my dissertation, "The Pirate Nest: The Impact of Piracy on Newport, Rhode Island and Charles Town, South Carolina 1670–1740" (Ph.D. diss., Harvard University, 2006), under the guidance of Laurel Thatcher Ulrich, Joyce Chaplin, and Jill Lepore.

1. Nuala Zahedieh, "Trade, Plunder, and Economic Development in Early English Jamaica, 1655–89," *Economic History Review* 39, no. 2 (May 1986): 205–22.

2. For more on the Indian slave trade, see Alan Gallay, *The Indian Slave Trade: The Rise of the English Empire in the American South, 1670–1717* (New Haven: Yale University Press, 2002).

3. For example, three vessels left Charles Town in 1687 headed for the South Sea "but were beaten back by foul weather at Magellan's strait, and forced into Providence." Lt. Gov. Molesworth to William Blathwayt, December 7, 1687, in *CSPC, 1685–1688*, no. 1555; Sir Thomas Lynch to the Lords of Trade and Plantations, September 12, 1683, CO 1/52, no. 95.

4. Sir Thomas Lynch to Secretary Leoline Jenkins, July 26, 1683, in *CSPC, 1681–1685*, no. 1163; Sir Thomas Lynch to Lords of Trade and Plantations, February 28, 1684, in *CSPC, 1681–1685*, no. 1563.

5. Lt. Gov. Molesworth to William Blathwayt, October 5, 1686, in *CSPC, 1686–1688*, no. 897.

6. Paper submitted to the Commissioners of Customs by Edward Randolph, August 17, 1696, in *CSPC, 1696–1697*, no. 149i; see also CO 5/1287, p. 101–2, 127, March 21, 1698.

7. *Representation of Mr. Byrd Concerning Proprietary Governments* (1699), Brock Collection, Huntington Library, San Marino, Cal., mss. 744; Reports of typical Red Sea pirate ventures that began or ended in Charles Town are in Names of fifteen Red Sea pirates who came to Pennsylvania from South Carolina in 1692, August 17, 1696, in *CSPC, 1696–1697*, no. 149x; Memorial of Sir Robert Robinson to the King, November 23, 1696, in *CSPC, 1696–1697*, no. 416; Examination of John Dann, mariner, of Rochester, August 3, 1696, in *CSPC, 1696–1697*, no. 517iv.

8. Lt. Gov. Nicholson to Lords of Trade and Plantations, July 16, 1692, in *CSPC, 1689–1692*, no. 2344; for more estimates see Gov. the Earl of Bellomont to Secretary Vernon, January 3, 1701, in *CSPC, 1701*, no. 7; Randolph, *A Discourse About Pyrates* (1696), Ms. GOS 9, National Maritime Museum, Greenwich, U.K.

9. George F. Steckley, "Litigious Mariners: Wage Cases in the Seventeenth-Century Admiralty Court," *Historical Journal* 42, no. 2 (June 1999): 319.

10. For example, See Shirley Hughson, *Blackbeard and the Carolina Pirates* (Hampton, Va.: Port Hampton Press, 2000), 12; Louis B. Wright, *South Carolina* (New York: Norton, 1976), 16.

11. Quoted in Oldmixon, *The British Empire in America* (London: 1708), 336.

12. Frank J. Klingberg, ed., *Carolina Chronicle: The Papers of Commissary Gideon Johnston 1707–1716* (Berkeley: University of California Press, 1946), 22.

13. For example see Marcus Rediker, *Villains of All Nations* (Boston: Beacon Press, 2004); Rediker and Peter Linebaugh, *The Many-Headed Hydra* (Boston: Beacon Press, 2001); Gabriel Kuhn, *Life under the Jolly Roger* (Oakland, Cal.: PM Press, 2010).

14. The most infamous was Captain Coxon: William Blathwayt to Lord Craven, Whitehall, August 31, 1682, CO 1/49, nos. 40, 40i; Journal of Lords of Trade and Plantations, August 31, 1682, CO 391/4, pp. 50–52.

15. Lords Proprietors to Gov. James Colleton, March 3, 1687, in *CSPC, 1685–1688*, no. 1161; See also Lords Proprietors to Gov. James Colleton, October 10, 1687, in *CSPC, 1685–1688*, no. 1457.

16. Lt. Gov. Nicholson to Lords of Trade and Plantations, July 16, 1692, in *CSPC, 1689–1692*, no. 2344.

17. Symon Musgrave to [Governor Sir Thomas Lynch?], September 29, 1682, in *CSPC, 1681–1685*, no. 709; also Sir Thomas Lynch to Secretary Sir Leoline Jenkins, November 6, 1682, no. 769; Sir Thomas Lynch to the Lord President of the Council, June 20, 1684, no. 1759; Lieutenant Governor Hender Molesworth to William Blathwayt, February 3, 1684, no. 2067.

18. J. Leitch Wright Jr., "Andrew Ranson: Seventeenth Century Pirate?," *Florida Historical Quarterly* 39, no. 2 (October 1960): 142.

19. Private Instructions of the Lords Proprietors to Seth Sothell, November 8, 1691, CO 5/288, pp. 52, 196.

20. Lords Proprietors to Paul Grimball, October 17, 1687, in *CSPC, 1685–1688*, no. 1465; Sirmans, *Colonial South Carolina*, 41; Earl of Craven to Lords of Trade and Plantation, May 27, 1684, in *CSPC, 1681–1685*, no. 1707.

21. Earl of Shaftesbury to the Governor and Council at Charles Town, June 10, 1675, in *CSPC, 1675–76*, no. 581.

22. Fundamental Constitutions of Carolina, January 12, 1682, in *CSPC, 1681–1685*, no. 359; Fundamental Constitutions of Carolina, August 17, 1682, no. 656. See also nos. 496–98 and no. 807.

23. Nairne, quoted in *Selling a New World*, ed. Jack Greene (Columbia: University of South Carolina Press, 1989), 44, 46, 48–49.

24. Sir Richard Kyrle came from Ireland but died soon after his arrival, so John Archdale was the only governor to sail across the Atlantic with the intention of becoming governor.

25. Gary L. Hewitt, "The State in the Planter's Service," in *Money, Trade, and Power: The Evolution of Colonial South Carolina's Plantation Society*, ed. Jack P. Greene, Rosemary Brana-Shute, and Randy Sparks (Columbia: University of South Carolina Press, 2001), 59.

26. Robert M. Weir, *Colonial South Carolina: A History* (Columbia: University of South Carolina Press, 1997), 39; Lords Proprietors of Carolina to Paul Grimball, October 6, 1690, in *CSPC, 1689–1692*, no. 1094; Lords Proprietors of Carolina to [Gov. Colleton?], October 18, 1690, in *CSPC, 1689–1692*, no. 1118.

27. *An Essay on Currency, Written in 1732* (Charles Town, 1734). One observer described the currency of Charles Town in 1710 as composing French Pistoles, Spanish and Arabian Gold, Dutch and German dollars, Peruvian and Mexican pieces of eight, but there was very "little English money": Greene, *Selling a New World*, 57. See also Gov. the Earl of Bellomont to the Board of Trade, June 22, 1700, in *CSPC, 1700*, no. 580.

28. Wood, *Black Majority* (New York: Knopf, 1975), 44.

29. Sir Thomas Lynch to Lords of Trade and Plantations, September 29, 1682, CO 1/49, no. 66.

30. Lords Proprietors to Gov. Joseph West, March 13, 1685, in *CSPC, 1685–1688*, no. 59.

31. Lords Proprietors of Carolina to Gov. Joseph Morton, February 15, 1686, in *CSPC, 1685–1688*, no. 568; Lords Proprietors to Gov. Colleton, March 3, 1687, in *CSPC, 1685–1688*, no. 1165; Instructions to James Colleton, March 3, 1687, CO 5/288, p. 51.

32. Sir Thomas Lynch to Lords of Trade and Plantations, February 28, 1684, in *CSPC, 1681–1685*, no. 1563. Sir Leoline Jenkins to the Governors of all the Colonies, March 24, 1684, in *CSPC, 1681–1685*, no. 1605.

33. See Acts of the Privy Council (Colonial), February 27, 1683–84, vol. 2, no. 142; Lords Proprietors of Carolina to the Governor of Carolina, March 13?, 1684, in *CSPC, 1681–1685*, no. 1588. There are different antipiracy acts from 1685 to 1687. See *Statutes at Large*, 2:7–9, 25–27.

34. *Statutes at Large*, 2:9–10.

35. Lords Proprietors to Gov. Morton, April 22, 1686, in *CSPC, 1685–1688*, no. 639.

36. Lords Proprietors to Gov. Colleton, March 3, 1687, in *CSPC, 1685–1688*, no. 1161.

37. Gov. Richard Cony to the Earl of Sunderland, December 2, 1686, in *CSPC, 1685–1688*, no. 1029.

38. [Unknown] to Seth Sothell, [1688?], in *CSPC, 1685–1688*, no. 1962.

39. Instructions to Gov. James Colleton, March 3, 1687, in *CSPC, 1685–1688*, no. 1165.

40. Lords Proprietors to the Governor, Deputies, and Officers of South Carolina, May 27, 1691, in *CSPC, 1689–1692*, no. 1535; Hughson, *Blackbeard*, 29.

41. See Declaration of Captain George St. Loe respecting Bermuda, November 27, 1687, in *CSPC, 1685–1688*, no. 1533; Haskett to the Board of Trade, July 13, 1702, in *CSPC, 1702*, no. 746.

42. The Lt. Gov. Francis Nicholson to Lords of Trade and Plantations, June 10, 1691, in *CSPC, 1689–1692*, no. 1583.

43. Gov. Francis Nicholson to the Board of Trade, August 20, 1698, *Archives of Maryland* (Baltimore: Maryland Historical Society, 1883–), 23:488–503.

44. Lords Proprietors to Seth Sothell, May 13, 1691, in *CSPC, 1689–1692*, no. 1498.

45. Crown instructions to colonial governors bypassed proprietary colonies like South Carolina. See Labaree, *Royal Instructions*, 1:212.

46. Memorandum of Lords of Trade and Plantations, February 27, 1684, in *CSPC, 1681–1685*, no. 1560. See also no. 1561, no. 1578, no. 1582.

47. Jeremiah Basse to William Popple, July 26, 1697, *Documents Relating to the Colonial History of the State of New Jersey* (Trenton: New Jersey Historical Society, 1880–1928), 2:157–58.

48. Lords Proprietors of Carolina to the Deputies and Council of South Carolina, April 12, 1693, in *CSPC, 1693–1696*, no. 270; Lords Proprietors write to Carolina, April 10, 1693, in CHJ; *Commissions and Instructions from the Lords Proprietors to Public Officials of South Carolina, 1685–1715*, ed. A. S. Salley (Columbia: Historical Comission of South Carolina, 1916), 63.

49. Lords Proprietors to Governor Colleton, March 3, 1687, in *CSPC, 1685–1688*, no. 1161.

50. Circular letter from the King, October 13, 1687, in *CSPC, 1685–1688*, no. 1463.

51. Lords Proprietors to [Gov. Colleton], October 10, 1687, in *CSPC, 1685–1688*, no. 1457.

52. Lords Proprietors to Governor James Colleton, March 3, 1687, in *CSPC, 1685–1688*, no. 1165; Instructions to James Colleton, March 3, 1687, CO 5/288, p. 51.

53. Christopher Hill, *The World Turned Upside Down*, (New York: Viking, 1972), 217–19; J. M. Beattie, *Crime and the Courts in England 1600–1800* (Princeton: Princeton University Press, 1986), 314.

54. Frederick B. Tolles and E. Gordon Alderfer, eds., *The Witness of William Penn* (New York: Macmillan, 1957), 85–86; Craig Horle, "Judicial Encounters with Quakers, 1660–1688," *Journal of the Friends Historical Society* 54, no. 2 (1977).

55. Lords Proprietors to Governor of Carolina, September 30, 1683, in *CSPC, 1681–1685*, no. 1284.

56. William Nelson, *Americanization of the Common Law* (Cambridge: Harvard University Press, 1975), 165–66, 3–4; Hendrik Hartog, "Distancing Oneself from the Eighteenth Century," in Hendrik Hartog, ed., *Law in the American Revolution and the Revolution in the Law* (New York: New York University Press, 1981), 241.

57. Sirmans, "Politics in Colonial South Carolina: The Failure of Proprietary Reform, 1682–1694," *WMQ* 23, no. 1 (1966): 34–35; Lords Proprietors write to Carolina, April 10, 1693, in CHJ; John Oldmixon, *British Empire*, 493; See Jack P. Greene, ed., *Selling a New World*, 48–49; see also Thomas Nairne to [Earl of Sunderland?], July 28, 1709, in *CSPC, 1708–1709*, no. 662.

58. Lords Proprietors of Carolina to the Deputies and Council of South Carolina, in *CSPC, 1693–1696*, April 12, 1693 no. 270; Lords Proprietors write to Carolina, April 10, 1693, in CHJ, no. 1, p. 58.

59. Proposals for a Jury Act, November 21, 1695, in CHJ, no. 1, p. 58.

60. Governor Markham to William Penn, February 13, 1697, in *CSPC, 1697–1698*, no. 76xii.

61. Edward Randolph to William Popple, May 12, 1698, in *CSPC, 1697–1698*, no. 451.

62. *Representation of Mr. Byrd Concerning Proprietary Governments* (1699), Huntington Mss., BR 744.

63. Lieut. Gov. Nicholson to Lords of Trade and Plantations, November 13, 1691, in *CSPC, 1689–1692*, no. 1897.

64. Gov. the Earl of Bellomont to the Board of Trade, August 28, 1699, in *CSPC, 1699*, no. 746. Letters describing the incident are in the Records of the Lords Proprietors of Carolina and the Bahamas, CO 5/289, f. 26, 35, 69, 72; Inhabitants of the Bahamas Islands to the Board of Trade, April 7, 1702, in *CSPC, 1702*, no. 307; The Case of Nicholas Trott the elder, Esq., Late Gover. of the Bahama Islands Relating to the Ship Charles I's Fancey Henry Every, Sloane Manuscripts, British Library, 2902, f.270.

65. India Office Records, British Library, H/36 p. 199; *The Tryals of Joseph Dawson, Edward Forseith, William May, William Bishop, James Lewis, and John Sparkes for several piracies and robberies...* (London, 1696).

66. See Hanna, "The Pirate Nest," 174–217

67. Randall Bridwell, "Mr. Nicholas Trott and the South Carolina Vice Admiralty Court: An Essay on Procedural Reform and Colonial Politics," *South Carolina Law Review* 28 (1976): 184.

68. Records clearly report the attendance of "Nicholas Trott, senior and junior." Journal of Lords of Trade and Plantations, December 20, 1692, in *CSPC, 1689–1692*, no. 2698; see also no. 2700; William Popple of the Board of Trade distinguished between the "Trott who resides now in Carolina" as someone of "good Charact'r" as opposed to the Trott who was "formerly Governor of the Bahama Islands" who "lives under many ill Imputations" in a letter dated March 5, 1701, in BPRO-SC, 27:2. For confusion, see Oldmixon, *British Empire in America*.

69. A further list of officers suggested for the Admiralty Courts in the Colonies, August 10, 1696, in *CSPC, 1696–1697*, no. 120v; L. Lynn Hogue, "Nicholas Trott: Man of Law and Letters," *SCHM* 76, no. 1 (January 1975): 29.

70. Sirmans, *Colonial South Carolina*, 49, 52–53, 76.

71. October–November, 1700, in CHJ; *Statutes at Large*, 1:446–47.

72. Joseph Morton to the Board of Trade, August 29, 1701, in *CSPC, 1701*, no. 804; Robert Quarry to the Lords of the Admiralty, August 28, 1701, in *CSPC, 1701*, no. 798.

73. *Commissions and Instructions from the Lords Proprietors*, 133–35, 138–39.

74. Gov. the Earl of Bellomont to Mr. Secretary Vernon, January 3, 1701, in *CSPC, 1701*, no. 7.

75. Deposition of Laurence Waldron, barber-chyrurgeon, May 17, 1709, in *CSPC, 1708–1709*, no. 908ii.

76. Edward Randolph to the Board of Trade, February 19, 1701, in *CSPC, 1701*, no. 180.

77. Joseph Morton to the Board of Trade, August 29, 1701, in *CSPC, 1701*, no. 804.

78. Gov. Moore to Gov. Nicholson, August 12, 1701, in *CSPC, 1701*, no. 1042xid.

79. Hogue, "Nicholas Trott," 11.

80. Joseph Morton to [Francis Nicholson?], August 21, 1701, in *CSPC, 1701*, no. 1042xia; Sirmans, *Colonial South Carolina*, 82.

81. Col. Quary to the Board of Trade, March 26, 1702, in *CSPC, 1702*, no. 260; Col. Quary to the Board of Trade, June 5, 1700, in *CSPC, 1700*, no. 500; see *South Carolina Historical Society Collections*, 2:205; Leo Francis Stock, ed., *Proceedings and Debates of the British Parliaments respecting North America* (Washington, D.C.: Carnegie Institution of Washington, 1930), 3:19.

82. June 17, 1707, in CHJ.

83. Representatives of South Carolina to the Earl of Bathe, February 20, 1702, in *CSPC, 1702*, no. 38i; Charles W. Arnade, *The Siege of St. Augustine in 1702* (Gainesville: University of Florida Press, 1959).

84. Col. Quary to the Board of Trade, October 15, 1703, in *CSPC, 1702–1703*, no. 1150.

85. Hanna, "The Pirate Nest," chapter 7.

86. Report of Col. Wm. Rhett to the Commissioners of Customs, October 3, 1716, *Calendar Of Treasury Papers, 1714–1719, preserved in the Public Records Office* (London: Public Record Office, 1883), no. 40.

87. Thomas Nairne to [Earl of Sunderland?], July 28, 1709, in *CSPC, 1708–1709*, no. 662.

88. *Statutes at Large*, 7:440–41; see L. Lynn Hogue, "An Edition of 'Eight Charges Delivered . . . by Nicholas Trott, Esq.'" (Ph.D. diss., University of Tennessee, 1972). The original is in the Charleston Historical Society. See also Hogue, "Nicholas Trott," 25–34.

89. *Statutes at Large*, 7:446, 465–66.

90. Sirmans, *Colonial South Carolina*, 106.

91. Lords Proprietors of Carolina to the Deputies and Council of South Carolina, April 9, 1709, in *CSPC, 1708–1709*, no. 455.

92. Wood, *Black Majority*, 131; Sheridan, *Sugar and Slavery*, 249–53.

93. *American Weekly Mercury*, January 2, 1721. See also June 2, 1720, June 16, 1720, and July 13, 1721.

94. See Col. Jenings to the Board of Trade, March 21, 1709, in *CSPC, 1708–1709*, no. 421. For example, the governor of Bermuda felt pressure to let pardoned pirates have their booty for fear that they might instigate a slave uprising. Colonel Bennet to William Popple, 1718, Bermuda Records, CO 37/10 f.9; List of negroes etc. taken to St. Augustine, December 5, 1722, in *CSPC, 1722–1723*, no. 427iv; Gov. Nicholson to the Governor of St. Augustine, March 12, 1721, in *CSPC, 1722–1723*, no. 427xxix; Instructions for Francis Young, May 9, 1722, in *CSPC, 1722–1723*, no. 130i.

95. July 12, 1716, in *BPRO-SC*, vol. 20.

96. See Lindley S. Butler, *Pirates, Privateers, and Rebel Raiders of the Carolina Coast* (Chapel Hill: University of North Carolina Press, 2000), 25–50.

97. *A General History of the Pyrates*, ed. Manuel Schonhorn (Mineola, N.Y.: Dover, 1999), 302–3.

98. *Boston News-Letter*, December 29, 1718; Carolina Council Minutes, CO 5/427, f. 4.

99. Charles Johnson, *The General History of the Pyrates* (London, 1724), 91.

100. Once more the statute referred to such a trial as "the court of admiralty sessions." *Statutes at Large*, 7:41; see High Court of Admiralty Records 1/55 f. 1–4, National Archives, U.K.

101. *Boston News-Letter,* November 24, 1718.

102. *The Tryals of Major Stede Bonnet and other Pirates* (London, 1719); Johnson, *General History,* 103–12.

103. Sir Robert Phillimore, *Commentaries on International Law* (Philadelphia, 1854), 1:286–87; Edwin D. Dickinson, "Is the Crime of Piracy Obsolete?," *Harvard Law Review* 38, no. 3 (January 1925): 337–39, 342, 351; Francis Hargrave, ed., *A Complete Collection of State Trials,* 4th ed., 11 vols. (London: Printed by T. Wright for C. Bathurst and others, 1776–81), 6:155–88; Thomas Bayly Howell, ed., *Cobbett's Complete Collection of State Trials,* 33 vols. (London: Printed by T.C. Hansard for Longman, Hurst, Rees, Orme, and Brown, 1809–26), 15:1231–1302.

104. Sirmans, *Colonial South Carolina,* 116; Sherman, *Robert Johnson,* 37.

105. Stock, *Proceedings,* 5:127; A 1979 article by Peter Hoffer and N. E. H. Hull claimed Trott was an early example of impeachment in America, but John E. Douglass cleared this up in "Impeaching the Impeachment: The Case of Chief Justice Nicholas Trott of South Carolina," *SCHM* 84, no. 2 (April 1993): 102–16.

106. South Carolina Sessional Papers, August 16, 1721, CO 5/425 p. 60; Testimonials to Thomas Curphey, November, 1722, in *CSPC, 1722–1723,* no. 368i–iii.

107. Messrs. Buck, Harris and Hyde to the Board of Trade, June 11, 1723, in *CSPC, 1722–1723,* no. 579; Gov. Nicholson to the Board of Trade, August 21, 1723, in *CSPC, 1722–1723,* no. 687.

108. Petition of Capt. James Sutherland to the King, May 8, 1730, in *CSPC, 1730,* no. 216, no. 216i–ii.

109. Quoted in Oldmixon, *British Empire;* Sirmans, *Colonial South Carolina,* 162.

Part Four
Aftermaths

Forging Alliances

The Impact of the Tuscarora War on North Carolina's Political Leadership

CHRISTINE STYRNA DEVINE

During the winter of 1712, South Carolinian John Barnwell and his army of Indian recruits marched to Bath County, North Carolina, to help defend their northern neighbor from warring Tuscaroras and their Indian allies.[1] South Carolina officials sent the troops after receiving an urgent request for aid from the North Carolina government. As South Carolina forces campaigned against the Lower Towns of the Tuscaroras, Colonel Barnwell chronicled his thoughts on the Indians and North Carolinians. Throughout his journal, Barnwell expressed admiration for the formidable defense works and bravery of the "heathen" enemy. His impressions of North Carolina's political leaders and inhabitants, however, were less favorable. Barnwell partly attributed the inability of his army to capture the Tuscarora stronghold of Fort Hancock to the "base, cowardly" behavior of the local militia, who ran away and refused to fight. He also harshly criticized the colony's political leaders, many of whom resided in Albemarle County and thus were not directly affected by the Indian attacks. Barnwell accused North Carolina officials of being more preoccupied with personal "controversies" than with providing him with much-needed supplies. The South Carolina leader described his peers as lacking the refinement and civil deportment expected of men in leadership roles. In one entry Barnwell reported that members of the Lower House and Council celebrated his truce with the Indians of Fort Hancock "with such plenty of punch that they voted, acted, signed, and stripped stark naked and boxed it fairly two and two, all the same day."[2]

John Barnwell was one of several colonial outsiders who portrayed eighteenth-century North Carolina as a colony governed by inept leaders incapable of forming stable political institutions. Although Barnwell and other commentators had their own political agendas when writing about early North Carolina, their writings have become the basis for the standard historical narrative of early North Carolina's political development. This paper suggests that while North Carolina did suffer from a considerable degree of political unrest and factionalism in the late seventeenth and early eighteenth centuries, it experienced an important period of stable leadership and institutional growth following the outbreak of the colony's greatest political and economic crisis, the Tuscarora War. During that conflict, a group of prominent Anglican merchant-planters from Albemarle County formed a relatively stable and cohesive political bloc and continued to dominate political affairs in the colony until the mid-1720s. While attacks by the warring Tuscaroras and their Indian allies threatened to destroy the colony, it also created a set of circumstances conducive to the Albemarle elite's regional politics and their commercial and religious interests. Albemarle leaders quickly capitalized on the Indians' devastation of southern settlements and the unpopularity of Quakers and their pacifist beliefs to take charge of the government and eliminate the rival Quaker-Bath faction. These elites used their dominance in the Council and influence with the Lower House to enact policies that promoted commercial and institutional growth as well as their own personal interests.

Early North Carolina leadership and the impact of the Tuscarora War on the colony's political and economic development have received only cursory treatment from scholars. The limited scholarly literature on early North Carolina is due in part to the paucity of both government and personal records from the period. Political and constitutional historians such as Jack Greene were among the first scholars to examine North Carolina's political development in the context of institutional growth and leadership throughout the English colonies. They concluded that North Carolina, unlike colonies such as Virginia and South Carolina, continued to experience severe political unrest during the eighteenth century that hampered the formation of self-governing institutions. These historians attributed the colony's stunted political growth to the absence of a stable and cohesive group of leaders. Greene and several other scholars noted that the colony enjoyed a period of political harmony between 1714 and 1725, during which time the North Carolina Lower House expanded its powers in key areas of public finance, expenditures, and legislative apportionment. They did not explain, however, what factors or individuals might have initiated this important phase in the colony's history.[3] A closer examination of leadership and legislation from that period indicates that political stability and growth occurred as a result of the ascendancy of an influential group of leaders from Albemarle County in the provincial government. The Albemarle elite were able to solidify their power as a result of the outbreak of the Tuscarora War, which provided them the opportunity to take control of the Council and use their political leverage to implement legislation that expanded the powers of the colonial assembly and promoted their political and economic interests. These findings suggest that while early North Carolina politics was tumultuous for much of the eighteenth century, the colony did experience a period of stable political leadership in the wake of the war that had far-reaching consequences for its institutional and commercial growth.

While the war provided a small cadre of leaders with the opportunity to dominate the government, other factors contributed to their political and commercial success. Jacqueline Wolf and Charles Lowry's research on the distribution of wealth in proprietary North Carolina indicates that those who held local and provincial political office came from the wealthiest minority of land- and slaveholders in the colony, whereas the vast majority of colonists were small farmers with few or no slaves. They also found that over half of the officeholders were members of the Church of England, suggesting that religious affiliation was an important factor in the pursuit of status and power. Wolf and Lowry attributed much of North Carolina's political unrest and factionalism in the early eighteenth century to the influx of new colonists whose commercial ambitions and, in some cases, dissenting religious beliefs, challenged those of more established Albemarle leaders.[4]

While Lowry and Wolfe's work shows that landed and personal wealth were important traits of early North Carolina leaders, further research suggests that political success, especially during and after the war, depended on other factors as well. Albemarle leaders cultivated political support within the community by providing an array of financial and legal services to their less affluent neighbors. These interpersonal relationships were a necessary step in building a strong social and political network. North Carolina leaders also increasingly turned to group-oriented politics as a means of increasing their political leverage. Beginning in the early eighteenth century, certain pro-Anglican leaders began to use religion as a political tool to generate group unity and to discredit their Quaker political rivals. These leaders intensified their political attacks on Quakers following the outbreak of the Tuscarora War and succeeded in enacting legislation that eliminated members of that religious sect from political office for the remainder of the proprietary period. After the war the Albemarle elite continued to work together to pass laws that brought greater commercial wealth to themselves and the colony.

Despite their efforts to keep their political competitors at bay, the Albemarle elite ultimately failed to build a long-lasting political dynasty. Albemarle leaders found it increasingly difficult to maintain their political hegemony as new settlers migrated into the lower Cape Fear region and the territory west of Albemarle Sound after the war. Historians A. Roger Ekirch and Brad Wood first identified the regional limitations of political power in North Carolina in their examination of colonial society and politics during the royal period. Both scholars argued that North Carolina's unique and varied geography, coupled with the different ethnic makeup and economies of the Albemarle and Cape Fear regions, fostered the growth of a regional rather than provincial political leadership.[5] This study builds on their work and shows that the Tuscarora War not only promoted the growth of regional leadership in Albemarle County but also led to the development of the lower Cape Fear and its emergence as a distinctive region with its own culture and leadership. Brad Wood points out in his study of the lower Cape Fear that the influx of colonists from different cultural backgrounds, coupled with the growth of a staple crop economy and transatlantic trade in the lower Cape Fear, led to the formation of a unique society and group of leaders whose wealth and ambition rivaled that of the Albemarle elite.[6] The ascendancy of the Cape Fear planters paralleled the slow decline of the Albemarle faction, which continued to lose political ground as a result of growing internal divisions and the deaths of certain prominent members. By the time the Crown took control of the colony in 1729, lower Cape Fear leaders had begun to challenge the power of the established Albemarle elite, plunging the colony into a new era of regional strife and political factionalism.

Reconstructing the political careers and lives of early North Carolina leaders is a difficult endeavor at best. Few legislative records have survived, making it difficult to trace membership in the Lower House or gain a complete understanding of that body's proceedings. Council minutes, on the other hand, exist for twenty-three of the years during this span of time, providing an almost continual record of membership. This study subsequently focuses on those individuals who ultimately received appointments to the Council, the most powerful political body in the colony during the proprietary period. Since few journals or personal letters of colonists have survived from the period, information on local leadership for this study comes from Council minutes, court records, land grants, tax lists, and shipping information gained from naval office lists and the *Boston Newsletter*. After 1694 the number of higher court records increases dramatically, providing valuable information about the economic activities and multiple legal and financial roles leaders played within the community. The court records also identify leaders who, besides serving in the provincial government, also held important positions of power within the court system. The letter book of Thomas Pollock also provides insights into the personal political thoughts and business dealings of perhaps the most powerful leader of the Albemarle elite.

Provincial and local records for the late seventeenth and early eighteenth centuries indicate that most individuals who ultimately gained political office came to the colony seeking new political and economic opportunities. The most successful colonists were those who either brought with them or quickly acquired the resources needed to invest in commercial ventures and increase their material wealth. Besides acquiring land, many ambitious newcomers also became entrepreneurs involved in various aspects of the coastwise and transatlantic trade. Thomas Pollock was an immigrant from Glasgow, Scotland, who traveled throughout British North America as a coastwise merchant before settling as a planter and merchant in Chowan precinct in the 1680s. Pollock suffered considerable financial losses during his first years in Albemarle as a result of fluctuating markets, lack of salt to preserve pork, and the raids of Spanish privateers. By 1700, however, Pollock had not only recovered his losses but was well on his way to becoming one of the most successful and powerful merchant-planters in the colony. Besides producing naval stores, provisions, and deer skins, Pollock acquired his own vessels and marketed his goods throughout the English colonies. Pollock also increased his wealth and status by renting his slaves to other planters, extending credit to other colonists, and serving as an attorney and executor for merchants and planters within and outside of northern Carolina.

Pollock's political career paralleled his rising material gains. After his settlement in Albemarle, proprietor Lord Craven appointed Pollock as his deputy on the Grand Council, a position he held continuously from 1694 to 1708. Pollock also was elected to the assembly and served as a justice in the General Court until 1698, when proprietary deputies no longer automatically sat on the court. Although his early religious affiliation is not clear, Pollock became one of the first colonists to serve as a vestryman for the Anglican parish in Chowan precinct during the early eighteenth century. At the beginning of the Tuscarora War, Pollock was an established member of the provincial government and one of the wealthiest men in the colony, with more than twenty slaves and over several thousand acres of land.[7]

Some merchant-planters came to northern Carolina for religious as well as economic reasons. The proprietors' policy of religious toleration attracted a steady flow of Quakers into the northern precincts in the late seventeenth and early eighteenth centuries, including several individuals who became prominent merchant-planters and officeholders. While few Quaker merchants achieved the same degree of economic wealth as their Anglican peers, they still owned more real and personal property than the average colonist.[8] John Hawkins was a Quaker who fled England in the late seventeenth century and settled in Pasquotank precinct, where he became an elder in the Pasquotank Monthly Meeting. During his lifetime Hawkins acquired a respectable estate of at least six hundred acres of land and several slaves. He also was part owner of a vessel and marketed his own goods as well as those of other colonists. Hawkins's important roles as Quaker elder, merchant-planter, and justice in the Pasquotank precinct court may explain why he was chosen by various individuals to act as their attorney, witness, and administrator in the local and provincial courts. Perhaps the greatest affirmation of Hawkins's status in colonial society was his appointment to the Council in 1707.

Another Quaker, Gabriel Newby, achieved even greater wealth. Newby participated in the coastwise trade, although he appears to have been a captain or commander rather than owner of vessels. He also amassed a considerable estate of nine hundred acres of land and more than six slaves before dying in 1735.[9] Like Hawkins, Newby also was chosen to serve on the Council. The appointment of Hawkins and Newby to the most powerful political body in the colony reflected growing Quaker participation in colonial government during the early eighteenth century.

Several merchant-planters who came to northern Carolina also hoped to pursue new trade and investment opportunities in Bath County. Beginning in the early eighteenth century, a growing number of colonists began to settle along the rivers and inlets of Bath County and formed their own commercial network.[10] Christopher Gale was one of several colonists who came to Bath County to participate in the skin and fur trade. Unlike most colonists, Gale arrived in the colony with the personal resources needed to become a significant trader and merchant. Gale's family was part of the English gentry, and several of his relatives held positions of power within the Church of England. After arriving in the colony, Gale improved his economic and political fortunes considerably in 1702 by marrying Sarah Lakar Harvey, the widow of former deputy governor Thomas Harvey. This marriage provided him with more political and commercial connections, which he used to become a leading Indian trader and merchant in Bath County. Only three years after his arrival, Gale had expanded his trade in skins and furs to include more distant western tribes such as the Cherokees and Catawbas. During this time, Gale also became active in the coastwise trade with Virginia and England. In 1703 Deputy Governor Robert Daniel named Gale to serve as a justice on the General Court. The appointment marked the beginning of a judicial career that would continue until the end of the proprietary period and make Gale one of the most powerful individuals in the colony.[11]

Among the most successful merchant-planters in North Carolina was Edward Moseley. Moseley arrived in Chowan precinct in 1704 with no real or personal property and no familial or commercial ties. Within a year of settling in North Carolina, Moseley succeeded in securing a considerable fortune in land and tenements by marrying Madame Anne Walker, the widow of the former deputy governor of Albemarle, Henderson Walker. Immediately following his betrothal, Moseley gained appointments to the Council, precinct court, and Chowan vestry. He also won election to the Lower House in 1708 and served frequently in that office for the rest of his life. Though he initially settled in Albemarle County, Moseley quickly turned his attention to the development of the southern frontier, especially the lower Cape Fear, and pursued land and trade deals in various regions of the colony. Moseley's unbridled ambition and early success may be one of the reasons he and other leaders such as Thomas Pollock ultimately did not become long-lasting allies in the government.[12]

In certain respects North Carolina leaders during the late seventeenth and early eighteenth centuries shared common traits with their social and political counterparts in Virginia and Maryland.[13] Many, although not all, of these leading colonists came from middling planter and/or merchant families in Virginia and the British Isles and used their connections to further their commercial interests and political goals. Furthermore Chesapeake and northern Carolina leaders did not limit their economic activities to agricultural pursuits but rather were entrepreneurs who invested in a wide range of business ventures and facilitated local exchange within the community by collecting debts, extending credit, and serving as attorneys and witnesses for business associates.[14]

Despite the similarities, North Carolina leaders differed from the Virginia and Maryland elite in two important ways. By the first decade of the eighteenth century, many members of the Chesapeake elite were native born and came from a select group of families that had formed strong bonds through intermarriage and trade. These men also reaffirmed their social position by assuming leadership roles within the local Anglican churches. They built churches, served as vestrymen, and attended church services in order to affirm their position within the emerging social hierarchy of plantation society. Most North Carolina leaders, on the other hand, were recent immigrants to the colony and shared few personal ties with one another or had only recently married into an established family. Furthermore, until the beginning of the eighteenth century, neither English nor Anglican officials had made a concerted effort to build churches or establish a strong religious presence in North Carolina. Leaders thus were not initially able to use the established church as a means of building their social network or cultivating political unity within their ranks.

The absence of Anglican churches in North Carolina stood in contrast to the rapid establishment of Quaker meetings in Albemarle County. Unlike Anglican officials, Quaker leaders in North Carolina benefited from a strong social and religious network. Although they tended to have less landed and personal wealth than their Anglican counterparts, members of the Society of Friends formed tight-knit communities and had the potential to derail the economic and political ambitions of non-Quaker leaders. The Reverend Mr. James Blair informed his superior in England that, unlike Anglican colonists, the Quakers acted unanimously in political decisions, and "stand truly to one another in whatsoever may be their interest." Various officials and Anglican ministers also reported that the number of Quaker officeholders was steadily increasing during the late seventeenth and early eighteenth centuries. Extant Council records between 1693 and 1708 indicate that at least one Quaker, and sometimes several, sat on the Council. In 1703 former deputy governor Henderson Walker and the Reverend Mr. James Blair reported that at least half the delegates in the Lower House were members of the Society of Friends. Although Walker and Blair may have overstated their case, their concern suggests that Quaker influence in the provincial government was growing and presented a threat to Anglican leaders.[15]

The growing political power and material wealth of Quakers prompted Thomas Pollock and other Albemarle leaders to work together to eliminate their political rivals. Fear of a powerful Quaker bloc drove Anglican officials in the Council and Lower House to pursue religious and apportionment policies intended to undercut the political power of Quaker officeholders as well as officials who favored the development of territories south of Albemarle Sound. The General Assembly first displayed its pro-Anglican leanings in 1701, when it passed a vestry act providing for the establishment of Anglican vestries, churches, and clergy, and imposed a poll tax on all colonists to fund such an effort. Although the act did not limit dissenting groups' political rights, it probably was meant to rally and unify political and religious opponents of the Quakers. The proprietors ultimately defused what might have been a politically explosive situation when they declared the law null and void. The vestry act, however, did lead to greater efforts to establish the Anglican Church within the colony. One month after the bill's passage, Deputy Governor Henderson Walker, Thomas Pollock, and several other members of the Council formed a vestry in Chowan precinct and served as vestrymen or churchwardens. By 1703 several other vestries had been established in the other "chief precincts" of Albemarle County.[16]

Anti-Quaker leaders ultimately gained the political ammunition they needed to oust their rivals from office when Robert Daniel, a devout Anglican, was chosen as deputy governor of North Carolina in 1703. After assuming office Daniel set out to dismantle the Quaker bloc in the government by enforcing a 1702 Privy Council order requiring all individuals holding political office to swear allegiance to Queen Anne or forfeit their position. He upheld the order with the knowledge that members of the sect were morally opposed to taking oaths or swearing. Encouraged by Daniel's actions, anti-Quaker forces in the North Carolina assembly succeeded in passing another vestry act that required elected representatives to receive the sacrament of the Eucharist in the Anglican Church before taking office.[17]

Those leaders who sought to dismantle the Quaker bloc also joined forces to limit the number of Bath County representatives in the Lower House. Following the creation of Bath County in 1696, the proprietors initially ordered that Bath precincts elect two representatives to the Lower House while Albemarle districts could send five delegates. Although the proprietors attempted to implement a more equitable system in their 1698 constitution, Albemarle officials refused to ratify the document or accept the new apportionment policy. When representatives from the Bath-Pamlico region petitioned the Upper House in 1704 for equal representation with the northern precincts, the Council insisted on upholding the earlier apportionment policy limiting southern representation to two delegates per precinct.[18]

Northern, pro-Anglican leaders' ability to garner support in both the Upper and Lower Houses suggests that they were forming a more unified front in dealing with political opponents. Thomas Pollock revealed this new group-oriented approach to politics when he advised fellow councilor William Glover in 1709 to refrain from seeking the support of political newcomers because in doing so, "some mistake might fall out in the management [of the government], which might tend to the disadvantage of our cause." Pollock also identified other officials who shared the same goals as himself and Glover. Nathaniel Chevin, Thomas Boyd, and William Maule were among the confidantes and colleagues of Pollock in the struggle with southern and Quaker leaders. Besides serving in the Council, these men also held important positions within the colonial court system and later served as vestrymen in local Anglican churches. William Maule was the only political newcomer in the group who quickly acquired power after emigrating from Scotland in 1709. Maule's friendship with fellow Scotsman Thomas Pollock led to his rapid ascendancy as a prominent merchant-planter and leader within Albemarle.[19]

Albemarle leaders' efforts to eliminate their political rivals from the government led to the formation of an opposing political group that included prominent Quaker leaders, Bath County residents, and several powerful Albemarle leaders, including Edward Moseley, who supported southern expansion. Political factionalism peaked during the first decade of the eighteenth century as the two factions vied for control of the government. At the center of the this political maelstrom was Thomas Cary, a South Carolina merchant who was appointed deputy governor of North Carolina in 1705. Cary attempted to maintain control by allying himself with whichever group of leaders appeared to hold the balance of power within the government at the time. After receiving his commission, Cary initially sided with Anglican officials and enforced laws that excluded Quakers from holding political office. These discriminatory policies prompted prominent Quaker residents and other opponents of the Albemarle faction to form their own political coalition. This group included Quakers such as John Hawkins and Gabriel Newby, Bath County settlers, and several Albemarle leaders such as Edward Moseley. Political factionalism intensified in 1707 following the proprietors' appointment of a new Council composed of five individuals, three of whom were Quakers and one of whom advocated southern expansion. Cary added fuel to the political fire by changing his allegiances and ingratiating himself with the new Council, which eventually chose him to be their president.[20]

The pro-Quaker Council immediately faced various challenges to their power and unity. Leaders of the Albemarle faction responded to the new government by refusing to recognize its legitimacy and forming their own de facto government. The greatest political threat to the Quaker coalition, however, was its loss of internal unity. The different religious backgrounds and regional interests of the Quaker-Bath faction rendered the alliance a tenuous one at best. The fragility of the Quaker-Bath alliance quickly became evident in 1709 when a bill calling for the creation of a new southern county came before the Upper House. The Council's rejection of the bill alienated Bath County representatives and supporters of southern expansion in the Lower House.[21] This suggests that while members of the Quaker coalition shared the common goal of stopping certain Albemarle leaders from dominating the government, certain individuals did not necessarily support southern expansion. The alliance formed by Quakers, southern leaders, and northern opponents of the Albemarle elite began to disintegrate when regional issues became the main foci of political debate.

For two years, the pro-Quaker Council and Albemarle faction remained locked in a power struggle, with neither one able to displace the other. Albemarle leaders regained political ground in 1711 with the arrival of a new deputy governor, Edward Hyde. Soon after his arrival in the colony, Hyde revealed his political leanings when he appointed Pollock and several members of the Albemarle faction to his council. The restoration of these leaders, along with the election of a new assembly, led to a series of legislative acts aimed at destroying the Quaker-Bath coalition. Along with reenacting earlier vestry laws, the assembly nullified all court actions filed during Cary's presidency and banned Cary, Edward Moseley and other supporters from serving in the government. This discriminatory legislation caused Cary and other members of the coalition to rise up and attack Hyde and members of the Council who lived in Albemarle County. When the Virginia government sent marines to put down the revolt, Cary and several of his commanders fled to Virginia, where they were captured and sent to England for trial.[22]

The rebellion underscored the unstable nature of political factions and leadership in northern Carolina. It also exposed the weakness of the government and rendered the colony vulnerable to enemy attack. The Lower Towns of the Tuscaroras recognized that the North Carolinians were unable to defend themselves and on the morning of September 22, 1711, decided to wage a series of devastating attacks on the newly established Swiss and German settlements near New Bern and plantations along the Pamlico River.[23] Hyde and the new Council attempted to organize the militia and send relief to war-stricken settlers. Their efforts, however, were seriously hindered by still-smoldering religious and regional tensions as well as a yellow fever epidemic that was sweeping through the colony. More disconcerting was the refusal of Quaker burgesses to pass bills for military and provisional aid and accusations that certain government officials were selling war provisions rather than sending them to the troops and southern colonists.[24]

The government's inability to secure adequate supplies and troops to defend the colony forced Hyde to seek aid from the proprietors and neighboring colonies. Neither the proprietors nor Virginia ultimately sent aid. South Carolina, on the other hand, responded quickly and decisively. South Carolina leaders agreed to send Colonel John Barnwell and several hundred South Carolina Indians in the fall of 1711 to subdue the warring Tuscaroras and their allies.[25] When Barnwell's truce with the Tuscaroras at Hancock's fort ultimately fell apart, the South Carolina officials agreed to send another expedition led by Colonel James Moore. In March 1713 Moore and his Indian allies attacked Neoheroka, one of the major strongholds of the lower Tuscarora towns, killing 558 Indians and capturing at least 392 prisoners. That battle marked the beginning of the end of the war. On April 14, 1713, North Carolina concluded a treaty with the remaining Tuscaroras from the Lower Towns, thus ending the war as well as the threat of another major Indian uprising in eastern North Carolina.[26]

Even as Albemarle officials struggled to defend the colony, they also rigorously pursued legislative measures to either destroy or limit the political power of their political and religious rivals. During the war the Council imposed a fine on Quakers and any other colonists who refused to support the war effort and required all residents to pay dues to local Anglican parishes. In 1715 the General Assembly passed "An Act for the Liberty of Conscience," which extended religious liberty to Quakers yet banned them from holding political office, serving on juries, and giving evidence in court.[27] This law proved highly effective in eliminating Quakers from serving in political office and on local courts. Based on the names and biographical information of members of the council from 1711 to 1729, not one member of the Society of Friends served on the executive board after the enactment of the law. The few legislative records that survive from the period indicate that only one burgess had the same surname as a former Quaker official, suggesting that Quaker membership in the Lower House had declined as well.[28]

The Quaker coalition received yet another blow to its legitimacy when one of its most prominent members, Edward Moseley, was found guilty of conducting inaccurate and illegal surveys of the proprietors' land while serving as surveyor general. Hyde and the pro-Albemarle Council ordered him not only to pay back all the fees he received but also to give a £500 bond as security for future good behavior. Despite his conviction, Moseley remained a powerful political figure and foe of the Albemarle elite. He responded to the government's orders by refusing to pay the fees or post bond and continued to expand his land and slaveholdings to become perhaps the wealthiest man in the colony by the end of the proprietary period.[29] The incident, however, contributed to disunity and tensions within the Quaker-Bath coalition.

Quaker influence in the government also declined as a result of the loss of leaders and constituents. Quaker leadership ranks were diminished by death, disownment from the Society of Friends, and the decision of individuals to leave public office. Two of the four Quakers who served on the Council in the late seventeenth century and early eighteenth centuries died before the end of the war. Emmanuel Lowe, a high-ranking Quaker who participated in Cary's Rebellion, was disowned by the Yearly Meeting for his involvement in the uprising. Other prominent Quaker officials such as Gabriel Newby and John Hawkins faded into political obscurity following the capture of Cary and his followers.[30] The Quaker bloc also most likely lost the support of a large number of southern constituents and leaders when its members refused to aid the southern settlements during the war.

Albemarle leaders also benefited from the widespread destruction incurred by the southern settlements. The Tuscaroras focused the majority of their attacks on Bath County settlements, leaving Albemarle County relatively unscathed. The devastation around New Bern and the town of Bath was so extensive that it took almost two decades for the area to recover. Many of the colonists who survived the initial attacks left their homes and, in some cases, the colony. The county's loss of population and preoccupation with recovery rendered southern residents less of a political threat than before the war.[31]

The dismantling of the Quaker–Bath County bloc removed a major obstacle to the Albemarle elite's efforts to gain control of the government. Beginning with the Tuscarora War and continuing until the mid-1720s, Thomas Pollock and his supporters in the Council dominated the government. These men, with the support of leaders in the Lower House, enacted laws that led to greater institutional and commercial development of the colony as well as their own interests. The ascendancy of the Albemarle elite can be traced through the Council and higher court records. During this period Council membership ranged between five and eight councilors along with the governor or acting governor of the colony. Between 1711 and 1722, fifteen different individuals served as councilors. Fourteen of the men who served on the Council during this period were living in the colony prior to the war and had already held one or more political offices. Of the fourteen, Thomas Pollock, Tobias Knight, Nathaniel Chevin, Francis Foster, Christopher Gale, Richard Sanderson Jr., and William Reed had served as a councilor or burgess prior to the outbreak of the war. Chevin, Foster, and Sanderson also held positions in their precinct courts and the General Court before being chosen to serve on the Council. Perhaps more importantly, these seven officials served on the Council for between eight and ten consecutive years during this period, providing the Council with an unprecedented degree of stability and political experience.

Several councilors during this period also served as acting governors when the appointed executive died in office. When Hyde passed away in 1712, Pollock became the acting governor of North Carolina, providing the faction with even greater leverage. After Charles Eden passed away in 1722, the council for a second time chose Pollock to act as governor until the proprietors could commission another one. When Pollock died the same year, his successor was William Reed, another long-standing member of the Council and member of the Albemarle elite.

The Albemarle elite who served on the Council were members of the Anglican Church and, with the exception of one individual, served as vestrymen in Albemarle County. This trend marks an important development in the nature of leadership in North Carolina. The Albemarle faction had "found religion" insofar as they recognized church membership as an important political tool to increase their power and form greater social bonds with other members of the community. Most leaders also continued to participate in various economic activities rather than pursue a single occupation. Several individuals, like earlier leaders, worked as merchant-planters. Richard Sanderson Jr. and Frederick Jones were sons of merchant-planters and pursued careers in the same areas. Sanderson produced and sold livestock and carried on his father's lucrative mercantile business with Bermuda, the West Indies, and other English colonies. At one point in his career, Sanderson owned three vessels.[32] William Reed's occupation is not clear, although the fact that he served with Sanderson and Jones as a commissioner to establish the boundary between Virginia and North Carolina suggests that he had a firsthand knowledge of the land and waterways that comes with involvement in trade. These individuals, along with Thomas Pollock, reflected the ongoing influence of prominent merchant-planters within the government.

Various pieces of legislation enacted during and after the war exemplifies the considerable political leverage Albemarle leaders wielded in the government, and how they used their power to further their political and commercial interests. In 1715 the Lower House passed a statute that not only asserted its right to determine apportionment in the colony but also continued its discriminatory practice of denying Bath County and other new areas of settlement equal representation with Albemarle. Northern leaders in the assembly succeeded in limiting southern representation until the end of the proprietary period despite the expansion of settlement south and west of Albemarle. According to the list of burgesses attending the April 1726 meeting of the Lower House, only five of the twenty-eight members were from southern precincts.[33]

Albemarle leaders also took advantage of their hegemony within the government to pursue various economic initiatives that benefited their business interests as well as the overall commercial development of the colony. During the war the assembly for the first time printed and distributed paper money in the colony. The Lower House continued to enact laws for the printing and retiring of paper money, culminating in the circulation of £40,000 in bills by 1729. It also levied new taxes and duties and created the bureaucracy needed to oversee revenue collection. The primary purpose of the revenues was to serve as collateral for the new paper money.[34]

The Lower House also worked with the Council on legislation intended to improve the infrastructure of the colony. Between 1715 and 1729, the General Assembly enacted a series of laws calling for the construction and maintenance of roads and navigational improvements with the stated purpose of encouraging domestic and foreign trade. These laws sparked a road construction boom, especially in Albemarle County. By the end of the proprietary period, major roads connected all major areas of settlement, with at least five roads running between Virginia and North Carolina and a road connecting the Cape Fear region with Albemarle Sound.[35] The government's efforts to improve North Carolina's financial system and transportation network, coupled with the removal of a major Indian enemy from the central coastal plains, encouraged new settlers to migrate to the colony. The colony's population increased gradually between 1715 and 1720 and then suddenly tripled between 1720 and

1728. The population boom contributed to the expansion of the domestic economy by increasing the pool of small producers and attracting new merchants and capital to the colony.[36]

Perhaps the greatest indicator of economic growth during the period of Albemarle dominance was the significant increase in the coastwise trade. According to shipping reports in the *Boston Newsletter*, the number of foreign vessels sailing to and from North Carolina between 1716 and 1720 increased fourfold in comparison to the five-year period before the war. This trend continued until the end of the proprietary period, with the volume of New England–North Carolina trade peaking at an annual average of fifty-five ships between 1720 and 1725. North Carolina continued to be New England's primary southern trading partner after the war, with the number of ships sailing between North Carolina and New England twice that of Virginia and three times the number of ships traveling between South Carolina and New England.[37]

Among the greatest beneficiaries of the colony's commercial growth were members of the Albemarle elite. While the majority of North Carolinians remained small landowners with no slaves, merchant-planters such as Thomas Pollock and Richard Sanderson expanded their landed and personal wealth substantially in the last fifteen years of proprietary control. In 1717 Pollock paid poll taxes for thirty-one individuals and owned over thirty thousand acres of land. At the time of his death, Pollock had acquired seventy slaves and increased his landholdings to over fifty thousand acres.[38] Fellow councilor Richard Sanderson also acquired extensive wealth in comparison to most North Carolinians. Although he lived on the Little River in Perquimans precinct, Sanderson acquired extensive landholdings that included Ocracoke Island and Cape Lookout and other plantations in Perquimans precinct. He used his land to raise livestock as well as crops, which he shipped to Bermuda and the West Indies. When he died Sanderson owned at least fourteen slaves, two sloops, and various pieces of furniture and dishware that reflected his material success.[39]

The Albemarle elite's accumulation of wealth and power after the war did not ensure their position within the provincial government or lead to the formation of the type of political dynasties that came to characterize the Chesapeake and other colonies. Thomas Pollock and his supporters found it increasingly difficult to maintain cohesion and power as wealthy political newcomers, especially from South Carolina, settled in the colony. Among the most prominent members of this group were Maurice and Roger Moore, two brothers from South Carolina who initiated settlement near the mouth of the Cape Fear River in 1725. Maurice Moore first came to North Carolina in 1712 to help fight the Tuscaroras. After the war he settled in Albemarle County, where he married Elizabeth Lillington Swann, the widow of an Albemarle politician and daughter of a former Council member. Moore's marriage to Elizabeth also brought Moore into direct contact with Edward Moseley, who was married to

Elizabeth's sister.⁴⁰ By the mid-1720s, other members of the Moore clan and their relatives began to settle in the lower Cape Fear region. "The Family," as they became known, gained political clout in North Carolina not only as a result of their material wealth and important mercantile connections but also because of their intermarriage and business relations with certain Albemarle leaders who supported southern expansion.⁴¹

The dominance of Pollock and his supporters in the Council during and immediately after the Tuscarora War caused Moseley and Moore to seek positions in other important political bodies and provincial offices. After serving two terms as councilor between 1705 and 1708, Moseley lost his seat and was not reappointed until 1723. His fifteen-year absence from the Council at the same time Thomas Pollock and other Albemarle elite dominated that political body suggests that Moseley was not in the same political camp as other councilors. After 1708 Moseley focused his efforts on building a political power base in the Lower House. He not only succeeded in being elected to that body but also served as speaker of the house, first in 1708 and again from 1715 to 1723. Both Moseley and Maurice Moore also increased their political influence and material wealth when the Lower House appointed them to new political posts created to oversee the collection of duties and taxes as well as the printing and distribution of paper money.⁴²

As their political clout increased, Moseley and Moore began to challenge the power of Pollock and the Albemarle faction. The first attack occurred in 1718, when Moseley and Moore set out to destroy the reputation of Governor Eden and councilor Tobias Knight, both of whom were considered allies of Thomas Pollock and other elite members of the Council. Moseley and Moore accused both men of conspiring with the infamous pirate Edward Teach. Their determination to prove their case against the two men led them to break into the house of the secretary of the colony to confiscate Council records they believed contained evidence of Eden's and Knight's illegal activities. They failed in this attempt and were tried by the General Court for their actions. The court inflicted the harshest penalty on Edward Moseley, the most powerful of the conspirators. He was ordered to pay a considerable fine and was banned from political office for three years as a punishment for his role in the affair.⁴³

The Albemarle faction also lost a major source of power and unity in 1722 with the death of Thomas Pollock, its most prominent and powerful leader. The proprietors further undermined the Albemarle hegemony by increasing the number of councilors from six to twelve and appointing three leaders of the Cape Fear faction—Maurice Moore, Edward Moseley, and Arthur Goffe—to the new council. The Albemarle elite also may have found it difficult to maintain their dominant position as a result of the appointment of several councilors with strong familial and political ties with Christopher Gale, a well-known political maverick in the colony. The appointment of these men disrupted the political unity the Council had achieved during the previous decade.

At the same time they altered the membership of the Council, the proprietors appointed George Burrington governor of the colony. Burrington's land policies and shifting loyalties led to further dissension among the Albemarle elite and contributed to their loss of political power. Burrington took the bold step of ignoring the proprietary ban on land sales and began to issue blank patents or "warrants" for lands, especially to his southern allies.[44] Rather than challenging Burrington's decision, however, members of the Council not only accepted it but called for the establishment of a standard fee for the executive every time he signed a warrant. This shift in attitude among some northern leaders may indicate that they realized they could no longer stop the settlement of Bath County or that they hoped to personally benefit from the sale of land. In any case, by acquiescing to southern expansion, they lost one of the main issues that had united them in the past. To make matters worse, Burrington granted substantial tracts of land to Moore and members of extended family in order to gain the support of Cape Fear planters.[45]

Burrington's replacement, Sir Richard Everard, cause further factional unrest by displaying the same vindictive and duplicitous behavior as Burrington. After arriving in the colony in 1725, Everard appeared to side with leaders of the Albemarle faction. In accordance with the proprietors' orders, Everard purged the Council of Burrington's cronies, Moseley, Moore, and Goffe. He also refused to convene the newly elected Lower House, which contained members related to Moore and Moseley. Everard and Albemarle leaders attempted to further undermine the growing political power of the lower Cape Fear faction by using their control of the judicial system to bring bogus lawsuits against various individuals and illegally imprisoning them.[46] Finally, the governor, with the support of the Council, attempted to silence Burrington and members of the Cape Fear faction who had been elected to the Lower House by constantly dissolving, disrupting, delaying, or proroguing the assembly during its sessions.

Despite these actions southern expansionists remained entrenched in the government. Their growing power base coincided with the loss of unity and membership in the Albemarle faction. Governor Everard ensured the ascendancy of the lower Cape Fear leaders when he switched his political allegiances and sided with the new coalition after 1728. Everard revealed his new loyalties when he resumed the practice of issuing warrants, giving especially large grants to members of the Cape Fear faction. Of the thirty-five individuals who received blank patents for Cape Fear lands, fifteen were family members or close friends of Maurice Moore. Grants to these individuals accounted for eighty thousand of the 115,000 acres sold during Everard's administration. Everard's fickle politics caused the Albemarle faction to splinter as northern leaders leveled verbal attacks and accusations against the governor and their former political allies. By 1728 this powerful coalition of wealthy Cape Fear colonists and

Albemarle leaders succeeded in breaking the Albemarle hegemony within the North Carolina government.[47]

The emergence of an elite group of Albemarle leaders during the early eighteenth century marked a unique and important event in the colony's early political development. While the Tuscarora War posed a serious threat to the survival of the government, it also provided certain individuals from Albemarle County with the opportunity to eliminate their political rivals and grab the reins of power within the government. This small group of men, led by Thomas Pollock, dominated the Council and gained support in the Lower House to enact legislation that promoted commercial and institutional growth as well as their personal interests. It is ironic that these developments, along with the opening of lands formerly occupied by the defeated Tuscarora Lower Towns and their allies, attracted ambitious and wealthy South Carolinians as well as prominent Albemarle merchant-planters like Edward Moseley to settle in the lower Cape Fear region. By the end of the proprietary period, the balance of power within the provincial government had shifted in favor of the Cape Fear faction, marking the end of the Albemarle hegemony and initiating a new phase of regional politics in North Carolina.

Notes

1. John Barnwell, "Journal of John Barnwell," *VMHB* 5, no. 4 (April 1898): 391-402, and 6, no. 1 (July 1898):42-55, esp. 5:392-96.

2. Barnwell, "Journal," 6: 44–47, 48–49.

3. Jack Greene, *The Quest for Power: The Lower House of Assembly in the Southern Royal Colonies, 1689–1776* (Chapel Hill: University of North Carolina Press, 1963), 20–42, 73, 115–17, 148–51, 174, 211, 233–35, 337–38; Jack Greene, "The Growth of Political Stability: An Interpretation of Political Development in the Anglo-American Colonies, 1660–1760," in *The American Revolution: A Heritage of Change*, ed. John Parker and Carol Urness (Minneapolis: Associates of the James Ford Bell Library, 1975), 40–52; Jack Greene, *Negotiated Authorities, Essays in Colonial Political and Constitutional History* (Charlottesville: University of Virginia Press, 1994), 147–62; Clarence Ver Steeg, *Origins of a Southern Mosaic: Studies of Early Carolina and Georgia* (Athens: University of Georgia Press, 1975), 54–57; Jack M. Sosin, *English America and Imperial Inconsistency: The Rise of Provincial Autonomy, 1696–1715* (Lincoln: University of Nebraska Press, 1985), 96.

4. Recent works by Noelleen McIlvenna and Jonathan Bard claim that the majority of early settlers chose to be subsistence farmers as a result of their belief in the radical political and social philosophy of the English Levelers. They argue that the colony enjoyed social and political harmony until the early eighteenth century, when ambitious newcomers gained political control and attempted to create a more traditional social and political order. Charles Lowry, "Class, Politics, Rebellion, and Regional Development in Proprietary North Carolina, 1697–1720" (Ph.D. diss., University of Florida, 1979); Jacquelyn H. Wolf, "The Proud and the Poor:

The Social Organization of Leadership in Proprietary North Carolina, 1663–1729" (Ph.D. diss., University of Pennsylvania, 1977); Noelleen McIlvenna, *A Very Mutinous People: The Struggle for North Carolina, 1660–1713* (Chapel Hill: University of North Carolina Press, 2009), 13–70; Jonathan Edward Bard, "The Sinke of America: Society in the Albemarle Borderlands," *NCHR* 87, no. 1 (January 2010): 1–27.

5. A. Roger Ekirch, *"Poor Carolina": Politics and Society in Colonial North Carolina, 1729–1776* (Chapel Hill: University of North Carolina Press, 1981), 38–39; Bradford J. Wood, *This Remote Part of the World: Regional Formation in the Lower Cape Fear, North Carolina, 1725–1775* (Columbia: University of South Carolina Press, 2004), 6, 21–22, 145–47, 167–68.

6. Wood, *This Remote Part of the World*, 17–25, 89–126, 167–70.

7. *CRNC* (2nd ser.), 2:lxiii–lxxiv; 3:xl–xli; General Court Minutes, May 31, 1691, in *CRNC* (2nd ser.), 3:20–21; General Court Records, April–June, 1697, in *CRNC* (2nd ser.), 3:38–40; General Court Records, March 1698, in *CRNC* (2nd ser.), 3:180; General Court Records, July–August, 1700, in *CRNC* (2nd ser.), 3:394–95; General Court Records, March 1701, in *CRNC* (2nd ser.), 3:434–35; General Court Records, July 1702, in *CRNC* (2nd ser.), 4:36; Virginia Naval Office List, CO5/1306; Thomas Pollock to Mr. Hamilton, January 19, 1719, Pollock Letterbook, Private Manuscripts, at NCSA; Robert E. Moody, "Massachusetts Trade with Carolina," *NCHR* 20, no. 3 (July 1943): 47–53.

8. Lowry, "Class, Politics, Rebellion, and Regional Development," 112–13.

9. *DNCB*, 6:39–40; *DNCB*, 3:73; *DNCB*, 4:363; Gabriel Newby, loose will, March, 1735, Pasquotank precinct, Secretary of State's Office, at NCSA.

10. Roy Merrens, *Colonial North Carolina in the Eighteenth Century: A Study in Historical Geography* (Chapel Hill: University of North Carolina Press, 1964), 19–20; Lawson, *New Voyage*, xxii–xxiv; Herbert Paschal, *A History of Colonial Bath* (Raleigh: Edwards and Broughton, 1955), 1, 3–4.

11. North Carolina Council Journal, January 16, 1703, in *CRNC*, 1:575; *DNCB*, 2:261–63.

12. *DNCB*, 4:332–33.

13. Trevor Burnard, *Creole Gentlemen: The Maryland Elite, 1691–1776* (New York: Routledge, 2002), 4–14, 20–30, 96, 114, 171, 207; Emory Evans, *A "Topping People": The Rise and Decline of Virginia's Old Political Elite, 1680–1790* (Charlottesville: University of Virginia Press, 2009), 1–20, 92–93; Lorena S. Walsh, "The Development of Local Power Structures: Maryland's Lower Western Shore in the Early Colonial Period," in *Power and Status: Officeholding in Colonial America*, ed. Bruce C. Daniels (Middletown, Conn.: Wesleyan University Press, 1986), 65.

14. Kristi Rutz-Robbins, "Colonial Commerce: Race, Class, and Gender in a Local Economy, Albemarle County, North Carolina, 1663–1729" (Ph.D. diss., Michigan State University, 2003), 1–8, 24–30, 34, 50–67, 98–124.

15. General Court Records, September 26–29, 1694, in *CRNC*, 1:405–10, 423; February 25–March 1, 1695, in *CRNC*, 1:442–51; Palatine's Court, December 9, 1696, in *CRNC*, 1:472; General Court Records, May 28, 1697, in *CRNC*, 1:486; Henderson Walker to the Bishop of London, October, 21, 1703, in *CRNC*, 1:571–73; Mr. Blair's Mission to North Carolina, January, 1704 to [unknown], in *CRNC*,

1:600–603; Mr. Adams to the Secretary, September 18, 1708, in *CRNC*, 1:686–87; Mr. Gordon to the Secretary, May 13, 1709, in *CRNC*, 1:600–603, 708–15; Stephen B. Weeks, *Southern Quakers and Slavery* (Baltimore: Johns Hopkins University Press, 1896), 50–51; Donald V. Dowless, "The Quakers of Colonial North Carolina, 1672–1789 (Ph.D. diss., Baylor University, 1989), 84–167.

16. Vestry Book, Chowan Precinct, December 15, 1701, in *CRNC*, 1:543–45; Mr. Blair's Mission to North Carolina, April 12, 1703, in *CRNC*, 1:600–603.

17. Proprietors to Nathaniel Johnson, June 18, 1702, CO5/289, *Carolina Proprietary Entry Book of Commissions, Instructions, Etc.*, microfilm reel Z.5.106N, 47–47b, at NCSA; An Act for the More Effectual Preservation of the Government, 1704, in *CRNC*, 2:863–82.

18. Palatine's Court, December 9, 1696, in *CRNC*, 1:472; *CRNC* (2nd ser.), 1:234, 237; Petition of Some Members of the House of Burgesses to the Governor and Council, n.d., in *NCHGR*, 3:74–75; North Carolina Council Minutes, December 3, 1705, in *CRNC*, 1:629.

19. Thomas Pollock to President Glover, April 16, 1710, in *CRNC*, 1:725–26; Thomas Pollock to Mr. Chevin and Mr. Boyd's, April 16, 1710, in *CRNC*, 1:723–24; *DNCB*, 1:366, 202, 203, 3:380.

20. *DNCB*, 1:38–39; Mr. Gordon to the Secretary, May 13, 1709, in *CRNC*, 1:709; Proclamation Making Void All Offices, n.d., in *NCHGR*, 3:261; Grand Assembly Meeting, November 10–19, 1709, in *Old Albemarle County North Carolina, Miscellaneous Records, 1678 to circa 1737*, ed.Weynette P. Haun (Durham, N.C.: Weynette P. Haun, 1982), 37–38; Grand Assembly Meeting, November 10–19, 1709, in Haun, *Old Albemarle County*, 46–47; Petitions of William Lewis to the Deputy Governor and Council, n.d., in *NCHGR*, 3:260; Spotswood to the Lords Proprietors, July 28, 1711, in *CRNC*, 1:795, Edward Hyde to the Lords Proprietors, August 22, 1711, in *CRNC*, 1:801–2.

21. Colonel Jenings to the Council of Trade and Plantations, September 20, 1708, in *CSPC*, 24:95–98; Message from the Council to the Lower House, November 1709, in Haun, *Old Albemarle County*, 180.

22. Minutes of the Proprietary Board, December 7, 1710, CO5/292, *Carolina Proprietary Entry Book of Commissions*, 35–36; *DNCB*, 3:246; Letter from the President and Council of North Carolina to Colonel Spotswood, June 29, 1711, in *CRNC*, 2:761; Mr. Urmstone's Letter, July 7, 1711, in *CRNC*, 1:768; Copies of an Address and Two Acts of Assembly to the Board of Trade, July 25, 1711, in *CRNC*, 1:784–87; Colonel Spotswood to the Board of Trade, July 25, 1711, in *CRNC*, 1:780–81; Mr. Dennis to the Secretary, September 3, 1711, in *CRNC*, 1:803–4; Acts Passed in North Carolina, 1711, in *CRNC*, 1:787–94.

23. Colonel Spotswood to the Board of Trade, October 15, 1711, in *CRNC*, 1:810; Colonel Thomas Pollock to Governor Spotswood, April 1713, in *CRNC*, 2:31, 39; De Graffenried Manuscript, n.d., in *CRNC*, 1:939, 955.

24. Pollock to the Lords Proprietors, September 20, 1711, Pollock Letterbook; Mr. Christopher Gale to [unknown], November 2, 1711, in *CRNC*, 1:825–27. [Thomas Pollock] to Lord Carteret, September 20, 1712, in *CRNC*, 1:877; Governor Hyde to the Governor and Council of South Carolina, 1712, in *CRNC*, 1:898–99; Corn lists, n.d., 1715–1716, in Colonial Court Records, Taxes, and Accounts, 1669–1754, at

NCSA; Thomas Pollock to Governor Spotswood, January 1713, in *CRNC,* 2:4; Pollock Letterbook; Reverend Raisnford to the Secretary of the S.P.G., February 17, 1713, in *CRNC,* 2:16; Mr. Urmstone to the Secretary of the S.P.G., June 12, 1714, in *CRNC,* 2:130–32; De Graffenried Manuscript, n.d., in *CRNC,* 1:948.

25. Mr. Spotswood to Lord Dartmouth, February 8, 1711, CO 5/1316, microfilm reel M-239, Virginia Colonial Records Project, Colonial Williamsburg Foundations Library, 314–16; Virginia Lower House Minutes, November 15, 1712, in *JHBV,* 1:27; South Carolina Assembly Minutes, August 8, 1712, *Records of the States of the United States,* ed. William S. Jenkins (Library of Congress, 1949), (microfilm), South Carolina Assembly, 1a; Virginia Lower House Minutes, November 21–24, 1712, in *JHBV,* 1:36–37; South Carolina Assembly Minutes, October 26–November 8, 1711, *Records of the States of the United States,* South Carolina Assembly, 1a; Barnwell, "Journal," 5:391–94; Hyde's Private Instructions to Mr. Foster, 1712, in *CRNC,* 1:900.

26. Barnwell, "Journal," 5:39; and 6:43–44; Colonel Spotswood to the Board of Trade, July 26, 1712, in *CRNC,* 1:861–63; Governor Pollock to [unknown], December 23, 1712, in *CRNC,* 1:892–94; Thomas Pollock to Governor Spotswood, January 15, 1713, in *CRNC,* 2:4; Letter from Colonel Moore to President Pollock, March 27, 1713, *SCHGM* 10, no. 1 (January 1909): 39; W. Stitt Robinson, *The Southern Colonial Frontier, 1607–1763* (Albuquerque: University of New Mexico Press, 1979), 111 (map).

27. Cushing, *The Earliest Printed Laws,* 2:11–13.

28. Members of the Lower House of Assembly, 1715, CO 5/293, microfilm reel z.5.22, 157b; List of Members of the Lower and Upper House, 1729, CO5/293, 137; Journal of the Lower House, April 1726, in *CRNC,* 2:608; Pasquotank Monthly Meeting, April 17, 1713, in *CRNC,* 2:36.

29. The General Assembly of North Carolina to the Lords Proprietors, July 25, 1711, in *CRNC,* 1:786; An Act for Redressing Several Grievances, Abuses, and Illegal Proceedings, 1711, in *CRNC,* 1:791–94; An Act for the Liberty of Conscience, 1715, in *CRNC,* 23:11.

30. *DNCB,* 1:9–10; 3:73; North Carolina Council Minutes, July 4, 1712, in *CRNC,* 1:855; Weeks, *Southern Quakers and Slavery,* 166; Loose Wills, Emmanuel Lowe, 1727, Pasquotank Precinct, Secretary of State, at NCSA; Loose Wills, Gabriel Newby, Pasquotank Precinct, 1734/35, North Carolina Secretary of State, at NCSA.

31. Pollock to the Lords Proprietors, September 20, 1712, in *CRNC,* 1:873–74; Colonial Spotswood to the Board of Trade, February 1713, in *CRNC,* 2:13; Reverend Raisnford to the Secretary of the S.P.G., February 17, 1713, in *CRNC,* 2:16; Reverend Urmstone to the Secretary of the S.P.G., September 22, 1714, in *CRNC,* 2:143–44; Alonzo T. Dill, "Eighteenth-Century New Bern: A History of the Town and Craven County, Part IV, Years of Slow Development," *NCHR* 22, no. 4 (October 1945): 465.

32. *DNCB,* 1:179, 202–3, 366; *DNCB,* 2:228–29, 260–61, 312; *DNCB,* 3:317–18, 380–81; *DNCB,* 4:101, 260–64; *DNCB,* 5:9, 116–17, 187, 283.

33. Instructions to Captain Henry Wilkinson, n.d., in *CRNC,* 1:333–38; North Carolina Lower House Journal, April, 1726, in *CRNC,* 1:608; General Court

Minutes, July, 1727, in *CRNC* (2nd ser.), 6:414–17; David Corbitt, *The Formation of North Carolina Counties, 1663–1943* (Raleigh: State Department of Archives and History, 1950), xv; Greene, *Quest for Power,* 174–83.

34. Governor George Burrington to the Lords Proprietors of Trade and Plantations, May 19, 1733, *CRNC,* 3: 484-86; John Cushing, ed. *The Earliest Printed Laws of North Carolina,* 2 vols. (Wilmington, Del.: Michael Glazier, 1977), 2: 20-29, 171-72, 175-80, 187-89; John J. McCusker, *Money and Exchange in Europe and America, 1600–1775: A Handbook* (Chapel Hill: University of North Carolina Press, 1978), 215; Pollock to [unknown], September 15, 1719, Pollock Letterbook.

35. F. W. Clonts, "Travel and Trade in Colonial North Carolina," *NCHR* 3, no. 1 (January 1926) 25–35; Cushing, *The Earliest Printed Laws,* 2:99, 208–10; Cummings, *Early Maps,* Plate IV.

36. Craven County Tax List, 1719, *Journal of North Carolina Genealogy* 9, no. 1 (Spring/Summer 1963): 2835–36; Currituck County 1715 Tax Lists, *Journal of North Carolina Genealogy* 10, no. 2 (Summer 1964): 1279–83; Perquimans County 1720 Tax List, *Journal of North Carolina Genealogy* 16, no. 1 (Spring/Summer 1970): 2484–89; Chowan County 1720 Tax List, *Journal of North Carolina Genealogy* 16, no. 2 (Fall/Winter 1970): 2553–59; Beaufort Precinct Tax List, 1717, *Journal of North Carolina Genealogy* 9, no. 2 (Summer 1963): 1124; Chowan County 1717 Tax List, *Journal of North Carolina Genealogy* 6, no. 4 (December 1960): 741–45; General Court Records, July 1722, in *CRNC* (2nd ser.), 5:316–17; General Court Records, October 1725, in *CRNC* (2nd ser.), 6:169–70; General Court Records, October 26, in *CRNC* (2nd ser.), 6:307; General Court Records, October 1728, in *CRNC* (2nd ser.), 6:528–29; James Shepherd and Gary Walton, *Shipping, Maritime Trade, and the Economic Development of Colonial North America* (Chapel Hill: University of North Carolina Press, 1966), 6–24.

37. *Boston Newsletter,* 1704–29, microfilm, Omohundro Institute of Early American History and Culture, Williamsburg, Virginia.

38. Chowan County 1717 Tax List, *Journal of North Carolina Genealogy* 6 (December 1960): 742; J. Bryan Grimes, ed., *North Carolina Wills and Inventories* (Baltimore: Genealogical Publishing, 1967), 313–20, 342–47.

39. *DNCB,* 5:283; Richard Sanderson's Will, 1733, Secretary of State Wills, 1722–1735 (Perquimans), Will Book 3, at NCSA.

40. *DNCB,* 4:65–66, 303–4.

41. Wood, *This Remote Part of the World,* 15–24; *DNCB,* 4:303–4; 332–33.

42. Proprietors to Christopher Gale, May 19, 1709, CO 5/289, *Carolina Proprietary Entry Book of Commissions,* 107b–108b; *CRNC* (2nd ser.), 3:xliii; Cushing, *Earliest Printed Laws,* 2:99, 208–10; Journal of the Lower House, February, 1714, in Haun, *Old Albemarle County,* 189; Meeting of the General Assembly, August 20, 1720, in Haun, *Old Albemarle County,* 119; Meeting of the General Assembly, July 31, 1720, in Haun, *Old Albemarle County,* 120–21; North Carolina Council Journal, August, December 1721, in *CRNC,* 2:389, 397, 425; Lords Proprietors to George Burrington, June 3, 1723, CO 5/291, in *Carolina Proprietary Entry Book of Commissions,* 46–63; Minutes of the Proprietary Board, May 7, 1726, CO 5/292, in *Carolina Proprietary Entry Book of Commissions,* 152–14; North Carolina Council Minutes, February 21, 1728, in *CRNC,* 2:726–29; Greene, *Quest for Power,* 39–53.

43. General Court Records, July 1–November 3, 1719, in *CRNC*, 5:199–202, 206–8; North Carolina Council Minutes, July 17, 1725, in *CRNC*, 2:566–68; North Carolina Council Minutes, October 25, 1725, in *CRNC*, 2:573; Journal of the Lower House, November, 1725, in *CRNC*, 2:575–76; North Carolina Council Minutes, January, 1726, in *CRNC*, 2:605; Journal of the Lower House, April, 1726, in *CRNC*, 2:608; Journal of the Lower House, November, 1727, in *CRNC*, 2:117.

44. Minutes of the Proprietary Board, CO 5/293, in *North Carolina: Original Correspondence. Board of Trade, 1730–1731*, microfilm reel Z.5.22, 96–97, at NCSA; North Carolina Council Minutes, April 4, 1722, in *CRNC*, 2:454; North Carolina Council Minutes, June 14, 1722, in *CRNC*, 2:458; North Carolina Council Minutes, September 7, 1722, in *CRNC*, 2:460; Lords Proprietors to George Burrington, June 3, 1723, in *Carolina Proprietary Entry Book of Commissions*, CO 5/291, 46–63; North Carolina Council Minutes, July, 1724, in *CRNC*, 2:532.

45. North Carolina Council Minutes, April 3, 1724, in *CRNC*, 2:563; North Carolina Council Minutes, April 15, 1724, in *CRNC*, 2:528–30; North Carolina Council Minutes, October 29, 1724, in *CRNC*, 2:541; Minutes of the Proprietary Board, January 21, 1725, CO 5/292, in *Carolina Proprietary Entry Book of Commissions*, 149; Christopher Gale to the Lords Proprietors, 1725, in *CRNC*, 2:561–62; E. Lawrence Lee, *The Lower Cape Fear in Colonial Days* (Chapel Hill: University of North Carolina Press, 1965), 94.

46. Journal of the North Carolina Lower House, April 1726, in *CRNC*, 2:613–16.

47. North Carolina Council Minutes, July 17, 1725, in *CRNC*, 2:566; North Carolina Council Minutes, July 20, 1725, in *CRNC*, 2:568; North Carolina Council Minutes, October 5, 1725, in *CRNC*, 2:571; Journal of the Lower House, November 1, 1725, in *CRNC*, 2:575; Journal of the North Carolina Lower House, April 1726, in *CRNC*, 2:613–16, 621–22; North Carolina Council Minutes, February 1728, in *CRNC*, 2:724–25; John Lovick, Secretary of North Carolina, to the Council of Trade, December 12, 1728, in *CSPC*, 36:272–75; *DNCB*, 1:283–84; Lee, *The Lower Cape Fear*, 102, 104.

"The Indians that live about Pon Pon"

John and Mary Musgrove and the Making of a Creek Indian Community in South Carolina, 1717–1732

STEVEN C. HAHN

John and Mary Musgrove are best known as the bicultural Anglo-Creek couple who, as interpreters, diplomats, and traders to the Creek Indians, were instrumental to the establishment of the Georgia colony. What has often been overlooked is that this same couple played an important role in South Carolina's early history as the founders of a small but strategically important community of Creek Indians in Colleton County, South Carolina—referred to locally as the "Indians that live about Pon Pon." Established in 1717 on lands owned by John and Mary Musgrove, this community transformed the Musgrove estate into a multicultural enclave that bridged Indian and English worlds and—for a brief period of time—defied the region's emerging ethic of racial separation.

While at one level it is true that the Yamasee War permanently altered the relationship between English colonists and Indians, the Pon Pon community's history suggests a degree of continuity between pre- and postwar patterns of cross-cultural interaction. Leery authorities from London to Coweta may have preferred that their respective peoples keep their distance from one another, but the personal relationships established before the war between traders and Indians nevertheless persisted. Moreover these personal relationships were embodied quite literally by *mestizos* like the Musgroves, who returned to their prewar homes at Pon Pon and emerged as important go-betweens for Carolina and the Creek nation. As was the case before the war, a degree of ambivalence characterized the relationship between Indians and colonists living on Carolina's southern border. Harmonious at times and acrimonious at others, their story offers lessons about the potential and limits of cross-cultural accommodation on the southern frontier in the early eighteenth century.

A World That Was Lost

The Yamasee War has been rightfully viewed as a watershed event in the early history of the Carolinas, in part because it promoted a recalibration of all manner of cross-cultural interaction between British subjects and their former

Indian allies. Weeks, months, and perhaps even years in the making, Indian dissatisfaction with the Carolina trade regime steadily increased due to the Indians' accruing debt, trader belligerence, and the inability of governing officials to address Indian grievances. The critical moment came on Good Friday 1715, when the Yamasee and Creek Indians began killing English ambassadors at the Yamasee town of Pocataligo and later directed their wrath at the Carolina settlements, thus beginning a war involving most of the southern Indian nations that lasted for more than two years.

Among the living witnesses to these events was a factor for a London mercantile firm named Charles Rodd, who penned one of the earliest (and most often cited) accounts of the outbreak of the "Indian War."[1] When viewed from one perspective, Rodd's account chronicles the final, violent collapse of a thirty-year relationship—built on trade, warfare, diplomacy, and intermarriage—between two mutually irreconcilable peoples. Rodd draws sharp distinction, for example, between the instigators of the violence, "the Indians," and its (mostly British) victims. Because the antagonists rejected what in Rodd's view were sincere peace overtures, he depicts the Indians as "devils," and "infamous criminals." Rodd's account likewise suggests that the feelings were mutual. Not only did the Indians torture pitilessly some of Carolina's agents, but also (so Rodd claims) they raped English women and pillaged settlers' farms, all while "dancing in a grotesque fashion, and uttering loud cries of joy."

The tendency to differentiate between antagonists and protagonists and to fixate on acts of violence is understandable when chronicling a war. But postbellum perspectives on the conflict tend to obscure a more complicated antebellum reality.[2] Indeed reading Rodd's account backward rather than forward in time exposes a world that was lost on South Carolina's southern frontier, one defined by the intimacy between rather than the separation of Indian and English peoples.[3] For one thing, Rodd indicates that the Carolinians dismissed early rumors of the Indian uprising, which is suggestive of the degree of trust they placed on their allies. Most important, at Pocataligo the Indians' deception would not have been possible had not both parties already been on intimate and familiar terms. By sharing drinks and talking together the night before the massacre, the agents and Indian leaders behaved much as they had done in the past. Business "as usual," as Rodd would have it. Predictably the Indian War brought much of that world to an end by enforcing a degree of separation (in some cases welcome on both sides). But that fact should not lead us to assume that such an outcome was inevitable, because many individuals on the southern frontier—Mary and John Musgrove included—lived lives that hinted at different, though unrealized possibilities for the future.

Mary Musgrove, the daughter of deerskin trader Edward Griffin and a Creek woman, grew into adulthood in a world that bridged her Creek and English heritages. After spending the first seven to ten years of her life in the Creek nation, Mary was brought by her father to Pon Pon, South Carolina, to have her educated and baptized. While the mestizo children of deerskin traders might be found anywhere in the colony, it just so happened that an unusually high concentration of them lived at Pon Pon, in the frontier parish of St. Bartholomew's in Colleton County, which Mary called home for a quarter century.

Mary (Griffin) Musgrove was one of several mestizo youths living at Pon Pon when the war broke out, most of them the offspring of local Indian traders. These individuals probably came to the colony at roughly the same time, lived in relative proximity to one another, and experienced together many of the formative experiences of youth, including schooling and baptism. Though we cannot identify this cohort precisely, circumstantial evidence allows us to hazard a few informed guesses as to their identities. Most probably it included Mary's brother, Edward Griffin, who appears to have been baptized (hence his Christian name), was capable of speaking passable English, and lived within the colony's borders as a young adult. Another was Thomas "Tommy" Jones, the son of an Indian trader by that same name. Like the Griffin siblings, Jones was half-Creek, related to Mary by blood, and later followed her to Georgia. Added to their number was James Welch and an unnamed brother, the "half breed" sons of trader/explorer Thomas Welch, who pioneered South Carolina's trade with the Chickasaws around the turn of the century.[4] John Musgrove, meanwhile, probably grew up on his father's estate in Berkeley County, but he would have had ample opportunity to interact with mestizos at Pon Pon due to his father's trade and livestock interests. Close in age if not blood, these individuals remained on intimate terms throughout their lives, a product of their common backgrounds and of the bonds forged in youth.

The presence of a visible bicultural youth population at Pon Pon testifies to the fact that the boundary between colonial and Indian lands was porous from the very beginning. Indians living on the colony's southern borders, particularly the Yamasees, frequently crossed into the settlements, perhaps to hunt, fish, trade or to meet with the governor in Charles Town. In addition to the Yamasee reservation near Port Royal, several other small tribes lived within the settlements, such as the Cusabo, whose reservation placed them squarely within the bounds of Colleton County. The porousness of the southern frontier, though, cut both ways. English traders and Indian agents frequented Indian country regularly, but there were also settlers who lived more or less permanently on Indian lands (admittedly sometimes to the Indians' chagrin) and thus closer to Indians than to other English colonists. Some of them were traders or agents, such as Thomas Nairne and William Bray, each of whom took up tracts of Yamasee lands adjacent to Granville County and were, quite literally, living amongst them when the war broke out in 1715. Others were aspiring planters, such as Joseph Bryan, who also squatted on Yamasee land and happened to become the progenitor of a family dynasty that continued to push elsewhere into Indian country to the eve of the American Revolution.[5]

Given the physical proximity of many of South Carolina's English and Indian frontier inhabitants, it is not surprising to find that their work and subsistence habits tended to rub off on one another. St. Bartholomew's parish resident John Norris, for example, indicated that Indians often worked for their English neighbors as commercial hunters and insinuated that the colonial diet assimilated with that of the Indians.[6] For their part, local Indians at times were willing to adjust their own work and subsistence habits in conformity with those of their English neighbors. Some Indians may have tried their hands at plantation agriculture.[7] A few Yamasees even appear to have owned livestock, such as one man who sought compensation from the South Carolina government for "some hogs" confiscated by an English army that descended on St. Augustine in 1702.[8]

In particular, military service drew English and Indian men into tight company. During a Spanish invasion of South Carolina in August 1706, militia leaders recruited Indians to repulse a hostile party that landed on James Island. The Indians accorded themselves well in that encounter, so the following April the South Carolina assembly implemented a defense policy whereby Indians were called on to help man various ranger posts.[9] The Edisto Island post, for example, was to have one white man and two Indians, whereas at Port Royal, Thomas Nairne was to direct a scout boat manned by four Indians and two white men.[10] While we may never know precisely how those multicultural units interacted, the long, monotonous routines of scouting together in isolation may have enabled them to learn a bit of each other's language, share food, work together, and perhaps engage in more meaningful conversations.

Indeed Indian and English men seem to have had ample opportunity to interact, not simply while working in defense or in the deerskin trade, but also in social settings. Convivial drinking, for example, was common among frontier men of both cultures. Much of this drinking no doubt occurred in Indian towns but also seems to have been tolerated, perhaps even promoted, in colonial settlements. In May 1714 one enterprising individual, John Jordine, set up a "punch house for the Indians" at Cochran's Point, at Port Royal. South Carolina authorities later reprimanded Jordine, not because he had sold alcohol to the Indians, but because he had no license from the government to do so.[11] Evidently authorities saw nothing in itself strange about a white barkeeper cultivating an Indian clientele.

This is not to romanticize the relationship between Indians and English colonists as being universally amicable. As the outbreak of war attests, that was far from the case. Yet even when parsing through the journals of the South Carolina Indian commissioners, which record the myriad complaints of Indians against the traders and white neighbors, one cannot help but notice the degree of intimacy between them that provided the context for their grievances. The traders' chronic physical abuse of the Indians, for instance, is symptomatic of familiarity rather than strangeness. Indian complaints against the traders could likewise assume a familial dimension, as when the traders abused their Indian spouses, divorced them, or tried to make wives of unwilling women. Keeping in mind this more nuanced view of the antebellum context, it is possible to reframe the Yamasee War as a conflict between intimate acquaintances, and in some cases between neighbors, rather than one between two cultures that misunderstood each other and could not bridge their cultural differences.

As is often the case in wars pitting former allies against one another, one detects a degree of ambivalence in its conduct. While some at Pocotaligo beat the drums of war, there were a number of individuals who tried to minimize its effects or avoid bloodshed altogether. Some no doubt pursued this course of action for strategic reasons, as many Indians already knew and feared the capabilities of the South Carolina war machine. But also Indians sought to limit bloodshed for emotional reasons, stemming from their personal attachments to particular colonists they considered friends. Some Indians likewise had relatives, "mixed blood" or not, living within the Carolina settlements and wished to spare them from the violence that was about to be unleashed.

It is therefore important to note that several Indians tried to warn their English friends ahead of time of the imminent danger they were in, thereby betraying the secrecy of war plans being hatched at Pocotaligo. Such was the case with a Yamasee Indian named Cuffy, who warned the wife of Port Royal trader William Bray of Creek Indian plans to "cut off" the traders and later to attack the settlements.[12] Likewise an Apalachicola man informed trader Samuel Warner of a Creek Indian plan to begin attacking "upon the first affront from any of the Traders." Most interesting perhaps is the story of trader John Fraser, who had befriended a Yamasee Indian named Sanute. Several weeks before the beginning of the war, Sanute paid a visit to Fraser's wife, washed her face and hands with water and herbs, and then declared "for the future, he would communicate to her all he knew in his heart." Sanute returned to Mrs. Fraser's house about nine days before the massacre at Pocotaligo and related to her in detail that the Indians, in conjunction with the Spanish, had formed a vast conspiracy to wage war against the Carolinians. The Frasers, like several others given advance warning, seemed not to believe these warnings and did too little, too late to alert their neighbors.[13]

In addition to giving advance warning to their English friends, there seems to have been a significant number of Indians who were reluctant to wage war against the Carolinians. The Yamasees, most agreed, struck the "first blow," but even among them we find hints that a minority disagreed with the hostile course of action that had been taken. S.P.G. minister Gideon Johnston, for example, reported a rumor that some Yamasee warriors refused to partake in the war against the South Carolinians.[14] Following the war Creek Indians tried to exonerate themselves by shifting the weight of the blame onto the Yamasees. Emperor Brims, among others, accused them of dragging his people into the conflict, as if the Creeks had had second thoughts about using military force all along.

Nor did those who took up arms kill English settlers indiscriminately, as there are many instances where Indian leaders sheltered their friends or others they considered "good" people. Writing over sixty years after the war, historian Alexander Hewatt recounted several instances in which the Indians had spared the lives of English colonists, suggesting that only "such as had no friends among them [the Indians] were tortured in the most shocking manner."[15] Women, in particular, seem to have been spared, such as "Mrs. Sisson" and one "Mrs. McCartney," who the Yamasees captured and carried to St. Augustine, as well as the wife of William Bull, who survived for more than two years as a prisoner among the Creeks.[16]

It is remarkable that several Indian traders also survived the war due to the protection as "prisoners" they received from the Indians. Trader John Chester and one other man, for example, endured among the Creeks for two years before the Creeks sent them back to the colony in the spring of 1717, much to the astonishment of South Carolina authorities, who had long given them up for dead.[17] Also improbable was the survival of Port Royal planter Hugh Bryan, who was captured soon after the initial massacre at Pocotaligo. Rather than kill him outright or subject him to torture, the Yamasees carried him to St. Augustine, where he languished for the better part of a year. While there, a Yamasee chief known as the Huspaw King looked after his well-being, causing Bryan to relate after his eventual return to the colony that the Huspaw King "has all along been a friend to the English saving his life when a great many others were cruelly put to death by ye Indians in cold blood."[18]

Only in retrospect of the violence begun in 1715, then, does Anglo-Indian relationship that preceded it assume the character of a black-and-white confrontation between irreconcilable foes. The war's English survivors, and historians who have written in their behalf, have tended to emphasize the military conflict and political breakdown between the South Carolinians and Indians, thereby characterizing the antebellum years as a prelude to the great "Indian War." While justifiable from one perspective, doing so has had the adverse effect of obscuring the varying shades of gray that was the cultural and social matrix for many a frontier life, Mary and John Musgrove's among them. We therefore have found it hard to imagine a world in which Indians learned to speak English and, conversely, in which English farmers learned to plant and eat Indian foods. Theirs was a world in which Indian and English people called each other neighbors, and, on occasion, learned to love one another. Mary and John Musgrove were the living embodiments of these processes. That the Indian War brought this world to a rather abrupt end must have been, for them and for others like them, a bitter pill to swallow.

A World (Partially) Restored

Following the Yamasee War, both South Carolina and Creek leaders took decisive measures to eliminate the intimacy and fluidity that had characterized their prewar relationship. South Carolinians, still reeling from the attacks that wiped out two parishes, established a ring of forts on the colony's borders to prevent future Indian incursions and to defend themselves against the Spanish or French, with whom the Creeks and other tribes were now allied. Three of these forts in particular were intended to protect the colony's southwest border: Fort Moore (opposite present-day Augusta, Georgia); Palachacola Fort, on the Savannah River; and Fort King George, built in 1721 at the mouth of the Altamaha River. Each was fortified, armed, and garrisoned with a small company of men. These forts, and others like them elsewhere in the colony, also served as a place of respite for several companies of rangers and militiamen employed to search the countryside for any sign of danger, come as it may from Indians, Spaniards, or rebellious slaves.[19]

The Creek Indians likewise attempted to create a buffer between themselves and the colonists. Anticipating English reprisals, in 1716 the Creeks scattered in several towns along the Ocmulgee, Oconee, and Savannah Rivers relocated to their former territory on the Chattahoochee.[20] More than a year later, the Creeks agreed to a peace treaty that established a boundary between them and the English at the Savannah River. As it applied to the Creeks, the treaty forbade them from crossing to the river's north bank. South Carolinians were conversely prohibited from settling south of the river, and from bringing their livestock there.[21]

These defensive measures and the mutually agreed-on buffer zone drawn at the Savannah River reflect more than just a preoccupation with security. Also important was a heightened sensitivity about race, particularly among white South Carolinians, who increasingly came to view both Indians and Africans as a fifth column that threatened the colony's internal stability. Much has previously been written on the subject of race as it applies to white Carolinains' views of African slaves.[22] But whereas the story of South Carolina's "black majority" is well known, significantly less attention has been given to the status of Indians within the colony and to what degree racial anxiety among whites was a product of their interaction with them. Recently William Ramsey has argued persuasively that the Yamasee War deserves emphasis as an important catalyst for white South Carolinians' racial attitudes. Ramsey notes that anti-Indian rhetoric became more pervasive in the speeches of South Carolina's leaders during the war, and that the practice of enslaving Indians declined precipitously over the next decade.[23] Most telling, perhaps, was the South Carolina legislature's "comprehensive set of race-based responses" that were intended to promote the viability and growth of the colony's white population.[24]

Together the growth of the colony's black numerical majority and the protections devised to buttress the white minority's numbers and legal status contributed to a process we might call the "whitening and blackening" of South Carolina. This left little room conceptually for Indians, who were to play little to no role in the new order of plantation agriculture. Yet the colony was not in a position to entirely dispense with local Indian allies, who served as scouts, messengers, and, what is most important, as a fighting force to oppose Spanish and Yamasee invasions or to capture runaway slaves. Thus South Carolina's emerging racial order of black and white left just enough wiggle room for the continued presence of Indians. However, the need to distinguish between the colony's friends and foes subjected all Indians to white scrutiny, a process Ramsey describes as "an early exercise in 'racial profiling,'" in which South Carolina became "a testing ground for new racial definitions, boundaries, and policies that set the tone for the colony's plantation regime."[25] In this context, then, emerged the small but strategically important Indian/mestizo community that took up residence on or near John Musgrove's land and whose members were often referred to as "the Indians at Pon Pon."

The Pon Pon Indians' saga begins with the marriage of John and Mary Musgrove, which most likely occurred sometime in early 1717, and under the auspices of the church. Shortly after their nuptials, John began looking for a suitable property for breeding livestock and on February 5, 1717, purchased five hundred acres of land near the "Round-O" Savannah in St. Bartholomew's parish, Colleton County.[26] This coincided with the influx of mestizos who had lived at Pon Pon before the war, like Mary's brother Edward, her half-Creek kinsman "Tommy" Jones, and the Welch brothers—pioneers of a sort. These bicultural children, now young adults, were well positioned to fill the void left by the parish's white inhabitants. Not only did ties to their mothers' communities uniquely position them to serve as cultural intermediaries, but also their bicultural upbringings made them socially adroit in a variety of contexts, enough, it seems, to overcome the racial profiling to which their white neighbors subjected them. In addition this mestizo cohort suffered disproportionately from Indian attacks, both during the Yamasee War and the long war of reprisal that followed. They seem consequently to have developed an unequivocal hatred for the Yamasees, or at least those they held responsible for killing their fathers and for throwing their lives in general disarray. In this they found common cause with white South Carolinians.

Whether or not John ever intended for his Indian relatives to move with him is difficult to judge. But just as kinship connected Pon Pon's mestizo community, kinship also factored heavily in attracting both Creeks and Yamasees to the area. Musgrove's "uncle" from Apalachicola, Whitlemico, appears to have been the first to arrive at Pon Pon, shortly after John's land purchase. Following him to St. Bartholomew's was a Creek man named Oweeka, a warrior who earned praise from the South Carolina government on several occasions for his exploits against the Yamasees. Circumstantial evidence suggests that these men attracted a handful of followers over the years, most of whom were Creek, but also others, like one "Wehomee," who were Yamasee. As permanent unisex Indian settlements were unheard of, we may assume that theirs also included women and children. And even a conservative estimate of their numbers—say, twenty-five—would seem to indicate a substantial presence in a parish that was so thinly populated.

Another factor drawing Indians to the area was the former Yamasee reservation adjacent to Port Royal. Though South Carolina officials considered it "abandoned," the Yamasee reserve continued to attract both Creek and Yamasee Indians for many years. Some came there with the peaceful intent to trade or hunt. Others lurked in the area plundering English settlements. All Indians might have agreed, though, that they had a right to those lands, as did one Yamasee man who claimed that "he had as much right to the land as we [the English] for land was free as Air & water to everybody."[27] It is important that the main path running through the former Yamasee reserve connected the Palachacola Fort on the Savannah River to Pon Pon. It served on the one hand as a thoroughfare for Indian visitors to Charles Town, not to mention Yamasee war parties. Conversely that same path allowed the Pon Pon Indians easy access not only to Palachacola Fort, but also to Port Royal and the interior. As a consequence, much of the Pon Pon Indians' activity seems to have taken place on or near that path, which enabled them to move readily between South Carolina and the Creek nation.[28] The Pon Pon Indians, then, did not remain isolated in St. Bartholomew's parish but instead ranged far and wide, in war and in peace, to create a considerable sphere of interaction.

The Pon Pon Indian community's existence, however, should be considered more broadly than as only evidence for the permeability of South Carolina's southern frontier. In addition, their presence would have had profound social implications and may help to explain how the Musgroves managed to retain the cultural trappings of "Creekness." For example, it is likely that the Creek language remained much in use on the Musgrove estate, as neither Whitlemico, Oweeka, nor any of the community's other members are on record as knowing how to speak English. John and Mary, then, would have been required to speak—and therefore retain—their native language, which is perhaps why the couple could be classified as "additive" bilinguals who acquired a second language without losing the ability to use their first. In addition to language, we may also imagine that certain aspects of Creek ritual life persisted at the Musgroves' estate, as likely did Creek oral traditions, and culinary and medicinal practices. It is therefore plausible to assume that John and Mary had ample opportunity to partake of the culture into which they were born—even as proximity to their English neighbors and the demands of business required them to present themselves more or less as English.

In some important ways St. Bartholomew's parish was a likely place for this unique community to find a home. The parish's total destruction during the Yamasee War had essentially returned it to frontier conditions, as Indians burnt the main bridge across the Edisto, limiting settler access to St. Bartholomew's and other southward parishes. Death and out-migration of the civilian population reduced the parish's population essentially to zero, and Yamasee attacks there persisted for more than a decade after the war's supposed "end" in 1717, making it a dangerous place to live. As a consequence, even in 1721 only forty-seven "free" heads of household (along with 144 slaves) lived in St. Bartholomew's, scattered thinly over the more than thirty-six thousand acres of the parish's taxable land.[29]

The dearth of white inhabitants may have been one of the parish's attractive features, in that it lent to the Indians a measure of invisibility. It is important that white people living in St. Bartholomew's may have welcomed the Pon Pon Indians because of their defense needs. By March 1717 the Pon Pon region had become a war zone again, when an Indian war party made a brazen incursion into the heart of St. Bartholomew's parish, killing trader William Steads at his "cowpen" near the Edisto River, afterward murdering William Saunders and his wife.[30] This same party appears to have remained active in late March and early April, as rumors of a "small parcel of sculking Indians" operating on "the other side of Pon Pon" continued to haunt colony officials.[31]

Within a couple of years, Whitlemico, Oweeka, and several of the Pon Pon mestizos were making themselves useful to the colony in its fight against the Yamasees at St. Augustine. Among the first to recognize their potential utility as a military force was Captain John Barnwell, commander of a small garrison at Port Royal, who had the unenviable task of defending the colony's southern frontier. In April 1719 Barnwell employed several of these Creek Indians to accompany him to the St. Mary's River, from which he sent three Creek runners to make contact with the Huspaw King, the Yamasee instigator of the recent war. In accordance with his instructions from the South Carolina government, Barnwell sent the three Indian men to invite the Huspaw King to make peace, and return to his vacated town in South Carolina. The Huspaw King refused, however, and Barnwell's Creek informants warned him of an imminent attack against Carolina. "Pon Pon I fear [for] much," Barnwell wrote, after receiving word that the Yamasees intended specifically to attack there.[32]

That summer the Yamasees struck, not at Pon Pon, but at the home of George Burrows on Hilton Head Island. The Yamasees took Mrs. Burrows prisoner, killing their child, two of their servants, and a neighbor named Mrs. McCord.[33] Mr. Burrows later sailed to St. Augustine under a flag of truce to free his wife but was detained there by the Spanish, causing Barnwell to organize yet another war party to render justice. At Port Royal, Barnwell gathered an impressive contingent of Creek Indians, who traveled with him by water to St. Augustine. The composition of the Creek leadership, which Barnwell identified in some detail, reveals the Pon Pon community's kinship ties to John and Mary Musgrove. The main fighting force consisted of forty to fifty "Creek Indians," all commanded by Oweeka. Musgrove's uncle, Whitlemico, was Oweeka's second in command. Also fighting under their leadership was John Musgrove and Mary's brother, Edward Griffin, both described as "half breed or mustees." Joining them was a lone "whiteman" named Melvin, probably William or

John Melvin, both of whom lived near Musgrove in St. Bartholomew's parish.[34] While it is improbable that forty to fifty Creek men, with their families, lived in St. Bartholomew's permanently, their presence nevertheless suggests that the Musgroves attracted them there on at least a temporary basis. Their presence confirms, too, the existence of a dependable path of communication between the Musgrove estate and the Creek nation.

It is likewise the case that some of Musgrove's friends and relatives were well connected to the Yamasees through intermarriage. In fact the Pon Pon Indians' forays against the Yamasees seem to have been conducted for reasons that were as much personal and familial as they were for the colony's defense. Moreover their stated goals suggest a kind of nostalgia for the prewar status quo, in which Yamasee and Creek Indians lived amicably in proximity to the South Carolinians. Concerning the April foray to Florida, for instance, three Creek men described as being "related to the Huspaw King" initiated the proposal to venture to St. Mary's, assuring South Carolina officials that they "could prevail with the Huspaw King to desert the Spaniards & bring over the Yamasee Indians with him to come & make a Peace with us [the English] & return to their former obedience under this Government."[35] They failed, but the September expedition is even more revealing in that some of the Creek Indians who fought under Oweeka were more concerned with retrieving "relatives" who still lived among the Yamasees.[36]

That self-interest spurred the actions of the Pon Pon Indians on one occasion suggests the probability that self-interest would govern their actions in the future. In this we see the seeds of potential conflict with the white colonists of South Carolina, particularly because each side held mutually opposing views of the southern frontier's destiny. For their part, most white South Carolinians desired to stabilize the frontier, so as to facilitate European settlement and the expansion of the plantation system, and to bring law and order to the colony's outlying areas. Pon Pon's Indians, in contrast, preferred the status quo, which enabled them move about undetected, in order to go to war, to hunt and fish, or to engage in illicit trade with welcoming white neighbors. The relationship between the Pon Pon Indians and their white neighbors turned on this axis, with periods of mutual accommodation punctuated by episodes mutual hostility. As a result, white South Carolinians and the Pon Pon Indians came to look on each other with suspicion, making both sides ambivalent about their proximity to one another.

The first sign of open hostility between the Pon Pon Indians and white Carolinians appears in the first week of 1722. On January 5 the Commons House of Assembly sent a message to Governor Francis Nicholson, imploring him to enforce the article of the Indian Trade Act that prohibited Indians from coming into the settlements. Creek and other Indians were then known to advance into the colony "under the colour of trading," only to turn on the inhabitants by stealing their cattle, by enticing their slaves to run away, and by committing unspecified "disturbances & mischiefs" at Port Royal. Moreover the Commons House message makes it clear that the man they held responsible for this mischief was John Musgrove's uncle Whitlemico, and they demanded that the governor order him and "his people . . . who now live on the other side of Pon Pon River" out of the settlement.[37]

That white South Carolinians engaged in a form of racial profiling to distinguish between its Indian friends and foes living in Pon Pon, however, can be gleaned from the different way the authorities handled Oweeka. Oweeka, by contrast, had recently proven his loyalty to the English by fighting against the Yamasees again at St. Augustine, causing the house to recommend that he be offered "further encouragement" to continue his fight. Taking the house's advice, the South Carolina Council promptly drafted a resolution offering to bring "Oweka and his people" to Charles Town, desiring the governor to "Treat him and them and make a present of such of his majesty's stores . . . from the government."[38]

The problem, as Whitlimico and Oweeka knew, and as the South Carolina government came to understand, was that the Pon Pon Indians had little control over Creek and Yamasee interlopers who came to visit them. Whitlemico later explained this to Governor Nicholson, when he begged him to rescind the order of banishment and allow him to "live on his cozen's [Musgrove's] land as he has done these four or five years past." Whitlemico promised good behavior and vowed "to suffer no Indians to come to him," suggesting that his Indian guests had instigated the recent mischief at Port Royal. Convinced of Whitlemico's "good character," Governor Nicholson recommended that the Commons House rescind the order for his banishment, which it did, on the condition that he follow through with his promise not to receive Indian visitors.[39]

As it turned out, Whitlimico was never able (or perhaps willing) to stem the flow of Indians into South Carolina, in particular a small gang made up of Creeks and Yamasees led by an Apalachicola chief named Cherokeeleechee. On record as having done much "harm" to the English during the Yamasee War, Cherokeeleechee remained something of a renegade after the war's supposed conclusion, settling with a pro-Spanish band of followers at the convergence of the Flint and Chattahoochee Rivers. Although the Creeks and Carolinians were officially at peace, Cherokeeleechee nevertheless carried on a clandestine war against the English by using the pretence of trade to gain admission to the area surrounding Port Royal. Providing cover were the Pon Pon Indians, who may have assisted Cherokeeleechee directly, or at least served him as unwitting accomplices. Why the Pon Pon Indians were willing to tolerate, perhaps even conspire with Cherokeeleechee's gang may be explained, in part, by the common Apalachicola origins that members of both groups shared. Most important, one of Cherokeeleechee's "relatives" was none other than Oweeka.[40] We may infer, then, that many, if not most, of the Pon Pon Indians were in some way related to Cherokeeleechee's gang, perhaps even John Musgrove, whose own ties to the Apalachicolas ran deep—at times, uncomfortably so.

The activities of Cherokeeleechee's gang in South Carolina first came to light in February 1723, when the South Carolina council complained of the recent murder of Port Royal Island planter David Duvall. Investigations later revealed that the murder was "likely done by Cherokeeleechee" and members of his "gang," several of whom lingered in the vicinity of Port Royal well into the summer.[41] At that point the gang's leadership fell on Istoweekee, a Yamasee man whose reputation for trouble was notorious among Port Royal planters. By June rumors that Istoweekee was being harbored by Hilton Head Island planter William Blakeway surfaced. According to one report, at Blakeway's Istoweekee kept a canoe, which he used to ferry over "several of the outlaying Pallacola Indians" to Port Royal, where they traded (illegally) with one Mr. Cullam. Later Istoweekee's gang appeared on Parris Island, terrorizing its inhabitants and luring slaves away from their masters' plantations. South Carolina authorities eventually captured Istoweekee and three other members of his gang, which consisted of another man and two women. John Barnwell later interrogated Istoweekee and, perhaps against his better judgment, sent him out of the colony. Barnwell also arrested William Blakeway for sheltering Istoweekee, but was forced to free him due to a "want of white evidence" to convict.[42]

Istoweekee's escapades in the summer of 1723 reveal the often-hidden complexities of life on the southern frontier and its racial fluidity. Istoweekee's interrogator, John Barnwell, complained that this "was now the fifth time he gave this trouble," indicating not only that he had been detained and released several times before, but also that his white friends, like William Blakeway, could not have cared less about his bad reputation. In fact Istoweekee later claimed that he ventured into the colony not on his own initiative, but rather upon the invitation of several Port Royal planters who wanted to trade with him. That Istoweekee's gang included two women suggests that they at one point had peaceful intentions, and that they had a lingering presence in South Carolina.

Moreover the identity of Istoweekee's Indian acquaintances indicates the breadth of the Indian networks then developing in the colony. For example, that network may have included some of the Indians living at Pon Pon, blithely referred to as the "outlaying Palachacolas" whom Istoweekee was known to ferry to Port Royal. Istowekee's network extended even to the Upper Creeks. The other Indian man captured along with him on Parris Island, in fact, was a well-known friend of the colony's named Hoboyhatchey, a headman from the Upper Creek village of Okchay, on the Coosa River.[43]

Of importance is that these Indians' networks also seem to have included Indian and "mustee" slaves, which undermined the ability of South Carolina planters to hold Indians in bondage and perhaps accelerated the institution's demise following the Yamasee War. At times the influence of free Indians on the enslaved was direct. Both Whitlemico and Istoweekee were accused of encouraging runaways, and Cherokeeleechee was known to have one "runaway" as a member of his gang. At other times the influence may have been indirect in that the presence of mobile "free" Indians inspired the slaves to gain their own freedom and provided cover that made it easier for them to move about without arousing suspicion. This latter scenario perhaps explains how in 1723 a group of Indian and mustee slaves fled from South Carolina only to turn up starving in the vicinity of Fort King George in July. The ringleader was a mustee slave from a Stono River plantation, who encouraged four other men (three from Colleton County plantations) to make their unsuccessful attempt for freedom at St. Augustine.[44]

Adding to this complex pattern of Indian mobility and interaction are the officially sanctioned visits of Creek leaders, many from Coweta, who made a habit of resting at Pon Pon before heading into Charles Town. For example, when Brims's "son" Ouletta came to Charles Town to meet Governor Nicholson in 1721, reports tracking his whereabouts indicated his "intent" to stop at Pon Pon.[45] When Ouletta again met with Nicholson the following year he took the same route and spent more than three months at Pon Pon, giving him ample opportunity to visit the Musgroves.[46] That the Coweta leadership regarded the Musgroves' home a destination on their way to Charles Town may be confirmed by a visit made by Chigelly and Ouletta in October 1723. Evidently the pair spent about nine days with the Musgroves, as indicated by John's later request for compensation for "dieting" (that is, boarding) them.[47] Moreover, as high-level Coweta leaders made at least two more visits to South Carolina in 1727 and 1728, it is difficult to imagine the Musgroves and other Indians at Pon Pon not somehow making contact with them.[48]

While the South Carolinians may have found the Pon Pon Indians' contact with the Coweta leadership convenient as a means of advancing Indian diplomacy, it is also the case that the government feared their interaction. The main reason was that the Pon Pon Indians' proximity to Charles Town and the outlying settlements enabled them to serve as the eyes and ears for Creek leaders—spies. Their continued interaction therefore guaranteed that any news from the colonies could easily reach the Creek nation, free and unfiltered through the fog of diplomacy in which the colony's Indian agents typically engaged. Just as often, communication between Pon Pon and the Creek nation allowed for the proliferation of rumors and innuendo, which complicated diplomacy for both sides. Particularly important to the spread of information were the mestizos living at Pon Pon, many of whom spoke English and at least one Indian tongue. At times, the Pon Pon mestizos seem to have deliberately spread information that contradicted the government's officially sanctioned speeches. On one noteworthy occasion Thomas Jones "the half breed" spread word in Coweta that the South Carolina government had given "no talk to kill the

Yamasees," when in fact the Carolinians had been encouraging the Creeks for years to do so. Consequently Jones's false words made it difficult for at least one Creek leader, who complained of appearing as a "lyer" when he tried to recruit Coweta warriors to fight against them.[49] Nor was even John Musgrove immune from the temptation to spread dangerous rumors. At some point in the summer of 1723, Musgrove returned to Coweta spreading a story that the Cowetas had spurned recent peace overtures made to them by the South Carolina government. Ouletta later reported that Musgrove said he had "heard that the Cowetas were to make the path bloody and that the said Ouletta [speaking] had despised the English talk; and scorned the presents given him" the year before.[50] Ouletta later denied the accusation and had to make yet another visit to Charles Town to smooth over Coweta's then-rocky relationship with South Carolina officials.

The loose lips of the Pon Pon Indians were clearly on the mind of South Carolina Indian agent Tobias Fitch when he conducted the second of two agencies to the Creeks in 1726. Writing from the Creek nation, Fitch confided that "I find that the Indians that live about Pon Pon are very pernicious to our interest here," mentioning one unnamed individual who "confuses the people, by telling them the prices of goods, in the settlement."[51] Such information was potentially damaging, as it made it easy for Indians to calculate the traders' profit margins, giving them leverage to bargain for better prices. More than two months later, at a general meeting held in Tuckabatchee, Fitch raised the issue again, making good on his vow to "complain to them of their people who reside among us and if possible put a stop to any more going down."[52] That Fitch recorded no Indian response to this complaint perhaps indicates the Creeks' unwillingness to do so.

Even more damning were the recent deeds of the Pon Pon Indians. Up to that point, colonial officials had tended to blame others for the various insults committed by Indians against the plantations. It became difficult for the Pon Pon Indians to evade suspicion however, when in the middle of August 1726, six Indians murdered a man and his wife on Hilton Head Island. Two weeks later, the same party moved inland, killing John Edwards and absconding with the slaves at his Ashepoo River plantation.[53] South Carolina officials almost immediately suspected Cherokeeleechee's hand at work and later organized a small war party to "bring in [his] head."[54] But by then Carolina officials had begun to connect the dots in a way that suggested the Pon Pon Indians' complicity in the murders. Edwards's plantation, for instance, was less than a day's walk from the Musgrove lands in St. Bartholomew's, a fact that must have first raised suspicions.[55] Council president Arthur Middleton likewise perceived that "the mischief is done by the stragling Creeks, that live in those lower parts & seldom go up to their nation." Middleton identified the leader as "the relation of one [Oweeka]," a discovery that seemed to implicate the Pon Pon Indians. Consequently Middleton ordered agent Fitch to inform the

Creeks of the recent "mischief" and to "press them to put a stop to them." To prevent future attacks, he urged the Creeks to "send for all their people up that live about Pon Pon, and all other parts" and order them home to the Creek villages. At that point Middleton was clearly serious about his desire for the Pon Pon Indians to depart the colony, warning that he would take "another course with them" (that is, one involving force) if they failed to do so.[56]

In St. Bartholomew's, these and like incidents contributed to a mounting climate of anxiety, which found expression in the various petitions for relief its residents sent to governing officials in Charles Town.[57] We can only guess, but this climate of anxiety must have had some impact on the lives of Mary and John Musgrove, as well as the Creek Indians who lived at Pon Pon. How was it possible for the Musgroves to avoid suspicion when it had become readily apparent that Indians living on their land (and perhaps related to them) had a hand in so many recent murders and violations of settler property? The answer may be found in the manner and intensity with which Musgrove and others from the Pon Pon community demonstrated their "English" credentials, in their dress, mannerisms, and economic pursuits, and, most important, in their war exploits. This latter attribute can be seen in John's response, and that of other mestizos, to a series of crises involving the Creek Indians that confronted the colony between 1727 and 1732. On multiple occasions, John Musgrove acted in a manner that demonstrated his loyalty to the government and that his interests were the same as those of any white South Carolinian. Perhaps John's motivation sprang from an anxiety about his ambiguous racial origins, and he found that his service to South Carolina "whitened" him in the eyes of his neighbors. Perhaps he was simply trying to protect his Indian relatives and make up for their bad behavior. Perhaps John even had come to identify with his late father and his white neighbors at St. Bartholomew's and, at certain moments, viewed Indians as much a menace as did they.

The first such crisis requiring John Musgrove's intervention began in the summer of 1727. At the beginning of August, trader Matthew Smallwood's Indian slave named "Jack," demonstrating his own loyalty to the colonists, reported that some Creek Indians had robbed his master's trading house located near the forks of the Altamaha River, killing Smallwood and several others in the process.[58] Immediately upon hearing word of the murders, the Commons House of Assembly sent a messenger to Pon Pon to contact John Musgrove and James Welch, asking them to go to the forks to investigate the situation. The Commons House judged the two men "proper for that service" because they were the most capable of a "[quick] dispatch."[59] The messenger might also have made a verbal agreement with the two men for financial compensation, as both later received fifty pounds for their service.[60] Musgrove and Welch promptly set out to for the forks and returned on September 21 to Charles Town, where they confirmed before government officials the destruction of Smallwood's store.

While on one level a practical decision based on their knowledge of Indian languages and the terrain, the appointment of Musgrove and Welch for this mission also indicates the degree of trust colony officials placed in the two men. While both were away at the forks, in fact, the Commons House's Committee of Indian Affairs made plans to have Musgrove and Welch command a war party consisting of twenty white men and whatever "Chickesaws and neighbouring Indians can be gott" to fall upon the Yamasees, who were leading suspects in Smallwood's murder.[61] The house clearly had faith not only that white soldiers would follow their lead in battle, but also in their ability to secure the loyalty of Indians. Welch, they expected, could recruit a few of the Chickasaws (then living at the Palachacola fort). Musgrove, it was assumed, would hold sway over some of the more loyal Pon Pon Indians, who were already working as auxiliaries to one of the ranger units operating in St. Bartholomew's.[62]

Conversely Musgrove's and Welch's zealous response to the call of duty suggests more than a pecuniary interest, but rather a genuine willingness to assist the colony in its time of need. For one thing, the two men carried out their mission to the forks with great efficiency, making the round trip in just a few weeks and providing a detailed report on the condition of Smallwood's store. Most telling, perhaps, was Musgrove's willingness to implicate the Creeks in Smallwood's murder. In their report to the South Carolina council, Musgrove and Welch mentioned two separate "paths" leading away from Smallwood's store, which the murderers must have used in their return home. One path pointed vaguely south in the direction of Cherokeeleechee's village or St. Augustine. The other, Musgrove must have confided with some regret, led west in the direction of the Lower Creeks, one report indicating that the guilty included warriors that "belong[ed] to Chigelly" of Coweta.[63]

The evidence that Musgrove and Welch obtained thus seemed to reveal a conspiracy involving the Yamasees, Cherokeeleechee's gang, and the Lower Creeks, which influenced the colony's plans to retaliate. Initially the South Carolina government proposed sending a small war party under Musgrove and Welch to fall upon on the Yamasees, while a larger force of three hundred white men was to march through the Lower Creek villages and proceed south to attack Cherokeeleechee. Colony officials later revised these plans and instead decided to apply most of the colony's force against the Yamasees near St. Augustine. Musgrove and Welch, then, were to lead a smaller party of Indians through Creek territory and attack the Yamasees by land from the northwest. In addition to this show of force, South Carolina authorities took diplomatic measures by appointing Fort Moore commander Charlesworth Glover as agent to the Creeks. Glover's job consisted in part of bringing the Creeks to "reason" and recruiting some of them to assist the colony in its impending attack on the Yamasees.[64]

As on previous occasions, Musgrove served the colony loyally and well during Glover's agency, as did several others drawn from Pon Pon's mestizo and

Indian community. For his part, Musgrove worked in the employ of Glover for six months beginning in November 1727, presumably assisting him in turning the Creeks against the Yamasees. The following February, Glover commissioned him and one other Indian known as the Tuckesaw King to command a party of thirty warriors to attack the Yamasees at St. Augustine. Though they arrived two days after Captain John Palmer's larger force laid waste to the Yamasee villages, they nevertheless returned that April to Glover bearing two Yamasee scalps.[65] Musgrove then escorted a large Creek delegation to Port Royal later that spring, where Coweta chiefs Brims and Chigelly were regaled with food, drink, and presents. Though he did not end up in Musgrove's war party, James Welch also contributed handsomely to the effort against the Yamasees by joining one of John Palmer's companies, which also included several of St. Bartholomew's white residents, such as John and William Melvin.[66] Most conspicuous, perhaps, in assisting the colony was Oweeka, who served along with several other Indians as auxiliaries to John Palmer and seems to have played an important role in bringing the Yamasees to heel. Colonial officials, in fact, singled him out for being "serviceable in several expeditions against the Yamasees." On May 3, 1728, Oweeka attended a session of the Commons House of Assembly, which rewarded him not only with a laudatory oration, but also with a new a gun, a fine sword with a brass handle, and a new suit of clothes, for which the house paid a bit extra to have trimmed in lace.[67]

If at one level the involvement of Pon Pon's men served the interest of the South Carolina colony, it should also be stressed that they had their own reasons for fighting the Yamasees. If, in fact, some of the perpetrators of the Smallwood murders "belonged to Chigelly," then it would appear that Musgrove and others perhaps were running interference in their behalf by turning the colony's attention against the Yamasees, thus diverting suspicion away from Coweta. Indeed John Musgrove's attempt to recruit Creek warriors to assist him at St. Augustine may have served a similar purpose, by illustrating Creek loyalty to the English.

But the Pon Pon Indians were, after all, victims of Yamasee attacks and likely found common cause in suffering along with their white neighbors. Yamasee attacks had gone on for a long time but were also important in the immediate context of the 1728 campaigns and may explain the zealous service of Musgrove, Welch, and Oweeka. In fact by late August 1727, during the absence of Musgrove and Welch, reports surfaced of Indians "lurking upon the borders of our settlements on Pon Pon River," where they had begun "harassing" the people who lived there.[68] The same party that killed Smallwood, it seems, later advanced into Colleton County, killing two planters named Henry Mushoe (Michaux) and Hezekiah Wood, and carrying away ten of their slaves. Shortly thereafter Captain John Bull, one of St. Bartholomew's more eminent planters, organized a retaliatory party that chased the Yamasees, killing six (and one Spaniard) and earning the approbation of the colony's leaders.

The Indian threat continued well into the following year, and by February St. Bartholomew's residents had to abandon their homes and live "three four or five families together," leaving their plantations exposed to plunder.[69]

Nor had St. Bartholomew's residents much reason to return to their plantations in March, when the discovery of several "tracks" of Indians in the "southward" parts kept everyone there on the defensive and in a "naked and defenceless condition."[70] Things had gotten so bad that in April residents of both Colleton County parishes, St. Paul's and St. Bartholomew's, petitioned the governor to implement a comprehensive relief package, which included the printing of more paper money and the reduction of court fees. The petitioners justified such measures on the grounds that they were a "frontier province and are forced to stand as a barrier to North America" against its European and Indian foes. John Musgrove was absent at the time the petition circulated, but we might imagine that he would have set his mark to it had he been at home. Signatories included several men who lived near him, such as John Jackson, Moses Martin, and James Buer, as well as his next-door neighbor, Bryan Kelley.[71]

Following the pacification of the Yamasees in 1728, St. Bartholomew's parish seems to have enjoyed better times, as little to no violence occurred for several years thereafter. But, as if to prove that history repeats itself, in the summer of 1732, another violent encounter on the frontier drew Musgrove yet again into the colony's service. On August 16, 1732, reports surfaced that two traders named Shaw and Sanders had been killed near the Flint River. Consistent with the recent Smallwood murders, it appeared that the guilty party consisted of Yamasees, as well as a few Creeks, led by one "Malatchi" who was said to be the "son" of Brims of Coweta. As they had four years before, South Carolina officials tapped Charlesworth Glover to serve as Indian agent, ordering him first to round up some Yuchis at the Palachacola fort and then find John Musgrove to "attend him with the head men of those Creeks who reside at Yamacraw," where the Musgroves had moved but two months before. From there, they were to proceed first to Fort Moore and then to the Creek nation, where Glover stayed until October.[72]

The appearance of Creek complicity in the murder of Shaw and Sanders turned the colony's attention again to Pon Pon and its Indian inhabitants. Statements made at the time indicate, too, that frontier security required colony officials to engage in racial profiling to determine just which of the Creeks living there were friendly, and which were hostile. Fitting into the latter category was a group of Creek Indians that had "lately come into the settlement" that June to sign a peace treaty with Governor Robert Johnson, all evidence indicating that at least a few of them lingered there into August. The Commons House promptly sent a company of rangers to visit the out settlements at Pon Pon to encourage the settlers to "keep their settlement a good watch" and to order the Creeks to "depart as soon as possible." Not all Creeks were ordered to depart, however, for among the more trustworthy were those Indians who made South Carolina their permanent home and in whom the government placed greater trust. For this reason, the house ordered the ranger captains to recruit "Wehomee the Yamasee and the other Creek fellow [Whitlemico] who have been long in the settlements" to stay and "make them as serviceable as possible on all occasions."[73]

As it turned out, however, neither the rangers nor Wehomee and his Creek accomplice could fully bring order to the Pon Pon area. Just three weeks later, St. Bartholomew's planter William Cattell reported an attack on his plantation carried out by "some Creek Indians who for some years past have resided in the settlements." In addition to driving away an overseer and slave, the Indians "robbed his house, destroyed his corn, and broke down his fences." Long practiced in making arrangements to secure the Pon Pon area, the house promptly ordered ranger captain William McPherson to take a detachment of his men and "take or kill the said Indians."[74] The record is silent as to if or how McPherson carried out this order. But the event nevertheless confirms the enduring fluidity of South Carolina's southern frontier and the ambivalence with which Indians and white people continued to regard each other after John and Mary Musgrove's departure from the scene. Suspicions remained between Indians and colonists, even after fifteen years of living in close proximity to one another in St. Bartholomew's.

In retrospect, the Pon Pon Indians' story is important because it adds nuance to our understanding of South Carolina's early frontier history and the development of southern race relations. While the Yamasee War may constitute a significant fault line, it is likewise the case that personal connections enabled some individuals to repair the rift between Indians and colonists that the war had opened. Likewise the very existence of the Pon Pon Indian community and the high degree of mobility exercised by its members offers evidence that the southern frontier remained permeable, despite attempts by governing officials to solidify the boundary between Indian country and the colony. As a consequence of that permeability English colonists and Creek Indians interacted more often than we might imagine, leading to fluctuating episodes of cooperation and conflict that influenced regional patterns of racial ideology and diplomacy. Furthermore the presence of Indians on the Musgrove lands was important at a cultural level, mainly in the localized persistence of Creek ritual life, subsistence patterns, and language.

For the Musgroves in particular, the presence of Creek Indians on their property had the profound effect of preparing them for the work of cultural mediation in which they engaged throughout their lives. Not only did John and Mary master the delicate balancing act of living between two cultural systems, but also the Pon Pon Indians constituted a speech community that enabled Mary and John to maintain the use of their first language—Muskogee—which later propelled them into positions of authority as interpreters in Georgia. Looking ahead, we can see that the establishment of the Musgroves' trading post among Creek immigrants at Yamacraw Bluff (Savannah, Georgia) in 1732 resembled past patterns of settlement and interaction set in St. Bartholomew's parish. Though difficult to prove conclusively, it is reasonable to suspect that at least a few of the Pon Pon Indians joined the Musgroves at Yamacraw.

Looking ahead further still, the maturation of the Deep South's plantation system required the solidification of the boundaries between Indian country and the colonies and also amplified the importance of racial hierarchies that had once been less well defined. South Carolina officials (indeed all white Carolinians) consequently recalibrated their relationships with local Indians. While small, politically subjugated Indian communities would continue to live within the settlements, the future held no place for a group like the Pon Pon Indians, whose mobility and ties to Indians living in the interior made them a potential threat. Once an indelible part of the local social fabric, the Pon Pon Indian community became a dangerous anomaly at a time when the colony increasingly came to be defined in terms of white and black. Nevertheless their experience suggests that the Anglicization of South Carolina's southern frontier occurred more gradually than has been imagined, and remained incomplete even in the 1730s, when the process began anew farther south at Yamacraw Bluff.

Notes

1. George Rodd to his employer in London, May 8, 1715, in *CSPC*, 28:167.

2. Verner Crane, *The Southern Frontier, 1670–1732* (Tuscaloosa: University of Alabama Press, 2004), 162–86; Stephen J. Oatis, *A Colonial Complex: South Carolina's Frontiers in the Era of the Yamasee War, 1680–1730* (Lincoln: University of Nebraska Press, 2004); William Ramsey, *The Yamasee War: A Study of Culture, Economy, and Conflict in the Colonial South* (Lincoln: University of Nebraska Press, 2008).

3. Joshua Piker, "Colonists and Creeks: Rethinking the Pre-revolutionary Southern Backcountry," *JSH* 70, no. 3 (August 2004): 503–40.

4. For sources identifying mestizos of the Pon Pon community, see James Oglethorpe to William Bull, December 29, 1739, in *Appendix to the Report of the Committee of Both Houses of Assembly of the Province of South Carolina, appointed to Enquire into the Causes of the Disappointment of Success, in the Late Expedition against St. Augustine* (London: J. Roberts, 1743), 4; John Barnwell to Robert Johnson, [no date] ca. October, 1719, in BPRO-SC, 8:1; *South Carolina Council Journal* (hereafter SC-CJ), August 3, 1727, in CO 5/429, p. 5; *South Carolina Gazette*, December 23–30, 1732, no. 50.

5. Alan Gallay, *The Formation of a Planter Elite: Jonathan Bryan and the Southern Colonial Frontier* (Athens: University of Georgia Press, 1989), 6–14.

6. John Norris, "Profitable Advice for Rich and Poor," in *Selling a New World: Two Colonial South Carolina Promotional Pamphlets*, ed. Jack P. Greene (Columbia: University of South Carolina Press, 1989), 89, 109, 112.

7. Letter of John Stewart to William Dunlop, June 23, 1690, in J. G. Dunlop and Mabel Weber, "Letters from John Stewart to William Dunlop," *SCHGM* 32, no. 2 (April 1931): 94.

8. Minutes, February 17, 1703, in *JCHA 1703*, 48.

9. Nicholas Trott, "An Account of the Invasion of South Carolina by the French & Spaniards," August 24–September 6, 1706, Ms. 43/703 at SCHS.

10. Minutes, April 11, 1707, in CHJ, 149–51.

11. Minutes, May 20, 1714, in *JCIT*, 75.

12. Minutes, August 12, 1715, in CHJ, 5:434.

13. Alexander Hewatt, *An Historical Account of the Rise and Progress of the Colonies of South Carolina and Georgia*, vol. 1 (London: Alexander Donaldson, 1779), 215–17.

14. Edgar L. Pennington, "The South Carolina Indian War of 1715, as Seen by the Clergymen," *SCHGM* 32, no. 4 (October 1931): 256–57.

15. Hewatt, *Historical Account*, 1:221.

16. Ibid., 1:222, 240–41.

17. Minutes, March 22, 1717, in *JCIT*, 169; Joseph Boone to the Board of Trade, April 26, 1717, and Richard Beresford to the Board of Trade [same date], in BPRO-SC, 7:15–21.

18. [Benjamin Godin, Ralph Izard, and Edward Hyrne] Committee of the Assembly of Carolina to Messers Boone and Beresford, August 13, 1716, in CSPC, 29:219–20.

19. Crane, *Southern Frontier*, 187–205; Oatis, *Colonial Complex*, 147–49, 266–68.

20. Mark Boyd, "Diego Pena's Voyage to Apalache and Apalachicola in 1716," *Florida Historical Quarterly* 28 (July, 1949): 1–27.

21. Mary Bosomworth, Memorial to Alexander Heron, August 10, 1749, and Malatchi's Speech to Alexander Heron, December 7, 1749, in *Early American Indian Documents: Treaties and Laws, 1607–1789*, ed. John Juricek, vol. 11, *Georgia Treaties, 1733–1763* (Frederick, Md.: University Press of America, 1989), 141, 149.

22. Peter Wood, *Black Majority: Negroes in South Carolina from 1670 through the Stono Rebellion* (New York: Norton, 1996), 324.

23. Ramsey, *Yamasee War*, 159; Minutes, May 6, 1715, in CHJ, 4:196.

24. Ramsey, *Yamasee War*, 168, *Statutes at Large*, 646–47. For additional laws, see "Law to Determine Eligibility for Political Participation," July 29, 1717, and "Law to Regulate the Indian Trade, 1719," in *Early American Indian Documents: Treaties and Laws, 1607–1789*, vol. 16, *Carolina and Georgia Laws, 1733–1763*, ed. Alden Vaughan and Deborah A. Rosen (Frederick, Md.: University Publications of America, 1989), 202, 222 (hereafter *EAID-SC/GA*); Law to Encourage the Importation of Irish Servants, 1717, *Statutes at Large*, 3:2.

25. Ramsey, *Yamasee War*, 159–60.

26. Thomas and Elizabeth Jones to John Musgrove, Lease and Release, February 4–5, 1716/17, in South Carolina Register of the Province, Conveyance Book F (unpaginated), Microfilm Reel ST 0756, at SCDAH.

27. John Barnwell to Governor Francis Nicholson, September 17, 1723, in BPRO-SC, 10:150.

28. "Law to Strengthen Forts and Promote Indian Trade," ca. July 1722, in *EAID-SC/GA*, 252.

29. South Carolina census, January, 1721, in Governor Francis Nicholson Papers, MS Am 1455, no. 17, Harvard University Houghton Library.

30. Lords Proprietors to the Board of Trade, March 29, 1717, in *BPRO-SC*, 7:17.

31. Lords Proprietors to the Board of Trade, April 24, 1717, in *BPRO-SC*, 7:20.

32. John Barnwell to Robert Johnson, April 20, 1719, in *BPRO-SC*, 7:186.

33. Hewatt, *Historical Account*, 1:221–22, 240–41.

34. John Barnwell to Robert Johnson, [no date] ca. October, 1719, in *BPRO-SC*, 8:1–5

35. William Rhett to William Rhett Jr., April 28, 1719, in *BPRO-SC*, 7:188.

36. John Barnwell to Robert Johnson, [no date] ca. October, 1719, in *BPRO-SC*, 8:1–5.

37. *SC-CJ*, January 5, 1721/22, in CO 5/425, f. 219, f. 223.

38. Ibid.

39. *SC-CJ*, March 8, 1721/22, in CO 5/425, f. 287.

40. *SC-CJ*, September 3, 1726, Arthur Middleton to Tobias Fitch, [same date], in CO 5/429, 16. For evidence indicating Cherokeeleechee's culpability for the 1726 murders, see *SC-CJ*, November 17, 1726, Letter of Tobias Fitch to George Chicken, October 30, 1726, in CO 5/429, f. 76.

41. *SC-CJ*, February 11, 1722/3, in CO 5/425, f. 391.

42. John Barnwell to Gov. Francis Nicholson, September 17, 1723, in *BPRO-SC*, 10:148–52.

43. Ibid.

44. Letter of John Woort, July 30, 1723, in *BPRO-SC*, 10:128.

45. Journal of the Grand Council of South Carolina, June 28–July 11, 1721, John Green Transcripts, Ms. 34/0367 at SCHS.

46. *SC-CJ*, February 7, 1721/2, in CO 5/425, f. 237.

47. *SC-CJ*, October 3, 1723, in CO 5/427, p. 3; *JCHA February 7 and 14, 1723/4*, in CO 5/427, f. 176, 191; *SC-CJ*, February 15, 1723/4, in CO 5/427, p. 79.

48. *SC-CJ*, January 25–26, 1726/7, in CO 5/387, 237–47. For the 1728 visit and Musgrove's apparent role in escorting the Creeks to Port Royal, see, *JCHA July 15, 1731*, in CO 5/432, f. 61, p. 119; South Carolina Treasurer, Reports of Public Accounts, Ledger "C," November [date illegible, ca. 1728], f. 123, Microfilm Reel ST 0750 at SCDAH.

49. Gerard Monger to Governor Nicholson, September 24, 1723, in *BPRO-SC*, 10:157.

50. Ouletta's Speech, October 25, 1723, in *BPRO-SC*, 10:175.

51. *SC-CJ*, September 1, 1726, Letter of Tobias Fitch to Governor Nicholson, dated August 1, 1726, in CO 5/429, p. 15.

52. *SC-CJ*, November, 17, 1726, Letter of Tobias Fitch to Arthur Middleton, dated October 30, 1726, in CO 5/429, f. 76.

53. *SC-CJ*, September 3, 1726, Arthur Middleton's Letter to Tobias Fitch [same date], in CO 5/429, p. 16; *SC-CJ*, December 1, 1726, in CO 5/429, f. 85.

54. *SC-CJ*, November, 17, 1726, Letter of Tobias Fitch to Arthur Middleton, dated October 30, 1726, in CO 5/429, f. 76.

55. John Washington, Plat for 640 Acres in Colleton County, August 17, 1711, Colonial Plat Books (Copy Series), 11:523, at SCDAH.

56. SC-CJ, September 3, 1726, Letter of Arthur Middleton to Tobias Fitch, in CO 5/429, p. 16.

57. SC-CJ, October 7, 1726, in CO 5/429, p. 28–29. For a later petition, see JCHA May 8, 1731, in CO 5/432, f. 33; JCHA November 18, 1731, in CO 5/433, f. 2; SC-CJ, February 3, 1726/7, in CO 5/429, f. 135; SC-CJ, February 1 and 9, 1727/8, in CO 5/430, f. 4, 7; "The Representation and Petition of the Inhabitants of the Parishes of St. Paul's and St. Bartholomew's Conjoyned," April 5, 1728, in BPRO-SC, 13:19–25.

58. SC-CJ, August 2 and August 3, 1727, in CO 5/429, pp. 2–5.

59. SC-CJ, August 3, 1727, in CO 5/429, p. 5.

60. SC-CJ, September 30, 1727, in CO 5/429, p. 25; JCHA July 15, 1727; South Carolina Treasury, Reports of General Accounts, Ledger C, f. 29, at SCDAH.

61. SC-CJ, August 26, 1727, in CO 5/429, p. 18.

62. SC-CJ, August 24, 1727, in CO 5/429, p. 8.

63. Oboyhatchey, King of the Abecas to Arthur Middleton, September 13, 1727, in BPRO-SC, 13:71; SC-CJ, September 21, 1727, in CO 5/429, p. 10.

64. Steven C. Hahn, *The Invention of the Creek Nation, 1670–1763* (Lincoln: University of Nebraska Press, 2004), 139–48.

65. Charlesworth Glover, Journal, in BPRO-SC, 13:113, 129, 163.

66. Muster Rolls for Palmer Raid, 1728, in BPRO-SC, 13:194.

67. JCHA May 3, 1728, in CO 5/430, p. 90; South Carolina-Treasury, Reports of General Accounts, Ledger C, f. 106, 110, at SCDAH.

68. Speech of Arthur Middleton, SC-CJ, August 24, 1727, in CO 5/429, p. 8.

69. Arthur Middleton to the Board of Trade, June 13, 1728, in BPRO-SC, 13:61.

70. JCHA March 20, 1727/8, in CO 5/430, p. 67.

71. "The Representation and Petition of the Inhabitants of the Parishes of St. Paul's and St. Bartholomew's Conjoyned," April 5, 1728, in BPRO-SC, 13:19–25.

72. SC-CJ, August 16, 1732, in CO 5/434, f. 1–2; SC-CJ, September 6, 1732, in CO 5/434, f. 2.

73. SC-CJ, August 16, 1732, in CO 5/434, f. 1.

74. SC-CJ, August 30, 1732, in CO 5/434, f. 2.

Contributors

IAN BEAMISH is a graduate student in history at Johns Hopkins University. He is currently working on his dissertation, titled "Saving the South: Printing Agricultural Improvement in the American South, 1819–1870." It focuses on cotton plantations in order to examine the links between the emergence of a Southern agricultural literature, scientific agriculture, rational management, and changes in plantation and slave management.

ERIC E. BOWNE is an assistant professor of anthropology at Arkansas Tech University, where he teaches Native American culture, history, and archaeology. He is the author of *The Westos Indians: Slave Traders of the Early Colonial South*. His second book, *A Guide to the Chiefdoms of the Ancient South*, will be published in the spring of 2013.

JAMES TAYLOR CARSON is chair of the Department of History at Queen's University in Kingston, Ontario. His many publications related to Native American history and the history of the early southeast include *Making an Atlantic World: Circles, Paths, and Stories from the Colonial South* and *Searching for the Bright Path: The Mississippi Choctaws from Prehistory to Removal*. Between 2007 and 2010 he served as executive editor of the journal *Native South*.

CHRISTINE STYRNA DEVINE received her Ph.D. in history from the College of William and Mary. Her dissertation is "The Winds of War and Change: The Impact of the Tuscarora War on Proprietary North Carolina, 1690–1729." She has taught at Kutztown University and the University of Mary Washington. Her professional interests include historical archaeology and public history. She currently serves on the board of the Albemarle Charlottesville Historical Society and the Albemarle County Historic Preservation Committee.

S. MAX EDELSON is an associate professor of history at the University of Virginia. He is the author of *Plantation Enterprise in Colonial South Carolina*. His current research examines cartography and empire in British North America and the West Indies in the generation before the American Revolution. He is also developing MapScholar, a web tool for publishing digital cartographic collections.

STEPHEN FEELEY grew up in Norcross, Georgia, and graduated from Davidson College in North Carolina in 1996. He spent a year at the University of Swansea,

Wales, as a Rotary Ambassadorial Scholar before beginning graduate studies at the College of William and Mary. In 2007 he completed his dissertation, entitled "Tuscarora Trails: Indians, Migrations, and Constructions of Eighteenth-Century Frontiers." He is currently an associate professor of history at McDaniel College.

STEVEN C. HAHN is an associate professor of history at St. Olaf College. His research interests involve the native peoples of the colonial southeast, and he has published two books: *The Invention of the Creek Nation* and *The Life and Times of Mary Musgrove*. He lives in Northfield, Minnesota.

MARK G. HANNA is an assistant professor of history at the University of California in San Diego, where he teaches courses on the history of early America, the Atlantic World, global piracy, and the age of sail. He is currently nearing completion of his first book manuscript, *The Pirates' Nests: Piracy and the Formalization of the First British Empire*.

MATTHEW JENNINGS is an associate professor of history at Macon State College in Macon, Georgia, where he teaches courses on colonialism, early America, Native American, and African American history. His first book, *New Worlds of Violence*, was published in 2011 by the University of Tennessee Press. He also contributed to Robbie Ethridge and Sheri Marie Shuck-Hall's *Mapping the Mississippian Shatter Zone*. His collection of William Bartram's writings on southeastern Indians, *The Flower Hunter and the People,* is slated for publication in spring 2013. Matt is currently writing on the Native American presence at Ocmulgee and Thomas Paine's ideas regarding Native Americans.

MICHELLE LEMASTER is an associate professor of history at Lehigh University, specializing in colonial and American Indian history. Her book *Brothers Born of One Mother: British–Native American Relations in the Colonial Southeast* investigates the role that ideas about gender and family played in shaping intercultural relations in the Lower South.

ALEXANDER MOORE is a student of eighteenth-century South Carolina and of southern art history. A documentary editor, he has published editions of letters of Thomas Nairne, Native American treaties, letters and speeches of John C. Calhoun, and letters of the South Carolina artist Anna Heyward Taylor. His 1991 doctoral dissertation was a study of the Proprietary Revolution of 1719 in South Carolina. He is the author of *The Fabric of Liberty: The Society of the Cincinnati of the State of South Carolina*.

GREGORY E. O'MALLEY is an assistant professor of history at the University of California, Santa Cruz. He is the author of an article, a forthcoming book chapter, and several book reviews on the slave trade. He is currently nearing completion of his first book manuscript, *Final Passages: The British Intercolonial Slave Trade, 1619–1807*.

JUSTIN ROBERTS is an assistant professor of history at Dalhousie University in Halifax, Nova Scotia. His articles have been published in the *William and Mary*

Quarterly, Historical Geography, and *Slavery and Abolition.* He has a book forthcoming entitled *Slavery and the Enlightenment in the British Atlantic, 1750–1807.* It explores the impact of Enlightenment ideas on plantation management and slave work routines with a particular focus on Barbados, Jamaica, and Virginia. He is currently working on the historical geography of sugar agriculture in the Danish Caribbean and on population management in the seventeenth-century English Caribbean.

HANNO T. SCHEERER received his M.A. in American history from the John F. Kennedy Institute for North American Studies at the Free University of Berlin, Germany. He specializes in colonial and early American history and wrote his M.A. thesis on the South Carolina Revolution of 1719. Currently he is a research associate at the University of Trier, Germany. He is in the process of completing his dissertation on land appropriation in Ohio's Virginia Military District, 1787–1810.

JESSICA STERN is an associate professor of history at California State University, Fullerton. She has published a series of articles and essays on southeastern Native American and British settler production, exchange, and consumption of cross-cultural goods. An article related to her next project, an intellectual biography of Roger Williams, appeared in the fall 2011 issue of *Early American Studies.*

BRADFORD J. WOOD is a professor of history at Eastern Kentucky University and the author of *This Remote Part of the World: Regional Formation in Lower Cape Fear North Carolina, 1725–1775.* He is also the editor of the letters of the merchant and planter James Murray. His research focuses on the North Carolina tidewater during the colonial period.

INDEX

Abaco Island, Bahamas, 258
Acadia, 34; *see also* Nova Scotia
Act for the Liberty of Conscience, 331
Adair, James, 175
Addison, Joseph, 266
Adena civilization, 190
Admiralty, 299–300, 304, 306, 310; *see also* courts
Africa, 16, 131, 235–42, 244, 246–48, 300
Africans, 2–6, 10–12, 14, 16, 33, 61, 118–20, 124, 128–34, 213, 217–18, 220, 234–49, 262, 265, 349; *see also* slave trade, slavery
Aja people, 237
Akan people, 237
Alabama, 78
Algiers, 298
Allen, Andrew, 281, 284
Altamaha (Yamasee headman), 124
Altamaha chiefdom, 81
Altamaha River, 28, 39, 41, 43, 349, 358
Albemarle, George Monck, Duke of, 57, 257–59
Albemarle, North Carolina, 6–7, 15, 29–32, 166, 211–28, 321–37
Albemarle, the, 58
alcohol, 100, 121, 153, 346
"Amaira," 168
Amory, Jonathan, 304
Anglican, 15, 82, 133, 211–12, 221–23, 226, 257, 300, 322–23, 325–29, 331–32
Angola, 234, 239, 249
Anne, Queen, 263, 328
Antigua, 51, 55, 58, 223, 243
Apalachee Indians, 87, 127, 164, 197, 200, 202–3
Apalachee province, 35, 81, 88–89, 125–26, 164, 170, 172, 203

Apalachicola, 81–82, 87–89, 347, 350, 354–55
Appalachian Mountains, 28, 43, 78, 86
Archdale, John, 276, 297
Ashepoo River, 38, 357
Ashley River, 30–32, 58, 63, 82, 166
Assembly, Commons House of (North Carolina), 142, 322, 324–29, 331–33, 335–37; Commons House of (South Carolina), 16, 98, 100–1, 104, 106, 108, 128–29, 167, 169, 176, 273–87, 301, 305–6, 307–10, 353–54, 358–61; Upper House of (North Carolina), 328; Upper House of (South Carolina), 100
Atlantic, 7, 17, 27, 30, 37, 40, 42–43, 49–50, 128, 171, 195, 213–14, 220, 227–28, 235, 239–40, 297; coast, 28, 35, 43, 190; economy, 15, 30, 32; slave trade, 16, 216, 227, 234–35, 237–38, 241, 243–49; World, 15–16, 142, 227, 295
Atlantic Ocean, 33, 35, 41, 43
Augusta, 349
Austria, 264
Ayubale, 126
Azila, Margravate of, 39–40

Bacon, Nathanial, 85
Bacon's Rebellion, 85, 140, 148, 191
Bahamas, 16, 214, 256–68, 296, 298–301, 303–4, 306–7, 309–10
Bambara, 246
Bank Bill, 279, 285
Barbadian, *see* Barbados
Barbados, 16, 49–65, 97, 127, 129, 212, 215–16, 236–39, 243, 247, 257, 260, 295–97, 300, 309
Barnwell, John, 40–41, 43–44, 146–48, 150, 168–70, 176, 178, 186–89, 191,

Barnwell, John (*continued*)
  193, 195–205, 224–25, 321, 330, 352, 355
Baron, Samuel, 284–86
Bath, North Carolina, 192, 195, 198, 202, 222–24, 321–22, 325–26, 328–33, 336
Bay of Campeche, 295
Bay River Indians, 202
Bear River Indians, 148, 151, 191–92
Belgra plantation, 211–13, 215, 222, 226
Beresford, Richard, 276
Berkeley, Governor William (of Virginia), 57, 85, 260
Berkeley, Lord John, 257
Berkeley County, South Carolina, 31, 300, 343
Bermuda, 58, 258–59, 262, 301, 304, 333–34
Bight of Biafra, 234–35, 237–38, 242, 245, 248
Bight of Benin, 237–38, 244–45
Bishop of Durham Clause, 258
Blackbeard, *see* Teach, Edward
Blaeu, Willem, 31
Blair, Rev. James, 327
Blake, Governor Joseph (of South Carolina), 262, 304–6
Blakeway, William, 355
Blathwayt, William, 8, 29
Blome, Richard, 30
Blount, "King" Tom (Tuscarora headman), 150–54, 192, 195, 198, 202–3, 224–25
Blue Ridge Mountains, 190
Board of Trade, 8, 27, 36, 40–44, 100, 175, 259, 261–62, 264, 266–67, 281, 283–86, 301, 306–7
Bonnet, Stede, 240, 266, 278, 309–10
Bonny, Anne, 240
Boone, John, 82–83, 276, 302
Boone, Joseph, 129, 285
Boston, Mass., 214–15, 217, 307
Boyd, Thomas, 328
Bray, William, 345, 347
Brayne, Henry, 58
Brazil, 50, 52, 141
Breholt, Captain John, 305
Brice, [?], 199

Bridgetown (Barbados), 297
Brims (Creek headman), 347, 356, 361
Bristol, 267
Britain, 8–9, 13, 28, 35–36, 39, 41–41, 102–5, 215, 264, 275, 278, 283–85, 287
buccaneers, 51, 53; *see also* pirates
Buer, James, 361
Bulkley, Thomas, 262
Bull, Captain John, 360
Bull, Stephen, 122, 131
Bull, William, 196, 287, 348
Burrington, Governor George (of North Carolina), 247, 336
Burrows, George, 352
Burrows, Mrs. [?], 352
Bushel's Case, 302
Bryan, Hugh, 348
Bryan, Joseph, 345
Byrd, William I, 77–78
Byrd, William II, 28, 106, 296, 303

Cahokia, 190
"Callabar," 248
Callihaun, Daniel, 101–2
Canada, 128, 189
Cape Canaveral (Florida), 35
Cape Cod, 240
Cape Fear, 29–30, 54, 226–27, 257, 323–24, 326, 333–37
Cape Hatteras, 33
Cape Henry (Virginia), 35
Cape Lookout, 334
Captain Jack (Esaw headman), 196
captive, 33, 59, 78, 83, 118, 122, 124–26, 141, 145–47, 164–65, 168, 170, 175, 187, 190, 196–97, 200–2, 223, 234–38, 240–45, 248; *see also* slavery
Cardross, Henry Erskine, 3rd Baron of, 63, 124–25
Carib Indians, 53
Caribbean, 6, 16, 33, 43, 49, 51–56, 58, 60, 62–63, 65, 75, 118, 153, 212, 236–41, 243–45, 257–58, 261, 263–66
Carlisle, the, 305–6
Carolana, 258
Carolina, the, 58, 75
Carteret, John, *see* Granville
Carteret, Nicholas, 121, 174

Carteret, Sir George, 257
Cary, Thomas, 193, 211, 222, 224, 226, 329–30
Cary's Rebellion, 2, 7, 11, 15, 141, 144, 146, 211–12, 222–24, 226, 331
Catawba Indians, 41–42, 196, 224, 326
Catechna (Tuscarora town), 1–2, 144–47, 151, 190, 193, 199, 200, 203, 205
Catechna Alliance, 141, 146–53
Cattell, William, 362
cattle, 37, 54, 146, 153, 194, 246, 280, 353; *see also* livestock
Chaplin, John, 124
Charles I, King, 28, 258
Charles II, King, 6, 28–30, 119, 258–59, 298
Charles Town, Bermuda, 258, 261–62; *see also* Nassau
Charles Town, on Cape Fear, 29–31
Charles Town (Charleston), South Carolina, 2, 6, 11, 30–32, 34–35, 37–38, 40–42, 50, 54, 58, 61–63, 75–76, 79, 82–83, 85–89, 119, 121–24, 126–27, 129, 131, 164, 186, 203, 234, 243, 248, 262–63, 273, 275, 277, 281–85, 287, 295–98, 300, 303, 305–11, 345, 351, 354, 356–58
Charlesfort, 265
Charlestown Harbor, 29
charter, 8, 28–29, 37, 39–40, 43, 118–20, 260–61, 263–64, 274, 299; for the Bahamas, 257–63, 266–67
Chatouka (Coree town), 143, 146, 192
Chattahoochee River, 81, 86–89, 349, 354
Chehaw River, 38
Cherokee Indians, 9, 11, 42, 103, 127–29, 134, 174–75, 178, 203, 326
Cherokee War, 178
Cherokeeleechee (Creek headman), 354–57, 359
Chesapeake, 33–34, 77–78, 118, 212–13, 217, 235, 243, 297, 310, 326–27, 334
Chester, John, 348
Chestowa (Yuchi town), 103
Chevin, Nathaniel, 328, 332
Chickasaw Indians, 35, 102, 172, 174, 345, 359
Chicken, Colonel George, 107, 281

Chigelly (Creek headman), 356, 359–60
Chisca Indians, 81
Choateehee (Cherokee town), 174–75
Choctaw Indians, 35, 41, 172
Chowan County, North Carolina, 222
Chowan Indians, 142
Chowan precinct, 324–26, 328
Chowan River, 211
Church Acts, 263–64, 279
Church of England, *see* Anglican
Civil War, English, 51–52, 302
Clarendon, Edward Hyde, Earl of, 258, 260
Clarendon County, South Carolina, 31
Clarke, Governor Robert (of Bahamas), 261
Clutterboake, Thomas, 54–55
Cochran's Point, 346
Cofitachequi, 31, 75, 77, 81, 167
Cole and Bean, the, 306
Colleton, James, 301–3
Colleton, John, 56, 58
Colleton, Sir Peter, 30, 64, 257, 261, 301
Colleton, Thomas, 58
Colleton County, South Carolina, 31, 343, 345, 350, 356, 360–61
Colleton family, 257
Colone (Creek Indian town), 88
Columbus, Christopher, 186–87, 191, 203
Combahee Indians, 31
Combahee River, 37–38, 167
Comberford, Nicholas, 28
Commissioners of the Indian Trade, 100–4
Commons House, *see* Assembly
Company of Barbadian Adventurers, 54, 59, 257
Company of Eleutherian Adventurers, 258–60
Concessions and Agreements, 120, 257, 259
Conestoga (Indian town), 144
Congregationalists, *see* Puritan
Conseillere, Benjamin de la, 284
Convention of the People, 256, 273, 277, 281
Cooper, Anthony Ashley, *see* Shaftesbury
Cooper River, 30–32, 58, 63, 82

Coosa River, 355
Coosawhatchie River, 38
Cope, John (Tuscarora), 226
Coree Indians, 141, 143–44, 146–48, 151, 191–94, 202–3
Coree Tom, 145
corn (maize), 32, 98, 106, 122, 133, 147, 187, 190–91, 194, 196, 198–99, 216, 220–21, 224, 362
Coronelli, Vincenzo Maria, 34
cotton, 57, 259
council (of North Carolina), 211–12, 227, 321–22, 324–32, 335–37; (of South Carolina), 33, 76, 82–85, 119, 167, 236, 274, 276–77, 298, 300–2, 306, 308, 310, 354
court, 214, 219–20, 324–26, 329–32, 361; Chancery (North Carolina), 219; General (of North Carolina), 325–26, 332, 335; (vice)admiralty, 283, 302, 304–7, 309
Cove Indians, 203
Coweta (Creek town), 81, 87–89, 343, 355, 357, 359–61; see also Creek Indians
Coxon, John, 261, 299
Crane, James, 284
Craven, Earl William, 257, 325
Craven, Governor Charles (of South Carolina), 169, 225, 279, 285
Crawley, Mr. [?], 106
Creek Indians, 9–10, 35, 42, 73, 81, 89–90, 101, 123, 125–29, 134, 164, 169–70, 174–75, 177–78, 343, 344–45, 347–63
Crisp, Edward, 34–35, 38–39
Cromwell, Oliver, 51–52, 223, 258
Cromwell, Richard, 258
Cross, Mr. [?], 303
Crown, of Great Britain, 2, 36–37, 40, 43, 53, 119, 221, 241, 243, 256, 261–64, 266–67, 275, 283, 287, 296–99, 301, 303–4, 306–7, 310, 324
Cuba, 259, 300
Cuffy (Yamasee), 347
Cullam, Mr. [?], 355
Cullen, Thomas, 214
Culpeper, John, 30
Cunaba Tom, 176, 195

Cusabo Indians, 9–10, 30–32, 98, 168, 345
Cussita Indians, 78, 81–82, 87–89; see also Creek Indians
Customs, Commissioners of, 286

Danes, 298
Daniel, Robert, 125, 143, 164, 326, 328
Daytona Beach, 119
Deane, James, 284
Dearsley, Richard, 61
deerskins, 33, 41, 73, 78, 80, 82, 85, 88–89, 97–98, 101, 106–7, 118, 121–22, 190–91, 266, 325, 326, 344–46
disease, 10, 14, 53, 55, 118, 122, 172–73, 191
Dismal Swamp, 214
Doctor's Common, 304
Dominica, 53
Dorrell, John, 259–60
Dover, 214
Drake, Sir Francis, 265
Dry, Captain William, 281
Dummer, Joseph, 264
Dunlop, William, 168, 170, 176
Dutch, 28, 34, 50–53, 55–56, 58, 241
Duvall, David, 355

East India Company, 296
Eden, Governor Charles, 227, 308, 332, 335
Edisto Indians, 79, 346
Edisto Island, 262
Edisto River, 32, 35, 37–38, 351–52
Edwards, John, 357
Election Law, 276, 278, 282, 287
Eleuthera Island, Bahamas, 258
England, 27–28, 35, 41, 55, 58, 64, 73–75, 82, 89, 97–100, 104, 109, 171, 211, 236, 257–62, 274–76, 278–80, 283–85, 287, 299, 301–3, 308–9, 323, 325–27, 330
Esaw Indians, 167, 196–97, 200, 202
Evans, John, 107–8
Everard, Sir Richard, 336
Every, Captain [?], 303–4
Exclusion and Establishment Acts, see Church Acts

Fellows, James, 308
Fenwick, Colonel John, 281
firearms, 10, 74, 78–80, 82–84, 88–89, 103, 121–22, 125, 168, 177, 220, 249; see also guns
Fitch, Tobias, 357
Flamborough, the, 310
Flint River, 361
Florida, 9, 28–29, 33–35, 41, 43, 54, 74, 78, 81, 118, 125, 164, 168, 175, 177, 203, 259, 296, 300, 353
Fort Christanna (Virginia), 149
Fort Hancock (Tuscarora), 321, 330
Fort King George, 28, 41, 349, 356
Fort Moore, 349, 359, 361
Foster, Francis, 332
Fox, George, 29
France, 29, 36, 40, 259, 264; see also French
Frank (slave woman), 220
Fraser, John, 347
Fraser, Mrs. [?], 347
French, 28, 34–36, 38, 40–44, 90, 102, 118, 125, 128, 147, 165, 169, 172, 174, 241, 265, 285, 307; Huguenots, 6, 32, 33, 192, 265, 303, 308, 349; in Caribbean, 51, 53, 55–56, 58, 261, 263, 298; in Louisiana, 9, 28, 41; see also France
Fundamental Constitutions, 6, 120, 129, 257, 260, 299

Gale, Christopher, 169, 176, 326, 332, 335
Gambians, 235, 241, 247; see also Senegambia
Garden, Alexander, 133
Gascoyne, Joel, 31, 63, 64
George I, King, 267, 273, 278
Georgia, 28, 39, 41–43, 78, 81, 83, 86, 125, 343, 345, 349, 363
German, 6, 143, 188, 192–3, 194, 200, 201, 205, 211, 280, 284, 330
Gibbon, William 284
Gibbs family, 257
Gils, Tom (Seneca), 176
Glasgow, 214, 324
Glorious Revolution (in England), 5, 7–9, 296

Glover, Charlesworth, 359–61
Glover, Governor William (of North Carolina), 222, 226, 328
go-betweens, 73, 75–76, 343
Godin, Benjamin, 284–85
Godin, Stephen, 280, 283–86
Goffe, Arthur, 335–36
Gold Coast, 237–38, 242, 244–45, 248
Goose Creek, 38, 63–64
Goose Creek men, 7, 63, 82–85, 87, 122, 300, 303, 306
Gordon, William, 221
Graffenried, Christoph von, 1, 144–48, 152, 192–94, 201–2, 211
Grammont, Captain [?], 296
Grand Council, see council (of South Carolina)
Granville, John Carteret, 2nd Earl of, 215, 227, 266
Granville County, South Carolina, 38, 345
Graves, John, 262, 264
Great Tellico (Cherokee town), 174
Grenada, 53
Grey, James, 133
Greyhound Galley, the, 240
Griffin, Edward, Jr., 345, 350, 352
Griffin, Edward, Sr., 344
Guale, 81, 83, 86, 121, 124
Guiana, 52
Guinea, 308
Gulf Coast, 28, 35, 41, 190, 240
Gulf of Mexico, 43
Gullah, 249
guns, 77–78, 81–84, 99, 122, 165–66, 168, 174, 177, 187, 189, 194, 198, 220, 360; see also firearms
half-breed, see mestizo
Hall, Captain Jacob, 296
Hancock, "King" (Tuscarora headman), 145–47, 150–53, 188, 192–93, 195, 197, 199, 201–2
Harry (slave), 200, 202–3
Hart, Charles, 286
Harvey, Sarah Lakar, 326
Harvey, Thomas, 326
Havana, Cuba, 164, 263
Hawkins, [?], 219–20
Hawkins, John, 265, 325, 329, 331

headrights, 59, 61, 218, 260
Heath, Sir Robert, 28, 258
Henry VIII, King, 308
Herbert, John, 40, 174–75
Hewatt, Alexander, 348
Hickahaugau (Westo town), 79–80, 83, 86
Hilton, William, 29, 54–55, 59
Hilton Head Island, 29, 352, 357
Hoboyhatchey (Creek headman), 355
Holland, 260, 264; see also Dutch
Hondius, Jocodos, 31
Hopewell, 190
Horne, Robert, 29
Hornigold, Benjamin, 266
House of Commons (British), see Parliament
House of Lords (British), 262–63, 303; see also Parliament
Huguenots, 6, 32–33, 192, 265, 284; see also French
Huspaw King, 348, 352–53
Hutchinson's store, 131
Hyde, Edward, see Clarendon
Hyde, Governor Edward (of North Carolina), 150, 193, 211–12, 222–23, 226, 330–32

Ichisi chiefdom, 81
Igbos, 235, 237–38, 248
Import Duty Act, 275–78, 282
India, 303–4
Indian Forster (Tuscarora headman), 101–2
Indian Ocean, 296, 301
Indian slave trade, see slavery
Indian trade, 7, 10–15, 33, 37, 73, 77–78, 84, 119, 128–29, 141, 146, 148–49, 170, 172, 174–75, 220–21, 280–81, 296, 327, 343, 346; proprietary monopoly on, 73, 82–84, 99–100, 104; public monopoly on, 106–7, 109, 275, 284–85; regulation of, 7, 11, 97–109, 122, 275, 282; see also traders
Indian Trade Act, 275, 285, 353
Innennits (Tuscarora town), 197
Inner Temple, 304–5
Inns of Court, 304
intermarriage, 73–75, 87, 89, 105, 165–66, 177, 327, 344, 347, 353

Ireland, 58, 126, 195, 275
Iroquois Indians, 121–23, 140, 144, 154, 190, 203, 226
Islam, 246, 296
Isthmus of Darien (Panama), 295, 298
Istoweekee (Yamasee), 355–56

Jack (Indian slave), 358
Jackson, Andrew, 177–78
Jackson, John, 361
Jamaica, 49, 51, 53, 56–57, 236–41, 243, 245, 247, 260, 295, 297, 300, 308
Jamaica Act, 296, 300
James II, King, 7–8, 260–62, 302
James Island, 346
Jamestown (Virginia), 190–91
John and Thomas, the, 58
Johnson, Captain Charles, 310
Johnson, Elias (Tuscarora), 189–91, 202–5
Johnson, Governor Nathaniel (of South Carolina), 171, 263, 283
Johnson, Governor Robert (of South Carolina), 42, 256, 266, 277–79, 281, 283, 285–86, 309–10, 361
Johnston, Rev. Gideon, 347
Jones, Frederick, 332–33
Jones, Governor Cadwallader (of Bahamas), 77, 262
Jones, Thomas, 345, 350, 356–57
Jordine, John, 346

Kelly, Bryan, 361
Kennedy, Captain [?], 240
Kenta (Tuscarora town), 196
Kiawah (Kussoe town), 30
Kidd, William, 240
Kiffin, William, 260
King Philip's War (New England), 4, 39, 140
King Street (in Charleston), 42
Knight, Tobias, 332, 335
Kongo, kingdom of, 131–32, 239, 249
Koromantin (on Gold Coast), 237

Lake Oneida, 154
Laurens, Henry, 234, 243, 248
Lawson, John, 1, 33, 74, 129, 142–46, 170, 176, 192–94

Lear, John, 219
Leeward Islands, 53–54, 56, 58, 75, 223
LeJau, Francis, 130, 133
Lesser Antilles, 240
Lilburne, Governor Richard, 261
Lisle, Guillaume de, 34
Little River, 324
livestock, 1, 32, 52–53, 170, 223, 237, 260, 333–34, 345–46, 349, 350; see also cattle
Locke, John, 30, 58, 259–60, 299, 302
Logan, George, 281
London (England), 8, 32, 55, 86, 266–67, 276, 282–86, 304, 308, 310, 343–44
Long, Alexander, 102–4, 106, 108
Lords of Trade and Plantations, 29, 259, 261; see also Board of Trade
Lorey, Captain [?], 176
Louisiana, 9, 28, 40–41, 125
Lowe, Emmanuel, 331
Loyd, John, 284
lumber, 32, 53; see also timber
Lynch, Governor Thomas (of Jamaica), 56, 241, 295

Machapunga Indians, 143, 148, 191–92
Macon trading house, 89
Madagascar, 305–6
maize, see corn
Malatchi (Creek headman), 361
Manuel (slave), 219
maps, 13, 27–44, 62–64, 280
marriage, Anglo-Indian; see intermarriage
Martin, Moses, 361
Maryland, 243, 298, 301, 326–27
Massachusetts, 258, 264
Matheos, Antonio, 87–88
Mather, Cotton, 188
Mathews, Maurice, 32, 63, 71, 82
Mattamuskeet Indians, 141, 146, 148, 191–92
Maule, William, 328–29
Maynard, Captain James, 266
McCartney, Mrs. [?], 348
McCord, Mrs. [?], 352
McPherson, William, 362
Medway, 55
Meherrin Indians, 9, 148–49, 220–21
Melvin, John, 352–53, 360

Melvin, William, 352–53, 360
Mercator, Gerardus, 28
merchant-planter, 322, 324–26, 329, 332, 334, 337; see also planter
merchants, 15, 50, 53, 58–59, 61–64, 103, 105–6, 108, 214–15, 217, 222, 234, 239–40, 243–44, 247–48, 266–67, 274, 276, 279–87, 297–98, 300, 311, 325
mestizo, 343, 345, 347, 350, 352, 355–56, 358–59
Mexico, 190, 300
Michel, Franz Ludwig, 143
microbes, see disease
Middle Passage, 237, 246
Middleton, Arthur, 62, 357–58
militia, 38, 129, 131–32, 149–50, 169, 171, 195, 223, 249, 321, 330, 346, 349
Mississippian civilization, 122, 172
Mississippi River, 34–37, 41
Mobile, 169, 203
Modyford, Governor Thomas (of Jamaica), 51–52, 56
Moll, Herman, 28, 36–37, 39, 43
Monck, George, see Albemarle
Montgomery, Sir Robert, 39–40
Moore, James, Jr., 1, 129, 150–51, 169–70, 175, 178, 203, 224–25, 277, 330
Moore, James, Sr., 9, 60, 82–83, 89, 125–28, 164–65, 167–72, 175, 177–78, 267, 306–7
Moore, Maurice, 334–36
Moore, Roger, 334–35
Morden, John, 32–34, 38–39
Morgan, [?], 300
Morgan, Henry, 295
Morris, Lewis, 53
Morton, Governor Joseph (of South Carolina), 262, 300–1, 304–6
Moseley, Edward, 326, 329–31, 334–37
Moxon, Joseph, 29
Musgrove, Captain John (Sr.), 101
Musgrove, John (Jr.), 343–45, 348, 350–63
Musgrove, Mary, 343–45, 348, 350–52, 356, 358, 361–63
Mushoe (Michaux), Henry, 360
muskets, see firearms
Muskogee, see Creek Indians

Muslim, *see* Islam
mustee, *see* mestizo

Nairne, Thomas, 1, 35–37, 40, 74, 102, 126, 164, 167, 169, 171–72, 174, 345–46
Nansemond Indians, 149
Narhantes (Tuscarora town), 168, 170, 176, 195–97, 198
Narragansett Indians (New England), 217
Narragansett River (New England), 212
Nasaw (Catawba town), 41–42
Nassau, Bahamas, 258, 263, 266–67
naval stores, 216, 227, 245, 266, 280, 324
Navigation Acts, 8, 56, 260, 265
Needham, James, 77–78
Neoheroka (Tuscarora town), 1, 140, 150–51, 203, 224, 330
Neuse Indians, 141, 148, 151, 191, 193, 202–3
Neuse River, 1, 140, 143–44, 147, 152, 176, 187–88, 192–93, 195, 203, 212, 223, 227
Nevis, 53, 55, 75
New Bern, North Carolina, 1, 143, 146, 188, 192–95, 198, 201–2, 3331
New England, 4, 51, 54, 57, 128, 140, 203, 214, 215, 217, 248, 264, 334
New France, 28, 34
New London, Connecticut, 214
New London (Willtown), South Carolina, 32
New Mexico, 124
New Providence, Bahamas, 214, 258, 260–62, 267, 296, 307–8, 310
New River (North Carolina), 33, 78
New York, 56, 226
Newby, Gabriel, 325, 329, 331
Newfoundland, 34, 37
Nicholson, Governor Francis (of South Carolina) (also Lt. Gov. of Virginia and Maryland), 40–41, 256, 297–98, 301, 303, 310, 353–54, 356
Nightingale v. Bridges, 100
Niquisalla (Guale headman), 124
Niquisaya (Yamasee headman), 87
Norris, John, 346
"Notche" Island, 167

Nottaway Indians, 148–49
Nova Scotia, 34, 36

Occaneechee Indians, 78, 83, 85, 191
Occaneechee Path, 78
Ochese Indians, *see* Creek Indians
Ocmulgee River, 89, 349
Oconee River, 349
Ocracoke Island, 334
Ocute chiefdom, 81
Ogeeche River, 43
Ogilby, John, 30–31
Oglethorpe, James, 43, 177–78
Okchay (Creek town), 355
Oldmixon, John, 303
Ortelius, Abraham, 28
"Ottoe" Island, 167
Ouletta (Creek headman), 356–57
Outer Banks, North Carolina, 28, 215
Oweeka (Creek warrior), 350–54, 357, 360
Owen, William, 98, 166
Oxford, 310
Oyster Point, 58, 63, 296

Pacific Ocean, 119, 265, 295
Palachacola Fort, 349, 351, 359, 361
Palachacola Indians, 355
Palatine, *see* German
Palmer, Captain John, 360
Pamlico Indians, 151, 193, 202
Pamlico River, 140, 151, 188, 192, 198, 200, 212, 223, 328, 330
Parke, Governor Daniel (of Leeward Islands), 223
Parliament (of Great Britain), 8, 100, 102, 256, 258, 262, 264, 281, 283–84, 298, 303–5, 308
Parris Island, 355
Pasquotank precinct, 325
pasturage, 54, 57
Peedee Indians, 196
Penn, William, 302, 306
Pennsylvania, 144, 203, 212, 303, 306
Pentocolo (cacique of Apalachicola), 87–88
Pequot War (in New England), 140
Perce, Mrs. [?], 201
Percival, Andrew, 78–79, 85

Perquimans precinct, 334
Peterba King (Indian headman), 176, 195
Petit Guavre, 298
piracy, *see* pirates
pirates, 8, 15, 120, 142, 239–41, 243, 260–61, 263–66, 273, 278, 295–311; rhetorical, 154
Piscataqua River (New England), 214
plantation(s), 2–3, 6, 10–12, 15, 27, 32, 35–39, 50, 55, 57, 59–60, 62, 97, 119–21, 127–29, 131, 133–34, 143, 212–14, 216–21, 227, 234, 237, 249, 280–81, 295–96, 327, 330, 334, 346, 349–50, 355–57
plantation system, *see* plantation(s)
planters, 6–7, 15–16, 31–32, 36, 39, 50–53, 57, 59, 61–64, 82–83, 104, 106, 118–19, 121–23, 125, 128–31, 133, 148, 168, 213, 216, 218–19, 227, 234–35, 237, 242–43, 247–48, 274, 278, 280–82, 284, 286–87, 297, 311, 325, 336, 348, 355, 360, 362
Pocahontas, 145
Pocotaligo (Yamasee town), 1–2, 37, 344, 347–48
Pollock, Governor Thomas (of North Carolina), 15, 150–53, 211–228, 324–29, 332–35, 337
Pollock, Thomas, Jr., 227
Pon Pon, South Carolina, 13, 343–63
Popple, Henry, 42–44
Port Royal, 28–30, 37, 58, 73, 75, 86, 99, 124, 262, 345–48, 352, 354–55, 360
Port Royal (Jamaica), 295–96
Port Royal Indians, 75–76, 90
Port Royal River, 38
Port Royal, the, 58
Porter, Edmond, 224
Portugal, 265
Portuguese, 51, 131, 241
Powhatan Indians, 77, 140, 145, 190–91
privateer, 75, 236, 261, 263, 265–66, 295, 298–300, 302–4, 306, 324; *see also* pirates
Privy Council, 259, 266–67, 283, 285, 328
Proprietors, 2, 6–7, 10–11, 15–16, 29–31, 33, 36, 40, 42–43, 50, 56–59, 64, 73, 75–77, 79, 81–82, 84, 86, 98–101, 106–7, 119–23, 167, 174, 215, 221, 256–58, 260–63, 266–67, 273–87, 296–300–4, 306–8, 310, 325, 328, 330–31, 336
Protectorate (Cromwell's), 51–53, 223, 258–59
provisions, 53, 76, 98, 106, 146–47, 151, 167–69, 197, 216, 223–24, 245, 259–60, 264–65, 296, 324, 330
Public Receiver Act, 278
Puritans, 258
Purrysburg, South Carolina, 42

Quakers, 6, 29, 142, 211, 214, 221–22, 224, 225–26, 306, 322–23, 325, 327–32
Quary, Robert, 300–1, 306–7
Quash, 130
Queen Anne's Revenge, the, 240
Queen Anne's War, 9, 35, 127, 171, 263, 265
Quelch, Captain John, 307
Quintyne family, 257

Rackam, John (Jack), 240
Randolph, Edward, 303–5
Read, Mary, 240
Red Sea, 296–97, 302–3, 305
Reed, William, 332–33
Restoration, 51, 54, 258, 260
Revolution, American, 11, 274, 345
Revolution of 1719, 2, 8, 11, 16, 27, 40, 107, 256–57, 260, 268, 273–87
Rhett, William, 266, 276, 278, 280–81, 284, 286, 305, 307, 309
rice, 11, 15, 17, 32, 35–37, 118, 128, 133–34, 216, 218, 243, 246–48, 266, 280, 308
River May, *see* Savannah River
Roanoke Island, 29, 126
Roanoke River, 29, 152
Robin, "King" (Indian headman), 176, 195
Rodd, Charles, 344
Rogers, Governor Woodes (of Bahamas), 266–68
Rowden, Isaac, 220
Royal African Company, 243, 300, 308
rum, 77, 146, 245; *see also* alcohol

runaways, 9, 130, 142–43, 148, 152, 205, 219–20, 300, 350, 356

St. Augustine, Florida, 9, 32, 35, 43, 75, 79, 81, 85, 119, 125–27, 164, 191, 217, 298, 300–1, 307, 346, 348, 352, 354, 356, 359–60
St. Bartholomew's parish, 345–46, 350–53, 357–63
St. Giles planation, 79, 80
St. Helena Indians, 167
St. Johns River, 164
St. Kitts, 55, 243
St. Lawrence River, 34, 36
St. Lucia, 49, 51, 53–55, 57–58
St. Mary's River, 352–53
St. Paul's parish, 361
St. Thomas, 298
St. Vincent, 53
Sanders, Mr. [?], 361
Sanderson, Richard, Jr., 332–34
Sanford, Robert, 74
Santa Catalina de Afuyca (Ajoyca), 124–25
Santa Catalina de Guale, 83
Santee Indians, 33, 127
Santee River, 32–33, 35, 38–39
Sanute (Yamasee), 347
Saponi Indians, 149
Satuache (mission town), 81
Saunders, William, 352
Savannah, Georgia, 363
Savannah Indians, 10–11, 32–33, 80, 84, 86, 99, 122–23, 128, 217
Savannah River, 31–32, 38–40, 42–43, 79, 167, 349, 351
Saxapahaw Indians, 169, 187, 196, 205
Sayle, William, 258–60
Scotland, 124, 214, 227, 324, 329
Scottish, 13, 53, 63, 124, 164, 175, 214, 262, 299
Scots, *see* Scottish
sea islands, 35, 86, 123
Searle, Robert, 75
Seneca Indians, 193, 201; *see also* Iroquois
Senegambia, 238, 242–43, 244–48
servants, 51–52, 54–55, 60–61, 142, 211, 217–18

Settlement Indians, 32, 127, 129, 167
Sewee Indians, 169
Shadoo Indians, 54
Shaftesbury, Anthony Ashley Cooper 3rd Earl of, 64, 76–80, 84, 86, 98, 120, 122, 257, 258–60, 299
Shaw, Mr. [?], 361
Shelton, Richard, 276
Shenkingh, Bernard, 38
Shoreham, the, 308
Shubrick, Richard, 284
Sierra Leone, 245, 247
Siouian Indians, 147
Sisson, Mrs. [?], 348
Skene, Alexander, 281–82
Skiascasea (Cherokee headman), 103
slave trade, *see* slavery
slaves, *see* slavery
slavery, 36, 39, 42, 50, 52–53, 59–61, 212–14, 219, 221–22, 226, 275, 286, 295–96, 308, 323, 325, 331, 334, 350, 356, 360; African, 5–6, 9, 10, 12, 16, 33–34, 78, 118, 119, 128–34, 144, 147, 194, 200, 205, 216–18, 220, 227, 234–49, 262, 265, 300–1, 349; Indian, 10–11, 33, 35, 63, 73, 78–85, 88, 97, 118–19, 121–24, 126–29, 140, 146–47, 151, 164, 168, 172–75, 177–78, 195, 198–99, 203, 217–18, 220–21, 225, 237, 349, 355; rhetorical, 307
Slockum, Samuel, 142
Smallwood, Matthew, 358–59, 361
Smith, John, 31, 145, 188
Society for the Propagation of the Gospel, 310, 347
Somers Island Company, 258–59
Sothell, Governor Seth (of North Carolina), 215, 298
Soto, Juan de, 122, 191
South Sea, 298
Spain, conflict with, 73–74, 89, 264–65, 301; Indian allies of, 164; land claims by, 29, 36, 54, 86; peace with, 295; threats from, 259; *see also* Spanish
Spaniards, *see* Spanish
Spanish, 10, 12, 36, 42, 74–76, 79–81, 83, 86–90, 118–20, 134, 147, 164–66, 174, 215, 241, 247, 265, 285, 298, 300, 302, 308, 324, 353; alliances with

Indians, 76, 86, 88, 164; conflict with, 2, 10, 127, 164, 167–68, 170, 172, 262, 267–68, 301, 307, 346–47, 350; in Caribbean, 51, 53, 58, 261, 263; in Florida, 9, 28, 32, 35, 41, 74, 78, 81, 118, 125, 127, 164, 217, 259; Indian enemies of the, 124; land claims of, 3, 9, 43, 58; missions (to Indians), 9–10, 12, 31, 35, 74, 76, 78, 81, 85, 87–89, 118, 121, 123–28, 134, 164, 170, 203; money, 295; threat from, 9, 40, 44, 76, 81, 125, 263, 266–67, 273, 277–78, 296, 310, 349; trade with Indians, 74, 80, 102; *see also* Spain
Spanish Main, 51, 53, 295
Spotswood, Governor Alexander (of Virginia), 142, 147, 149–52, 154, 175, 192, 195, 223, 225, 310
Steads, William, 352
Stegge, Thomas, 77
Stephens, [?], 219–20
Stono Island (Wadmalaw Island), 38
Stono Rebellion, 130–32, 249
Stono River, 32, 38, 76, 356
Strode, John, 58
Stuart Town, 63, 124–25, 262
sugar, 6, 15, 49–58, 64, 127, 203, 216, 237, 245, 295
Surinam, 49, 51–58
Susquehanna Indians, 30, 78, 83
Susquehanna River, 144, 154
Sutherland, Captain James, 310
Swann, Elizabeth, 334
Swedish, 28
Swiss, 1, 6, 42, 143, 192, 194, 201, 330

Talaje (mission town), 81
Talapoosa Indians (Creek), 35, 203
Tallahassee, Florida, 81
Tar River, 198
Tasquiqui (Creek Indian town), 88
Taylor, [?], 201
Teach, Edward, 240, 308, 335
Tennessee River, 35
Thames River, 267
Thornhill, Sir Robert, 283
Thornton, John, 32–34, 38–39, 64
Three Brothers, the, 58
timber, 51, 54, 57–58; *see also* lumber

Timucua Indians, 124–25, 164
tobacco, 14, 57, 191, 216, 220, 259
Tomahitan Indians, 78, 83
torture, 1, 126–27, 144–45, 150, 170, 176, 196, 199, 202, 298, 344, 348
traders, to Indians, 10–11, 13, 15, 35–37, 73–74, 79, 83, 87–88, 98–108, 124–25, 164, 169–71, 175–76, 344–45, 347–48, 352, 358, 361
treaties, Anglo-Indian, 83, 120, 123, 140–54, 171
Treaty of Tordesillas, 186
Treaty of Utrecht, 37, 263–64, 308
Trent River, 143
Trott, Governor Nicholas (Bahamas), 262, 303–4
Trott, Nicholas (the younger), 276–77, 279, 304–10
Tuckabatchee (Creek town), 357
Tuckesaw King, 360
Tuscarora Indians, 1, 9, 14, 33, 101, 140–54, 168–69, 212–13, 321–22, 334; Lower Towns of, 203, 321, 330, 337; Upper Towns of, 141, 148–50, 154, 176–77, 186–205, 224–26, 331
Tuscarora War, 1–2, 4, 10–11, 14, 39, 140–54, 168–70, 175–76, 186–205, 223–27, 321–23, 325, 331–32, 335, 337

Ucouhnerunt (Tuscarora town), 150–51, 198
Urmston, John, 211–12, 223

Vane, Charles, 240, 308
Vaughan, Sir John, 302
Vera Cruz, 241, 295, 300
violence, 2–3, 10, 12, 15, 32, 38, 140–41, 144–45, 154, 211, 219, 348; cultures of, 14, 118–34
Virginia, 6, 28–29, 31, 33–36, 41–43, 51, 56, 61, 76–79, 83, 85, 87, 106–7, 119, 122, 140–42, 144–45, 147–52, 154, 168, 175, 188, 190–93, 195, 203, 214–17, 220, 223, 225, 235, 246, 260, 266, 285, 296–98, 301, 303, 306, 308, 310, 322, 326–27, 330

Walker, Anne, 326

Walker, Henderson, 326–28
Walrond, Humphrey, 52
Wando River, 32
War of the League of Augsburg, 171
War of the Quadruple Alliance, 264, 267
War of the Spanish Succession, *see* Queen Anne's War
Waraperes Indians, 196
Warner, Samuel, 347
Warner, Thomas, 53
Wateree King (Indian headman), 176, 195, 196
Webb, Nicholas, 308
Weetox Indians, 202
Wehomee (Yamasee), 350, 362
Wehuna (North Carolina Indian), 142
Welch, [?] (son of Thomas), 345, 350
Welch, James, 345, 350, 358–60
Welch, Thomas, 345
Wentworth, Hugh, 259–60
West, Capt. [?], 153
West, Governor Joseph (of South Carolina), 60, 62–63, 166, 260
West Indies, 32, 203, 213, 216, 225, 248, 283, 295–96, 308, 333–34; *see* also Caribbean
Westbrooke, Caleb, 124
Westminster, 260
Westo Indians, 9, 11, 31–33, 73, 78–87, 89, 98–100, 121–23, 128, 134, 167, 174, 217, 248
Westo War, 10, 84–85, 100, 104, 118–23
Westobau River, *see* Savannah River
Whitehall, 260, 262
Whitlemico, 350–52, 354, 356, 362

Whydah, the, 240
Williamson, Dove, 200
Willoughby, Governor Francis (of Barbados), 50, 52–56
Wimbee Indians, 168
Windward Coast (of Africa), 234, 245
Windward Islands, 53
Winiaw Indians, 169, 196
Wolof, 246
Wood, Abraham, 77–78
Wood, Hezekiah, 360
Woodward, Dr. Henry, 13, 73–90, 104, 122, 124
Wragg, Samuel, 308
Wright, John, 1, 102

Yamacraw, 361, 363
Yamasee Indians, 1, 9, 37–39, 42, 73, 81, 86–88, 100, 106, 121–25, 127–28, 147, 164, 168, 170, 175, 177–78, 187, 196–200, 202–3, 205, 217, 224, 227, 244, 263, 277, 343, 345–47, 350–55, 357, 359–62
Yamasee Land Act, 275
Yamasee Lands, Act to Encourage the Settlement of, 275
Yamasee War, 1–2, 4, 7, 10–11, 13, 16, 27, 34, 37–40, 42–43, 84, 104, 106–8, 121, 128, 140, 174, 264, 273, 275, 280–81, 283–86, 343–44, 347–49, 351, 354, 356
Yeamans family, 257
Yeamans, John, 56, 77
Yonge, Francis, 274–78
Yuchi Indians, 103, 361

CPSIA information can be obtained at www.ICGtesting.com
Printed in the USA
LVOW06*0312240913

353787LV00005B/9/P